For Dan Ellis,

a great Dean, mentor and friend; with many thanks for your support of my work on the international criminal court, and for building a great law school!

With best and warm wishes,

St. Louis, Mo
February 20, 2002

INTERNATIONAL
AND
COMPARATIVE
CRIMINAL
LAW SERIES

THE INTERNATIONAL CRIMINAL COURT AND THE TRANSFORMATION OF INTERNATIONAL LAW: JUSTICE FOR THE NEW MILLENNIUM

Leila Nadya Sadat

Transnational Publishers, Inc.
Ardsley, New York

Published and distributed by Transnational Publishers, Inc.
410 Saw Mill River Road
Ardsley, NY 10502, USA

Phone: 914-693-5100
Fax: 914-693-4430
E-mail: info@transnationalpubs.com
Web: www.transnationalpubs.com

Library of Congress Cataloging-in-Publication Data

Sadat, Leila Nadya.
The International Criminal Court and the transformation of international law : justice for the new millennium / by Leila Nadya Sadat.
p. cm. — (International and comparative criminal law)

Includes bibliographical references and index.
ISBN 1-57105-133-3
1. International Criminal Court–Rules and practice. 2. Criminal procedure (International law) 3. International offenses. I. Title. II. Series.
K5000 .S23 2001
341.7'7–dc21 2001047650

Manufactured in the United States of America

To Sam and Kyra, that there might be Peace in their time.

TABLE OF CONTENTS

PREFACE

This book is the fruit of many years of work on the International Criminal Court. The impetus for its writing came from my dear and now departed friend Edward Wise, a great scholar in international criminal law and a wonderful man I miss very much. I wish he could have read and critiqued the manuscript, for it would have benefitted enormously from his wisdom. It is based upon my first-hand observations of the work of the Preparatory Committee, the Preparatory Commission and the Diplomatic Conference, as well as the innumerable conversations I had with delegates both during meetings and subsequently. It has been enriched by the many conferences on the ICC I have been privileged to attend, particularly those in Siracusa, Italy convened by Professor M. Cherif Bassiouni and the wonderful seminar organized by William Schabas at the National University of Ireland in Galway, the many interviews I have had with personnel of the ICTY and ICTR, and the keen insights and extraordinary knowledge of the members of the International Law Association (American Branch) International Criminal Court Committee I have had the honor to chair.

The work is not intended as a treatise, but as a synthesis and analysis of many major features of the Court's Statute, features that highlight its contribution to the transformation of international law. Many of the theoretical constructs in it are new—some are bold, and I hope they will inspire debate. It is intended for use as both a text and a reference work, and will hopefully assist and inspire the reader to learn more about this extraordinary new international institution. I do not hide my bias in favor of the Court's establishment and the principles of justice and peace its creation represents; but I have offered gentle critiques where the Statute's text falls short of the lofty goals stated in the Treaty's preamble. Being educated and trained in both the United States and France I have tried to bring a comparative law perspective to this study, but much more could of course be done in this regard, and readers from other national legal systems will have much to contribute to future editions of this work and to the literature on the Court generally.

The book could not have been completed without the help of family, friends, colleagues, students and institutional support, and there are many to whom I owe a great deal. The work was directly supported by a generous grant from the United States Institute of Peace, as well as research assistance provided by the Washington University School of Law. Both Dorsey D. Ellis, Jr., the Law School's former Dean, and Joel Seligman, the current Dean, have been enthusiastic supporters, and I thank them greatly. Thanks also to the many research assistants I have had who have worked on this project over the years, and particularly to Scotty Allen, Micaela Ashe, Richard Carden, Theresa Clark, Mario Loyola, Sujeet Mehta, Kevin Ray, and Rachel Storch, as well as to my faculty assistants Josephine Hobbs, Beverly Owens and Pamela Williams who stoically endured what seemed like hundreds of re-writes and revisions. The NGO Coalition for an International Criminal Court rendered extraordinary assistance in obtaining documents and other information, and especially gracious were the many colleagues who took time out of their busy schedules to read and comment on drafts of this and earlier works, especially Kelly Askin, Kathy Brickey, Roger Clark, Frances Foster, George Edwards, Steve Legomsky, Lynn Lopucki, Darryl Robinson, Michael Scharf, Alfred Rubin, Edward Wise, and John Washburn. Finally, this book could never have been completed without the love and support of my family: my parents, my children, and most especially my husband, Andrew Ruben, who unselfishly and painstakingly read the entire manuscript and offered me encouragement when I faltered. Yet even with all this assistance the usual disclaimers, of course, apply—any mistakes or errors in the work are entirely my own.

FOREWORD

The Treaty of Rome of July 18, 1998 establishing an International Criminal Court (ICC), is likely to go down in history as the date when international criminal law came of age.

Since the signing of the Rome Treaty, three major works have been published. Two are experts' commentaries on the Statute's provisions edited by Professors Triffterer and Lee, while the third book is authored by Professor William Schabas.

Professor Leila Sadat's well-written and highly-documented book is, however, the first comprehensive authored text on the history of the ICC's Statute and a commentary on its text. But it is also more than that.

This book, whose contents and structure are described by the author in her Introduction, starts with three chapters that deal essentially with the historic evolution of international criminal justice. The author's description of this evolution argues for the values and policies of accountability which are needed in order to achieve justice and peace. Though the facts are not new, their presentation is articulate, precise and succinct. This part on its own could almost be a separate book on international criminal justice.

A discussion of the relationship between the ICC, the United Nations, and States follows. It is a premise to the notion of complementarity. Only then does the author go into her analysis of the different parts of the statute as they relate to jurisdiction, crimes and penalties, general principles of criminal law and responsibility, procedural aspects, and the court's processes. This chapter also includes the state cooperation regime and enforcement. Professor Sadat concludes with her assessment of the codification compromises made in the Rome Treaty, and a discussion of "what is in and what is out." She aptly ends with a chapter that takes us into the future, but more importantly, shows that the ICC is but only a window to the future.

This is not only a book about the ICC but also about international criminal law. In the first chapter, the author points out that the journey of international criminal law began in 1899, more than a century ago, but is not yet completed. Indeed, we have yet to complete the transformation from a culture of impunity to a culture of accountability. The author's description of the pursuit of international criminal justice through the complementarity of international tribunals and national criminal justice systems is amply documented. The overall purpose, as she explains, is to develop a big enough net through which few perpetrators of international crimes will fall and evade accountability.

The first impulse for contemporary international criminal justice came after World War I, but its thrust was weak and short-lived. The aftermath of World War II took it to a new level, but it was still viewed as one-sided. Some called it "victors' vengeance," even though those who were prosecuted at the Nuremberg and Tokyo trials were war criminals. The question is not whether they were fairly tried, but whether the system as a whole is fair when it excludes violators on the victors' side. She traces the history and details of establishing the ICC from WWI, through Nuremberg and Tokyo, the bleak years of the Cold War, and the final stretch in 1992 when the Security Council established the Commission of Experts [Security Council Resolution 780 (1992)] to Investigate Violations of International Humanitarian Law in the Former Yugoslavia. It was the first time since Nuremberg and Tokyo that an international criminal investigating body was established. The Commission's compilation of evidence of criminality was a factor in bringing about the establishment of the International Criminal Tribunal for the Former Yugoslavia [ICTY] (1993). These events broke the psychological barrier that seemed to hold back the international community from its ability to pursue international criminal justice. Shortly thereafter, the Security Council established the International Criminal Tribunal for Rwanda [ICTR] (1994). As other atrocities in various parts of the world became known—Sierra Leone, East Timor, to name only a few—it became clear that the Security Council could not re-invent an *ad hoc* post-conflict justice formula every time a conflict occurred during which violations of international humanitarian law took place. The logic of a permanent International Criminal Court imposed itself. But legal logic and politics are not always compatible.

Between 1995 and 1998, an elaborate and complex draft ICC statute was developed by dedicated government delegates, while a consensus among governments and international civil society was being forged. Its purpose was to not only serve justice but also peace. Professor Sadat retraces this travailed historical evolution, which was fraught with difficulties. As she observes, on the one side stood the political opposition of some governments and, on the other, the complex task of codifying substantive and procedural international criminal law as well as devising modalities of cooperation and enforcement. This was a task of a scale never before undertaken. She describes the preparatory work done in 1995 by the General Assembly's *ad hoc* Committee for the Establishment of an International Criminal Court, followed from 1996 to 98 by that of the General Assembly's Preparatory Committee for the Establishment of an

International Criminal Court. It was not, however, until December of 1997 that the convening of a diplomatic conference became reasonably certain. This left only four months in 1998 for the work of the Preparatory Committee to be completed. It was a considerable challenge in view of the many political and technical difficulties that remained to be overcome. By the end of April, 1998—barely six weeks before the convening of the diplomatic conference—the draft statute which governments would have to consider in Rome for a short five weeks consisted of 116 articles contained in 173 pages, riddled with some 1300 parenthetical brackets for optional provisions and word choices. Some of these were so complex that only a few of the experts who had followed the preceding three years' work could understand it.

The negotiating process in Rome was extraordinary in many respects. The author captures so well the mood of the place and its people, as well as the difficulties that were faced in bringing about the conclusion of the Rome Treaty on July 17, 1998.

Some 5000 delegates attended the first week of the Diplomatic Conference. Most, in the opinion of inside observers, had not read the draft statute. After a week of speeches by delegation heads, it was clear that the work on the Statute had only begun. By the third week, the task appeared impossible, and many delegates already spoke of another diplomatic conference. But a few dedicated delegates worked assiduously—some on the political side of the issue, others, like the Drafting Committee—on the technical legal side. Their cumulative efforts brought about this unique result, but not without cost to the technical legal accuracy and precision of some of the provisions contained in the statute. For example, the definition of aggression was postponed for lack of political consensus. In addition, genocide was defined as in the 1948 convention without filling its gaps (i.e., non-inclusion of social and political groups), and crimes against humanity became a menu of what appear to be human rights violations and war crimes—other than grave breaches of the Geneva conventions—requiring much more specificity. Subsequently, as the author points out, the "elements of crimes," as elaborated by the Preparatory Commission established by a resolution of the Diplomatic Conference, did not produce the expected precision and detail needed to fill the gaps and clarify any overlap in crimes.

Nevertheless, overlaps and gaps exist in three categories of crimes: genocide, crimes against humanity, and war crimes, which are now considered to cumulatively constitute the core crimes of international humanitarian law. But their legal contexts differ. "Grave breaches" of the Geneva Convention and Protocol I apply to conflicts of an international character, while the provisions of Common Article 3 of the Geneva Convention and Protocol II of the Geneva Conventions apply to conflicts of a non-international character. Genocide and crimes against humanity apply in times of war as well as in times of peace, but many of the same acts fall under more than one, or all three, of these crimes. Nevertheless, as evidenced by the jurisprudence of the ICTY and ICTR, there is confusion as to whether these crimes can be charged alternatively or cumulatively, and whether there can be multiple conventions and consecutive sentences for more than one of these crimes when the underlying facts are the same. This situation reflects a lack of understanding of what the Romanist-Civilist legal systems consider to be *concours d'infractions*. Regrettably, the ICC's Statute does not address this problem, even though it contains a provision prohibiting *ne bis in idem*.

The author's coverage of the "crimes within the jurisdiction of the Court" (Articles 5, 6, 7 and 8), and their "Elements" (Article 9) as elaborated by the U.N.'s Preparatory Commission, is incisive, critical and instructional.

The ICC's general principles of criminal responsibility or the general part (Part III of the ICC's Statute) is a comparative criminal law codification that leaves something to be desired. Admittedly, it is a difficult task, and the negotiators in Rome did their best in light of their expertise as diplomats, and considering the limited time they had at their disposal. Thus, they produced a text that is unsatisfactory—according to standards of comparative criminal law experts—and that left—in one aspect at least—a significant gap by not adopting a provision on the "material element" (because of inability to reach political consensus). Some commentators even question the validity of a provision on self-defense that may justify a certain type of self-defense in protection of property that would otherwise be deemed a war crime. Because the Diplomatic Conference gave no mandate to the Preparatory Commission to elaborate on the contents of the general part, as in the case of the "crimes," the opportunity to fill in some gaps was lost. The author reveals some of the weaknesses in the "general part."

The same is true with respect to the procedural part, which is also an exercise in comparative criminal procedure integration. The drafters freely mixed the adversary-accusatorial and inquisitorial models and processes. The "Rules of Procedure and Evidence" elaborated by the Preparatory Committee offer an additional level of detail. The result is an unparalleled mixture that produces what—to paraphrase Charles Dickens—became the best and the worst of all worlds. The procedural norms contain the best guarantees for the rights of the defense, but they also provide for a lengthy and cumbersome process that is likely to cause extensive delays and extraordinary costs to administer that type of justice.

Lastly, the "enforcement part" (Part IX of the ICC Statute), overly deferential to the sovereignty concerns of states, places the ICC in the position of having to deal exclusively through national legal systems based on existing national laws and procedures. Thus, the ICC's enforcement will only be as good as the national system called upon to enforce its orders and to assist it in connection with the various modalities of cooperation that the Statute describes. Presumably, national implementing legislation is to address these issues, but I doubt that they will.

This book's unquestioned strength lies in its substantive international criminal law aspects as it relates to the history of international criminal justice, the evolution of the ICC's process, its negotiating history, the jurisdictional aspects, crimes and relations with state-parties and non-state parties.

For years to come, commentators and writers will offer their insights and views as to what actually happened in Rome or on the way to Rome. This is inevitable in view of the historical significance of the event and the absence of an authoritative legislative history. Professor Sadat was a close observer of each step of the ICC process from 1995-1998, during which time she also assumed an active leadership role in the community of scholars interested in the ICC. Prior to the Rome Conference, she was the editor of 13 *bis Nouvelles Etudes Pénales, Observations on the Consolidated International Criminal Court Before the Final Session of the Preparatory Commission* (1997). She had also contributed her thoughts to the negotiating process by proposing a *Model Draft Statute* which was published in 13 *Ter Nouvelle Etudes Pénales* (1998). Professor Sadat attended the Rome Conference as a delegate of the International Law Association (American Branch).

The author has been noted in the last few years for her scholarly work in connection with "crimes against humanity" prosecutions in France as an outgrowth of WWII events that occurred during that country's occupation and the collaboration of its Vichy regime with Nazi Germany. Recently she became a contributing author to the second edition of the U.S.'s first casebook on international criminal law along with Professors Paust, Gurulé, Zagaris, Williams, and myself.

Some thirty years ago, when I picked up the torch of the ICC from my predecessors in the Association Internationale de Droit Pénal, there were very few who believed in the realization of that goal, and even fewer who were willing to dedicate themselves to it. As the international community moved forward and the goal became achievable, more joined the ranks. Later, when the prospects became politically likely, there was a groundswell of support. Until 1994, there were no more than five major non-governmental organizations in the world with a commitment to the establishment of an ICC. By the time the diplomatic conference took place, there were more than three hundred such NGOs, and today there are close to 1000 of them supporting the ICC. The few scholars who, from the 1920s into the 1990s have consistently worked in support of the ICC, have been joined by hundreds of scholars from all over the world. In universities across the globe numerous masters theses and doctoral dissertations are written about international criminal law and the ICC. Among these contemporary students, many will become tomorrow's scholars, and their future work in support of international criminal justice will be that much more significant because of their early interest in it.

Human nature being what it is, the few parents of the past will soon be relegated to the footnotes of history, while the more recent putative ones seek recognition, and the ones to come will necessarily seek to reshape what they have inherited.

The idea, which at one time could count only a few among its parents, now has thousands in the academic world and among activists in international civil society. That is the hallmark of an idea whose time has come. Now, one of our colleagues adds her important scholarly contribution to the work of others, and the torch passes on.

In the meantime, the ICC will enter into effect, probably at the end of 2002. Its beginning will be difficult as with every new institution. But, it will move forward and deal with its problems. In time, it will be one of the world's most important international institutions, and most observers will never know how arduous a task it was to bring it about and how long it took. Professor Sadat's book and other writings will then become important records of history. In the meantime, this book will serve an important contemporary need.

Chicago, September 29, 2001
M. Cherif Bassiouni*

* Professor of Law, President, International Human Rights Law Institute, DePaul University; President, International Association of Penal Law; President, International Institute of Higher Studies in Criminal Studies; Drafting Committee, U.N. Diplomatic Conference on the Establishment of the ICC; Chairman, United Nations Security Council Committee to Investigate Human Rights Violations in the Former Yugoslavia

CHAPTER 1

AN UNEASY REVOLUTION

> *Many thought, no doubt, that the horrors of the Second World War—the camps, the cruelty, the exterminations, the Holocaust—could never happen again. And yet they have. In Cambodia, in Bosnia and Herzegovina, in Rwanda. . . . Genocide—the destruction of an entire people on the basis of ethnic, of national origins—is now a word of our time, too, a stark and haunting reminder of why our vigilance must be eternal.*
>
> —Kofi Annan
> Secretary-General of the United Nations

From June 15 through July 17, 1998, representatives of 160 countries,[1] closely watched by 250 non-governmental organizations (NGOs),[2] met in Rome to negotiate a Treaty that would establish a permanent international criminal court. The weather was hot, the mood alternated between exhilaration and anxiety, the work was hard. Issues that had been debated for more than two years during the Preparatory Committee meetings leading up to the Rome Conference[3] remained on

1. *Rome Statute*, Annex II.

2. *Rome Statute*, Annex IV. One hundred and thirty-seven NGOs were officially credentialed at the Conference; however, nearly 250 NGOs were actually represented in Rome. M. Cherif Bassiouni, *Historical Survey: 1919–1998, in* STATUTE OF THE INTERNATIONAL CRIMINAL COURT: A DOCUMENTARY HISTORY 1, 26 n. 135 (M. Cherif Bassiouni, ed., 1998). In addition to the NGOs, representatives of 16 intergovernmental organizations, 5 specialized agencies, 9 United Nations programs and the Palestinian people attended the conference. *Rome Statute*, Annex III.

3. In 1995 the Security Council established the Preparatory Committee to "prepar[e] a widely acceptable consolidated text of a convention for an international criminal court as a next step towards consideration by a conference of plenipotentiaries. . . ." U.N. GAOR 50/46, 50th Sess., at 2, U.N. Doc. A/Res/50/46 (1995). Following adoption of the Rome Statute, the Diplomatic Conference of Plenipotentiaries established a Preparatory Commission to continue the work of

the table unresolved.[4] The starting point of the negotiations was a complex consolidated text containing 116 articles, including some 1300

---

the Preparatory Committee and the Conference on the development of an International Criminal Court. The Preparatory Commission is charged with drafting the Rules of Procedure and Evidence (RPE), Elements of Crimes, a relationship agreement between the Court and the United Nations, basic principles of the headquarters agreement, financial regulations and rules, an agreement on the privileges and immunities of the Court, a budget for the first financial year, and the rules of procedure of the Assembly of States Parties. *Final Act of the United Nations Diplomatic Conference of Plenipoteniaries on the Establishment of the International Criminal Court on 17 July 1998*, at Annex I, Resolution F, U.N. Doc. A/CONF.183/10.

4. Open to all members of the United Nations as well as members of specialized agencies, the Preparatory Committee held six official meetings at the United Nations Headquarters in New York City from March 25 to April 12, and August 12 to 30, 1996, from February 11 to 21, August 4 to 15, and December 1 to 12, 1997, and from March 16 to April 3, 1998. For a summary of these Preparatory Committee proceedings see *Report of the Preparatory Committee on the Establishment of an International Criminal Court (Proceedings of the Preparatory Committee during March–April and August 1996)*, Vols. I & II, U.N. GAOR, 51st Sess., Supp. No. 22, U.N. Doc. A/51/22 (1996); *Decisions Taken by the Preparatory Committee at its Session Held from 11 to 21 February 1997*, U.N. Doc. A/AC.249/1997/L.5 (1997); *Decisions Taken by the Preparatory Committee at its Session Held from 4 to 15 August 1997*, U.N. Doc. A/AC.249/1997/L.8/Rev.1 (1997); *Decisions Taken by the Preparatory Committee at its Session Held from 1 to 12 December 1997*, U.N. Doc. A/AC. 249/1997/L.9/Rev.1 (1997); *Report of the Preparatory Committee on the Establishment of an International Criminal Court*, U.N. Doc. A/CONF.183/2/Add.1 (1998); *Report of the Inter-Sessional Meeting from 19 to 30 January 1998 in Zutphen, The Netherlands*, U.N. Doc. A/AC.249/1998/L.13 (1998). In addition, several informal inter-sessional meetings took place resulting in revised drafts of the Statute. The International Institute of Higher Studies in Criminal Sciences (ISISC) in Siracusa, Italy hosted four of these inter-sessional meetings held from December 3 to 8, 1995, July 10 to 14, 1996, May 29 to June 4, 1997 and November 17 to 21, 1997. M. Cherif Bassiouni, *Historical Survey: 1919–1998, in* STATUTE OF THE INTERNATIONAL CRIMINAL COURT: A DOCUMENTARY HISTORY 1, 24 (M. Cherif Bassiouni, ed., 1998). The final intersessional meeting, held in Zutphen, the Netherlands, in January 1998, produced the Zutphen Intersessional Draft. *Report of the Intersessional Meeting From 19 to 30 January 1998 in Zutphen, the Netherlands*, U.N. Doc. A/AC.249/1998/L.13 (1998). For a chronology of the Preparatory Committee process, as well as the Diplomatic Conference, *see generally* Fanny Benedetti & John L. Washburn, *Drafting the International Criminal Court Treaty: Two Years to Rome and an Afterword on the Rome Diplomatic Conference*, 5 GLOBAL GOVERNANCE 1 (1999). On the Conference's procedure and organization see Roy S. Lee, *The Rome Conference and its Contribution to International Law, in* THE INTERNATIONAL CRIMINAL COURT: THE MAKING OF THE ROME STATUTE 1, 13–26 (Roy S. Lee, ed., 1999); M. Cherif Bassiouni, *Historical Survey: 1919–1998, in* STATUTE OF THE INTERNATIONAL CRIMINAL COURT: A DOCUMEN-

phrases in brackets.[5] It was extremely difficult to read, let alone understand.

The Conference was held in the United Nations Food and Agricultural Organization building (*la FAO* in Italian), a large, rather plebeian structure from the Mussolini period, with a splendid view of *Il Palatino* from the top floor terrace. Colorful flags surrounding the building flew high under a brilliant blue sky, as each delegation and many individuals who had been involved in the task of establishing a permanent international criminal court made moving speeches at the opening Plenary Sessions. Amnesty International set up a tent for information and publicity purposes a few hundred yards away, and the Italian-based Transnational Radical Party, in addition to papering the city with posters,[6] supplied each delegation with a small plastic briefcase containing literature and a transistor radio so that the Conference could be followed live on *Radio Radicale 2*. Delegates shuttled back and forth between Committee of the Whole meetings, Working Group meetings, and informal consultations, feverishly trying to complete the Statute in the time allotted,[7]

TARY HISTORY 1, 26–33 (M. Cherif Bassiouni, ed., 1998). *See also* Mahnoush H. Arsanjani, *The Rome Statute of the International Criminal Court*, 93 AM J. INT'L L. 22 (1999); M. Cherif Bassiouni, *Negotiating the Treaty of Rome on the Establishment of an International Criminal Court*, 32 CORNELL INT'L L. J. 443 (1999); Philippe Kirsch & John T. Holmes, *The Rome Conference on an International Criminal Court: The Negotiating Process*, 93 AM. J. INT'L L. 2 (1999); Mauro Politi, *Le Statute de Rome de la Cour Pénale Internationale: Le point de vue d'un négociateur*, 1999 REVUE GÉNÉRALE DE DROIT INTERNATIONAL PUBLIC 817; John Washburn, *The Negotiation of the Rome Statute for the International Criminal Court and International Lawmaking in the 21st Century*, 11 PACE INT'L L. REV. 361 (1999).

5. M. Cherif Bassiouni, *Historical Survey: 1919–1998, in* STATUTE OF THE INTERNATIONAL CRIMINAL COURT: A DOCUMENTARY HISTORY 1, 26 (M. Cherif Bassiouni, ed., 1998). Brackets were used by the Preparatory Committee to indicate proposed text as an option for the delegates to consider. The 128-article Rome Statute is much more complex and twice as long as the 60-article ILC Draft on which it was based.

6. The posters announced the conference and added, "We expect concrete results."

7. The thirteen parts of the draft statute were divided among different working groups chaired by coordinators that worked feverishly to complete the text in the allotted time. The Working Groups reported back to the Committee of the Whole which in turn referred completed articles or portions of articles to the Conference's Drafting Committee. The Conference was managed by a Bureau chaired by Canadian Philippe Kirsch, elected to replace the Chair of the Preparatory Committee's Bureau, Adriaan Bos, who had taken ill. The difficult and sensitive nature of the negotiations meant that with only two days remaining, the Statute's adoption was still in question. The Bureau decided that rather than report to the plenary that a second session would have to be held, which

while NGO representatives observed, discussed and participated in the negotiations from their Headquarters in the *FAO's* aptly named Sudan room.

As is by now well-known, after five weeks of grueling negotiations, the Diplomatic Conference adopted a Statute for the Court in an emotional vote of 120 to 7, with 21 countries abstaining.[8] The United States, whose delegation was instrumental in the development of the Statute throughout the Preparatory Committee meetings and the Rome Conference, was one of the seven countries voting against the Treaty.[9]

The adoption of the International Criminal Court Statute is the culmination of a Century of hard work and false starts. As the Preamble to the Treaty notes, the purpose of the Court is to end impunity for the perpetrators of "atrocities that deeply shock the conscience of humanity."[10] And the Twentieth Century has been witness to atrocities on a truly unprecedented scale: an estimated 170 million human beings have died in more than 250 conflicts since World War II, a grim testament to the fail-

---

many feared could delay the creation of the Court indefinitely, it would attempt to present a "package deal" to the delegates. This package, which was the product of intense negotiations and judicious compromises particularly as regards Part 2 of the Statute, was designed to reach widespread agreement, which it did. *See generally* Phillippe Kirsch & John T. Holmes, *The Rome Conference on an International Criminal Court: The Negotiating Process*, 93 AM. J. INT'L L. 2 (1999); John T. Washburn, *The Negotiation of the Rome Statute for the International Criminal Court and International Lawmaking in the 21st Century*, 11 PACE INT'L L. REV. 361 (1999); U.N. Dept. Of Public Information, *International Criminal Court: Some Questions and Answers #3* (undated), *at* <http://www.un.org.law.icc.statute/iccq&a.htm>.

8. M. Cherif Bassiouni, *Historical Survey: 1919–1998*, *in* STATUTE OF THE INTERNATIONAL CRIMINAL COURT: A DOCUMENTARY HISTORY 1, 31–33 (M. Cherif Bassiouni, ed., 1998). Both India and the United States attempted to amend the package proposed by the Bureau on the last night of the conference with what one author has dubbed "killer amendments," intended to completely thwart the passage of the piece of legislation. John T. Washburn, *The Negotiation of the Rome Statute for the International Criminal Court and International Lawmaking in the 21st Century*, 11 PACE INT'L L. REV. 361, 372 (1999). Norway blocked the proposed amendments, which reopened highly controversial points and would likely have defeated the Statute entirely, by offering "no-action" motions, which the Conference approved.

9. The United States requested the vote. Because it was unrecorded, it is unclear which States voted no, in addition to the United States, although China, India, Iraq, Israel, Libya, Qatar, and Yemen are among the most likely candidates, according to discussions with delegates and observers at the time.

10. *Rome Statute*, preamble.

ure of the international community to create a viable mechanism to prevent aggression and enforce international humanitarian law.[11]

It was thus appropriate and somehow fortuitous that the Diplomatic Conference was held in Rome. Once the center of an empire that stretched, during the Hadrianic period, across an area the size of the Continental United States and Alaska,[12] Rome is a city rich in historic and cultural treasures. It has also been devastated repeatedly by war. Sacked by Alaric in 410 A.D., then by Gaiseric in 457 A.D., Rome fell from its previously proud status to a medieval city "with seedy streets, derelict temples and ever more churches."[13] The city was invaded again in 1527 by Charles V of France, whose army of some 20,000 soldiers, in a beastly display of cruelty and barbarism, ransacked and looted the city and besieged Pope Clement and many of his Cardinals in *Castel Sant'Angelo*, even after a truce had been agreed upon.[14] In the last Century, Rome, like Paris, fell to Nazi Germany and felt both the "fist of the invader and the heel of the collaborator."[15] So what delegate, gazing out over *Il Palatino* and the ruins of the Forum, or seeing *Castel Sant'Angelo* and recalling the Pope's cruel imprisonment, could not feel the weight of history upon him or her, or understand the historic purpose for which all were gathered? Indeed, what better place in which to argue, on behalf of humanity, that the excesses of war should be restrained by the Rule of Law?

Given the unsuccessful history of previous efforts to establish an international criminal court, and the tepid support of many of the major powers during the Preparatory Committee meetings leading up to the Diplomatic Conference,[16] the adoption of the Statute by the Diplomatic Conference came as a surprise. It can be credited, at least in part, to the enormous lobbying and informational efforts of NGOs, which conducted a tireless campaign in support of the Court[17] and came together in a new

---

11. M. Cherif Bassiouni, *The Normative Framework of International Humanitarian Law: Overlaps, Gaps and Ambiguities*, 8 TRANSNAT'L L. & CONTEMP. PROBS. 199, 203 (1998).

12. DEREK WILLIAMS, THE REACH OF ROME xviii (1988).

13. *Id.* at 285.

14. E.R. CHAMBERLIN, THE SACK OF ROME 9, 154–92 (1979).

15. MELTON S. DAVIS, WHO DEFENDS ROME 476 (1972).

16. The address by the Honorable Bill Richardson, United States Ambassador to the United Nations, to the Diplomatic Conference, stated that the United States remained "cautiously optimistic" as to the possibility that the Conference's outcome would be successful.

17. The NGOs were particularly effective in lobbying via use of e-mail and the internet. *See, e.g., Rome ICC Treaty Conference: Welcome to the CICC's Web Page on the Rome Treaty Conference* (visited July 21, 1999) <http://www.igc.org/icc/rome/index.html>; *No Peace Without Justice: International Campaign for the*

example of global civil society.[18] Some NGOs were large human rights organizations such as Amnesty International, Human Rights Watch, and Lawyers Committee for Human Rights. Others were religious organizations (Quaker, Unitarian, and Jewish groups, to name a few), academic institutions,[19] or even individuals who went to Rome not as official representatives of governments or NGOs, but out of a sense of deep commitment to the goals the ICC was intended to promote.[20] The NGO movement was able to amass its strength through the formation of a coalition, the Coalition for an International Criminal Court (CICC), that originated under the auspices of the World Federalist Movement and ultimately grew from 30 to 800 NGOs from all over the world.[21] The CICC was able to influence the treaty-making process substantially, particularly

---

Establishment of the International Criminal Court and Support of the Ad Hoc International Tribunals for the Former Yugoslavia and Rwanda (visited July 21, 1999) <http://www.stm.it/npwj> (No Peace Without Justice (NPWJ) website). These organizations, among many others, were very active during the years prior to Rome. NPWJ, in association with Inter Press Service (IPS), published both electronic, *see* IPS, *TerraViva, The Conference Daily Newspaper* (visited July 21, 1999) <http://www.ips.org/icc>, and hard copy versions of *TerraViva*, a daily newsletter, during the Rome Conference. The United Nations also created an official website for the Rome Conference.

18. By "civil society," I refer to "uncoerced [networks of] human association . . . formed for the sake of family, faith, interest, and ideology." Michael Walzer, *The Concept of Civil Society, in* TOWARD A GLOBAL CIVIL SOCIETY 7 (Michael Walzer, ed., 1995). The term "global" adopts the terminology of Professor Falk (and others) who, while recognizing the difficulty of determining what "society" one is exactly referring to, given the weakness of international networks when compared to their national homologs, nevertheless suggests that one can identify "[international] social forces that respond to the patterns of behavior associated with the phenomena of economic globalization." Richard Falk, *Global Civil Society: Perspectives, Initiatives, Movements*, 26 OXFORD DEV. STUD. 99 (1998). For Professor Falk, global civil society "refers to the field of action and thought occupied by individual and collective citizen initiatives of a voluntary, non-profit character both within states and transnationally." *Id.* at 100. This definition would describe the character of the NGOs in Rome. *See also* Richard Falk, *The Nuclear Weapons Advisory Opinion and the New Jurisprudence of Global Civil Society*, 7 TRANSNAT'L L. & CONTEMP. PROBS. 333 (1998); Richard Falk & Andrew Strauss, *On the Creation of a Global Peoples Assembly: Legitimacy and the Power of Popular Sovereignty*, 36 STAN. INT'L L. 191 (2000).

19. The International Law Association (American Branch), for example, which the author represented, as chair of its ICC Committee.

20. *See generally* Fanny Benedetti & John L. Washburn, *Drafting the International Criminal Court Treaty: Two Years to Rome and an Afterword on the Rome Diplomatic Conference*, 5 GLOBAL GOVERNANCE 1, 3 (1999).

21. *Id.* at 22.

as it came to form an alliance with the so-called "like-minded" States.[22] This group of States, although individually holding quite divergent views on many issues, were united in their view that the Court's ultimate establishment was a priority,[23] and emerged as an important component of the Conference's ultimate success. Finally, strong support from many European countries and other traditional U.S. allies rallied the West behind the Court despite the opposition of the United States.[24] As of this

---

22. In addition to the Like-Minded Group, States coalesced into different groups depending upon the issue involved. The permanent members of the Security Council had the strongest solidarity on two points: preserving a strong role for the Council vis-à-vis the Court, and excluding nuclear weapons from those weapons that would ultimately be prohibited by the Statute. Opposing the P-5 were States that were extremely suspicious of the Council and which insisted upon the inclusion of nuclear weapons among the weapons ultimately prohibited (including India, Mexico and Egypt). On other issues, States took positions that generally transcended the caucuses that characterize the General Assembly and grouped togehter based upon common interests. Phillippe Kirsch & John T. Holmes, *The Rome Conference on an International Criminal Court: The Negotiating Process*, 93 AM. J. INT'L L. 2, 4 (1999); John T. Washburn, *The Negotiation of the Rome Statute for the International Criminal Court and International Lawmaking in the 21st Century*, 11 PACE INT'L L. REV. 361, 367 (1999).

23. This group of States tended to act in concert during the meetings of Preparatory Committee and in Rome. *See* M. Cherif Bassiouni, *Historical Survey: 1919–1998, in* STATUTE OF THE INTERNATIONAL CRIMINAL COURT: A DOCUMENTARY HISTORY 1,25 (M. Cherif Bassiouni, ed., 1998). The like-minded group became increasingly powerful as the treaty-making process continued. Fanny Benedetti & John L. Washburn, *Drafting the International Criminal Court Treaty: Two Years to Rome and an Afterword on the Rome Diplomatic Conference*, 5 GLOBAL GOVERNANCE 1, 30–31 (1999). It originated with 42 States and grew considerably thereafter to more than sixty members. *Id.* This group had been formed during the Ad Hoc Committee's work by a handful of Western European and Latin American states that were frustrated by the opposition of the major powers to the establishment of the ICC. It did not include any of the permanent members of the Security Council until the United Kingdom joined it after the Labor Party's victory in British elections. Mahnoush H. Arsanjani, *The Rome Statute of the International Criminal Court*, 93 AM. J. INT'l L. 22, 23 (1999). Because the group "was the only one with an operational strategy," it was clearly the moving force behind the Conference's successful conclusion. Fanny Benedetti & John L. Washburn, *Drafting the International Criminal Court Treaty: Two Years to Rome and an Afterword on the Rome Diplomatic Conference*, 5 GLOBAL GOVERNANCE 1, 30–31 (1999).

24. Another important element of the Statute's negotiation was the presence of powerful caucuses, such as the Women's Caucus for Gender Justice in the International Criminal Court, the Children's Caucus and the Victims Caucus who often served as expert consultants to delegates on particular issues. On the Women's Caucus, *see generally* Kelly D. Askin, *Crimes within the Jurisdiction of the International Criminal Court*, 10 CRIM. L. F. 33, 45 (1999).

writing, one-hundred thirty-nine States have signed the Statute, and thirty-seven States have ratified it.[25]

The International Criminal Court is the last great international institution of the Twentieth Century. It is no exaggeration to suggest that its establishment could reshape our thinking about international law. For if many aspects of the Rome Treaty demonstrate the tenacity of traditional Westphalian notions of State sovereignty, there are nonetheless elements of supranationalism and efficacy in the Statute that could prove extremely powerful. Not only does the Statute place State and non-State actors side-by-side in the international arena, but the Court will put real people in real jails. Indeed, the establishment of the Court raises hopes that the lines between international law on the one hand and world order on the other are blurring, and that the normative structure being created by international law might one day influence or even restrain the Hobbesian order established by the politics of States.

This book examines the organization, operating principles and substantive law of the Court. The study suggests that the negotiation and adoption of the Rome Treaty has worked a quiet, albeit uneasy, revolution that has the potential to profoundly transform the landscape of international law. Yet no revolution would be complete without a counterrevolution, and many aspects of the Statute reflect the constraints of classical international law that did not yield to the forces of innovation and revolution at Rome.[26] This is not surprising, for if State sovereignty (and particularly its expression as nationalism) is often blamed for the violent condition of world affairs, international governance is not necessarily looked upon as a superior alternative.[27] This tension is evident in

---

25. *The Coalition for the International Criminal Court (CICC) Web site: Rome Statute Signature and Ratification Chart*, <http://www.igc.org/icc/rome/html/ratify.html> (last update July 17, 2001). As of July 19, 2001, the following States have ratified the Statute: Andorra, Antigua & Barbuda, Argentina, Austria, Belgium, Belize, Botswana, Canada, Costa Rica, Croatia, Denmark, Dominica, Fiji, Finland, France, Gabon, Germany, Ghana, Iceland, Italy, Lesotho, Luxembourg, Mali, Marshall Islands, The Netherlands, New Zealand, Norway, Paraguay, San Marino, Senegal, Sierra Leone, South Africa, Spain, Sweden, Tajikistan, Trinidad and Tobago, Venezuela.

26. As Justice Higgins has so eloquently written, "[C]onsent and sovereignty are constraining factors against which the prescribing, invoking, and applying of international law norms must operate." ROSALYN HIGGINS, PROBLEMS AND PROCESS: INTERNATIONAL LAW AND HOW WE USE IT 1 (1994).

27. *See, e.g.*, DAVID W. ZIEGLER, WAR, PEACE, AND INTERNATIONAL POLITICS 163–79 (7th ed. 1997) (noting that there is little consensus supporting a world government, that it would require a great deal of police power that would pose its own dangers, and suggesting that regional integration may be a happy medium).

every part of the Statute's adoption and operation: its organizational and institutional structure, substantive law, rules of procedure and enforcement regime.

Chapter 2 examines the ICC's evolutionary path through the Twentieth Century, for, in spite of the Statute's revolutionary aspects, it is the fruit of intellectual and creative energies that have been at work for some time. The journey begins with the formalities that attended the 1899 Hague Peace Conference and the classic ideas of sovereignty that prevailed at the time: that Heads of State were accountable to no one but their own people; that all States are juridically equal; and that States are subject to no law to which they do not consent. The erosion of these axioms of State sovereignty throughout the ensuing hundred years was a necessary precondition to the creation of the international criminal court, but it took two world wars and other bloody conflagrations for the process to run its course. Exploring just how difficult it was for the Rome Treaty to be drafted and adopted suggests that if the road to Rome was long and difficult, the journey to the seat of the Court at the Hague[28] may be equally arduous.

Chapter 3 examines the justifications offered for the Court's establishment, as well as the expectations its establishment may create. Premised on the view that there can be no real or lasting peace without justice, the Court is seen by its supporters as a critical step towards combating impunity for international crimes in order to deter their commission in the future and to bring peace and solace to their victims. The long term consequences of the culture of impunity that has existed until now has created the impression that "extermination, deportation, and wanton destruction," are within a ruler's range of viable options.[29] Changing the normative discourse of international relations so that rulers who commit atrocities become international pariahs, rather than tolerated, or even admired, despots, is critically important to influencing their behavior. Establishing the Court as a permanent international institution, with jurisdiction over crimes committed anywhere in the world, not just in particular locations, is seen as a key component of this endeavor.

Others question the premise that punishment and prosecution may lead to deterrence, and suggest that trading peace for justice is sometimes required to end a conflict. Leaving aside the unsavory element of *realpolitik*, it is often postulated that even if the use of the criminal law is an appropriate remedy for the commission of war crimes and atrocities,

---

28. *Rome Statute*, art. 3(1).

29. Payam Akhavan, *Beyond Impunity: Can International Criminal Justice Prevent Future Atrocities?*, 95 AM. J. INT'L L. 7, 13 (2001).

national prosecutions and truth commissions may do more to bring about peace and reconciliation than international criminal trials. Chapter 3 explores the contours of this debate and concludes that the case for international criminal trials is a strong one. The current situation is clearly unacceptable, and most national legal systems are unable to address the problem of mass atrocities, committed either on their own territories or abroad, having neither the political will nor the capacity to do so. While the Court will not be a panacea for the world's ills, its establishment takes an important step towards addressing its problems.

Chapter 4, on institutional structure, outlines some of the innovations (and restrictions) incorporated within the Statute. In particular, it highlights the significance of the decision to establish the Court as a free-standing institution outside the United Nations system, addresses some of the strengths and weaknesses of the Court's four organs, and considers the role of the Assembly of States Parties. A study of the Court's structure reveals the fundamental tension between the desire of States Parties to retain control of the Court and the Court's need for independence to preserve the integrity of the judicial process. The Framers[30] were largely successful in establishing an institutional structure and procedural regime that would be a true hybrid, not based entirely upon either the adversarial or inquisitorial systems, but combining what is hoped will be the most useful elements of both. They also opted for an institution that would operate relatively free from concerns about nationality—the nationality of the judges, prosecutors, victims and defendants is virtually irrelevant to proceedings before the Court, meaning that the justice dispensed will be truly universal in character.

Chapter 5 explores the general principles underlying the jurisdiction of the Court, the effectuation and expression of the complementarity principle in the Court's Statute, and the manner in which cases will come before the Court. This is perhaps the core of the revolution worked in Rome: the prescriptive jurisdiction of the international community and the adjudicative jurisdiction of the Court itself are premised on transfor-

30. The term "Framers" is used in a non-technical sense, but with full cognizance of its constitutional connotations. The term "drafters" was originally employed, but was rejected as technically incorrect, for the actual drafters of the Statute were the 25 members of the Drafting Committee who were charged with the elaboration of the text but were not given discretion as to matters of substance. While aspects of the Statute are legislative in nature, other aspects of the Rome Treaty are clearly constitutional, for in addition to articulating substantive norms of international criminal law, the Statute is also the constituent document of a new international organization.

mative redefinitions of those principles in current international law. Indeed, as explored below, through a rather astonishing mutation, jurisdictional principles concerning "which State" may exercise its authority over particular cases have been transformed into norms establishing the circumstances under which the international community may prescribe rules of international criminal law and punish those who breach those rules. The repartition of competences between national and international jurisdictions incorporated in the Statute as a matter of prescriptive and adjudicative jurisdiction may presage a quasi-federal organization of international legal authority in the future.[31]

In contrast, the Court's enforcement jurisdiction is paltry, at best, suggesting the unease of the States Parties to the Statute with the revolution they wrought. While they boldly proclaimed the right of the international community to prescribe, and, for the most part, suggested that jurisdiction to adjudicate followed in principle, they in no manner followed suit in terms of enforcement. Here classic paradigms of sovereignty, in which each State is master of its own territory, prevailed. To put it another way, if the Framers were willing to permit the intangible presence of the law to permeate State borders, the reception offered to those whose duty it was to enforce that law was much chillier. Finally, the Framers' distrust of their new creation is evidenced by the extremely complex and potentially burdensome procedural regime governing challenges to jurisdiction and admissibility, which may ultimately prevent the Court from efficiently fulfilling its primary mission to administer justice.

Chapter 6 explores the definitions of the crimes within the Court's jurisdiction, as well as the penalty provisions of the Statute. It should be noted at the outset that the Statute may be viewed as an international criminal code created in the absence of an international legislature. Yet, one of the classic objections to the establishment of an international criminal court has been the absence of an international sovereign power with the authority to exert prescriptive jurisdiction over the human beings of the world. The delegates in Rome, sensitive to questions about the legitimacy of their undertaking, were generally quite conservative in crafting the definitions of crimes, and for the most part adhered to existing treaties, or in the absence of treaties, fairly well-established principles of customary international law. But in fact, as I have noted elsewhere, the Rome Conference was a quasi-legislative process during which the international community "legislated" by a non-unanimous vote. It is possible, of course, to view the government representatives in Rome merely as scribes writing

31. The European Union offers a useful comparison, although in the case of the Court, the organization is implicit rather than explicit.

down existing customary international law, rather than legislators prescribing new laws for the international community. Indeed, this is partly true, as all revolutions build upon pre-existing ideas. But it would be disingenuous to suggest that the Rome process was in no way legislative, given that most of the crimes were very poorly defined in customary international law. Moreover, even where there was general agreement on the existence of a particular crime, drafting the Statute required clarifying and elucidating the precise content of the offense in a way that often moved the "law" of the Statute far beyond existing customary international law understandings.

Descriptions of international conferences at the turn of the Century emphasized how they differed from Parliamentary assemblies. James Scott, a U.S. delegate to the Second Hague Peace conference, while recognizing that the "international statute" was "[g]radually and unconsciously" replacing customary international law, nevertheless noted that although an international conference is "a deliberative body, it is not a parliament."[32] Studies by the United Nations suggest that although voting is employed in some multilateral conferences, the default position calls for making decisions by consensus or unanimity if the conference rules are silent.[33] In Rome, there is no doubt that voting was employed, albeit ironically at the behest of the United States which attempted twice to *defeat* the Statute by putting it to a vote (once to table; a second time on the merits).[34] Although most delegates to the Conference do not believe that they were innovating at Rome, the fact that the process was "quasi-legislative"[35] is confirmed by the coercive nature of the substantive law adopted. For even the United States, one of the most outspoken critics of the Diplomatic Conference, has conceded the propriety of the Security Council applying, to citizens of party and non-party States alike, the substantive criminal law embodied in the Statute.

---

32. JAMES BROWN SCOTT, I THE HAGUE PEACE CONFERENCES OF 1899 AND 1907 36 (1909).

33. *See Review of the Multilateral Treaty-Making Process*, U.N. Doc. ST/LEG/SER.B/21 (1985), at 34.

34. Giovanni Conso, *Looking to the Future, in* THE INTERNATIONAL CRIMINAL COURT: THE MAKING OF THE ROME STATUTE 471, 472–73 (Roy S. Lee, ed., 1999).

35. My use of the term "legislative" is tempered by the addition of "quasi," for two principal reasons: *First*, the entire process was an unconscious one and the body constituted was certainly not a legislature in any formal sense, nor, as evidenced by conversations with delegates, did those participating consider themselves to be members of a legislature; *Second*, the law "created" by the diplomatic conference is subject to the very cumbersome second stage of ratification prior to its entry into force.

If this is correct, the political legitimacy of the Statute rests not on any classic theory of contract between absolute sovereigns (treaty-making) but on some other grounds.[36] From this perspective, it cannot be denied that the adoption of the ICC statute represented an extraordinary moment for international law.[37] The Rome Conference is not the first time that this shift towards quasi-legislative rule making by international conferences has appeared (see, for example, the Law of the Sea Conference), but the ICC process seemed different in degree, perhaps due to the participants' breadth of moral agreement and commitment.[38] Indeed, the Rome Conference, unlike the Hague Conferences of a century before, did not represent an exercise in multilateral treaty-making of a contractual nature,

---

36. Scholars have been observing shifts in sovereignty paradigms for some time now. For a sample of the literature on this issue, *see, e.g.*, Martin A. Rogoff, *Interpretation of International Agreements by Domestic Courts and the Politics of International Treaty Relations: Reflections on Some Recent Decisions of the United States Supreme Court*, 11 AM. U. J. INT'L L. & POL'Y 559, 624–55 (1996); Anne-Marie Slaughter, *International Law in a World of Liberal States*, 6 EUR. J. INT'L L. 503 (1995). *See generally* John O. McGinnis, *The Decline of the Western Nation State and the Rise of the Regime of International Federalism*, 18 CARDOZO L. REV. 903 (1996); Panel, *The Transformation of Sovereignty*, 88 AM. SOC'Y INT'L L. PROC. 1 (1994); Conference, *Sovereignty in the North American Context and in a Changing World*, 20 CAN.-U.S. L.J. 1 (1994).

37. Elsewhere I have argued that Rome was a "Grotian Moment" (a redefining moment) in international law. It was also a constitutional moment of sorts—in which the peoples of the world, as well as, or in spite of, their governments, constructed a new constitutional conception of the international legal order. *See* Leila Nadya Sadat & S. Richard Carden, *The New International Criminal Court: An Uneasy Revolution*, 88 GEO. L. J. 381 (2000). *See also* Richard Falk, *The Grotian Moment: Unfulfilled Promise, Harmless Fantasy, Missed Opportunity?*, 13 INT'L INSIGHTS 3 (1997); Richard Falk, *The Grotian Quest, in* INTERNATIONAL LAW: A CONTEMPORARY PERSPECTIVE 36 (Richard Falk et al. eds., 1985); Saul Mendlovitz & Merav Datan, *Judge Weeramantry's Grotian Quest*, 7 TRANSNAT'L L. & CONTEMP. PROBS. 401, 402 (1997) (defining "Grotian Moment").

38. *See also* Oscar Schacter, *The U.N. Legal Order: An Overview, in* 1 UNITED NATIONS LEGAL ORDER 1, 29 (Oscar Schacter & Christopher C. Joyner, eds., 1995) (noting that U.N. decision-making processes are "essentially political processes, but they are shaped by the conditions of quasi-parliamentary procedures and the mandates of constituent instruments"); *cf.* Robert Y. Jennings, *Treaties, in* INTERNATIONAL LAW: ACHIEVEMENTS AND PROSPECTS 135, 148 (Mohammed Bedjaoui, ed., 1991) (positing that a new way of making and developing general international law is likely to evolve through the multilateral treaty-making process; however, the parts of treaties that have *per se* general application, including non-parties, must be readily identifiable and distinguishable). For a discussion of the quasi-legislative effect that General Assembly Resolutions may have if certain conditions are met, see generally FARHAD MALEKIAN, THE MONOPOLIZATION OF INTERNATIONAL CRIMINAL LAW IN THE UNITED NATIONS: A JURISPRUDENTIAL APPROACH 76–81 (2d ed. 1995).

in which unanimity of decision-making is the fundamental feature.[39] As a result, several countries that felt entitled to a veto were outvoted.[40] This supranationalism pervades the Statute and is evidenced by the fact that the Assembly of States Parties established by the Statute[41] will take decisions on which a consensus cannot be reached by a two-thirds majority, or even a simple majority, in most cases.[42] It is also apparent in the decision of the Framers to give the Court, rather than States, the final word in interpreting the Statute[43] on such issues as burden of proof,[44] admissibility,[45] and the admission of evidence.[46]

In addition to analyzing the status of the definitions of crimes as law, Chapter 6 also suggests a methodology to separate the jurisdictional from

---

39. *See generally* IAN BROWNLIE, PRINCIPLES OF PUBLIC INTERNATIONAL LAW 607–40 (5th ed. 1998); LORD MCNAIR, THE LAW OF TREATIES 1–236 (1961); Paul Szasz, *General Law-Making Processes, in* 1 UNITED NATIONS LEGAL ORDER 35, 39–41 (Oscar Schacter & Christopher C. Joyner, eds., 1995) (arguing that recent treaties are not "contractual in a normal sense," but instead tend to be more "law-making" or "law-expressing" in nature).

40. This loss of power seemed particularly problematic for the United States. Indeed, the reaction of the United States, which tried to put the Statute to a vote twice, only to be resoundingly defeated, is reminiscent of the "empty chair" policy of France under President DeGaulle in the early days of the European Community's existence. GEORGE A. BERMANN ET AL., CASES AND MATERIALS ON EUROPEAN COMMUNITY LAW 54 (1993).

41. *Rome Statute*, art. 112; *see also* Figure 6.

42. *Rome Statute*, art. 112(7). While the delegates to the Rome Conference consistently asserted that they were not "legislating," the Rome Statute is fundamentally coercive and thus can be considered a law-making treaty. *See generally* Paul Szasz, *General Law-Making Processes, in* 1 UNITED NATIONS LEGAL ORDER 35 (Oscar Schacter & Christopher C. Joyner, eds., 1995).

43. Subject, of course, to the oversight of the Assembly of States Parties. *Rome Statute*, art. 112(2)(b).

44. *Rome Statute*, art. 66. The Court will determine the meaning of reasonable doubt, as well as the punishment a defendant receives, for example, without reference to national law. Contrast in this regard articles 77 and 78 of the Rome Statute with article 47 of the 1994 ILC Draft Statute (permitting the Court to have reference to national law in sentencing). The only substantive role reserved for national law by the Rome Statute is the provision in article 21 that the Court may apply "general principles of law *derived by the Court* from national laws of legal systems of the world. . .". *Rome Statute*, art. 21(1)(c) (emphasis added). As a matter of procedure, however, State cooperation will largely be governed by national law.

45. *Rome Statute*, art. 17(1).

46. *Id.* art. 69(4). Conversely, article 69(8) provides that the Court shall not rule on the application of a State's national law when deciding the relevance or admissibility of evidence collected by a State. *Id.* art. 69(8).

the material elements of the crimes so as to effectuate, as a matter of substantive international criminal law, the repartition of prescriptive jurisdictional competence effected by the Statute. This could have important consequences for the pleading and proving of elements of offenses, and could streamline the caseload of the Court considerably by eliminating the need to relitigate jurisdictional elements (such as whether a state of armed conflict existed, for example) more than once.

With respect to aggression, although the International Military Tribunal at Nuremberg labeled aggressive war the "supreme international crime," containing within itself the "accumulated evil of the whole,"[47] the international community has been unable to achieve consensus as to what the elements of the crime of aggression are, and when criminal responsibility for the offense should attach. Moreover, the right to use force in self-defense (and, in earlier times, to pursue political or other agendas) is one of the most cherished prerogatives of the State. Although many fervently argued that omitting aggression from the ICC's jurisdiction would mark a retreat from the Nuremberg principles, others countered that its inclusion could scuttle the Court entirely. Through a clever compromise, the Rome Statute includes aggression, but leaves it undefined and, therefore, unimplemented for the time being.[48]

In addition to defining the crimes within the Court's jurisdiction, the Framers applied their energies to elaborating a system of general rules pertaining to the imposition of criminal responsibility and the defenses thereto. Chapter 7 explores the general principles underlying the Rome Treaty, including the legality principle and the sources of law to be considered in the Statute's interpretation and application. The tremendous complexity of this part of the Statute cannot be overestimated. Among other things, the Framers were required to weld common and civil law

47. Judgment of October 1, 1946, International Military Tribunal, Judgment and Sentences, 41 AM. J. INT'L L. 172, 186 (1947).

48. Jurisdiction over the crime of aggression cannot be implemented without the Statute's amendment, which, at the earliest, may take place seven years after its entry into force. *See Rome Statute*, arts. 5(2), 121, 123. The adoption of amendments to the Statute absent consensus among the States Parties requires a two-thirds majority vote. If seven-eighths of the States Parties adopt an amendment, any State Party that did not accept it may withdraw from the Statute with immediate effect by giving notice no later than one year after the amendment enters into force, subject to the withdrawal provisions in article 127(2). *Rome Statute*, art. 121(6). All amendments to article 5 enter into force for those States that adopt the amendment one year after the deposit of their instruments of acceptance or ratification. *See id.* art. 121(5). The Court may not exercise jurisdiction over a crime covered by such an amendment if that crime is committed by a national of or on the territory of a State that did not accept the amendment. *Id.*

principles into an amalgam suited to the needs of international justice, establish a system that would preserve judge's prerogatives without undermining either the principle of legality or separation of powers, and grapple with extraordinarily difficult terminological debates. For the most part, these issues were resolved successfully.

Chapter 8 takes up the Statute's procedural regime. One of the major differences between the substantive provisions of the Statute and its procedural regime is the degree of flexibility enjoyed by the Framers in its formulation. As Chapter 5 explores, the Statute's regime of universal international jurisdiction required the Framers to adhere relatively faithfully to existing customary international and treaty norms, permitting only small innovations in terms of "progressive development" of the law. Procedure, however, was quite a different matter. Thus, unlike the substantive law explored in Chapter 6, and the general part of the Statute discussed in Chapter 7, we find in the Statute's procedural regime a fairly dramatic departure from past precedent. Indeed, the resulting regime in the Rome Statute is quite unlike any of its predecessors, including the procedural rules of the ICTY and ICTR.

In particular, the delegates noted the need to avoid excessive reliance on the common law legal tradition, as the ILC Draft had done, and lend balance to the Statute by drawing inspiration from the Civil law and, to a much lesser degree, other legal traditions.[49] They also needed to insure that the procedures adopted would adequately protect the rights of the defendant, and strike an appropriate balance between the requisite independence of the Court and the sovereignty of States.[50] Finally, they were

---

49. *Id.*; Silvia A. Fernández de Gurmendi, *The Process of Negotiations, in* THE INTERNATIONAL CRIMINAL COURT: THE MAKING OF THE ROME STATUTE 217, 220–24 (Roy S. Lee, ed., 1999). Particularly as regards terminology, the ILC's draft was quite common law in orientation. Prosecution began upon the establishment of a "prima facie case," and the filing of an "indictment" with the Registrar. *1994 ILC Draft Statute*, art. 27(1). This is also true of the two ad hoc tribunals. *ICTY Statute*, art. 18(4); *ICTR Statute*, art. 17(4), which, in response to criticisms that their procedures were excessively adversarial, have adopted at least some rules attempting to strike a better balance between the two. JOHN R.W.D. JONES, THE PRACTICE OF THE INTERNATIONAL CRIMINAL TRIBUNALS 163 (2000). Some disputes over terminology have been resolved in a purely cosmetic manner. Thus, although the ICC Statute avoids the term "prima facie," the concept, which was defined in ICTY Rule 47(A) as "reasonable grounds for believing that a person has committed a crime within the jurisdiction of the Court," reappears as the verbatim text of article 58(1)(a) of the Rome Statute.

50. One departure from the ad hoc tribunals practice suggested by the Ad Hoc Committee, for example, was to have the Rules of Procedure and Evidence prepared and adopted by the States Parties to the Treaty rather than the Court's

required to craft a Statute that would accomplish all of the above in enough detail so as to satisfy each position, without including levels of unnecessary detail that would render the Statute, which was after all a Constitutive document, unduly encumbered by minutiae that could make it impossibly long, difficult to negotiate, overly complex, and, because of the relatively cumbersome amendment process, insufficiently flexible to meet the continually changing needs of a fledgling institution.

The long and protracted negotiations of the procedural aspects of the Statute, and the efforts of the delegates intimately involved, were largely successful in achieving these goals. The Statute is rich in complexity without being overly verbose; elements of the civil and common law traditions have been blended in a way that would appear to suit the needs of an international criminal justice system; and defendants, as well as those persons under investigation by the Court, should be well-protected by the extensive panoply of rights contained in the Statute. The one glaring but perhaps inevitable exception to the Statute's overall success was the extensive concessions required to the sovereignty of States, which are particularly apparent in Part 9 of the Statute on International Cooperation and Judicial Assistance, and Part 10 on Enforcement.

Chapter 9 considers the relationship between the Court and its elaboration of international criminal law ("Rome law") and law "outside" the Rome treaty regime. The prospect of drafting a Statute for the ICC presented a unique opportunity to codify, advance, and refine the existing law.[51]

At the very least, an advantage of codifying the law would be that State practice arguably inconsistent with the normative principles of customary law would not comprise evidence that the custom was no longer accepted, but would, instead, constitute a breach of the norm.[52] As the negotiation of the ICC treaty proceeded, however, the disadvantages of

---

judges. *Report of the Ad Hoc Committee on the Establishment of an International Criminal Court*, U.N. GAOR, 50th Sess., Supp. No. 22, U.N. Doc. A/50/22 (1995) at para. 129. Another crucial issue for many States was the protection of information they considered essential to their national security, an issue not taken up here, but which engendered much controversy during the Statute's negotiation. *See*, Donald K. Piragoff, *Protection of National Security Information, in* THE INTERNATIONAL CRIMINAL COURT: THE MAKING OF THE ROME STATUTE 270–94 (Roy S. Lee, ed., 1999).

51. Pursuant to article 13 of the U.N. Charter, the General Assembly can "initiate studies . . . encouraging the progressive development of international law and its codification . . .". U.N. CHARTER art. 13.

52. One of the most articulate and thorough treatments of the interaction between treaty law, state practice, and custom can be found in the *Nicaragua* case before the International Court of Justice. Case Concerning Military and Paramilitary Activities in and Against Nicaragua (Nicaragua v. U.S.) (Merits) 1986 I.C.J. 14.

codification also became clear. Indeed, it began to seem that there might be a fundamental incompatibility between the political agendas of States and the process of codifying, in a progressive manner, the customary international law of war and crimes against humanity. Thus, the codification process was fated to produce a text that represented a set of political compromises, rather than a new set of progressive norms criminalizing behavior on a broad scale.[53]

Seemingly to ensure that the codification of some international criminal law in the ICC Statute would not negatively impact either the existing customary international framework or the development of new customary law, a unique provision was introduced during the Preparatory Committee's negotiations on the ICC. This proposal eventually became article 10 of the Court's Statute, and provides: "[n]othing in this Part of the Statute shall be interpreted as limiting or prejudicing in any way existing or developing rules of international law for purposes other than this Statute."[54]

If it is correct that the prescriptive norms of the Statute are universal in application, it appears paradoxical that article 10 of the Statute expressly attempts to deny them the status of custom, at least insofar as they might restrict existing or developing rules of customary international law, which would also bind all States. Chapter 9 explores this apparent contradiction and concludes that having law inside the ICC Statute differ from the law outside the Statute is inevitable. Countries may decide to advance the substance of the laws of war and humanity beyond the collection of compromises codified in the Rome Statute. Customary international law is both the product and the source of this evolution, although it is unclear whether in the long run, the international community may be able to have it both ways, asserting that universal "laws" made by treaty may differ from universal "laws" established by custom.

The overwhelming vote of the delegates to the Diplomatic Conference to approve the ICC Treaty opened a window to the future.[55] The substan-

---

53. There was little agreement during the drafting process as to whether a codification of international law "should merely declare and systematize existing rules or also include 'progressive development' [of international law]" as the United Nations Charter and Statute of the International Law Commission contemplate. Otto Triffterer, *Article 10, in* COMMENTARY ON THE ROME STATUTE OF THE INTERNATIONAL CRIMINAL COURT 316 (Otto Triffterer, ed., 1999).

54. A similar provision, article 80, was introduced in respect of the penalties provisions of the Statute, the negotiation of which also required a great deal of compromise.

55. Fanny Benedetti & John L. Washburn, *Drafting the International Criminal Court Treaty: Two Years to Rome and an Afterword on the Rome Diplomatic Conference*, 5 GLOBAL GOVERNANCE 1, 34 (1999).

tive law, institutional structure, procedures and foundations of the Court establish an extraordinarily rich and complex legal regime. Indeed, it is arguable that the contribution that the Statute and its adoption have made and will make to international law is separate from the question whether the Court is ultimately successful. The pace of ratifications has exceeded most expectations, and current predictions suggest that the Court's Statute will enter into force sometime in 2002. Yet the Revolution wrought by the Diplomatic Conference was in no sense an easy one, and the political will that carried the day in Rome must be translated into financial and logistical support if the Court is to succeed. As humanity struggles to overcome its darkest impulses in this new millennium, impulses that led not only to the slaughter of hundreds of millions during the Twentieth Century, but threaten our very survival, the creation of effective international institutions and regimes is essential. The fact of the Statute's adoption, as well as its normative content, demonstrate our willingness and ability not only to survive, but to evolve. It is conceivable, perhaps, that we have reached a stage during which a quantum leap in our thinking and behavior has become possible—enabling us to transform the prohibitions on the commission of genocide, war crimes, crimes against humanity and aggression into real tools to deter the cruel and the powerful. The journey from the Hague to Rome was long and arduous; it is to be hoped that the journey back to the Hague will be shorter, less encumbered, and ultimately successful. Humanity deserves no less.

CHAPTER 2

HISTORICAL EVOLUTION

> *If . . . the purpose of our endeavors is to create a better world . . . [w]e require . . . in effect, an understanding of those elements of structure that resist change, as well as a feel for the possibilities of innovation that lie within the shadowland cast backward by emergent potential structures of power. Only within this shadowland, if at all, is it possible to discern "openings" that contain significant potential for reform . . . .*
>
> —Professor Richard Falk, *The Grotian Moment*

The International Criminal Court's evolution over the course of the Twentieth Century took place in four distinct stages: the idea's emergence following the two Hague Conferences; its embodiment in the two international military tribunals at Nuremberg and Tokyo during the Second World War; the struggle to establish the Court during the post-war and cold war period; and, finally, the establishment of the two ad hoc tribunals and the negotiations and proposals leading to the adoption of the Court's Statute at the Diplomatic Conference in Rome. The journey was long and slow, with many false starts along the way. It began at the Hague and will end there with the Court's eventual establishment, most likely in the year 2002. In each stage, detailed proposals for the Court's structure and operation were issued. Although most were discarded, each contributed to the institution that ultimately emerged at Rome; an institution that, in many respects, can trace its revolutionary impact to its evolutionary origins.

I. EMERGENCE: 1899–1945

On August 24, 1898, the Russian Minister of Foreign Affairs proposed to Czar Nicholas II that the governments of the world tackle the problems stemming from the arms build-up in recent years.[1] The result was the Peace Conference held in the Hague in 1899. Unlike the Rome Conference held nearly 100 years later, very few nations attended, no women were present, and the proceedings were highly formal and conducted in relative secrecy. Twenty-six countries (out of fifty-nine claiming independent sovereignty) were represented by one hundred delegates who included in their ranks diplomats, statesmen, publicists, lawyers and technical and scientific experts.[2] Although the Conference was unsuccessful in reaching agreement on any general arms limitation, three conventions *were* adopted relating to the peaceful settlement of disputes (which established the Permanent Court of Arbitration), the laws and customs of war on land, and maritime warfare.[3]

A second peace conference was held in 1907. The conference was called at the initiative of the Inter-Parliamentary Union which was meeting in St. Louis, Missouri, the site of the 1904 World's Fair. The meeting unanimously adopted a resolution which was sent to President Roosevelt. At the President's suggestion, the Czar once again sent an invitation to the governments of the world to assemble at The Hague for a second peace conference.[4] Forty-four countries sent delegates this time, construction of the Peace Palace began, and the Conference concluded successfully with the adoption of thirteen Conventions (three of which revised the 1899 Conventions), including Convention (IV) Respecting the Laws and Customs of War on Land.[5]

---

1. WILLIAM I. HULL, THE TWO HAGUE CONFERENCES AND THEIR CONTRIBUTIONS TO INTERNATIONAL LAW 2–3 (Boston, 1908). *See also* JAMES BROWN SCOTT, I THE HAGUE PEACE CONFERENCES OF 1899 AND 1907 (1909); JOSEPH H. CHOATE, THE TWO HAGUE CONFERENCES (1913).

2. George H. Aldrich and Christine M. Chinkin, *Symposium: The Hague Peace Conferences*, 94 AM. J. INT'L L. 1, 1 (2000).

3. *Id.* at 10, 35–36. Convention [No. I] Regarding the Pacific Settlement of International Disputes, July 29, 1899, 32 Stat. 1779, 1 Bevans 230; Convention [No. II] with Respect to the Laws and Customs of War on Land, with annex of regulations, July 29, 1899, 32 Stat. 1803, 1 Bevans 247; Convention [No. III] for the Adaptation to Maritime Warfare of the Principles of the Geneva Conventions of 22 August 1864, July 29, 1899, 32 Stat. 1827, 1 Bevans 263. The Conference also adopted three Declarations.

4. WILLIAM I. HULL, THE TWO HAGUE CONFERENCES AND THEIR CONTRIBUTIONS TO INTERNATIONAL LAW 4–5 (Boston, 1908).

5. Convention [No. IV] Respecting The Laws and Customs of War on Land, Oct. 18, 1907, art. 2, 36 Stat. 2277, T.S. No. 539, 1 Bevans 631. On the Hague Conventions generally, *see* Detlev F. Vagts, *The Hague Conventions and Arms Control*, 94 AM. J. INT'L L. 31 (2000).

The treaties signed at the Hague were silent as to whether or not particular uses of force were lawful. They regulated only the *means* an actor could employ in achieving his military objectives once the decision to use force had already been made. Moreover, the self-congratulatory feelings following the two Hague Peace Conferences quickly dissipated as a century of bloody warfare transpired, each conflict followed by the adoption of new treaties condemning the wrongs that had just occurred. These instruments, as well as the customary international law that developed alongside them, came collectively to constitute and be known as international humanitarian law. Several of the new instruments regulated not only the *jus in bello* but also the *jus ad bellum*. In particular, the League of Nations Charter purported to restrain the use of force by replacing unilateral decision making with a weak version of collective security. These efforts, however, were largely ineffective.

The attempts to regulate warfare that emerged from the two Hague Conferences were constrained by notions of State sovereignty prevalent at the time: First, that the ruler of a State exercises sole authority over the territory of that State; second, that all States are juridically equal; third, that States are not subject to any law, other than their own, to which they do not consent.[6] Thus, Hague Convention IV contemplated that only the parties to the treaty would be bound by the rules of war therein, and then only if "all the belligerents were parties."[7] In addition, the only remedy for a breach of the Convention was State responsibility and a right to compensation inuring to the injured party, "if the case demands."[8] The language of the Martens Clause which provided that in cases not included in the Hague Regulations, "the inhabitants and the belligerents remain under the protection and the rule of the principles of the law of nations, as they result from the usages established among civilized peoples, from the laws of humanity, and the dictates of the public conscience,"[9] suggests that the States Parties conceded that some law lay outside the four corners of the treaty. Nevertheless, no thought was given to criminal responsibility for violations of the treaty's proscriptions.

By the end of World War I, however, when the "world lay breathless and ashamed"[10] by the devastation of a war characterized by bitter savagery

6. ANTHONY C. AREND & ROBERT J. BECK, INTERNATIONAL LAW AND THE USE OF FORCE: BEYOND THE U.N. CHARTER PARADIGM 16 (1993).

7. Convention [No. IV], art. 2.

8. *Id.* art. 3.

9. *Id.* preamble.

10. WILLIAM I. HULL, THE TWO HAGUE CONFERENCES AND THEIR CONTRIBUTIONS TO INTERNATIONAL LAW 1 (Boston, 1908) (describing the first quarter of the *Nineteenth* Century).

and monstrous slaughter, the idea that some *criminal* liability might be imposed for acts of war beyond the pale surfaced. This concept departed dramatically from Hague law and ideas of sovereignty firmly held by virtually all at the time. Nevertheless, following World War I it was seriously proposed that war crimes prosecutions occur. Over American objections, the Commission on the Responsibility of the Authors of the War and on the Enforcement of Penalties[11] proposed the formation of an international "high tribunal" for the trial of "all enemy persons alleged to have been guilty of offenses against the laws and customs of war and the laws of humanity."[12] After difficult negotiations, articles 227, 228 and 229 of the Treaty of Versailles provided for a "special tribunal" that would try the German Emperor, William II of Hohenzollern, for the "supreme offence against international morality and the sanctity of treaties."[13] The trial never occurred, however, as the Netherlands refused to extradite William II. Indeed, the whole effort was generally considered a fiasco.

Following this attempt to establish an international criminal tribunal, proposals for the establishment of a permanent international criminal court issued from many quarters. None was successful. The Advisory Committee of Jurists of the League of Nations submitted a Resolution (*Voeu*) to establish a High Court of International Justice, composed of one member from each State, which would be "competent to try crimes constituting a breach of international public order or against the universal law of nations, referred to it by the Assembly or by the Council of the League of Nations."[14] The Resolution was ultimately ignored. The International Law Association (ILA) adopted a statute for an international

---

11. The Commission was established at the plenary session of the Preliminary Peace Conference in 1919. *Historical Survey of the Question of International Criminal Jurisdiction: Memorandum Submitted by the Secretary General*, at 7, U.N. Doc. A/CN.4/7/Rev.1, U.N. Sales No. 1949.V.8 (1949).

12. *Commission on the Responsibility of the Authors of the War and on Enforcement of Penalties: Report Presented to the Preliminary Peace Conference*, 14 AM. J. INT'L L. 95, 123 (1920).

13. Treaty of Peace Between the Allied and Associated Powers and Germany, June 28, 1919, art. 227, *reprinted in* 11 MARTENS NOUVEAU RECUEIL (Ser. 3) 323 (Fr.). The Tribunal was to be international in character, being composed of five judges appointed, one each, by the United States, Great Britain, France, Italy and Japan, respectively. *Id.*

14. *Procès-verbaux* of the proceedings of the Advisory Committee of Jurists, 1920, p. 503. For a discussion of the *voeu* and its fate in the League of Nations, see Manley O. Hudson, *The Proposed International Criminal Court*, 32 AM. J. INT'L L. 549, 550 (1938); Lord Phillimore, *An International Criminal Court and the Resolutions of the Committee of Jurists*, 1922–23 BRIT. Y.B. INT'L L. 79.

criminal court in 1926, as did the International Association of Penal Law in 1928. Both drafts envisaged that the court would be a division of the Permanent Court of International Justice, and both proposed the trial of States as well as individuals. Neither draft was ever officially considered.

The idea was again revived after the assassination of King Alexander of Yugoslavia in 1934, and in 1937 a convention was opened for signature on the creation of an international criminal court that would try persons accused of offenses established in the Convention for the Prevention and Punishment of Terrorism. Because the proposed court's subject matter jurisdiction was limited and relatively well-defined, it avoided many of the objections raised to earlier proposals. Nevertheless, the convention was signed by only thirteen nations, and never entered into force.[15]

During this phase of the ICC's history, three major obstacles arose. First, the question of sovereignty was still omnipresent. An international court that could try and sentence individuals was incompatible with the notion that international law governs only inter-State relations. Closely related to objections concerning national sovereignty was a proposed "right" to be judged by one's own people according to domestic law, rather than by foreigners under international law.

Second, critics pointed to the absence of positive law with which potential defendants could be charged. Some argued that there could be no international criminal law because there was no international sovereign power. As a corollary, it was asked *"Faut-il avoir la Cour avant la Loi, ou la Loi avant la Cour?"* Although many scholars answered that the ICC would function as kind of common law court, meaning that the code need not precede the Court's establishment, this notion ultimately ran afoul of three countervailing trends: an increasing awareness of the need for fairness in criminal proceedings; the establishment of legal positivism as the prevailing conception of legitimate lawmaking; and, as an additional dimension of the sovereignty concern, the reluctance of States to surrender sovereignty to the court if the crimes were not clearly defined in advance.

Finally, not all agreed that an international criminal court could help prevent war, which was a fundamental premise of the court's establishment. Of course, no one seriously suggested that the proposed court alone

---

15. Convention for the Creation of an International Criminal Court, *opened for signature*, Nov. 16, 1937, LEAGUE OF NATIONS O.J. Spec. Supp. 156 (1938); League of Nations Doc. C.547(I)M.384(I)1937V (never entered into force), *reprinted in* 7 INTERNATIONAL LEGISLATION (1935–1937), at 878 (Manley O. Hudson ed., 1941). *See also Historical Survey of the Question of International Criminal Jurisdiction: Memorandum Submitted by the Secretary General*, at 16, U.N. Doc. A/CN.4/7/Rev.1, U.N. Sales No. 1949.V.8 (1949).

could prevent war. Rather, they hoped that the court's establishment would contribute to that goal. But some contended that the court would actually worsen international relations:

> This Court would render a peace impossible. When the soldiers and sailors had finished fighting, when hostilities were over and the soldiers and sailors on both sides were ready to shake hands with one another, as they are today, the lawyers would begin a war of accusation and counter accusation and recrimination. Such a war would render a peace of reconciliation impossible.[16]

II. THE NUREMBERG AND TOKYO TRIALS

The atrocities of the Second World War rekindled interest in the establishment of a permanent international criminal court. Once again, a variety of proposals ensued. Hans Kelsen, in *Peace Through Law*, proposed the punishment of war criminals by an international criminal tribunal;[17] the International Commission for Penal Reconstruction and Development issued a report (but no definite proposal) discussing the possibility of establishing an international criminal court; and the United Nations War Crimes Commission, established by a conference of the Allied Governments to investigate war crimes, drafted a convention for the establishment of a United Nations war crimes court to try war criminals.[18]

One of the more detailed statutes was the proposal of the London International Assembly established in 1941 under the auspices of the League of Nations. Like the ICC established at Rome, the court proposed by the Assembly would have heard only cases in which "no domestic court of any one of the United Nations has jurisdiction to try the accused and . . . [is] in a position and willing to exercise such jurisdiction."[19] The

16. Leila Sadat Wexler, *The Proposed Permanent International Criminal Court: An Appraisal*, 29 CORNELL J. INT'L L. 665, 672 (1996) (quoting remarks of Sir Graham Bower to the 1926 meeting of the International Law Association). To this, one member retorted "the honorable gentleman seems to forget that behind the shake hands [sic] there are millions of mourning widows and crying orphans." *Id.*

17. HANS KELSEN, PEACE THROUGH LAW 110–24 (Garland, 1973).

18. *Historical Survey of the Question of International Criminal Jurisdiction: Memorandum Submitted by the Secretary General*, at 19–20, U.N. Doc. A/CN.4/7/Rev.1, U.N. Sales No. 1949.V.8 (1949). *See also* TELFORD TAYLOR, THE ANATOMY OF THE NUREMBERG TRIALS 26 (1992).

19. *Historical Survey of the Question of International Criminal Jurisdiction: Memorandum Submitted by the Secretary General*, at 98, U.N. Doc. A/CN.4/7/Rev.1, U.N. Sales No. 1949.V.8 (1949).

court would have had jurisdiction only over a fairly loosely defined set of "war crimes."[20] One interesting aspect of the Statute that set it apart from other efforts was the provision for an international constabulary charged with the "execution of the orders of the Court and of the Procurator General [of the Court]."[21]

The model statutes proposed by jurists gave way to the pressure of political events, however, and the Charters of the Nuremberg and Tokyo tribunals took their place. Although not the first international criminal trials in history,[22] the Nuremberg and Tokyo trials are the first major precedents of our time. Much less weight is generally accorded to the decision of the International Military Tribunal for the Far East than to Nuremberg for a variety of reasons, including the perception that the Tokyo proceedings were substantially unfair to many of the defendants. Indeed, its example is primarily relevant in considering what a credible international criminal justice system ought *not* to look like.[23]

---

20. *Id.* art. 2.

21. *Id.* art. 25. *See* Leila Sadat Wexler, *The Proposed Permanent International Criminal Court: An Appraisal*, 29 CORNELL J. INT'L L. 665, 672 n. 41 (1996).

22. Precedents as early as the trial of Conradin von Hohensafen in Naples in 1268 who was convicted of waging an unjust war, and in 1474 of Peter von Hagenbach in Austria who was arraigned before a tribunal of twenty-eight judges drawn from States opposing the Burgundians who had appointed him to force the Austrian town of Briesach to submit to Burgundian rule, have been cited. *See* M. Cherif Bassiouni, *The Time has come for an International Criminal Court*, 1 IND. INT'L & COMP. L. REV. 1 (1991); Timothy L.H. McCormack, *From Sun Tzu to the Sixth Committee: The Evolution of an International Criminal Law Regime, in* THE LAW OF WAR CRIMES: NATIONAL AND INTERNATIONAL APPROACHES 37–39 (Timothy L.H. McCormack & Gerry J. Simpson, eds., 1997). *See also* M. Cherif Bassiouni, *From Versailles to Rwanda in Seventy-Five Years: The Need to Establish a Permanent International Criminal Court*, 10 HARV. HUM. RTS. J. 11 (1997).

23. The Tokyo proceedings were conducted by the International Military Tribunal for the Far East, which was established by a Special Proclamation issued by General Douglas MacArthur as the Supreme Commander for the Allied Powers. *See* Special Proclamation: Establishment of an International Military Tribunal for the Far East, Jan. 19, 1946, T.I.A.S. No. 1589, at 3, 4 Bevans 20. The Tribunal established consisted of eleven members, nine of whom had signed Japan's surrender agreement, and two others, India and the Philippines, who were added due to their status as members of the Far Eastern Commission. M. Cherif Bassiouni, *From Versailles to Rwanda in Seventy-Five Years: The Need to Establish a Permanent International Criminal Court*, 10 HARV. HUM RTS. J. 11, 31–32 (1997). The proceedings were generally considered to be procedurally, as well as substantively, unfair. *Id.* at 33. *See generally* B.V.A. RÖLING & ANTONIO CASSESE, THE TOKYO TRIAL AND BEYOND (1993); Elizabeth S. Kopelman, *Ideology and International Law: The Dissent of the Indian Justice at the Tokyo War Crimes Trial*, 23 N.Y.U. J. INT'L L. & POL.

Nuremberg, however, was clearly a watershed event in the ICC's progression from the drawing board to concrete reality. As is well known, upon winning the war, the victors decided to try the Axis leaders. The Allies had announced their intentions in the Declaration of St. James in 1942 and at Moscow, in 1943, but the decision to hold a trial was not a foregone conclusion. Indeed, it took a great deal of convincing, this time by the Americans of their British allies, to hold trials rather than summarily execute the Nazi leaders.

The International Military Tribunal at Nuremberg was constituted by an international agreement signed by the four Allied powers on August 8, 1945.[24] The Agreement was originally signed by the United States, the Provisional Government of the French Republic, the United Kingdom and the Union of Soviet Socialist Republics. Subsequently, nineteen other nations signed it as well. Known as the London Accord, the agreement stated the Allies' intention to try "war criminals whose offenses have no particular geographical location, whether they be accused individually or in their capacity as members of organizations or groups or in both capacities."[25] Annexed to the London Accord was the Charter of the International Military Tribunal.[26] The thirty articles of the Charter addressed the Tribunal's composition, rules of procedure and jurisdiction. They also defined, in summary fashion, the law to be applied.

Pursuant to article 6, the defendants, were arraigned on three charges: crimes against peace, war crimes and crimes against humanity. The Charter provided that the defendants were individually responsible for the commission of such crimes, notwithstanding their position as Head

---

373 (1991). Moreover, the allies' legacy in Japan is particularly problematic when one considers that on the very day the London Charter was signed, the United States dropped an atomic bomb on the Japanese city of Nagasaki, immediately killing at least 70,000 individuals. Gerry J. Simpson, *War Crimes: A Critical Introduction, in* THE LAW OF WAR CRIMES: NATIONAL AND INTERNATIONAL APPROACHES 4 (Timothy L.H. McCormack & Gerry J. Simpson, eds., 1997).

24. The Agreement for the Prosecution and Punishment of Major War Criminals of the European Axis, Charter of the International Military Tribunal, August 8, 1945, 8 U.N.T.S. 279, *reprinted in* 39 AM. J. INT'L L. 257 (Supp. 1945). *See generally The Charter and Judgment of the Nuremberg Tribunal: History and Analysis: Memorandum Submitted by the Secretary General*, at 3, U.N. Sales No. 1949.V.7 (1949).

25. The Agreement for the Prosecution and Punishment of Major War Criminals of the European Axis, Charter of the International Military Tribunal, August 8, 1945, art. 1, 8 U.N.T.S. 279, *reprinted in* 39 AM. J. INT'L L. 257 (Supp. 1945).

26. The Agreement for the Prosecution and Punishment of Major War Criminals of the European Axis, Charter of the International Military Tribunal, August 8, 1945, 8 U.N.T.S. 279, *reprinted in* 39 AM. J. INT'L L. 258 (Supp. 1945).

of State or the fact that the defendant may have acted pursuant to an order of his Government or of a superior.[27] The Charter also experimented with the idea of group liability and conspiracy charges. These concepts proved difficult to apply and dropped out of future proposals for the ICC.

Of the twenty-two individual defendants tried by the IMT, nineteen were found guilty and three were acquitted.[28] Although the criminal procedures employed by the IMT fall considerably short of modern standards, the trials were generally considered to have been conducted in a manner that was fair to the defendants, suggesting that international criminal trials need not be inherently unfair nor impossible to conduct in a manner satisfactory to jurists from diverse legal systems. It is indisputable, however, that the vanquished were tried by judges representing only the nationalities of the victors, and there is little doubt that the Tribunal was influenced by the political and psychological stress of the war.[29]

In issuing its judgment after nine months of trial, the Tribunal addressed many of the defendants' objections to the Tribunal's jurisdiction and the law it was asked to apply. First, the Tribunal rejected the defendants' arguments based on State sovereignty, holding that individuals, including Heads of State, and those acting under orders, could be criminally responsible under international law. In a now-famous phrase, the Tribunal stated: "[c]rimes against international law are committed by men, not by abstract entities, and only by punishing individuals who commit such crimes can the provisions of international law be enforced."[30]

Second, the Tribunal affirmed the primacy of international law over national law: "[T]he very essence of the Charter is that individuals have international duties which transcend the national obligations of obedience imposed by the individual State."[31] Thus the Nuremberg judgment seemed to lay to rest, at least as a practical matter, the theory that the constitution of an international criminal tribunal impermissibly contravenes the sovereignty of States *per se*. Of course, arguments may be made that

---

27. *Id.* arts. 6, 8.

28. Judgment of October 1, 1946, International Military Tribunal, Judgment and Sentences, 41 AM. J. INT'L L. 172, 333 (1947). Twelve were sentenced to death by hanging, three were sentenced to life imprisonment, and the others were sentenced to terms of imprisonment ranging from ten to twenty years.

29. *See, e.g.*, M. CHERIF BASSIOUNI, CRIMES AGAINST HUMANITY IN INTERNATIONAL CRIMINAL LAW 4, 12–13 (2d ed. 1999). One of the principal criticisms leveled at the Nuremberg and Tokyo trials was their ad hoc nature. Indeed, they represented "a conflict between legality and power." *Id.* at 37.

30. Judgment of October 1, 1946, International Military Tribunal, Judgment and Sentences, 41 AM. J. INT'L L. 172, 221 (1947).

31. *Id.*

this was possible only because of Germany's unconditional surrender (and subsequent loss of sovereignty to the Allies), but that contention is more persuasive as an explanation for the de facto power of the Allies to establish the tribunal and try the defendants than as an inherent limitation on the power of the Allies to try a suspect for committing an international crime (admittedly, very loosely defined) by establishing an international tribunal.[32]

Third, by holding that individuals may be liable for initiating a war, as well as for the means used in conducting it, the IMT established the wrongfulness of aggression. In this way, not only the *jus in bello* was criminalized but the *jus ad bellum*, which represents a quantum leap forward from the steps taken at the Hague half a century earlier.

The IMT Charter and Judgment are often criticized for being merely a (retroactive) *droit ad hoc*.[33] Indeed, as the defendants argued before the IMT, prior to the Charter's signature, for the most part no instrument specifically proscribed their conduct. This was particularly true as regards crimes against humanity. Moreover, even where an international instrument did exist, such as the Kellogg-Briand pact, which was relied upon to establish the crimes against peace charge, the treaty instrument cited did not penalize individual behavior, but was either silent as to the remedy for breach or contemplated only State responsibility.

Nonetheless, having embodied its judgment in a legal precedent, the Tribunal arguably created the positive law thought to be lacking prior to its existence.[34] As Robert Jackson, Chief Prosecutor for the United States of America, noted (quoting Justice Benjamin Cardozo), the power of precedent is the power of the "beaten path."[35] And while the IMT's judgment is not legally *binding* upon either municipal or international courts, its moral force is clear. Freed from its original limitations, the Nuremberg judgment has come to embody the idea that war as a means of solving interstate conflict is morally, legally, and politically wrong.

---

32. *See also* Egon Schwelb, *Crimes Against Humanity*, 1946 BRIT. Y.B. INT'L L. 178, 210–11.

33. CLAUDE LOMBOIS, DROIT PÉNAL INTERNATIONAL 157 (1979).

34. As Professor Meron has observed, in contrast to the ICTY, the IMT "paid little attention to the process or rationale by which various provisions of humanitarian conventions were transformed into customary law." Theodor Meron, *The Role of Custom in the Formation of International Humanitarian Law*, 90 AM. J. INT'L L. 238, 239 (1996).

35. ROBERT H. JACKSON, THE NÜRNBERG CASE xv (New York, 1971).

III. THE POST-WAR PERIOD

Nuremberg helped overcome objections to an international criminal court based on sovereignty. But the use of ad hoc tribunals such as the IMT raises several problems.[36] First, no matter how "fair" the actual trial proceedings, ad hoc tribunals give the impression of arbitrary and selective prosecution. This charge was leveled at both the Nuremberg and Tokyo Tribunals and is a recurring complaint about the International Criminal Tribunals for the Former Yugsolavia (ICTY) and Rwanda (ICTR), where both defendants and commentators have raised the issue of the tribunals' legitimacy. Of course, the ICTY and ICTR, unlike the IMT at Nuremberg (and the IMTFE at Tokyo), are not military tribunals but were established by Security Council Resolution. Moreover, the judges are not the nationals of victorious powers passing judgment on the vanquished, but are drawn from many nations. Nevertheless, the creation of ad hoc tribunals by the Security Council is arguably nondemocratic in that it denies most States a "vote" on the court's establishment, and circumvents the right of nations to engage in a debate about their cession of sovereignty.[37]

Second, there is the problem of delay. Ad hoc tribunals represent a post hoc mechanism that takes time to establish—time during which evidence may be destroyed and additional lives lost. A permanent tribunal would provide the international community with an existing mechanism able promptly to investigate and prosecute reported war crimes and other atrocities.

Finally, and perhaps most critically, ad hoc tribunals fail to build the kinds of institutional memory and competence that are the hallmark of a permanent court. Each time prosecutors must be found, staff must be assembled and trained, and judges must be procured who are willing and able to leave their existing commitments, and who may have little or no experience in international criminal law. These problems might not only damage the ad hoc court's ability to conduct an effective prosecution and

---

36. Ruth Wedgwood, *The Case for a Permanent War Crimes Court*, THE CHRISTIAN SCIENCE MONITOR, Aug. 16, 1995, at 19.

37. Christopher L. Blakesley, *Obstacles to the Creation of a Permanent War Crimes Tribunal*, 18 FLETCHER FORUM WORLD AFF. 77 (1992). On the ICTY, *see generally* VIRGINIA MORRIS & MICHAEL P. SCHARF, AN INSIDER'S GUIDE TO THE INTERNATIONAL CRIMINAL TRIBUNAL FOR THE FORMER YUGOSLAVIA (1995); M. CHERIF BASSIOUNI & PETER MANIKAS, THE LAW OF THE INTERNATIONAL CRIMINAL TRIBUNAL FOR THE FORMER YUGOSLAVIA (1996). On the ICTR *see generally* VIRGINIA MORRIS & MICHAEL P. SCHARF, THE INTERNATIONAL CRIMINAL TRIBUNAL FOR RWANDA (1998).

trial, but could also adversely affect the rights of the defendant. The latter is particularly likely when hasty recruitment results in inexperience and unthinking zeal in those investigating, prosecuting and judging the accused.

Thus it is not surprising that immediately after World War II, the United Nations considered the establishment of a permanent international criminal court. The subject was raised in connection with the formulation and adoption of the Genocide Convention in 1948. Yet although the Genocide Convention was adopted relatively quickly, efforts to create the international criminal tribunal envisaged in article VI of the Convention failed. Indeed, the reference to an international penal tribunal now found in article VI had been deleted from earlier drafts, and was restored only after extensive debate.[38]

In a resolution accompanying the adoption of the Genocide Convention, the General Assembly invited the newly-established International Law Commission, along with its work on the codification of international criminal law, to "study the desirability and possibility of establishing an international judicial organ for the trial of persons charged with genocide or other crimes over which jurisdiction will be conferred upon that organ by international conventions."[39] It also requested the Commission to consider the possibility that this might be accomplished through the creation of a Criminal Chamber of the International Court of Justice. Thus instructed, the ILC embarked upon what would prove to be a long and frustrating endeavor. Although the international community adopted a series of instruments in addition to the Genocide Convention following World War II that not only prohibited the worst atrocities, but also required States to impose criminal sanctions on those responsible for their commission,[40] there was no mechanism for ensuring that they do so, and

---

38. The Soviet delegation, in particular, objected to the creation of an international penal jurisdiction on the grounds that it would violate national sovereignty. Others felt that the organization of an international criminal court was premature either because there existed no international criminal law or because there existed as yet no international enforcement mechanism. Upon the insistence of the French delegation and after a compromise proposal made by the U.S. representative, who suggested that the jurisdiction of the proposed international penal tribunal become optional, the provision was restored. On the Genocide Convention and its elaboration and interpretation *see generally* WILLIAM A. SCHABAS, GENOCIDE IN INTERNATIONAL LAW (2000).

39. *Prevention and Punishment of the Crime of Genocide*, G.A. Res. 260B(III), 2 UNITED NATIONS RESOLUTIONS, SERIES I: RESOLUTIONS OF THE GENERAL ASSEMBLY 241 (Dusan J. Djonovich, ed., 1973).

40. The Convention Against Torture or other Cruel, Inhuman or Degrading Treatment or Punishment, G.A. Res. 39/46, 39 U.N. GAOR Supp. (No. 51) at 197,

the International Law Commission was unable to advance the international criminal court proposal very far.

The ILC ultimately voted at its Second Session in 1950 to support the desirability and feasibility of creating an international criminal court. However, an examination of the Summary records and Reports on the topic shows that the Commission was deeply divided on this subject. Indeed, two separate reports were submitted to the Commission on the international criminal court, one supporting the court's establishment and a second rejecting it.

The first report, by Ricardo Alfaro, concluded that an ICC was both "desirable" and "possible."[41] Very few elements of Alfaro's report ultimately appear in the Rome Statute, particularly his proposal that the "international organ of penal justice" would exercise its jurisdiction over States as well as individuals. The report penned by Emil Sandström took the opposite approach. Sandström concluded that although the creation of an international criminal court was possible, it was not desirable.[42] Indeed, Sandström opined that the creation of such a court would "do more harm than good."[43] After heated debate, the ILC voted 8–1, with two

U.N. Doc. A/39/51 (1984); Convention on the Suppression and Punishment of the Crime of Apartheid, U.N. GAOR Supp. (No. 30), at 75, U.N. Doc. A/9030 (1973); and the grave breaches regime of the four Geneva Conventions of 1949. The Conventions provide that the High Contracting Parties "shall be under the obligation to search for persons alleged to have committed, or to have ordered to be committed, such grave breaches, and shall bring such persons, regardless of their nationality, before its own courts . . . [or] hand such persons over for trial to another High Contracting Party." Geneva Convention for the Amelioration of the Condition of the Wounded and Sick in Armed Forces in the Field, Aug. 12, 1949, art. 49, 75 U.N.T.S. 31, 62; Geneva Convention for the Amelioration of the Condition of Wounded, Sick and Shipwrecked Members of Armed Forces at Sea, Aug. 12, 1949, art. 50, 75 U.N.T.S. 85, 116; Geneva Convention Relative to the Treatment of Prisoners of War, Aug. 12, 1949, art. 129, 75 U.N.T.S. 135, 236; Geneva Convention Relative to the Protection of Civilian Persons in Time of War, Aug. 12, 1949, art. 146, 75 U.N.T.S. 287, 386. Building upon the Nuremberg precedent, some of these instruments target not only a State's treatment of foreigners or the nationals of another State, but a State's mistreatment of its own citizens. The Genocide Convention goes even further and criminalizes non-State action that amounts to genocide, as well.

41. Ricardo J. Alfaro, *Question of International Criminal Jurisdiction*, U.N. Doc. No. A/CN.4/15 (1950), *reprinted in* [1950] 2 Y.B. INT'L L. COMM'N 1, U.N. Doc. A/CN.4/SER.A/1950/Add.1, at 17.

42. Emil Sandström, *Question of International Criminal Jurisdiction*, U.N. Doc. No. A/CN.4/15 (1950), *reprinted in* [1950] 2 Y.B. INT'L L. COMM'N 18, U.N. Doc. A/CN.4/SER.A/1950/Add.1, at 23.

43. *Id.*

abstentions, that it was *desirable* to establish an international penal judicial organ, and 7–3, with one abstention, that its establishment was *possible*.[44]

Although the Commission ultimately adopted a Draft Code of Offenses Against the Peace and Security of Mankind in 1954,[45] the General Assembly removed the question of the court which might enforce such a code from the ILC and vested it in a committee composed of the representatives of seventeen Member States.[46] As was later pointed out, the General Assembly's action involved a reversal of roles that was curious: it had asked a body of jurists a political question (whether the creation of the court was desirable) and had subsequently entrusted a political body with the technical task of elaborating a draft statute.[47]

The Committee on International Criminal Jurisdiction met in Geneva during the month of August, 1951, by the end of which it had agreed to a draft statute (the Geneva draft) for an international criminal court. The Committee was careful to point out that it did not consider its terms of reference to include the issue of the *desirability* of the court's establishment; rather, its task was to elaborate concrete proposals for the consideration of the General Assembly to permit it "to appreciate the full scope of the problems involved."[48]

A detailed examination of the Committee's work reveals many features that reappeared in the 1994 ILC draft statute and ultimately the 1998 Rome Statute. To begin with, although the Committee felt that the most satisfactory course would be to establish the court as an organ of the United Nations, in light of the practical difficulties involved in amending

44. *Report of the International Law Commission to the General Assembly*, U.N. GAOR Supp. (No. 10), U.N. Doc. No. A/1316 (1950), *reprinted in* [1950] 2 Y.B. INT'L L. COMM'N 364, 374–78, U.N. Doc. A/CN.4/SER.A/1950/Add.1.

45. *Report of the International Law Commission Covering the Work of its Sixth Session*, 3 June–28 July 1954, 9 U.N. GAOR, Supp. (No. 9), U.N. Doc. No. A/2693 (1954), *reprinted in* [1953] 2 Y.B. INT'L L. COMM'N 195, U.N. Doc. A/CN.4/SER.A/1954/Add.1.

46. *International Criminal Jurisdiction*, G.A. Res. 489 (V), reprinted in 3 UNITED NATIONS RESOLUTIONS, SERIES I: RESOLUTIONS OF THE GENERAL ASSEMBLY 151 (Dusan J. Djonovich, ed., 1973).

47. *Summary Records of the Thirty-Fifth Session*, [1983] 1 Y.B. INT'L L. COMM'N, U.N. Doc. A/CN.4/SER.A/1983 at 21, paraphrasing CLAUDE LOMBOIS, DROIT PÉNAL INTERNATIONAL 83 (1979).

48. *Report of the Committee on International Criminal Jurisdiction on its Session Held from 1 to 31 August 1951*, U.N. GAOR, 7th Sess., Supp. (No. 11), U.N. Doc. A/2136 (1952) at 2, para. 11. The Committee members also made it clear that no member of the Committee would be committing his government to any of the Committee's decisions by participating in the Committee's deliberations and voting on the draft texts. *Id.* at para. 12.

the Charter, and the legal difficulties one might encounter in attempting to establish the court by General Assembly Resolution, the Committee ultimately recommended the court's establishment by multilateral convention.[49] This was the solution ultimately adopted at Rome. Although it was, as a practical matter, perhaps the only means to ensure the Court's timely establishment it has had the arguably negative effect of placing the Court and its operations outside the United Nations system, a point discussed further in Chapter 4.

The court was envisaged by the Committee as a "semi-permanent" institution that would hold sessions only when matters before it required consideration,[50] an idea that the ILC retained in subsequent incarnations of the court's Statute, but which was ultimately discarded at Rome. In addition, like the Rome Statute, the Committee's report provided that the court should hear cases against natural persons only, including heads of state and agents of governments.[51] The question of the criminality of States thus disappeared permanently from the agenda.

The proposed court's subject matter jurisdiction was limited to international crimes "provided in conventions or special agreements among States parties" to the Statute. This seemed to exclude many of the most serious international crimes, including aggression, from the proposal, although the opacity of the formula leaves matters quite unclear. Finally, cases could proceed only if the State or States of the accused's nationality, and the State or States in which the crime was alleged to have been committed, expressly conferred jurisdiction upon the court.[52] In addition, jurisdiction was subject to prior approval by the General Assembly. These elements of the 1951 Draft were not retained at Rome, at least not as initially proposed.

Very few Member States commented upon the proposed statute. The United Kingdom expressed the view that "the whole project [was] fundamentally unsound."[53] The French and Dutch delegations were more optimistic, and the General Assembly requested the formation of another seventeen Member State committee to re-examine several of the issues and prepare another report.[54] The second Committee met in New York

---

49. *Id.* at 3.

50. *Id.* art. 3.

51. *Id.* art. 25.

52. *Id.* art. 27. This declaration could either be made prior to the crime's commission or afterwards by special agreement or unilateral declaration. *Id.* art. 26.

53. *Comments Received from Governments Regarding the Report of the Committee on International Criminal Jurisdiction*, U.N. GAOR, 7th Sess., Annex 2, Agenda Item 52, at 1, U.N. Doc. A/2186 and Add.1 (1952), at 16.

54. *International Criminal Jurisdiction*, G.A. Res. 687 (VII), *reprinted in* 4 UNITED

during the summer of 1953 and issued its report with an amended version of the Statute annexed thereto.[55] The 1953 Committee modified the Geneva text in some respects, although not fundamentally.

The 1951 and 1953 Committee Reports were never implemented for lack of a political consensus on the desirability of creating an international criminal court. Instead, the idea stalled in the United Nations for more than thirty-five years. The General Assembly, which had postponed consideration of the Draft Code of Offences until a definition of aggression could be adopted, took twenty years to complete this task, despite several excellent reports on the topic by the International Law Commission.[56] Moreover, even after General Assembly Resolution 3314 had defined aggression, the body which should determine whether an act of aggression had been committed remained unclear. The preamble to Resolution 3314 specified that the Security Council would determine whether a "threat to the peace, breach of the peace or act of aggression" had occurred, in connection with the Council's responsibility to maintain or restore international peace and security. However, it remained ambiguous as to the relationship between such a breach of the peace and aggression as a criminal offence, simply labeling aggression "a crime against international peace."[57] The proper resolution of this question is still uncertain, as we shall see when we return to the question of aggression in Chapter 6.

The legal and political complexities of the ICC's establishment,[58] as well as the stalemate in the United Nations resulting from the Cold War, rendered action on the Draft Code of Crimes and the international criminal court virtually impossible, although the Draft Code remained on the General Assembly's agenda. But with the gradual thawing of East-West

---

NATIONS RESOLUTIONS, SERIES I: RESOLUTIONS OF THE GENERAL ASSEMBLY 147 (Dusan J. Djonovich, ed., 1973).

55. *Report of the 1953 Committee on International Criminal Jurisdiction*, 27 July–20 August 1953, U.N. GAOR, 9th Sess., Supp. (No. 12), U.N. Doc. A/2638 (1954).

56. *Definition of Aggression*, G.A. Res. 3314 (XXIX), *reprinted in* 15 UNITED NATIONS RESOLUTIONS, SERIES I: RESOLUTIONS OF THE GENERAL ASSEMBLY 392 (Dusan J. Djonovich, ed., 1974).

57. *Id.* at Annex, art. 5(2).

58. As noted earlier, the court would often be trying heads of State or other State officials, a highly sensitive and political question. In addition, the court's successful operation would ultimately require some cession of national criminal jurisdiction, as well as extensive cooperation by national authorities. *See* Roy S. Lee, *The Rome Conference and its Contributions to International Law, in* THE INTERNATIONAL CRIMINAL COURT: THE MAKING OF THE ROME STATUTE 1, 5–6 (Roy S. Lee, ed., 1999).

relations, work on the international criminal court resumed. In 1981, the General Assembly again requested the ILC to work on the Draft Code of Crimes.[59] Upon resuming work on the Draft Code, members of the Commission pointed out the need to establish a mechanism for the Code's eventual implementation,[60] and repeatedly asked the General Assembly whether the ILC should prepare an international criminal court statute.[61] Finally, on December 9, 1988, the Assembly asked the ILC to consider the question of the Code's implementation,[62] and in 1989 specifically requested the International Law Commission to address the question of establishing an international criminal court.

The 1989 resolution was introduced by a coalition of sixteen Caribbean and Latin American nations led by Trinidad and Tobago.[63] Because their primary concern was the problem of extraditing and prosecuting international narco-terrorists, the resolution went on to specify that the ILC should specifically address the crime of illicit trafficking in narcotic drugs across national frontiers, and presumably discuss the international criminal court (or other trial mechanism) in that context.[64]

---

59. *Draft Code of Offenses Against the Peace and Security of Mankind*, G.A. Res. 36/106, U.N. GAOR, Dec. 10, 1981.

60. *See, e.g.*, Doudou Thiam, Special Rapporteur, *First Report on the Draft Code of Offenses Against the Peace and Security of Mankind*, U.N. GAOR, 35th Sess., U.N. Doc. No. A/CN.4/364 (1983), at paras. 63, 67 (suggesting that the ILC should seek the General Assembly's opinion on the need for an international criminal court to enforce the code); *Summary Records of the Thirty-Fifth Session, reprinted in* [1983] 1 Y.B. INT'L L. COMM'N, U.N. Doc. A/CN.4/SER.A/1983, at 38, ¶ 16 ("[I]t would be inadvisable, if not dangerous, to make the code applicable to individuals without, at the same time, establishing an international criminal court.").

61. *Report of the International Law Commission Covering the Work of its Thirty-Fifth Session* 3 May–22 July 1983, 38 U.N. GAOR, Supp. (No. 10), U.N. Doc. No. A/38/10 (1983), *reprinted in* [1983] 2 Y.B. INT'L L. COMM'N 1, U.N. Doc. A/CN.4/SER.A/1983/Add.1 (Part 2), at para. 69. *See also, Report of the International Law Commission Covering the Work of its Thirty-Eighth Session,* 5 May–11 July 1986, 41 U.N. GAOR Supp. (No. 10), U.N. Doc. No. A/41/10 (1986), *reprinted in* [1986] 2 Y.B. INT'L L. COMM'N 1, U.N. Doc. A/CN.4/SER.A/1986/Add.1 (Part 2).

62. *Draft Code of Crimes Against the Peace and Security of Mankind*, G.A. Res. 43/164, U.N. GAOR, 43d Sess., Supp. (No. 49) at 280, U.N. Doc. A/43/49 (1988).

63. Their initiative is described in *Summary Records of the Forty-Second Session*, [1990] 1 Y.B. INT'L L. COMM'N, U.N. Doc. A/CN.4/SER.A/1990, at 39, para. 24.

64. *International Criminal Responsibility of Individuals and Entities Engaged in Illicit Trafficking in Narcotic Drugs Across National Frontiers and Other Transnational Criminal Activities: Establishment of an International Criminal Court with Jurisdiction Over Such Crimes*, G.A. Res. 44/39, U.N. GAOR, 44th Sess., Supp. (No. 49), U.N. Doc. A/44/49 (1989), at 311.

The ILC provisionally adopted a Draft Code of Crimes in 1991[65] and, in its forty-fourth session in 1992, created a working group on an international criminal court. The Working Group produced an extensive report outlining the general bases upon which, in its opinion, the establishment of the ICC could proceed.[66] The ILC adopted the basic propositions of the Working Group, as follows:

- an international criminal court should be established by a statute in the form of a treaty agreed to by States Parties;
- at least in the first phase of its operations, the court should exercise jurisdiction only over private persons as distinct from States;[67]
- the court's jurisdiction should be limited to crimes of an international character defined in specified international treaties in force. These should include the crimes defined in the draft Code of Crimes against the Peace and Security of Mankind (upon its adoption and entry into force), but should not be limited to the Code. It should be possible for a State to become a party to the Statute without thereby becoming a party to the Code;
- the court would essentially be a facility for States Parties to its statute (and on defined terms, other States). In the first phase of its operations, at least, it should not have compulsory jurisdiction, in the sense of a general jurisdiction which a State party to the statute is obliged to accept *ipso facto* and without further agreement;
- in the first phase of its operations, at least, the court would not be a standing full-time body. On the other hand, its constituent instrument should not be a mere draft or proposal,

---

65. *Report of the International Law Commission Covering the Work of its Forty-Third Session*, 29 April–19 July 1991, 46 U.N. GAOR, Supp. (No. 10), U.N. Doc. No. A/46/10 (1991), *reprinted in* [1991] 2 Y.B. INT'L L. COMM'N 1, U.N. Doc. A/CN.4/SER.A/1991/Add.1 (Part 2).

66. Annex, Report of the Working Group on the Question of an International Criminal Jurisdiction, at 58. *Report of the International Law Commission Covering the Work of its Forty-Fourth Session*, 4 May–24 July 1992, 47 U.N. GAOR, Supp. (No. 10), U.N. Doc. No. A/47/10 (1992), *reprinted in* [1992] 2 Y.B. INT'L L. COMM'N 1, U.N. Doc. A/CN.4/SER.A/1992/Add.1 (Part 2).

67. While the term "private persons" could be read as excluding public officials, the working group's report included a footnote referencing the Commission's draft code of crimes which had always referred to "individuals" (as opposed to legal entities), presumably the meaning intended here.

which would have to be agreed on before the institution could operate. Thus the statute should establish a legal mechanism which could be available to be called into operation as and when required;

. . . .

- whatever the precise structure of the court or other mechanism, it must guarantee due process, independence and impartiality in its procedures.[68]

Not all the Commission's members were pleased with the relatively modest proposals made by the Working Group. But, as the Group's chairman, Abdul Koroma, pointed out, the proposals represented a compromise between those who would have gone much further and those who felt that nothing should be done at all.[69] With the exception of the Court's jurisdiction, which was expanded in the 1994 Draft Statute, these proposals (which were themselves largely based on the work of the 1951 and 1953 Committees) were substantially adopted in the 1994 Draft Statute issued by the ILC. Many found their way into the Rome Statute, as well.

IV. THE APPIAN WAY

Following the Commission's report, the General Assembly granted the ILC a mandate to elaborate a draft statute "as a matter of priority,"[70] although many countries (including the United States) did not support the Draft Code of Crimes.[71] The project gained momentum after the creation of the ICTY by the Security Council.[72] The adoption of the ICTY's

---

68. *Report of the Working Group on the question of an International Criminal Jurisdiction, in Report of the International Law Commission on the work of its forty-fourth session*, 47 U.N. GAOR, Supp. (No. 10), U.N. Doc. No. A/47/10 (1992), *reprinted in* [1992] 2 Y.B. Int'l L. Comm'n 1, U.N. Doc. A/CN.4/SER.A/1992/Add.1 (Part 2), at 58 (footnotes omitted).

69. *Id*. at 6–7. *See also id*. para. 19.

70. *Report of the International Law Commission on the Work of its Forty-fourth Session*, G.A. Res. 47/33, U.N. GAOR, 47th Sess., Supp. (No. 49), at 287, U.N. Doc. A/RES/47/33 (1992).

71. *Comments and Observations on the Draft Code of Crimes Against the Peace and Security of Mankind Adopted on First Reading by the International Law Commission at its Forty-Third Session*, U.N. Doc. A/CN.4/448 and Add.1 (1993).

72. The ICTY was Established by S.C. Res. 808, U.N. SCOR, 3175mtg. at 2, U.N. Doc. S/Res/808 (1993). Pursuant to Resolution 808, the Secretary-General prepared a report containing comments on the articles of the statute of the tribu-

Statute not only suggested that a permanent court was needed, but that governments, including the United States, might be willing to support its establishment, at least under certain circumstances.[73] The creation of the ICTR shortly thereafter[74] underscored the aching need for the establishment of an international institution that could address serious violations of international humanitarian law. The successes of the two tribunals demonstrated the feasibility of international criminal prosecutions. Moreover, even the problems they faced in recruiting top-flight prosecutors and judges, obtaining suitable facilities for their work, financing their activities, and obtaining custody of suspects, as well as the allegations of corruption that beset the Rwanda tribunal, did not dampen enthusiasm for the ICC. Rather, they highlighted the urgent need for a permanent institution.

The International Law Commission considered two draft statutes before finally adopting a 60-article version in 1994.[75] Aware of the politics involved and perhaps wary of having its work shelved once again, the Commission took no position on some of the more difficult questions involved in drafting the Statute (such as the definitions of crimes and financing of the court), or deferred to State sovereignty on other issues (such as jurisdictional regimes and organizational structure). The ILC envisaged a court with jurisdiction over both treaty crimes and violations of international humanitarian law, that would act only when cases were submitted to it, and was, in all instances except for Security Council referrals, completely dependent on State consent for its operation. In fact, the State consent regime and system of jurisdictional reservations contem-

---

nal. The tribunal's state appears in an Annex to the Secretary-General's report. *Report of the Secretary-General Pursuant to Paragraph 2 of Security Council Resolution 808*, U.N. Doc. S/25704/Add.1/Corr. 1 (1993). The Security Council adopted the Secretary-General's draft of the statute without change in Resolution 827. S.C. Res. 827, U.N. SCOR, 3217th mtg., U.N. Doc. S/Res/827 (1993).

73. From its modest and somewhat troubled beginnings the ICTY has grown into a thriving international organization, employing more than 1000 staff members from over 70 countries, and expending more than U.S. $ 100 million annually. Kelly Dawn Askin, *The ICTY: An Introduction to its Origins, Rules and Jurisprudence, in* ESSAYS ON ICTY PROCEDURE AND EVIDENCE IN HONOUR OF GABRIELLE KIRK MCDONALD 13, 17 (Richard May, et. al., eds., 2000). Although the Tribunal initially had difficulties obtaining custody of its indictees, it recently scored an enormous moral and legal victory when former Yugoslav President Slobodan Milosevic was handed over to it for trial.

74. Established by Security Council Resolution 955. S.C. Res. 955, U.N. SCOR, 49th Sess., 3453rd mtg., at 2, U.N. Doc. S/Res/955 (1994).

75. *Report of the International Law Commission on the work of its Forty-Sixth Session*, U.N. GAOR, 49th Sess., Supp. No. 10, U.N. Doc. A/49/10 (1994).

plated by the Commission probably would have completely crippled the proposed court, except for those rare cases involving affirmative action by the Security Council. The basic premise upon which the ILC proceeded was that the court should "complement" national prosecutions, rather than replace them; that it should try only those accused of the most serious violations of international criminal law, in cases in which national trials would not occur, or would be ineffective. The ILC did not consider the court to be an institution that would unify or construct international criminal law, and thus did not grant the court any advisory jurisdiction, although there had been some discussion among Commission members as to the desirability of doing so.[76]

In its 1994 draft, the ILC proposed that the court should have four organs: a Judicial branch with a pretrial and appellate division; a Registry, a Procuracy, and a Presidency. It also provided that only States Parties and the Security Council could refer matters to the court, thereby excluding victims and the General Assembly from direct access. Finally, the proposed draft would have permitted the court's organs, with the exception of the Registry, to function only "intermittently," meaning that this new "permanent" institution was, as conceived by the Commission, only a "stand-by" court in fact.[77]

The ILC's Draft Statute was returned to the United Nations' General Assembly for consideration, and the General Assembly then established an Ad Hoc Committee, which met twice in 1995 to review the Commission's report.[78] The Ad Hoc Committee, ably chaired by Adriaan Bos, the Legal Advisor of the Ministry of Foreign Affairs for the Netherlands, rendered its report in late 1995, which became the basis for the work of the Preparatory Committee established by the General Assembly to consider the Statute.[79] While the Ad Hoc Committee focused on the general question whether the establishment of the Court was a viable possibility, the Preparatory Committee turned its attention to the text itself.[80] The Preparatory Committee, open to all members of the United Nations as well as members of specialized agencies, was charged with "preparing a

76. *Report of the International Law Commission on the work of its Forty-Second Session*, 45 U.N. GAOR, Supp. (No. 10), at 155, U.N. Doc. No. A/45/10 (1990), *reprinted in* [1990] 2 Y.B. INT'L L. COMM'N 1, U.N. Doc. A/CN.4/SER.A/1990/Add.1 (Part 2), at 24–25.

77. Daniel H. Derby, *An International Criminal Court for the Future*, 5 TRANSNAT'L L. & CONTEMP. PROBS. 307, 311 (1995).

78. U.N. GAOR, 6th Comm., 49th Sess., U.N. Doc. A/49/738 (Nov. 23, 1994).

79. *1994 ILC Draft Statute*, at 51.

80. Mahnoush H. Arsanjani, *The Rome Statute of the International Criminal Court*, 93 AM. J. INT'L L. 22, 22 (1999).

widely acceptable consolidated text of a convention for an international criminal court as a next step towards consideration by a conference of plenipotentiaries."[81] In 1996 and 1997, the Preparatory Committee held six official sessions, each lasting approximately two weeks, and several inter-sessional sessions.[82] Finally, in April 1998 it issued a consolidated text of a draft Statute for the consideration of the Diplomatic Conference later that summer.[83]

As Chapter 1 relates, the Diplomatic Conference to consider the April Draft Statute was held in Rome from June 15 to July 17, 1998.[84] Five weeks of difficult negotiations culminated in a 128-article Statute that reflected nearly a Century of work. In retrospect, the Rome Conference may have been the natural destination of the journey begun in 1899 at the Hague, but its successful conclusion was in no way inevitable. As others have noted, the "change in the political climate and in the attitude by governments towards an ICC was extraordinary."[85] Moreover, if the road to Rome was long and difficult, the journey from Rome to the seat of the

81. *Establishment of An International Criminal Court*, G.A. Res. 50/46, U.N. GAOR 50th Sess., U.N. Doc. A/RES/50/46 (1995).

82. In addition to several inter-sessional meetings held at the International Institute of Higher Studies in Criminal Sciences (ISISC) in Siracusa, Italy, members of the Bureau and working group coordinators held an important inter-sessional meeting from January 19–30, 1998 in Zutphen, the Netherlands, which resulted in the issuance of an important interim draft. M. Cherif Bassiouni, *Historical Survey: 1919–1998, in* STATUTE OF THE INTERNATIONAL CRIMINAL COURT: A DOCUMENTARY HISTORY 1, 24 (M. Cherif Bassiouni, ed., 1998).

83. For an excellent analysis of the Preparatory Committee's work, see M. Cherif Bassiouni, *Historical Survey: 1919–1998, in* STATUTE OF THE INTERNATIONAL CRIMINAL COURT: A DOCUMENTARY HISTORY 1 (M. Cherif Bassiouni, ed., 1998).

84. On the Conference's procedure and organization see Roy S. Lee, *The Rome Conference and its Contributions to International Law, in* THE INTERNATIONAL CRIMINAL COURT: THE MAKING OF THE ROME STATUTE 1, 13–26 (Roy S. Lee, ed., 1999); M. Cherif Bassiouni, *Historical Survey: 1919–1998, in* STATUTE OF THE INTERNATIONAL CRIMINAL COURT: A DOCUMENTARY HISTORY 1, 26–33 (M. Cherif Bassiouni, ed., 1998). *See also* Mahnoush H. Arsanjani, *The Rome Statute of the International Criminal Court*, 93 AM. J. INT'L L. 22 (1999); M. Cherif Bassiouni, *Negotiating the Treaty of Rome on the Establishment of an International Criminal Court*, 32 CORNELL INT'L L. J. 471 (1999); Philippe Kirsch & John T. Holmes, *The Rome Conference on an International Criminal Court: The Negotiating Process*, 93 AM. J. INT'L L. 2 (1999); John Washburn, *The Negotiation of the Rome Statute for the International Criminal Court and International Lawmaking in the 21st Century*, 11 PACE INT'L L. REV. 361 (1999).

85. M. Cherif Bassiouni, *Historical Survey: 1919–1998, in* STATUTE OF THE INTERNATIONAL CRIMINAL COURT: A DOCUMENTARY HISTORY 1, 18 (M. Cherif Bassiouni, ed., 1998).

Court at the Hague[86] will not be completed with ease. One of the major obstacles is the refusal of the United States to join this new international institution. There is no doubt that the failure of the United States to support the League of Nations contributed to the ultimate demise of that institution, and one wonders whether a lack of U.S. support could significantly diminish the ICC's chances of success. Although the Clinton administration ultimately signed the Treaty in a dramatic move on December 31, 2000, the last day the Statute was open for signature,[87] the Bush administration has hardened the U.S. position on the Court, moving from an attitude of cautious engagement to one of outright opposition.[88] This is unfortunate from the Court's perspective, for U.S. participation would mean much, both practically (in terms of enforcement, financing and logistical support) and morally to the fledgling Court.

Even assuming U.S. participation to be irrelevant to the ultimate success or failure of the institution, however, as some do,[89] 60 States must rat-

---

86. *Rome Statute*, art. 3(1).

87. *Rome Statute*, art. 125(1). *See, e.g.*, Thomas E. Ricks, *U.S. Signs Treaty on War Crimes Tribunal*, THE WASHINGTON POST, at A1, January 1, 2001.

88. The Bush administration has stated that it will not forward the ICC Treaty to the Senate. Barbara Crossette, *Powell Pledges Strong Support for Wide Spectrum of U.N. Activities*, THE NEW YORK TIMES, at A15, February 15, 2001. In addition, stung by the ouster of the United States from the Human Rights Commission, the House of Representatives voted to withhold $244 million in arrears from the U.N. and to restrict U.S. cooperation with the ICC. Maggie Farley, *Action on U.N. Dues Dismays Envoys*, LOS ANGELES TIMES, at A3, May 11, 2001, *available in* Lexis, Nexis Library, News Group File. The money was released just as this book was going to press in response to to the September 11, 2001 attacks on the World Trade Center and the Pentagon.

89. In a recent article Ambassador David Scheffer, who headed the United States' delegation in Rome, wrote in support of the Court, stating:

> The world is changing. The International Criminal Court will be established, soon. We have to decide whether we stand for the rule of law or squirm in the face of it. If we cannot stand for the proposition that heinous crimes against humankind will be answered and build the institutions to do that job in a very complex world, then our leadership in promoting the rule of law abroad will decline rapidly and the value of our own principles will erode. Others will take the lead.

David J. Scheffer, *A Negotiator's Perspective on the International Criminal Court*, 167 MILITARY L. REV. 1, 7 (2001). Elsewhere I have argued, along the lines of Samuel Huntington, that the United States' defeat at Rome suggests that it no longer exercises an unchallenged hegemony over world affairs. Leila Nadya Sadat & S. Richard Carden, *The New International Criminal Court: An Uneasy Revolution*, 88 GEO. L. J. 381, 447–57 (2000). *See* Samuel P. Huntington, *The Lonely Superpower*, 78

ify the Treaty[90] before the Court can come into existence. Moreover, before the Court can exercise its functions, the Preparatory Commission established by the Diplomatic Conference at Rome[91] must complete draft texts of Rules of Procedure and Evidence (RPE), the Elements of Crimes,[92] the relationship agreement between the Court and the United Nations, basic principles of the headquarters agreement, financial regulations and rules, an agreement on the privileges and immunities of the Court, a budget for the first financial year, and the rules of procedure of the Assembly of States Parties.[93]

As of this writing, the Preparatory Commission has held seven sessions and has successfully completed the Draft Rules of Procedure and Evidence and the Elements of Crimes, the text of which are found in Appendices 2 and 3, respectively. It has also made significant progress towards completion of the other documents and agreements required to bring the Court into operation,[94] as well as starting to build a consensus

---

FOREIGN AFF. 35, 35–37 (1999). Although I adopt Huntington's terminology distinguishing between the bipolar system of the Cold War era and the emergent Post-Cold War multipolar system, I do not adopt his analysis, which he grounds on fundamental divisions between cultures or "civilizations," which themselves strongly resemble larger versions of sovereign nation States. *See id.* at 45–46 (identifying cultural differences between countries with similar interests as reason for continued U.S. preeminence). For a more complete discussion see generally SAMUEL P. HUNTINGTON, THE CLASH OF CIVILIZATIONS AND THE REMAKING OF WORLD ORDER (1996). For a sampling of the extensive literature on the topic *see generally* BENJAMIN R. BARBER, JIHAD VS. MCWORLD (1995), LEA BRILMAYER, AMERICAN HEGEMONY: POLITICAL MORALITY IN A ONE-SUPERPOWER WORLD (1994); THOMAS L. FRIEDMAN, THE LEXUS AND THE OLIVE TREE: UNDERSTANDING GLOBALISM (1999); and PAUL KENNEDY, THE RISE AND FALL OF THE GREAT POWERS: ECONOMIC CHANGE AND MILITARY CONFLICT FROM 1500 TO 2000 (1987).

90. *Rome Statute*, art. 126(1).

91. *Final Act*, Annex I, Resolution F, para. 1. The Preparatory Commission consists of representatives of States which signed the Final Act of the Conference and other States which were invited to participate in the Conference. Under Paragraph 4 of General Assembly resolution 55/155, the Secretary-General was requested to reconvene the Preparatory Commission for an additional session in 2001, from September 24 to October 5, 2001.

92. *Final Act*, Annex I, Res. F, cl. 5. The resolution required the draft texts of Elements of Crimes and Rules of Procedure and Evidence to be finalized by June 30, 2000.

93. *Id.* at Annex I, Resolution F, para. 5.

94. These include a draft relationship agreement between the Court and the United Nations, U.N. Doc. PCICC/2001/WGICC-UN/RT.1/Rev.1, March 8, 2001, the draft financial regulations and rules of the Court, U.N. Doc. PCNICC/2001/WGFIRR/RT/Rev.1, March 7, 2001; a Draft agreement on the privileges and

on the definition of aggression. The Preparatory Commission's success, as well as the significant number of signatures and ratifications received to date, suggests that the Court may become operational as soon as July 2002. Of course, the two principal obstacles to the Court's successful operation—the State sovereignty paradigm and the political will to overcome it—raise concerns about the Court's future effectiveness. Indeed, the international community's failure to adequately support the ad hoc Tribunals[95] counsels caution in predicting the Court's ultimate success. Nevertheless, although the Court's future is impossible to predict, its establishment, after a century of travail, is an extraordinary achievement.

immunities of the Court, U.N. Doc. PCNICC/2001/WGAPIC/RT.1, March 8, 2001; and the Draft Rules of Procedure of the Assembly of States Parties, U.N. Doc. PCNICC/2001/WGRPASP/L.1, December 20, 2000. As of this writing, the headquarters agreement and the budget for the first year had not yet been addressed, but work on those documents will begin at the eighth session of the Preparatory Commission to be held from September 25 to October 5, 2001.

95. Michael P. Scharf, *The Tools for Enforcing International Criminal Justice in the New Millennium: Lessons from the Yugoslavia Tribunal*, 49 DEPAUL L. REV. 925 (2000).

CHAPTER 3

PURSUING INTERNATIONAL JUSTICE

Together we must rid this planet of the obscenity that a person stands a better chance of being tried and judged for killing one human being than for killing 100,000.

—Jose Avala Lasso
United Nations High Commissioner for Human Rights

As the preamble to the Rome Statute states, the establishment of the International Criminal Court was a direct response to the "unimaginable atrocities" of the Twentieth Century. According to the Framers, this response was required by our common humanity[1] and the threat that these crimes pose to international peace and security.[2] These two principles, which the Statute invokes to justify the jurisdiction of the international community over individuals in the legal sense,[3] also provide the Court with its *raison d'être*—the rule of law is offered as an antidote to the chaos of war; justice[4] is offered as a necessary, if not necessarily a sufficient, condition for peace.[5] Indeed, this is the foundational principle of the

---

1. *Rome Statute*, preamble, cl. 1. The Statute speaks of the "common bonds" that unite all peoples.
2. *Id.* cl. 3.
3. This point is taken up in Chapter 5.
4. *See also* CARLOS SANTIAGO NINO, RADICAL EVIL ON TRIAL x (Yale, 1996); GARY JONATHAN BASS, STAY THE HAND OF VENGEANCE 10–20 (Princeton, 2000). In addition to this foundational premise, the Statute contains several other principles of justice: that the accused shall be fairly treated, in accordance with due process of law, an idea taken up again in Chapter 8; that the victims of international crime shall be able to participate in the process of criminal justice and receive reparations for the harm they have suffered; and that the officers of the Court shall perform their functions impartially and in accordance with the law of the Statute and its ancillary instruments.
5. Peace building has many components, particularly in civil conflicts where there are "no border[s] to separate [former] antagonists." Ruth Wedgwood & Harold K. Jacobson, *Foreword: Symposium: State Reconstruction After Civil Conflict,*

Court's establishment, namely the notion that the punishment of those who commit crimes within the jurisdiction of the Court may prevent the reoccurrence of similar crimes in the future.[6]

Societies in transition and international negotiators, however, are often tempted to suggest that justice should be traded, or at least postponed, in exchange for peace. Prosecuting perpetrators of human rights atrocities from a former regime, it is argued, may plunge fragile societies back into chaos or bring about an endless cycle of recrimination. Indeed, it is sometimes suggested that criminal trials may do more harm than good. Challenges to full accountability come in many guises: amnesties, truth commissions, and realpolitik.[7] Each of these is a variation on a common theme: is obtaining justice consistent with the restoration of peace?

I. FOUNDATIONS: ACCOUNTABILITY

The most obvious response to the atrocities of the Twentieth Century would have been to stop them before they occurred or while they were occurring,[8] and there have been efforts to establish international "police forces" capable of doing so. Unfortunately, the international legal community has not yet developed either the political institutions or the legal and logistical infrastructure to effectively halt or prevent grave disturbances of international *ordre public*. Moreover, to hope that the international community will acquire the capacity to prevent the commission of atrocities in the near future seems unrealistic.[9] Even well-developed

---

95 AM. J. INT'L L. 1, 1 (2001). These include disarming the antagonists and restoring order, social reconstruction, rebuilding shattered economies, stabilizing political systems, rebuilding infrastructure, and repatriating refugees. *See* AN AGENDA FOR PEACE: PREVENTIVE DIPLOMACY, PEACEMAKING AND PEACE-KEEPING [Report of the Secretary-General pursuant to the state adopted by the summit meeting of the Security Council on Jan. 31, 1992], U.N. Doc. A/47/277-S/2411 (1992), U.N. Sales No. E.95.I.15 (1995). This chapter focuses only on the question of legal accountability, not the other elements involved in restoring peace.

6. *Rome Statute*, preamble, cl. 5.

7. For the view that State sovereignty is the principle obstacle to the enforcement of international humanitarian law, see Antonio Cassese, *Reflections on International Criminal Justice*, 61 MOD. L. REV. 1 (1998).

8. W. Michael Reisman, *Legal Responses to Genocide and Other Massive Violations of Human Rights*, 59 L. & CONTEMP. PROBS. 75, 75 (1996).

9. *But see* Payam Akhavan, *Justice and Reconciliation in the Great Lakes Region of Africa: The Contribution of the International Criminal Tribunal for Rwanda*, 7 DUKE J. COMP. & INT'L L. 325, 328 (1997) (arguing that because cataclysmic violence requires extensive planning it is both foreseeable and preventable). *See also* Hansjörg

national legal systems are often unsuccessful in combating criminal behavior *ex ante*, at least in democratic countries where most members of society are relatively free to travel and organize their affairs unfettered by government interference. It is only *after* behavior becomes problematic that governments intervene in the name of public safety; indeed, the largely retroactive operation of the law means that criminal behavior is generally not averted before the fact, and is only occasionally thwarted during the perpetration of the offense. Democratic societies respond to the tension between the need for order and the imperative of freedom by attempting to induce citizens to exercise self-restraint in the hope that most citizens will not commit crimes most of the time. Societies engage in norm-building that involves proscribing certain conduct and punishing breaches of those proscriptions with either civil or criminal sanctions. The intention is to deter potential offenders through inculcation of the norms and to instill general respect for the rule of law. While the various components of international "society" form a less cohesive body than the individuals and entities which constitute national or local communities, the international community has nevertheless come to hold similar aspirations for international law. Bereft of *ex ante* solutions and convinced for the most part that ignoring mass atrocities is ultimately unacceptable,[10] the international community has searched for *post hoc* mechanisms that might, at the international level, bring about some of the benefits generally believed to inure to society from the making and enforcing of rules of law.

One of the primary obstacles to establishing the rule of law at the international level has been the culture of impunity that has prevailed to date. Genocidal leaders flaunt their crimes openly, unconcerned about international reaction, which they suspect will range from wilful blindness (at best, from their perspective) to diplomatic censure (at worst). Yet as U.N. High Commissioner for Human Rights, Mary Robinson, has observed:

> Where domestic law and order has broken down, individuals may feel that they can commit even the most atrocious crimes without fear of legal sanction. When this happens, there is an urgent need to re-establish the principle of individual responsibility for

---

Strohmeyer, *Collapse and Reconstruction of a Judicial System: The United Nations Missions in Kosovo and East Timor*, 95 AM. J. INT'L L. 46 (2001) (advocating the establishment of a standby network of lawyers, judges and military forces to assist in post-conflict reconstruction).

10. *See, e.g.*, MARTHA MINOW, BETWEEN VENGEANCE AND FORGIVENESS: FACING HISTORY AFTER GENOCIDE AND MASS VIOLENCE 4 (1998).

> crimes. If serious human rights violations are not addressed and a climate of impunity is permitted to continue, then the effect will be to stoke the fires of long term social conflict. Where a community splits along religious or ethnic lines, such conflict can vent itself through cycles of vengeance over decades, and even centuries.[11]

As others have noted, the long term consequences of a culture of impunity have "created a political climate in which extermination, deportation, and wanton destruction" lie within a ruler's range of viable options.[12] The remedy proposed has been the establishment of international legal regimes and, more recently, international institutions, that can bring about the transition from a culture of impunity to one demanding accountability. Although mechanisms such as Truth Commissions, reparations to victims and civil proceedings have been proposed and used to address the problems suffered by societies victimized by mass atrocities, a cornerstone of the effort to combat impunity has been the traditional framework of the criminal law: the condemnation of certain behavior as *criminal*, not simply a breach of treaty or customary international law obligations, and the imposition of individual criminal responsibility.[13]

This use of the criminal law is not accidental. Standard criminology was developed in the context of behavior that attacks norms established by the State, not in the context, as is so often the case in international crimes, of normatively unacceptable behavior *by* the State. Nevertheless, the international community, frustrated with the inability of civil sanc-

---

11. Mary Robinson, *Genocide, War Crimes, Crimes Against Humanity* 23 FORDHAM INT'L L. J. 275, 277–78 (1999).

12. Payam Akhavan, *Beyond Impunity: Can International Criminal Justice Prevent Future Atrocities?*, 95 AM. J. INT'L L. 7, 13 (2001).

13. In 1996 the United Nations Commission on Human Rights issued a report to which was attached a set of principles defining and attacking the culture of impunity. The report defined impunity as "the impossibility, *de jure* or *de facto*, of bringing the perpetrators of human rights violations to account whether in criminal, civil, administrative or disciplinary proceedings since they are not subject to any inquiry that might lead to their being accused, arrested, tried and, if found guilty, convicted, and to reparations being made to their victims." *Question of the Impunity of Perpetrators of Human Rights Violations (Civil and Political)* U.N. Doc. E/CN.4/Sub.2/1997/20 (1997), at Annex II, Definitions, A. Although it appears to leave room for a variety of legal responses to the commission of atrocities, by referring to "criminal, civil, administrative or disciplinary proceedings," the definition clearly contemplates that "criminal proceedings" are the most appropriate response to atrocity.

tions, military reprisals and the doctrine of State responsibility to deter atrocities,[14] has increasingly moved towards a criminal model that treats the commission of atrocities as unacceptably disruptive behavior, for which *individual* offenders must be tried and punished.[15] Modern theories of criminal justice generally justify the punishment of criminals either on the basis of some benefit society can expect to receive as a result—to deter other criminals or to rehabilitate or incapacitate the offender (utilitarian theory), or because the criminal "deserves" punishment for the injury he has inflicted on society (retributive justice).[16] Both utilitarian and retributive aspirations are found in international criminal justice. Certainly it is hoped, although not empirically demonstrable, that erecting a system of international criminal justice (including national and international prosecutions) will prevent the reoccurrence of abuses and assist in repairing the havoc wreaked upon society thereby.[17] Indeed, this is the Statute's chief premise. Some support for its validity is found in early studies of the effects of the two ad hoc tribunals, which have suggested that because the violence in both cases was deliberately and systematically induced by unscrupulous leaders, a viable threat of punishment may have a positive and deterrent effect.[18] In addition, the criminal justice apparatus is also designed to ensure respect for the rule of law as a value in and of itself.[19]

---

14. Antonio Cassese, *On the Current Trends Towards Criminal Prosecution and Punishment of Breaches of International Humanitarian Law*, 9 EUR. J. INT'L L. 2, 3–4 (1998); Leila Nadya Sadat, *The Establishment of the International Criminal Court: From the Hague to Rome and Back Again*, 8 DET. J. INT'L L. & PRAC. 97, 102–07 (1999).

15. *See* Theodor Meron, *Is International Law Moving Towards Criminalization?*, 9 EUR. J. INT'L L. 18 (1998).

16. Leila Nadya Sadat, *Reflections on the Trial of Vichy Collaborator Paul Touvier for Crimes Against Humanity in France*, 20 J. L. & SOC. INQUIRY 191, 210 (1995). Retributive justice has many variants, as wonderfully explained in Joshua Dressler, *Hating Criminals: How can Something That Feels so Good be Wrong?*, 88 MICH. L. REV. 1448, 1451–53 (1990) *reviewing* JEFFRIE G. MURPHY & JEAN HAMPTON, FORGIVENESS AND MERCY (CAMBRIDGE, 1988). The most widely supported variant is what he calls "negative retributivism," which holds that it is morally wrong to punish an innocent person even if society might benefit from the action (but does not require the guilty be punished, which "positive retributivism" does). *Id.* at 1451. For a critique of modern retributive theory, see David Dolinko, *Three Mistakes of Retributivism*, 39 U.C.L.A. L. REV. 1623 (1992).

17. Stanley Cohen, *State Crimes of Previous Regimes: Knowledge, Accountability and the Policing of the Past*, 20 J. L. & SOC. INQUIRY 1, 22 (1995).

18. Payam Akhavan, *Beyond Impunity: Can International Criminal Justice Prevent Future Atrocities?*, 95 AM. J. INT'L L. 7, 12 (2001).

19. Indeed, "the idea that wrongs should be redressed, that reparation should be made to the injured is among the most venerable and most central of

Finally, by channeling accountability and punishment through an official mechanism, society hopes to avoid individual vigilantism, as well as to provide an impartial forum where individuals accused of crimes during a prior regime may be tried, with all the due process rights necessary to ensure that their treatment is not tantamount to a purge.[20] That is, the legitimacy of the trials require that the offenders receive all the benefits of due process and legality they themselves denied to their victims.[21] Public trials occurring in courts using rules of evidence and formalized procedures are invested with a solemnity and transparency often absent from other venues. Hopefully this not only provides a forum for the punishment of a particular defendant, but an arena in which the victims may be heard, and an "official" version of the truth recorded.[22] In addition, by employing the *criminal law*—the most coercive form of power generally available to a society to regulate social behavior—the international community (and its component States) is constructing a normative discourse that expresses deep condemnation of the behavior and support for its victims.

---

legal principles." Naomi Roht-Arriaza, *Punishment, Redress and Pardon: Theoretical and Psychological Approaches, in* IMPUNITY AND HUMAN RIGHTS IN INTERNATIONAL LAW AND PRACTICE 17 (Naomi Roht-Arriaza, ed., Oxford, 1995).

20. Purges have been another traditional response of societies in transition. As Professor Osiel notes, many societies have seen a "quick, decisive purge of enthusiastic collaborators" to be an effective alternative to criminal trials. Professor Osiel mentions Argentina and de-Nazification in Germany as examples, and notes the serious due process and other problems that attend the use of purges by a society. Mark J. Osiel, *Why Prosecute? Critics of Punishment for Mass Atrocity*, 22 HUM. RTS. Q. 118, 133 (2000). In post-War Europe they were common, the purge in France resulting in as many as 40,000 extrajudicial executions. Leila Nadya Sadat, *Reflections on the Trial of Vichy Collaborator Paul Touvier for Crimes Against Humanity in France*, 20 J. L. & SOC. INQUIRY 191, 197 n. 34 (1995). Indeed, the purge in France, while perhaps understandable, probably increased tensions in post-War France that, in combination with other factors, created a deep schism in French society that persists to this day. *See generally* JOHN F. SWEETS, THE POLITICS OF RESISTANCE IN FRANCE 213–17 (1976).

21. Stanley Cohen, *State Crimes of Previous Regimes: Knowledge, Accountability and the Policing of the Past*, 20 J. L. & SOC. INQUIRY 1, 22 (1995). For a critique of this position, suggesting that many safeguards afforded to defendants in national courts should not be extrapolated to the international arena, see Tom J. Farer, *Restraining the Barbarians: Can International Criminal Law Help?*, 22 HUM. RTS. Q. 90, 92–98 (2000).

22. For a superb treatment of many of the issues surrounding the use of criminal trials following mass atrocities see MARK OSIEL, MASS ATROCITY, COLLECTIVE MEMORY, AND THE LAW (1997).

II. ACCOUNTABILITY WITHOUT TRIALS? PEACE VS. JUSTICE

A. Truth Commissions and Amnesties

1. Truth Commissions

Truth commissions need not pose a challenge to accountability, for they do not prejudice the subsequent application of the criminal law. Indeed, truth commissions may facilitate accountability by serving as precursors to the adoption of measures of accountability that may include reparations, restitution, civil remedies, lustration laws, and even criminal prosecutions.[23] Rather than focusing on individual criminality, truth commissions attempt to focus on the overall pattern of abuses occurring under a prior regime. They are sometimes referred to as the "truth phase," after which the "justice phase" can begin.[24] The goal is to establish an accurate record of past atrocities, and to "lift the lid of silence and denial from a contentious and painful period of history."[25] In addition, truth commissions, unlike criminal trials, generally focus on the needs of victims, rather than the imperative of punishment.[26]

The Rome Statute in no way impedes the establishment of truth commissions, and it explicitly recognizes the rights of victims[27] in many

---

23. Many commentators position truth commissions as alternatives to prosecutions. But the question whether to establish a truth commission is quite separate from the issue whether any or all of the regimes' former leaders (or lower level offenders) will ultimately be prosecuted. *See* John Dugard, *Reconciliation and Justice: The South African Experience*, 8 TRANSAT'L L. & CONTEMP. PROBS. 277, 287 (1988); PRISCILLA B. HAYNER, UNSPEAKABLE TRUTHS: CONFRONTING STATE TERROR AND ATROCITY 87 (2001).

24. Stanley Cohen, *State Crimes of Previous Regimes: Knowledge, Accountability and the Policing of the Past*, 20 J. L. & SOC. INQUIRY 1, 12 (1995). As Professor Cohen notes, the truth phase of social transitions "is an onslaught on all [the] forms of denial—personal and collective, the conscious coverup and the convenient forgetting, the euphemistic renaming. This process can be as painful as its common metaphors imply: digging up graves, opening wounds." *Id.*

25. PRISCILLA B. HAYNER, UNSPEAKABLE TRUTHS: CONFRONTING STATE TERROR AND ATROCITY 25 (2001).

26. *Id.* at 28.

27. The term "victim" is defined in Draft RPE 85 as either "(a) natural persons who have suffered harm as a result of the commission of any crime within the jurisdiction of the Court" or "(b) organizations or institutions that have sustained direct harm to any of their property, which is dedicated to religion, education, art or science or charitable purposes, and to their historic monuments, hospitals and other places and objects for humanitarian purposes."

respects. While falling short of permitting victims to initiate cases as *parties civiles*, an option that many delegates argued strenuously for, the Statute requires the Prosecutor to take their interests into account in deciding whether or not to prosecute or investigate a particular person,[28] establishes a Victims and Witnesses Unit within the Registry,[29] allows them to participate at trial[30] and grants them a right to reparations.[31]

It is argued that truth commissions have generally had a positive effect, "often reducing tension and increasing national reconciliation, and perhaps increasing the understanding of and respect for human rights issues by the general public and political leaders alike."[32] Others emphasize their therapeutic powers, as a form of restorative justice, asserting that because victims may be able to narrate the account of their victimization without the cumbersome baggage and ritualized procedures of the criminal trial, they serve a "victim-centered" vision of justice much more than criminal trials could.[33] Nevertheless, truth commissions may threaten accountability where they are established by unrepentant governments to manipulate public perceptions at home or abroad, or represent an attempt to whitewash past atrocities, as was the case with the first truth commission established by Idi Amin in Uganda, in 1974, which was created partly as a result of international pressure and disregarded thereafter as Amin continued his brutal rule.[34] The same could be said, to a lesser degree, of

---

28. *Rome Statute*, arts. 53(1)(c), 53(2)(c).

29. *Id.* art. 43(6).

30. The Trial Chamber may refuse to accept an admission of guilt, when, *inter alia*, the Chamber believes that a "more complete presentation of the facts of the case is required in the interests of justice, in particular the interests of the victims . . . ." *Id.* art. 65(4). In addition, article 68 requires the Court to "take appropriate measures to protect the safety, physical and psychological well-being, dignity and privacy of victims and witnesses," *id.* art. 68(1), and may permit them to present their "views and concerns" where their "personal interests" are affected, so long as the manner in which they do so is not prejudical to or inconsistent with the rights of the accused and a fair and impartial trial. *Id.* art. 68(3).

31. *Id.* art. 75.

32. Pricilla B. Hayner, *Fifteen Truth Commissions—1974 to 1994: A Comparative Study*, 16 HUM. RTS. Q. 597, 610 (1994). Peter A. Schey, Dinah Shelton & Naomi Roht-Arriaza, *Addressing Human Rights Abuses: Truth Commissions and the Value of Amnesty*, 19 WHITTIER L. REV. 325, 337–38 (1997).

33. Elizabeth Kiss, *Reflections on Restorative Justice, in* THE MORALITY OF TRUTH COMMISSIONS: TRUTH V. JUSTICE 70–74 (Robert I. Rotberg & Dennis Thompson, eds., 2000).

34. Pricilla B. Hayner, *Fifteen Truth Commissions—1974 to 1994: A Comparative Study*, 16 HUM. RTS. Q. 597, 608 (1994). The Commission was known as the "Commission of Inquiry into 'Disappearances' of People in Uganda," held public

the truth commission established in Chad in 1990. Charged with the investigation of the Habré government's "Crimes and Misappropriations," the commission received space for its headquarters in the former secret detention center of the security forces where some of the worst abuses had occurred. This deterred many former victims from testifying before it. Moreover, although the commission "named names," and published a report, its findings were largely ignored and it has been suggested that the commission was primarily established to improve the new president's image.[35]

2. *Amnesties*

If the goal of truth commissions is remembrance, the purpose of amnesties is oblivion.[36] Derived from the Greek word *amnestia*, meaning forgetfulness, "[a]mnesty . . . connotes that the offender's crime has been overlooked because that course of action benefits the public welfare more than punishment would."[37] Unlike pardons, which imply forgiveness of

---

hearings concerning disappearances that had occurred under the Amin government, and issued a report which President Amin refused to publish. The four commissioners who sat on the Commission were targeted by the State for reprisals, and one was ultimately executed on false murder charges. *Id.* at 611–12. A second and better known truth commission was established in Uganda in 1986 which, although more active than the first commission, was beset with financial and logistical problems. II TRANSITIONAL JUSTICE: COUNTRY STUDIES 513–31 (Neil J. Kritz, ed., 1995). The report was issued in 1994 and has received little attention, as most copies are apparently languishing in Ugandan warehouses. Neil J. Kritz, *Coming to Terms with Atrocities: A Review of Accountability Mechanisms for Mass Violations of Human Rights*, 59 J. L. & CONTEMP. PROBS. 127, 142 (1996).

35. Pricilla B. Hayner, *Fifteen Truth Commissions—1974 to 1994: A Comparative Study*, 16 HUM. RTS. Q. 597, 607, 624–25 (1994). The United Nations, in its work on Impunity Guidelines, proposed a set of principles for the conduct of truth commissions that would set an internationally acceptable minimum standard for their operation. *See Set of Principles for the Protection and Promotion of Human Rights Through Action to Combat Impunity*, U.N. Subcommission for Prevention of Discrimination and Protection of Minorities, 48th Sess., Annex II, Agenda Item 10, at 12, U.N. Doc. E/CN.4/Sub.2/1996/18 (1996). For a critique of truth commissions see Mark J. Osiel, *Why Prosecute? Critics of Punishment for Mass Atrocity*, 22 HUM. RTS. Q. 118 (2000).

36. Fania Domb, *Treatment of War Crimes in Peace Settlements—Prosecution or Amnesty?*, 24 ISRAEL Y.B. HUM. RTS. 253, 253 (1994).

37. Daniel T. Kobil, *The Quality of Mercy Strained: Wrestling the Pardoning Power from the King*, 69 TEX. L. REV. 569, 576 (1991).

the offender and are generally particularized in nature, amnesties typically apply to groups of offenders, and neither eradicate the offense nor expunge the moral guilt that accompanies it.[38] They are thus practical, if somewhat unsatisfactory solutions to the problem of mass atrocities: Justice is traded for peace, or at least a temporary truce, in the hopes that the atrocities will end and that society will be able to move on.

Domestically, two principal justifications have been advanced for offering blanket amnesties for human rights violations committed by a regime in power against its citizens.[39] First, dictators and military leaders have often demanded impunity as a condition of relinquishing power.[40] In response, societies eager to end a conflict and fearful of repercussions may shy away from criminal trials or other proceedings to hold responsible those accused of committing human rights violations in the former regime. New governments may also feel too fragile to take on former dictators and their followers.[41] Thus, some societies emerging from periods of repression, such as El Salvador,[42] have offered blanket amnesties to perpe-

---

38. *Id.* at 575–577. Recent surveys of the pardoning power worldwide suggest that "this institution remains an integral part of the constitutional scheme in almost every jurisdiction." Leslie Sebba, *The Pardoning Power—A World Survey*, 68 J. CRIM. L. & CRIMINOLOGY 83, 120 (1977).

39. This section addresses blanket amnesties, that is, amnesties granted pursuant to a general law or decree that do not require the recipient to account in any way, through confession or other method, for the crime of which he or she is accused. Amnesties granted after a judicial or quasi-judicial official proceeding of some kind are similar to pardons, and are therefore considered in connection with the South African experience, outlined below.

40. *See* Michael P. Scharf, *The Amnesty Exception to the Jurisdiction of the International Criminal Court*, 32 CORNELL INT'L L. J. 507, 509 (1999) (arguing that civilian rule was restored to Haiti because the members of the military regime that had been accused of massive human rights abuses received amnesty for their crimes pursuant to the Governors Island Agreement negotiated in July 1993 under international auspices). *But see contra* Irwin P. Stotzky, *Haiti: Searching for Alternatives, in* IMPUNITY AND HUMAN RIGHTS IN INTERNATIONAL LAW AND PRACTICE 185, 189 (Naomi Roht-Arriaza, ed., Oxford, 1995) (stating that the "Governors Island Agreement was a total failure. Neither Cédras [the military leader] nor François resigned. Instead Cédras broke every part of the brokered deal and employed every kind of delay while subordinates known as attachés continued to terrorize the population," and that the only way the military leaders were ousted was the threat of invasion by the United States, which ultimately sent U.S. Troops to Haiti under an agreement that also required Cédras and François to leave their posts, and receive amnesty for their crimes).

41. Diane F. Orentlicher, *Settling Accounts: The Duty to Prosecute Human Rights Violations of a Prior Regime*, 100 YALE L. J. 2537, 2546 (1991).

42. Pricilla B. Hayner, *Fifteen Truth Commissions—1974 to 1994: A Comparative*

trators. Moreover, even without the passage of amnesty laws, nations may grant perpetrators amnesty *de facto* by simply failing to pursue them.[43]

Second, even if a new regime is committed to prosecuting past international crimes, it may face considerable obstacles in doing so. Rwanda is a case in point. As a result of the genocide, Rwanda lost over 80% of its justice system personnel, including judges and magistrates.[44] Moreover, the judicial system faced serious shortages of resources, basic facilities and equipment.[45] Rwanda attempted to address the problem, at least in part, by adopting a law under which the offenders would be punished that effectuated a four-part triage of offenses, ranging from the most serious "Category one" offenses,[46] to the least egregious "Category four" offenses, which for the most part involved crimes against property.[47] The law also provided for a "confession and guilty plea procedure" that would permit offenders in the second, third and fourth categories to obtain significant reductions in penalties in exchange for a full confession. At least some

---

Study, 16 HUM. RTS. Q. 597, 627–29 (1994). Professor Orentlicher notes that in addition to El Salvador, amnesty laws or decrees were adopted by Argentina, Brazil, Chile, Uruguay, Guatemala, Nicaragua, Namibia and Suriname. Diane F. Orentlicher, *Settling Accounts: The Duty to Prosecute Human Rights Violations of a Prior Regime*, 100 YALE L. J. 2537, 2548 n. 36 (1991).

43. In her classic study of 15 truth commissions, Priscilla Hayner notes that "prosecutions are very rare after a truth commission report; in most cases there are no trials of any kind, even when the identity of violators and the extent of the atrocities are widely known." Pricilla B. Hayner, *Fifteen Truth Commissions—1974 to 1994: A Comparative Study*, 16 HUM. RTS. Q. 597, 604 (1994). *See also* Diane F. Orentlicher, *Settling Accounts: The Duty to Prosecute Human Rights Violations of a Prior Regime*, 100 YALE L. J. 2537, 2548 n. 36 (1991) (noting that de facto immunity was conferred in the Philippines and Haiti).

44. Evelyn Bradley, *In Search for Justice—A Truth in Reconciliation [sic] Commission for Rwanda*, 7 J. INT'L L. & PRAC. 129, 140 (1998). Payam Akhavan, *Justice and Reconciliation in the Great Lakes Region of Africa: The Contribution of the International Criminal Tribunal for Rwanda*, 7 DUKE J. COMP. & INT'L L. 325, 339–40 (1997).

45. Evelyn Bradley, *In Search for Justice—A Truth in Reconciliation [sic] Commission for Rwanda*, 7 J. INT'L L. & PRAC. 129, 140 (1998).

46. Category one offenses include organizers or planners of the genocide, persons in positions of authority, and "notorious murderers who by virtue of the zeal or excessive malice with which they committed atrocities, distinguished themselves. . ." and persons who committed "acts of sexual torture." Organic Law on the Organization of Prosecution for Offences Constituting the Crimes of Genocide or Crimes Against Humanity Committed Since 1 October 1990 (Organic Law No. 8/96), art. 2, *reprinted in* VIRGINIA MORRIS & MICHAEL P. SCHARF, II THE INTERNATIONAL CRIMINAL TRIBUNAL FOR RWANDA 369, 371 (1998).

47. *Id.*

commentators have suggested that, unfortunately, the sheer numbers of prisoners (estimated to be more than 100,000 at times),[48] as well as the fact that the planners of the genocide are still reported to exert influence over the prison population,[49] have rendered the confession and guilt procedures ineffective.[50] Finally, many of the trials which have occurred under the new law have been severely criticized as unfair. Some defendants had little or no access to legal counsel during critical periods of the investigation or trial, trials were unduly rapid and conducted in an atmosphere hostile to the defendants, and death sentences were imposed and expeditiously carried out.[51] In such a case it is unclear whether imposing individual criminal responsibility is a viable strategy, an all-too common scenario in cases involving mass atrocities.[52] Of course, avoiding some of these difficulties was one reason establishing an international criminal tribunal for Rwanda appeared desirable.[53] However, that Tribunal has faced problems of its own.[54]

---

48. Christina M. Carroll, *An Assessment of the Role and Effectiveness of the International Criminal Tribunal for Rwanda and the Rwandan National Justice System in Dealing with the Mass Atrocities of 1994*, 18 Boston Univ. Int'l L. J. 163, 189 (2000) *citing* Amnesty International Report 1999: Rwanda (1999), *at* <http://www.amnesty.org/ailib/airesport/ar99/afr47.htm>.

49. If true, it is arguable that Rwanda would be worse off if it released prisoners still under the influence of the *génocidaires*. Indeed, it suggests that Rwanda must be constantly vigilant to avoid a resurgence of violence.

50. Evelyn Bradley, *In Search for Justice—A Truth in Reconciliation [sic] Commission for Rwanda*, 7 J. Int'l L. & Prac. 129, 135 (1998).

51. *Id.* at 144–45. Martha Minow, Between Vengeance and Forgiveness: Facing History After Genocide and Mass Violence 124–25 (1998).

52. Professor John Dugard suggests an alternative reason that criminal prosecutions may be thwarted following a transition to democracy: sufficient evidence may simply be unavailable to support a criminal conviction, given that the repressive regime in question may quite probably have operated under a shroud of secrecy that makes information gathering after the fact quite difficult. He suggests South Africa as a case in point. John Dugard, *Reconciliation and Justice: The South African Experience*, 8 Transat'l L. & Contemp. Probs. 277, 286–87 (1988).

53. Antonio Cassese, *Reflections on International Criminal Justice*, 61 Mod. L. Rev. 1 (1998); Payam Akhavan, *Justice and Reconciliation in the Great Lakes Region of Africa: The Contribution of the International Criminal Tribunal for Rwanda*, 7 Duke J. Comp. & Int'l L. 325, 336 (1997). *See also* Christina M. Carroll, *An Assessment of the Role and Effectiveness of the International Criminal Tribunal for Rwanda and the Rwandan National Justice System in Dealing with the Mass Atrocities of 1994*, 18 Boston Univ. Int'l L. J. 163 (2000).

54. For a critique of the Rwanda Tribunal see José Alvarez, *Crimes of State/Crimes of Hate: Lessons from Rwanda*, 24 Yale J. Int'l L. 365 (1999). For a more positive assessment see Payam Akhavan, *Beyond Impunity: Can International*

3. *The South African Exception*

The South African experience, as many have noted, is unique.[55] The political transition from an apartheid regime to a government guaranteeing full civil and political rights to all its citizens gave rise to the establishment of South Africa's Truth and Reconciliation Commission (TRC). As part of a negotiated settlement with the leaders of the apartheid regime, the 1993 interim Constitution for the Republic of South Africa called for amnesty to be granted "in respect of acts, omissions and offences associated with political objectives committed in the course of the conflicts of the past."[56] Implementing this provision led to extensive debate between those who favored, at one extreme, blanket amnesties, and those who were opposed to amnesties of any kind.[57] The TRC that was ultimately established[58] attempted to forge a compromise between

---

Criminal Justice Prevent Future Atrocities?, 95 AM. J. INT'L L. 7 (2001); Susan W. Tiefenbrun, *The Paradox of International Adjudication: Developments in the International Criminal Tribunals for the Former Yugoslavia and Rwanda, the World Court, and the ICC*, 25 N. CAROLINA J. INT'L L. & COMM. REG. 589 (2000).

55. On the South African experience generally, see, *e.g.*, RICHARD J. GOLDSTONE, FOR HUMANITY: REFLECTIONS OF A WAR CRIMES INVESTIGATOR 59–73 (Yale, 2000); John Dugard, *Reconciliation and Justice: The South African Experience*, 8 TRANSAT'L L. & CONTEMP. PROBS. 277 (1988); Lorna McGregor, *Individual Accountability in South Africa: Cultural Optimum or Political Facade?*, 95 AM. J. INT'L L. 32 (2001). Jeremy Sarkin, *The Trials and Tribulations of South Africa's Truth and Reconciliation Commission*, 12 SOUTH AFRICAN J. HUM. RTS. 617 (1996); Peter A. Schey, Dinah Shelton & Naomi Roht-Arriaza, *Addressing Human Rights Abuses: Truth Commissions and the Value of Amnesty*, 19 WHITTIER L. REV. 325 (1997); Justin M. Schwartz, *South Africa's Truth and Reconciliation Commission: A Functional Equivalent to Prosecution*, 3 DEPAUL DIG. INT'L L. 13 (1997).

56. The Constitution of the Republic of South Africa Act 200 of 1993, post-amble.

57. Jeremy Sarkin, *The Trials and Tribulations of South Africa's Truth and Reconciliation Commission*, 12 SOUTH AFRICAN J. HUM. RTS. 617, 620 (1996); John Dugard, *Reconciliation and Justice: The South African Experience*, 8 TRANSAT'L L. & CONTEMP. PROBS. 277, 279 (1988). Interestingly, prior to the political transition that finally occurred, it had been contemplated that the leaders of the apartheid regime would be tried either by an international criminal court, à la Nuremberg, or in States to which they might flee. Thus, the apartheid convention criminalized apartheid as a crime and provided for the trial of offenders either by States parties to the Convention or an international tribunal. John Dugard, *Reconciliation and Justice: The South African Experience*, 8 TRANSAT'L L. & CONTEMP. PROBS. 277, 290 (1988).

58. Law No. 34 of July 26, 1995 "Promotion of National Unity and Reconciliation Act" *available at* <http://www.truth.org.za.legal.act9534.htm> (visited July 6, 2000).

these two extremes.[59] Composed of three committees,[60] the TRC's mission was to "overcome the injustices of the past by promoting national unity and reconciliation,"[61] a goal to be achieved, according to the Promotion of National Unity and Reconciliation Act of 1995, which established the TRC, by accomplishing four tasks:

- to provide for the investigation and establishment of as complete a picture as possible of the nature, causes and extent of gross violations of human rights committed during the period from March 1, 1960 to December 6, 1993, as well as the fate or whereabouts of the victims of such violations;
- to grant amnesty to persons who make full disclosure of all the relevant facts relating to acts associated with a political objective committed in the course of the conflicts of the past during such period;
- to afford victims an opportunity to relate the violations they suffered and take measures aimed to grant reparation to and rehabilitate and restore the human and civil dignity of victims; and
- to make a report about such violations and victims and recommend measures aimed at preventing such violations in the future.[62]

Pursuant to the Act, amnesties may be granted only if the act, omission or offence was committed with a political objective, in the course of the conflicts of the past.[63] Moreover, the applicant for amnesty must make full disclosure of all relevant facts.[64] The grounds for determining whether a crime was committed with a political objective are similar to those used in extradition law to decide if "an offense in respect of which extradition is sought is a political offense."[65] As of November 1, 2000, of the 7112

59. John Dugard, *Reconciliation and Justice: The South African Experience*, 8 TRANSAT'L L. & CONTEMP. PROBS. 277, 292 (1988).

60. The Committee on Human Rights Violations, the Committee on Amnesty and the Committee on Reparation and Rehabilitation.

61. For the meaning of reconciliation in the South African context, *see* Abdullah Omar, *Truth and Reconciliation in South Africa: Accounting for the Past*, 4 BUFFALO HUM. RTS. L. REV. 5 (1997).

62. Law of 1995, preamble.

63. *Id.* section 20(1)(b).

64. *Id.* section 20(1)(c).

65. John Dugard, *Reconciliation and Justice: The South African Experience*, 8 TRANSAT'L L. & CONTEMP. PROBS. 277, 294 (1988).

amnesty applications that had been dealt with by the Amnesty Committee, only 849 had been granted in full, while another 54 had been granted in part.[66] Unlike blanket amnesties, the TRC's Amnesty Committee must make a particularized finding as to whether each individual seeking amnesty fulfills the legal criteria therefor. Those who do not come forward remain open to civil suits and criminal prosecutions.[67] Because the process became "judicialized" due to concerns about the due process rights of those named as alleged perpetrators, the TRC hearings and amnesty applications came "to resemble criminal trials, with both victims or their families and the alleged perpetrators of human rights violations represented by lawyers determined to drag out the examination and cross-examination of witnesses."[68]

The TRC submitted an initial five-volume report to President Nelson Mandela on October 28, 1998.[69] Public discussion of the Commission's work inside South Africa and abroad suggests that reactions to it have been mixed.[70] The failure of former President Pieter W. Botha and many former cabinet ministers and military officers to appear was disappointing, as was the acquittal of the former Minister of Defense, Magnus Malan, and his generals for murder arising from the KwaMakutha massacre. Moreover, most of those applying for amnesty were relatively low-level perpetrators, as opposed to high government officials.[71] On the other

---

66. *See* <http://www.truth.org.za/amntrans/index.htm> (last visited June 5, 2001). The Amnesty Committee completed its work at the end of May 2001, but its report was not yet available at the time of this writing. *Agence France Presse*, May 31, 2001, *available in* LEXIS, NEXIS Library, News Group File.

67. The difficulty of obtaining evidence suitable for prosecutions is often cited as another factor supporting the South African solution. Antonio Cassese, *Reflections on International Criminal Justice*, 61 MOD. L. REV. 1, 4 (1998) .

68. John Dugard, *Reconciliation and Justice: The South African Experience*, 8 TRANSAT'L L. & CONTEMP. PROBS. 277, 298 (1988).

69. *See* <http://www.polity.org.2a/govdocs/commissions/1887/trc/index.htm>. It is expected that an additional two-volume report will be completed by the TRC by the end of 2001. *Agence France Presse*, May 31, 2001, *available in* LEXIS, NEXIS Library, News Group File.

70. For a critique of the process see Peter A. Schey, Dinah Shelton and Naomi Roht-Arriaza, *Addressing Human Rights Abuses: Truth Commissions and the Value of Amnesty*, 19 WHITTIER L. REV. 325, 331–32 (1997); John Dugard, *Reconciliation and Justice: The South African Experience*, 8 TRANSAT'L L. & CONTEMP. PROBS. 277 (1988).

71. Peter A. Schey, Dinah Shelton and Naomi Roht-Arriaza, *Addressing Human Rights Abuses: Truth Commissions and the Value of Amnesty*, 19 WHITTIER L. REV. 325, 328 (1997). *But see* Abdullah Omar, *Truth and Reconciliation in South Africa: Accounting for the Past*, 4 BUFFALO HUM. RTS. L. REV. 5, 11 (1997) (stating that the TRC has enjoyed "overwhelming support" in South Africa).

hand, prosecutors have brought cases against many who did not apply for amnesty, suggesting that the TRC was not an attempt to whitewash crimes, but to give those who committed them with a political motive the opportunity to avoid criminal sanctions at the cost of making a full disclosure of the facts. As the South African Minister of Justice recently summed up:

> We have a tradition of violence, a culture of violence, a history of violence, a history of people taking the law into their own hands, and a history of people who have not been held accountable for what they did. . . . So ending violence is a priority. Ending the culture of violence is a priority. . . if we committed human rights violations during the course of conducting our struggle, we must be held accountable because that is the only way we will send a signal to our people that every person who commits a violation in the future will be held accountable. *That is the only way we will establish peace and stability in our country and create an environment of safety and security for all our people.*[72]

4. *The Validity of Amnesties in International Law*

The question arises whether amnesties for the crimes within the ICC Statute are valid under international law. As regards the validity of amnesties for war crimes, most commentators appear to distinguish between international and non-international armed conflict. With respect to international armed conflict, although amnesty clauses for war crimes committed in international armed conflict were generally incorporated in peace agreements prior to World War I,[73] they were vigorously rejected thereafter. The decision by the Allied powers to prosecute war criminals following both the First World War (with little actual success) and the Second World War brought about the expectation that war criminals would be punished. This expectation was codified in the four Geneva Conventions of 1949, and expanded upon in the 1977 Protocol Additional to the Geneva Conventions of 12 August 1949, and Relating to the Protection of Victims of International Armed Conflicts (Protocol I)[74] which

---

72. Abdullah Omar, *Truth and Reconciliation in South Africa: Accounting for the Past*, 4 Buffalo Hum. Rts. L. Rev. 5, 13–14 (1997) (emphasis added).

73. Fania Domb, *Treatment of War Crimes in Peace Settlements—Prosecution or Amnesty?*, 24 Israel Y.B. Hum. Rts. 253, 256–57 (1994).

74. Protocol Additional to the Geneva Conventions of 12 August 1949, and

extends the grave breaches regime substantially.[75] It is generally agreed that these Conventions are now a source of customary international law. Thus, while it is certainly possible that only the substantive provisions of the Conventions and not their procedural provisions have risen to the level of custom, most commentators have accepted that at least with respect to war crimes committed in international armed conflict that fall within the grave breaches regime, a fair (but not watertight) case can be made not only for the existence of a customary international law duty to prosecute or extradite the offender, but, as a corollary,[76] for a rule prohibiting blanket amnesties.[77]

As regards non-international armed conflicts, at least some take the view that general amnesties are not only permitted, but are encouraged by existing law.[78] This view relies upon article 6(5) of Protocol II relating

---

Relating to the Protection of Victims of International Armed Conflicts, June 8, 1977, 1125 U.N.T.S. 3.

75. Fania Domb, *Treatment of War Crimes in Peace Settlements—Prosecution or Amnesty?*, 24 ISRAEL Y.B. HUM. RTS. 253, 261 (1994); Michael Bothe, *War-Crimes in Non-International Armed Conflicts*, 24 ISRAEL Y.B. HUM. RTS. 241, 241 (1994) .

76. There are two related, yet distinct, issues raised by the question of amnesties. First, whether States have a duty to prosecute or extradite those who commit crimes for which there is universal jurisdiction. Second, even if no such duty exists, whether international law recognizes the legality of amnesties for such offenses. The two questions are often conflated, but they are distinct. One can answer the first question in the negative, for example, but still recognize that the absence of an affirmative obligation to prosecute does not permit States *carte blanche* in their reaction to the commission of mass atrocities. On the other hand, an affirmative duty to prosecute or extradite would appear to rule out the legality of amnesties.

77. Scholars are divided even as to this question, however. For a view that the duty imposed by the Geneva Conventions to prosecute or extradite offenders under the laws of war is part of customary international law, *see* YORAM DINSTEIN, LAWS OF WAR 275 (Hebrew, 1983); Fania Domb, *Treatment of War Crimes in Peace Settlements—Prosecution or Amnesty?*, 24 ISRAEL Y.B. HUM. RTS. 253, 263 (1994). Similarly, Professor Meron argues that every State has a duty to try or extradite those guilty of grave breaches, and has "the right, although probably not the duty, to prosecute [other] serious violations of the Geneva Conventions." Theodor Meron, *Is International Law Moving Towards Criminalization?*, 9 EUR. J. INT'L L. 18, 23 (1998). On the other hand, States have generally not complied with this obligation, thereby undermining its claim as custom. Antonio Cassese, *On the Current Trends Towards Criminal Prosecution and Punishment of Breaches of International Humanitarian Law*, 9 EUR. J. INT'L L. 2, 5 (1998); M. CHERIF BASSIOUNI & EDWARD M. WISE, AUT DEDERE, AUT JUDICARE: THE DUTY TO EXTRADITE OR PROSECUTE IN INTERNATIONAL LAW 44–46 (1995).

78. Fania Domb, *Treatment of War Crimes in Peace Settlements—Prosecution or Amnesty?*, 24 ISRAEL Y.B. HUM. RTS. 253, 266–67 (1994).

to the Protection of Victims of Non-International Armed Conflict, which provides:

> At the end of hostilities, the authorities in power shall endeavor to grant the broadest possible amnesty to persons who have participated in the armed conflict, or those deprived of their liberty for reasons related to the armed conflict, whether they are interned or detained.[79]

Many have argued that this language was intended to apply to those combating the State, not those acting as its agents.[80] Nonetheless, some courts have taken a different view. For example, a lower South African Court held that this provision permitted the South African TRC to grant amnesties in regard to human rights violations committed under the apartheid regime.[81] The South African Constitutional Court affirmed, stating:

> [in the case of] violent acts perpetrated during . . . conflicts which take place within the territory of a sovereign state in consequence of a struggle between the armed forces of that state and other dissident armed forces operating under responsible command, within such a state. . . there is no obligation on the part of a contracting state to ensure the prosecution of those who might have performed acts of violence or other acts which would ordinarily be characterized as serious invasions of human rights.[82]

This decision has been criticized on the grounds that it fails to analyze the crimes committed as crimes against humanity (of which apartheid is clearly one), and to establish whether there exists any customary international law duty to punish offenders of a prior regime for such crimes.[83] This criticism is consistent with the view that there is an

---

79. Protocol Additional to the Geneva Conventions of 12 August 1949, and Relating to the Protection of Victims of Non-International Armed Conflicts, June 8, 1977, art. 6(5), 1125 U.N.T.S. 609, 614.

80. Peter A. Schey, Dinah Shelton and Naomi Roht-Arriaza, *Addressing Human Rights Abuses: Truth Commissions and the Value of Amnesty*, 19 WHITTIER L. REV. 325, 340 (1997).

81. Case No. 4895/96, (South African Cape Provincial Div. Supreme Ct., May 9, 1996) *quoted in* Jeremy Sarkin, *The Trials and Tribulations of South Africa's Truth and Reconciliation Commission*, 12 SOUTH AFRICAN J. HUM. RTS. 617, 626–28 (1996).

82. Azanian Peoples Organisation (AZAPO) v. The President of the Republic of South Africa, 1996 (4) S.A.L.R. 671, para. 30 (South African Const. Ct.).

83. John Dugard, *Reconciliation and Justice: The South African Experience*, 8 TRANSAT'L L. & CONTEMP. PROBS. 277, 302 (1988).

international duty to punish offenders after a civil war as a necessary corollary of the need to protect human rights.[84]

With respect to crimes against humanity and genocide, some commentators have strenuously argued for the existence of a duty to investigate and punish human rights violations committed under a prior regime.[85] Certainly, the Genocide Convention and the Torture Convention suggest that a duty is assumed by States Parties to those conventions to pursue and punish (or extradite, in the case of the Torture Convention) those who violate the Conventions' terms.[86] Moreover, the United Nations has consistently maintained the position that amnesty cannot be granted in respect of international crimes such as genocide, crimes against humanity or other serious violations of international humanitarian law.[87]

As to a generalized customary international law rule requiring punishment, the evidence of State practice seems weak. As Professor Roht-Arrizia notes, in general, the human rights instruments that guarantee human beings a right to bodily integrity and to be free from torture and other abuses do not typically, by their terms, require States to investigate

84. Michael Bothe, *War-Crimes in Non-International Armed Conflicts*, 24 ISRAEL Y.B. HUM. RTS. 241, 248 (1994). Nonetheless, while one may argue that the distinction between international and non-international armed conflict is disappearing, it has not done so yet. *Accord*, Peter A. Schey, Dinah Shelton & Naomi Roht-Arriaza, *Addressing Human Rights Abuses: Truth Commissions and the Value of Amnesty*, 19 WHITTIER L. REV. 325, 339 (1997).

85. Diane F. Orentlicher, *Settling Accounts: The Duty to Prosecute Human Rights Violations of a Prior Regime*, 100 YALE L. J. 2537 (1991).

86. Article 3 of the Genocide Convention, provides that "genocide . . . is a crime under international law which they undertake to prevent and to punish." The convention is not based on a principle of universal jurisdiction, but of territorial jurisdiction; that is, pursuant to article 6 of the convention, those charged with genocide or similar acts "shall be tried by a competent tribunal of the State in the territory of which the act was committed, or by [an international penal tribunal]." Similarly, article 4 of the Torture Convention, requires States Parties to "ensure that all acts of torture are offences under [their] criminal law" and article 7 requires them to either extradite or prosecute alleged torturers. Thus, States Parties to these treaties would appear to be precluded from offering unconditional amnesties for the crimes within the jurisdiction of those instruments. Roman Boed, *The Effect of a Domestic Amnesty on the Ability of Foreign States to Prosecute Alleged Perpetrators of Serious Human Rights Violations*, 33 CORNELL INT'L L. J. 297, 318 (2000). However, even those treaties are unclear as to the precise modalities of such punishment. They would thus appear to leave a certain margin of appreciation to national legal systems in their implementation.

87. *Report of the Secretary-General on the Establishment of a Special Court for Sierra Leone*, U.N. SCOR, 55th Sess., U.N. Doc. S/2000/915, para. 22, October 4, 2000.

and prosecute abuses of rights.[88] A handful of decisions, however, emanating from the Human Rights Committee established to monitor compliance with the International Covenant on Civil and Political Rights and the Inter-American Court of Human Rights, charged with application of the American Convention on Human Rights, have imposed affirmative obligations on States to investigate human rights abuses stemming from provisions in the treaties that require States to respect and ensure to all persons subject to their jurisdiction the free and full exercise of the rights and freedoms contained in the treaties.[89] The European Court of Human Rights has, similarly, suggested that States have affirmative obligations to prevent and remedy breaches of the Convention, suggesting in one case that criminal prosecution could be required as part of that obligation.[90] Although these important decisions may signal a trend[91] or evidence Regional Custom, they would seem insufficient, without more, to establish that such a duty has crystallized into general customary international law.[92] Many countries have granted amnesties to the perpetrators of atrocities under a prior regime, and while a handful of national courts have overturned them, others have not.[93] As one writer notes, the international

88. Naomi Roht-Arrizia, *Sources in International Treaties of an Obligation to Investigate, Prosecute and Provide Redress, in* IMPUNITY AND HUMAN RIGHTS IN INTERNATIONAL LAW AND PRACTICE 28 (Naomi Roht-Arriaza, ed., Oxford, 1995).

89. *Id.* at 29–32. The leading case is *Velásquez Rodríguez*, Inter-Am. Ct.H.R. (Ser. C) No. 4 (1988) (July 29, 1988). *Velásquez* has been followed by the Inter-American Human Rights Commission to find that Chile's amnesty laws violated the right to judicial protection in the Convention, as well as the State's duty to "prevent, investigate and punish" any violations of the rights found in the Convention. *Garay Hermosilla et al. v. Chile*, Inter-Am.C.H.R., Report No. 36/96, para. 73 (Oct. 15, 1996).

90. *In the case of X and Y v. The Netherlands*, European Court of Human Rights, para. 27 (Feb. 27, 1985) (holding that the Netherlands was required to adopt criminal-law provisions to remedy sexual abuse of a mentally handicapped individual living in a home for mentally handicapped children because "the protection afforded by the civil law in [this] case is . . . insufficient. This is a case where fundamental values and essential aspects of private life are at stake. Effective deterrence is indispensable in this area and it can be achieved only by criminal-law provisions.")

91. This trend is reinforced by the Rome Statute's Preamble which proclaims that it is the "duty of every State to exercise its criminal jurisdiction over those responsible for international crimes."

92. *But see contra* Diane F. Orentlicher, *Settling Accounts: The Duty to Prosecute Human Rights Violations of a Prior Regime*, 100 YALE L. J. 2537, 2568–81 (1991); GEOFFREY ROBERTSON, CRIMES AGAINST HUMANITY: THE STRUGGLE FOR GLOBAL JUSTICE 248–53 (2000).

93. Peter A. Schey, Dinah Shelton & Naomi Roht-Arriaza, *Addressing Human Rights Abuses: Truth Commissions and the Value of Amnesty*, 19 WHITTIER L. REV. 325, 341–42 (1997).

community "warmly welcomed" the decision of South Africa to pursue a course involving conditional amnesties "thereby casting doubts on the existence of an obligation upon successor regimes to prosecute those suspected of having committed international crimes."[94]

The Rome Statute is explicit on certain challenges to accountability such as superior orders,[95] head of state immunity[96] and statute of limitations[97] but is silent with regard to amnesties.[98] Although the issue was raised during the Diplomatic Conference, no clear consensus developed among the delegates as to how the question should be resolved. This may suggest that customary international law simply has not crystallized on this point.[99] According to the Chairman of the Conference, the question was purposely left open by the Framers: while the Statute does not condone the use of amnesties by its terms, presumably the Prosecutor has the power to accept them if doing so would be "in the interests of justice."[100]

Although it is unclear whether international law clearly prohibits blanket amnesties for international crimes, it seems that if it does not already, it should. Indeed, as noted above, the United Nations has consistently maintained this position.[101] Blanket amnesties undermine the rule

94. John Dugard, *Reconciliation and Justice: The South African Experience*, 8 TRANSAT'L L. & CONTEMP. PROBS. 277, 279 (1988). While noting several flaws of the South African process, Professor Dugard suggests that it complies with international law by requiring that wrongdoers be held accountable by combining a truth commission, conditional amnesties and criminal prosecutions. *Id.* at 307. Moreover, the situation might have been different had South Africa, instead of adopting a course involving conditional amnesties, adopted a policy of blanket amnesties.

95. *Rome Statute*, art. 28.

96. *Id.* art. 27.

97. *Id.* art. 29.

98. For a good discussion of some of the issues raised by the Statute, see Michael P. Scharf, *The Amnesty Exception to the Jurisdiction of the International Criminal Court*, 32 CORNELL INT'L L. J. 507, 523–25 (1999).

99. The preamble to the Statute states that, "it is the duty of every State to exercise its criminal jurisdiction over those responsible for international crimes." However, this language is not implemented by any other article of the Statute.

100. *Rome Statute*, art. 53(1)(c). The delegates were largely unable to achieve consensus on the issues of pardons, commutations and amnesties. *See* John T. Holmes, *The Principle of Complementarity*, *in* THE INTERNATIONAL CRIMINAL COURT: THE MAKING OF THE ROME STATUTE 41 (Roy S. Lee, ed., 1999).

101. Although the difference may seem purely semantic, it would not appear correct to assert that if no international rule requires prosecution, a grant of amnesty with regard to that crime is valid under international law. Moreover, even if international law rule affirmatively prohibits a grant of amnesty, it would be incorrect to extrapolate from the absence of a prohibition the presence of a rule

of law, and are, for the most part, simply self-serving declarations by government officials exempting themselves from the reach of the law. They represent an attempt to trump the application of rules of law, and as such constitute a threat to both the legitimacy and the fairness of the rules.[102] Moreover, the argument that amnesties are necessary due to the sheer volume of potential criminal cases does not appear to refute the overwhelming evidence that addressing the past is necessary for countries to break vicious cycles of human rights abuses—that there can be no real peace without justice. As one Rwandan lawyer poignantly stated:

> We are in the process of falling into the trap that these murderers have set for us. This genocide is distinguished by the fact that a maximum number of people have been implicated in the killings—there is talk of a million killers. The Hutu extremists estimated that no court in the world could judge that many criminals, and they bet that they were going to get off. Are we going to say that they're right?[103]

Conditional amnesties, such as those granted in the South African case, are of a different kind, and would not appear to threaten accountability, but to bring it about using a variation of the criminal process. Yet, even the amnesty process in South Africa has been criticized and it is still too early to tell whether the use of limited amnesties is more effective than criminal trials in bringing about reconciliation. Although some have suggested that the South African effort was a creative response to past atrocities,[104] the response within South Africa has been mixed.[105] Due process

---

permitting the amnesty. Thus, I have argued that in the absence of a prohibition, blanket amnesties should presumptively be disfavored. Leila Nadya Sadat, *Universal Jurisdiction and National Amnesties, Truth Commissions and Other Alternatives to Prosecution: Giving Justice a Chance*, Princeton Project on Universal Jurisdiction (Princeton University, 2001). *Contra* Roman Boed, *The Effect of a Domestic Amnesty on the Ability of Foreign States to Prosecute Alleged Perpetrators of Serious Human Rights Violations*, 33 CORNELL INT'L L. J. 297 (2000).

102. *Cf.*, THOMAS M. FRANCK, FAIRNESS IN INTERNATIONAL LAW AND INSTITUTIONS 16 (1997).

103. Laurent Bijard, *Can Justice Be Done? Massacred: 1,000,000: Tried 0*, World Press Rev. (June 1996), at 7 (quoting Rwandan lawyer Frederic Mutagwera), cited in Evelyn Bradley, *In Search for Justice—A Truth in Reconciliation [sic] Commission for Rwanda*, 7 J. INT'L L. & PRAC. 129, 139 (1998).

104. MARTHA MINOW, BETWEEN VENGEANCE AND FORGIVENESS: FACING HISTORY AFTER GENOCIDE AND MASS VIOLENCE (1998).

105. In addition to the constitutional challenges brought against the amnesty laws, the families of many of those who were tortured and killed have objected to

concerns for perpetrators either named before the TRC or brought before the TRC have required the process be judicialized to the point that the proceedings resemble trials in fact. Moreover, the South African experience is unique in that the two sides negotiated a power transition without the intervention of a civil war and the victory of one side or the other. Where a country has emerged from a bloody genocide, as in Rwanda, the idea of amnesties, even conditional amnesties, for the perpetrators of genocide appears unthinkable, particularly for the leaders. If the international community truly believes that some behavior is *criminal*, indeed, pathological, with all that implies, amnesties would appear to be inconsistent with the re-establishment of peace and the rule of law. Even those ultimately supporting the use of conditional amnesties have suggested that criminal trials, particularly international criminal trials, may be appropriate for the leaders, while other mechanisms of accountability, including the use of conditional amnesties, truth commissions, lustration laws and reparations may be used for lower-level perpetrators.[106]

B. Realpolitik

The challenge from realpolitik is not the fear of a particular society from sitting dictators, or the problem of mass atrocities flooding an inadequate criminal justice system. Rather, international negotiators eager to bring about a settlement in the hopes of ending a bloody conflict will often ignore calls for justice.[107] Negotiators in the Bosnian conflagration thus felt obligated to treat with Slobodan Milosevic, in spite of expert opinion and substantial evidence that implicated his leadership in the ethnic cleansing operations of the former Yugoslavia. Similarly, the international community negotiated with Foday Sankoh to try to bring about a settlement in the Sierra Leone conflict.[108] In both cases, as is well known, the two leaders went on, not to bring peace to their nations, but to renew their

---

amnesty proceedings for the perpetrators of those who victimized their loved ones. John Dugard, *Reconciliation and Justice: The South African Experience*, 8 TRANSAT'L L. & CONTEMP. PROBS. 277, 301 (1988).

106. John Dugard, *Reconciliation and Justice: The South African Experience*, 8 TRANSAT'L L. & CONTEMP. PROBS. 277 (1988).

107. They argue that the "policies and practices of accommodation in the pursuit of political settlement conflict with legal accountability in the pursuit of retributive and restorative justice." M. Cherif Bassiouni, *Combating Impunity for International Crimes*, 71 U. COLO. L. REV. 409, 409 (2000).

108. See Peace Agreement Between the Government of Sierra Leone and the

attacks on their countrymen and women, attacks for which one leader was subsequently indicted and ultimately arrested[109] (the other may meet a similar fate).[110]

The case for trading justice for peace to bring about the international settlement of disputes is quite weak, however. In addition to the moral repugnancy of turning a blind eye to the commission of atrocities, it may well be contrary to self-interest. Examples such as Milosevic and Sankoh suggest that granting impunity, rather than definitively settling a conflict, simply encourages a resurgence of the criminal behavior. If one of the most important purposes of the criminal law is to remove dangerous individuals from society, it suggests that Slobodan Milosevic and Foday Sankoh should have been indicted and tried years ago.[111] Following the

---

Revolutionary United Front of Sierra Leone (July 7, 1999), <http://www.sierra-leone.gov.sl/peace_agreement.htm>.

109. Keith B. Richburg, *Milosevic in Hague Prison, Belgrade gets Aid Package*, INT'L HER. TRIB., June 30–July1, 2001, at 1.

110. Following the Lomé Peace Agreement, Sankoh continued his criminal behavior. He was ultimately arrested and now faces prosecution. A special court was proposed for Sierra Leone by the Security Council in Resolution 1315, S. C. Res. 1314 (2000), 14 August 2000, which was jointly established by an Agreement between the United Nations and the Sierra Leone government. *Report of the Secretary-General on the establishment of a Special Court for Sierra Leone, Statute of the Special Court*, U.N. SCOR, 55th Sess., U.N. Doc. S/2000/915, October 4, 2000. The Court has jurisdiction over crimes committed either under international or national law, *id*. art. 1, and will be composed of both international and Sierra Leonean judges, prosecutors and staff. In particular, the court will have a Chief Prosecutor appointed by the Secretary-General and a Deputy Prosecutor appointed by Sierra Leone in consultation with the United Nations. *Id*. art. 15. The court will be headquartered in Sierra Leone and will have jurisdiction over persons 15 or older. Fifteen to eighteen year old defendants will receive special protections in their trials and any sanctions imposed will be in the form of counseling, vocational training or approved schools, rather than custodial sentences. *Id*. art. 7(3)(a)–(f). *See generally* Konstantinos D. Magliveras, *The Special Court for Sierra Leone: A New Type of Regional Criminal Court for the International Community?*, 17 INT'L ENFORCEMENT L. REP. (Feb. 2001), *available in* LEXIS, Nexis Library, Secondary Legal Publications Group File. *See also* Babafemi Akinrinade, *International Humanitarian Law and the Conflict in Sierra Leone*, 15 NOTRE DAME J. L. ETHICS & PUB. POL. 391 (2001); Michael P. Scharf, *The Special Court for Sierra Leone*, ASIL Insight (Oct. 2000), *available in* <http://www.asil.org/insigh53.htm>.

111. Belatedly recognizing that fact, Sankoh and his followers are likely to be defendants before a new ad hoc tribunal currently being formed under the aegis of the Security Council. Security Council Resolution 1315, dated August 14th, 2000, provides for the establishment of an "independent special court" with jurisdiction over persons who bore the greatest responsibility for the commission of

de facto immunity Milosevic received at Dayton, he was indicted by the International Criminal Tribunal for the Former Yugoslavia in 1999, for war crimes and crimes against humanity subsequently committed in Kosovo. Indeed, one expert recently suggested that the ICTY's failure to indict Milosevic for crimes he allegedly committed in Bosnia empowered him to commit additional crimes in Kosovo.[112] Yet as late as Fall 2000, United Nations officials were suggesting that Milosevic would have to be granted immunity in order to convince him to step down.[113] Not only did this prove wrong, as he was removed during subsequent elections, but he was then indicted by the new government on charges of corruption.[114]

---

crimes against humanity, war crimes and other serious violations of international law, as well as crimes under relevant Sierra Leonean law committed within the territory of Sierra Leone. The Resolution specifically rejects amnesty for the perpetrators of such crimes in spite of the provisions of the Lomé Agreement, negotiated with Sankoh in 1999 to attempt to settle the conflict last year, that provide for amnesty, on the basis that the Secretary-General of the United Nations appended to his signature of the Agreement a statement that the United Nations holds the understanding that the amnesty provisions of the Agreement would not apply to the international crime of genocide, crimes against humanity, war crimes and other serious violations of international humanitarian law. S. C. Res. 1315 (2000), U.N. Doc. S/Res/1315 (2000), to be issued in U.N. SCOR, 55th Year, Resolutions and Decisions 2000.

112. Remarks of Professor Paul Williams, at *The International Criminal Court and American National Security*, given at American University Washington College of Law, Thursday, September 14, 2000. (As further evidence of the play of *realpolitik* in the Former Yugoslavia, it was reported that the United States was offering immunity to Milosevic in return for his relinquishing power in the Former Yugoslavia). Steven Erlanger, *U.S. Seeks Way Out for Milosevic*, INT'L HER. TRIB., June 19, 2000, at 1.

113. The U.N. Human Rights Commission's special rapporteur for the former Yugoslavia, Jiri Dientsbier, suggested that "the only possible deal, and the most important thing for Mr. Milosevic is to have guarantees that if he leaves power he will not be prosecuted and will not spend the rest of his life in prison." Bernard Kouchner, *Milosevic Must be Brought to Justice*, Press Release, UNMIK/PR/381, Oct. 5, 2000, *obtainable from* <http://www.un.org/peace/ kosovo/news/99/oct00.htm#Anchor16>.

114. Milosevic was jailed on charges "concerned with his financial dealings, causing damage to the Serbian economy and bringing instability to the country during the period of hyperinflation in the early 1990's." Carlotta Gall, *Milosevic Jailed In Belgrade On Financial Charges; Standoff Is Ended; Quick Transfer To Hague Unlikely*, INT'L HER. TRIB., April 2, 2001, at 1. Although, President Kostunica stated that "his country should not extradite former President Slobodan Milosevic to The Hague to face war crimes charges . . . ," Steven Erlanger, *Kostunica Says He's Opposed to Extradition of Milosevic*, INT'L HER. TRIB., April 3, 2001, Milosevic was

It is also difficult to imagine how it could lead to good law enforcement to offer deals to tyrants and the perpetrators of human rights atrocities, while refusing to treat with terrorists or hostage takers. In domestic law and in other areas of international criminal law, governments such as the United States have adopted a clear policy: no ransom for hostages deals,[115] and no immunity for terrorists.[116] Finally, if international law and State practice is increasingly moving towards rejecting blanket amnesties *per se*, and lower-level perpetrators are finding themselves in the dock in increasing numbers, it is difficult to support the notion that the leaders of a genocide or ethnic cleansing should receive immunity as a condition of their relinquishing power, while their followers will be prosecuted or otherwise held accountable.

III. GIVING JUSTICE A CHANCE

Most scholars have favored, and even advocated, adoption of the accountability paradigm in one form or another.[117] The strongest proponents of this view support not only the utility of criminal trials, but suggest a duty under both customary international law and treaties to try offenders or extradite them to jurisdictions where they will be tried.[118]

---

ultimately transferred to the Hague on June 29, 2001 by the Prime Minister Zoran Djindjic. Keith B. Richburg, *Milosevic in Hague Prison, Belgrade gets Aid Package*, INT'L HER. TRIB., June 30–July1, 2001, at 1.

115. The United States government took this position in the Philippines quite recently. The general view is that paying ransoms or granting immunity will encourage further hostage-taking.

116. The U.S. Department of State web site on counter terrorism sets out the basic policy of the U.S. government with respect to terrorists: "First, make no concessions to terrorists, and strike no deals; Second, bring terrorists to justice for their crimes." <http://www.state.gov/www/global/terrorism>.

117. *See, e.g.*, Payam Akhavan, *Justice in the Hague, Peace in the Former Yugoslavia*, 20 HUM. RTS. Q. 737, 746 (1999); M. Cherif Bassiouni, *Combating Impunity for International Crimes*, 71 U. COLO. L. REV. 409 (2000); Antonio Cassese, *Reflections on International Criminal Justice*, 61 MOD. L. REV. 1 (1998); Mark J. Osiel, *Why Prosecute? Critics of Punishment for Mass Atrocity*, 22 HUM. RTS. Q. 118, 133 (2000); Carlos S. Nino, *The Duty to Punish Past Abuses of Human Rights Put Into Context: The Case of Argentina*, 100 YALE L. J. 2619 (1991); CARLOS SANTIAGO NINO, RADICAL EVIL ON TRIAL x (Yale, 1996); Diane F. Orentlicher, *Settling Accounts: The Duty to Prosecute Human Rights Violations of a Prior Regime*, 100 YALE L. J. 2537 (1991); Naomi Roht-Arriaza, *State Responsibility to Investigate and Prosecute Grave Human Rights Violations in International Law*, 78 CAL. L. REV. 451 (1990).

118. Professor Diane Orentlicher, in particular, is identified with this posi-

Recently, however, the accountability paradigm has been challenged. Some are skeptical of the utility of international criminal trials, taking issue both with the normative claims for their value, as well as their actual impact.[119] Others are critical of the two ad hoc tribunals, particularly the ICTR, suggesting that international criminal trials may even undermine "the preservation of accurate collective memory, the national rule of law, [and . . .] the realization of justice."[120] A variant of this critique suggests that international law enforcement is so sporadic that it is unlikely to deter, and so plagued with "liberal" safeguards for criminal defendants, that international criminals, who often represent State power, are able to thwart the international tribunals' ability to mete out justice.[121] Finally, some recognize the value of criminal trials in theory, but suggest that truth commissions promote healing and truth telling and may be more useful than criminal trials which, they believe, may be divisive, expensive, and possibly unfair.[122]

Those who have critiqued the work of the ICTY and ICTR, or the inappropriateness of criminal trials generally, have traditionally suggested that arguments supporting the establishment of a system of international criminal justice lack empirical foundation. Deterrence, they argue, is unproven. Because deterrence is also largely unproven in domestic legal

---

tion, and has argued eloquently in favor of prosecution as a tool for reestablishing the rule of law. Diane F. Orentlicher, *Settling Accounts: The Duty to Prosecute Human Rights Violations of a Prior Regime*, 100 YALE L. J. 2537, 2547–49 (1991); M. CHERIF BASSIOUNI & EDWARD M. WISE, AUT DEDERE, AUT JUDICARE: THE DUTY TO EXTRADITE OR PROSECUTE IN INTERNATIONAL LAW 20–25 (1995). The reader should note, however, that Professor Orentlicher advocates a duty to *punish*; the *aut dedere aut judicare* principle set out by Professor Bassiouni is slightly different, being a duty to prosecute *or* extradite. Professors Wise and Bassiouni are not completely in agreement in their treatise on the subject. Professor Bassiouni argues that the principle is not only customary international law, but a *jus cogens* norm, while Professor Wise is skeptical with regard to both propositions.

119. David Wippman, *Atrocities, Deterrence, and the Limits of International Justice*, 23 FORDHAM INT'L L. J. 473 (1999).

120. José Alvarez, *Crimes of State/Crimes of Hate: Lessons from Rwanda*, 24 YALE J. INT'L L. 365, 385 (1999). Professor Alvarez is particularly critical of primacy jurisdiction whereby the ICTR can require defendants to be turned over to it.

121. Tom J. Farer, *Restraining the Barbarians: Can International Criminal Law Help?*, 22 HUM. RTS. Q. 90, 94–98 (2000).

122. Evelyn Bradley, *In Search for Justice—A Truth in Reconciliation [sic] Commission for Rwanda*, 7 J. INT'L L. & PRAC. 129 (1998). *See also* Mark A. Drumbl, *Punishment, Postgenocide: From Guilt to Shame to* Civis *in Rwanda*, 75 N.Y.U. L. REV. 1221 (2000).

orders,[123] it is not clear whether commentators relying on this argument believe that national, as well as international, criminal justice systems should be abandoned.[124] The key difference may be that if it is true that high probability of punishment generally deters more effectively than a severe sanction rarely applied,[125] the international criminal justice system has not yet reached the stage at which its deterrent value may be fairly assumed, largely due to problems of inter-State cooperation and State sovereignty. Yet if there appears to be little decisive evidence as to whether disclosing the truth about past abuses or punishing those responsible will necessarily deter future abuses, there is equally little proof that amnesties promote reconciliation whereas criminal trials provoke relapses.[126] Moreover, there is at least some evidence that the ICTY and ICTR have, if not specifically deterred the commission of particular international crimes, helped to bring about a change in perceptions—so much so that "accountability" is part of a new realism.

Yet even if neither the realists nor the international idealists may stake a clear claim to the truth, what appears to be at issue is a competition over the values underlying the normative claims. Those supporting the use of criminal trials believe (even if they cannot demonstrate empirically) that changing the prevailing discourse about the commission of mass atrocities by condemning the behavior as criminal and punishing those that can be brought to justice will, over time, bring about a decrease in the number of situations involving the commission of mass atrocities. Those rejecting the accountability paradigm tender the opposite view: that "evil will always be with us . . . and genocide and mass violence are [its] case in chief."[127] Indeed, some suggest that the evils perpetrated may be so terrible that "no legal norms . . . can cope."[128] It has also been argued that the much narrower scope of legal responsibility, as opposed to moral respon-

---

123. See Dan M. Kahan, *The Secret Ambition of Deterrence*, 113 HARV. L. REV. 414, 416 & n. 6 (1999) (noting that empirically, deterrence claims (in the United States) are speculative).

124. If they concede that empirical claims for deterrence in national legal systems are also speculative, but do not think that national criminal justice systems should be abandoned, the question is why they perceive deterrence to be crucial in justifying the existence of an international system of criminal justice.

125. Tom J. Farer, *Restraining the Barbarians: Can International Criminal Law Help?*, 22 HUM. RTS. Q. 90, 92 (2000).

126. Aryeh Neier, *What Should be Done About the Guilty*, THE NEW YORK REV. OF BOOKS, 1 Feb. 1990, at 35.

127. MARTHA MINOW, BETWEEN VENGEANCE AND FORGIVENESS: FACING HISTORY AFTER GENOCIDE AND MASS VIOLENCE 146 (1998).

128. JUDITH SHKLAR, LEGALISM: LAW, MORALS AND POLITICAL TRIALS 167 (1964).

sibility, may lead observers to regard the response of the law with suspicion, or even hostility.[129] Their solution then, is not to waste resources pursuing the offenders, but to establish mechanisms to comfort the victims.[130]

Yet, experience suggests that leaders who were never punished become increasingly emboldened by their apparent impunity. To reject an international paradigm of accountability in favor of "bottom-up" solutions ignores that it was the inability of national legal systems to address the problem of mass atrocities that goaded the international community into action in the first place. International law, as others have noted, can play a pivotal role in transitional justice. For successor regimes reeling from the shock of political upheaval, and faced with the problem that the conduct of perpetrators under the law of the former regime was not only condoned but was lawful behavior, international law may offer an "alternate construction of law that, despite substantial political change, is continuous and enduring."[131] Given that the move to exercise universal jurisdiction by States and the exercise of international universal jurisdiction by the international community began only a few years ago, it would appear injudicious to abandon the effort at this early stage of development.[132] The world has suffered from the reign of impunity since World War II, with the result of millions dead, raped, tortured or disappeared. Surely more evidence that the accountability paradigm is misguided would be necessary for the international community to conclude that it should so soon be abandoned.

---

129. Mark J. Osiel, *Why Prosecute? Critics of Punishment for Mass Atrocity*, 22 HUM. RTS. Q. 118, 127–28 (2000).

130. A different variant of this critique suggests that forgiveness may be more important to healing a society, a view often expressed by writers urging reevaluation of the values underlying the criminal justice system (both domestically and internationally). See Joshua Dressler, *Hating Criminals: How can Something That Feels so Good be Wrong?*, 88 MICH. L. REV. 1448 (1990); *cf.* Hilary Charlesworth and Christine Chinkin, *The Gender of Jus Cogens*, 15 HUM. RTS. Q. 63 (1993).

131. Ruti Teitel, *Transitional Jurisprudence: The Role of Law in Political Transformation*, 105 YALE L. J. 2009, 2028 (1997).

132. *Cf.* Theodor Meron, *Is International Law Moving Towards Criminalization?*, 9 EUR. J. INT'L L. 18, 30–31 (1998).

CHAPTER 4

ORGANIZATION AND INSTITUTIONAL STRUCTURE

This Tribunal, while it is novel and experimental, is not the product of abstract speculations nor is it created to vindicate legalistic theories. [It] represents the practical efforts of four of the most mighty of nations, with the support of seventeen more, to utilize International Law to meet the greatest menace of our times—aggressive war.

—Justice Robert H. Jackson
Chief Counsel for the United States at Nuremberg

In exploring the organization and institutional structure of the International Criminal Court, the many compromises that were necessary to bring States into agreement on the Court's establishment become apparent. Many of these reflect the fundamental tension between the desire of States Parties to retain control of the Court to protect their sovereignty, and the Court's need for independence so as to preserve the integrity of the judicial process. In addition, the Framers were required to establish an institutional structure and procedural regime that would be a true hybrid, neither based entirely upon the common law, nor the civil law, but combining what are hopefully the best elements of both.[1] Finally, nationality, either of the defendants or the Court's personnel, is virtually irrelevant to proceedings before the Court,[2] meaning that the (international) justice dispensed will be truly universal in character.

1. Non-Western legal traditions are not represented in the Statute to any significant degree. That does not mean the Statute is necessarily inconsistent with many non-Western legal traditions. Osama Ghanem Alobaidy, The International Criminal Court: An Arab Perspective in View of Islamic Law and the 1998 Rome Statute (2000) (unpublished J.S.D. dissertation, Washington University School of Law) (on file with the Washington University School of Law Library).

2. Bias based upon the nationality of decisionmakers is a charge often levelled at international institutions. By attempting to make the Court's personnel diverse in terms of national origin (based upon region), the Statute expressly

At the same time, the Framers were not writing on a blank slate—their ability to innovate was fettered by the need to observe political realities and constrained by the existing infrastructure of international law. Thus, although the Framers created a truly permanent entity rather than the stand-by institution proposed by the International Law Commission, fears of a strong Prosecutor and powerful judiciary caused them to limit both their independence of action and tenure in office.[3] Moreover, the Court's independence from, but many links to, the United Nations, through the Security Council, through the financing of the Court, and through the Relationship Agreement between the Court and the United Nations, renders the Court an important part of the United Nations system, and, at the same time, underscores its fragility. Indeed, the Court will be brought into what may very well be an uneasy relationship with the United Nations, with significant implications as to its financing, bureaucratic structure, control over prosecutions, and enforcement of its commands.

I. THE RELATIONSHIP OF THE COURT TO THE UNITED NATIONS

In establishing the Court by multilateral treaty, rather than as a United Nations organ, which presumably would have required amendment of the Charter, the international community made a practical decision.[4] Yet the implications of this choice are profound, affecting the Court's financing, bureaucratic structure and procedures, authority, and power. From a theoretical perspective, if the United Nations Charter is a nascent

---

rejects the notion that nationality may impute bias *per se*, but substitutes distribution requirements in order to reduce both the appearance and the potential reality of national bias playing a role in the actions of the Court's personnel. There are distribution requirements as to nationality and representativeness with respect to the selection of the Court's personnel. Once selected, however, the nationality of the Court's personnel is virtually irrelevant to the procedural regime and application of the substantive law.

3. They also provided for the establishment of an Assembly of States Parties to oversee the Court's operations, an entity similar to the oversight bodies recently established by other multilateral treaties.

4. *See* Roger S. Clark, *The Proposed International Criminal Court: Its Establishment and Its Relationship with the United Nations*, 8 CRIM. L. F. 411, 416 (1997) (Charter amendments are unacceptable because they may open up questions about the entire UN structure, including the Security Council's composition and the veto).

"Constitution," as some have argued,[5] it is not clear where the Rome Treaty fits in the existing structure. As the constitutive document of a new international institution in "relationship" with the United Nations, it might be considered to be a constitutional "end-run" around the United Nations system. Many delegations expressed concern during the Diplomatic Conference that they did not wish the ICC to reflect the balance of power in the United Nations—which they viewed as an anachronistic body in which a handful of States hold a disproportionate degree of power.[6] The Rome Statute reflects their concern and abandons the two-tier hierarchy of the United Nations, but perhaps at the cost of alienating the United States, which was particularly unhappy with its loss of control over the Court's jurisdiction.

Another aspect of establishing the ICC outside of the United Nations system is the possibility that the Rome Conference represented a Constitutional Moment in international law—a decision to reequilibrate the constitutional, organic structure of international law, albeit *sotto voce*.[7] The process by which the Statute was adopted, the Court's ultimate institutional structure, and the fact that it will have jurisdiction over individuals, not traditionally considered subjects of international law, all suggest an important shift in the substructure of international law upon which the Court's establishment is premised. Unable to effectuate the change explicitly, through formal amendment to the Charter, the international community, including not only States but global civil society, seized upon imaginative ways to bring about the shifts in constitutional structure necessary to permit international law to respond to the needs of international society and changing times.

This is not to suggest that the United Nations was not supportive of the ICC's establishment, or that the shift away from the United Nations was in any way complete. The logistical, technical, and moral support of the United Nations were critical to the success of the Diplomatic Conference,[8] and continue to be essential to the work of the Preparatory

---

5. Bardo Fassbender, *The United Nations Charter as Constitution of the International Community*, 36 COLUM. J. TRANSNAT'L L. 529, 531–32 (1998).

6. Roy S. Lee, *Introduction: The Rome Conference and its Contributions to International Law, in* THE INTERNATIONAL CRIMINAL COURT: THE MAKING OF THE ROME STATUTE 1, 24–25 (Roy S. Lee, ed., 1999).

7. *See, e.g.*, Bruce Ackerman, *Constitutional Politics/Constitutional Law*, 99 YALE L. J. 453 (1989) (describing the process by which constitutions may be amended by practice, not just by textual changes).

8. Fanny Benedetti & John L. Washburn, *Drafting the International Criminal Court Treaty: Two Years to Rome and an Afterward on the Rome Diplomatic Conference, in* 5 GLOBAL GOVERNANCE 1, 23–24 (1999).

Commission.[9] As the Draft Relationship Agreement between the United Nations and the International Criminal Court[10] provides, the relationship is to be "mutually beneficial . . . whereby the discharge of [their] respective responsibilities . . . may be facilitated."[11] The Relationship Agreement requires the two institutions to "cooperate closely,"[12] specifying the requirements as to cooperation between the Security Council and the Court,[13] the United Nations and the Prosecutor,[14] and granting the Court the right to attend and participate in the work of the General Assembly as an observer.[15] It also provides a mechanism for the submission of disputes relating to the interpretation or application of the Statute to the International Court of Justice for an advisory opinion,[16] and authorizes

---

9. As John Washburn writes, "the U.N. as a venue, institution, and community was . . . the primary shaper of the psychology of the negotiations. Many of the delegates, and almost all of the Secretariat officials and key Non-Governmental Organization . . . representatives knew each other personally or by reputation at the start of the negotiations. . . . Knowledge of each other's styles, personalities and abilities—both strengths and weaknesses, provided confidence, predictability and mutual forbearance." John Washburn, *The Negotiation of the Rome Statute for the International Criminal Court and International Lawmaking in the 21st Century*, 11 PACE INT'L L. REV. 361, 364 (1999).

10. U.N. Doc. PCNICC/2001/WGICC-UN/RT.1, March 7, 2001. This is the latest version of the Relationship Agreement, which will probably be finalized at the last meeting of the Preparatory Commission in 2001.

11. *Id.* preamble.

12. *Id.* art. 3.

13. *Id.* art. 4.

14. *Id.* art. 5.

15. *Id.* art. 9(1). Subject to the Rules of Procedure and Evidence, the United Nations has a reciprocal right to attend public hearings of the Chambers of the Court that relate to cases of interest to the organization. *Id.* at 9(3).

16. *Id.* art. 13; *see also Rome Statute*, art. 119(2). This proposal was discussed in the seventh session of the Preparatory Commission. A number of delegations and NGOs favored the idea of permitting the General Assembly's delegate to the Assembly of States Parties to seek ICJ advisory opinions directly rather than requiring the Assembly to go to the General Assembly in each case. In addition, questions were raised about the respective competencies of the ICJ and ICC to interpret international law and the Court's Statute. It was suggested that it might be more appropriate to delete this provision from the Relationship Agreement and conclude a supplementary agreement pursuant to article 19 of the Draft Relationship Agreement outlining the respective competencies of the two bodies. Jennifer Schense, NGO Coalition for an International Criminal Court, *Draft Report on the Seventh Session of the Preparatory Commission, February 26–March 9, 2001*, at 15.

the principle personnel of the Court to use the laissez-passer of the United Nations as a valid travel document.[17]

Finally, the Security Council will retain an important role with respect to the Court. First, the Security Council may refer cases to the Court acting under Chapter VII of the Charter.[18] Second, the Council may defer investigations or prosecutions under the Statute for a twelve-month period if it adopts a resolution to that effect, again relying upon Chapter VII of the Charter.[19] Third, the Court may inform the Security Council of a States' failure to cooperate with its requests pursuant to article 87 of the Statute.[20] Finally, although it is not yet certain, it is likely that the Security Council will need to make a preliminary determination as to aggression in a particular case prior to a charge involving that crime being justiciable before the Court.[21]

II. A HYBRID SYSTEM OF INTERNATIONAL CRIMINAL JUSTICE

A. Foundational Premises

The delegations that came together to craft the Rome Statute came from many different legal traditions and represented a myriad of national legal regimes, including, *inter alia*, countries in the civil law tradition, embodying most of Europe and Latin America as well as some African and Asian nations, countries adhering to the common law system including the United States, the United Kingdom and former Commonwealth nations, countries following Islamic law traditions including much of the Arab world, and countries representing socialist and post-socialist legal regimes, including Russia and China. This might lead one to expect a Court combining elements of these various systems, and, indeed, the States Parties to the Statute are required to take into account the need for "the representation of the principal legal systems of the world" in their

---

17. Draft Relationship Agreement, art. 17.

18. *Rome Statute*, art. 13(b). Draft Relationship Agreement, art. 4(1) provides for the transmittal of the Security Council's decision to refer a case to the Court by the Secretary-General.

19. *Id*. art. 16. Draft Relationship Agreement, art. 4(2) provides for the request for deferral to be transmitted to the President of the Court and the Prosecutor by the Secretary-General.

20. The mechanism for doing so is provided in article 4(3).

21. See Chapter 6, *infra*.

selection of the Court's judiciary.[22] Nevertheless, the negotiations centered around two principal models, the common and civil law systems, which are both, of course, largely Western legal traditions, although they have been exported to many other parts of the world, adapted to the needs of other countries, and modified accordingly. Partisans of the common law adversarial system found it difficult to conceive of the civil law inquisitorial model as either fair or efficient; partisans of the inquisitorial system felt the same way about the common law. Essentially, the Statute compromises by blending elements of both inquisitorial and adversarial procedural models, creating new procedures and institutions where neither model seemed apropos.

The Statute envisages that the Court will have four organs:[23] the Presidency, the Judiciary (which is composed of three divisions: Appeals, Trial, and Pre-Trial Divisions), the Office of the Prosecutor, and the Registry.[24] This is similar to the original structure proposed by the 1994 ILC Draft Statute, with the notable addition of a Pre-Trial Division, which is new.[25]

Although there is no provision for a public defender's office as an official organ of the Court, proposals were introduced into the Preparatory Commission to include a "defense unit" either within the Registry or as a separate entity, to function in accordance with the Rules of Procedure and Evidence (RPE).[26] The finalized draft text of the Rules of Procedure and Evidence adopted by the Preparatory Commission abandons the idea of a "defense unit" in favor of simply imposing certain responsibilities on the Registrar relating to the rights of the accused. Draft RPE 20 requires the Registrar to provide facilities, support and assistance to defense counsel, including the dissemination of information and case law of the Court, and RPE 21 requires the Registrar to create and maintain a list of defense coun-

---

22. *Rome Statute*, art. 36(8)(a)(i).

23. *See* Santiago Torres Bernárdez, *Subsidiary Organs, in* MANUEL SUR LES ORGANISATIONS INTERNATIONALES 108 (René-Jean Dupuy, ed., 1988).

24. *Rome Statute*, art. 34; *see also* Figures 2–4.

25. The Pre-Trial Division developed from the Netherlands' suggestion that an investigative judge be added to the original structure proposed. Leila Sadat Wexler, *The Proposed Permanent International Criminal Court: An Appraisal*, 29 CORNELL INT'L L. J. 665, 691 n. 153 (1996).

26. *See, e.g., Proposal submitted by Canada, France, Germany and the Netherlands in connection with article 43 of the Rome Statute of the International Criminal Court concerning the Rules of Procedure and Evidence as regards document PCNICC/1999/DP.1*, Preparatory Commission for the International Criminal Court, Working Group on Rules of Procedure and Evidence, U.N. Doc. PCNICC/1999/WGRPE(4)/DP.2 (1999).

sel, from which persons suspected of a crime who are to be questioned by the Prosecutor and the accused may "freely choose."[27] It remains to be seen how effective this solution will be. Assignment of defense counsel and their payment is crucial to preserving the rights of the accused—it also involves the payment of public funds which must be wisely administered.[28] The Defence Counsel Unit in the ICTY, for example, performs many tasks in addition to assignment and payment of counsel, including monitoring their qualifications, conducting training programs, reimbursing costs and expenses, monitoring ethical issues and imposing disciplinary measures.[29]

---

27. RPE 21(2). The rules address the problems raised before the ICTR in *Prosecutor v. Akayesu*. In that case, Jean-Paul Akayesu challenged the Registrar's decision to place a temporary ban on the assignment of French and Canadian defense attorneys, claiming that U.N. regulations necessitated geographic diversity at the Tribunal. *Ban on Canadian Lawyers at UN Court Lifted?, in* INTERNEWS REPORTS, *available at* <http://www.internews.org/activities?ICTR_reports/ICTR/ICTRnewsJul99.html> (visited May 24, 2001). Twenty-six genocide suspects awaiting trial protested the policy with a hunger strike, *22 Rwandan Detainees at the ICTR are Continuing their Hunger Strike*, FONDATION HIRONDELLE—AGENCE DE PRESSE HIRONDELLE À ARUSHA, October 27, 1998, *available at* <http://www.igc.org/wcw/ictr/news/news10-27.txt> (visited May 24, 2001) and Jean-Paul Akayesu brought the issue to the Appeals Chamber. Although the Appeals Chamber intially rejected the Registry's view, and determined that the accused could choose freely from among any counsel that was on the list, regardless of his or her nationality, the Appeals Chamber ultimately rejected his appeal, finding that the right to free counsel "does not confer the right to have counsel of one's own choice." Prosecutor v. Akayesu (Case No. ICTR-96-4-A), (ICTR Appeals Chamber, June 1, 2001).

28. Allegations were made in respect to the ICTY that defense counsel were entering into "fee-splitting" arrangements with their clients, and after an investigation by the United Nations Office of Internal Oversight, it was determined that fee-splitting arrangements had been entered into with former defense counsels at both Tribunals, and in some cases counsel had hired friends or relatives of their clients or, in the case of the ICTR, made arrangements for gifts to their clients, their clients' relatives and other forms of indirect support and maintenance. *Report of the Office of Internal Oversight Services on the investigation into possible fee-splitting arrangements between defence counsel and indigent detainees at the International Criminal Tribunal for Rwanda and the International Tribunal for the Former Yugoslavia*, U.N. Doc. A/55/759, February 1, 2001.

29. *Information Paper submitted by the delegations of Bosnia and Herzegovina, Canada, Colombia, Egypt, Portugal and Spain concerning Part 4 of the Rome Statute: Contributions of the Chambers of the International Tribunal for the Former Yugoslavia on the provisional rules of procedure and evidence for the court, submitted to the Preparatory Commission at its 13–31 March 2000 session*, U.N. Doc. PCNICC/2000/ WGRPE(4)/INF/1, April 5, 2000.

The Statute provides that the judges are all to be elected as full-time members of the Court,[30] and that the Prosecutor, Deputy Prosecutors,[31] and Registrar[32] shall also serve on a full-time basis. This was a major improvement over earlier proposals for the ICC, virtually all of which conceived of the Court as a "stand-by" institution,[33] whose personnel would largely be part-time.[34] The Statute also expressly addresses the need for continuing oversight by the States Parties by establishing an Assembly of States Parties, as noted below, and providing rules for its organization and operation.

The Rome Statute reflects the practical experience of the international community in the Yugoslavia and Rwanda Tribunals in several important ways. First, the Statute evinces a much greater concern for the problems unique to victims and witnesses than any of its predecessor instruments. Thus, one major change to the Registry, as originally conceived by the ILC in 1994, is the inclusion of a Victims and Witnesses Unit established in consultation with the Office of the Prosecutor.[35] This Unit will provide protective measures and security arrangements, counseling, and other appropriate assistance for witnesses, victims who appear before the Court, and others at risk by virtue of witness testimony. The Unit is to include staff with expertise in trauma, including trauma related to crimes of sexual violence.[36] Second, the Statute addresses gender-related crimes and crimes against children explicitly, as evidenced not only in the definition of crimes discussed in Chapter 6, but also in a specific command to the

30. *Rome Statute*, art. 35(1). There is a provision permitting the Presidency to reduce Judges' terms if the workload so warrants. *Id.* art. 35(3). Article 40(3) adds that judges "required to serve on a full-time basis shall not engage in any other occupation of a professional nature." *Id.* art. 40(3).

31. *Id.* art. 42(2).

32. *Id.* art. 43(5).

33. *See, e.g., 1994 ILC Draft Statute*, at 59, cmt., §3.

34. Under the scheme envisaged by the ILC in 1994, only the Registrar would have been a truly full-time member of the Court. Leila Sadat Wexler, *The Proposed Permanent International Criminal Court*, 29 Cornell Int'l L. J. 665, 695–96 (1996). Article 36 of the April Draft Statute also seemed to favor a part-time judiciary. *April Draft Statute*, art. 36.

35. *Rome Statute*, art. 43(6).

36. *Id.* Articles 16 through 18 of the Draft Rules of Procedure and Evidence address in greater detail the responsibilities of the Registrar with respect to victims and witnesses, and the functions and responsibilities of the Victims and Witnesses Unit. Draft Rule 19 provides several additional areas of expertise that the Victims and Witnesses Unit may wish its staff to have, including psychology in criminal proceedings, gender and cultural diversity, children, elderly persons, persons with disabilities, social work and counseling, and health care.

Prosecutor to appoint advisers with legal expertise on issues including, but not limited to, sexual and gender-based violence and violence against children.[37] Similarly, the Victims and Witnesses Unit is to include staff with expertise in, *inter alia*, trauma related to crimes of sexual violence. Indeed, the Rome Statute has a much stronger gender perspective throughout its text, as a result of the hard work of the Women's Caucus and many State delegations.[38] Third, the Statute recognizes the important role that gratis personnel have played in the two ad hoc tribunals (as well as some of the problems their seconding has presented for the tribunals as an administrative matter), and explicitly permits the Court to accept (exceptionally) the expertise of gratis personnel.[39] In particular, the Statute permits the Prosecutor to accept offers of gratis personnel directly, rather than requiring him or her to make arrangements through the Registry.[40]

Thus, the ICC Statute improves substantially on the two ad hoc tribunals in many ways. Yet in one respect the ICC will do no better, and may not even equal, its sister institutions, for it will operate not on the basis of primacy jurisdiction, but subject to the principle of complementarity. Neither the ICC nor the ad hoc tribunals have a police force to enforce their orders or arrest their defendants. This has been a recurring problem for the International Criminal Tribunal for Yugoslavia (ICTY).[41] However, whereas the two ad hoc tribunals, by virtue of their primacy jurisdiction, may require States to deliver defendants to them, the ICC cannot.[42]

---

37. *Rome Statute*, art. 42(9).

38. On gender crimes and perspectives in the Statute and its negotiation, *see generally* Dorean M. Koenig & Kelly D. Askin, *International Criminal Law and the International Criminal Court Statute: Crimes Against Women, in* II WOMEN AND INTERNATIONAL HUMAN RIGHTS LAW 3–29 (Kelly D. Askin & Dorean M. Koenig, eds., 2000). *See also* Rhonda Copelon, *Gender Crimes as War Crimes: Integrating Crimes against Women into International Criminal Law*, 46 MCGILL L. J. 217 (2000).

39. *Rome Statute*, art. 44(4). The Assembly of States Parties is directed to establish guidelines governing the employment of gratis personnel. *Id*. The use of seconded personnel in the ICTY and ICTR has led wealthy nations to be overly represented in the two tribunals because they are typically the only countries that can afford to send their personnel. This creates representational problems in the institutions, a problem that the ICC will wish to avoid.

40. *Id*.

41. *See, e.g.*, Minna Schrag, *The Yugoslav War Crimes Tribunal: An Interim Assessment*, 7 TRANSNAT'L L. & CONTEMP. PROBS. 15, 17 (1997).

42. *ICTY Statute*, art. 9(2); *ICTR Statute*, art. 8(2).

B. Structural Framework

1. The Judiciary

The eighteen judges of the Court[43] will be nominated and elected by secret ballot by the Assembly of States Parties.[44] They are each to be persons "of high moral character, impartiality and integrity who possess the qualifications required in their respective states for appointment to the highest judicial offices."[45] In choosing the judges, the Assembly is to "take into account" the need for gender balance, equitable geographical representation, and the representation of the principal legal systems of the world.[46] In addition, the "States Parties shall also take into account the need to include Judges with legal expertise on specific issues, including, but not limited to, violence against women or children."[47] Finally, at least nine of the judges must have "established competence [and experience] in criminal law and procedure,"[48] and five must have "established competence [and experience] in relevant areas of international law."[49] The areas specifically mentioned as "relevant" to the work of the Court include international humanitarian law and the law of human rights.[50]

The Statute's provisions on the judiciary are similar to the structure proposed by the ILC in 1994, although the Rome Statute is far more detailed.[51] By insisting on the permanence of the judiciary, at least as a presumption, however, the Rome Statute is a substantial improvement. In addition, consonant with the Framers' vision of a Court dispensing uniform and universal international justice, the Statute, unlike the ILC draft, does not automatically disqualify judges on the basis of their nationality,

---

43. *Rome Statute*, art. 36(1). Under paragraph 2 of article 36, the number of judges may be increased, if necessary, by the Assembly of States Parties acting on a proposal by the Presidency.

44. *Id.* art. 36(6). The judges elected shall be those who obtain the highest number of votes and a two-thirds majority of States present and voting.

45. *Id.* art. 36(3).

46. *Id.* art. 36(8)(a).

47. *Id.* art. 36(8)(b).

48. Article 36(5) requires that at least nine members of the Court have knowledge as well as experience as "judge, prosecutor, advocate or in other similar capacity, in criminal proceedings." *Rome Statute*, art. 36(3)(b)(i).

49. *Id.* arts. 36(3)(b)(ii), 36(5).

50. *Id.* art. 36(3)(b)(ii).

51. There is very little in the Draft Rules of Procedure and Evidence on the judiciary. Rules 4 and 5(a) address plenary sessions of the judges and the solemn undertaking to be made by the judges, respectively.

but adopts a more flexible approach, permitting a judge's disqualification on a case-by-case basis if his or her "impartiality might reasonably be doubted" or if he or she was previously involved in that case before the Court or in a related criminal case at the national level.[52] Although the Rome Statute permits the Assembly of States Parties to place other grounds for disqualification in the Rules of Procedure and Evidence, making it possible for a *per se* rule regarding nationality to reappear in this way, Draft RPE 34, on disqualification of a judge, the Prosecutor, or a Deputy Prosecutor, contains no such rule.[53] The Statute takes a similar, but not identical, approach to the Prosecutor and Deputy Prosecutors.[54]

As finally adopted, the Rome Statute, like the 1994 ILC Draft, provides that each of the judges elected to the Court will serve one, nonrenewable, nine-year term.[55] The Commission's 1993 Draft had provided

---

52. *Rome Statute*, art. 41(2)(a). *But see 1994 ILC Draft Statute*, art. 9(7) ("[n]o judge who is a national of a complainant State or of a State of which the accused is a national shall be a member of a chamber dealing with the case").

53. Draft RPE 34 sets out four additional grounds for disqualification, in addition to those found in the Statute, including: a personal interest in the case; involvement in legal proceedings in which the person being investigated or prosecuted was or is an opposing party; performance of functions prior to taking office during which he or she could be expected to have formed an opinion on the case, the parties, or their lawyers, which objectively, could affect his or her impartiality; and public expressions of opinion that could adversely affect his or her impartiality. Interestingly, Draft RPE 34's predecessor contained a footnote noting that "it was generally understood that, under certain circumstances, nationality could be taken into consideration as a ground on which the person's impartiality might reasonably be doubted." *Mont Tremblant Draft*, Rule 4.30, n. 10. In its comments on the final rules, Singapore noted the deletion of the footnote, but also that the text of the rule remained unchanged. *NGO Coalition for an ICC, Report of Outcome of the Key Issues at the Fifth PrepCom*, June 6, 2000.

54. *Rome Statute*, art. 42(7). The Prosecutor and Deputy Prosecutors are to be of different nationalities. *Id.* art. 42(2). However, the Prosecutor and Deputy Prosecutors shall not automatically be disqualified from acting in respect of complaints involving a person of their own nationality, as they would have been under the ILC Draft Statute. *Compare 1994 ILC Draft Statute*, art. 12(5) ("The Prosecutor and Deputy Prosecutor shall not act in relation to a complaint involving a person of their own nationality."), *with Rome Statute*, art. 42(7) (they shall be disqualified from a case if "their impartiality might reasonably be doubted" or "they have previously been involved in any capacity in that case before the Court or in a related criminal case at the national level involving the person being investigated or prosecuted"). Unlike the judiciary, however, the Statute does not specifically provide for additional cases of disqualification to be specified in the Rules of Procedure and Evidence. Nevertheless, Draft RPE 34 (on disqualification) covers judges, Prosecutors and Deputy Prosecutors by its terms.

55. *Id.* art. 36(9)(a).

for a 12-year term, which the Commission shortened in response to criticism from some States.[56] During the Statute's negotiation, some delegations proposed that judges' terms of office be renewable either once or more than once, either for nine years or some shorter period,[57] along the lines of the judges of the World Court. This viewpoint was ultimately rejected on the grounds that the ICC, being a criminal court, was not comparable to the International Court of Justice.[58] In addition, others pointed to the electioneering involved in the selection of judges to the World Court, arguing that the Court would simply become too politicized were judges able to stand for more than one term.[59] While these concerns are understandable, the Statute may prejudice the capacity of the Court to build institutional memory and competence by limiting judges' terms. Moreover, judicial legitimacy, or the ability of a court "to command acceptance and support from the community so as to render force unnecessary," is predicated, at least in part, on the continuity of the Court's composition over time,[60] in part because this permits the Court to develop a jurisprudence which is constant and coherent.

Apart from issues of personnel, developing consistency in its judgments will be critical to the Court's perceived legitimacy. The Rome Statute permits the issuance of majority and minority views by the Trial[61] and Appeals Chambers,[62] and allows the issuance of separate opinions (on questions of law only) by judges in the Appeals Chamber.[63] This may not be an advantage to the Court in establishing either the credibility or authority of its decisions. Although many of the common law delegations present in Rome strongly advocated the right of dissent, it is not part of the judicial traditions of many parts of the of the world, particularly those

56. *1994 ILC Draft Statute*, at 51.

57. *Zutphen Intersessional Draft*, art. 30[6](6); *April Draft Statute*, art. 37(10).

58. Medard R. Rwelamira, *Composition and Administration of the Court*, *in* THE INTERNATIONAL CRIMINAL COURT: THE MAKING OF THE ROME STATUTE 153, 156 (Roy S. Lee, ed., 1999).

59. Roger S. Clark, *Commentary on Parts 1 and 4 of the Zutphen Intersessional Draft: Establishment of the Court and Composition and Administration of the Court*, *in* OBSERVATIONS ON THE CONSOLIDATED ICC TEXT BEFORE THE FINAL SESSION OF THE PREPARATORY COMMITTEE, 13*bis* NOUVELLES ÉTUDES PÉNALES 55, 66 n. 37 (Leila Sadat Wexler, special ed., 1998).

60. Laurence R. Helfer & Anne-Marie Slaughter, *Toward a Theory of Effective Supranational Adjudication*, 107 YALE L.J. 273, 284 (1997).

61. *Rome Statute*, art. 74(5).

62. *Id.* art. 83(4).

63. *Id.*

influenced by French law.[64] The standard reason for permitting dissent is clarification of the majority opinion and development of the law.[65] Judge Shahabuddeen, formerly of the International Court of Justice,[66] wrote a thoughtful essay on the issue, approving of separate opinions for these and other reasons,[67] and the ICJ has a venerable tradition of permitting judges to write separately.[68] Yet, it has often been suggested that the European Court of Justice has been highly successful precisely because, among other things, judges are not permitted to issue separate opinions meaning that the position of individual judges on a specific case or issue is not made public.[69] One great difficulty the World Court has faced is that

---

64. Kurt H. Nadelmann, *The Judicial Dissent: Publication v. Secrecy*, 8 AM. J. COMP. L. 415 (1959).

65. Those supporting the right of dissent argue that dissents may be prophetic in nature, serving as a beacon to later courts; may aid the growth of the law or allow new and radical ideas time to mature and ripen; may contribute to the integrity of the judical function; may promote accountability by forcing the majority to provide a satisfactory rationale; or may be declaratory in nature, identifying the limit and contours of the majority decision as well as possible loopholes and end-runs. *See, e.g.*, William J. Brennan, *In Defense of Dissents*, 50 HASTINGS L. J. 671 (1999). In addition, dissents permit the judge to vote his or her conscience and make his or her views fully known. But dissents serve less lofty purposes as well. Indeed, one judge from the ICTY confided to the author that another "plus" of the right to dissent was its value as a bargaining chip used to induce one's colleagues to compromise to reach consensus in issuing a judgment by threatening to write a dissent if they did not. Others have noted that dissents may undermine the legitimacy or authority of decisions, that preparation of dissents may waste scarce judicial resources, and finally that dissents may impair collegiality and lead to a fractious atmosphere among judges, or, even worse, be written for egoistic or aggrandizing reasons. *See, e.g.*, Ruth Bader Ginsburg, *Remarks on Writing Separately*, 65 WASH. L. REV. 133 (1990); Rory K. Little, *Reading Justice Brennan: Is There a "Right" to Dissent?*, 50 HASTINGS L. J. 683 (1999); Karl M. Zobell, *Division of Opinion in the Supreme Court: A History of Judicial Disintegration*, 44 CORNELL L. Q. 186 (1959).

66. Judge Shahabuddeen is now a member of the ICTY Appeals Chamber.

67. MOHAMED SHAHABUDDEEN, PRECEDENT IN THE WORLD COURT 177–208 (1996).

68. IJAZ HUSSAIN, DISSENTING AND SEPARATE OPINIONS AT THE WORLD COURT (1984).

69. *See generally* GEORGE A. BERMANN, ET. AL., CASES AND MATERIALS ON EUROPEAN COMMUNITY LAW 70 (1993). As the authors note, however, some judges have done important and influential academic writing while on the ECJ. *See also* Leila Sadat Wexler, *The Role of the European Court of Justice on the Way to European Union*, *in* EUROPE AFTER MAASTRICHT: AMERICAN AND EUROPEAN PERSPECTIVES 159, 160 (Paul Michael Lützeler, ed., 1994). On the European Court of Justice generally *see, e.g.*, WERNER FELD, THE COURT OF THE EUROPEAN COMMUNITIES: NEW DIMENSION IN INTERNATIONAL ADJUDICATION 99–100 (1964); Jean Paul Jacqué & Joseph H.H. Weiler, *On*

on many occasions a judge's position is predictable in light of his or her nationality.[70] Insulating the International Criminal Court from this potential criticism would have been useful. Finally, even studies of common law courts have suggested that unanimity, or near unanimity, in decision-making may be one of the most important factors in establishing judicial legitimacy,[71] making the choice at Rome to permit dissents and minority views potentially troubling.[72]

Once elected, the judges of the Court are to organize themselves into divisions[73] and elect the members of the Presidency.[74] As shown in Figure 3, the Court will have an Appeals Division, consisting of one appeals chamber with five judges, including the President; a Trial Division, consisting of at least six judges, further divided into Trial Chambers of three judges each; and a Pre-Trial Division of not less than six judges that is further divided into Pre-Trial Chambers of one or three judges, depending

---

the Road to European Union—A New Judicial Architecture: An Agenda for the Intergovernmental Conference, 27 COMMON MKT. L. REV. 185 (1990); Maurice Lagrange, *La Cour de Justice des Communautés Européennes: du plan Schuman à l'union européenne*, 14 REVUE TRIMESTRIELLE DE DROIT EUROPÉEN 2 (1978); Joseph H.H. Weiler, *The Transformation of Europe*, 100 YALE L. J. 2403 (1991).

70. *See, e.g.*, Edith Brown Weiss, *Judicial Independence and Impartiality: A Preliminary Inquiry, in* THE INTERNATIONAL COURT OF JUSTICE AT A CROSSROADS 123, 124–126 (1987) (quoting a study suggesting that regular and ad hoc judges vote for their own national government approximately 80% of the time, but noting that judges will oppose their own governments in certain cases). *See also* SHABTAI ROSENNE, THE WORLD COURT: WHAT IT IS AND HOW IT WORKS 71 (1989).

71. For example, in *Brown v. Board of Education*, 347 U.S. 483 (1954), and *Cooper v. Aaron*, 358 U.S. 1 (1958), both early desegregation cases, the United States Supreme Court thought it necessary to the Court's legitimacy to issue a single, undivided opinion, due to the controversial nature of the case. Scott C. Idleman, *A Prudential Theory of Judicial Candor*, 73 TEX. L. REV. 1307, 1389–91 (1995). The Court also spoke with one voice in *United States v. Nixon*, 418 U.S. 683 (1974), and in fact, in the early years of the Marshall Court, unanimity was the rule, a tradition that became the norm for more than a century. Laura Krugman Ray, *Justice Brennan and the Jurisprudence of Dissent*, 61 TEMPLE L. REV. 307, 308 (1988).

72. Virtually all of my common law colleagues disagree with this assessment, arguing for the value of dissents in clarifying the law. Dissents and separate opinions clearly render judicial decisions more transparent, exposing to public view the court's reasoning on particular issues, and even particular judges' opinions on particular issues. I do not question the utility or value of dissent in the American legal tradition; rather, I suggest that in the context of the ICC, the costs associated with its use may outweigh the benefits.

73. *Rome Statute*, art. 39(1).

74. *Id*. art. 38(1).

on the functions the Pre-Trial Chamber is exercising.[75] Judges will not rotate between the appellate and trial divisions, a feature of the ad hoc tribunals that has been criticized.[76]

The Rome Statute, in adding a Pre-Trial Division to the judiciary's organization, reduced many of the roles given the Presidency in the ILC version by transferring those functions to the Pre-Trial Division.[77] It also added to the functions of judging and deciding cases the "*mise en état*" of the case by having a Pre-Trial Chamber, composed of either one or three judges,[78] actively involved in the organization and supervision of the case by the Prosecutor during the pre-trial phase. As others have noted, it was imperative to shorten the time it took to try each case before the Court. Otherwise, with only two trial chambers, it could take up to 25 years to try

---

75. *Id.* arts. 34(b), 39(1), 39(2)(b).

76. The group of experts appointed to review the operation and functioning of the International Tribunals proposed that judges be assigned to either the appeals chamber or the trial chamber for the duration of their terms, avoiding intermingling between chambers that could unintentionally tend to influence the outcome of appeals. *Report of the Expert Group to Conduct a Review of the Effective Operation and Functioning of the International Tribunal for the Former Yugoslavia and the International Criminal Tribunal for Rwanda*, at Recommendation 18, paras. 105–06, U.N. Doc. A/54/634 (1999). Judges in the Rwanda Tribunal, unlike the judges of the ICTY, may rotate between Trial Chambers but not between the Appeals Chamber and the Trial Chambers. Rules and Procedure and Evidence of the Rwanda Tribunal, Rule 27 (2001). For a critique of the rotation principle in the ICTY see VIRGINIA MORRIS & MICHAEL P. SCHARF, I AN INSIDER'S GUIDE TO THE INTERNATIONAL CRIMINAL TRIBUNAL FOR THE FORMER YUGOSLAVIA 150 (1995); for a discussion of the principle's effect in the Rwanda Tribunal see VIRGINIA MORRIS & MICHAEL P. SCHARF, I THE INTERNATIONAL CRIMINAL TRIBUNAL FOR RWANDA 356–60 (1998).

77. For example, under the ILC Draft, the Prosecutor's decision not to prosecute a case was reviewable by the Presidency. *1994 ILC Draft Statute*, art. 26(5). Under the Rome Statute, the decision not to prosecute is within the purview of the Pre-Trial Chamber. *Rome Statute*, art. 53(3).

78. Article 39(2)(b)(iii) provides that the Pre-Trial Chamber shall be composed of either three or one judge of the Pre-Trial Division, in accordance with the Statute and the Rules of Procedure and Evidence. One is required to consult each particular article to know whether a single judge may act, or a three judge chamber is required. Draft RPE 7(3) permits the Pre-Trial Chamber, either on its own motion or at a parties request, to take action as a three judge chamber, rather than by a single judge. In addition, Draft RPE 7(2) provides that in cases in which a single judge is to act, in accordance with article 39(2)(b)(iii) of the Statute, the judge shall be chosen on the basis of "objective pre-established criteria." Both rules respond to the concerns, raised by some States, that a single judge should not have the power to make important decisions.

the crimes committed during a genocide, a result that would be undesirable from both a legal and political point of view.[79] The Pre-Trial Division will oversee each case, from the initial decision whether to open an investigation[80] until confirmation of the charges, after which time the accused will be committed to a Trial Chamber for trial.[81] Among other functions, the Pre-Trial Division will determine whether a reasonable basis exists for the Prosecutor to proceed *proprio motu*,[82] hear preliminary rulings on admissibility and challenges to admissibility or jurisdiction prior to trial,[83] authorize the Prosecutor to conduct investigations on the territory of a State,[84] issue orders and warrants, provide for the protection and privacy of victims and witnesses, preserve evidence, protect persons who have been arrested or have appeared in response to a summons, protect national security information,[85] and confirm the charges against the accused.[86] The Statute also permits a Pre-Trial Chamber to authorize the Prosecutor to investigate on the territory of a State Party without its cooperation if the State is clearly unable to execute a request for cooperation because the mechanisms of judicial cooperation are unavailable (i.e., the State has essentially collapsed).[87]

The addition of the Pre-Trial Division represents a victory for countries in the civil law tradition who felt that the Court, as originally conceived, tracked the common law model too closely. Indeed, the Court's statute melds the common and civil law traditions nicely: the Prosecutor retains his or her independence of action for the most part (that is, there is

---

79. Gilbert Bitti, Ministère de la Justice (France), Remarks at the Colloquium on the International Criminal Court (Sept. 16–22, 1998, Siracusa, Italy). Excessive trial times have also been noted in the two ad hoc Tribunals, and were the subject of much of the expert group's report. Report of the Expert Group to Conduct a Review of the Effective Operation and Functioning of the International Tribunal for the Former Yugoslavia and the International Criminal Tribunal for Rwanda, U.N. Doc. S/2000/597. The experts suggested, *inter alia*, that stipulations as to factual matters not in dispute, increased use of provisions governing judicial notice, the use of written deposition testimony, better case management, increased judicial control over proceedings, and more efficient motions practices could significantly reduce the time it takes to try cases. *Id.* paras. 36–101.

80. *Rome Statute*, art. 15(4).

81. *Id.* art. 61(7).

82. *Id.* arts. 15(4), 53(2). Article 57(2)(a) requires a majority for decisions under article 15.

83. *Id.* arts. 15(3), 17–19, 57(2).

84. *Id.* arts. 54(2)(a), 57(2).

85. *Id.* art. 57(3)(c).

86. *Id.* art. 61.

87. *Id.* art. 57(3)(d).

no judge actually functioning as a *juge d'instruction*, in the French sense),[88] but the judicial branch has supervisory powers over the proceedings to better ensure prosecutorial accountability, evidentiary integrity and fairness to the accused, as well as the protection of victims and potential witnesses. The only difficulty in the approach taken is that the functions and operation of the judicial divisions are spread throughout the Statute, and finding their respective roles and operational guidelines can be confusing to the uninitiated.[89] By its unwillingness to create a truly strong and independent judiciary, the Diplomatic Conference may also have unwittingly deprived the Court of an important bulwark against the politicization of cases.

2. *The Presidency*

As mentioned earlier, the addition of the Pre-Trial Division eliminated many functions assigned to the Presidency by earlier drafts of the Statute. Nevertheless, the Presidency, composed of a President and two Vice-Presidents, still retains a certain importance. First, the judges composing the Presidency, who are elected by an absolute majority of their peers,[90] are the only judges required by the Statute to serve full-time.[91] The Presidency is responsible for the proper administration of the Court, with the exception of the Office of the Prosecutor,[92] and, in that regard, decides when and to what extent the remaining judges shall be required to serve on a full-time basis, as well as whether an increase in the number of judges is required by the Court.[93] The Presidency is also required to draw

---

88. Article 56 creates an exception to this principle and permits a judge to observe personally and make recommendations or orders regarding the collection and preservation of evidence, and the questioning of persons, if an investigative opportunity arises that is unique and requires rapid action. *Id.* art. 56(2)(e). However, all actions that take place within the territory of a State are subject to the State cooperation regime. *See infra* Chapter 8.

89. For example, the functions of the Pre-Trial Chamber are contained in articles 15, 18, 53, and 56–61, among others. In addition, some articles, such as article 19 on challenges to the jurisdiction of the Court or the admissibility of a case, apply to "the Court" in general, without reference to a particular Division. *Rome Statute*, art. 19.

90. *Rome Statute*, art. 38. They are elected for a three year term or until the end of their term of office as judges. They may be re-elected once.

91. *Id.* art. 35(2).

92. *Id.* art. 38(3)(a).

93. *Id.* art. 36(2).

up a draft Code of Professional Conduct for counsel,[94] and carry out such other duties as the Statute may assign.[95] Finally, the Draft Rules of Procedure and Evidence assign many additional functions to the Presidency, such as the functions assigned to the Court under Part 10 of the Statute (on enforcement).[96]

3. *The Office of the Prosecutor*

Defining the powers of the Prosecutor was a highly contentious issue during the Preparatory Committee's meetings, specifically with respect to whether the Prosecutor should be able to act *proprio motu* or *ex officio*, that is, on his or her own motion, in bringing cases to the Court. This issue created a deep schism among the delegates to the Preparatory Committee, with many smaller nations, some European nations, and most NGOs strongly supporting a Prosecutor able to act independently of State referral,[97] and many larger countries, including most of the permanent five members of the Security Council, opposing an independent Prosecutor.[98] Many States were concerned that the independent prosecutor could become an "independent counsel for the universe," unaccountable to anyone and liable to file complaints against States on the basis of political prejudices rather than legal concerns. However, numerous procedural safeguards are built into the Statute to prevent the Prosecutor from abusing his or her power.

---

94. Draft RPE 8. The Presidency is to do so on the basis of a proposal made by the Registrar, and after having consulted with the Prosecutor.

95. *Rome Statute*, art. 38(3)(b).

96. Draft RPE 199.

97. The issue arose at The Preparatory Committee (IV) in August 1997, during discussions on article 23 of the ILC Draft. Supporters of an independent Prosecutor included Germany, Finland, Norway, Costa Rica, Tanzania, South Korea, Italy, Austria, Trinidad & Tobago, Argentina, Greece, Switzerland, Liechtenstein, and New Zealand. LAWYER'S COMMITTEE FOR HUMAN RIGHTS, THE INTERNATIONAL CRIMINAL COURT TRIGGER MECHANISM AND THE NEED FOR AN INDEPENDENT PROSECUTOR (July 1997); HUMAN RIGHTS WATCH, COMMENTARY FOR THE AUGUST 1997 PREPARATORY COMMITTEE MEETING ON THE ESTABLISHMENT OF AN INTERNATIONAL CRIMINAL COURT: MATERIALS FOR WORKING GROUPS 1 AND 2 (1997). The Lawyer's Committee for Human Rights wrote a second paper to refute the idea that an independent Prosecutor would be uncontrollable. LAWYER'S COMMITTEE FOR HUMAN RIGHTS, THE ACCOUNTABILITY OF AN EX OFFICIO PROSECUTOR (Feb. 1998).

98. Opponents of an independent Prosecutor during the fourth session of the Preparatory Committee included the United States, the Russian Federation, China, France, Israel, India, Malaysia, Egypt, and Syria. The United Kingdom appeared to be undecided.

Pursuant to article 42 of the Statute, the Office of the Prosecutor is to be independent from the other organs of the Court.[99] The Statute also provides that no member of the Office shall seek or act on instruction from any external source. The Prosecutor is responsible for receiving referrals and substantiated information on crimes within the jurisdiction of the Court, for examining those referrals and for conducting investigations and prosecutions.[100] Like the judges, the Prosecutor and Deputy Prosecutors will be elected by the Assembly of States Parties, and will serve one nonrenewable, nine-year term.[101]

The Prosecutor and Deputy Prosecutors are to be of different nationalities.[102] However, the Prosecutor and Deputy Prosecutors shall not automatically be disqualified from acting in respect of complaints involving a person of their own nationality, as they would have been under the ILC Draft Statute.[103] Unlike the judiciary, however, the Statute does not specifically provide for additional cases of disqualification to be specified in the Rules of Procedure and Evidence, although it is hard to see why they could not be if the Assembly of States Parties so desired.

As a response to the concerns about the unchecked power of an independent Prosecutor, the Rome Statute contains a complex procedure by which the Pre-Trial Chamber is to closely supervise cases in which the Prosecutor exercises his or her *proprio motu* investigation powers. As shown in Figure 8, the Prosecutor may commence an investigation only if both he or she and the Pre-Trial Chamber (composed of three judges) have determined that a "reasonable basis" exists to initiate the investigation.[104] Reasonable basis is not a defined term, *per se*, in the Statute, but article 53 suggests that a finding of reasonable basis has three elements: (a) there is a reasonable basis to believe that a crime within the jurisdiction of the Court has been or is being committed; (b) the case is or would be

---

99. *Rome Statute*, art. 42(1).

100. RPE 10 also requires the Prosecutor to be responsible for the retention, storage and security of information and physical evidence obtained in the course of investigations by his or her Office.

101. *Rome Statute*, art. 42(4). A shorter term may, however, be decided upon at the time the Prosecutor or Deputy Prosecutors are elected. Election is by an absolute majority of the Assembly of States Parties.

102. *Id*. art. 42(2).

103. *Compare 1994 ILC Draft Statute*, art. 12(5) ("The Prosecutor and Deputy Prosecutor shall not act in relation to a complaint involving a person of their own nationality."), *with Rome Statute*, art. 42(7) (they shall be disqualified from a case if "their impartiality might reasonably be doubted" or "they have previously been involved in any capacity in that case before the Court or in a related criminal case at the national level involving the person being investigated or prosecuted").

104. *Rome Statute*, art. 15(3), (4).

admissible under article 17; (c) the investigation serves the interests of justice, taking into account the gravity of the crime and the interest of victims.[105] This somewhat circular definition would appear to be further modified by the provision that, in addition to considering the admissibility of a case under article 17 and the interests of justice, the Prosecutor should consider whether there is "a sufficient legal or factual basis to seek a warrant or summons under article 58."[106]

If a State or the Security Council refers a situation, however, the matter is referred to the Court under article 13(a) or under article 13(b), respectively, and the Prosecutor is to initiate an investigation pursuant to article 53, unless there is no reasonable basis to proceed under the Statute.[107] The Statute permits the Pre-Trial Chamber to order an investigation or prosecution to proceed if the Prosecutor's decision not to do so is based solely on a determination that the prosecution would not serve the interests of justice.[108]

4. *The Registry*

The Registry is the organ of the Court for non-judicial matters.[109] While the Registry fills an administrative rather than a judicial or prosecutorial role, care must be taken not to underestimate its power, for it is co-equal to the other organs of the Court.[110] Far more than a "Clerk's" office, the Registry is likely to have a fairly extensive staff responsible for wide-ranging duties that will impact the effective functioning of the Court in many ways. The Registries of the ad hoc Tribunals, for example, provide legal services to the Chambers, administer the budget of the tri-

---

105. *Rome Statute*, art. 53(1). Draft RPE 48 makes clear that "reasonable basis" in article 15 of the Statute is to be determined with regard to the criteria contained in article 53(1).

106. *Id*. art. 53(2)(a).

107. *Id*. art. 53(1).

108. *Id*. art. 53(3)(b).

109. *Rome Statute*, art. 43(1). The Presidency is responsible for judicial administration. *Id*. art. 38(3)(a).

110. Moreover, the Tribunals have a single administrative office for both the Prosecutor and the Judges, unlike national legal systems where each branch of the criminal justice system has its own administrative organization tailored to its specific needs. Report of the Expert Group to Conduct a Review of the Effective Operation and Functioning of the International Tribunal for the Former Yugoslavia and the International Criminal Tribunal for Rwanda, at para. 22, U.N. Doc. S/2000/597.

bunals, maintain the library and court records, language, conference and translation services, maintain and oversee the detention units, and procure and maintain the tribunals' facilities and equipment, such as courtrooms and vehicles used by investigators.[111] In addition, they are the Tribunals' link to the outside world, maintaining a press office and the court records,[112] and are responsible for maintaining a list of defense counsel, a function that has generated both controversy in and criticism of the Rwanda Tribunal.[113] Indeed, there have been numerous conflicts between the Judges, Prosecutor and the Registrar in both the ICTR and ICTY over many of these issues.[114]

The Registry of the ICC is presided over by the Registrar, a full-time member of the Court,[115] who is elected by the Judges for a five-year term.[116] Election is by absolute majority of the Judges, taking into consideration the recommendation of the Assembly of States Parties.[117] The Registrar may be re-elected once.[118] If necessary, the Judges may elect a

---

111. VIRGINIA MORRIS & MICHAEL P. SCHARF, I THE INTERNATIONAL CRIMINAL TRIBUNAL FOR RWANDA 396–98 (1998); VIRGINIA MORRIS & MICHAEL P. SCHARF, I AN INSIDER'S GUIDE TO THE INTERNATIONAL CRIMINAL TRIBUNAL FOR THE FORMER YUGOSLAVIA 168–70 (1995).

112. The Registry of the ICTY makes court documents available to the press and interested scholars and publishes a monthly bulletin which is available by subscription. *Id.* at 398. The Bulletin currently has 799 total subscribers, of which 543 receive the publication in English, 177 in French, and 79 in both languages.

113. The refusal of the Registrar to permit the accused at the Rwanda Tribunal to choose the counsel of their choice led to a hunger strike, and ultimately a challenge in the Appeals Chamber.

114. In 1997, the ICTR Registrar took the position that the President of the Tribunal had no authority over its activities. The United Nations' Office of Internal Oversight Services took an opposing view, namely that the President was responsible for supervising the activities of the Registry. The U.N. Office of Legal Affairs then took a middle position, suggesting that the "supervisory role of the President should be understood in a general sense of oversight, rather than direct authority or responsibility." VIRGINIA MORRIS & MICHAEL P. SCHARF, I THE INTERNATIONAL CRIMINAL TRIBUNAL FOR RWANDA 398–99 (1998). The difficulties have not stopped however; more recently, the Judges and the Prosecutor criticized the Registrar for exceeding his power by issuing a letter of safe conduct to Bernard Ntuyahaga, after he was released by the Tribunal, so that he could stand trial in Belgium. *Rwanda Genocide Court Still Quarrelling Over Suspect's Release*, AFR. NEWS SERV., Apr. 16, 1999, *available in* AFRNS, 1999 WL 14357132.

115. *Rome Statute*, art. 43(5).

116. *Id.* art. 43(4).

117. *Id.*

118. *Id.* art. 43(5).

Deputy Registrar to assist the Registrar.[119] The Deputy Registrar serves a five-year term, unless the Judges decide on a shorter tenure at the time of election, and need not be a full-time member of the Registry.[120] The Registry is responsible for keeping the Court's records,[121] proposing Staff Regulations, which detail the terms of employment of all staff members, including the Prosecutor's staff,[122] and for proposing a draft Code of Professional Conduct.[123] The Registry is also responsible for the establishment and operation of the Victims and Witnesses Unit,[124] as well as supervising and facilitating the assignment of defense counsel.

C. The Assembly of States Parties

The Rome Statute adds another institution to the structure envisaged by the 1994 ILC Draft: the Assembly of States Parties. Although the establishment of the Assembly of States Parties was not envisaged by the International Law Commission in its 1994 draft statute, the idea was generally well-received following a French proposal introduced in the Preparatory Committee during 1996,[125] to establish an *Assemblée Générale* as an oversight body of States Parties for the Court. Because the delegates did not focus on it, it did not appear in interim drafts of the Statute, however, but finally appeared in the April Draft Statute submitted to the Diplomatic Conference in 1998.[126] Although not stated to be one of the four "official" organs of the Court,[127] it is, as shown in Figure 6, extremely important as the Court's *organe plénier* charged with overseeing its opera-

119. *Id.* art. 43(4).

120. *Id.* art. 43(5).

121. Draft RPE 15.

122. *Rome Statute*, art. 44(3). The Prosecutor and the President must agree to the regulations, and the Assembly of States Parties must approve them.

123. Draft RPE 8.

124. *Rome Statute*, art. 43(6).

125. *Preparatory Committee on the Establishment of an International Criminal Court, 12–30 August 1996, Drafts Statute of the International Criminal Court, Working paper submitted by France*, U.N. Doc. A/AC.249/L.3 (1996). Article 2 of the French draft proposed the establishment of a "General Assembly of the States Parties."

126. *April Draft Statute*, art. 102.

127. As others have noted, the Assembly's legal status, whether a de facto "organ" of the Court or not, is not altogether clear. Claus Kreß & Kimberly Prost, *Article 87: Requests for Cooperation: General provisions, in* COMMENTARY ON THE ROME STATUTE OF THE INTERNATIONAL CRIMINAL COURT 1055, 1063 (Otto Triffterer, ed., 1999).

tions and functioning.[128] It will not only consider the work of the Preparatory Commission in establishing the Court, but will also provide management oversight, act on the budget, decide whether to alter the number of the judges, adopt the Elements of Crimes and the Rules of Procedure and Evidence,[129] and take up amendments to the Statute.[130] In addition, the Assembly of States Parties will elect the Judges, Prosecutor, and Deputy Prosecutors. It may remove them as well.[131] The Statute provides that the Assembly will have a Bureau, consisting of a President, two Vice-Presidents and 18 members,[132] which shall "assist the Assembly in the discharge of its responsibilities."[133] The Assembly may also establish subsidiary bodies as may be necessary "in order to enhance its efficiency

---

128. *See* Ignaz Seidl-Hohenveldern, *Les organes des organisations internationales: organes pléniers, in* MANUEL SUR LES ORGANISATIONS INTERNATIONALES 81 (René-Jean Dupuy, ed., 1988).

129. *Rome Statute,* arts. 112(2)(a), (b), (d), (e), 9, 51 (respectively). During the Statute's negotiation, the possibility for the Assembly to grant pardons arose, but was ultimately rejected. *See Zutphen Intersessional Draft,* art. 89[60], n. 340. *See also* S. Rama Rao, *Financing of the Court, Assembly of States Parties and the Preparatory Commission, in* THE INTERNATIONAL CRIMINAL COURT: THE MAKING OF THE ROME STATUTE 399, 409–10 (Roy S. Lee, ed., 1999).

130. A State Party may propose amendments seven years after the Statute enters into force. *Rome Statute,* art. 121(1). Adoption of the amendment, absent consensus among the States Parties, requires a two-thirds majority vote of States Parties. *Id.* art. 121(3). If seven-eighths of the States Parties adopt an amendment, any State Party that did not accept the amendment may withdraw from the Statute with immediate effect by giving notice no later than one year after the amendment enters into force, subject to the withdrawal provisions in article 127(2). *Id.* art. 121(6). All amendments to article 5 enter into force for those States that adopt the amendment one year after the States deposit instruments of ratification. *Id.* art. 121(5). The Court may not exercise jurisdiction over a crime covered by such an amendment if that crime is committed by a national of or on the territory of a State that did not accept the amendment. *Id.* art. 121(5).

131. *Id.* arts. 36, 42(4), 46(2). As shown in Figure 5, the Statute provides for removal of the officers of the Court in cases of serious misconduct or a serious breach of his or her duties, or where the individual can no longer exercise the functions required by the Statute. *Id.* art. 46(1). Disciplinary measures may be taken for less serious misconduct. *Id.* art. 47.

132. *Id.* art. 112(3). The members of the Bureau are elected for three-year terms. *Id.* art. 112(3)(a). In addition, the Bureau shall have a representative character, taking into account, in particular, equitable geographical distribution and the adequate representation of the principal legal systems of the world. *Id.* art. 112(3)(b).

133. *Id.* art. 112(3)(c). Detailed provisions regarding the Bureau's operation can be found in Draft RPASP 29–33.

and economy."[134] Finally, the Draft Rules of the Assembly provide for the creation of a Secretariat for the Assembly to, *inter alia*, receive, translate, reproduce and distribute documents, reports and decisions of the Assembly and its subsidiary bodies; interpret speeches at meetings; prepare and print its records (if so requested); and serve as custodian for its documents and archives.[135]

The Assembly of States Parties perfectly illustrates the tension in the Statute between State sovereignty and the emerging international order. Certain aspects of the Assembly's operation suggest a retention of the sovereignty paradigm. This is particularly evident in article 119's provision that disputes between two or more States regarding interpretation of the Statute that do not involve "the judicial functions of the Court" are to be decided first by negotiation, and if that is unsuccessful, then by the Assembly.[136] Presumably the negotiations would be intergovernmental rather than supranational, although the Statute is unclear as to whether the Assembly could vote to impose a solution on one of the States involved.[137] In addition, the Assembly operates on a one-seat, one-vote basis, and all decisions are to be taken by consensus if possible.[138] Finally, it is not clear whether the meetings of the Assembly will be open to the public and whether NGOs and other interested observers will be permitted to participate or observe.[139]

---

134. *Id.* art. 112(4). *See also* Draft RPASP 79–80. The Working Group on Financial Regulations and Rules of the Preparatory Commission has proposed the Establishment of a Committee on Budget and Finance to "provide an appropriate mechanism for the budgetary and financial review and monitoring of the resources of the International Criminal Court, including those of the Assembly." U.N. Doc. PCNICC/2001/WGFIRR/RT.2/Rev.1, March 7, 2001.

135. Draft RPASP 36. It is not clear what the relationship of the Bureau and the Secretariat will be.

136. *Rome Statute,* art. 119. The Assembly may, in turn, refer the case to the International Court of Justice. *Id.* art. 119(2). This provision is now implemented in article 13 of the Draft Relationship Agreement, but has been the subject of some controversy during the Preparatory Commission's discussions.

137. It is unclear what effect an interpretation of the Statute between two governments, arrived at by negotiation, would have on the uninvolved States Parties, although presumably it would not bind them in any way.

138. *Rome Statute,* art. 112(7); Draft RPASP 59–62. The Draft Rules propose that a quorum for opening a meeting is the presence of one third of the States Parties participating in the session. The quorum for voting consists of an absolute majority of the States Parties. Draft RPASP 43.

139. Draft RPASP 41 provides that meetings of the Assembly shall be held in public unless the Assembly decides that exceptional circumstances require they

Yet the Assembly's operation is also consistent with the recent trend away from unanimity as the basis of international decision-making,[140] for where States are unable to achieve a consensus[141] decisions are to be taken by either a two-thirds majority or a simple majority, depending on the question addressed.[142] Consistent with the principle of sovereign equality, no weighting of votes is present. Rather, smaller States have the same voting power as larger States. Yet because larger States generally have greater populations, and are often required (under current rules) to contribute a great deal more in the way of financial support to the Court,[143] a legitimate question exists as to whether a new paradigm for international assemblies, based upon some sort of weighted voting system, is in order.[144] To achieve such a result, however, would require States to explicitly acknowledge the erosion of sovereignty implicit in the formation and governance of international organizations, something that many States have been unwilling to do.

---

be held in private. However, meetings of the Bureau and subsidiary bodies are to be held in private unless the body in question decides otherwise.

140. N.D. WHITE, THE LAW OF INTERNATIONAL ORGANIZATIONS 73 (1996).

141. As Professor White notes, unanimity should not be confused with consensus. The latter typically refers to "'the making of decisions without a vote and without formal objection by any member state.'" *Id. quoting* H. G. SCHERMERS, INTERNATIONAL INSTITUTIONAL LAW 393 (2d ed., 1980).

142. *Rome Statute*, art. 112(7).

143. The contributions of the States Parties to the Court are to be determined in accordance with a scale that will be based on the current scale used by the United Nations. *Id.* art. 117. This would seem to be inconsistent with the idea of a one-seat, one-vote system, indicating that a weighted voting system, such as the qualified majority method used by the European Union might be appropriate. EC Treaty, art. 205. *Accord* N.D. WHITE, THE LAW OF INTERNATIONAL INSTITUTIONS 76 (1996). For a discussion of the methods that the United Nations system has used in addressing the inequities of a one-State, one-vote system, see Paul Szasz, *General Law Making Process, in* 1 UNITED NATIONS LEGAL ORDER 48–50 (Oscar Schacter & Cristopher C. Joyner, eds., 1995).

144. Of course, the problem is how to apportion the weight—by population, financial contribution, GDP, power or some other basis.

CHAPTER 5

UNIVERSAL INTERNATIONAL JURISDICTION

> *If we are ever to develop an orderly international community based upon a recognition of human dignity it is of the utmost importance that the necessary punishment of those guilty of atrocities be as free as possible from the ugly stigma of revenge and vindictiveness. Justice must be tempered by compassion rather than by vengeance.*
>
> —In re *Yamashita*
>
> Dissenting Opinion of Mr. Justice Murphy

The general principles underlying the jurisdiction of the Court, the effectuation and expression of the complementarity principle in the Court's Statute, and the manner in which cases will come to the Court and be decided, are, perhaps, the core of the revolution worked in Rome: the prescriptive jurisdiction of the international community and the adjudicative jurisdiction of the Court are premised on transformative redefinitions of those principles in current international law. Indeed, through a rather astonishing mutation, jurisdictional principles concerning "which State" may exercise its authority over particular cases have been transformed into norms establishing the circumstances under which the international community may prescribe rules of international criminal law and punish those who breach such rules. The repartition of competences between national and international jurisdictions that is incorporated in the Statute as a matter of prescriptive and adjudicative jurisdiction presages a quasi-federal organization of international legal authority in the future.[1]

In contrast, the Court's enforcement jurisdiction is paltry, at best, suggesting the unease of the States Parties to the Statute with the revolution they wrought. While they boldly proclaimed the right of the international

1. The European Union offers a useful comparison, although in the case of the Court, the organization is implicit rather than explicit.

community to prescribe, and, for the most part, suggested that jurisdiction to adjudicate followed in principle, they in no manner followed suit in terms of enforcement. Here, classic paradigms of sovereignty, in which each State is master of its own territory, prevail. To put it another way, if the Framers were willing to permit the intangible presence of the law to permeate State borders, the reception they offered those whose duty it was to enforce that law was much chillier. Finally, the Framers' distrust of their new creation is evidenced by the extremely complex and potentially burdensome procedural regime governing challenges to jurisdiction and admissibility, which may prevent the Court from efficiently fulfilling its primary mission to administer justice.

I. SCOPE OF THE COURT'S JURISDICTION

A. Jurisdiction *ratione temporis, ratione loci,* and *ratione personae*

Under article 11 of the Statute, the Court's jurisdiction is limited to crimes committed after the Statute enters into force.[2] This precludes the transfer of cases from the two ad hoc tribunals to the Court, an option that had been considered earlier in the Statute's negotiation. The decision to make the Court's jurisdiction prospective only will disappoint some who thought that the Court might be a forum in which to redress old wrongs. On the other hand, it has undoubtedly increased the number of States willing to ratify the Statute.[3]

---

2. For States becoming parties after the Statute's entry into force, the Court may exercise jurisdiction only with respect to crimes committed after the entry into force of the Statute with respect to that State, unless the State declares otherwise. *Rome Statute*, art. 11(1), 11(2).

3. The Zutphen Intersessional Draft contained a version of article 11 that would seemingly have permitted the transfer of cases from an ad hoc tribunal established by the Security Council as regards crimes committed before the entry into force of the Statute upon a decision of the Security Council. *Zutphen Intersessional Draft*, art. 8[21ter]. The provision, which reappeared essentially unchanged in the April Draft Statute, was confusing however, and the current redaction is much clearer. Leila Sadat Wexler, *Commentary on Parts 1 and 2 of the Zutphen Intersessional Draft: Establishment of the Court, Complementarity, Jurisdiction and Admissibility, in* OBSERVATIONS ON THE CONSOLIDATED ICC TEXT BEFORE THE FINAL SESSION OF THE PREPARATORY COMMITTEE, 13*bis* NOUVELLES ÉTUDES PÉNALES 17, 22 (Leila Sadat Wexler, special ed., 1998).

The geographic scope of the Court's jurisdiction, *ratione loci*, varies depending on the mechanism by which the case comes to the Court. In the event that the Security Council refers the matter, jurisdiction covers the territory of every State in the world, whether or not the State in question is a party to the Statute.[4] If the matter is referred by a State Party or initiated *proprio motu* by the Prosecutor, however, the Court's jurisdiction is more restricted. In such instances, jurisdiction extends to the territory of a non-party State only if that State consents to the jurisdiction of the Court, and either the acts were committed in the territory of the consenting State or the accused is a national of the consenting State.[5]

The Statute provides for jurisdiction *ratione personae* over natural persons only (thereby excluding organizations or States).[6] The ILC, in early discussions on the question of an international criminal court, proposed adding State culpability.[7] The idea was rejected as "science fiction."[8] Finally the Court's jurisdiction is limited to persons eighteen years or older.[9] Interestingly, the Rome Statute expressly avoids referring to the age limit in the Statute as an age of criminal responsibility. Rather, in order to accommodate sharp differences of view as to the appropriate age of criminal responsibility, as well as the argument that many atrocities are committed by minors, the Statute takes the view that the age threshold is jurisdictional in nature, rather than normative. Thus, as Per Saland has noted in his commentary on article 11, it can be argued that the provision

---

4. *Rome Statute*, art. 13(b). Because the Security Council will refer cases only under its Chapter VII powers, referral to the Court, like the establishment of the two ad hoc tribunals, is presumably a measure "not involving the use of force" that the Security Council may adopt to maintain international peace and security. *See* Prosecutor v. Tadić (Case No. IT-94-1-AR72), Decision on the Defence Motion for Interlocutory Appeal on Jurisdiction (ICTY Appeals Chamber Oct. 2, 1995).

5. *Rome Statute*, arts. 4(2), 12(2).

6. *Id.* arts. 1, 25(1). The Statute does not permit trials in absentia. Thus, the Court must always have the defendant in its custody to obtain personal jurisdiction, in the sense that U.S. lawyers use the term. *Id.* art. 63(1).

7. Leila Sadat Wexler, *The Proposed Permanent International Criminal Court: An Appraisal*, 29 CORNELL INT'L L. J. 665, 678 n. 75 (1996).

8. *Id.* at 680 n. 88.

9. *Rome Statute*, art. 26. As noted in the commentary to the Zutphen Intersessional Draft, art. 20[E] n. 92, the age of criminal responsibility varies widely among States. Article 1 of the Convention on the Rights of the Child defines a "child" as a human being younger than eighteen. Convention on the Rights of the Child, Nov. 20, 1989, G.A. Res. 44/25, U.N. GAOR, 44th Sess., Supp. No. 49, art. 1, U.N. Doc. A/44/49 (1989), *reprinted in* 28 I.L.M. 1456 (1989). The Convention prohibits life imprisonment without parole and the death penalty for children convicted of crimes. *Id.* art. 37(a). The ILC's 1994 Draft was silent on the age of criminal responsibility.

neither prejudices whatever age of responsibility exists in national systems, nor condones offenses by minors.[10]

B. Jurisdiction *ratione materiae*

As shown in Figure 1, the Rome Statute extends the Court's subject matter jurisdiction to four crimes:[11] genocide, crimes against humanity, war crimes, and aggression.[12] Jurisdiction is without reservation (subject to the State consent regime and complementarity principle, as detailed below), with two exceptions. First, a State may opt out of the war crimes jurisdiction of the Court as regards its nationals or crimes committed on its territory for seven years after the Statute enters into force for that State.[13] Second, the Statute does not define aggression. Article 5(2) provides that the Court shall exercise jurisdiction over that crime once it has been defined.

The ICC's jurisdiction as ultimately constituted is narrower than the jurisdiction originally contemplated by article 20 of the ILC Draft Statute, which provided that the Court would also be able to hear cases involving treaty crimes.[14] Restricting subject matter jurisdiction in this way was largely positive, for it permitted the Diplomatic Conference to strengthen the compulsory nature of the Court's jurisdiction, which, as originally conceived by the International Law Commission, was largely optional.[15] Because the Preparatory Committee also felt strongly that the Court's

---

10. Per Saland, *International Criminal Law Principles, in* THE INTERNATIONAL CRIMINAL COURT: THE MAKING OF THE ROME STATUTE 189, 201(Roy S. Lee, ed., 1999).

11. *Rome Statute*, art. 5.

12. It is interesting to note that the delegates chose not to reserve an article in the definition of crimes section for aggression. The definition of aggression must be adopted in accordance with articles 121 and 123 of the Statute, which detail the process of amending the Statute.

13. *Rome Statute*, art. 124. The opt-out was of particular importance to many States such as the United States and France, as the Statute provides that no reservations are permitted. *Rome Statute*, art. 120. The United States desired, but did not obtain, a similar ten-year opt-out provision respecting crimes against humanity. Although the war crimes opt-out has been severely criticized in many quarters, over the anticipated long life of the Court's existence it is probably of minor importance, particularly as the opt-out will not apply in the event the Security Council refers a situation to the Court. Thus far only France has invoked the war crimes opt-out in ratifying the Statute.

14. *1994 ILC Draft Statute*, art. 20.

15. Leila Sadat Wexler, *The Proposed Permanent International Criminal Court: An Appraisal*, 29 CORNELL INT'L L. J. 665, 699 (1996).

Statute should define the crimes within its jurisdiction, rather than simply list them, as the ILC had done,[16] inclusion of some of the treaty crimes was problematic given difficulties in reaching a consensus on their definition.[17] Recognizing, however, that treaty crimes present serious problems for the international community and that some countries felt particularly strongly about their inclusion, Resolution E, which was adopted by the Diplomatic Conference in its Final Act, provides that the issues of terrorism and drug crimes should be taken up at a Review Conference, with a view to their ultimate inclusion in the jurisdiction of the Court.[18]

II. FOUNDATIONS OF THE COURT'S JURISDICTION

A. Jurisdiction to Prescribe

One intriguing aspect of the Rome Treaty, which underscores its nature as a constitutive document, is that it combines jurisdiction to prescribe, jurisdiction to adjudicate, and jurisdiction to enforce all in one instrument. And it is perhaps the implementation and implications of the jurisdictional theories of the Statute that are its most revolutionary features. For, through a rather extraordinary process, these three jurisdictional categories classically known to international law have been transformed from norms providing "*which State* can exercise authority over whom, and in what circumstances,"[19] to norms that establish under

---

16. *See* Chapters 6 and 9.

17. As the International Law Association (American Branch) Committee noted in its initial report on the ILC draft, the inclusion of treaty crimes had the potential to complicate the Court's jurisdictional regime, involve the creation of special chambers, and require a filtering mechanism to assure that States did not dump insignificant cases on the Court. Nevertheless, the Committee supported the inclusion of at least some treaty crimes within the Court's initial jurisdiction. Leila Sadat Wexler, *First Committee Report on Jurisdiction, Definition of Crimes and Complementarity, in* THE INTERNATIONAL CRIMINAL COURT: OBSERVATIONS AND ISSUES BEFORE THE 1997–98 PREPARATORY COMMITTEE; AND ADMINISTRATIVE AND FINANCIAL IMPLICATIONS, 13*ter* NOUVELLES ÉTUDES PÉNALES 163, 164–65 (M. Cherif Bassiouni, ed., 1997). For a good discussion of the treatment of treaty crimes during the Rome Statute's negotation, see Herman von Hebel & Darryl Robinson, *Crimes Within the Jurisdiction of the Court, in* THE INTERNATIONAL CRIMINAL COURT: THE MAKING OF THE ROME STATUTE 79 (Roy S. Lee, ed., 1999).

18. *Final Act*, Annex I, Res. E.

19. ROSALYN HIGGINS, PROBLEMS AND PROCESS: INTERNATIONAL LAW AND HOW WE USE IT 56 (1994) (emphasis added).

what conditions *the international community*, or more precisely the States Parties to the Treaty, may prescribe international rules of conduct, adjudicate breaches of those rules, and enforce those adjudications. This section will focus on prescriptive jurisdiction. Jurisdiction to adjudicate and jurisdiction to enforce are addressed below.

As classically defined, jurisdiction to prescribe refers to the manner in which the international community makes "its law applicable to the activities, relations, or status of persons, or the interests of persons in things. . . ."[20] The Rome Statute does this by embodying prescriptive norms for the international community as a matter of substantive criminal law. The delegates' willingness to engage in such an exercise overcame one of the major historical objections to an international criminal court: the absence of international criminal law with which potential defendants could be charged.[21] Moreover, the elaboration and adoption of an international criminal code as part of the Rome Treaty was perhaps the least controversial of the three jurisdictional axes within the Rome Statute, for the four categories of crimes within the Statute were considered *jus cogens* norms by most writers,[22] even though their precise definition had not yet been completely agreed upon by all States. That is, even without complete accord on the definitional content of each offense, States generally seemed confident as to the propriety of defining them as a matter of treaty law at the Diplomatic Conference.

The use of the treaty as the legal vehicle by which the crimes were defined, however, should not obscure the innovative nature of the process used. Indeed, it must be recognized that to the extent the Rome Con-

---

20. RESTATEMENT (THIRD) OF THE FOREIGN RELATIONS LAW OF THE UNITED STATES § 401(a) (1987). *See also* Michael Akehurst, *Jurisdiction in International Law*, 1972–1973 BRITISH Y.B. INT'L L. 145, 179.

21. Leila Sadat Wexler, *The Proposed Permanent International Criminal Court: An Appraisal*, 29 CORNELL INT'L L. J. 665, 717–20 (1996).

22. *See, e.g.*, M. Cherif Bassiouni, *The Normative Framework of International Humanitarian Law: Overlaps, Gaps and Ambiguities*, 8 TRANSNAT'L L. & CONTEMP. PROBS. 199, 201–02 (1998). It would be overbroad, however, to state categorically that there is complete agreement on the *jus cogens* nature of the crimes, particularly as regards aggression, which some contend has not even been defined in international law. Christian Tomuschat, *Crimes Against the Peace and Security of Mankind and the Recalcitrant Third State*, 24 ISRAEL Y.B. HUM. RTS. 41, 52 (1994) (arguing that "the international community . . . is not really convinced that a universally acknowledged class of crimes against peace entailing individual criminal responsibility exists"). On the nature of *jus cogens* obligations generally see A.J.J. de Hoogh, *The Relationship between* Jus Cogens, *Obligations* Erga Omnes *and International Crimes: Peremptory Norms in Perspective*, 42 AUSTRIAN J. PUBL. INTL' L. 183 (1991).

ference was actually a quasi-legislative process by which the international community "legislated" by a non-unanimous vote, the political legitimacy of the norms must rest not on a theory of contract (treaty-making) but on some other grounds. Elsewhere I have argued that this marked a "Constitutional Moment" of sorts, a sea-change in international law-making with which political theory and institutional form has not caught up.[23] For present purposes, it suffices to say that the power and legitimacy of these norms was premised on the well-accepted theory of universal inter-State jurisdiction that derives from the idea that when criminal activity rises to a certain level of harm (the gravity idea threaded through the Statute), or sufficiently important interests of international society are threatened, any State may apply its laws to the act, "even if it occurred outside its territory, even if it has been perpetrated by a non-national, and even if its nationals have not been harmed by [it]."[24]

Universal inter-State jurisdiction is predicated on at least two ideas. First, that some crimes are so heinous that they offend the interest of all humanity — indeed, they imperil civilization itself.[25] Thus, any State may, as humanity's agent, prosecute and punish the perpetrators.[26] Second, these crimes are often committed by States or those in control of a State, and are therefore likely to go unpunished by the territorial State. In a world in which very few States are likely to prosecute non-nationals for atrocities, having a theory of "absolute" universal jurisdiction, that is, universal jurisdiction subject to no limitations borne from prudential concerns, makes sense.[27] But if many States adopt legislation to punish

---

23. Leila Nadya Sadat & S. Richard Carden, *The New International Criminal Court: An Uneasy Revolution*, 88 Geo. L. J. 381, 394–95 (2000).

24. Rosalyn Higgins, Problems and Process: International Law and How We Use It 57 (1994); *see also* Restatement (Third) of the Foreign Relations Law of the United States § 404 (1987) (noting that States may define punishments for offenses which are of "universal concern"). *See generally* Kenneth C. Randall, *Universal Jurisdiction Under International Law*, 66 Tex. L. Rev. 785 (1988).

25. Kenneth C. Randall, *Universal Jurisdiction Under International Law*, 66 Tex. L. Rev. 785, 803 (1988).

26. *See, e.g.*, Restatement (Third) of the Foreign Relations Law of the United States § 404 and comments (1987). For the view that war crimes may not be subject to universal jurisdiction, see D. W. Bowett, *Jurisdiction: Changing Patterns of Authority over Activities and Resources*, 1982 British Y. B. Int'l L. 1, 12–13.

27. See also the work of Professor Marc Henzelin, dividing universal jurisdiction into three categories: the principle of unilateral universal jurisdiction, used in a similar sense to what I have termed "absolute" universal jurisdiction, Marc Henzelin, Le principe de l'universalité en droit pénal international 63 (2000); the principle of delegated universal jurisdiction, by which one State has delegated to another its criminal jurisdiction, *id.* at 71; and the principle of absolute universal

perpetrators of international crimes, and then begin to assert jurisdiction over such offenders, international law will have to establish some reasonable and principled rules to resolve otherwise difficult conflicts of jurisdiction.[28]

This theory of universal inter-State jurisdiction was extended in Rome, following the precedent of Nuremberg and the two ad hoc Tribunals, to a principle of *universal international jurisdiction*[29] which would permit the international community as a whole, in certain limited circumstances, to supplement, or even displace,[30] ordinary national laws of territorial application[31] with international laws that are universal in thrust and unbounded in geographical scope.[32]

The Treaty's preamble articulates the two bases upon which jurisdiction is predicated, namely our "common humanity" and the threat that these crimes pose to international peace and security.[33] Yet the Statute does not propose a bright line test for sorting the international from the national; that is, there is no "interstate commerce clause requirement" such as we find in U.S. federal criminal law, nor is there a "subsidiarity principle," such as we find in the delimitation of competencies in the European Union between the Communities and the Member States. That

---

jurisdiction, according to which the State exercises its jurisdiction in execution of a transcendent obligation, natural law or divine right. *Id.* at 81.

28. Work on this project has already begun. *See* Princeton Project on Universal Jurisdiction, Working Papers, January 26–27, 2001 (Princeton University).

29. The novelty of this theory is underscored by the fact that international law textbooks invariably treat international jurisdictional rules as rules governing the repartition of competences *between States. See, e.g.*, LOUIS HENKIN ET AL., INTERNATIONAL LAW 821 (2d ed. 1987) ("International law has not yet developed a comprehensive set of rules defining with reasonable precision all forms of jurisdiction that may be exercised by states and other international legal persons."); *see also* MARK W. JANIS & JOHN W. NOYES, INTERNATIONAL LAW 609–57 (1997); COVEY T. OLIVER ET AL., THE INTERNATIONAL LEGAL SYSTEM 133–215 (4th ed. 1995).

30. National law is displaced if it is inconsistent with international law.

31. Territoriality is the most obvious nexus. Nationality, passive personality, effects, and the protective principle are also either recognized or asserted to be legitimate bases upon which States may assert jurisdiction to prescribe. *See* RESTATEMENT (THIRD) OF THE FOREIGN RELATIONS LAW OF THE UNITED STATES § 402 (1987).

32. The theoretical basis upon which the Framers rested this jurisdiction is unclear because it was not explict. It is probably closest to Henzelin's principle of absolute universal jurisdiction. MARC HENZELIN, LE PRINCIPE DE L'UNIVERSALITÉ EN DROIT PÉNAL INTERNATIONAL 81 (2000).

33. *Rome Statute*, preamble, cls. 1 & 3.

is because the Statute does not focus on this issue at all, leaving it essentially up to the complementarity principle and State consent regime to sort permissible from impermissible assertions of the Court's jurisdiction (to adjudicate). The one explicit clue is the Treaty's command that the Court is to exercise its jurisdiction only in cases involving "the most serious crimes of concern to the international community as a whole."[34] This phrase combines both a substantive limit on the Court's jurisdiction with its underlying premise—that in a world of conflicting "sovereigns," both territorial (States) and non-territorial (the international community as a whole), some system must be adopted to sort permissible from impermissible assertions of jurisdiction (to prescribe). As Professor Georges Levasseur noted some years ago, the problem is essentially akin to one of conflict of laws: international criminal law as a body of law may apply where an "individual's behavior (whether a national or a foreigner) has troubled the *ordre public* of a country other than his own."[35]

As will be shown below, the complementarity principle and State consent regime will generally restrain the exercise of the Court's prescriptive jurisdiction such that the Court's reach does not exceed what reasonable theories of power distribution and lawmaking authority between "sovereigns" suggest the proper sphere of the Court's authority should be—but it would have been useful for the Statute to have been more explicit on this point. For, without a doubt, there will be cases in which complementarity will not pose an obstacle to jurisdiction but which the Court should dismiss as inadmissible, because it would be unreasonable for the Court, as an instrument of the international legal order, to exercise jurisdiction over the case.[36] Moreover, it will likely increase the moral and political legitimacy of the Court to do so—if it is seen as an institution willing to exercise self-restraint and be constrained by fidelity to law, it may improve its credibility with State governments, skeptical of international power and meddling in otherwise domestic affairs.

34. *Rome Statute*, art. 5(1); *see also id*. art. 1.

35. Georges Levasseur, *Les crimes contre l'humanité et le problème de leur prescription*, 93 J. DU DROIT INT'L [J.D.I.] 259, 267 (1966).

36. For example, there could be cases of isolated war crimes in a particular armed conflict in which no State was able or willing to prosecute, but which might not rise to the level of gravity contemplated by the Statute.

B. Jurisdiction to Adjudicate

1. General Principles

Although the three separate components of jurisdiction—jurisdiction to prescribe, jurisdiction to adjudicate, and jurisdiction to enforce—are not always congruent,[37] jurisdiction to adjudicate generally follows jurisdiction to prescribe, subject to a rule of reasonableness. By "jurisdiction to adjudicate," I mean "to subject persons [and in particular criminal defendants] or things to the process of [the ICC]."[38] According to the American *Restatement on Foreign Relations (Third)*, "[a] State may exercise jurisdiction through its courts to adjudicate with respect to a person or thing if the relationship of the State to the person or thing is such as to make the exercise of jurisdiction reasonable."[39] This principle generally applies in the ICC as well, with three major caveats. First, the State consent regime (explained below) excludes certain cases from the Court's judicial jurisdiction even though prescriptive jurisdiction exists. Second, the complementarity principle removes another set of cases due to a different set of prudential concerns. Finally, if a defendant has already been tried for the conduct that is the subject of the complaint against him or her in the Court, the principle of *ne bis in idem* applies to remove the case from the Court, as a human rights protection afforded to the defendant that renders an otherwise justiciable case inadmissible.[40]

In all three instances, the Rome Treaty removes a case from the Court, even though, as a matter of substantive law, the ICC Statute would otherwise apply to the conduct in question. Thus, if the defendant's conduct is also being regulated (or he or she is being pursued) by a State, the ICC must relinquish jurisdiction over the case if the State so desires. In some instances, this will be true even though it might seem more appropriate for the ICC to pursue the case. Similarly, if the Prosecutor or a State files a complaint with the Court, a State consent regime attaches that again may divest the Court of jurisdiction to adjudicate. Finally, although the Statute outlaws genocide and crimes against humanity, a regime transitioning from a genocidal past may decide on amnesty and reconciliation instead of criminal prosecutions. This seems to be permitted by the Statute

---

37. Restatement (Third) of the Foreign Relations Law of the United States 230–31 (1987).

38. *Id.* § 401(b).

39. *Id.* § 421(1).

40. *Rome Statute*, arts. 17 (admissibility), 20 (*ne bis in idem*).

which is "creatively ambiguous" on this point, according to Philippe Kirsch, who presided over the Rome Conference as the Chair of the Committee of the Whole.[41] It is hotly contested, however, when and under what conditions amnesties are permissible either as a matter of international law, or under the Statute.[42]

This deference to State sovereignty seems derived from two separate concerns. First, there is an unease with the nature of the law being made. Legal theory and political reality conceive of international law-making as predominantly contractual and consensual. Yet, while the Rome Treaty takes the form of a contract between States it was clearly conceived as a codification of custom and indeed of *jus cogens* crimes. In cases involving a Security Council referral, the Statute's scope is unbounded by geography.[43] Thus, even though article 10 attempts to separate the Statute from customary international law existing outside the Statute's application, and each definition of crimes purports to define the law only "for purposes of this Statute," the Statute, as all have admitted, and to which some countries, including the United States, have strenuously objected, applies to non-party State nationals in certain circumstances, and can be applied by

---

41. *See* Michael P. Scharf, *Justice vs. Peace, in* THE UNITED STATES AND THE INTERNATIONAL CRIMINAL COURT 186 (Sarah B. Sewall & Carl Kaysen, eds., 2000).

42. For a discussion of this issue see Diane F. Orentlicher, *Settling Accounts: The Duty to Prosecute Human Rights Violations of a Prior Regime*, 100 YALE L.J. 2537 (1991); Naomi Roht-Arriaza, *State Responsibility to Investigate and Prosecute Grave Human Rights Violations in International Law*, 78 CAL. L. REV. 449 (1990); Leila Nadya Sadat, *Universal Jurisdiction and National Amnesties, Truth Commissions and Other Alternatives to Prosecution: Giving Justice a Chance*, Princeton Project on Universal Jurisdiction (Princeton University, 2001); Michael P. Scharf, *Swapping Amnesty for Peace: Was there a Duty to Prosecute International Crimes in Haiti?*, 31 TEX. INT'L L. J. 1 (1996).

43. It has been argued that the U.N. Charter is no more binding on non-signatories than any other treaty. *See, e.g.*, Herman Mosler, *The International Society as a Legal Community, in* 140 RECUEIL DES COURS 1, 205–07 (1974). Most writers, however, do not share that view, *see, e.g.*, Bardo Fassbender, *The United Nations Charter as Constitution of the International Community*, 36 COLUM. J. TRANSNAT'L. L. 529, 574–78 (1998), and appear to accept the suggestion that the U.N. Charter establishes a constitution of the international community: a constitution which "every State is bound to observe irrespective of its own will." *Id.* at 549. The States gathered in Rome seemed to take the latter view by making the Statute's application universal in cases involving Security Council referrals under Chapter VII. Indeed, as Professor Tomuschat notes, the U.N. Security Council has addressed its binding decisions to "all States" since it imposed an arms embargo on South Africa in 1977 by Resolution 418. Christian Tomuschat, *Crimes Against the Peace and Security of Mankind and the Recalcitrant Third State*, 24 ISRAEL Y.B. HUM. RTS. 41, 42 n. 5 (1994).

the Security Council to all the human beings of the world. In other words, there is a schizophrenia about the status and binding effect of the prescriptive norms that the text attempts to redress by, in certain limited cases, deferring to the sovereignty of States.

Second, there are legitimate questions involving finite resources. It is both logical and appropriate for States, rather than the ICC, to prosecute cases where they are willing and able to do so. Certainly States have better developed systems of criminal justice, and, insofar as the crimes may have been committed on their territories, will not have the difficulties that the ICC is certain to face in terms of gathering evidence, conducting investigations, and arresting suspects. Moreover, although jurisdiction to adjudicate will generally follow jurisdiction to prescribe, it may be more acceptable (and will be more practical) to exercise judicial jurisdiction where there are clear links to the forum State in respect of the persons, interests, relations, or activities involved.[44]

Finally, the question of *ne bis in idem* raises human rights concerns central to the establishment of a new system of international criminal justice sensitive to the need to meet international human rights standards.

2. *Universal Jurisdiction and State Consent*

Under the 1994 ILC Draft Statute, only States and the Security Council could lodge complaints with the Court.[45] As noted earlier, the Rome Statute also permits the Prosecutor to bring cases before the Court on his or her own initiative.[46] The ILC Draft originally conceived of four separate jurisdictional hurdles that would be prerequisites to the exercise of the Court's jurisdiction in any particular case:[47]

---

44. *Cf.* RESTATEMENT (THIRD) OF THE FOREIGN RELATIONS LAW OF THE UNITED STATES 231 (1987).

45. *1994 ILC Draft Statute*, art. 23, 25.

46. *Rome Statute*, arts. 13(c), 15(1). Private individuals and NGOs may not file complaints directly with the Court (there is thus no right to proceed as a *partie civile*, in the French sense), although the Prosecutor may receive information from NGOs or other reliable sources concerning the possible commission of crimes potentially within the Court's jurisdiction. *Id.* art. 15(2). The ILC and most State delegations consistently took the position that individuals should not be able to bring cases to the Court. Leila Sadat Wexler, *The Proposed Permanent International Criminal Court: An Appraisal*, 29 CORNELL INT'L L. J. 665, 696 n. 181, 699 n. 197 (1996).

47. Interestingly, the jurisdictional predicates clearly seem to apply to an indictment against a particular individual, as the Statute refers to "person" in article 21(1). *Rome Statute*, art. 21(1). Article 23(1) on Security Council referrals, how-

- First, none of the crimes except genocide were within the Court's "inherent" jurisdiction (*compétence propre*), but instead were subject to a complex regime of State consent that was bypassed only in cases referred to the Court by the Security Council;[48]
- Second, States could (again, except in the case of a Security Council referral) limit the jurisdiction of the Court accepted by them in advance by lodging a declaration to that effect with the depositary;[49]
- Third, the Security Council had to make a determination of aggression for a complaint on that basis to be receivable (*recevable*) by the Court. Furthermore, the Security Council, if it was dealing with a "situation" involving a threat to or breach of the peace or an act of aggression under Chapter VII of the Charter, could stop a prosecution from being "commenced";[50]
- Fourth, assuming subject matter jurisdiction (*compétence*) to be generally present, all cases had to be "admissible" (*admissible*) in keeping with the principle of complementarity on which the Statute of the Court was predicated.[51]

The combination of these four jurisdictional predicates would have rendered the Court quite powerless over most international crimes, even those of extreme gravity, unless the Security Council referred a matter to the Court. To many observers, this would have been unsatisfactory, for often the Security Council cannot reach agreement as to the proper disposition of a particular situation. Moreover, most States are not members of the Council.

The Rome Statute responds to many of these concerns. In the words of one of the delegates at Rome, the Framers rejected a "Court à la carte."

---

ever, refers to jurisdiction over the "crimes in article 20" if a "matter" is referred to the court. *Id.* art. 23(1). Presumably, however, the Court would then have jurisdiction over the person charged with those crimes as well. The ILC assumed that the Court would only have personal jurisdiction over individuals, and that jurisdiction would be effected by the arrest of the suspect, given that the Statute essentially forbids trials *in absentia*. *Report of the International Law Commission on the Work of its 46th Session*, U.N. GAOR, 49th Sess., Supp. No. 10, at para. 58, U.N. Doc. A/49/10 (1994). The Rome Statute follows this approach.

48. *1994 ILC Draft Statute*, arts. 21, 22, 25.
49. *Id.* art. 22.
50. *Id.* art. 23(3).
51. *Id.* art. 35.

The Statute now requires all States Parties to accept the Court's inherent jurisdiction[52] over all crimes in article 5, subject to the seven year opt-out for war crimes.[53] It also no longer permits reservations with respect to the Court's jurisdiction over particular offenses.[54] Moreover, it reduces, but in no way eliminates, the power of the Security Council over ongoing proceedings by permitting the Council to interfere only if it adopts a resolution under Chapter VII requesting the Court not to commence an investigation or prosecution, or to defer any proceeding already in progress.[55] Finally, the ILC requirement of a Security Council determination as to aggression[56] is now uncertain,[57] an important point should this crime eventually be brought within the Court's jurisdiction.

There continues to be a great deal of discussion as to whether jurisdiction in the Statute is "universal" or consent-based.[58] Most of the confusion has been generated by a failure to separate the principles of jurisdiction upon which the Statute is premised from the regime governing the exercise of jurisdiction by the Court in particular cases. Indeed, jurisdiction over particular cases is premised on three principles which are widely accepted in international law. First, and foremost, is the universality principle, which thus operates not only as a principle of prescriptive jurisdiction, but of adjudicative jurisdiction, as well. If the Security Council refers a case to the Court, the Court may be asked to pass judgment on the commission of crimes anywhere in the world. The consent of no State is required, even as to the nationals of States not party to the Court's Statute. This is uncontroversial except insofar as the universality principle has been extended from a principle governing inter-State

---

52. "Inherent jurisdiction" is not the equivalent of primacy jurisdiction. Admissibility and complementarity are still limits on the exercise of jurisdiction in a particular case, even with respect to crimes over which there is inherent jurisdiction.

53. *Rome Statute*, art. 124.

54. *Id.* art. 12(1).

55. *Id.* art. 16.

56. *1994 ILC Draft Statute*, art. 23.

57. The Assembly of States Parties, however, will probably reintroduce this requirement when adopting the definition of aggression. *See infra* Chapter 6.

58. The U.S. position, for example, is that the Court does not exercise "universal jurisdiction," but that the jurisdictional regime is nevertheless improper because the nationals of non-party States may find themselves before the Court even if their State of nationality objects. David J. Scheffer, Speech at the Twelfth Annual U.S. Pacific Command International Military Operations and Law Conference, at 20 (Hawaii, Feb. 23, 1999), *available in* <http://www.state.gov/www/policy_remarks/1999/990223_scheffer_hawaii.html>.

relations to one of general prescriptive international law, as discussed above. Even this, however, is not unprecedented, for it is presumably the jurisdictional basis upon which the ICTY and ICTR Statutes were premised.[59] Indeed, although some countries, particularly the United States, have objected to the assertion of jurisdiction by the Court over the nationals of States not parties to the Court's Statute, it has been accepted ever since Nuremberg that, with respect to the establishment of courts for the trial of international crimes over which there exists universal jurisdiction, States may do together what any one of them could have done separately.[60]

If the Prosecutor or a State refers the case, however, although the universality principle does not disappear, layered upon it is a State consent regime based on two additional principles (which are disjunctive) of jurisdiction: the territorial principle and the nationality principle. Thus, as shown in Figure 7, the Court has jurisdiction over cases referred by States Parties (or the Prosecutor *proprio motu*) so long as either the territorial State *or* the State of the accused's nationality is *either* a party to the Statute or has accepted the jurisdiction of the Court.[61]

---

59. *See ICTY Statute; ICTR Statute.*

60. Delegation of Samoa to the Fourth Preparatory Committee, *Note on (Inherent) Jurisdiction and State Consent*, at 5 (Aug. 7, 1997) (on file with author); Judgment of October 1, 1946, International Military Tribunal Judgment and Sentence, 41 AM. J. INT'L L. 172 (1947). An earlier precedent for the exercise of universal adjudicative jurisdiction is cited by Professor Randall. He notes that several nineteenth Century slave trading treaties entered into by Great Britain with other nations created tribunals jointly administered by the parties to the treaties. Kenneth C. Randall, *Universal Jurisdiction Under International Law*, 66 TEX. L. REV. 785, 799 (1988).

61. *Rome Statute*, art. 12(2). The Statute seemingly permits States to consent to jurisdiction in a particular situation without subjecting themselves to jurisdiction in the same case. *See id.* art. 12(3). This is contrary to the Framers' intent as well as the ILC's 1994 Draft Statute (as was noted by the Chair of the drafting committee, Professor M. Cherif Bassiouni, in his remarks at the annual meeting of the American Society of International Law, Spring 1999), which did not permit States the benefits of the Statute without accepting the burdens. It was the subject of four proposals presented to the Preparatory Commission by France, Australia, the United States, and Bosnia-Herzegovina, respectively. LAWYERS COMMITTEE FOR HUMAN RIGHTS, ISSUES OF JURISDICTION AND ADMISSIBILITY IN THE RULES OF PROCEDURE AND EVIDENCE 2 (2000). The problem was ultimately corrected by Draft RPE 44(2) which requires the Registrar to inform States lodging a declaration with the Court pursuant to article 12(3) that the consequence of making such a declaration is acceptance of the Court's jurisdiction with respect to the situation in question.

One might argue that because States may certainly theoretically exercise jurisdiction concurrently with the ICC over the crimes within the Court's Statute, the State consent regime simply serves as a conflicts of jurisdiction principle: unless the Security Council asserts the need to refer the case to the Court because there has been a threat to world peace and security, States and the ICC may wrangle over which entity will prosecute the cases within the Court's prescriptive jurisdiction. Moreover, a State may, in limited circumstances, prevent the ICC from moving forward by withholding its consent. In addition, States that are not parties to the Statute may refuse their consent at least as to crimes committed on their territories, or by their nationals on the territories of States also not parties and which do not consent.

It is more likely, however, that the State consent regime was retained as a concession to the sovereignty of States, for the ends sought by the Statute are imperfectly addressed by the means chosen. First, the Statute stops short of permitting custodial States to consent to jurisdiction. That is, if a defendant of a State not party to the Statute travels to a State party to the Statute, the State to which the potential defendant has traveled may not serve as a jurisdictional nexus to the ICC, even though it could, under well-accepted principles of universal jurisdiction, try the defendant itself. The human rights community desperately fought, albeit unsuccessfully, to include the custodial State as a jurisdictional nexus to prevent the phenomenon of "traveling tyrants,"[62] able to travel to any State (other than the territorial State) so long as they avoid States that join the ICC. Second, under the State consent regime, unlike the complementarity system, the State withholding its consent need not make any effort to try the defendant(s) involved itself. So, absent a Security Council referral, many of the most egregious cases will not be prosecuted by anyone. This result was certainly not required by any principle of jurisdiction; if it is conceded that the international community has jurisdiction to prescribe (and the Statute is admittedly schizophrenic on this point), jurisdiction to adjudicate should follow, subject to the conflict of jurisdictions principles and reasonableness limitations one naturally expects with respect to any exercise of jurisdiction by any "sovereign."

---

62. The phrase was coined by Jelena Pejic, who represented the Lawyer's Committee for Human Rights in Rome.

3. Complementarity with State Judicial Systems

Both the preamble to the Statute and article 1 express a fundamental principle of the Rome Statute: that the Court is to be "complementary" to national criminal jurisdictions.[63] While complementarity is not defined (and indeed, there is no general "definition" section in the Statute, although there are definitional provisions within particular articles),[64] an analysis of the articles on admissibility demonstrates that complementarity does not mean "concurrent" jurisdiction (which it arguably could have under the ILC's original conception). Instead the Court may exercise jurisdiction only if: (1) national jurisdictions are "unwilling or unable" to; (2) the crime is of sufficient gravity; and (3) the person has not already been tried for the conduct on which the complaint is based.[65]

Complementarity has a substantive component, a procedural component, and a component that we may think of as "political," or "prudential" for lack of a better term.[66] The procedural aspect of complementarity is embodied in the regime of admissibility to which all cases are subject, and which is discussed below. The prudential aspect refers to the policy choices made in determining which cases should be in the ICC, rather than national courts, which means that some cases that are clearly within the Court's jurisdiction (prescriptively) will not be heard by the Court. As discussed earlier, the governments that gathered in Rome struggled to find a neutral and principled manner to determine what kind of cases this new international institution should hear. Those cases were deemed (by the Framers) to be instances in which national courts are unwilling to or unable to proceed. The Framers could have been bolder, of course. Having flexed their muscles in defining the crimes, they could have given the Court jurisdiction over all the cases conceivably within its purview. But to do so would most likely have made the Treaty unacceptable to many States. Choosing to limit the Court's jurisdiction was, therefore, probably wise; where complementarity has more unfortunate consequences, however, is in the enforcement area and the State cooperation regime, difficulties discussed both in the next section of this Chapter as well as in Chapter 8, below.

---

63. *Rome Statute*, preamble, art. 1.

64. *See, e.g.*, *id.* art. 7(2) (containing definitions respecting the definition of crimes against humanity outlined in paragraph 1 of the same article).

65. *Rome Statute*, art. 17(1); *see also* Figure 9.

66. Leila Nadya Sadat, Panel Discussion, *Association of American Law School Panel on the International Criminal Court*, 36 AM. CRIM. L. REV. 223, 248 (1999).

C. Jurisdiction to Enforce

As classically conceived, jurisdiction to enforce concerns rules governing the enforcement of law by a State through its courts, as well as through executive, administrative, and police action.[67] If we extrapolate from this principle to the enforcement power of the ICC, we see that this third jurisdictional component of the Statute is by far the weakest. Indeed, the Court's enforcement jurisdiction is so feeble that it has the potential to completely undermine the efficacy of the Court, which, in other respects (such as institutional structure and definition of crimes), is likely to be quite strong.

To begin with the most obvious point, the ICC has no police force.[68] Indeed, it was unthinkable to propose one either before or during Rome, although there was at least some precedent for doing so.[69] But the orders of the Court, whether they be arrest warrants, judgments, orders to seize assets, or sentences, will need to be enforced. The delegates were not unaware of the problem and many provisions of the Statute address it directly.[70] But virtually all of them are premised on three principles. First,

---

67. RESTATEMENT (THIRD) OF THE FOREIGN RELATIONS LAW OF THE UNITED STATES § 401(c) (1987). By "jurisdiction to enforce," I mean jurisdiction "to induce or compel compliance or to punish noncompliance with [the orders and decisions of the ICC]."

68. As one French writer has pointedly remarked, the Court represents "*justice sans police*." Jean-Eric Schoettl, *Décisions du Conseil Constitutionnel: Cour pénale internationale*, L'ACTUALITÉ JURIDIQUE—DROIT ADMINISTRATIF 230 (Mar. 20, 1999).

69. Leila Sadat Wexler, *The Proposed Permanent International Criminal Court: An Appraisal*, 29 CORNELL J. INT'L L. 665, 673 n. 41 (1996) (discussing the proposed statute of the London International Assembly which provided for an international constabulary charged with the "execution of the orders of the Court and of the Procurator General [of the Court]").

70. See, for example, *Rome Statute*, art. 70, which permits the Court to exercise jurisdiction over offences against its administration of justice, subject to conditions that are now set out in Draft RPE 162–69. Article 70 requires States Parties to extend their criminal laws penalizing offenses against their own investigative or judicial processes to similar offenses against the Court, but notes that international cooperation "under this article shall be governed by the domestic laws of the requested State." *Id*. art. 70(2). Thus, even this jurisdiction in aid of enforcement is strongly dominated by reference to State law insofar as its execution is concerned. Article 71 permits the Court to sanction persons present before it who disrupt its proceedings or deliberately refuse to comply with its directions by "administrative measures other than imprisonment." This section, which seems to allow the Court some direct enforcement power, appears to apply only to persons actually in front of the Court, and again would presumably require State cooperation if the sanctions were somehow directly unenforceable.

the Court may not compel compliance, either of individuals or of States, with its orders. That is, it may not compel the appearance of witnesses or the execution of arrest warrants, and it may not seize bank accounts or government documents of its own accord. There is no subpoena power;[71] and there is no writ of mandamus. Second, the Court will not be permitted to sanction States directly for noncompliance with the Statute or its orders. Rather, the Court will be required to make findings of noncompliance and direct those to the Assembly of States Parties, or to the Security Council, if the Security Council referred the case to the Court.[72] Finally, the personnel of the Court will have no right, in most cases, to proceed directly to the execution of their duties on the territories of States, but will work through the authorities present in the requested State and will be subject to national law. There are three important exceptions to this. First, pursuant to article 56, a judge from the Court may be present "to observe and make recommendations or orders regarding the collection and preservation of evidence and the questioning of persons."[73] Second, the Prosecutor may be authorized by the Pre-Trial Chamber to take "specific investigative steps" within the territory of a State Party without the cooperation of the State, if the State is clearly unable to execute requests for cooperation because its judicial system has collapsed.[74] Finally, pursuant to article 99(4), the Prosecutor may under limited circumstances execute specific requests for assistance (other than arrest warrants) directly on the territory of a State Party, if they require no compulsory measures.[75]

Even this brief review of the Court's enforcement jurisdiction suggests that the Statute will be much less revolutionary in practice than in theory. Indeed, it suggests the unease of the States Parties with the revolution they wrought. While they boldly proclaimed the right of the international community to prescribe, and, for the most part suggested that jurisdiction to adjudicate followed in principle, they in no manner followed suit in terms of enforcement. Here, classic paradigms of sovereignty in which each State is master of its territory prevail. To put it another way, if the Framers were willing to permit the intangible presence of the law to

---

71. The concept of subpoena power at the international level has proven controversial. *See* Prosecutor v. Blaskić (Case No. IT-95-14), Judgment on the Request of the Republic of Croatia for Review of the Decision of Trial Chamber II of July 18, 1997 (ICTY Appeals Chamber, Oct. 29, 1997).

72. *Rome Statute*, art. 87(7); *see also* Figure 20.

73. *Rome Statute*, art. 56(2)(e).

74. *Id.* art. 57(3)(d).

75. The Statute specifically includes "the interview of or taking evidence from a person on a voluntary basis," and "the examination without modification of a public site or other public place." *Rome Statute*, art. 99(4).

permeate State borders, the reception they were willing to offer those charged with enforcing that law was much chillier. Given the difficulty that the two ad hoc tribunals, and the ICTY in particular, have had with the arrest of suspects and the conduct of investigations, even when backed with the power of the Security Council, the ICC's ability to effectively enforce international criminal law remains an open question.

III. CHALLENGES TO JURISDICTION AND ADMISSIBILITY

A. Procedural Requirements

Seemingly as the *quid pro quo* for obtaining a Prosecutor with (limited) independent powers of action and for vigorously pruning the State consent regime, the Rome Statute contains an extremely complex procedure for challenging jurisdiction and admissibility. Essentially, at every stage of the proceeding up to trial, including the vetting of the case by the Pre-Trial Chamber if the Prosecutor is investigating *proprio motu*,[76] challenges to admissibility and jurisdiction are permitted, and, for the most part, are subject to interlocutory appeal.[77] Given that at most stages of the proceedings there are several parties (including the Court) with a right of challenge, it is likely that the Court will be spending a great deal of time on motions relating to admissibility and jurisdiction. While it was important to preserve the principle of complementarity and to verify the Court's jurisdiction in all cases, it is quite possible that motions on jurisdiction and admissibility will hamper the efficient functioning of the Court. It is all too easy for disputes about jurisdiction to be abused and thereby overshadow the principal purpose of the Court, which is to administer justice. Because issues of jurisdiction and admissibility are so important, and because the complex and burdensome procedural regime established should easily assuage States' fears that the Court will be an easy means for the filing of political cases, it is discussed in fairly extensive detail below.

Pursuant to article 19, the Court must satisfy itself that it has jurisdiction in any case before it. It *may* on its own motion determine the admissibility of a case under article 17.[78] The Statute thus appears to treat jurisdiction (*ratione materiae*) differently from admissibility. The text is not

76. *Rome Statute*, art. 15(4).

77. Decisions of the Pre-Trial Chamber under article 15 regarding authorization of an investigation do not appear to be subject to interlocutory appeal. *See id*. arts. 15, 82. *Cf*. Draft RPE 50(5).

78. *Rome Statute*, arts. 17, 19(1).

clear whether, in the case of a Security Council referral, the complementarity regime is bypassed (although the case certainly would be on a "fast track" with respect to challenging admissibility because article 18 would not apply). Given that the Prosecutor is under an independent obligation to determine admissibility in all cases, however, including cases referred to the Court by the Security Council, it seems clear that jurisdiction and admissibility (as defined in article 17) are mandatory requirements from the Prosecutor's perspective for all prosecutions before the Court, although admissibility (but not jurisdiction) may in fact be waivable by other parties, as explained below.[79]

Admissibility is defined in article 17 of the Statute. Essentially, as shown in Figure 9, cases are inadmissible in four situations: (1) the case is being investigated by a State with jurisdiction, (2) the case has been investigated by a State with jurisdiction which has decided not to prosecute, (3) the person has already been tried for the conduct which is the subject of the complaint, or (4) the case is of insufficient gravity to warrant pursuit. Each of these categories is subject to further explication in the Statute.[80]

With respect to investigation or prosecution, State action will render a case inadmissible, unless the State is unwilling or unable *genuinely* to carry out the investigation or prosecution.[81] Unwillingness, in turn, is defined as situations in which the proceedings were undertaken "for the purpose of shielding the person concerned from criminal responsibility," where "there has been an unjustified delay in the proceedings [that is] inconsistent with an intent to bring the person concerned to justice," or where "the proceedings were not, or are not being, conducted independently or impartially" *and* in a manner that is consistent "with an intent to bring the person concerned to justice." Inability to prosecute does not raise quite the same problem, for the Statute is clear that inability concerns the total or substantial collapse of a State's judicial system. In making a determination of

---

79. Although a rule was proposed that would require the Pre-Trial Chamber authorizing an investigation pursuant to article 15 to consider the case's ultimate admissibility, it was criticized on the grounds that it could lead to unnecessary delay, Lawyers Committee for Human Rights, Issues of Jurisdiction and Admissibility in the Rules of Procedure and Evidence 4 (2000), and was ultimately deleted. On the other hand, article 53 (on reasonable basis) clearly requires the Prosecutor to consider admissibility before launching an investigation.

80. *Rome Statute*, art. 17; *see also* Figure 9. An extensive debate took place during the Preparatory Commission meetings as to whether the Rules of Procedure and Evidence should articulate admissibility criteria, or factors to be considered by the Court in making determinations under article 17. Indeed, the discussions revisited many of the battles fought at Rome.

81. *Rome Statute*, art. 17(1)(a)–(b).

"unwillingness" the Court is admonished by the Statute to "hav[e] regard to the principles of due process recognized by international law."[82]

The term "genuinely" was drawn from the Zutphen Intersessional Draft. It is problematic for two reasons. First, it permits a State to prevent a case from proceeding before the Court merely by launching an investigation. Indeed, although the word "genuinely" appears to require some good faith element on behalf of the State, it is perfectly proper under the Statute for a State to open an investigation for the sole purpose of depriving the ICC of jurisdiction, so long as the State does not exhibit "unwillingness" in doing so (or its "inability" is not apparent).

Second, the use of the word "genuinely" may create ambiguities. Does "genuinely" refer to situations where the State's motives are not "genuine" (i.e., are duplicitous or disingenuous) or situations where the State is "really" unable or unwilling to prosecute? Since the terms "unwilling" and "unable" are defined in paragraph 2, it might have been clearer if the qualification of "genuineness" had been deleted.[83]

The ILC did not include within the definition of admissibility situations involving the previous trial of the individual brought before the Court. This section in the Rome Statute,[84] which was also present in the Zutphen Intersessional Draft,[85] is a clear improvement over the original. Moreover, the Statute indicates that it is most certainly the Court, not the State that previously tried the accused, which has the final say as to the effect the previous trial has before the ICC.[86]

Finally, the Statute has always had threaded through it the idea of gravity—that the Court should hear only the most serious cases of truly international concern.[87] This was the International Law Commission's position, and it remains true in the Rome Statute. Nevertheless, gravity is not a defined term and it is presumably up to the Court (the Rules are silent on this point) to elaborate its meaning over time. One clue perhaps, as noted earlier, is in the precatory *chapeau* to article 8 (War crimes) which

82. *Rome Statute*, art. 17(2).

83. Leila Sadat Wexler, *Commentary on Parts 1 and 2 of the Zutphen Intersessional Draft: Establishment of the Court, Complementarity, Jurisdiction and Admissibility*, *in* OBSERVATIONS ON THE CONSOLIDATED ICC TEXT BEFORE THE FINAL SESSION OF THE PREPARATORY COMMITTEE, 13*bis* NOUVELLES ÉTUDES PÉNALES 17, 24 (Leila Sadat Wexler, special ed., 1998). According to one delegate, the term "genuinely" modifies "carry out" and was specifically placed where it was to avoid splitting an infinitive.

84. *Rome Statute*, art. 17(1)(c).

85. *Zutphen Intersessional Draft*, art. 11(1)(c).

86. *Rome Statute*, arts. 17(1)(c), 20(3).

87. *See, e.g., Rome Statute*, preamble, arts. 1, 5.

suggests that war crimes are particularly appropriate subjects for the Court's jurisdiction if they are part of a plan or policy or are committed on a large-scale basis.[88] This *chapeau*, combined with the "widespread or systematic" requirement in crimes against humanity[89] and the idea of the "group" in genocide,[90] suggests that at least one element of gravity is scale—that is, the magnitude or widespread nature of the crimes may be an element of their admissibility before the Court (if not their jurisdiction). Another criterion could be how heinous the offense is. A final factor might be the need to distinguish "major" war criminals from "minor" offenders who should be tried locally, as was done at Nuremberg.[91] The Statute now contains extremely high threshold and intent requirements for the substantive offenses, indicating an intent to prosecute major offenders (essentially leaders) rather than followers. This may prove problematic in operation, for in many cases, particularly if a State's judicial system has collapsed, the ICC should be able to try more, rather than fewer, participants in mass crimes, hopefully without being overwhelmed. Achieving this balance was one of the most difficult tasks of the Framers. Understanding the delicate compromise reached is equally difficult, for the Statute does not address the problem explicitly, but only indirectly through the concept of "gravity" and the jurisdictional and material elements of the *chapeaux* of the crimes against humanity and war crimes articles.

B. The Relationship Between Jurisdiction *ratione materiae* and Admissibility

The question remains as to the relationship between jurisdiction and admissibility. The Rome Statute is somewhat opaque as to whether admissibility is a waivable procedural objection or a fundamental requirement of the Court's pursuit of a case. This point was made in the discussions of the Zutphen Intersessional Draft, which included a footnote querying whether a State could waive complementarity-related admissibility requirements.[92] Presumably the requirements of gravity and *ne bis in idem* are important to the *validity* of any prosecution before the Court, and to this extent seem at least quasi-jurisdictional.[93] But objections based on the inves-

88. *Id.* art. 8(1).

89. *Id.* art. 7.

90. *Id.* art. 6.

91. *See* Judgment of October 1, 1946, International Military Tribunal, Judgment and Sentence, 41 AM. J. INT'L L. 172 (1947).

92. *Zutphen Intersessional Draft*, art. 11, at 140 n. 53.

93. Challenges after the commencement of the trial may only be based on article 17(1)(c) (*ne bis in idem*), *Rome Statute*, art. 19(4).

tigation or prosecution of the case by the State do not appear to affect the Court's power in such a fundamental manner and should be waivable, subject to the Prosecutor's duty not to go forward with inadmissible cases,[94] and to the Court's discretionary power to dismiss cases that are being pursued elsewhere.[95] A study of articles 18 and 19, which govern challenges to admissibility, supports this view, as explained below.[96]

The Statute contains two articles (articles 18 and 19) permitting challenges to jurisdiction and admissibility by States.[97] As shown in Figure 10, in cases referred by States or the Prosecutor *proprio motu*, article 18 requires the Prosecutor to notify States Parties and those States that would normally exercise jurisdiction over the crimes concerned of investigations commenced or about to be commenced. Those States have a limited time to decide to investigate,[98] and if they do, the Prosecutor must defer to the investigating State, unless the Pre-Trial Chamber holds otherwise.[99] The Pre-trial Chamber's decision is subject to appeal, and if appealed, counts as the State's one attack on admissibility unless there is a subsequent change of circumstances or additional significant facts are raised.[100]

In all other cases (Security Council referrals and cases in which States do not open investigations in response to a Prosecutor's notification), article 19 applies. Article 19 permits several parties, in addition to the Court and the Prosecutor, to bring challenges: (1) "an accused or a person for whom a warrant or summons has been issued," (2) a State with jurisdiction that has prosecuted or investigated or is prosecuting or investigating the crime, or (3) "a State from which acceptance of jurisdiction is required under article 12."[101] Each party may challenge jurisdiction only once, except by leave of the Court in exceptional circumstances.[102] Parties must bring challenges prior to the commencement of the trial or risk losing

94. *Id.* art. 53(1)(b), (2)(b).

95. *Id.* art. 19(1).

96. Although article 17 states that the Court "shall determine that a case is inadmissible" if the requirements of article 17 have been met, this phrase must be read in conjunction with the first sentence of article 19, which requires the Court to satisfy itself as to jurisdiction, but makes *sua sponte* determinations of admissibility purely discretionary. *Id.* arts. 17, 19(1).

97. These are complemented by Draft RPE 31 to 62.

98. The time is limited to one month from the date on which the notice was received. *Rome Statute*, art. 18(2).

99. *Id.*

100. *Id.* art. 18(7).

101. That is, the territorial State or the State of the accused's nationality, which it will be recalled, accept jurisdiction either by declaration or by becoming Parties to the Statute. *Id.* art. 19(2); *see also* Figure 11.

102. *Rome Statute*, art. 19(4).

them (subject to special permission, and only on grounds of *ne bis in idem* if the challenge is to admissibility, rather than jurisdiction).[103] Thus, the Court could hear many jurisdictional challenges at the outset of each case, each of which would presumably be appealable, and which could slow down the proceedings considerably. In addition, challenges by States suspend the Prosecutor's investigation of the case,[104] subject to the Prosecutor's right to seek permission from the Court to pursue certain investigative measures to preserve evidence and prevent the absconding of persons.[105]

The Statute is unclear as to whether challenges to admissibility and jurisdiction must be brought together, that is, whether both (together) "may be challenged only once," or whether *each* may be challenged once in separate proceedings. By interpreting the Statute with the efficiency of the Court in mind, however, two conclusions as to the proper procedures can be drawn. First, it would seem necessary to require parties to bring their admissibility challenge at the same time as their jurisdictional challenge (except on grounds of *ne bis in idem*), although it might be necessary to permit jurisdictional challenges subsequent to the bringing of admissibility challenges, since the former go to the Court's power over the case. Second, if several States have the right to bring a challenge and one of those States proceeds to challenge the jurisdiction of the Court (or the admissibility of the case), it is arguable that the remaining States should not be permitted to bring additional challenges except on different grounds.[106] This would have been a useful clarification for the Rules of Procedure and Evidence and should be resolved in favor of requiring parties to bring all their procedural challenges at once, subject to challenges on grounds which, if proven, would either vitiate the Court's power over the case or render it fundamentally unfair.

---

103. *Id.*

104. *Id.* art. 19(7).

105. *Id.* art. 19(8). This right applies only if the Prosecutor has already requested a warrant of arrest with respect to the person in question.

106. *Zutphen Intersessional Draft*, art. 12(3), at 143 n. 67. The notes also point out that the Statute is silent as to the consequences that flow from a failure of a State to make a timely challenge. It seems fairly clear, however, that the State simply loses the ability to challenge the proceedings on those grounds.

CHAPTER 6

THE LAW OF THE STATUTE

The greatest human torment is to be tried without the benefit of law.

—Albert Camus, *La Chute*

One of the thorniest questions that arose in the elaboration of the Rome Statute was which crimes would be included within the jurisdiction of the Court. The International Law Commission's 1994 Draft Statute originally proposed the inclusion of two distinct categories of crimes. The first included genocide, aggression, serious violations of the laws and customs applicable in armed conflict and crimes against humanity.[1] The second category consisted of "treaty crimes"—offenses criminalized under various treaty regimes, including terrorism and drug trafficking, as well as apartheid and grave breaches of the four 1949 Geneva Conventions.[2] The first category of crimes were referred to by the Commission as the "core" crimes,[3] and were subject to a different jurisdictional regime than the

1. *1994 ILC Draft Statute*, art. 20(a)–(d).
2. *Id.* art. 20(e). The treaty crimes were included based upon two criteria:
   (a) that the crimes are themselves defined by the treaty so that an international criminal court could apply that treaty as law in relation to the crime, subject to the *nullum crimen* guarantee . . .
   (b) that the treaty created either a system of universal jurisdiction based on the principle *aut dedere aut judicare* or the possibility for an international criminal court to try the crime, or both, thus recognizing clearly the principle of international concern.

Id. at 78.

3. I adopt this terminology, while recognizing that others believe strongly that terrorism and drug trafficking should be included in the list of core crimes. *See* Herman von Hebel & Darryl Robinson, *Crimes within the Jurisdiction of the Court, in* THE INTERNATIONAL CRIMINAL COURT: THE MAKING OF THE ROME STATUTE 79, 81–82 (Roy S. Lee, ed., 1999).

treaty crimes, rendering the Statute's operation highly complex.[4] Although the Preparatory Committee's discussions of the Court's jurisdiction *ratione materiae* always included both categories of crimes, it seemed apparent as the negotiations proceeded that a majority of States leaned towards limiting the Court's jurisdiction to the core crimes,[5] the solution ultimately adopted at Rome.[6]

The concern remained, however, whether to include the crime of aggression in the Court's Statute. Many argued that a failure to include aggression would mark a retreat from the principles laid down by the International Military Tribunal at Nuremberg. In addition, any deterrent effect the Court might have would arguably be undermined if those who started a conflict were insulated from punishment. On the other hand, defining aggression has historically presented a nearly insurmountable task for the international community. Moreover, the probable involvement of the Security Council could encourage arbitrary and political application of the law, thereby undermining the Court's credibility.[7] The Diplomatic Conference finessed the question by including the crime in the Statute but leaving it undefined and therefore nonjusticiable for the time being.

Finally, having decided to include three of the four "core" crimes in the Statute right away, the delegates in Rome were faced with the particularly difficult job of defining those crimes.[8] In 1926, the International Law

---

4. Leila Sadat Wexler, *The Proposed Permanent International Criminal Court: An Appraisal*, 29 CORNELL INT'L L. J. 665, 687–91 (1996).

5. Herman von Hebel & Darryl Robinson, *Crimes within the Jurisdiction of the Court, in* THE INTERNATIONAL CRIMINAL COURT: THE MAKING OF THE ROME STATUTE 79, 85–87 (Roy S. Lee, ed., 1999).

6. As a concession to the States who felt very strongly that at least terrorism and international narcotics trafficking should be within the Court's jurisdiction, the Diplomatic Conference adopted a Resolution recommending that a Review Conference take up their future inclusion in the Statute. *Final Act*, Resolution E.

7. Leila Sadat Wexler, *International Law Association (American Branch) Committee on a Permanent International Criminal Court, First Committee Report on Jurisdiction, Definition of Crimes and Complementarity*, 25 DENVER J. INT'L L. & POLICY 221, 223–24 (1997) (Rapporteur's Report).

8. The ILC, as noted earlier, did not define the crimes listed in its 1994 Draft, because historically the Draft Code and Court Statute had proceeded as separate tasks of the Commission. In addition, the Commission feared that defining the crimes would render the Statute politically unpalatable and therefore unsuccessful, as this problem had plagued efforts to establish a permanent international criminal court since Versailles. The Commission took the position that it would neither define nor codify crimes under general international law; rather, it viewed the statute as "primarily an adjectival and procedural instrument." *1994 ILC Draft*

Association queried, "*Faut-il avoir la Cour avant la Loi, ou la Loi avant la Cour?*"[9] In 1996 (seventy years later!), the Preparatory Committee answered that both the law and the blueprint for the Court would be prepared simultaneously. Thus began the monumental task of achieving in only fourteen weeks of preparatory sessions,[10] several intersessional meetings,[11] and five weeks of diplomatic wrangling, a consensus among States that the ILC had been unable to achieve with its Draft Code of Crimes in the fifty years since the inception of the project.[12] The Framers' task was further complicated by various factors: the political agendas of States and the NGO community; the absence of any neutral legal principles to guide the drafting process, which in no way constituted "codification" in the civil law sense;[13] the difficult task of working with some crimes, such as crimes against humanity, which were not yet precisely defined in international law; a general lack of technical expertise,[14] particularly on the

---

Statute, art. 20, cmt., §4; *see also* Leila Sadat Wexler, *The Proposed International Criminal Court: an Appraisal*, 29 CORNELL INT'L L. J. 665, 691 (1996). Scholars have, for the most part, criticized the Commission for this position. *See, e.g.*, M. Cherif Bassiouni, *Historical Survey: 1919–1998, in* STATUTE OF THE INTERNATIONAL CRIMINAL COURT: A DOCUMENTARY HISTORY 1, 12 (M. Cherif Bassiouni, ed., 1998); Leila Sadat Wexler, *International Law Association (American Branch) Committee on a Permanent International Criminal Court, First Committee Report on Jurisdiction, Definition of Crimes and Complementarity*, 25 DENVER J. INT'L L. & POLICY 221, 224–25 (1997) (Rapporteur's Report). Yet the decision to proceed without definitions does not appear either illogical or in contravention of the legality principle. Indeed, the "codification" achieved in the Statute, while sufficient for the Court's purposes, may not be either optimal or required. *See* Jordan J. Paust, *Nullem Crimen and Related Claims, in* THE INTERNATIONAL CRIMINAL COURT: OBSERVATIONS AND ISSUES BEFORE THE 1997–98 PREPARATORY COMMITTEE; AND ADMINISTRATIVE AND FINANCIAL IMPLICATIONS 275 (Association Internationale de Droit Pénal, Nouvelles Études Pénales No. 13) (M. Cherif Bassiouni, ed., 1997).

9. "Shall the Court precede the Law, or the Law precede the Court?" INTERNATIONAL LAW ASSOCIATION, REPORT OF THE THIRTY-FOURTH CONFERENCE 182 (1927).

10. M. Cherif Bassiouni, *Historical Survey: 1919–1998, in* STATUTE OF THE INTERNATIONAL CRIMINAL COURT: A DOCUMENTARY HISTORY 1, 22 (M. Cherif Bassiouni, ed., 1998).

11. *See, e.g., Zutphen Intersessional Draft.*

12. Leila Sadat Wexler, *The Proposed Permanent International Criminal Court: An Appraisal*, CORNELL INT'L L. J. 665, 676–85 (1996). *See generally* Rosemary Rayfuse, *The Draft Code of Crimes Against the Peace and Security of Mankind: Eating Disorders at the International Law Commission*, 8 CRIM. L. F. 43 (1997).

13. *See, e.g.*, JOHN HENRY MERRYMAN, THE CIVIL LAW TRADITION 27–34 (1969).

14. There were, of course, many experts present. However, they tended to focus on their particular areas of expertise, and not on the task of legal codification and construction of the institution as a whole.

part of countries which were unable to afford large delegations that included legal counsel; and the need to work with great speed in several languages at once.

This Chapter explores the substantive law of the Statute: the definition of crimes, and the punishments therefor.[15] The discussion focuses on the elements of each crime that are jurisdictional in nature (that is, which render it an international crime, as opposed to a municipal crime), as well as the overall pattern of analysis the Statute mandates in applying a given crime to a perpetrator's particular conduct. Finally, because the purpose of the Court is not just to elucidate more complete definitions of crimes, but to punish those who commit them, Part II takes up the question of penalties.

I. CRIMES WITHIN THE COURT'S JURISDICTION

A. Aggression: The Supreme International Crime

The Nuremberg judgment declared aggression to be "not only an international crime; [but] the supreme international crime differing only from other war crimes in that it contains within itself the accumulated evil of the whole."[16] Following World War II, this prohibition against aggressive war was embodied in article 2(4) of the United Nations Charter,[17] not

15. Sentencing as a matter of procedure is taken up in Chapter 8.

16. Judgment of October 1, 1946, International Military Tribunal Judgment and Sentences, 41 AM. J. INT'L L. 172, 186 (1947). Article 6(a) of the IMT Charter defined the "planning, preparation, initiation or waging of a war of aggression" as a crime against peace. For the historical development of the crime of aggression, see, e.g., Leila Nadya Sadat & S. Richard Carden, *The New International Criminal Court: An Uneasy Revolution*, 88 GEO. L. J. 381, 438–442 (2000); Christian Tomuschat, *Crimes Against the Peace and Security of Mankind and the Recalcitrant Third State*, 24 ISRAEL Y.B. HUM. RTS. 41, 50–53 (1994); Vladan A. Vasilijevic, *Crimes Against Peace: Between the Past and the Future*, 43 JUGOSLOVENSKA REVIJA ZA MEDUNARODNO PRAVO 425 (1996); BENJAMIN B. FERENCZ, 2 DEFINING INTERNATIONAL AGGRESSION: THE SEARCH FOR WORLD PEACE—A DOCUMENTARY HISTORY AND ANALYSIS (1975); AHMED M. RIFAAT, INTERNATIONAL AGGRESSION: A STUDY OF THE LEGAL CONCEPT: ITS DEVELOPMENT AND DEFINITION IN INTERNATIONAL LAW (1979).

17. U.N. CHARTER art. 2, para. 4. Article 2(4) of the Charter requires all Member States to "refrain in their international relations from the threat or use of force against the territorial integrity or political independence of any state, or in any other manner inconsistent with the Purposes of the United Nations." *Id.* Although the United States' delegation suggested defining aggression in the Charter, this proposal was rejected. *See* BENJAMIN B. FERENCZ, AN INTERNATIONAL CRIMINAL COURT 137–38 (2 vols., 1980).

as a matter of criminal law, but as a fundamental norm of international law binding all States.[18] Yet, the Charter does not define the crime, and arriving at one has posed a seemingly intractable problem for the international community. The General Assembly adopted a definition by consensus in 1974[19] that contained a non-exhaustive list of seven acts a State could commit that would be considered "acts of aggression."[20] In addition, article 5(2) of the definition provides that a "war of aggression" is a crime against peace, and that aggression gives rise to "international responsibility."[21] Yet although this definition has been "on the books" since 1964, it has not been employed either in criminal proceedings, or

---

18. This statement assumes the view that the Charter binds even States that are not members of the United Nations, at least as to measures involving the maintenance of international peace and security. U.N. CHARTER art. 2, para. 6. For a discussion of this issue, which is not without controversy, see Chapter 5.

19. *Definition of Aggression*, G.A. Res. 3314 (xxix), 29 U.N. GAOR Supp. No. 31, at 142, U.N. Doc. A/9631 (1974).

20. Article 3 provides:

> Any of the following acts, regardless of a declaration of war, shall, subject to and in accordance with the provisions of article 2, qualify as an act of aggression:
>
> (a) The invasion or attack by the armed forces of a State of the territory of another State, or any military occupation, however temporary, resulting from such invasion or attack, or any annexation by the use of force of the territory of another State or part thereof;
>
> (b) Bombardment by the armed forces of a State against the territory of another State or the use of any weapons by a State against the territory of another State;
>
> (c) The blockade of the ports or coasts of a State by the armed forces of another State;
>
> (d) An attack by the armed forces of a State on the land, sea or air forces, or marine and air fleets of another State;
>
> (e) The use of armed forces of one State which are within the territory of another State with the agreement of the receiving State, in contravention of the conditions provided for in the agreement or any extension of their presence in such territory beyond the termination of the agreement;
>
> (f) The action of a State in allowing its territory, which it has placed at the disposal of another State, to be used by that other State for perpetrating acts of aggression against a third State;
>
> (g) The sending by or on behalf of a State of armed bands, groups, irregulars or mercenaries, which carry out acts of armed force against another State of such gravity as to amount to the acts listed above, or its substantial involvement therein.

Definition of Aggression, art. 3. Article 4 notes that the list is not exhaustive. *See id.* art. 4.

21. *Id.* art. 5(2).

even by the Security Council to any significant degree.[22] Efforts to define the crime by the International Law Commission fared no better, and in 1996, after fifty years of work, the Commission simply included it, undefined, as article 16 of the Draft Code of Crimes Against the Peace and Security of Mankind.[23]

It is thus unsurprising that criminalizing aggression in the Rome Statute proved difficult. Although the Statute reaffirms the illegality of aggression in principle,[24] implementing jurisdiction over the crime was the source of significant disagreement.[25] Indeed, inclusion of aggression in the Statute threatened to derail the entire process. During the

---

22. It was not used in the Security Council's resolution condemning the Iraqi invasion of Kuwait, and authorizing Member States to "use all necessary means" to achieve an Iraqi withdrawal, for example, see S.C. Res. 678, U.N. SCOR, 45th Sess., 2963d mtg., U.N. Doc. S/RES/678 (1990), nor was it included in the Statutes of the two ad hoc tribunals, although, at least in the case of the ICTY, there was certainly a good case for doing so. It could have been particularly helpful in the case of the former Yugoslavia to pinpoint responsibility for the decision to commit ethnic cleansing and carrying out plans to do so. Christian Tomuschat, *Crimes Against the Peace and Security of Mankind and the Recalcitrant Third State*, 24 ISRAEL Y.B. HUM. RTS. 41, 52 (1994). As Professor Tomuschat notes, others have argued the contrary: that omitting aggression from the Statute of the ICTY was required in order to insulate it from "the political issues surrounding the conflict." James C. O'Brien, *The International Tribunal for Violations of International Humanitarian Law in the Former Yugoslavia*, 87 AM. J. INT'L L. 639, 645 (1993).

23. *Draft Code of Crimes Against the Peace and Security of Mankind*, art. 16, U.N. Doc. A/CN.4/L.532 (1996). Article 16 provides: "An individual who, as leader or organizer, actively participates in or orders the planning, preparation, initiation or waging of aggression committed by a State shall be responsible for a crime of aggression."

24. *Rome Statute*, preamble.

25. It is not clear whether the prohibition against use of force embodied in article 2(4) of the U.N. Charter remains a norm of international law. For an argument that article 2(4) may not represent customary international law, see Thomas M. Franck, *Who Killed Article 2(4): Changing Norms Governing the Use of Force by States*, 64 AM. J. INT'L L. 809 (1970); Anthony Clark Arend, *International Law and the Recourse to Force: A Shift in Paradigms*, 27 STAN. J. INT'L L. 1, 42–45 (1990). *But see* Louis Henkin, *The Reports of the Death of Article 2(4) are Greatly Exaggerated*, 65 AM. J. INT'L L. 544, 544, 547 (1971); Oscar Schachter, *In Defense of International Rules on the Use of Force*, 53 U. CHI. L. REV. 113, 128–31 (1986). The International Court of Justice has taken the position that the prohibition on the use of force in article 2(4) and the General Assembly definition of aggression represent customary international law and that departures should be considered breaches rather than repudiations of the norm. Case Concerning Military and Paramilitary Activities in and Against Nicaragua (Nicaragua v. U.S.) (Merits) 1986 I.C.J. 14, paras. 186, 195.

Preparatory Committee meetings leading up to the Statute's adoption, several proposals were made for defining and including aggression in the Statute.[26] The political obstacles to its incorporation, however, were so extensive that even some of the human rights NGOs were uncomfortable insisting upon its inclusion.[27] Negotiations during the Conference on the question of aggression were heated, and there was little consensus on either the crime's definition or the appropriate trigger mechanism to accompany its inclusion.[28] In a clever compromise initiated, in part, by the German government's submission of a paper on aggression,[29] as well as the urging of the non-aligned States,[30] the Statute includes aggression as one of the crimes within the Court's jurisdiction,[31] but leaves it undefined. The Treaty specifies that the Court may not exercise jurisdiction over aggression until the Assembly of States Parties defines it, which cannot

---

26. The *Zutphen Intersessional Draft* proposed a non-exhaustive enumerated list for defining aggression that combined language from the Nuremberg Charter and the General Assembly definition. *Zutphen Intersessional Draft*, art. 5[20]. The first part of the article is similar to Control Council Law 10. The April Draft contained three different options, including a general definition with no list of prohibited acts (which was proposed by Germany), and an enumerated, non-exhaustive list of aggressive acts. A third option would not have required a definition of aggression as this question would simply be left to the Security Council. *April Draft Statute*, at 12–14. The second approach was the most widely supported prior to the Rome Conference, Herman von Hebel & Darryl Robinson, *Crimes within the Jurisdiction of the Court, in* THE INTERNATIONAL CRIMINAL COURT: THE MAKING OF THE ROME STATUTE 79, 83 (Roy S. Lee, ed., 1999).

27. Scholars were similarly divided. *See, e.g.*, Leila Sadat Wexler, *International Law Association (American Branch) Committee on a Permanent International Criminal Court, First Committee Report on Jurisdiction, Definition of Crimes and Complementarity*, 25 DENVER J. INT'L L. & POLICY 221, 223–24, 226 (1997) (Rapporteur's Report) (noting a split among members of the International Law Association (American Branch) Committee on a Permanent International Criminal Court as to whether to include aggression in the Court's Statute).

28. *Aggression Splits the Rome Conference*, ON THE RECORD, June 19, 1998, at 4–5.

29. The German Proposal on Aggression, German Delegation to the United Nations Diplomatic Conference of Plenipotentiaries on the Establishment of an International Criminal Court, *Crime of Aggression* (June 18, 1998) relied on Option 3 of the *April Draft Statute*, art. 5.

30. Herman von Hebel & Darryl Robinson, *Crimes within the Jurisdiction of the Court, in* THE INTERNATIONAL CRIMINAL COURT: THE MAKING OF THE ROME STATUTE 79, 85 (Roy S. Lee, ed., 1999); Kelly Dawn Askin, *Crimes within the Jurisdiction of the International Criminal Court*, 10 CRIM. L. F. 33, 35 (1999).

31. *Rome Statute*, art. 5(1)(d).

occur until seven years after the Statute enters into force.[32] Interestingly, the delegates chose not to reserve an article in the Statute for the definition of aggression.

Because of the crime's central importance, the Preparatory Commission embarked upon the task of defining aggression almost immediately, even though its ultimate inclusion in the Statute would be years away, at best. At the second meeting of the Preparatory Commission, arrangements were made regarding discussions on aggression. It was agreed that a working group on the crime would be established, but without prejudice to completing the work on the Elements of Crimes and Rules of Procedure and Evidence which, as required by Resolution F of the Diplomatic Conference[33] had to be, and were, completed by June 30, 2000.[34] A coordinator for the work was appointed, Tuvako Manongi of the United Republic of Tanzania, and in addition to compiling reference material on prior definitions of the crime,[35] the Working Group met several times during the March and June 2000 sessions of the Preparatory Commission to address both the issues of the crime's definition and the trigger mechanism by which it would be brought to the Court. The coordinator presented a paper setting out the general issues for consideration in the third week of the March 2000 session, but the consensus was that significant differences of views remained present among the delegates, and the coordinator was encouraged to prepare a new and more restrictive consolidated text for the June 2000 session.[36] When the issue was

32. *Rome Statute*, art. 5(2), 121, 123.

33. *United Nations Diplomatic Conference of Plenipotentiaries on the Establishment of an International Criminal Court*, U.N. Doc. A/CON.181/10, July 17, 1998.

34. *Proceedings of the Preparatory Commission at its second session (26 July–13 August 1999)*, Preparatory Commission for the International Criminal Court, para. 8, U.N. Doc. PCNICC/1999/l.4/Rev.1 (1999). In addition, many countries submitted proposed definitions. *See Compilation of Proposals on the Crime of Aggression, submitted at the Preparatory Committee on the Establishment of an International Criminal Court (1996–1998), the United Nations Diplomatic Conference of Plenipotentiaries on the Establishment of the International Criminal Court (1998), and the Preparatory Commission for the International Criminal Court (1999)*, U.N. Doc. PCNICC/ 1999/INF/2 (1999). For a description of the difficulties engaged by the Preparatory Commission, and a suggestion for future discussions, see Benjamin B. Ferencz, *Can Aggression be Deterred by Law*, 11 PACE INT'L L. REV. 344, 352–353 (1999).

35. *See, e.g., Reference Document on the Crime of Aggression, Prepared by the Secretariat*, Working Group on the Crime of Aggression, U.N. Doc. PCNICC/ 2000/WGCA/INF/1, June 17, 2000.

36. Jennifer Schense, NGO Coalition for an International Criminal Court, *Draft Report on the Fourth Session of the Preparatory Commission, March 13–31, 2000*, at 20–21.

brought back to the Working Group in June, significant disagreement again reappeared. Questions remain as to the right of States to act in their own self-defense, whether aggressive *acts* may be criminalized, or only aggressive *war*,[37] and whether a Security Council determination of a State's aggression must precede any complaint brought before the ICC against individual defendants for the crime. Both the language of article 5(2) and many delegations appear to support a requirement that the Security Council make a finding of aggression prior to its justiciability by the Court,[38] although many other delegations have expressed deep opposition to any influence that the Security Council might exercise over proceedings in the Court. The issue returned to the Preparatory Commission during the Fall of 2000, and a Consolidated text ensued,[39] which was considered by the working group at the Spring session in 2001. A new coordinator was appointed, Silvia Fernandez de Gurmendi of Argentina, and during the Spring session a compromise was submitted that would permit the U.N. General Assembly to request the International Court of Justice to determine whether an act of aggression has been committed if the Security Council did not act in a particular case.[40] While this proposal

---

37. *See, e.g., U.S. Statement on the Crime of Aggression, submitted to the Preparatory Commission for the International Criminal Court*, June 26, 2000 (suggesting that only wars of aggression and not acts of aggression were clearly criminalized by G.A. Resolution 3314, and that the ICC Statute should be similarly limited).

38. The ILC draft required a preliminary finding of aggression by the Security Council prior to bringing cases before the Court which included that crime. *1994 ILC Draft Statute*, art. 23(2). The Rome Statute is less clear on this point. Article 5(2) provides that the definition shall be adopted and conditions shall be set out "under which the Court shall exercise jurisdiction with respect to this crime. [This] provision shall be consistent with the relevant provisions of the Charter of the United Nations." *Rome Statute*, art. 5(2). Most believe that this language is a direct concession to the Security Council's responsibility (and right) to act and make determinations as to cases involving aggression. Herman von Hebel & Darryl Robinson, *Crimes within the Jurisdiction of the Court, in* THE INTERNATIONAL CRIMINAL COURT: THE MAKING OF THE ROME STATUTE 79, 85 (Roy S. Lee, ed., 1999). The Statute's opacity on this point is one of the reasons proffered by the U.S. government for voting against the Treaty. *See* Statement of David J. Scheffer, Ambassador-at-Large for War Crimes Issues and Head of the U.S. Delegation to U.N. Diplomatic Conference on the Establishment of a Permanent International Criminal Court, Before the Committee on Foreign Relations of the U.S. Senate, July 23, 1998, *reprinted in* 1998 WL 425945, 21 (F.D.C.H.).

39. *Proceedings of the Preparatory Commission at its sixth session (27 November–8 December 2000)*, Annex V, Crime of Aggression, U.N. Doc. PCNICC/2000/L.4/Rev.1.

40. *Preparatory Commission for the International Criminal Court, Working Group*

engendered some support, a consensus on the issue is far from certain. Thus, for the time being, aggression, while illegal in principle, remains non-justiciable in practice.[41]

B. Genocide, Crimes Against Humanity, and War Crimes

1. *Interpreting and Applying the Definitions*

As for the crimes which are currently included in the Court's Statute, the Statute defines them against the backdrop of five basic principles.

First, each crime is defined only "[f]or the purpose of this Statute."[42] Thus, the Statute does not, by its terms, purport to be a codification of international criminal law or international humanitarian law, although the definitions largely reflect existing law and will be universally applied through Security Council referrals to the Court. The approach of the Framers is consistent with the ICC's predecessor instruments, including the Statutes of the ICTY and ICTR,[43] and the IMT Charter at Nuremberg.[44]

Second, to address the possibility that the definitions could nevertheless be construed as new codifications of customary international law, particularly if applied universally through a Security Council referral, article

---

on the Crime of Aggression, Proposal submitted by Bosnia and Herzegovina, New Zealand and Romania, art. 4, U.N. Doc. PCNICC/2001/WGCA/DP.1, Feb. 23, 2001. The proposal provides that if the Security Council has made no determination under article 39 of the Charter as to the existence or otherwise of an act of aggression and has not invoked article 16 (of the Statute) within 12 months from the date of notification by the Court, the "Court may notify the General Assembly of the situation . . . and invite the General Assembly to request the International Court of Justice, in accordance with Article 96 of the Charter, to give an advisory opinion on the legal question of the existence or otherwise of an act of aggression by the State concerned."

41. Christian Tomuschat, *Crimes Against the Peace and Security of Mankind and the Recalcitrant Third State*, 24 ISRAEL Y.B. HUM. RTS. 41, 52 (1994) (arguing that "the international community . . . is not really convinced that a universally acknowledged class of crimes against peace entailing individual criminal responsibility exists").

42. *Rome Statute*, arts. 6 (genocide), 7(1) (crimes against humanity), and 8(2) (war crimes).

43. Minna Schrag, *The Yugoslav War Crimes Tribunal: An Interim Assessment*, 7 TRANSNAT'L L. & CONTEMP. PROBS. 15, 16–17, 22 nn. 5–6 (1997).

44. Article 6 of the Charter, however, was less clear in this regard. The Agreement for the Prosecution and Punishment of Major War Criminals of the European Axis, Charter of the International Military Tribunal, August 8, 1945, art. 6, 8 U.N.T.S. 279, *reprinted in* 39 AM. J. INT'L L. 257 (Supp. 1945).

10 of the Statute provides: "Nothing in this Part shall be interpreted as limiting or prejudicing in any way existing or developing rules of international law for purposes other than this Statute."[45] While the intent of article 10 was to prevent the Statute's restrictive definitions from creeping into customary international law, this proviso could arguably prevent broader definitions or new crimes (forced pregnancy, for example[46]) from being asserted as part of new customary international law as well. To the extent that the Statute is widely ratified, however, even the inclusion of article 10 will not prevent States, or other tribunals, from eventually arguing that the Statute's definitions represent customary international law. The combination of principles one and two suggests that the Statute, to paraphrase the International Military Tribunal at Nuremberg Charter, is both the "expression of international law existing at the time of its creation" and, at the same time, "a contribution to international law."[47] It also suggests that the international community eventually might not be able to have it both ways, asserting that universal "laws" made by treaty may differ from universal "laws" established by custom. Indeed, another of Rome's revolutionary contributions is its subtle challenge to the authoritativeness and continuing relevance of customary international law. This point is taken up again in Chapter 9.

Third, the definitions in the Statute are not self-contained. Rather, article 9 of the Statute requires the Elements of Crimes to be elaborated and adopted by a two-thirds majority of the Assembly of States Parties. These Elements are to "assist the Court in the interpretation and application" of articles 6, 7, and 8, which define the three crimes currently within the Court's jurisdiction.[48] Article 9 does not mention aggression, but presumably, once defined by the Assembly of States Parties, it would include Elements as well.[49] The addition of the new crimes, many of which were avidly desired as improvements over the past list of crimes, as well as the

45. *Rome Statute*, art. 10.

46. Forced pregnancy is in article 7 (1)(g) as a crime against humanity, and articles 8(2)(b)(xxii) and 8(2)(e)(vi) as a war crime. It is defined in article 7(2)(f) as "the unlawful confinement, of a woman forcibly made pregnant, with the intent of affecting the ethnic composition of any population or carrying out other grave violations of international law." *Rome Statute*, art. 7(2)(f). Because of fears that this crime could affect national laws against abortion, however, paragraph 7(2)(f) adds, "[t]his definition shall not in any way be interpreted as affecting national laws relating to pregnancy." *Id. See generally* KELLY DAWN ASKIN, WAR CRIMES AGAINST WOMEN 273–76 (1997).

47. Judgment of October 1, 1946, International Military Tribunal, Judgment and Sentences, 41 AM. J. INT'L L. 172, 186, 216–17 (1947).

48. *Rome Statute*, art. 9.

49. The United States took this position in the June 2000 Session of the

vagueness of the existing list, troubled many delegations. This not only led to the adoption of a list of definitions for the Court to apply, such as the definition of gender discussed below, but the adoption of Elements for each crime. While it is understandable that States wished to know in advance what they were contracting for, the definition of the crimes in the Statute should be read in light of the existing customary and treaty-based understandings of international humanitarian law. The Elements should follow the same principle, and although they will hopefully remove some of the ambiguities in the Statute, they should not be the focus of a further attempt to narrow the Court's jurisdiction beyond what was already negotiated in Rome.[50] Draft elements for genocide, crimes against humanity and war crimes were finalized by the Preparatory Commission on June 30, 2000, and are included in the Annex at the end of this text.[51] In addition to clarifying some of the definitions in the Statute (although many of the Elements simply repeat the Statute's text, and are thus redundant), the Elements complement the Statute on certain points. In particular, the general introduction to the Elements provides that mental elements involving value judgments, such as "inhumane" or "severe," do not require the perpetrator to have personally completed the particular value judgment unless otherwise indicated.[52] In addition, the Elements make clear that the same conduct may constitute one or more crimes, a point we will revisit in Chapter 7. Finally, and importantly, the text makes clear that intent and knowledge may be inferred from relevant facts and circumstances.[53] This has been a critical issue in cases before the two ad hoc tribunals, where the level of proof required to establish intent has been the subject of much debate.[54] Some of the Elements, however, arguably restrict the reach of the Statute,[55] and it will be interesting to see how the Court ultimately recon-

---

Preparatory Commission. *U.S. Statement on the Crime of Aggression, submitted to the Preparatory Commission for the International Criminal Court*, June 26, 2000.

50. *Cf.* M. Cherif Bassiouni, *The Normative Framework of International Humanitarian Law: Overlaps, Gaps and Ambiguities*, 8 TRANSNAT'L L. & CONTEMP. PROBS. 199, 202 (1998) (norms regarding crimes against humanity contain ambiguities because governments are not particularly inclined to criminalize the conduct of their high officials).

51. Finalized draft text of the Elements of Crimes, Preparatory Commission for the International Criminal Court, U.N. Doc. PCNICC/2000/INF/3/Add.2, July 6, 2000.

52. Draft Elements of Crimes, General Introduction, para. 4.

53. *Id.* para. 3.

54. Prosecutor v. Tadić (Case No. IT-94-1-T), Opinion and Judgment, paras. 675–680 (ICTY Trial Chamber II, May 7, 1997).

55. *See, e.g.*, Element 7(1)(i) (enforced disappearance of persons) (requiring the perpetrator effectuating the arrest to be aware of the fact that the arrest would

ciles the Elements with the Statute, if the two appear to conflict.[56]

Fourth, all definitions must be read in conjunction with Part 3 of the Statute on General Principles of Criminal Law.[57] In particular, article 22(2) provides that definitions of crimes shall be "strictly construed and shall not be extended by analogy."[58] Furthermore, article 30 requires the material elements of the crime to be committed with "intent" and "knowledge."[59] The Draft Elements provide that exceptions to the article 30 standard will be indicated where applicable.[60]

Fifth, the combination of the restrictive *chapeaux*, high thresholds for intent, the language of the Preamble, and the gravity requirement for admissibility suggests that the Statute is oriented towards the prosecution of "major" criminals, not their subordinates or other lesser offenders. This is consistent with the approach taken in establishing international criminal tribunals since Nuremberg.

Keeping these basic principles in mind, I now turn to an examination of the three crimes currently defined in the Statute.

2. Genocide

Sometimes referred to as "the crime of crimes,"[61] genocide was established as a form of crime against humanity in order to criminalize the eradication of ethnic minorities.[62] Its criminalization in the Rome Statute

---

be followed in the ordinary course of events by a refusal to acknowledge the deprivation of freedom or to give information on the fate or whereabouts of the arrestee); Element 7(1)(h) (persecution) (limiting the grounds to those "universally" recognized as impermissible under international law).

56. Pursuant to article 9(3) of the Statute, the Elements must be consistent with the Statute, which presumably must govern the Court's analysis in each case.

57. *See* Chapter 7, *infra*.

58. Paragraph 2 continues: "In case of ambiguity, the definition shall be interpreted in favour of the person being investigated, prosecuted or convicted." *Rome Statute*, art. 22(2).

59. *Id*. art. 30(1). Article 30 defines both "intent" and "knowledge," noting that the definitions are for "purposes of this article." *Id*. art. 30(2), (3). Article 31 addresses grounds for excluding criminal responsibility. *See id*. art. 31.

60. Draft Elements of Crimes, General Introduction, ¶ 2.

61. Prosecutor v. Kambanda (Case No. ICTR-97-23-S), Judgment and Sentence, para. 16 (ICTR Trial Chamber I, Sept. 4, 1998); Prosecutor v. Serashugo (Case No. ICTR-98-39-S), Sentence, para.15 (ICTR Trial Chamber I, Feb. 5, 1999). This is Professor Schabas' view, who argues that genocide is at the "apex of the pyramid" of international crimes. WILLIAM A. SCHABAS, GENOCIDE IN INTERNATIONAL LAW 9 (2000).

62. WILLIAM A. SCHABAS, GENOCIDE IN INTERNATIONAL LAW 9 (2000).

was a foregone conclusion, and indeed it was the one crime that the International Law Commission felt was so broadly accepted by the international community that the Commission's 1994 Draft Statute included it within the "inherent jurisdiction" of the Court, not dependent on the consent of States.[63] Following the ILC's proposal, the Rome Statute incorporates wholesale article II of the Genocide Convention,[64] which has generally been accepted as part of customary international law.[65] Although many hoped that the negotiation of the ICC Treaty would present the opportunity to expand the Genocide Convention, so that at least political and social groups could be added to article II,[66] an omission that most commentators have viewed with dismay,[67] faced with objections from many States, the delegates eventually decided not to "repair" the conventional definition of genocide, but to leave it as is.[68] Persecutions based on political grounds are instead treated as crimes against humanity under article 7(1)(h) of the Statute.[69]

---

63. *1994 ILC Draft Statute*, arts. 21(1)(a), 25(1). *See also* Leila Sadat Wexler, *The Proposed Permanent International Criminal Court: An Appraisal*, 29 CORNELL INT'L L. J. 665, 696 (1996).

64. One change the Rome Statute effects is to move article III of the Convention, which deemed punishable not only genocide, but also associated crimes, including conspiracy to commit genocide, attempted genocide, direct and public incitement to genocide, and complicity to article 25 of the Statute, as part of the General Part. This means, however, that the Draft Elements of Crimes do not address the interpretation of the crimes in article III of the Convention. On the Convention's origins and negotiating history, see WILLIAM A. SCHABAS, GENOCIDE IN INTERNATIONAL LAW 14–101 (2000).

65. *Reservations to the Genocide Convention*, International Court of Justice [1951] I.C.J. Rep. 15, at 23 ("the principles underlying the Convention are principles which are recognized by civilized nations as binding on States, even without any conventional obligation.")

66. *Zutphen Intersessional Draft*, at 5 n. 11.

67. *See, e.g.*, Lori Lyman Bruun, *Beyond the 1948 Convention—Emerging Principles of Genocide in Customary International Law*, 17 MD. J. INT'L L. & TRADE 193, 204, 206–07 (1993); Matthew Lippman, *The Convention on the Prevention and Punishment of the Crime of Genocide: Fifty Years Later*, 15 ARIZ. J. INT'L & COMP. L. 415, 455, 464, 504–05, 512 (1998); Beth Van Schaack, *The Crime of Political Genocide: Repairing the Genocide Convention's Blind Spot*, 106 YALE L. J. 2259, 2269, 2271, 2290–91 (1997). *But see* WILLIAM A. SCHABAS, GENOCIDE IN INTERNATIONAL LAW 114 (2000) (arguing that "[d]iluting the definition, either by formal amendment of its terms or extravagant interpretation of the existing text, risks trivializing the horror of the real crime when it is committed.").

68. Herman von Hebel & Darryl Robinson, *Crimes within the Jurisdiction of the Court*, *in* THE INTERNATIONAL CRIMINAL COURT: THE MAKING OF THE ROME STATUTE 79, 89 (Roy S. Lee, ed., 1999).

69. *Rome Statute*, art. 7(1)(h).

Other discussions during the negotiations aimed to narrow the Convention definition. For example, one issue that arose during Preparatory Committee meetings was whether the words "intent to destroy, in whole or in part . . . a group" required a specific intent to destroy more than a small number of individuals who are members of the group.[70] This interpretation would have been contrary to the approach taken in many domestic prosecutions for crimes against humanity, which sometimes involved attacks against small numbers of citizens, carried out within a broader context.[71] The final text of the Rome Statute makes no such restriction; the Elements are silent on the issue.

The apparent absence of controversy over the definition of genocide should not give rise to a false sense of comfort with respect to either the crime's definition or its application by the Court. The Convention's implementation was virtually non-existent for the first fifty years of its existence, leaving genocide poorly defined in international law. Although the Convention was adopted in 1948, the first conviction for genocide was not obtained until 1998, when the ICTR rendered the *Akayesu* decision.[72] Many questions concerning the nature of the groups protected by the Convention, the mental element required for conviction of the crime,[73] and the kinds of acts capable of giving rise to criminal liability for the crime[74]

---

70. *Zutphen Intersessional Draft*, at 121 n. 10.

71. Jordan J. Paust, *Commentary on Parts 1 and 2 of the Zutphen Intersessional Draft, in* OBSERVATIONS ON THE CONSOLIDATED ICC TEXT BEFORE THE FINAL SESSION OF THE PREPARATORY COMMITTEE, 13*bis* NOUVELLES ÉTUDES PÉNALES 27, 27–28 (Leila Sadat Wexler, special ed., 1998); *see also* MODEL DRAFT STATUTE FOR THE INTERNATIONAL CRIMINAL COURT BASED ON THE PREPARATORY COMMITTEE'S TEXT TO THE DIPLOMATIC CONFERENCE, ROME, JUNE 15–JULY 17, 1998 (Association Internationale de Droit Pénal, Nouvelles Études Pénales No. 13*ter*) (Leila Sadat Wexler, ed., 1998).

72. Prosecutor v. Akayesu (Case No. ICTR-96-4-T), Judgment (ICTR Trial Chamber I, Sept. 2, 1998). The first case brought to the International Court of Justice seeking enforcement of the Convention was brought in 1993 by Bosnia-Herzegovina against the Federal Republic of Yugoslavia. For a history of the case, see William L. Hurlock, *The International Court of Justice: Effectively Providing a Long Overdue Remedy for Ending State-Sponsored Genocide (Bosnia-Herzogovina v. Yugoslavia)*, 12 AM. U. J. INT'L L. & POL'Y 299 (1997).

73. Prosecutor v. Rutaganda (Case No. ICTR-96-3-T), Judgment and Sentence, paras. 59–63 (ICTR Trial Chamber I, Dec. 6, 1999).

74. Whether acts of sexual violence may constitute genocide, for example, was controversial. The ICTR resolved the question in the affirmative. Prosecutor v. Akayesu (Case No. ICTR-96-4-T), Judgment, paras. 731–34 (ICTR Trial Chamber I, Sept. 2, 1998) ("with regard, particularly to the acts . . . [of] rape and sexual violence, the Chamber wishes to underscore the fact that in its opinion, they constitute genocide in the same way as any other act as long as they were committed with the specific intent [required]. . . . Sexual violence was a step in the process of

have been left open, even by the Draft Elements for the crime which were adopted by the Preparatory Commission in fairly short order.[75]

For example, the Draft Elements contain no definition of "group" to guide the Court. The identification of the groups protected by the Convention plagued not only the Convention's drafters,[76] but latter-day courts such as the ICTR, leading Trial Chamber I of the Rwanda Tribunal to declare in the *Rutaganda* decision that "there are no generally and internationally accepted precise definitions [of the concepts of national, ethnical, racial and religious groups]."[77] *Rutaganda* is the third in a series of decisions from the ICTR addressing the issue whether Rwanda's Hutu and Tutsi appellations denoted different "groups" within the Convention's terms. In each case, starting with the *Akayesu* decision rendered in 1998, the Tribunal concluded that Hutu and Tutsi were different ethnic groups, even though it arguably stretched the definition of the term considerably in doing so, since they share the same nationality, race, religion (for the most part), language, and culture.[78] In the *Akayesu* decision, the Tribunal appeared to reject the view that the four groups listed in the definition were exclusive, holding that the intent of the drafters of the Genocide Convention was "clearly to protect any stable and permanent group."[79] At the same time, due perhaps to the *nullum crimen* principle and the controversial nature of its holding, the Tribunal declined to extend its definition to its logical conclusion and find that additional groups are protected by analogy, preferring instead to reach the desired result by finding that the Tutsi were an ethnic group given the context of the situation in Rwanda.[80] This case law would not bind the ICC, of course, but it

---

destruction of the Tutsi group—destruction of the spirit, of the will to live, and of life itself.")

75. The Draft Elements contain four footnotes intended to clarify issues that arose during the Preparatory Commission's discussions. Importantly, they specify that rape and other forms of sexual violence may constitute "serious bodily or mental harm," and give broad readings of the terms "conditions of life" and "forcibly transferred" children. They leave the issue of the mental element "to be decided by the Court on a case-by-case basis." Draft Elements of Crimes, article 6, Introduction.

76. William A. Schabas, Genocide in International Law 102–14 (2000).

77. Prosecutor v. Rutaganda (Case No. ICTR-96-3-T), Judgment and Sentence, para. 55 (ICTR Trial Chamber I, Dec. 6, 1999).

78. Johan D. van der Vyver, *Prosecution and Punishment of the Crime of Genocide*, 23 Fordham Int'l L. J. 286, 302–04 (1999).

79. Prosecutor v. Akayesu (Case No. ICTR-96-4-T), Judgment, para. 710 (ICTR Trial Chamber I, Sept. 2, 1998).

80. Prosecutor v. Akayesu (Case No. ICTR-96-4-T), Judgment, paras. 510–14

suggests that even with the adoption of "Elements" by the Assembly of States Parties, many interpretative difficulties will remain. It may also indicate, as might the Preparatory Commission's silence on the issue, that a certain discomfort remains as regards the narrow definition of genocide in article II of the Convention. Strict constructionists have argued that ethnic cleansing in Bosnia, the killing fields of Cambodia, and many other cases of mass atrocities in which thousands or even millions have been killed escape the Convention's terms.[81] Although some have argued that this narrow view of the Convention is proper,[82] that perspective is not widely shared. Adopted more than 50 years ago as a compromise text that protected only limited categories of victims from the evil of decimation, it

---

(ICTR Trial Chamber I, Sept. 2, 1998). Professor van der Vyver argues that the ICTR's approach, which required the group to be "stable," i.e., determined by birth, rather than a "mobile" group one might join by choice such as a political or economic group, would cover the protection of homosexuals or other institutional groups, if not as part of the ICC Statute, then under national implementation of the Genocide Convention, which may be broader than the Convention's terms. Johan D. van der Vyver, *Prosecution and Punishment of the Crime of Genocide*, 23 FORDHAM INT'L L. J. 286, 305–06 (1999). In a subsequent decision, the ICTR held the Tutsi were an "ethnic group," Prosecutor v. Kayishema and Ruzindana (Case No. ICTR-95-1-T), Judgment, para. 98 (ICTR Trial Chamber II, May 21, 1999), but at the same time took the position that one determines group identity by looking only to the perpetrator's subjective point of view of the victim. *Kayishema*, para. 131–32. Finally, in *Rutaganda*, the ICTR accepted the definition of the crime (presumably including the definition of "group") articulated in *Akayesu*, but articulated a two-pronged approach to the problem of group identity, examining first the perpetrator's subjective intent; second, the objective nature of the group according to its political and cultural context. Prosecutor v. Rutaganda (Case No. ICTR-96-3-T), Judgment and Sentence, paras. 56–58 (ICTR Trial Chamber I, Dec. 6, 1999). The ICTY appeared to take the same approach in its first case involving the crime of genocide. Prosecutor v. Jelesić (Case No. IT-95-10-T), Judgment, paras. 69–72 (ICTY Trial Chamber I, Dec. 14, 1999). Professor Schabas takes the same approach. WILLIAM A. SCHABAS, GENOCIDE IN INTERNATIONAL LAW 109–110 (2000).

81. Yoram Dinstein, for example, takes the view that only Rwanda and the holocaust represents "true" cases of genocide. *Remarks of Professor Yoram Dinstein*, Lester B. Pearson Canadian International Peacekeeping Training Centre, Montréal, Canada, November 19–20, 1999. Others have, of course, argued otherwise. General Assembly Resolution 47/121, adopted by a recorded vote with 102 for, 0 against, and 57 abstentions, for example, states that "ethnic cleansing" in the former Yugoslavia is a "form of genocide." G.A. Res. 121, U.N. GAOR, 47th Sess., 91st plen. mtg., U.N. Doc. A/RES/47/121 (1992). On ethnic cleansing generally, see Jennifer Jackson Preece, *Ethnic Cleansing as an Instrument of National-State Creation: Changing State Practices and Evolving Legal Norms*, 20 HUMAN RTS. Q. 817 (1998).

82. WILLIAM A. SCHABAS, GENOCIDE IN INTERNATIONAL LAW 9 (2000).

is difficult both for the lay person and the lawyer to understand how the deliberate killing of one million or more Cambodians is less criminal than the extermination of European Jews by the Nazis during World War II. It is no answer to suggest that "in any hierarchy, something must sit at the top,"[83] nor is it obvious why it would "trivialize" the crime of genocide[84] for it to encompass mass killings and exterminations of all kinds. Instead, it may be that a more modern approach to the crime is warranted, given our understanding that all group identity is an "imagined reality"[85] and the sad recognition that it is the very process of apportioning ourselves into groups that leads to discrimination and hate in the first place. The ICC may find itself torn between an anachronistic text trapped in an historic past and the aspirations and thinking of present and future times.

3. *Crimes Against Humanity and War Crimes*

a. *Jurisdictional Elements and Constitutive Elements of Offenses*

The Statute adopted by the Diplomatic Conference is a montage of historically-based texts, massaged during difficult political negotiations, that improved the existing law in some respects, but left it either unchanged or more restrictive in other cases.[86] One particularly thorny problem left unresolved by the Statute, for example, is its failure to distinguish jurisdictional from material elements of offenses. By jurisdictional elements, I mean elements that must be established in order for the Court to have jurisdiction over the crime. By material elements, I mean the traditional elements of the underlying crime that render an individual criminally liable, i.e. the *actus reus* and *mens rea* or the *élément materiel* and the *élément moral*.[87] The confusion was no doubt a direct result of the

---

83. *Id.*

84. *Id.* at 150.

85. BENEDICT ANDERSON, IMAGINED COMMUNITIES: REFLECTIONS ON THE ORIGIN AND SPREAD OF NATIONALISM (Rev. ed. 1991).

86. Jordan J. Paust, *Commentary on Parts 1 and 2 of the Zutphen Intersessional Draft, in* OBSERVATIONS ON THE CONSOLIDATED ICC TEXT BEFORE THE FINAL SESSION OF THE PREPARATORY COMMITTEE, 13*bis* NOUVELLES ÉTUDES PÉNALES 27, 27–39 (Leila Sadat Wexler, special ed., 1998).

87. For an American, this distinction is perhaps best understood by analogy to U.S. federal criminal law. The majority of federal criminal law arose from Congress's power to regulate interstate commerce. NORMAN ABRAMS & SARA SUN BEALE, FEDERAL CRIMINAL LAW AND ITS ENFORCEMENT 16 (2d ed. 1993). Thus, many federal crimes contain an "interstate commerce" element that must be established

unconscious manner by which theories of universal jurisdiction were converted from international law norms addressing the distribution of competences between States to a norm of international law addressing the negotiation of competence between the international legal order and national legal systems.

Jurisdictional elements are generally found in the *chapeaux* of the articles defining the crimes. The question arises in war crimes, for example, as to whether an offense was committed in an armed conflict, and whether that armed conflict was international or non-international in character. Should the Prosecutor have to re-establish the existence of an armed conflict in each case? This is arguably a jurisdictional element that, once established, applies to a given situation[88] in its entirety and should not be relitigated. This application of a form of "estoppel by judgment"[89] is appropriate for two main reasons. First, estoppel on jurisdictional elements is necessary to provide consistency in the judgments of the Court. If the Court were to find that the jurisdictional element was satisfied in one case and then find that it was not established in a later case arising from the same situation, the judgment in the initial case would be brought into question. This could diminish the credibility of the Court. Second, because the Court will necessarily address numerous crimes arising from the same situation, requiring the Prosecutor to establish the same jurisdictional element in each case would unnecessarily hinder the efficiency of the Court in addressing these situations.

Similarly, it is not clear whether the burden of proof that the Prosecution should bear as to the jurisdictional elements should be their establishment beyond a reasonable doubt. It is true that article 67(1)(i) guarantees that the accused shall not "have imposed on him or her any reversal of the burden of proof or any onus of rebuttal." Yet surely some defenses, particularly those peculiarly within the control of the accused, should not be for the Prosecutor to disprove, but for the accused to establish, at least insofar as making out a prima facie case.[90] Moreover, jurisdictional elements, unlike material elements, go to the power of the Court

---

as a prerequisite to the jurisdiction of the federal courts, in addition to the elements required for the underlying crime. Another example is the jurisdiction of the federal courts over crimes committed on federal property; in these cases the commission of the crime on federal property constitutes the jurisdictional element.

88. I use "situation" as it is used in the Statute to indicate the overall context within which individual crimes have been or are being committed. *Rome Statute*, arts. 13–14.

89. BLACK'S LAW DICTIONARY 551 (6th ed., 1990).

90. An earlier version of the Draft Elements included a paragraph that was ultimately deleted, containing the following provision:

to hear individual cases arising out of a situation referred to the Court, not to the guilt or innocence of a particular accused.[91]

b. Crimes Against Humanity

Defining crimes against humanity presented one of the most difficult challenges at Rome, for no accepted definition existed, either as a matter of treaty or customary international law.[92] Indeed, of the several definitions that have been "promulgated," no two are alike. The Tokyo Charter and Control Council Law No. 10 differed slightly from the Nuremberg version; the ICTY provision on crimes against humanity differs from all of its predecessors; and the ICTR version is different from the ICTY version.[93] Municipal law applications of the crime have also varied from State to State.[94] Finally, the International Law Commission has adopted various formulations, none of which has been particularly well-received.[95]

> Consistent with the general principles of law defined in article 30, it is presumed that all conduct described in the elements must be intentionally committed and the elements do not repeat the general intent implied in each action. Likewise, the elements presume that the conduct is not otherwise legally justified under applicable law referred to in article 21, paragraph 1 (b) and (c) of the Statute. Hence, the element of "unlawfulness" that exists in the Statute and in the jurisprudence of many of these offences has not been repeated in the elements of crimes. Absence of a lawful justification for a particular action need not be proved by the Prosecutor unless the issue is raised by the accused.

This language may suggest that at least some of the delegates believe that it is for the Prosecutor, not the accused, to bear the burden even as regards excuses or justifications. *Proceedings of the Preparatory Commission at its second session (26 July–13 August 1999)*, Preparatory Commission for the International Criminal Court, U.N. Doc. PCNICC/1999/l.4/Rev.1 (1999). This point is taken up again in Chapters 7 and 8.

91. Determining whether an intent requirement exists for jurisdictional elements of crimes is a more difficult problem. *Cf.* U.S. MODEL PENAL CODE §§ 1.13, 2.02 (1998) (noting that intent is required for material elements, which are defined as those not involving jurisdiction).

92. STEVEN R. RATNER & JASON S. ABRAMS, ACCOUNTABILITY FOR ATROCITIES IN INTERNATIONAL LAW 45–48 (1997).

93. Many would argue that none of them accurately represents the full scope of the crime in customary international law.

94. STEVEN R. RATNER & JASON S. ABRAMS, ACCOUNTABILITY FOR ATROCITIES IN INTERNATIONAL LAW 51–55 (1997); *see also* LAW OF WAR CRIMES: NATIONAL AND INTERNATIONAL APPROACHES (Timothy L.H. McCormack & Gerry J. Simpson, eds., 1997).

95. *See generally* Rosemary Rayfuse, *The Draft Code of Crimes Against the Peace*

The disparity in definitions underscores the two major problems in defining the scope of crimes against humanity: first, distinguishing the crime from war crimes and from crimes under domestic law;[96] second, determining which acts are punishable under international law as a matter of individual criminal responsibility, as opposed to State responsibility for violations of human rights.[97] The Rome Statute attempts to address both problems through an extensive *chapeau*. The text is quite restrictive in overall character, although two positive outcomes should be noted. First, the Rome Statute does not require any nexus to an "armed conflict."[98] Although some delegations in Rome repeatedly urged retention of the

---

and Security of Mankind: Eating Disorders at the International Law Commission, 8 CRIM. L. F. 43, 63–68 (1997); Leila Sadat Wexler, *The Proposed Permanent International Criminal Court: An Appraisal*, 29 CORNELL INT'L L. J. 665, 690–91 (1996). The variations in definition led Professor M. Cherif Bassiouni to propose the elaboration and adoption of a specialized convention to systematize and codify crimes against humanity. Professor Bassiouni's proposal would have addressed both the *actus reus* requirements (on which there is relatively general agreement) and questions of *mens rea*, the statute of limitations, and other important issues. M. Cherif Bassiouni, *"Crimes Against Humanity": The Need for a Specialized Convention*, 31 COLUM. J. TRANSNAT'L L. 457, 483–86 (1994).

96. Leila Sadat Wexler, *The Interpretation of the Nuremberg Principles by the French Court of Cassation: From Touvier to Barbie and Back Again*, 32 COL. J. TRANSNAT'L L. 289, 309–10 (1994).

97. STEVEN R. RATNER & JASON S. ABRAMS, ACCOUNTABILITY FOR ATROCITIES IN INTERNATIONAL LAW 49 (1997).

98. In this way the Rome Statute is more liberal than the ICTY Statute, which retained the armed conflict nexus. In the *Tadić* case, the Appellate Chamber questioned the armed conflict nexus, pointing out that it was "settled" that "crimes against humanity do not require a connection to international armed conflict. Indeed . . . customary international law may not require a connection between crimes against humanity and any conflict at all." Prosecutor v. Tadić (Case No. IT-94-1-AR72), Decision on the Defence Motion for Interlocutory Appeal on Jurisdiction, para. 141 (ICTY Appeals Chamber, Oct. 2, 1995). Trial Chamber II had difficulty applying the requirement, noting that, although it was unclear, the armed conflict requirement should probably be interpreted narrowly, to require only a temporal and geographic link rather than a substantive link between the criminal act and the armed conflict. In addition, the tribunal held that "the act and the [armed] conflict must be related, [i.e.,] . . . must not be done for purely personal motives of the perpetrator." Prosecutor v. Tadić, (Case No. IT-94-1-T), Opinion and Judgment, paras. 633–34 (ICTY Trial Chamber II, May 7, 1997). This holding was reversed by the Appeals Chamber, which refused to add to the requirement that the crimes be related to an attack on a civilian population of which the accused was aware (i.e., he knew his crimes were so related), the requirement that the act must not have been committed for the purely personal motives of the perpetrator. Prosecutor v. Tadić, (Case No. IT-94-1-A), Judgment,

words "armed conflict," which was a bracketed option in the Zutphen Intersessional Draft and the April Draft Statute,[99] that proposal was properly defeated as contrary to the weight of judicial decisions, national legislation, and other authority.[100]

Second, absent from the *chapeau* is any requirement that the crimes be committed as part of an attack based on political, philosophical, racial, ethnic, religious, or other grounds.[101] Instead, the Statute maintains the historic difference between "murder-type" crimes and "persecution-type" crimes that originated with article 6(c) of the IMT Charter.[102] In this way

---

paras. 271–72 (ICTY Appeals Chamber, July 15, 1999). For an analysis of the Trial Chamber's decision, see Jose E. Alvarez, *Rush to Closure: Lessons of the Tadić Judgment*, 96 MICH. L. REV. 2031 (1998) and Michael P. Scharf, *Trial and Error: An Assessment of the First Judgment of the Yugoslavia War Crimes Tribunal*, 30 N.Y.U. J. INT'L L. & POL. 167 (1997–98).

99. *Zutphen Intersessional Draft*, at 132, art. 5[20]; *April Draft Statute*, at 26, art. 5.

100. Although the words appear in the ICTY Statute, and the Nuremberg prosecutions required a nexus to the war, this nexus is more properly thought of as jurisdictional, rather than a substantive element of the crime. Thus, this nexus was omitted from ICTR Statute, and "widespread or systematic" was substituted in its stead; *see* STEVEN R. RATNER & JASON S. ABRAMS, ACCOUNTABILITY FOR ATROCITIES IN INTERNATIONAL LAW 56–57 (1997) (concluding that although "the question is not free of doubt, the trend of decision since Nuremberg appears to have severed the bond between crimes against humanity and war crimes or crimes against the peace, and to have accepted that acts may be deemed crimes against humanity without any link to armed conflict, international or internal").

101. Earlier versions of the Statute had this as a bracketed option. *Zutphen Intersessional Draft*, at 132, art. 5[20]; *April Draft Statute*, at 26, art. 5.

102. Article 6(c) of the IMT Charter made the distinction, but scholars have since debated its meaning. *See, e.g.*, M. CHERIF BASSIOUNI, CRIMES AGAINST HUMANITY IN INTERNATIONAL CRIMINAL LAW 327–28 (2d ed., 1998); Roger S. Clark, *Crimes Against Humanity*, *in* THE NUREMBERG TRIAL AND INTERNATIONAL LAW 177 (George Ginsburgs & V.N. Kudriavtsev, eds., 1990); Egon Schwelb, *Crimes Against Humanity*, 23 BRIT. Y.B. INT'L L. 178, 188, 193 (1946); Leila Sadat Wexler, *The Interpretation of the Nuremberg Principles by the French Court of Cassation: From Touvier to Barbie and Back Again*, 32 COL. J. TRANSNAT'L L. 289, 309–10 (1994); *see also* STEVEN R. RATNER & JASON S. ABRAMS, ACCOUNTABILITY FOR ATROCITIES IN INTERNATIONAL LAW 63–64 (1997) (arguing that "the law appears to admit of two interpretations": either that all crimes against humanity require some underlying motive that identifies the victim as a member of a particular group, or that some crimes are so horrendous in and of themselves that motive is irrelevant). The second interpretation is probably the better view. Leila Sadat Wexler, *The Interpretation of the Nuremberg Principles by the French Court of Cassation: From Touvier to Barbie and Back Again*, 32 COL. J. TRANSNAT'L L. 289, 359–60 (1994).

the Statute tracks the ICTY approach (which was confirmed by the Appeals Chamber in the *Tadić* case)[103] and appears consistent with the weight of authority on this point. The Statute, however, reinserts the linkage later by requiring that the crime of persecution be committed in connection either with another crime against humanity or any other crime within the jurisdiction of the Court.[104]

Article 7 contains four separate preconditions that must be satisfied before jurisdiction attaches in a particular case in which crimes against humanity are charged.[105] Some appear to be purely jurisdictional, mean-

---

103. Although ICTY Trial Chamber II held that "discriminatory intent [is required] for all crimes against humanity under Article 5," Prosecutor v. Tadić (Case No. IT-94-1-T), Opinion and Judgment, paras. 650–52 (ICTY Trial Chamber II, May 7, 1997), the Appeals Chamber reversed this holding. Prosecutor v. Tadić (Case No. IT-94-1-A), Judgment, para. 305 (ICTY Appeals Chamber, July 15, 1999).

104. *Rome Statute*, art. 7(1)(h). The Statute also contains additional grounds for persecutions of groups, including political, cultural, and gender groups.

105. An example perhaps best demonstrates the limitations imposed on the Treaty's definition by the several requirements of the *chapeau*. Consider the two bombings in 1998 by the United States in Afghanistan and the Sudan. *See, e.g.*, James Bennet, *U.S. Cruise Missiles Strike Sudan and Afghan Targets Tied to Terrorist Network*, N.Y. TIMES, Aug. 21, 1998, at A6. These acts, whether or not lawful uses of force under international law generally, probably are not crimes against humanity within the meaning of the Rome Statute (I do not opine on whether they might be so considered under the broader customary international law definition of the crime, or under municipal law definitions). First, it would be straining the ordinary meaning of the text to argue that two acts satisfy the requirement that the crimes be "widespread," particularly in light of the qualifying language in paragraph 2 that "multiple" acts must be committed for an "attack" against a civilian population to count as a crime against humanity (and they certainly are not "systematic" in the ordinary sense of that word, particularly when its Nuremberg origins are considered). Multiple may mean "more than one" (i.e., two attacks suffice), which is a plausible interpretation of the English text, X THE OXFORD ENGLISH DICTIONARY 83–85 (2d ed. 1991), but a less plausible reading of the French text, 1 LE PETIT ROBERT DICTIONNAIRE DE LA LANGUE FRANÇAISE 1243 (2d ed. 1992). Second, the attacks were not committed "against a civilian *population*" but against two discrete targets. Finally, even if one could consider these actions attacks on a civilian population, there would have to be evidence of a "state or organizational policy" to commit these crimes to bring them within the jurisdiction of the Court. Conversely, the attacks of September 11, 2001 on the World Trade Center and the Pentagon would appear to satisfy the multiple requirements of the *Chapeau*. Finally, *assuming* the four preconditions are satisfied, an individual defendant may be criminally liable even if he or she commits only one of the acts listed in article 7(1); *see* Prosecutor v. Tadić (Case No. IT-94-1-T), Opinion and Judgment, paras. 648–49 (ICTY Trial Chamber II, May 7, 1997).

ing that once they have been proved as regards a particular situation, they need not be reestablished *ab initio* with respect to each defendant. Others, however, are material elements of the offense, meaning that they must be committed with intent or knowledge on the part of the defendant,[106] and proven with particularity in each case. The text is essentially a codification of compromises between those who thought the Statute was too innovative in character and too broad in its reach, and those who thought it did not go far enough.

First, the Statute requires commission of the crime as part of a "widespread *or* systematic attack."[107] This predicate, which is arguably jurisdictional in nature,[108] is also found in the ICTR Statute, and was a compromise between the position of the ICTY Statute, which contains no threshold,[109] and those who thought the requirements of "widespread" and "systematic" should be cumulative, rather than disjunctive. The Statute thus adopts the position taken by most recent authorities, including the ICTY in the *Tadić* case, that these requirements are alternatives.[110]

---

106. *Rome Statute*, art. 30.

107. *Id.* art. 7(1).

108. The Draft Elements take the position that this is an element of each offense, which indicates an intent to require the Prosecutor to prove this in respect to each defendant accused of crimes against humanity before the Court. Surely, however, if the Court is hearing several cases arising from the same situation, the Prosecutor need not re-establish the fact that the attack was "widespread or systematic" in each case, which would be enormously time consuming and a potential waste of resources.

109. Professor Paust argues that the proper approach is to have no threshold at all. Jordan J. Paust, *Commentary on Parts 1 and 2 of the Zutphen Intersessional Draft*, *in* OBSERVATIONS ON THE CONSOLIDATED ICC TEXT BEFORE THE FINAL SESSION OF THE PREPARATORY COMMITTEE, *13bis* NOUVELLES ÉTUDES PÉNALES, 27, 39 (Leila Sadat Wexler, special ed., 1998) (arguing with respect to the Zutphen Intersessional Draft that these words "would be severely and unnecessarily limiting of and threatening to accountability").

110. Prosecutor v. Tadić (Case No. IT-94-T), Opinion and Judgment, paras. 647–48 (ICTY Trial Chamber II, May 7, 1997). The ICTR recently defined widespread as "massive, frequent, large scale action, carried out collectively with considerable seriousness and directed against a multiplicity of victims." Prosecutor v. Akayesu (Case No. ICTR-96-4-T), Judgment, para. 580 (ICTR Trial Chamber I, Sept. 2, 1998). "Systematic" means "thoroughly organised and following a regular pattern on the basis of a common policy involving substantial public or private resources." *Id.* The Draft Elements do not address the language "widespread or systematic" directly, but state "[a]ttack directed against a civilian population in these context elements is understood to mean a course of conduct involving the multiple commission of acts referred to in article 7, paragraph 1, of the Statute. . . ."

Second, the attack must be against a "civilian population."[111] To the extent that the widespread/systematic nature of the criminal pattern of activity actually defines what is meant by targeting a "population," as some have argued,[112] this second element of the *chapeau* is either redundant or is intended to focus on the "civilian" aspect of the phrase. Although this requirement has a considerable historical pedigree,[113] it has proven problematic in application, for it often requires courts to draw unseemly distinctions between civilian and non-civilian victims of atrocities. Such distinctions, although understandable from a legal perspective, are indefensible from a moral perspective, and incomprehensible as a matter of common sense.

For example, in the *Barbie* case, a French court of appeals found that a charge against Klaus Barbie, based on allegations that he had tortured and killed Professor Gompel, a Jewish member of the French Resistance, had to be dropped because it was not clear whether Gompel had been arrested "in his capacity as a Jew," or in his capacity as a member of the Resistance.[114] The *Tadić* decision also wrestled with this element of the offense, asking, first, what the character of the targeted population must be; and second, how it would determine "whether an individual victim qualifies as a civilian such that acts taken against the person constitute crimes against humanity" in a particular case. The ICTY thus recognized that the "civilian population" requirement has both a jurisdictional aspect that looks at the nature of the atrocities as a whole, and a particularized material aspect that looks at the nature of the act and the status of the victim in a particular case. One definition of civilian would restrict crimes against humanity "to inhumane acts committed against civilians as opposed to members of the armed forces."[115] Another approach would be to take the view that crimes against humanity were applicable in all cases where the perpetra-

---

111. *Rome Statute*, art. 7(1). Some delegations supported deletion of the words "civilian population" as too limiting.

112. STEVEN R. RATNER & JASON S. ABRAMS, ACCOUNTABILITY FOR ATROCITIES IN INTERNATIONAL LAW 57 (1997).

113. The term was employed in the Agreement for the Prosecution and Punishment of Major War Criminals of the European Axis, Charter of the International Military Tribunal, August 8, 1945, art. 6(c), 8 U.N.T.S. 279, *reprinted in* 39 AM. J. INT'L L. 257 (Supp. 1945).

114. Leila Sadat Wexler, *The Interpretation of the Nuremberg Principles by the French Court of Cassation: From Touvier to Barbie and Back Again*, 32 COLUM. J. TRANSNAT'L L. 289, 339 (1994). The Court of Cassation ultimately reversed this holding.

115. Prosecutor v. Tadić (Case No. IT-94-1-T), Opinion and Judgment, paras. 636, 640 (ICTY Trial Chamber II, May 7, 1997) (internal quotations omitted).

tor and the victim were of the same nationality, regardless of the whether the victim were civilian or military. The tribunal took the first approach, with the caveat that the targeted population need not be completely civilian in nature, but "predominantly" civilian. Thus, the presence of non-civilians in an otherwise civilian population does not change the character of the population, even if members of the population are actively involved in a resistance movement.[116]

This approach mitigates, but does not avoid, having to draw distinctions that may in application become unseemly based upon the characterization of a particular victim as a combatant or noncombatant. One can easily imagine situations in which massacres and other atrocities are occurring in a country, but not at the level of armed conflict necessary to enable the war crimes provisions of article 8 to apply. If some of those massacred are part of a nascent armed opposition to the government forces engaging in the atrocities, and others are their unarmed family members, for example, it does not seem reasonable to distinguish between the victims of the massacre. Instead, the entire event should be characterized as a "crime against humanity." Indeed, to the extent crimes against humanity were conceived of to fill the gap left by the laws of war, it would be regressive for the ICC Statute to permit such a distinction to remain in this case. It may be that adopting a definition of "civilian" that tracks the idea of "noncombatant" in the Geneva Convention, while not ideal, will at least provide consistency. If Geneva law does not apply because there is no armed conflict, presumably no one in the conflict could be considered "noncivilian" for purposes of article 7.

Third, the crime must be committed "with knowledge of the attack [directed against any civilian population]."[117] This is clearly a material element of the offense.[118] For not only must the Prosecutor demonstrate that the defendant committed the criminal act (such as murder or extermination) in the context of an attack on a civilian population, but also that the defendant must personally have known about the larger context in which the attack was occurring. From article 30(3) (mental element), it appears that this knowledge, which the Statute equates to "awareness,"

116. *Id*. paras. 636, 638. *See also id*. para. 643; accord Prosecutor v. Mkskić, Radić, and Sljivancanin (Case No. IT-95-13-R61), Review of the Indictment Pursuant to Rule 61 of the Rules of Procedure and Evidence (ICTY Trial Chamber I, Apr. 3, 1996), *cited in* Prosecutor v. Tadić (Case No. IT-94-1-T), Opinion and Judgment, para. 643 (ICTY Trial Chamber II, May 7, 1997).

117. *Rome Statute*, art. 7(1).

118. Thus, the Draft Elements of Crimes rightly include this provision with regard to each crime within the Statute.

must be subjectively demonstrated, rather than merely inferred from circumstantial evidence.[119]

Finally, the attack must involve "a course of conduct involving the multiple commission of acts . . . against any civilian population *pursuant to or in furtherance of a State or organizational policy to commit such attack*."[120] The Rome Statute thus takes a middle road between those who argue and the case law which suggests, that government action, and indeed a governmental policy, are necessary prerequisites to the commission of a crime

---

119. *Id.* art. 30(3). The Statute appears similar in this regard to the U.S. Model Penal Code, which defines knowingly as:

> A person acts knowingly with respect to a material element of an offense when: (i) if the element involves the nature of his conduct or the attendant circumstances, he is aware that his conduct is of that nature or that such circumstances exist; and (ii) if the element involves a result of his conduct, he is aware that it is practically certain that his conduct will cause such a result.

U.S. MODEL PENAL CODE § 2.02(2)(b) (1997). The Model Penal Code thus proposes a subjective test. U.S. MODEL PENAL CODE § 2.02 explanatory notes on section (Official Draft and Revised Comments 1985). If the Statute's application is limited only to the organizers of the plan, this intent and knowledge requirement is perhaps appropriate. It will, however, make it difficult to reach other participants in the plan—camp guards, mid-level civil servants, and other essential cogs in the criminal machine—who will simply claim they had no knowledge of the overall plan. *See, e.g., Papon*, Cour d'assises de la Gironde, Apr. 2, 1998 (acquitting Vichy bureaucrat who signed deportation orders for 1600 Jews of murder as a crime against humanity for failure to prove complicity in the Nazi "final solution"). *But see* Regina v. Finta [1994] 1 S.C.R. 701, 816–20 (acquitting Hungarian gendarmerie officer who participated in implementing the Baky Order as part of the Nazi "final solution" of crimes against humanity notwithstanding the court's finding that intent could be inferred from the circumstances surrounding the crime). The term "knowledge" may be further elaborated in the Elements of Crimes adopted by the Assembly of States Parties, and could improve this situation. Contrast, for example, Trial Chamber II's opinion in the *Tadić* case, holding that "knowledge and intent can be inferred from the circumstances," citing the *Mauthausen* case to the effect that all those who were employed at, or resided in, the Mauthausen Concentration Camp must have acquired a definite knowledge of the criminal practices and activities therein existing. Prosecutor v. Tadić (Case No. IT-94-1-T), Opinion and Judgment, para. 676 (ICTY Trial Chamber II, May 7, 1997); *see also* Prosecutor v. Akayesu (Case No. ICTR-96-4-T), Judgment, para. 693 (ICTR Trial Chamber I, Sept. 2, 1998) (finding knowledge to have existed by allowing acts of sexual violence to take place on premises where the defendant was located or in the presence of the defendant).

120. *Rome Statute*, art. 7(2)(a) (emphasis added).

against humanity, and authorities that require no such linkage.[121] Although there does not appear to be a "State-action" requirement *per se*, there does need to be some plan on behalf of some entity. The abolition of the strict "State action" requirement is an important contribution to international humanitarian law. It is illogical to require State action for crimes against humanity but not for genocide; and it would also significantly hinder prosecutions for atrocities committed in civil wars or other situations, in which identification of the offending "State" is difficult to make.[122] While the Statute is thus progressive in this respect, the introductory paragraph of the Draft Elements adds language that is restrictive. Although noting that the attack in question need not be military in nature, during the Preparatory Commission the issue arose whether a State's failure to prevent an attack on a civilian population could satisfy the Statute's policy requirement. The Draft Elements adopted by the Preparatory Commission at its June 2000 Session took the position that a government's failure to act was not, in most instances, sufficient to satisfy the Statute's policy requirement. Thus, paragraph three of the Elements' introduction provides: "It is understood that 'policy to commit such attack' requires that the State or organization *actively promote or encourage such an attack* against a civilian population."[123] A footnote adds: "Such a policy may, in exceptional circumstances, be implemented by a deliberate failure to take action, which is consciously aimed at encouraging such attack. *The existence of such a policy cannot be inferred solely from the absence of governmental or organizational action*."[124] The NGO Community objected strenuously to the inclusion of this language in the Elements, noting that in many cases crimes against humanity have been committed with the "toleration, acquiescence, endorsement or indirect or implicit encouragement or promotion of State authorities."[125] This being the case, addition of the restrictive lan-

121. *See generally* STEVEN R. RATNER & JASON S. ABRAMS, ACCOUNTABILITY FOR ATROCITIES IN INTERNATIONAL LAW 64–67 (1997).

122. Leila Sadat Wexler, *The Interpretation of the Nuremberg Principles by the French Court of Cassation: From Touvier to Barbie and Back Again*, 32 COL. J. TRANSNAT'L L. 289, 360 (1994); *see also* Prosecutor v. Tadić (Case No. IT-94-1-T), Opinion and Judgment, paras. 653–55 (ICTY Trial Chamber II, May 7, 1997); STEVEN R. RATNER & JASON S. ABRAMS, ACCOUNTABILITY FOR ATROCITIES IN INTERNATIONAL LAW 67 (1997) (suggesting that linkage to State action is now outdated). *But see* M. Cherif Bassiouni, *The Normative Framework of International Humanitarian Law: Overlaps, Gaps and Ambiguities*, 8 TRANSNAT'L L. & CONTEMP. PROBS. 199, 209–11 (1998) (noting that State action is a distinguishing characteristic of crimes against humanity).

123. Draft Elements of Crimes, article 7, Introduction, para. 3 (emphasis added).

124. *Id.* n. 6 (emphasis added).

125. HUMAN RIGHTS WATCH, COMMENTARY TO THE PREPARATORY COMMISSION ON

guage in the Elements could seriously curtail the ability of the Prosecutor to bring cases, as well as increase the evidentiary burden upon him or her considerably in trying to establish that a particular attack was actively encouraged or promoted by a State. This is because much of the non-circumstantial information which could establish the nature of the State or organizational policy will be in the hands of the State or organization and will be acquired only with difficulty by the Court's personnel.[126]

The Rome Statute also requires that a defendant act pursuant to or in furtherance of the (State or organizational) plan, of which he or she has knowledge.[127] Apparently, the delegates agreed with a French line of cases, stretching from *Barbie*[128] to *Papon*,[129] which distinguish murder, war crimes, and crimes against humanity from each other by focusing not only on the context within which the crime occurred and the status of the victim, but also on the mental intent of the perpetrator.[130] In addition, it is important to demonstrate that the act of the defendant has been accomplished as a part of the plan, and not for purely personal motives.[131] Finally, while the existence of the plan or policy appears to be a jurisdictional element,[132] establishing that the defendant acted in furtherance of it or pursuant to it is clearly material.

THE INTERNATIONAL CRIMINAL COURT, ELEMENTS OF CRIMES AND RULES OF EVIDENCE AND PROCEDURE 5 (June 2000).

126. *Id.* at 5–6.

127. The intent requirement is imposed by article 30 of the Statute, which requires that material elements be committed with intent and knowledge. *Rome Statute*, art. 30(2)(a).

128. Oct. 6, 1983, Cass. Crim., 1984 D.S. Jur. 113, Gaz. Pal. Nos. 352–54, at 710 (Dec. 18–20, 1983), 1983 J.C.P. II G, No. 20,107, J.D.I. 779 (1983); Jan. 26, 1984, Cass. Crim., 1984 J.C.P. II G, No. 20,197 (Note Ruzié), J.D.I. 308 (1984); Dec. 20, 1985, Cass. Crim., 1986 J.C.P. II G, No. 20,655, J.D.I. 127 (1986); and June 3, 1988, Cass. Crim., 1988 J.C.P. II G, No. 21,149 (Report of Counselor Angevin).

129. Cour d'assises de la Gironde, Apr. 2, 1998.

130. One Trial Chamber of the ICTY has noted that the policy element is important to establish international jurisdiction over the crimes: "[T]he reason that crimes against humanity so shock the conscience of mankind and warrant intervention by the international community is because they are not isolated, random acts of individuals but rather result from a deliberate attempt to target a civilian population." The Prosecutor v. Tadić (Case No. IT-94-1-T), Opinion and Judgment, para. 653 (ICTR Trial Chamber II, May 7, 1997).

131. *Id.* para. 656.

132. In an important decision the ICTY held that the policy "need not be formalized and can be deduced from the way in which the acts occur." Prosecutor v. Tadić (Case No. IT-94-1-T), Opinion and Judgment, para. 653 (ICTY Trial Chamber II, May 7, 1997). Thus, potential criminals cannot shield themselves from liability simply by refusing to articulate their inhumane policies.

With respect to the list of criminal acts, the Rome Statute retained those offenses historically considered crimes against humanity under the IMT Charter and its successor instruments, and added several more: the forcible transfer of population;[133] "severe deprivation of physical liberty in violation of fundamental rules of international law;"[134] "sexual slavery, enforced prostitution, forced pregnancy, enforced sterilization, or any other form of sexual violence of comparable gravity;"[135] and the crime of apartheid.[136] The Statute also includes the residual category of "other inhumane acts" (which has been traditionally part of crime against humanity's various manifestations), but further qualifies it by specifying that these acts must be "of a similar character intentionally causing great suffering, or serious injury to body or to mental or physical health."[137] The enforced disappearance of persons was also added as a crime,[138] partly in response to the problem of the *desaparecidos* (political prisoners who are arrested and then disappeared). The inclusion of this provision further supports the decision of the Framers not to require any nexus to armed conflict from the definition of crimes against humanity, as these disappearances often occur in the absence of any conflict, whether internal or international. The *desaparecidos* could pose problems for the Court, however, both in terms of caseload and application of the non-retroactivity provisions of the Statute, should the Court adopt the position taken by many human rights activists that past disappearances are "ongoing crimes" until solved.[139] The Draft Elements do not appear to support this view, providing: "This crime falls under the jurisdiction of the Court only if the [widespread or systematic] attack [against a civilian population] . . . occurs after the entry into force of the Statute."[140]

As noted above, several new crimes involving sexual violence were added to "rape,"[141] some of which became controversial during the

133. *Rome Statute*, art. 7(1)(d).

134. *Id.* art. 7(1)(e). This was added to "imprisonment," which appears in the Statutes of the ICTR and ICTY.

135. *Id.* art. 7(1)(g).

136. *Rome Statute*, art. 7(1)(j).

137. *Id.* art. 7(1)(k). Aside from adding yet another intent requirement, the limiting language is so vague as to be subject to a variety of interpretations.

138. *Id.* art. 7(1)(i).

139. Alejandro Kirk, *Desaparecidos, A Festering Wound*, TERRAVIVA, June 24, 1998, at 4.

140. Draft Elements of Crimes, element 7(1)(i) n. 24.

141. The Draft Element for rape, article 7(1)(g)–1, indicates that the crime is gender-neutral.

Statute's negotiation. For example, an interesting debate arose during the informal consultations on article 7(1)(g) concerning the language "of comparable gravity" after the words "sexual violence." Although several States suggested its deletion, other countries protested, arguing that, in the absence of such language, sexual harassment or genital mutilation could be crimes within the Statute's reach. In addition, many States expressed concern that the inclusion of forced pregnancy as a crime could be interpreted as a pro-abortion position. In response, article 7(2)(f) states that forced pregnancy shall "not in any way be interpreted as affecting national laws relating to pregnancy."[142]

Concerns about the inclusion of gender-based crimes sharply divided delegates at the Rome Conference. Some of the discussions took place in connection with the elaboration of the non-discrimination paragraph in article 21(3) (on applicable law), which is taken up in Chapter 7. Other debates surfaced in defining article 7, on crimes against humanity, both because it is the only article in the Statute with any definitions at all, and because that article is the first time the term "gender" appears in the Statute.[143] Some delegations felt that the Rome Statute should use the generally accepted United Nations definition of the term "gender." Opponents of this view felt that the term as used was too broad, and might be taken to condone homosexuality and abortion, or, even worse, suggest that laws prohibiting the same could be criminally suspect under the Statute. The discussions on this issue were protracted, and, as one delegate notes, "ensued in all levels of the Conference—the formal debates, informal debates, bilateral corridor negotiations between delegations and discussions between delegations and NGOs."[144] After informal negotiations (during which the atmosphere became so tense that the Chairman adjourned the meeting, asked NGO representatives to leave, and then resumed discussions),[145] the definition finally adopted provides: "For the purpose of this Statute, it is understood that the term 'gender' refers to the two sexes, male and female, within the context of society. The term 'gender' does not indicate any meaning different from the above."[146]

---

142. *See Enforced Pregnancy Issue Turns into Abortion Debate*, TERRAVIVA, June 25, 1998, at 7.

143. Cate Steains, *Gender Issues*, *in* THE INTERNATIONAL CRIMINAL COURT: THE MAKING OF THE ROME STATUTE 357, 371 n. 44 (Roy S. Lee, ed., 1999).

144. *Id*. at 373.

145. Per Saland, *International Criminal Law Principles*, *in* THE INTERNATIONAL CRIMINAL COURT: THE MAKING OF THE ROME STATUTE 189, 216 (Roy S. Lee, ed., 1999). According to some observers, it is not clear whether the NGO representatives were the cause of the tension.

146. *Rome Statute*, art. 7(3).

How this provision will ultimately be interpreted by the Court remains to be seen. Some argue that the definition in article 7(3) differs from sex discrimination by taking the modern view that "sex is not simply a biological matter but involves the social construction of roles and power differentials."[147] Yet it is clear that many delegations agreed to the term's inclusion in the Statute based on a very different view of its meaning—that the language refers not to a "modern" view of gender (which may be quite fluid), but to a more traditional perspective that would not render laws banning homosexuality, for example, capable of qualifying for persecution-based crimes pursuant to article 7(g) of the Statute.[148] The beauty, and the difficulty, of the compromise language employed is that while it was crafted to appease two irreconcilable points of view, both sides may assert that the definition as adopted reflects their understanding of the term.[149]

c. *War Crimes*

The war crimes section of the Statute is extensive, and the battle over which crimes should be included was protracted. The Rome Statute is much more detailed than any of the predecessor instruments, which has the virtue of making it more complete and the defect of expressly excluding certain very serious threats to international peace and security. Without entering into great detail, it is worth making a few general points about the crimes included in (and left out of) article 8.

---

147. Margaret McAuliffe deGuzman, *Article 21: Applicable Law, in* COMMENTARY ON THE ROME STATUTE OF THE INTERNATIONAL CRIMINAL COURT 435, 446 (Otto Triffterer, ed., 1999).

148. For the view that the definition does not permit arguments based upon cultural relativity, but requires the Court to give the term gender a broad reading, see Kelly D. Askin, *Crimes within the Jurisdicton of the International Criminal Court*, 10 CRIM. L. F. 33, 48 (1999).

149. Given the difficulty that the term engendered during the discussions at Rome, it is unsurprising that it is very sparingly employed in the Draft Elements of Crimes adopted by the Preparatory Commission, and remains "unclarified" by the Elements. The only references to "gender" in the Elements appear in footnote 15 on the Elements of Crimes Against Humanity, specifying that, with regard to article 7(1)(g) (on the crime of rape), "invasion" of a person's body by a perpetrator was a term employed "to be broad enough to be gender-neutral" (the same language appears in footnotes 50 and 62 on war crimes), and with regard to article 7(1)(h) (on the crime of persecution), the targeting of a group based on gender for persecutions referred to "gender as defined in article 7, paragraph 3" of the Statute.

First, in spite of some ambiguity in article 8(2)(b), it appears that war crimes cannot be committed within the meaning of the Rome Statute unless an armed conflict exists. That is, the Statute does not appear to criminalize uses of force (which may nevertheless be illegal under article 2(4) of the UN Charter, or under some other provision of international law) that occur outside a state of armed conflict.[150] This interpretation is consistent with the purpose of the Court, which is to prosecute only the "most serious crimes of concern to the international community as a whole."[151] Second, article 8 grants the Court jurisdiction over war crimes "*in particular* when committed as part of a plan or policy or as part of a large-scale commission of such crimes."[152] This language was developed during the Preparatory Committee's discussions of war crimes and appeared as an option in earlier drafts of the Statute.[153] The phrase retained is not as limiting as some of its earlier incarnations in that it does not *require* the Court to restrict its jurisdiction to cases involving large-scale commission of war crimes or cases involving plans or policies to commit war crimes.[154] Indeed, it is not clear precisely what this phrase means, except perhaps as a guide to the Court in determining the gravity of a case for admissibility purposes pursuant to article 17(1)(d) of the Statute.[155]

The Statute elaborates in four paragraphs the substance of the war crimes within the Court's jurisdiction. Article 8(2)(a) incorporates Grave Breaches of the Geneva Conventions of 12 August 1949, and is uncontroversial. As others have noted, the use of the formula "namely" suggests that the list of grave breaches in the Statute is exhaustive, not merely illustrative.[156]

---

150. Thus, the two U.S. air strikes in Afghanistan and the Sudan referred to earlier, even if illegal uses of force, would not by themselves give rise to criminal responsibility under the Rome Statute.

151. *Rome Statute*, art. 5(1).

152. *Id.* art. 8(1) (emphasis added).

153. *See Zutphen Intersessional Draft*, at 131; *April Draft Statute*, art 5.

154. This was Option 1 in the Zutphen Intersessional Draft and the April Draft Statute. *See April Draft Staute*, art. 5. Option 3 had no provision on threshold. *Id.*

155. *Rome Statute*, art. 17(1)(d). It may also go to determining, as per article 5, which crimes are "the most serious crimes of concern to the international community as a whole." *Id.* art. 5(1).

156. *See, e.g.*, Jordan J. Paust, *Commentary on Parts 1 and 2 of the Zutphen Intersessional Draft, in* OBSERVATIONS ON THE CONSOLIDATED ICC TEXT BEFORE THE FINAL SESSION OF THE PREPARATORY COMMITTEE, *13bis* NOUVELLES ÉTUDES PÉNALES 27, 29 (Leila Sadat Wexler, special ed., 1998). Compare article 3 of the ICTY Statute (incriminating violations of the laws or customs of war), which uses the language

Article 8(2)(b) covers "other serious violations of the laws and customs applicable in international armed conflict, *within the established framework of international law*."[157] This phrasing is a bit cumbersome and presumably requires that an international armed conflict exist before acts under article 8(2)(b) can become criminal. This would be consistent with the decision of the appellate chamber in the *Tadić* case which asserted that international humanitarian law does not apply in the absence of an armed conflict.[158] It also appears to meet the Statute's intent. One could argue that crimes committed during uses of force which fall short of international armed conflict are within the scope of article 8(2)(b), for the language is really quite different from the other three operative paragraphs of article 8. To do so, however, would strain the meaning of the Statute, and the Draft Elements confirm that a state of "armed conflict" must exist for war crimes to be committed within the meaning of article 8. The subsections often begin with the word "intentionally," in spite of article 30's requirement that all material elements of the offense be committed with intent and knowledge for criminal liability to attach. This redundancy, though inelegant, is probably not fatal.[159]

"shall include, but not limited to," *with* Prosecutor v. Tadić (Case No. IT-94-1-AR72), Decision on the Defence Motion for Interlocutory Appeal on Jurisdiction, para. 87 (ICTY Appeals Chamber, Oct. 2, 1995) (interpreting the article as providing a list that was "merely illustrative, not exhaustive").

157. *Rome Statute*, art. 8(2)(b).

158. Prosecutor v. Tadić (Case No. IT-94-1-AR72), Decision on the Defence Motion for Interlocutory Appeal on Jurisdiction, para. 67 (ICTY Appeals Chamber, Oct. 2, 1995).

159. An earlier version of the Elements included a paragraph that was ultimately deleted, which attempted to resolve this ambiguity, as follows:

> Consistent with the general principles of law defined in article 30, it is presumed that all conduct described in the elements must be intentionally committed and the elements do not repeat the general intent implied in each action. Likewise, the elements presume that the conduct is not otherwise legally justified under applicable law referred to in article 21, paragraph 1 (b) and (c) of the Statute. Hence, the element of "unlawfulness" that exists in the Statute and in the jurisprudence of many of these offences has not been repeated in the elements of crimes. Absence of a lawful justification for a particular action need not be proved by the Prosecutor unless the issue is raised by the accused. *Proceedings of the Preparatory Commission at its second session (26 July–13 August 1999)*, Preparatory Commission for the International Criminal Court, U.N. Doc. PCNICC/1999/l.4/Rev.1 (1999).

As in article 8(2)(a), the list in article 8(2)(b) is probably exclusive. This is demonstrated by the use of the word "namely" before the list of acts, as well as the provision in article 8(2)(b)(xx) that particular weapons, not already listed in article 8(2)(b),[160] are not prohibited unless they are "subject to a comprehensive prohibition" *and* on a list adopted in an annex by amendment of the Statute.[161] The absence of weapons of mass destruction such as chemical, biological, and nuclear weapons from the list in article 8(2)(b) was a political compromise and represented a great disappointment.[162]

Articles 8(2)(c) and 8(2)(e) address armed conflict not of an international character. Their inclusion, even if imperfect, represents a great success, for many States at the conference (and throughout the Preparatory Committee's meetings) expressed a desire to completely exclude war crimes committed in internal conflict from the Statute.[163] The International

---

160. Such as flattening or expanding bullets. *Rome Statute,* art. 8(2)(b)(xix).

161. *Id.* art. 8(2)(b)(xx). This language is somewhat vague, but presumably expresses the Framers' intent to require the existence of a treaty prohibiting use of a weapon prior to inclusion of that weapon in the annexed list. It is also representative of a view of international law taken by the nuclear weapons states in the *Nuclear Weapons Advisory Opinion,* with which the International Court of Justice essentially agreed, that what is not expressly prohibited is permitted. It is important to note, however, that even if a particular weapon is not prohibited *per se,* use of that weapon is still subject to the principles of proportionality, necessity, and the distinction between civilians and combatants. The choice of the Framers to require an express list of weapons prohibited *per se* is consistent with the principle of legality that requires potential offenders to be on notice of their crimes.

162. The absence of land mines is equally troubling. *See* Convention on the Prohibition of the Use, Stockpiling, Production and Transfer of Anti-Personnel Mines and on Their Destruction, *opened for signature* Dec. 3, 1997, 36 I.L.M. 1507 (1997) (entered into force Mar. 1, 1999). Their inclusion may, however, be reconsidered at the Review Conference. Another controversy that erupted during the Conference was the inclusion in article 8(2)(b)(viii) of the crime of transferring "directly or indirectly, by the Occupying Power of parts of its own civilian population into the territory it occupies, or the deportation or transfer of all or parts of the population of the occupied territory within or outside this territory." The incorporation of this provision, which is similar to article 49 of the 1949 Geneva Convention on the Protection of Civilians, caused Israel to vote against the Statute. *UN Diplomatic Conference Concludes in Rome with Decision to Establish Permanent International Criminal Court,* Press Release L/ROM/22, July 17, 1998, at Explanations of Vote.

163. The inclusion of common article 3 in the Statute, *Rome Statute,* art. 8(c), is not particularly controversial. However, the list of crimes in article 8(e), which covers much of Protocol II to the Geneva Conventions, as well as some new crimes, was hotly controverted.

Committee of the Red Cross and the United States' delegation fought consistently for its inclusion,[164] however, and ultimately prevailed, although the Statute is not as broad with regard to criminalizing offenses committed in internal armed conflicts as it is with regard to crimes committed in international armed conflict.

The Draft Elements for war crimes adopted by the Preparatory Commission contain few surprises, and for the most part track the Statute. One exception is the final element for each offense which provides that the perpetrator must be "aware of factual circumstances that established the existence of an armed conflict." Concerns that this element might impose an undue burden on the Prosecutor, as well as concerns that this would permit those who commit acts illegal in any context, such as torture or rape, to escape liability because they believed they were committing the crime during a civil disturbance rather than an armed conflict caused the Preparatory Commission to insert a provision in the introductory paragraph, as follows:

> There is no requirement for a legal evaluation [or awareness] by the perpetrator as to the existence of an armed conflict or its character as international or non-international;
>
> . . . .
>
> There is only a requirement for the awareness of the factual circumstances that established the existence of an armed conflict that is implicit in the terms "took place in the context of and was associated with" [an international or non-international armed conflict].[165]

It is not clear whether this language, which is not free from ambiguity, properly addresses this concern, or how the Court will ultimately interpret it. As previously noted, the existence (or absence) of an armed conflict should be a jurisdictional and not a material element of the offense, and the defendant's knowledge or awareness of it should be immaterial so long as there is some nexus between the armed conflict and the crime.[166]

---

164. Kelly D. Askin, *Crimes within the Jurisdicton of the International Criminal Court*, 10 CRIM. L. F. 33, 55–56 (1999).

165. Draft Elements of Crimes, war crimes, introductory paragraph.

166. This is the position taken by the ICTY in Prosecutor v. Tadić (Case No. IT-94-1-T), Opinion and Judgment, paras. 572–73 (ICTY Trial Chamber II, May 7, 1997); Prosecutor v. Delalić (Case No. IT-96-21-T), Judgment, paras. 193–98 (ICTY Trial Chamber II, Nov. 16, 1998); Prosecutor v. Furundzija (Case No. IT-95-17/1-T), Judgment, paras. 60–65 (ICTY Trial Chamber II, Dec. 10, 1998).

A second area of concern is the proportionality provision of the Statute, addressed by article 8(2)(b)(iv) (war crime of excessive incidental death, injury, or damage). Some delegations and the human rights NGOs were relatively unhappy with the Statute's provision on proportionality on the ground that it was weaker than existing customary international law and therefore more favorable to disproportionate uses of force. The Element adopted for this crime engendered additional concerns,[167] as the footnote included to "explain" the text provides:

> The expression "concrete and direct overall military advantage" refers to a military advantage that is foreseeable by the perpetrator at the relevant time. Such advantage may or may not be temporally or geographically related to the object of the attack. The fact that this crime admits the possibility of lawful incidental injury and collateral damage does not in any way justify any violation of the law applicable in armed conflict. It does not address justifications for war or other rules related to *jus ad bellum*. It reflects the proportionality requirement inherent in determining the legality of any military activity undertaken in the context of an armed conflict.[168]

While admonishing potential defendants against using the Statute's relatively generous provisions on proportionality not to excuse the commission of war crimes, the language of the footnote, by referring to advantage that is "foreseeable" and may or may not be "temporally or geographically related to the attack," would appear to be inconsistent with the Statute's requirement that the advantage be "concrete and direct."

II. PENALTIES

The penalties provisions of the Statute, like the definitions of crimes, were quite difficult to negotiate. Although most delegates agreed that the punishment should fit the crime, the idea of what punishment might be fitting varied considerably from State to State.[169] In addition, as noted in

---

167. HUMAN RIGHTS WATCH, COMMENTARY TO THE PREPARATORY COMMISSION ON THE INTERNATIONAL CRIMINAL COURT, ELEMENTS OF CRIMES AND RULES OF EVIDENCE AND PROCEDURE 17 (June 2000).

168. Draft Elements of Crimes, art. 8(2)(b)(iv) n. 36.

169. *See generally*, Payam Akhavan, *The International Criminal Tribunal for Rwanda: The Politics and Pragmatics of Punishment*, 90 AM. J. INT'L L. 501 (1996); William A. Schabas, *Sentencing by International Tribunals: A Human Rights Approach*,

Chapter 3, it is not clear what theory of punishment the Statute employs—making it less evident what punishments are appropriate in particular cases. Balancing the need for flexibility in sentencing with the need for clarity, both as a matter of legality as well as political compromise, article 77 of the Statute specifies the three punishments permitted by the Statute[170] while still leaving the Court's judges relatively free to apply particular punishments in individual cases.[171] Importantly, unlike the Statutes of the two ad hoc tribunals, the Court may not take into account national provisions on punishment or sentencing. Instead, the Statute envisages a universal and uniform penalty and sentencing procedure that should ensure the equal treatment of all defendants before the Court. In order to preserve national prerogatives, however, a feature of the Court that many delegations insisted upon, article 80 of the Statute provides that "Nothing in this Part affects the application by States of penalties prescribed by their national law, nor the law of States which do not provide for penalties prescribed in this Part." This proviso, which is more fully discussed below, ensures, along with the principle of complementarity, that should a country wish a specific punishment to be available in a particular case (such as the death penalty), it can do so by asserting jurisdiction and trying the particular individual in its national courts.[172]

The primary punishment envisioned by the Statute is imprisonment for a term of up to thirty years.[173] No minimum sentences are suggested by the text,[174] nor are specific sentences proposed for particular crimes,[175]

---

7 DUKE J. COMP. & INT'L L. 461 (1997); Dirk van Zyl Smith, *Life Imprisonment as the Ultimate Penalty in International Law: A Human Rights Perspective*, 9 CRIM. L. F. 5 (1999).

170. Punishments proposed but ultimately rejected include the death penalty and loss of suspension of rights, disqualification from office and disenfranchisement.

171. Because the language of article 77 is arguably permissive (the Court "may impose one of the following penalties . . .") it might be argued that the penalties in the Statute are not exclusive, and that judges might impose other penalties not found in article 77, whether more or less severe. Given the negotiating history of the text, however, such a conclusion is unlikely at least as to penalties expressly rejected by the delegates, such as the death penalty. It does not appear that the application of penalties not clearly rejected by the Diplomatic Conference is precluded, however, and it will remain for the Court to interpret this provision in the future.

172. The import of article 80 is considered in connection with article 10 in Chapter 9.

173. *Rome Statute*, art. 77(1)(a).

174. *See, e.g., Zutphen Intersessional Draft*, art. 68[A](a) ("a definite term of imprisonment between [20] and [40] years . . .); *April Draft Statute*, art. 75(a) (same language).

175. Rolf Einer Fife, *Penalties, in* THE INTERNATIONAL CRIMINAL COURT: THE MAKING OF THE ROME STATUTE 319, 327 (Roy S. Lee, ed., 1999).

proposals that were made and ultimately rejected by various delegations during the Statute's negotiation.[176] Rather, the length of a given sentence is left to the discretion of the judges, subject to two qualifications. First, the maximum sentence of thirty years may only be extended to life imprisonment in cases of "extreme gravity."[177] Second, because many delegations felt that life imprisonment was excessively severe, and indeed, the Constitutions of many countries prohibit it, article 110 of the Statute imposes a mandatory review (but not a mandatory reduction) of the sentence after twenty-five years to determine if the sentence should be reduced.[178] Other sentences are to be reviewed by the Court after the person has served two-thirds of his or her time. The factors to be considered by the Court in reviewing sentences are enumerated in article 110(4), and include the person's cooperation with the Court, as well as any "clear and significant change of circumstances sufficient to justify the reduction of sentence."[179]

In addition to imprisonment, the Court has the power to impose fines,[180] or to order the forfeiture of proceeds, property and assets derived directly or indirectly from the crime.[181] Draft Rule 146 provides that in determining whether to order a fine, and in fixing the amount of the fine, the Court shall determine whether imprisonment is a sufficient penalty, taking into account the financial capacity of the person, including any orders for forfeiture or reparation, as well as whether and to what degree the crime was motivated by personal financial gain.[182] Finally, the Court may also order fines or forfeited proceeds transferred to the Trust Fund established pursuant to article 79.[183]

---

176. *Id.* at 330–35.

177. *Rome Statute*, art. 77(1)(b). The second condition for its imposition is the requirement that the Court consider the "individual circumstances of the convicted person." *Id.*

178. *Id.* art. 110(3).

179. *Id.* art. 110(4).

180. *Id.* art. 77(2)(a).

181. Forfeiture of instrumentalities of crime was rejected by the Framers, however, for it would have "given rise to a number of difficult legal and practical issues, in particular concerning title to the instruments used in committing crimes . . . which may typically be State property governed by rules of State immunity." Rolf Einer Fife, *Penalties, in* THE INTERNATIONAL CRIMINAL COURT: THE MAKING OF THE ROME STATUTE 319, 333 (Roy S. Lee, ed., 1999).

182. Draft RPE 146(1). The Rule specifies that the fine may not exceed 75 per cent of the convicted person's identifiable assets, after deduction of an appropriate amount to satisfy the financial needs of the convicted person and his or her dependants. Failure to pay the fine may result in an extension of the term of imprisonment. Draft RPE 146(5).

183. *Rome Statute*, art. 79(2).

One punishment rejected by the Framers was the death penalty, despite strong support from many delegations for its inclusion.[184] Its supporters argued that the death penalty has been accepted in international law since the Nuremberg and Tokyo trials, and is found in many national laws. Indeed, countries supporting the application of the death penalty felt it was an essential component of deterrence, one of the principle rationales for the Court's establishment. They also argued strenuously that its omission from the Statute would render the Court less effective. In addition, they noted the contradiction present in having the leaders or planners of a campaign of genocide, ethnic cleansing or war crimes face a maximum penalty life imprisonment in the Hague, while their followers would possibly receive death sentences in national trials.[185]

Opponents of the death penalty were vehement in their opposition on both legal and humanitarian grounds. To begin with, States parties to the 1989 Second Optional Protocol to the International Covenant on Civil and Political Rights argued that they could not support the Court's Statute if it included the death penalty, nor could States Parties to the 1969 American Convention on Human Rights, which prohibits States from restoring the death penalty once they have abolished it.[186] In addition, many States, particularly members of the Council of Europe,[187] might be

---

184. *See, e.g., Report of the Preparatory Committee on the Establishment of an International Criminal Court, Volume I (Proceedings of the Preparatory Committee during March–April and August 1996)*, ¶ 306, U.N. GAOR, 51st Sess., Supp. No. 22, U.N. Doc. No. A/51/22; *Report of the Ad Hoc Committee on the Establishment of an International Criminal Court*, ¶ 187, U.N. GAOR, 50th Sess., Supp. No. 22, U.N. Doc. A/50/22 (1995). One proposal which appeared in the Zutphen Intersessional Draft was to retain the death penalty as an option in case of aggravating circumstances and when the Trial Chamber finds it necessary in light of the gravity of the crime, the number of victims, and the severity of the damage. *Zutphen Intersessional Draft*, art. 68[A][(e) (Death penalty) Option 1].

185. This has already occurred in the case of Rwanda, leading one commentator to note the presence of "anomalies of inversion" where national and international courts have concurrent jurisdiction. *See* Madeline Morris, *The Trials of Concurrent Jurisdiction: The Case of Rwanda*, 7 DUKE J. COMP. & INT'L L. 349, 371 (1997).

186. American Convention on Human Rights, Nov. 22, 1969, art. 4(3), S. TREATY Doc. No. 95–2, 1144 U.N.T.S. 144, 145 ("the death penalty shall not be reestablished in states that have abolished it.").

187. Protocol No. 6 to the European Convention For the Protection of Human Rights and Fundamental Freedoms, art. 1, *opened for signature* Apr. 28, 1983, EUROP. T.S. NO. 114, 22 I.L.M. 538 (1983) ("The death penalty shall be abolished. No one shall be condemned to such penalty or executed."). *See also*, Second Optional Protocol to the International Covenant on Civil and Political Rights, art. 1(1), *opened for signature* Dec. 15, 1989, 29 I.L.M. 1464 (1990) ("No one within the Jurisdiction of a State Party to the present Protocol shall be executed.").

prevented from surrendering suspects to the Court or otherwise cooperating with it if the death penalty were included in the Statute.[188] In a similar vein, there were arguments that the prohibition against the death penalty had become increasingly widespread, suggesting its acceptance as a new rule of customary international law. Finally, it was argued that application of the death penalty was inhumane and immoral, and that its imposition upon the defendants before the Court would undermine the very principles of justice the Court's establishment was intended to promote.

In the final analysis, the availability of a sentence of life imprisonment won over those delegations that felt that application of the death penalty was a necessary deterrent; the absence of the death penalty no doubt persuaded those opposed even to life imprisonment on humanitarian grounds (as well as legal principles) to compromise on the issue of life imprisonment to reach a consensus. As a final concession to strong national feelings on this subject, article 80 provides that "nothing in this Part affects the application by States of penalties prescribed by their national law, nor the law of States which do not provide for penalties prescribed in this Part."[189] This "non-prejudice" clause underscores the sentiment of the States Parties to the Treaty that the penalties provisions, like the definitions of crimes, are for purposes of the ICC Statute only, and do not embody progressive developments that may be considered new formulations of customary international law (some would even argue that they do not embody current international law). As noted with regard to the definitions of crimes, the fact that the Statute has universal application in cases referred to the Court by the Security Council probably required this result. Moreover, although the absence of the death penalty from the Court's Statute might make it a more desirable venue for trial for certain defendants than their own countries, leading them to engage in "forum shopping," the Court must relinquish cases that a national court wishes to try under the principles of complementarity, making it unlikely that individuals would ever avoid the reach of their own government. This should prevent the kind of adverse publicity and disrespect for the Court that could otherwise ensue.

One last point regarding penalties under the Statute is worth noting. In the *Tadić* case, which was the first case tried before the ICTY, Trial

---

188. The United Nations Model Treaty on Extradition contains a death penalty exemption clause. Model Treaty on Extradition, Dec. 14, 1990, art. 4(d), U.N. GAOR, 45th Sess., 68th plen. mtg., U.N. Doc. A/RES/45/116 (1990) ("Extradition may be refused . . . [i]f the offense for which extradition is requested carries the death penalty under the law of the requesting State. . . .").

189. *Rome Statute*, art. 80.

Chamber II systematically imposed longer sentences for crimes against humanity than for war crimes.[190] This approach reflects the view, shared by many, that the crimes are not of equal gravity but form a "hierarchy of evils"[191] to be punished according to their gravity, with genocide at the top, crimes against humanity in the middle, and war crimes at the bottom. The problem with this approach, which attempts to apply legal distinctions to identical and horrific factual situations, has already been alluded to above in the discussion of genocide and crimes against humanity. As Judge Li wrote in his separate and dissenting opinion in the *Erdemović* case,

> . . . I submit, in the first place, that the gravity of a criminal act, and consequently the seriousness of its punishment, are determined by the intrinsic nature of the act itself and not by its classification under one category or another. Take the present case: the Appellant killed seventy to one hundred innocent Muslim civilians. Whether his criminal act is classified under crimes against humanity or war crimes, the harm done to individuals and society is exactly the same, neither an iota more or less. Then, why should he be punished more severely if his criminal act is subsumed under crimes against humanity and not war crimes?[192]

The Appeals Chamber of the Yugoslavia Tribunal ultimately adopted this view in its judgment on Tadić's appeal of his sentence, holding that there was "in law no distinction between the seriousness of a crime against humanity and that of a war crime,"[193] thereby rejecting the notion of a hierarchy *per se*, and focusing instead on the particular conduct of the accused and the circumstances of the case. This approach seems generally preferable, and the Rome Statute follows it in refusing to attach specific penalties to particular crimes. It would seem unlikely for the Court to imply gradations of penalties where none were included in the Statute, but this, of course, remains to be seen. Draft RPE 145, "Determination of Sentence," lists as aggravating circumstances, *inter alia*, commission of the crime for any motive involving discrimination on any of the grounds

---

190. Prosecutor v. Tadić (Case No. IT-94-1-T), Sentencing Judgment, para. 74 (ICTY Trial Chamber II, May 7, 1997).

191. The phrase is Professor Roger Clark's.

192. Prosecutor v. Erdemović (Case No. IT-96-22-A), Separate and Dissenting Opinion of Judge Li, para. 19 (ICTY Appeals Chamber, Oct. 7, 1997).

193. Prosecutor v. Tadić (Case No. IT-94-1-A), Judgment in Sentencing Appeals, para. 69 (ICTY Appeals Chamber, Jan. 26, 2000).

referred to in article 21, paragraph 3, i.e., age, race, color, language, religion or belief, political or other opinion, national, ethnic or social origin, wealth, birth or other status. This may permit the Court to sanction genocide and crimes against humanity more severely than other crimes, at least on a case-by-case basis.

CHAPTER 7

GENERAL PRINCIPLES OF INTERNATIONAL CRIMINAL LAW

Justice cannot be for one side alone, but must be for both.

—Eleanor Roosevelt

Historically, a major impediment to the establishment of a permanent international criminal court was the absence of any international criminal law with which to charge potential defendants. With the gradual codification of crimes following the Second World War in various treaty instruments and later in the Statutes of the ICTY and ICTR, this situation improved and attention soon turned to a slightly different problem. Advocates for an ICC realized that even assuming a consensus could be reached on the definitions of crimes, no system of general rules existed to address issues such as who could be liable for the crime and what defenses there might be to its commission. Erecting a true system of international criminal justice, it seemed, required writing a complete international criminal code, a task substantially complicated by a lack of consensus among legal systems on solutions to particular questions and the absence of an extensive jurisprudence and experience to draw upon.

One solution would have been to leave this endeavor to the judges that might one day sit in the Hague. This approach was generally thought to be unsatisfactory, however, and efforts were undertaken by various non-governmental organizations,[1] as well as the International Law

1. *See, e.g.*, AIDP DRAFT INTERNATIONAL CRIMINAL CODE (1980); M. CHERIF BASSIOUNI, A DRAFT INTERNATIONAL CRIMINAL CODE AND DRAFT STATUTE FOR AN INTERNATIONAL CRIMINAL TRIBUNAL (1987); *Draft Statute for an International Criminal Court: Suggested Modifications to the 1994 ILC Draft Prepared by a Committee of Experts*, Done in Siracusa/Freiburg/Chicago, January 31, 1996; *1994 ILC Draft Statute for an International Criminal Court With Suggested Modifications (Updated Siracusa-Draft) prepared by a Committee of Experts*, Done in Siracusa/Freiburg/Chicago, March 15, 1996.

Commission,[2] to develop and systematize international criminal law principles. Because the Commission had bifurcated work on the Code and the Court, however, the sixty articles of its 1994 draft statute for the Court, while considerably more detailed than the Nuremberg or Tokyo Charters, contained only a few provisions embodying general principles of criminal law.[3] During negotiations on the Rome Treaty, delegations expressed discomfort with the ILC's laconic approach, and developed and inserted into the Statute a detailed part on general principles of international criminal law. In so doing, the Framers were concerned with the principle of legality, as we shall see below. In addition, they were concerned with constitutional form and function. For, as one expert wrote:

> The principle [of legality] rests in part on the judgment that it is for legislators (or their international equivalent) rather than judges to settle questions about what kinds of conduct will be proscribed. In this aspect, the legality principle is a congener of the political doctrine of separation of powers. The principle rests in part on a sense that fixed rules are required if we are to realize the ideal of treating like cases alike, and that this ideal is particularly important when it comes to imposing criminal penalties. It rests in part on the sense that, especially in criminal cases, it is important to apply impersonal rules articulated beforehand without regard to the particular persons to whom they will be applied.[4]

Thus, much of this part of the Statute,[5] together with articles 20 (on *ne bis in idem*) and 21 (on applicable law), raises quite profound questions about the role and powers of international judges as well as the status of their opinions as law. Drafting it also required careful consideration, *ex ante*, of the elements an effective *international* system of criminal justice requires in order to empower the prosecution, respect the fundamental

---

2. The Commission included several articles on general principles in its Draft Code of Crimes. *Draft Code of Crimes against the Peace and Security of Mankind, Report of the International Law Commission on the work of its forty-eighth Session*, U.N. GAOR 51st Sess., Supp. No. 10, A/51/10 (1996).

3. *See, e.g.*, the articles on the principle of legality, *1994 ILC Draft Statute*, art. 39, and *non bis in idem*. *Id.* art. 42.

4. Edward M. Wise, *General Rules of Criminal Law, in* THE INTERNATIONAL CRIMINAL COURT: OBSERVATIONS AND ISSUES BEFORE THE 1997–98 PREPARATORY COMMITTEE; AND ADMINISTRATIVE AND FINANCIAL IMPLICATIONS, 13*ter* NOUVELLES ÉTUDES PÉNALES 267, 272–73 (M. Cherif Bassiouni, ed., 1997).

5. Because the age of criminal responsibility (article 26) was discussed earlier (see Chapter 5), it will not be reviewed here.

rights of the accused, maintain the universality and impartiality of the ICC as an international forum, and at the same time make appropriate concessions to the sovereignty of States. Moreover, questions arose as to how these provisions of the Statute could be formulated so as to be understandable and accessible to individuals from vastly different legal traditions.

To avoid an undue bias in favor of any particular legal tradition, the Framers opted in several places to avoid terms of art belonging to a given legal system in favor of "neutral" language without content in any given system. This had the positive effect of facilitating the Statute's negotiation as a political matter, but will ultimately require the Court to engage in a great deal of interpretative work to clarify these areas of purposeful ambiguity. Finally, it remains to be seen how the rules and jurisprudence of the Court developed in regard to international criminal law principles will interact with the rules and procedures of national court systems. Certainly, the Statute's provisions will govern actions before the Court, and potentially proceedings of States Parties in national courts. However, to the extent the rules in question are ultimately taken to evidence customary international law, their reach may be even broader, a point taken up at the end of this Chapter.

I. FOUNDATIONS: LEGALITY AND APPLICABLE LAW

A. Applicable Law

Determining the sources of law that the Court could apply in carrying out its mission was no easy task.[6] The predecessor instruments of the ICC Statute—the Statutes of the ICTY and ICTR and the IMT and IMFTE Charters—were silent on this question, and left the judges to fend for themselves. This approach was considered unacceptable by most States with respect to the ICC, and, recognizing the importance of this issue, article 33 of the International Law Commission's 1994 Draft Statute for the International Criminal Court, entitled "applicable law," was elegant and straightforward. According to the text, the Court would apply "(a) this Statute; (b) applicable treaties and the principles and rules of general international law; and, (c) to the extent applicable, any rule of national law."[7] No hierarchy was formally specified for the three categories of sources

6. The Zutphen Intersessional Draft contained seven separate proposals on applicable law. *Zutphen Intersessional Draft Statute*, art. 14[33].

7. *1994 ILC Draft Statute*, art. 33.

available, although the commentary states that "[i]n the event of a conflict between national and international law, the latter . . . will prevail."[8] This suggests that the three sources were listed by the Commission in order of preference.

The Preparatory Committee and, ultimately the Diplomatic Conference, retained the structure generally proposed by the Commission, but expanded upon it considerably. Article 21, on applicable law, is comprised of three separate paragraphs that address not only the law the Court is to apply, but the legal status of the Court's decisions, as well as the obligation to respect fundamental principles of human rights. The first paragraph, article 21(1) provides:

> The Court shall apply:
>
> (a) In the first place, this Statute, Elements of Crimes and Rules of Procedure and Evidence;
> (b) In the second place, where appropriate, applicable treaties and the principles and rules of international law, including the established principles of the international law of armed conflict;
> (c) Failing that, general principles of law derived by the Court from national laws of legal systems of the world including, as appropriate, the national laws of States that would normally exercise jurisdiction over the crime, provided that those principles are not inconsistent with this Statute and with international law and internationally recognized norms and standards.

This paragraph clarifies any ambiguity in the Commission's draft by listing in order the sources of law to be applied by the Court.[9] Although facially straightforward in application, there are several important points to note with regard to its interpretation. To begin with, although a cursory reading of article 21(1)(a) might suggest that the Statute, the Elements and the Rules of Procedure and Evidence all possess the same legal status before the Court, article 9(3) (on Elements of Crimes) and article 51(5) (on the Rules of Procedure and Evidence) make it abundantly clear that in the event of a conflict, the Statute prevails.

---

8. *Id*. at 104.

9. This had been a major issue during the Preparatory Committee discussions of this article. *Report of the Preparatory Committee on the Establishment of an International Criminal Court*, U.N. GAOR, 51st Sess., Supp. No. 22, Vol. II, at 104–05, U.N. Doc. A/51/22 (1996).

As to sources of law outside the Statute, article 21(1)(b) addresses the relevance of international law as a source of law available to the Court. Conceptually, it seems appropriate for the ICC, as a Court of the international legal order, to refer to the sources of international law recognized in article 38 of the Statute of the International Court of Justice, namely treaties, customary international law, and general principles of law.[10] However, the question arose as to the relationship of the Statute to specific treaties such as the Vienna Convention on the Law of Treaties or the Torture Convention.[11] The delegates opted for a formulation that refers to "applicable" and not just "relevant" treaties, although it no doubt remains for the Judges to decide which treaties they may properly consider to be "applicable" in a particular case.[12] While many delegations expressed discomfort over leaving the Court's judges an extensive margin of interpretive discretion, ultimately they were content, or perhaps required, to use language that would permit the judges considerable leeway in considering which sources of international law could be appropriately applied[13] in a particular case.

Finally, article 21(1)(c) addresses the status of national law in the ICC. The ILC's 1994 Draft provided that a rule of national law could be applied if "applicable." This tautology papered over fundamental questions that were very important to many delegations negotiating the Treaty's text.[14]

---

10. *See generally* Margaret McAuliffe deGuzman, *Article 21, Applicable Law, in* COMMENTARY ON THE ROME STATUTE OF THE INTERNATIONAL CRIMINAL COURT 435, 436–39 (Otto Triffterer, ed., 1999).

11. Per Saland, *International Criminal Law Principles, in* THE INTERNATIONAL CRIMINAL COURT: THE MAKING OF THE ROME STATUTE 189, 214–15 (Roy S. Lee, ed., 1999).

12. The Framers' formulation is perhaps *maladroit*. By choosing the term "applicable" instead of "relevant," they apparently wished to avoid widespread references by the Court to treaties that might be relevant but would not apply to the accused's conduct, or to the procedures of the Court. A narrow reading of the term could prevent the Court from referring to the ICCPR or the European Convention on Human Rights on the grounds they are not "applicable," but only relevant. This would seem unnecessarily restrictive and unfortunate and would contradict the practice of the ICTY and ICTR which have looked to other international treaties and cases when faced with novel issues to decide. It is unlikely that the Framers wished to deprive the Court of the same possiblity and so it is unclear whether "applicability" may become much different from "relevant" when interpreted by the Judges.

13. *Rome Statute*, art. 21(1)(b).

14. Indeed, the degree to which an international criminal tribunal, or the ICC, should take account of or be subject to national law is one of the issues upon which the opinions of States varied most widely. Per Saland, *International Criminal Law Principles, in* THE INTERNATIONAL CRIMINAL COURT: THE MAKING OF THE ROME

The approach taken by article 21(1)(c) permits recourse to the national laws of particular States (in particular, those which would "normally exercise jurisdiction over the crime") only insofar as those principles are not inconsistent with either the Statute or international law. This language effected a compromise between the views of States wishing to tie the Statute's operation to the laws of a particular State or States,[15] and the views of States wishing the Court, as an international institution, to be autonomous.

The result is consistent with the general approach taken by the Framers to base the ICC on the principle of *délocalisation*—the law of the Statute and the Court and its operations are generally autonomous from national legal systems and their laws, except, as we shall see, with regard to State Cooperation. Articles 21(1)(b) and 21(1)(c) should assist the Court in this endeavor by permitting it to avoid situations of *non liquet* by apply-

---

STATUTE 189, 214–15 (Roy S. Lee, ed., 1999). The Statutes of the ICTY and the ICTR do not provide a particularly useful precedent on this question. They permit reference to national law (of the former Yugoslavia and Rwanda, respectively) with respect to sentencing of defendants convicted by the tribunals. *ICTY Statute*, art. 24(1); *ICTR Statute*, art. 23(1). They also refer to national law (of the State in which the convicted person is serving his or her sentence) in determining eligibility of the convicted person for pardon or commutation of sentence, subject to the caveat that a pardon or commutation of sentence may be granted by the Tribunal only if such is warranted in "the interests of justice and the general principles of law." *ICTY Statute*, arts. 27, 28; *ICTR Statute*, arts. 26, 27. The Tribunals' Statutes are otherwise silent on the issue of applicable law. Commentators have suggested that this confirms not only the applicability of international norms and standards, but the irrelevance of national legislation. VIRGINIA MORRIS & MICHAEL P. SCHARF, I THE INTERNATIONAL CRIMINAL TRIBUNAL FOR RWANDA 118–19 (1998). The ICC Statute removes the reference to national law with respect to penalties and sentencing found in the ICTY and ICTR Statutes, containing its own set of penalties in Part 7 of the Statute, as discussed in Chapter 6, and providing, in article 110, that the Court "alone" (with no mention of national law) shall "have the right to decide any reduction of sentence."

15. As one French commentator notes, this would have injected an element of State sovereignty back into the ICC Statute. WILLIAM BOURDON, LA COUR PÉNALE INTERNATIONALE 110–11 (Seuil, 2000). Proposal 1 for article 14[33], on applicable law, in the *Zutphen Intersessional Draft*, specified a hierarchy of national laws to be applied in the event the Statute did not contain "the necessary provision to be applied." The proposal referred the Court to the national law of the territorial State, the State of the accused's nationality, or there being none, permanent residence, and, absent any of the above, the national law of the custodial State, in that order. This proposal, which was retained as Option 2 in the *April Draft Statute*, did not receive broad support, and was ultimately rejected. *April Draft Statute*, at n. 62.

ing either treaty or customary international law or, like the ICJ, deriving general principles of (international criminal) law from national laws, to fill in the *lacunae* sure to exist in the application of the Statute.[16]

Paragraph 21(2) of the Statute addresses the issue of *stare decisis* and the role of the Court's own jurisprudence as a source of law. The text had no predecessor in the ILC's 1994 Draft, and is the result of a proposal proffered by the government of Singapore that expressed the view that the Court "may," but is not required, to apply its own decisional law.[17] This article is quite different from article 59 of the Statute of the International Court of Justice, which expressly denies the case law of the World Court any formal status as a source of law.[18] Although one might perceive in this difference an "evolution in the attitude of the world community" towards judicial law-making,[19] it is more probably a practical position that recognizes that even if the ICJ's opinions do not have the force of law as to non-parties, in practice the court tends to follow them.[20] That is, the distinction between precedential and non-precedential systems of law, so important in theory, may be less important in fact.[21] This provision may also take on a certain importance given the variation between the definitions of crimes in the ICC Statute and in other treaties and customary international law, which will require the Court to develop an interpretation of its Statute

---

16. Margaret McAuliffe deGuzman, *Article 21, Applicable Law, in* COMMENTARY ON THE ROME STATUTE OF THE INTERNATIONAL CRIMINAL COURT 435, 443 (Otto Triffterer, ed., 1999). Of course, the availability of applicable law has not prevented the ICJ from issuing judgments of *non liquet*. *Cf.* Legality of the Threat or Use of Nuclear Weapons, Advisory Opinion, 1996 ICJ 226 (July 8).

17. Per Saland, *International Criminal Law Principles, in* THE INTERNATIONAL CRIMINAL COURT: THE MAKING OF THE ROME STATUTE 189, 215 (Roy S. Lee, ed., 1999). This language appeared as Proposal 6 (to article 14[33], on applicable law) in the *Zutphen Intersessional Draft Statute*, and remained unchanged in the *April Draft Statute* (article 20, on applicable law), and the *Rome Statute*.

18. Article 59 of the ICJ Statute provides "[t]he decision of the Court has no binding force except between the parties in respect of that particular case."

19. *See* Margaret McAuliffe deGuzman, *Article 21, Applicable Law, in* COMMENTARY ON THE ROME STATUTE OF THE INTERNATIONAL CRIMINAL COURT 435, 445 (Otto Triffterer, ed., 1999).

20. Jonathan I. Charney, *International Law and Multiple International Tribunals*, 271 RECUEIL DES COURS 101, 129 (1998).

21. *See, e.g.*, RUDOLF B. SCHLESINGER, HANS W. BAADE & PETER S. HERZOG, COMPARATIVE LAW 667–70 (6th ed., 1998). As others have noted, although civil law systems typically reject *stare decisis* as a formal matter, a consistent holding upon a particular question by a higher court may come to represent *une jurisprudence constante* that lower courts consider binding. Jonathan I. Charney, *International Law and Multiple International Tribunals*, 271 RECUEIL DES COURS 101, 358 (1998).

independent of outside sources.[22] Finally, maintaining the consistency of its jurisprudential view is an important element of the principle of legality, discussed below.

The closing paragraph of article 21 was introduced somewhat late in the negotiations,[23] and provides:

> The application and interpretation of law pursuant to this article must be consistent with internationally recognized human rights, and be without any adverse distinction founded on grounds such as gender as defined in article 7, paragraph 3, age, race, colour, language, religion or belief, political or other opinion, national, ethnic or social origin, wealth, birth or other status.[24]

The text was presumably intended to admonish the Court's personnel to observe standards of internationally recognized human rights, particularly the principle of non-discrimination. While the language appears uncontroversial, the word "gender" evoked strong negative reactions from several delegations, who felt it was a covert reference to homosexuality.[25] Their agreement to the paragraph's inclusion in article 21 was garnered only by the insertion of a definition of gender (in article 7(3), on crimes against humanity).[26]

B. The Principle of Legality

As expressed in the maxim *nullum crimen nulla poena sine lege*, it is now well-accepted that crimes must be defined in advance of the conduct sought to be punished.[27] Known as the "legality principle," this concept

---

22. WILLIAM BOURDON, LA COUR PÉNALE INTERNATIONALE 111 (2000).

23. The language is not found in the article on applicable law in the *Zutphen Intersessional Draft*, but in a footnote to article 25[L] (grounds for excluding criminal responsibility). *Zutphen Intersessional Draft*, n. 117.

24. *Rome Statute*, art. 21(3).

25. Per Saland, *International Criminal Law Principles, in* THE INTERNATIONAL CRIMINAL COURT: THE MAKING OF THE ROME STATUTE 189, 215–16 (Roy S. Lee, ed., 1999).

26. See the previous discussion of this issue in Chapter 6.

27. GASTON STEFANI, GEORGES LEVASSEUR & BERNARD BOULOC, DROIT PÉNAL GÉNÉRAL 95 (16th ed. 1997); M. CHERIF BASSIOUNI, CRIMES AGAINST HUMANITY IN INTERNATIONAL CRIMINAL LAW 123–76 (2d ed. 1999). Professor Bassiouni suggests, after an extensive study of several legal traditions, that the following general conclusions can be made about the status of the principle of legality in various legal traditions:

has constitutional foundations in many legal systems, and may be considered the "first principle" upon which a fair system of criminal justice is founded.[28] In addition to its importance in national legal systems, it is enshrined in several international instruments, including article 11(2) of the Universal Declaration of Human Rights[29] and article 15 of the International Covenant on Civil and Political Rights,[30] as well as several regional human rights Conventions.[31] As with so many aspects of the ICC Statute, however, although there may have been general agreement on *nullum crimen* as a concept, the difficulty was in the details. More specifically, international law appeared to take a looser view of the principle's specificity than many national legal systems (and scholars), and permitted

---

> 1—All the families of legal systems prohibit *ex post facto* criminal laws, but not all of them extend it to an absolute non-retroactive application of some penal aspects;
>
> 2—The principle of no crime without criminal law is widely recognized, and while in some systems it prohibits reliance on judicial analogy (i.e., the Romanist-Civilist-Germanic systems), in others it permits it (i.e., the common law, Islamic and Marxist-Socialist systems). But even in those families of systems which reject analogy in judicial interpretation, there still are some exceptions in certain national systems. Other national systems that profess to reject analogy altogether still make some exceptions.
>
> 3—The principle of no penalty without law is probably the one that is applied with the greatest diversity. In some systems judicial discretion is wide and includes indeterminate and alternative sentencing, while in others the judge can apply a sentence by analogy to another similar crime.

Id. at 137.

28. JOSHUA DRESSLER, UNDERSTANDING CRIMINAL LAW 29–35 (1998).

29. Article 11(2) provides: "No one shall be held guilty of any penal offence on account of any act or omission which did not constitute a penal offence, under national or international law, at the time when it was committed. Nor shall a heavier penalty be imposed than the one that was applicable at the time the penal offence was committed." Universal Declaration of Human Rights, art. 11(2).

30. "No one shall be held guilty of any criminal offence on account of any act or omission which did not constitute a criminal offence, under national or international law, at the time when it was committed. Nor shall a heavier penalty be imposed than the one that was applicable at the time when the criminal offence was committed. If subsequent to the commission of the offence, provision is made by law for the imposition of a lighter penalty, the offender shall benefit thereby." International Covenant on Civil and Political Rights, art. 15(1).

31. American Convention on Human Rights, art. 9; African [Banjul] Charter on Human and Peoples' Rights, art. 7(2); European Convention for the Protection of Human Rights and Fundamental Freedoms, art. 7(1).

crimes to be defined not only by Treaty, but by customary international law as well.[32]

Well aware of the critical importance of the principle of legality to the legitimacy of international prosecutions conducted by the ICC, the International Law Commission included an article on the legality principle in its 1994 draft. Because the Commission's view was that definitions of crimes would be incorporated by reference, rather than included in the Statute, the *nullem crimen* principle it included as article 39 of its 1994 Draft was quite broad, requiring only that the defendant be charged with an "act or omission [that] . . . constituted a crime under international law" at the time of its commission.[33] The approach of the Commission, while consistent with the general thrust of its draft, engendered several difficulties as the text wound its way through the negotiating process.

First, many were uncomfortable with a criminal court applying law that was uncodified. This could be a particular problem for the ICC given that the defendants would likely be facing judges with various methodologies and approaches to the derivation of customary international law.[34] Second, the delegates wished to know, in advance and with specificity, the elements of the crimes within the future Court's jurisdiction. Because the Court would potentially hear cases against high government officials, as noted earlier, States had every incentive to clearly delimit the Court's jurisdiction in advance. In addition to reasons of self-interest, States that become parties to the ICC Statute undertake certain obligations with respect to the Court, such as the requirement that they "cooperate fully with the Court in its investigation and prosecution of crimes within the jurisdiction of the Court."[35] Thus, the Statute's articulation of the legality principle not only protects the accused from possible overreaching by the Court's judges, but provides certainty to States as to the extent of their obligations under the Statute's provisions.[36] Finally, as noted in the intro-

---

32. STEVEN R. RATNER & JASON S. ABRAMS, ACCOUNTABILITY FOR HUMAN RIGHTS ATROCITIES IN INTERNATIONAL LAW 20 (1997).

33. *1994 ILC Draft Statute*, art. 39(a).

34. Bruce Broomhall, *Article 22, Nullum crimen sine lege, in* COMMENTARY ON THE ROME STATUTE OF THE INTERNATIONAL CRIMINAL COURT 447, 450–51 (Otto Triffterer, ed., 1999); STEVEN R. RATNER & JASON S. ABRAMS, ACCOUNTABILITY FOR HUMAN RIGHTS ATROCITIES IN INTERNATIONAL LAW 20 (1997); Edward M. Wise, *General Rules of Criminal Law, in* THE INTERNATIONAL CRIMINAL COURT: OBSERVATIONS AND ISSUES BEFORE THE 1997–98 PREPARATORY COMMITTEE; AND ADMINISTRATIVE AND FINANCIAL IMPLICATIONS, 13*ter* NOUVELLES ÉTUDES PÉNALES 267, 269 (M. Cherif Bassiouni, ed., 1997).

35. *Rome Statute*, art. 86.

36. Bruce Broomhall, *Article 22, Nullum crimen sine lege, in* COMMENTARY ON

ductory paragraphs of this Chapter, the legality principle operates as a constraint upon judges who might otherwise be tempted to expand definitions of crimes through an overly generous reading of their own jurisdiction. In national legal systems, the legality principle serves not only to protect individual rights, but functions as a principle of constitutional dimension that reinforces the separation of powers between the legislative, judicial and executive branches of government.[37] In the ICC Statute, it has a similarly dualistic role, serving as both a constitutional directive to the Court's various organs regarding their respective roles, as well as shielding the accused from retroactive prosecution or punishment.

The sole article in the ILC's 1994 Draft was considerably expanded in the Rome Statute, which includes three articles relating to the principle of legality—articles 22, 23 and 24. Article 22(1) restates the legality principle: that a person *shall not be criminally responsible* under the Statute unless the conduct in question constitutes a crime within the jurisdiction of the Court, at the time it takes place.[38] Article 23 adds that a "person convicted by the Court may be *punished* only in accordance with this Statute."[39]

THE ROME STATUTE OF THE INTERNATIONAL CRIMINAL COURT 447, 451 (Otto Triffterer, ed., 1999).

37. As one French court put it: *"La définition légale des infractions s'impose aux juges. Cette situation inhérente au principe de séparation des pouvoirs, ne saurait être analysée comme une atteinte à leur indépendance et à leur impartialité." See also* GASTON STEFANI, GEORGES LEVASSEUR & BERNARD BOULOC, DROIT PÉNAL GÉNÉRAL 96 (16th ed. 1997).

38. *Rome Statute*, art. 22(1) (emphasis added). Unlike the ILC 1994 Draft which referred to "act or omission," article 22(1) uses the term "conduct" which, according to Per Saland, who chaired the Working Group on Part 3, was a term proposed to avoid difficulties with delegations that wished not to place omissions on a par with acts. This difficulty resurfaced several times during the negotiations. Per Saland, *International Criminal Law Principles, in* THE INTERNATIONAL CRIMINAL COURT: THE MAKING OF THE ROME STATUTE 189, 195 (Roy S. Lee, ed., 1999). In addition, the final text diverges considerably from earlier drafts because earlier drafts reflected the uncertainty as to which crimes would be included within the jurisdiction of the Court and whether those crimes would be defined in the Statute itself. Once the decision was made to define the crimes in the Statute, and to exclude treaty crimes, the wording of this article could be, and was, considerably streamlined.

39. *Rome Statute*, art. 23 (emphasis added). This article was added by the Drafting Committee. *Report of the Working Group on General Principles of Criminal Law*, at 3, U.N. Doc. A/CONF. 183/C.1/WGGP/L.4 (June 18, 1998). One commentator suggests that article 23 serves not only as a check on the Court, but may also prevent States Parties from imposing additional punishment on defendants convicted by the Court, including, possibly, the imposition of civil sanctions.

These two fundamental principles are reinforced by three other provisions. First, article 22(2) provides that definitions of crimes shall be strictly construed and shall not be extended by analogy, with any ambiguity in meaning to be interpreted in favor of the accused.[40] This article is a direct rejection of common law (and Islamic law)[41] practice and an explicit constraint on the power of the Court's judges to interpret the definitions of crimes within the Statute. It also incorporates what is often referred to as the "principle of lenity"—the idea that when a criminal statute is subject to conflicting interpretations, it should be construed against the government.[42]

Second, and closely related to the principle of lenity, is the rule articulated in article 24(2) that "in the event of a change in the law applicable to a given case prior to a final judgment, the law more favorable to the person being investigated, prosecuted or convicted shall apply."[43] This is

---

William A. Schabas, *Article 23, Nulla poena sine lege, in* COMMENTARY ON THE ROME STATUTE OF THE INTERNATIONAL CRIMINAL COURT 463, 466 (Otto Triffterer, ed., 1999). It is not completely clear however, that this would necessarily be so.

40. *Rome Statute*, art. 22(2). See also the discussion of this point in Chapter 6.

41. Osama Ghanem Alobaidy, The International Criminal Court: An Arab Perspective in View of Islamic Law and the 1998 Rome Statute (2000) (unpublished J.S.D. dissertation, Washington University School of Law) (on file with the Washington University School of Law Library).

42. While not adopted by the United States Model Penal Code, JOSHUA DRESSLER, UNDERSTANDING CRIMINAL LAW 35 (1998); U.S. MODEL PENAL CODE § 1.02 (1985) (providing that criminal statutes should be construed according to their "fair import," and that ambiguities be resolved in a manner that further the general purposes of the Code and the special purposes of the particular provision involved), this principle is found in other common law countries, such as the United Kingdom, as well as continental practice. *See, e.g.*, N. CODE PÉN. (France) art. 111–4 ("*La loi pénale est d'interprétation stricte*"); N. CODE PÉN. (France) art. 112–1 (*Sont seuls punissables les faits constitutifs d'une infraction à la date à laquelle ils ont été commis. Peuvent seules être prononcées les peines légalement applicables à la même date. Toutefois, les dispositions nouvelles s'appliquent aux infractions commises avant leur entrée en vigeur et n'ayant pas donné lieu à une condamnation passée en force de chose jugée lorsqu'elles sont moins sévères que les dispositions anciennes.*) Some commentators suggest that the greater the severity of punishment, the more strictly the statute should arguably be construed. WAYNE R. LAFAVE & AUSTIN W. SCOTT JR., CRIMINAL LAW 78–79 (2d ed. 1986).

43. *Rome Statute*, art. 24(2). As one commentator notes, the language chosen suggests that this provision may be invoked at *any* stage of the proceedings, even post-conviction, provided that the finding of guilt is still susceptible to appeal under article 81. Raul C. Pangalangan, *Non-retroactivity ratione personae, in* COMMENTARY ON THE ROME STATUTE OF THE INTERNATIONAL CRIMINAL COURT 467, 473 (Otto Triffterer, ed., 1999). This provision appeared in brackets in the April Draft

an extension of the general rule that it is impermissible to adopt legislation either criminalizing acts which were legal when committed, or aggravating the crime or punishment therefor.[44] Given the extensive criticism and legal challenges which were raised before the IMT at Nuremberg, the IMFTE at Tokyo, and even the ICTY and ICTR, all of which applied law "enacted" retroactively to crimes committed prior to the adoption of the respective tribunals' statutes,[45] it is not surprising that the drafters of the Rome Statute occupied themselves with the issue of judicial, as well as legislative, retroactivity, and wished to shield the ICC from challenges raised on that basis.

Third, article 24(1) not only deprives the Court of jurisdiction over crimes committed prior to the Statute's entry into force, but provides that no person shall be criminally responsible under the Statute for conduct that occurs prior to the entry into force of the Statute.[46] This paragraph, which, on a first reading appears to duplicate article 11(1), differs in one important respect: article 11(1) refers to "crimes committed" whereas article 24(1) refers to "criminal conduct." This linguistic difference was not accidental—at stake was the treatment of so-called "continuous crimes" such as enforced disappearances, which might have begun prior to the Statute's entry into force, but continued thereafter. This was a major point

---

Statute, and the principle it embodies is accepted in many national legal systems. *See, e.g.*, N. CODE PÉN. (France) art. 112–1 (*Sont seuls punissables les faits constitutifs d'une infraction à la date à laquelle ils ont été commis. Peuvent seules être prononcées les peines légalement applicables à la même date. Toutefois, les dispositions nouvelles s'appliquent aux infractions commises avant leur entrée en vigeur et n'ayant pas donné lieu à une condamnation passée en force de chose jugée lorsqu'elles sont moins sévères que les dispositions anciennes.*) *See also* M. CHERIF BASSIOUNI, CRIMES AGAINST HUMANITY IN INTERNATIONAL CRIMINAL LAW 123–76 (2d ed. 1999).

44. This is required in the United States by Article I, Sections 9 and 10 of the United States Constitution, prohibiting the adoption of bills of attainder or *ex post facto* legislation. *See* Calder v. Bull, 3 U.S. (3 Dall.) 386, 398 (1798).

45. Of course, each of the tribunals in question sustained its own jurisdiction, leading to a general sense that the *nullum crimen* and *ex post facto* prohibitions applied to the substantive law, but not the procedural mechanisms adduced by governments (or the international community) to prosecute those laws. As the IMT stated "The Charter is not an arbitrary exercise of power on the part of the victorious nations, but . . . the expression of international law existing at the time of its creation, and to that extent is itself a contribution to international law." International Military Tribunal (Nuremburg), Judgment and Sentences, 41 AM. J. INT'L L. 172, 216 (1947). For a superb treatment of the problem of retroactivity in another context, see Peter E. Quint, *The Border Guard Trials and the East German Past—Seven Arguments*, 48 AM. J. COMP. L. 541 (2000).

46. *Rome Statute*, art. 24(1).

of controversy among delegations—although one could read article 11(1) as permitting the Court to pursue disappearances occurring prior to the Statute's entry into force on the grounds that the crime continues to be "committed" until the disappeared have been found, the use of the term "conduct" in article 24(1) suggests that conduct which led to the disappearances is outside the jurisdiction of the Court if it occurred prior to the Statute's entry into force. This was the view taken by the Preparatory Commission in the Draft Elements of Crimes,[47] and underscores that one of the political compromises required to bring the ICC into existence was the exclusion from its jurisdiction crimes committed, or conduct which transpired, prior to the Statute's entry into force.[48]

It is important to note that the principles of legality set forth in the Rome Statute govern the Court's operations and were not intended as codifications of those principles generally applicable to international criminal law as a matter of customary international law. Article 22(3) expresses this idea in a savings clause, providing: "This article shall not affect the characterization of any conduct as criminal under international law independently of this Statute."[49] This text resulted from a proposal made by the Austrian government, and incorporates two ideas. First, if, as others have noted, articles 22 through 24 arguably incorporate a "strict" understanding of the *nullum crimen* principle,[50] they depart dramatically from what many believed to be the content of the *nullum crimen* principle as a matter of *international* law, which, as a general matter, is more liberal than many national legal orders in its understanding of the strictures imposed by the legality principle on criminal prosecutions.[51] Article 22(3) arguably underlines this difference between the legality principle as a matter of international law (generally speaking), and the principle's enforcement and application by the Court as a matter of treaty law. Second, the provision reinforces article 10's insistence that the Statute in no way prejudices the existence or continuing development of customary international law outside the Statute, even though article 10, by its terms, excludes Part 3

---

47. Draft Elements of Crimes, art. 7(1)(i) n. 24.

48. Although this could remain an open question for the Court if the Assembly of States Parties takes a different view than the Preparatory Commission, the language appears restrictive rather than permissive in thrust.

49. *Rome Statute*, art. 22(3).

50. Professor Bassiouni appears to take a different view, suggesting that the ICC Statute's approach "is closer to the common law than to the Romanist-Civilist one." M. CHERIF BASSIOUNI, CRIMES AGAINST HUMANITY IN INTERNATIONAL CRIMINAL LAW 176 (2d ed. 1999).

51. Kai Ambos, *General Principles of Criminal Law in the Rome Statute*, 10 CRIM. L. F. 1, 2–5 (1999).

of the Statute entirely. Rather, the legality principle and definition of crimes within the Statute are "for the purposes of the Statute" only, and other definitions could be relied upon by States, regional tribunals, or the International Court of Justice, as Chapter 9 explores.[52]

II. *NE BIS IN IDEM*

This principle, which roughly corresponds in common law systems to the notion of double jeopardy,[53] has as its central tenet that no one should be twice judged for the same offense. Although it is less widely found in international instruments than the legality principle,[54] it is enshrined in article 14(7) of the International Covenant on Civil and Political Rights, which provides: "No one shall be liable to be tried or punished again for an offence for which he has already been finally convicted or acquitted in accordance with the law and penal procedure of each country."[55] Although it has been argued that this principle has not attained

---

52. Whether the Security Council retains any flexibility either as a legal or a practical matter to vary definitions of crimes from those now found in the Rome Statute remains to be seen.

53. Readers from the United States, however, should probably avoid drawing too many comparisons between the Rome Statute and U.S. law. United States' law permits jeopardy to "attach" earlier in criminal proceedings (at the stage when the jury is empaneled in jury trials, or when the first witness is sworn in bench trials, Crist v. Bretz, 437 U.S. 28 (1978); WAYNE R. LAFAVE & JEROLD H. ISRAEL, CRIMINAL PROCEDURE 1060 (2d ed. 1992)) than the ICC Statute (after acquittal or conviction). In addition, U.S. readers are often surprised to realize that acquittals may be appealed by the Prosecutor in the ICC (as is the case in many national legal systems). On the other hand, it is generally thought that the 5th amendment prohibition on double jeopardy does not forbid successive trials by different sovereigns (federal, as opposed to a state) for the same conduct, *see* Bartkus v. Illinois, 359 U.S. 121 (1959), whereas the ICC Statute does. WAYNE R. LAFAVE & AUSTIN W. SCOTT, JR., CRIMINAL LAW 126 (2d ed. 1986). The United States' Model Penal Code takes the position that successive prosecutions are a bar, even if occurring in different jurisdictions, subject to three exceptions: (1) the offense charged in the second proceeding requires proof of a fact not required by the other and the law defining each of such offenses is intended to prevent a substantially different harm or evil; or (2) the second offense was not consummated when the former trial began; or (3) the earlier acquittal, final order or judgment (for the accused) necessarily required a determination inconsistent with a fact that must be established for conviction of the offense for which the defendant is subsequently prosecuted. U.S. MODEL PENAL CODE § 1.08 (1985).

54. It is absent from the Universal Declaration of Human Rights, for example.

55. International Covenant on Civil and Political Rights, G.A. Res. 2200A

the status of a general rule of international law, particularly as regards retrials by different, as opposed to the same jurisdiction,[56] there was no question of leaving the Statute silent on this point. Because it was agreed during the Preparatory Committee's negotiations that *ne bis in idem* would be a ground of inadmissibility, and therefore closely linked to the Court's jurisdiction, the article was transferred during the Statute's negotiation from Part 3 of the Statute to Part 2, on jurisdiction, admissibility and applicable law.[57] I take it up here, rather than in Chapter 5, because of its close relationship to the principle of legality, and because it is typically found in the "general part" of most penal codes.

The International Law Commission included an article on *ne bis in idem* in its 1994 Draft Statute, which was largely based on similar articles in the ICTY and ICTR Statutes.[58] Article 42 of the Commission's draft shielded a person from a retrial in two situations: If proceedings were before the ICC and the accused had already been tried by another court "for acts constituting a crime of the kind referred to in article 20 [on crimes within the jurisdiction of the court]" or if proceedings were before a court other than the ICC and the accused had been already tried by the ICC. The prohibition only covered "trials," and, in the words of the Commission, only applied "where the first court actually exercised jurisdiction and made a determination on the merits with respect to the particular acts constituting the crime, and where there was a sufficient measure of identity between the crimes which were the subject of the successive trials."[59]

The Commission included two principal exceptions to article 42's operation: first, if the acts underlying the trial in the first court were characterized by that court as "ordinary crime[s] and not as a crime which is

---

(XXI), U.N. GAOR, 21st Sess., Supp. No. 16, art. 14(7), U.N. Doc. A/6316 (1966), 999 U.N.T.S. 171 (*entered into force* Mar. 23, 1976).

56. For a summary of this issue, see Immi Tallgren, *Article 20, Ne bis in idem, in* COMMENTARY ON THE ROME STATUTE OF THE INTERNATIONAL CRIMINAL COURT 419, 422–23 (Otto Triffterer, ed., 1999); AMNESTY INTERNATIONAL, THE INTERNATIONAL CRIMINAL COURT: MAKING THE RIGHT CHOICES—PART V 36 (1998).

57. *Zutphen Intersessional Draft*, at 145; John T. Holmes, *The Principle of Complementarity, in* THE INTERNATIONAL CRIMINAL COURT: THE MAKING OF THE ROME STATUTE 41, 56 (Roy S. Lee, ed., 1999); Immi Tallgren, *Article 20, Ne bis in idem, in* COMMENTARY ON THE ROME STATUTE OF THE INTERNATIONAL CRIMINAL COURT 419, 420 (Otto Triffterer, ed., 1999).

58. *ICTY Statute*, art. 10; *ICTR Statute*, art. 9. For a discussion of these articles of the ICTY and ICTR Statutes, *see* VIRGINIA MORRIS & MICHAEL P. SCHARF, I AN INSIDER'S GUIDE TO THE INTERNATIONAL CRIMINAL TRIBUNAL FOR THE FORMER YUGOSLAVIA 132–35 (1995); VIRGINIA MORRIS & MICHAEL P. SCHARF, I THE INTERNATIONAL CRIMINAL TRIBUNAL FOR RWANDA 343–47 (1998).

59. *1994 ILC Draft Statute*, at 117–18.

within the jurisdiction of the Court;" second, if the proceedings in the other court were not "impartial or independent or were designed to shield the accused from international criminal responsibility or the case was not diligently prosecuted."[60] The exceptions, like the principle itself, suggested that the ICC would have a certain autonomy from and primacy over national legal systems, stepping in where national justice had failed or was insufficient.

When the Preparatory Committee, and subsequently the Diplomatic Conference, took up the ILC Draft, it was generally agreed that the Statute's article on *ne bis in idem* should cover proceedings in the ICC that followed national prosecutions (article 20(3)), as well as proceedings in national courts that followed ICC prosecutions (article 20(2)).[61] In addition, even though the point might appear self-evident, a consensus emerged that the Statute should also address proceedings in the ICC that followed earlier ICC prosecutions (article 20(1)). But in determining the conditions under which the Statute's prohibition against double jeopardy would attach, three major points of controversy emerged.

First, the question arose whether the core event triggering application of the principle was two prosecutions for the *same crime* or two prosecutions for the *same conduct*. Interestingly, although paragraph two of article 20, which limits trials by other courts following trials in the ICC, refers to trial for "a *crime* referred to in article 5,"[62] paragraphs (1) and (3) refer to "*conduct*." The difference in wording reflects the fact that the Statute may only bind States to follow rules related to offenses specifically set out in the Statute,[63] and could consequently permit a person convicted for a crime by the ICC to be tried under national law for the same conduct (but different crimes).[64] In contrast, reference to the term "conduct" in the other two paragraphs of article 20, which govern subsequent proceedings in the

60. *Id.* arts. 42(a) & 42(b).

61. It should be noted that the Statute does not use the term "national," but only refers to "another court" suggesting that trials by regional courts or ad hoc tribunals are also covered by the Statute. Of course, with respect to all courts other than the ICC, a legal basis would be required for the application of the Statute to trials before that other court. With respect to national courts, since the Statute binds only States Parties, in the absence of a general rule of international law, presumably only States Parties are bound by the *ne bis in idem* provisions in the Statute, except insofar as a Security Council referral is involved, in which case a challenge to admissibility based on *ne bis in idem* grounds would presumably be valid, even if the original proceedings were in the courts of a non-State Party.

62. *Rome Statute*, art. 20(2) (emphasis added).

63. John T. Holmes, *The Principle of Complementarity, in* THE INTERNATIONAL CRIMINAL COURT: THE MAKING OF THE ROME STATUTE 41, 58 (Roy S. Lee, ed., 1999).

64. Immi Tallgren, *Article 20, Ne bis in idem, in* COMMENTARY ON THE ROME STATUTE OF THE INTERNATIONAL CRIMINAL COURT 419, 428 (Otto Triffterer, ed., 1999).

Court, suggests the Framers' intention to incorporate a fairly broad bar to successive prosecutions in the ICC arising out of a single set of facts.

Closely related to this question, several States wished the ICC Statute, like the ILC Draft and the Statutes of the two ad hoc tribunals, to exempt from article 20's protection national prosecutions that were based on crimes characterized (presumably by the prosecuting jurisdiction) as "ordinary crimes" (*crimes de droit commun*),[65] as opposed to international crimes.[66] Thus it was argued that a conviction for aggravated assault should not bar a subsequent prosecution for torture or inhuman treatment, given the different societal interests protected by the different crimes as well as the extreme gravity of the international crimes within the ICC's purview.[67] This argument ultimately failed, and the exception for ordinary crimes was deleted from the Statute.

The second issue was the question of "sham" prosecutions.[68] Because the provision on *ne bis in idem* was finalized along with the articles in Part 2, and the issue of national proceedings conducted in bad faith had already been carefully negotiated in connection with the adoption of article 17 (on admissibility), crafting this exception to *ne bis in idem* was much less difficult than it otherwise might have been.[69] Articles 20(3)(a) and 20(3)(b) contain language quite similar to article 17, providing that a person shall not be protected from a prosecution by the Court if the proceedings on which he or she is relying as a shield were either "(a) for the purpose of shielding the person concerned from responsibility," or "(b) [o]therwise were not conducted independently or impartially in accordance with the norms of due process recognized by international law and were conducted in a manner which, in the circumstances, was inconsistent with an intent to bring the person concerned to justice."[70]

The third and most controversial issue involved a proposal that would have created an additional exception to the *ne bis in idem* principle

65. Crimes within the jurisdiction of ordinary as opposed to specialized jurisdictions or crimes *de droit commun* in French law. GERARD CORNU, VOCABULAIRE JURIDIQUE 545 (1987).

66. This concept, familiar to many continental lawyers, but unknown to many other legal systems, was advocated by many on the basis that "common crimes" (such as assault, murder, rape, etc.) may not have the special characteristics of the crimes referred to in the Court's Statute.

67. *See 1994 ILC Draft Statute*, at 118.

68. Immi Tallgren, *Article 20, Ne bis in idem, in* COMMENTARY ON THE ROME STATUTE OF THE INTERNATIONAL CRIMINAL COURT 419, 431 (Otto Triffterer, ed., 1999). *1994 ILC Draft Statute*, at 70.

69. John T. Holmes, *The Principle of Complementarity, in* THE INTERNATIONAL CRIMINAL COURT: THE MAKING OF THE ROME STATUTE 41, 58 (Roy S. Lee, ed., 1999).

70. *Rome Statute*, art. 20(3).

for pardons, commutations of sentence or amnesties granted by a national jurisdiction in respect of someone before the Court. The provision appeared in brackets as article 19 in the penultimate version of the Statute, and provided:

> Without prejudice to article 18 [*Ne bis in idem*], a person who has been tried by another court for conduct also proscribed under article 5 may be tried by the Court if a manifestly unfounded decision on the suspension of the enforcement of a sentence or on a pardon, a parole or a commutation of the sentence excludes the application of any appropriate form of penalty.[71]

The purpose of the proposal was to fill any gaps in the complementarity regime that could arise as a result of someone being investigated or prosecuted in a manner that was apparently genuine (and thereby escape the jurisdiction of the ICC), only to find out that the individual had subsequently been pardoned and thereby escaped criminal responsibility. Although many delegations supported it, others were concerned about granting the Court this extensive power to "examine the administrative and political decision-making powers of a State and intervene if dissatisfied with the result."[72] As a result of the political and substantive objections to the provision, it was dropped from the Statute, leaving quite a potentially serious gap in the complementarity regime.[73]

Finally, although the ICC Statute requires States to desist from prosecutions that would violate article 20, the Court has no power to ensure that they do so. Nevertheless, although the Statute does not specify a particular remedy for violations of article 20, the Court could presumably apply the provisions of article 87(5) (for States not parties to the Statute) or article 87(7) (for States Parties to the Statute) on assistance to the Court,[74] which provide that upon a State's failure to comply with a request from the Court, the Court may make a finding to that effect, and refer the matter to the Assembly of States Parties or, if the Security Council referred the

---

71. *April Draft Statute*, art. 19.

72. John T. Holmes, *The Principle of Complementarity, in* THE INTERNATIONAL CRIMINAL COURT: THE MAKING OF THE ROME STATUTE 41, 59 (Roy S. Lee, ed., 1999).

73. *Id.* at 76–77. Holmes argues, however, that it may nevertheless be possible to challenge a pardon that was clearly tainted, given that the protection of article 20 is lost if the Prosecutor can show that the national proceedings were "for the purpose of shielding the person concerned." As Holmes acknowledges, this would be an "onerous task" for the Prosecutor; but suggests that "[t]he fact that a pardon or granting of parole took place shortly after a conviction may give rise to a presumption that the entire proceedings were not genuine." *Id.* at 77.

74. *Rome Statute*, art. 87(5) & (7).

case, to the Security Council.[75] On the other hand, in the opposite situation, where the first trial occurred in national courts and an individual seeks to invoke *ne bis in idem* either directly before the Court as a grounds of inadmissibility pursuant to article 17(1)(c) or before a national court as a shield to his or her surrender, pursuant to article 89(2), the accused should be afforded the full protection of the Statute, with all its procedural rights and the possibility of appeal.

III. GENERAL PRINCIPLES OF CRIMINAL RESPONSIBILITY

A. Individual Criminal Responsibility

Although the concept of individual responsibility for international law crimes has a venerable pedigree, it was not until the Nuremberg and Tokyo trials that it became "positive" law in modern times. The Nuremberg Charter[76] and judgment explicitly recognized individual liability for the commission of international crimes—as the Tribunal held in a now famous passage: "[t]he very essence of the Charter is that individuals have international duties which transcend the national obligations of

---

75. Rule 13 of the ICTY and ICTR address this specific point, and provides:

> When the President receives reliable information to show that criminal proceedings have been instituted against a person before a national court for a crime for which that person has already been tried by the Tribunal, a Trial Chamber shall, following *mutatis mutandis* the procedure provided in Rule 10, issue a reasoned order requesting the national court permanently to discontinue its proceedings. If the national court fails to do so, the President may report the matter to the Security Council.

The ICC's Draft Rules have no parallel provision. The only reference made to the *ne bis in idem* principle in the Draft Rules is found in Draft RPE 168 which extends the *ne bis in idem* principle to offenses against the administration of justice under article 70 of the Statute.

76. The Agreement for the Prosecution and Punishment of Major War Criminals of the European Axis, Charter of the International Military Tribunal, August 8, 1945, art. 6, 8 U.N.T.S. 279, *reprinted in* 39 AM. J. INT'L L. 257 (Supp. 1945). This was reaffirmed by the General Assembly when it adopted a Resolution affirming "the principles of international law recognized by the Charter of the Nuremberg Tribunal and the judgment of the Tribunal," principle 1 of which provided: "Any person who commits an act which constitutes a crime under international law is responsible therefor and liable to punishment." 1 U.N. GAOR (Part II) at 188, U.N. Doc. A/61/Add.1 (1946).

obedience imposed by the individual state."[77] The Statutes of the ICTY and ICTR also rely upon the principle of individual responsibility for international crimes and each have an article addressing the scope of individual criminal responsibility under their respective Statutes.[78] The International Law Commission did not include a general article on culpability in its 1994 Draft Statute, suggesting implicitly that the Statute applied only to "persons" (and not States or legal entities).[79] However, the ILC took up the question in its Draft Codes of Crimes, and included an article on individual responsibility therein.[80]

When this issue was addressed by the Preparatory Committee, first in informal consultations and subsequently in the Working Group on Part 3 at the third session of the Preparatory Committee in 1997, it proved so complex that it occupied fully half the Working Group's time.[81] Part of the difficulty was the great number of proposals received, which often contained very different conceptions of criminal responsibility, depending upon the jurisdiction from which they originated. Another difficulty was that this article originally combined not only principles of individual responsibility, but questions of *mens rea, actus reus,* and punishment. Finally, governments held widely divergent views on many issues such as the question of conspiracy, liability of legal entities, the criminality of incitement, and the inclusion (or exclusion) of omission as a separate basis for criminal responsibility.

The article as finalized is more extensive than any of its predecessor instruments, including article 2 of the 1996 Draft Code of Crimes, and many subsidiary questions, such as superior orders, command responsibility, mental element and punishment are now found in other articles of the Statute. Nevertheless, American readers, familiar with the Model Penal Code, or French readers, familiar with the *Code Pénal,* will find the article both too long and convoluted in some respects and too abbreviated in others. Too long, because it combines many ideas that in national legal systems would be the subject of separate provisions; too short because it leaves many questions unanswered (such as liability for omissions). It bears repeating that, as discussed in Chapters 5 and 6, the Framers were generally required to stay within the confines of what could be accepted

77. Judgment of October 1, 1946, International Military Tribunal, Judgment and Sentences, 41 AM. J. INT'L L. 172, 221 (1947).

78. *ICTY Statute,* art. 7; *ICTR Statute,* art. 6.

79. *1994 ILC Draft Statute,* art. 21(1) ("The Court may exercise its jurisdiction over a *person* with respect to a crime referred to in article 20 . . .") (emphasis added).

80. *ILC 1996 Draft Code of Crimes,* art. 2.

81. Per Saland, *International Criminal Law Principles, in* THE INTERNATIONAL CRIMINAL COURT: THE MAKING OF THE ROME STATUTE 189, 198 (Roy S. Lee, ed., 1999).

as existing customary international law. Thus, many innovations that would have made perfect sense if one was starting "from scratch," such as the inclusion of an article on omission, or the addition of incitement as a basis for the imposition of liability in respect of crimes other than genocide, were ultimately rejected by the Diplomatic Conference.

Paragraph 1 of article 25, on individual responsibility, limits its application to natural persons (18 or older)[82] only. Although some delegations argued vigorously for the inclusion of legal entities (other than States), ultimately no consensus could be reached on this point and the idea was dropped.[83] Although the criminal responsibility of States was never seriously considered by the Framers, paragraph 4 reaffirms that nothing in the ICC Statute affects their potential responsibility under international law.[84] Finally, paragraph 2 reiterates with regard to the ICC what has been generally accepted since Nuremberg: that "a person who commits a crime within the jurisdiction of the Court shall be individually responsible and liable for punishment in accordance with this Statute."[85]

It is perhaps the third paragraph of article 25, which combines not only the *actus reus* element of the crimes within the Court's jurisdiction, but the notion of attempt and levels of participation, that posed the greatest difficulty in its formulation. Subparagraphs (a), (b) and (c) of this paragraph provide, respectively, that a person shall be criminally liable if he or

---

82. *Rome Statute*, art. 26. See Chapter 5, *supra*.

83. Per Saland, *International Criminal Law Principles, in* THE INTERNATIONAL CRIMINAL COURT: THE MAKING OF THE ROME STATUTE 189, 199 (Roy S. Lee, ed., 1999); Kai Ambos, *Individual Criminal Responsibility, in* COMMENTARY ON THE ROME STATUTE OF THE INTERNATIONAL CRIMINAL COURT 475, 477–78 (Otto Triffterer, ed., 1999). The reasons generally advanced to support the liability of legal entities were that *first*, they had been included at Nuremberg and their exclusion from the ICC Statute would be a retreat from the Nuremberg Principles; *second*, that their inclusion could be quite important in terms of restitution and compensation orders for victims. *Id.* In commenting on this provision of the Statute, however, one author rejected the inclusion of legal entities other than States as practically difficult, due to the concept's absence from many legal systems, but noted the "moral[] obtuse[ness] for States to insist on the criminal responsibility of all entities other than themselves." MODEL DRAFT STATUTE FOR THE INTERNATIONAL CRIMINAL COURT BASED ON THE PREPARATORY COMMITTEE'S TEXT TO THE DIPLOMATIC CONFERENCE, ROME, JUNE 15–JULY 17, 1998, 13*ter* NOUVELLE ÉTUDES PÉNALES 42 (Leila Sadat Wexler, special ed., 1998).

84. *Rome Statute*, art. 25(4).

85. *Rome Statute*, art. 25(2).

86. *Id.* art. 25(a). This subparagraph also imposes liability whether the crime is committed "as an individual, jointly with another or through another person, regardless of whether that other person is criminally responsible." One commentator refers to this as a form of "co-perpetration," and suggests that the Statute has removed it from the concept of complicity and recognized it as an autonomous

she *commits* a crime;[86] *orders, solicits or induces the commission* of a crime which occurs or is attempted;[87] or, *aids, abets or otherwise assists in its commission* or attempted commission, including providing the means for its commission.[88] This is quite a bit different than any of the ICC's predecessor instruments, including the Statutes of the ICTY and ICTR tribunals.[89]

---

basis of liability, Kai Ambos, *Individual Criminal Responsibility, in* COMMENTARY ON THE ROME STATUTE OF THE INTERNATIONAL CRIMINAL COURT 475, 478–79 (Otto Triffterer, ed., 1999), akin perhaps to "common plan" liability in French law, but somehow different from crimes committed by groups, which are addressed in paragraph (d).

87. *Rome Statute*, art. 25(3)(b). Although one commentator has suggested that this article does not necessarily require a hierarchical relationship between the person ordering, soliciting or inducing and the person ordered, solicited or induced, while this may be true for "soliciting" or "inducing," it is hard to imagine many cases in which "orders" would be given (and followed) in the absence of such a relationship. *Accord* Prosecutor v. Rutaganda (Case No. ICTR-96-3-T), Judgment and Sentence, para. 39 (ICTR Trial Chamber I, Dec. 6, 1999) (holding that "in the opinion of the Chamber, ordering . . . implies a superior-subordinate relationship between the person giving the order and the one executing it, with the person in a position of authority using such position to persuade another to commit an offence.") It will ultimately be for the Court to determine whether "ordering" in article 25 means something different than "ordering" in article 28, which covers the responsibility of commanders and other superiors, and which appears to require a hierarchical relationship that explicitly requires the subordinate to be under the effective authority and control of the superior.

88. This subparagraph additionally requires that the person aid or abet "for the purpose of facilitating the commission" of the crime. *Rome Statute*, art. 25(c). The *1996 ILC Draft Code of Crimes* requires aiding and abetting to be committed "knowingly" and to "directly and substantially" assist in committing the crime. The Commission's report suggests that the contribution should facilitate the commission of the crime "in some significant way." *1996 Draft Code of Crimes*, at 31 (para. 11). Article 30 of the ICC Statute incorporates the "knowledge" element of the Commission's draft automatically, but it is interesting that the drafters rejected the "direct and substantial" requirement in formulating article 25 of the ICC Statute, particularly as the two ad hoc tribunals read this requirement into the ICTY and ICTR Statutes. *See, e.g.*, Prosecutor v. Tadić (Case No. IT-94-1-T), Opinion and Judgment, paras. 674, 688–92 (ICTY Trial Chamber II, May 7, 1997); Prosecutor v. Rutaganda (Case No. ICTR-96-3-T), Judgement and Sentence, para. 43 (ICTR Trial Chamber I, Dec. 6, 1999) (holding that although the person need not be present during the commission of the offence, "aiding and abetting include (sic) all acts of assistance in either physical form or in the form of moral support; nevertheless, it emphasizes that any act or participation must substantially contribute to the commission of the crime.")

89. Article 6(1) of the Rwanda Tribunal's Statute, for example, provides:

> A person who planned, instigated, ordered, committed or otherwise aided and abetted in the planning, preparation or execution of a crime

Two points bear noting with regard to subparagraphs (a) through (c). First, what will be immediately obvious to a lawyer from virtually any legal system is that although he or she may find the above categories of perpetrator recognizable, and find analogs in his or her own legal system,[90] the Framers' insistence on avoiding, as much as possible, the use of terms of art from any one legal system renders the categories of perpetrators contained in the Statute *sui generis*—equally comprehensible, and probably equally confusing, to all.

Second, the Statute is purposefully silent on the issue of omission as a basis for criminal liability. The ILC's 1994 Draft Statute generally employed the form "act or omission" when referring to the *actus reus* element of the Statute. During the Statute's negotiation, however, several delegations, and France in particular, objected to the inclusion of a general principle of criminal responsibility based on the concept of omission.[91] The Zutphen Intersessional Draft included a bracketed article entitled "Actus Reus (act and/or omission)," which provided for liability based on omissions.[92] Intractable difficulties in reaching agreement on this article led to its deletion, although certain elements were retained in what became the general article on individual criminal responsibility in the penultimate version of the Court's Statute. The omission section of this final draft was a bracketed paragraph which provided that a person is criminally liable if he or she "fails to prevent or repress the commission of such a crime in the circumstances set out in article 25 [on command/superior responsibility]."[93] This provision, too, was deleted, and the article on

---

> referred to in articles 2 to 4 of the present Statute, shall be individually responsible for the crime.

The ICC Statute resembles, somewhat, article 2(3) of the *1996 ILC Draft Code of Crimes*, but avoids many of the terms of art used by the Commission in its draft (such as conspiracy, a term unknown to many legal systems), as well as repeated references to the mental element required for each level of criminal participation, which were sprinkled throughout the Commission's draft, and have been largely (but not completely) eliminated in the Rome Statute by replacing all references to mental element with one global reference in article 30.

90. One category of culpability absent from the Statute is the "accessory after the fact," known to the common law, which punishes individuals who aid the perpetrator of a felony after the commission of the crime in order to hinder the felon's apprehension, conviction or punishment. WAYNE R. LAFAVE & AUSTIN W. SCOTT, CRIMINAL LAW 596 (2d ed. 1986).

91. Per Saland, *International Criminal Law Principles, in* THE INTERNATIONAL CRIMINAL COURT: THE MAKING OF THE ROME STATUTE 189, 212 (Roy S. Lee, ed., 1999).

92. *Zutphen Intersessional Draft*, art. 22[G]

93. *April Draft Statute*, art. 23(7)(c).

criminal responsibility now contains no explicit provision for omissions. Although liability for omissions is retained under article 28 of the Statute (responsibility of commanders and other superiors), the delegates' failure to reach a compromise text on its inclusion in article 25 may ultimately mean that liability for omission does not exist under the Statute. Although the ICTY and ICTR have implied liability for omissions from their Statutes (which are also silent on this question),[94] the legality principle in the Rome Statute is arguably more demanding than the parallel provision of its two sister institutions, specifically requiring, as we saw earlier, definitions of crimes to be "strictly construed" and forbidding extension "by analogy."[95]

Article 25(3)(d) embodies the drafters' compromise text on conspiracy. Because the concept is unknown to many legal systems, the Framers opted to eliminate the term from the text, making reference instead to the "commission or attempted commission of . . . a crime by a group of persons acting with a common purpose."[96] The language used was largely borrowed from the 1997 Convention for the Suppression of Terrorist Bombings,[97] which had been recently negotiated and addressed the issue of conspiracy. Although this paragraph has been criticized as failing to respect "basic dogmatic categories,"[98] there was probably little choice as to its formulation, given the widely disparate views on conspiracy liability in different legal systems. It also struck an acceptable balance between competing interests. On the one hand, it was critical to include liability for group participation, as many of the offenses criminalized by the Statute are collective crimes committed against groups. On the other hand, it was important to recognize and respect the basic premise of the Rome Statute that criminal responsibility is based upon personal moral culpability.

Article 25(e), which criminalizes "direct and public" incitement to commit genocide, simply relocates article 3(c) of the Genocide Convention

---

94. *See, e.g.*, Prosecutor v. Rutaganda (Case No. ICTR-96-3-T), Judgment and Sentence, para. 41 (ICTR Trial Chamber I, Dec. 6, 1999) (holding that "an accused may participate in the commission of a crime either through direct commission of an unlawful act or by omission, where he has a duty to act."); Prosecutor v. Delalić (Case No. IT-96-21-T), Judgment, para. 333 (ICTY Trial Chamber II, Nov. 16, 1998) (holding that "criminal liability may arise either out of the positive acts . . . or from . . . culpable omissions.").

95. *Rome Statute*, art. 22(2).

96. *Rome Statute*, art. 25(d). The 1996 Draft Code of Crimes includes no provision for group or conspiracy liability.

97. International Convention for the Suppression of Terrorist Bombings, art. 2(3)(c), U.N. GAOR, 52nd Sess., Annex, U.N. Doc. A/RES/52/164 (1998).

98. Kai Ambos, *Individual Criminal Responsibility*, *in* COMMENTARY ON THE ROME STATUTE OF THE INTERNATIONAL CRIMINAL COURT 475, 485 (Otto Triffterer, ed., 1999).

from the substantive definition of the crime found in article 6 of the Statute to a more appropriate location in article 25.[99] Its transfer, however, raised the question whether responsibility ought to be imposed for incitement as regards crimes other than genocide within the Statute. The 1996 Draft Code of Crimes included such a provision,[100] but achieving consensus on its inclusion in Rome proved unattainable, and the Statute retains liability for incitement only as regards the crime of genocide.[101]

Finally, the Statute includes a provision on the crime of attempt, which, although absent from earlier instruments such as the Nuremberg Charter, was included in the ILC 1996 Draft Code of Crimes.[102] Attempt is defined as "taking action that commences its execution by means of a substantial step, but the crime does not occur because of circumstances independent of the person's intentions."[103] The definition is quite similar to that found in French law.[104] The Framers of the Rome Statute added to this idea the requirement that a "substantial step" be taken by the actor to distinguish criminal acts from mere preparation, which is found, among other places in the United States' Model Penal Code. The Statute does not

---

99. *See Zutphen Intersessional Draft*, art. 5[20], n. 14.

100. *1996 Draft Code of Crimes*, art. 2(3)(f).

101. Per Saland, *International Criminal Law Principles, in* THE INTERNATIONAL CRIMINAL COURT: THE MAKING OF THE ROME STATUTE 189, 200 (Roy S. Lee, ed., 1999).

102. The IMT Charter and the Statutes of the two ad hoc tribunals include "planning" and "preparation," words that have been deleted from the Rome Statute, as culpable conduct, however.

103. *Rome Statute*, art. 25(3)(f).

104. Article 121–5 of the New French Criminal Code provides:

> *La tentative est constituée dès lors que, manifestée par un commencement d'exécution, elle n'a été suspendue ou n'a manqué son effet qu'en raison de circonstances indépendantes de la volonté de son auteur.*

N. CODE PÉNAL art. 121–5. This definition is virtually identical to the definition proposed in the 1996 Draft Code of Crimes. *1996 Draft Code of Crimes*, art. 2(3)(g). It also has similarities to United States law, and although considerably less detailed, would probably cover the three kinds of situations identified by the U.S. Model Penal Code:

> [T]hose where the actor's conduct would constitute the crime if the circumstances were as he believed them to be; those where the actor has completed conduct that he expects to cause a proscribed result; and those where the actor has not yet completed his own conduct, and the problem is to distinguish between acts of preparation and a criminal attempt.

U.S. MODEL PENAL CODE, Explanatory Note to § 5.01 (1985).

define what "substantial step" means,[105] presumably leaving it to the judges to do so in the future. However, the Model Penal Code defines a "substantial step" as conduct that is "strongly corroborative of the actor's criminal purpose,"[106] and lists seven actions which presumptively suffice:

> (a) lying in wait, searching for or following the contemplated victim of the crime;
> (b) enticing or seeking to entice the contemplated victim of the crime to go to the place contemplated for its commission;
> (c) reconnoitering the place contemplated for the commission of the crime;
> (d) unlawful entry of a structure, vehicle or enclosure in which it is contemplated that the crime will be committed;
> (e) possession of materials to be employed in the commission of the crime, that are specially designed for such unlawful use or that can serve no lawful purpose of the actor under the circumstances;
> (f) possession, collection or fabrication of materials to be employed in the commission of the crime, at or near the place contemplated for its commission, if such possession, collection or fabrication serves no lawful purpose of the actor under the circumstances;
> (g) soliciting an innocent agent to engage in conduct constituting an element of the crime.[107]

Although it would be inconsistent with its function as an international adjudicative body for the Court to rely on the law of any one particular jurisdiction, the above examples may be instructive to the Court in crafting its own concept of "substantial step."

Finally, the Statute incorporates a Japanese proposal to permit an actor to voluntarily abandon the criminal activity and thereby escape liability. This proviso was not in the ILC's 1996 Draft Code of Crimes, but resembles, once again, the language of the United States Model Penal Code, as well as the 1996 Siracusa Draft.[108]

---

105. *Id.* § 5.01(2).

106. *Id.*

107. *Id.*

108. U.S. Model Penal Code §5.01(4) (1985); Draft Statute for an International Criminal Court: Suggested Modifications to the 1994 ILC Draft Prepared by a Committee of Experts, Done in Siracusa/Freiburg/Chicago, January 31, 1996.

B. Irrelevance of Official Capacity

Following World War I, when the Commission on the Responsibility of the Authors of the War and on the Enforcement of Penalties proposed to try William II of Hohenzollern, the German Emperor, the American members of the Commission objected. They argued that although heads of State might be morally "responsible to mankind," legally they exercised sovereign rights conferred upon them by their subjects, to whom they were alone accountable.[109] The American view was ultimately rejected by the Commission,[110] and the principle that one's official position, whether as Head of State or otherwise, should not serve as a shield to the imposition of international criminal responsibility subsequently became well-established in international law.[111]

This rule was required for practical as well as theoretical reasons. First, once it was agreed that State sovereignty was no longer an absolute bar to the imposition of individual criminal responsibility, it seemed illogical to "pierce" the cloak of State immunity for some defendants, while at the same time retaining it for Heads of State or those acting on their behalf. As the Nuremberg Tribunal noted, "[h]e who violates the laws of war cannot obtain immunity while acting in pursuance of the authority of the State if the State in authorizing action moves outside its competence

109. *U.N. Secretary-General, Historical Survey of the Question of International Criminal Jurisdiction*, 58–60, U.N. Doc. A/CN.4/7/Rev.1, U.N. Sales No. V.8 (1949).

110. Articles 227, 228 and 229 of the Treaty of Versailles provided for a "special tribunal" that would try the Emperor for the "supreme offence against international morality and the sanctity of treaties." Treaty of Peace with Germany, June 28, 1919, art. 227, 2 Bevans 43, 136, *reprinted in* 11 MARTENS NOUVEAU RECEUIL (Ser. 3) 323 (Fr.). The trial never occurred, however, for the Netherlands refused to extradite William II.

111. Article 7 of the Nuremberg Charter provided that defendants' "official position . . . whether as Heads of States or responsible officials . . . shall not be considered as freeing them from responsibility or mitigating punishment." The corresponding article of the Tokyo Charter was much less categorical, providing that official position, while not "sufficient to free . . . an accused from responsibility for any crime with which he is charged, but . . . may be considered in mitigation of punishment. . . ." *IMFTE Charter*, art. 6. Subsequent texts have adopted the Nuremberg approach in their provisos on official position, and both the ICTY and ICTR Statutes provide that "official position . . . whether as Head of State or Government or as a responsible Government official, shall not relieve such person of criminal responsibility nor mitigate punishment." *ICTY Statute*, art. 7(2); *ICTR Statute*, art. 6(2). See also ANDRÉ HUET & RENÉE KOERING-JOULIN, DROIT PÉNAL INTERNATIONAL 54 (1994).

under international law."[112] Second, it would be incongruous to suggest that government officials or their subordinates might face international criminal liability, but that those directing their actions, and, most particularly, the Head of State or of Government, could assert immunity simply by virtue of his or her position. This would result in inequities in the application of the law, by allowing those who were arguably the most culpable to escape liability, and would seriously undermine any deterrent value that international criminal prosecutions might ultimately provide.[113]

Article 27 of the Rome Statute reflects this view of the law on official position, but is longer and more detailed than its predecessor instruments.[114] Paragraph 1 provides:

> This Statute shall apply equally to all persons without any distinction based on official capacity. In particular, official capacity as a Head of State or Government, a member of a Government or parliament, an elected representative or a government official shall in no case exempt a person from criminal responsibility under this Statute, nor shall it, in and of itself, constitute a ground for reduction of sentence.

This provision, of course, does not prevent the Court from imposing a more severe sentence on the basis of official position;[115] nor does it

---

112. Judgment of October 1, 1946, International Military Tribunal, Judgment and Sentences, 41 AM. J. INT'L L. 172, 186, 221 (1947).

113. The role of Head of State immunity in national prosecutions raises different questions than its treatment in international prosecutions. Because the rules governing international immunities are primarily derived from international law, the international community may determine when those immunities are no longer applicable, and apply that determination in an international forum such as the ICC. National courts, however, are more circumspect in their treatment of international immunities. Thus, domestic courts have demonstrated greater reluctance to pursue Heads of State, whether current or former. Thus, in Regina v. Bow Street Metro. Stipendiary Magristrate, *ex parte* Pinochet Ugarte, [1999] 2 W.L.R. 827 (H.L.), the House of Lords decided by a 6-1 majority that the Torture Convention excludes the invocation of immunity by former Heads of State and by their home State on their behalf, provided that the Convention is in force for the States concerned. The Law Lords declined to articulate a broad rule excluding Head of State immunity in all cases of international crimes, and none of the Law Lords suggested that serving Heads of State were subject to prosecution.

114. Although the International Law Commission included no provision on official position in its 1994 Draft Statute for the Court, it did include an article on official position in the 1996 Draft Code of Crimes, which was quite similar to the Statutes of the two ad hoc tribunals. *1996 Draft Code of Crimes*, art. 7.

115. Otto Triffterer, *Irrelevance of official capacity, in* COMMENTARY ON THE ROME

deprive those acting in their official positions of the defenses and justifications that any other accused has before the Court.[116] It simply removes from the accused's arsenal the defense that his or her official status should shield him or her from the Court's jurisdiction.

Finally, paragraph 2 of article 27 was added to address the possibility that defendants sought by the Court would seek to invoke Head of State or other immunities before national courts to avoid surrender to the Court. If States recognized official position as an absolute defense to criminal prosecution, the ICC's effectiveness would be considerably reduced in practice, for States would presumably be obliged not to surrender defendants to the Court if they were cloaked with diplomatic or other immunities under national or international law. Paragraph (2) attempts to resolve this problem, providing that "[i]mmunities or special procedural rules which may attach to the official capacity of a person, whether under national or international law, shall not bar the Court from exercising its jurisdiction over such a person."[117] This provision is consistent with the Nuremberg Judgment, which held that, at least as involves international criminal prosecutions, international legal obligations take precedence over national legal obligations. It is somewhat ambiguously drafted however, and may pose difficulties in practice when read in conjunction with article 98(1) of the Statute, which bars the Court from proceeding with a request for surrender or assistance which would require the requested State to "act inconsistently with its obligations under international law with respect to the State or diplomatic immunity of a person or property of a third State, unless the Court can first obtain the cooperation of that third State for the waiver of the immunity."[118] As the following Chapter suggests, a great deal of what the Rome Statute "giveth" in its first few Parts is "taken away" when it comes to enforcement and State cooperation. The relationship between article 27 and article 98(1) is a case in point.

STATUTE OF THE INTERNATIONAL CRIMINAL COURT 501, 511 (Otto Triffterer, ed., 1999).

116. *See infra* Chapter 7, Section IV.

117. *Rome Statute*, art. 27(2). The Preparatory Commission is currently engaged in adopting a *Draft Agreement on the Privileges and Immunities of the Court*, U.N. Doc. PNCICC/2001/WGAPIC/RT.1, March 8, 2001.

118. *Rome Statute*, art. 98(1). As Per Saland, who chaired the Working Group on Part 3 observes, article 98 was assigned to a different group, which could explain the discrepancy. In addition, unless the words "Third State" are limited to non-Party States, article 98(1) would appear to prohibit the Court from securing the presence of the accused in many, many cases, if he or she could invoke immunities in the Requested State that fall within the language of article 98(1). Per Saland, *International Criminal Law Principles, in* THE INTERNATIONAL CRIMINAL COURT: THE MAKING OF THE ROME STATUTE 189, 202 n. 25 (Roy S. Lee, ed., 1999).

Indeed, article 98 will bar the Court from exercising its jurisdiction in many cases unless the accused voluntarily surrenders, or is transferred to the Court without, or independent from, the Court's request.[119]

C. Responsibility of Commanders and Other Superiors

As we saw earlier, the Framers of the Rome Statute were uncomfortable including an article on *actus reus* in Part 3 of the Statute, in large part due to disagreements among delegates as to whether omissions, as well as acts, could give rise to criminal liability. The one area in which it was generally agreed that a failure to act could give rise to responsibility for the crimes within the jurisdiction of the Court was with regard to command responsibility, there being a general consensus that military commanders may be liable for the acts of their subordinates under certain conditions, even where they did not directly order the crimes to be committed. It would be hard to overstate the importance of this principle with regard to the crimes within the ICC's jurisdiction. As others have noted, someone who has the authority to prevent a crime and fails to do so is, to some extent, responsible for its commission. Moreover, if a commander learns that one of his or her subordinates has committed a crime and fails to punish it, he or she is not only condoning its commission, but "sending a signal that such crimes can be committed with impunity."[120] Although this principle was not explicitly included in the Nuremberg and Tokyo Charters, or in the Geneva Conventions, which imposed liability upon commanders only for the acts they committed or ordered, several post-

---

119. Article 98(2) permits the requested State to rely upon international agreements, in particular extradition treaties or similar instruments, that require permission of the State of the extraditee's nationality prior to the accused's extradition to a third State, or, in this case, the Court, as a grounds for refusing to surrender an individual to the Court. This provision became the subject of an extensive battle during the Preparatory Commission negotiations when the United States of America introduced a proposal to rely upon this article in order to avoid the surrender of any United States nationals to the Court without U.S. permission. The United States proposal was ultimately defeated and a relatively innocuous provision adopted as Draft RPE 195(2), which suggests that the Court has the burden to obtain the consent of the sending State under the conditions elaborated in article 98(2). The operation of this Rule could not deprive the Court of jurisdiction, as article 27(2) specifically preserves the Court's jurisdiction. Obviously, however, the presence of the accused would be difficult to obtain.

120. VIRGINIA MORRIS & MICHAEL P. SCHARF, I AN INSIDER'S GUIDE TO THE INTERNATIONAL CRIMINAL TRIBUNAL FOR THE FORMER YUGOSLAVIA 100–01 (1995).

World War II cases imposed liability for a commander's failure to control his troops, the most famous, and to some extent the most controversial of which was the *Yamashita* case, which held that even a commander without operational or administrative control of his forces could be liable for crimes committed by them due to his occupational or executive responsibility for the area in which they were stationed.[121]

This principle or some variant thereof was subsequently codified in several instruments, suggesting its widespread acceptance by the international community.[122] Thus article 86 of the First Protocol to the Geneva Conventions, entitled "Failure to act," imposes responsibility upon "superiors" if they "knew, or had information which should have enabled them to conclude in the circumstances at the time, that [a subordinate] was committing or was going to commit. . . a breach [of the Conventions or of this Protocol] and if they did not take feasible measures within their power to prevent or repress the breach."[123] This provision, which is generally thought to be more favorable to commanders than the *Yamashita* standard, is found in slightly different form in the Statutes of the two ad hoc tribunals,[124] as well as the International Law Commission's 1996 Draft Code of Crimes,[125] all three of which suggest, through their use of the term "superior" rather than "commander," their applicability to non-military officials.[126]

---

121. Japanese General Tomoyuki Yamashita was convicted by a United States Military Commission in Manila for failure to properly control his troops. *United States v. Yamashita*, 327 U.S. 1 (1946); Trial of General Tomoyuki Yamashita, United States Military Commission, Manila (8th October–7th December, 1945), 4 LAW REPORTS OF TRIALS 1 (1948).

122. Prosecutor v. Delalić (Case No. IT-96-21-T), Judgment, para. 340 (ICTY Trial Chamber II, Nov. 16, 1998).

123. Protocol I Additional to the Geneva Conventions of 12 August 1949, art. 86(2).

124. *ICTY Statute*, art. 7(3). *See also ICTR Statute*, art. 6(3) ("The fact that any of the acts referred to in . . . the present Statute was committed by a subordinate does not relieve his or her superior of criminal responsibility if he or she knew or had reason to know that the subordinate was about to commit such acts or had done so and the superior failed to take the necessary and reasonable measures to prevent such acts or to punish the perpetrators thereof.").

125. *1996 Draft Code of Crimes*, art. 6 ("The fact that a crime against the peace and security of mankind was committed by a subordinate does not relieve his superiors of criminal responsibility, if they knew or had reason to know, in the circumstances at the time, that the subordinate was committing or was going to commit such a crime and if they did not take all necessary measures within their power to prevent or repress the crime.").

126. *Final Report of the United Nations Commission of Experts Established*

When the Preparatory Committee for the International Criminal Court took up the question, three principle issues were raised: First, what standard would be set for imposing liability upon commanders; second, whether command responsibility would extend to civilians, and under what circumstances; finally, the more theoretical question whether command responsibility was an additional form of individual criminal responsibility, or simply a principle that commanders are not immune from the acts of their subordinates.[127]

As to the last point, the Framers ultimately opted for the view that responsibility of commanders and other superiors is an additional ground of criminal responsibility under the Statute with regard to crimes within the jurisdiction of the Court.[128] In addition, over the strong objections of China, but consistent with the views of most delegations, as well as the jurisprudence of the ICTY and ICTR,[129] the Statute adopted a formulation that included liability for both military and non-military superiors, but varies considerably the standard applicable to each.

The responsibility of military commanders is addressed by article 28(a), and imposes liability only if forces are under the commander's "effective command and control, or effective authority and control." This incorporates a test similar to the text of the two ad hoc tribunals, which have held that a superior may be liable only where he or she had the power to control the acts of his or her subordinates.[130] This requires either the de jure or de facto *direct* control by the commander of his or her forces, although one commentator suggests that it would include cases such as General Yamashita's, for example, where the forces committing the crimes may not be in the direct chain of command as an operational matter, but are under the general authority of a particular commander of an occupation zone.[131]

Pursuant to Security Council Resolution 780 (1992), U.N. SCOR, 54th Sess., Annex, para. 57, U.N. Doc. S/1994/674 (1994) ("The doctrine of command responsibility is directed primarily at military commanders . . . [p]olitical leaders and public officials have also been held liable under this doctrine in certain circumstances.").

127. *Zutphen Intersessional Draft*, art. 19[C], n. 90. *See also* Per Saland, *International Criminal Law Principles, in* THE INTERNATIONAL CRIMINAL COURT: THE MAKING OF THE ROME STATUTE 189, 202 (Roy S. Lee, ed., 1999).

128. *Rome Statute*, art. 28, first line.

129. *See, e.g.*, Prosecutor v. Delalić (Case No. IT-96-21-T), Judgment, paras. 356, 363 (ICTY Trial Chamber II, Nov. 16, 1998).

130. *See, e.g.*, Prosecutor v. Delalić (Case No. IT-96-21-T), Judgment, paras. 373, 377–78 (ICTY Trial Chamber II, Nov. 16, 1998).

131. William J. Fenrick, *Responsibility of commanders and other superiors, in* COMMENTARY ON THE ROME STATUTE OF THE INTERNATIONAL CRIMINAL COURT 515, 518

As regards non-military officials, article 28(b) provides that they too may be held criminally responsible for the crimes of their subordinates.[132] However, it imposes several additional requirements before culpability can be established. First, unlike the military commander who is held to a "knew or should have known" standard,[133] the civilian superior must either have known or "consciously disregarded information which clearly indicated, that the subordinates were committing or about to commit such crimes." Although authoritative sources such as the Commission of Experts for the Former Yugoslavia have recommended consideration of various factors to establish whether a commander must have known about the acts of his subordinates,[134] it is not clear whether they would

---

(Otto Triffterer, ed., 1999). The *Yamashita* precedent has been roundly criticized, however. *See, e.g.*, Gerry J. Simpson, *War Crimes: A Critical Introduction, in* THE LAW OF WAR CRIMES: NATIONAL AND INTERNATIONAL APPROACHES, at 2 (McCormack & Simpson, eds., 1997).

132. This is consistent with the jurisprudence of the ad hoc tribunals. *See, e.g.*, Prosecutor v. Aleksovski (Case No. IT-95-14/1-T), Judgment, paras. 75–76 (ICTY Trial Chamber I, June 25, 1999).

133. This has been likened to criminal negligence in common law systems. Edward M. Wise, *Commentary on Parts 2 and 3 of the Zutphen Intersessional Draft : General Principles of Criminal Law, in* OBSERVATIONS ON THE CONSOLIDATED ICC TEXT BEFORE THE FINAL SESSION OF THE PREPARATORY COMMITTEE, 13*bis* NOUVELLES ÉTUDES PÉNALES 43, 49 (Leila Sadat Wexler, special ed., 1998). Although the ICTY held that a superior may be criminally responsible only if some specific information was available to him which would provide notice of offenses committed by his subordinates, it also noted that its holding was limited to what it believed customary international law contained at the time, and suggested that the Rome Statute was broader. Prosecutor v. Delalić (Case No. IT-96-21-T), Judgment, para. 393 (ICTY Trial Chamber II, Nov. 16, 1998).

134. The factors are:

(a) The number of illegal acts;
(b) The type of illegal acts;
(c) The scope of illegal acts;
(d) The time during which the illegal acts occurred;
(e) The number and type of troops involved;
(f) The logistics involved, if any;
(g) The geographical location of the acts;
(h) The widespread occurrence of the acts;
(i) The tactical tempo of operations;
(j) The *modus operandi* of similar illegal acts;
(k) The officers and staff involved;
(l) The location of the commander at the time.

Final Report of the United Nations Commission of Experts Established Pursuant to Security Council Resolution 780 (1992), S/1994/674, May 27, 1994, at 17. These factors were cited by the ICTY in Prosecutor v. Delalić (Case No. IT-96-21-T),

suffice to meet the standard of known or "consciously disregarded" applicable to civilian superiors, which suggests a subjective determination of the perpetrator's state of mind.[135]

Second, the crimes must concern activities "that were within the effective responsibility and control of the superior," thereby possibly eliminating liability for activities that were only indirectly within the accused's control.[136] Because non-military subordinates, unlike their military counterparts, are not subject to the control of their supervisors outside of their work-related activities, it was no doubt necessary to distinguish between the two categories of putative defendants. The Court will be required to interpret these provisions in light of their object and purpose, and it will be interesting to see whether the civilian/military distinction effected by the Statute in theory is borne out by the practice of the Court in fact.

Finally, the relationship of article 30, on mental element, to article 28 is somewhat troublesome. Presumably the "knew or should have known" and "conscious disregard" standards in article 28 suggest something less than "intent," such as criminal negligence or recklessness, as to the commission of crimes by subordinates.[137] On the other hand, the Court could read articles 30 and 28 together, and require the Prosecutor to establish that the superior intentionally failed to act (within the meaning of article 30) in a situation where it was reckless (within the meaning of article 28) to do so. This interpretation seems unduly complex, however, particularly

---

Judgment, para. 386 (ICTY Trial Chamber II, Nov. 16, 1998), as circumstantial evidence which could establish a superior's knowledge of the offenses committed by his subordinates.

135. One commentator suggests that this standard is met if information exists, that was available to the superior, that clearly indicated a significant risk that subordinates were committing or were about to commit offences. It is irrelevant whether the supervisor availed himself of the information or not, there being a duty to inform oneself sufficiently. William J. Fenrick, *Responsibility of commanders and other superiors*, *in* COMMENTARY ON THE ROME STATUTE OF THE INTERNATIONAL CRIMINAL COURT 515, 521–22 (Otto Triffterer, ed., 1999). The ICTR, however, has taken a more cautious view, holding that the accused's mental intent must be so serious as to be tantamount to acquiescence or even malicious intent. Prosecutor v. Musema (Case No. ICTR-96-13-T), Judgment, para. 131 (ICTR Trial Chamber I, Jan. 27, 2000).

136. This authority "must involve . . . more than higher rank or grade. The superior must have control over the work of the subordinates and be able to give orders to the subordinates." Fenrick, *supra* at 520.

137. One commentator suggests that the standard in article 28 is something akin to recklessness. Per Saland, *International Criminal Law Principles*, *in* THE INTERNATIONAL CRIMINAL COURT: THE MAKING OF THE ROME STATUTE 189, 206 (Roy S. Lee, ed., 1999).

as article 30 itself notes that its application is only to provisions that do not "otherwise provide" for some mental element in their text.

D. Mental Element (article 30)

This provision of the Statute has no predecessors in any text. Neither the Statutes of the ICTY and ICTR nor the International Law Commission's 1996 Draft Code of Crimes (or 1994 Draft Statute) had any counterpart.[138] Yet very few issues were involved in its negotiation, delegates being in general agreement that criminal liability should not be imposed under the Statute without a showing of moral culpability on the part of the accused. The only real question for the Framers was defining what that level of culpability should be, and adopting a terminology mutually acceptable (even if mutually confusing) to delegates from diverse legal traditions.[139]

Article 30 as finally adopted is narrow in scope. It states that "unless otherwise provided, a person shall be criminally responsible and liable for punishment for a crime within the jurisdiction of the Court only if the material elements[140] are committed with intent and knowledge."

---

138. Article 2(3)(a) of the 1996 Draft Code of Crimes requires that crimes be committed "intentionally" for criminal responsibility to attach, but the Code contains no provision on *mens rea* as such.

139. For example, the title of the article, which was originally "mens rea," a common law term, was changed to "mental element." *See* Edward M. Wise, *Commentary on Parts 2 and 3 of the Zutphen Intersessional Draft: A Critical Introduction, in* OBSERVATIONS ON THE CONSOLIDATED ICC TEXT BEFORE THE FINAL SESSION OF THE PREPARATORY COMMITTEE, 13*bis* NOUVELLES ÉTUDES PÉNALES 43, 49 (Leila Sadat Wexler, special ed., 1998) (noting that actus reus and mens rea are common law terms ill-suited to international instruments).

140. The term "material elements" is not free from ambiguity. In French law, "material elements," or *élément matériel*, is one of the three elements required for a crime to be punishable, the other two being the *élément légal* and the *élément moral*. GASTON STEFANI, GEORGES LEVASSEUR & BERNARD BOULOC, DROIT PÉNAL GÉNÉRAL 31 (16th ed. 1997). Within the context of the ICC Statute, one commentator has suggested that it means something slightly different, referring to "the specific elements of the definition of the crimes as defined in articles 5 to 8. This refers to the conduct or action described in the definition, any consequences that may be specified in addition to the conduct, and any factual circumstances that qualify the definition." Donald K. Piragoff, *Mental Element, in* COMMENTARY ON THE ROME STATUTE OF THE INTERNATIONAL CRIMINAL COURT 527, 529 (Otto Triffterer, ed., 1999). This view appears overly broad. Within the context of the Statute, the question arises, for example, whether the crime was committed in international armed conflict. If

Thus, unless "otherwise provided,"[141] the Statute excludes other bases of culpability.[142]

The Statute defines intent in paragraph (2) and knowledge in paragraph (3), suggesting relatively straightforward, if narrow, definitions for both terms. "Intent," we are told, means:

> (a) In relation to conduct, that person means to engage in the conduct;
> (b) In relation to a consequence, that person means to cause that consequence or is aware that it will occur in the ordinary course of events.[143]

"Knowledge," on the other hand, means "awareness that a circumstance exists or a consequence will occur in the ordinary course of events,"[144] which suggests, somewhat confusingly, that knowledge is an element of intent.[145] Thus, although there was some debate in the

---

this was a material element of the offense, presumably the accused would need to intend to commit the crime in international armed conflict, perhaps an overly heavy burden for the prosecution to prove. In Chapter 6, I have argued that this is a jurisdictional requirement, essentially unrelated to a particular accused's mental state. The Draft Elements take an intermediate view, noting in the introduction to the war crimes elements, for example, that "there is no requirement for awareness by the perpetrator of the facts that established the character of the conflict as international or non-international." Thus although the Prosecutor would need to establish the international nature (or not) of the conflict, the perpetrator need only be "aware of factual circumstances that established the existence of an armed conflict." Draft Elements of Crimes, article 8(2)(a)(i)(5).

141. For example, article 28 appears to contain culpability requirements amounting to either criminal negligence or recklessness.

142. Proposals were made for the inclusion of recklessness and/or *dolus eventualis* as a basis for culpability sufficient for liability if other modes for culpability were not present or specified by the Statute. Report of the Preparatory Committee on the Establishment of an International Criminal Court, U.N. GAOR, 51st Sess., Supp. No. 22, U.N. Doc. A/51/22 (1996), Vol. II, pp. 92–93. However, these were ultimately defeated.

143. *Rome Statute*, art. 30(2).

144. *Id.* art. 30(3).

145. Professor Kai Ambos has argued that the definition fails to distinguish sufficiently between intent and knowledge, and confuses basic criminal law concepts found in German law (knowing and wanting, or *Wissen und Wollen*), as well as the U.S. Model Penal Code. Experts on French law have, similarly, criticized the ICTY's jurisprudence as failing to respect well-understood national categories of criminal law in favor of a hybrid international mixture. Catherine Elliott, *The French Law of Intent and its Influence on the Development of International Criminal Law*, 11 CRIM. L. FORUM 35 (2000).

Preparatory Committee as to whether the requirements of intent and knowledge should be disjunctive, rather than conjunctive, it would seem that the choice of the conjunctive formulation suggests that, in general, the Framers preferred to impose liability for the crimes within the jurisdiction of the ICC Statute only in cases of serious moral culpability. This would be consistent with the general purpose of the Statute, which is to prosecute those guilty of the "most serious crimes of concern to the international community as a whole,"[146] and could be seen as a rejection of holdings in the ICTY and ICTR to the contrary.[147] States could obviously impose culpability on lesser grounds in national prosecutions.

Finally, several definitions of crimes within the Statute include the word "intent" or "intentionally" in their text.[148] These include article 6, which refers to the "intent to destroy . . . a national, ethnical, racial or religious group,"[149] as one of the elements of genocide, and several of the war crimes provisions, for example, "intentionally directing attacks against the

146. *Rome Statute*, preamble.

147. Commentators have suggested that the language of the Rome Statute does not change existing international jurisprudence as to liability for aiding and abetting, for example. The ICTY has held that "a knowing participation in the commission of an offence" or "awareness of the act of participation coupled with a conscious decision to participate" is sufficient for accomplice liability under the ICTY Statute. Prosecutor v. Furundzjia (Case No. IT-95-17/1-T), Judgment, para. 241 (ICTY Trial Chamber II, Dec. 10, 1998). Thus, to be guilty of complicity for murder (as a crime against humanity) under the *Furundzjia* holding, the accomplice need not share the principal's intent to kill, but may be convicted on a much lesser showing of culpability. It is possible that the text of article 30 (requiring intent and knowledge), would exclude accomplice liability in this circumstance. One commentator, however, has suggested that because "'intent' may be satisfied by an awareness that a consequence will occur in the ordinary course of events," awareness that a consequence may occur fulfills the requirements of intent *and* knowledge. Donald K. Piragoff, *Mental Element, in* COMMENTARY ON THE ROME STATUTE OF THE INTERNATIONAL CRIMINAL COURT 527, 530 (Otto Triffterer, ed., 1999). Of course, the question then becomes, if they both mean the same thing, why did the Framers include them both in the Statute as conjunctive requirements?

148. Several of the war crimes also refer to "wilful" actions, or actions accomplished "willfully." *See, e.g.*, article 8(2)(a)(i) ("Wilful killing"); 8(1)(vi) ("Wilfully depriving . . ."). The elements for these crimes do not define "wilful" or "wilfully" and presumably article 30's mental element therefore applies. Because the Court is bound to follow the Statute before the Elements, it could, of course, decide that "wilful" killing means something different than murder ("intentional killing") as a crime against humanity, for example. This interpretation would appear overly complex, however, and it is not clear, at least *ex ante*, how it would further the purposes of the Statute to do so.

149. *Rome Statute*, art. 6.

civilian population,"[150] or "intentionally using starvation of civilians as a method of warfare."[151] While the use of intentionally in the latter cases is probably redundant,[152] as the term was found in the texts from which the definitions originated, the use of the term "intent" in the definition of genocide has generally been thought to connote "specific" as opposed to "general" intent, and it is not clear whether the definition in article 30 suffices in that case. The Preparatory Commission, apparently equally unsure of the relationship between article 30 and article 6, addressed this question somewhat obliquely in its Draft Elements of Crimes:

> Notwithstanding the normal requirement for a mental element provided for in article 30, and recognizing that knowledge of the circumstances will usually be addressed in proving genocidal intent, the appropriate requirement, if any, for a mental element regarding this circumstance will need to be decided by the Court on a case-by-case basis.[153]

IV. GENERAL PRINCIPLES EXCLUDING CRIMINAL RESPONSIBILITY AND OTHER DEFENSES

A. Grounds for Excluding Criminal Responsibility

This article of the Statute was one of the most difficult to negotiate,[154] and has been subject to a great deal of criticism after the fact.[155] The task

---

150. *Id.* art. 8(2)(b)(i).

151. *Id.* art. 8(2)(b)(xxv).

152. The Draft Elements of Crimes support this result. In the case of attacks on the civilian population, for example, they do not impose an additional "intent" requirement, but simply require that the accused intended (presumably as defined in article 30) the civilian population to be the object of the attack. Draft Elements of Crimes, Element 8(2)(b)(i).

153. Draft Elements of Crimes, Introduction to article 6.

154. Per Saland, *International Criminal Law Principles, in* THE INTERNATIONAL CRIMINAL COURT: THE MAKING OF THE ROME STATUTE 189, 206 (Roy S. Lee, ed., 1999).

155. *See, e.g.*, Kai Ambos, *General Principles of Criminal Law in the Rome Statute*, 10 CRIM. L. FORUM 1, 24–28 (1999); Albin Eser, *Grounds for excluding criminal responsibility, in* COMMENTARY ON THE ROME STATUTE OF THE INTERNATIONAL CRIMINAL COURT 537, 539 (Otto Triffterer, ed., 1999) (noting with respect to this article, that, while it has its merits, "its heading is misleading and its contents incomplete.") For the argument that international criminal law defenses should be derived inductively from the domestic legal principles of the major legal systems of the

of crafting an article (or several articles, as was originally proposed) that would specify the defenses, justifications and excuses to criminal responsibility to the mutual satisfaction of jurists from all the legal systems of the world, seemed virtually impossible. Moreover, the international case law was not yet extensive enough to provide much guidance. Article 31 as finally adopted acknowledges its own status as a work in progress—it provides texts for only four grounds for excluding criminal responsibility, while explicitly preserving the right of the Court's judges not only to "determine the applicability of the grounds for excluding criminal responsibility provided for in [the] Statute to the case before it,"[156] but to consider grounds "for excluding criminal responsibility other than those referred to in paragraph 1 [of article 31] where such a ground is derived from applicable law as set forth in article 21."[157] Moreover, article 31 notes that it is not an exhaustive list of grounds upon which criminal responsibility is excluded by the Statute, and several others are found elsewhere in the text.[158]

Article 31(1) enumerates just four grounds of exculpation that an accused may plead: (a) incapacity, which is essentially an "insanity" defense;[159]

---

world, see GEERT-JAN G.J. KNOOPS, DEFENSES IN CONTEMPORARY INTERNATIONAL CRIMINAL LAW 32–33 (2001).

156. *Rome Statute,* art. *31(2).*

157. *Id.* art. 31(3). Defenses neither excluded nor included in the Statute, and which might therefore one day fall within the proviso of article 31(3) include alibi (specifically referred to in Draft RPE 79(1)), consent of the victim, conflict of interests, reprisals, military necessity, the tu quoque argument, and diplomatic immunity. *See, e.g.,* Albin Eser, *Grounds for excluding criminal responsibility, in* COMMENTARY ON THE ROME STATUTE OF THE INTERNATIONAL CRIMINAL COURT 537, 543 (Otto Triffterer, ed., 1999). Article 31(3) also provides that the "procedures relating to the consideration of such a ground shall be provided for in the Rules of Procedure and Evidence." Accordingly, draft rules 79–81 were adopted by the Preparatory Commission to govern the procedures by which defenses are to be raised and pleaded. Rule 79 governs alibis and the defenses enumerated in paragraph (1), while Rule 80 addresses attempts to raise a defense under paragraph (3).

158. In his excellent commentary on this article, Professor Eser notes that in addition to the articles on superior orders (art. 33) and mistake of fact or law (art. 32), abandonment (art. 25(3)(f)) and exclusion of jurisdiction of persons under 18 (art. 26) should be considered additional grounds for the exclusion of criminal responsibility under the Statute. *See* Albin Eser, *Grounds for excluding criminal responsibility, in* COMMENTARY ON THE ROME STATUTE OF THE INTERNATIONAL CRIMINAL COURT 537, 541–42 (Otto Triffterer, ed., 1999).

159. Article 31(1)(a) states that criminal responsibility is excluded if the person "suffers from a mental disease or defect that destroys that person's capacity to appreciate the unlawfulness or nature of his or her conduct, or capacity to control his or her conduct to conform to the requirements of law." This provision was not

(b) intoxication;[160] (c) self-defense or defense of others, or, in the case of war crimes, of "essential" property;[161] and (d) duress.[162] Each was the

---

the subject of much debate, and remained unchanged following its adoption by the Preparatory Committee in December 1997. Decisions Taken by the Preparatory Committee at its Session Held from 1 to 12 December 1997, at 16, U.N. Doc. A/AC.249/1997/L.9/Rev.1 (1997). The article is relatively narrow in scope, and is quite similar to Section 4.01 of the U.S. Model Penal Code. Like the Model Penal Code, no effort was made to define the term "mental disease or defect;" unlike the Model Penal Code, however, the Rome Statute does not include any language as to what kind of behavior "mental disease or defect" might exclude. *See* U.S. MODEL PENAL CODE §401(2) (1985) ("mental disease or defect" does not include "an abnormality manifested only by repeated criminal or otherwise antisocial conduct.") For the argument that the Rome Statute may permit genetic or neurobiological defenses see GEERT-JAN G.J. KNOOPS, DEFENSES IN CONTEMPORARY INTERNATIONAL CRIMINAL LAW 253–54 (2001).

160. Intoxication proved quite difficult to negotiate because some governments wished to exclude any defense based on voluntary intoxication completely, while others did not. The resulting text attempted to "square the circle" by making the exception for involuntary intoxication as broad as possible, without totally excluding voluntary intoxication as a defense. Per Saland, *International Criminal Law Principles, in* THE INTERNATIONAL CRIMINAL COURT: THE MAKING OF THE ROME STATUTE 189, 207 (Roy S. Lee, ed., 1999). The last phrase of paragraph (b), requiring that voluntary intoxication may be an excuse if the accused did not know, or disregarded the risk, that as a result of the intoxication he or she was likely to engage in conduct likely to constitute one of the crimes within the Court's jurisdiction, is likely to give rise to substantial interpretative difficulties. *See* Albin Eser, *Grounds for excluding criminal responsibility, in* COMMENTARY ON THE ROME STATUTE OF THE INTERNATIONAL CRIMINAL COURT 537, 548 (Otto Triffterer, ed., 1999) (suggesting that even if a soldier committed murder, and was aware that he might do so as a result of drunkenness, voluntary intoxication would serve as a defense "as long as he was not aware of the genocidal or anti-humanitarian character of the murder in terms of article 6 or 7 of th[e] Statute.") Other commentators have suggested that this provision did not belong in the Statute, but should simply be an attenuating circumstance to be taken into account by the judge. WILLIAM BOURDON, LA COUR PÉNALE INTERNATIONALE 128 (2000). It is likely that judges coming from legal systems rejecting voluntary intoxication may reject Eser's analysis, and read the Statute more narrowly on this point.

161. This provision was uncontroversial insofar as it related to self-defense, but highly controversial as regards defense of property. Again, the compromise reached, which permits defense of property to exclude criminal responsibility in the case of war crimes, but not crimes against humanity or genocide, satisfied no one fully. Per Saland, *International Criminal Law Principles, in* THE INTERNATIONAL CRIMINAL COURT: THE MAKING OF THE ROME STATUTE 189, 208 (Roy S. Lee, ed., 1999).

162. This provision of the Statute is relatively complicated, because it combines the defenses of necessity and duress into one provision, arriving at a melange that resembles neither. Duress in the Rome Statute resembles the defini-

subject of protracted negotiations as delegates sought to elaborate a common text. Again, the definitions finally agreed upon are drawn from various legal systems to a certain degree, but track no one system exactly. It will thus fall to the Court to elaborate through its jurisprudence the detailed application of each section. In so doing, the Court may ultimately reconsider the fact that the Statute, by its terms, does not distinguish between grounds excusing responsibility (such as insanity), and those justifying the accused's actions (such as self-defense).[163] Although the distinction between justification and excuse is often overlooked, it is not always semantic. For example, conduct that is excused, such as killing due to insanity, is excused only as to the person who suffers from the excusing condition.[164] Their accomplice may not rely upon the insanity defense to escape responsibility for the killing; but should the killing be justified, i.e., in self-defense, the accomplice would ordinarily be justified in assisting

---

tion in the U.S. Model Penal Code as well as French law: "an affirmative defense that the actor engaged in the conduct charged . . . because he was coerced to do so by the use of, or a threat to use, unlawful force against his person or the person of another, that a person of reasonable firmness in his situation would have been unable to resist." U.S. MODEL PENAL CODE § 2.09 (1) (1985). *Compare* N. CODE PÉNAL art. 122–3 (Fr.) ("*N'est pas pénalement responsable la personne qui a age sous l'empire d'une force ou d'une contrainte à laquelle ell n'a pu résister.*"). However, the Rome Statute adds the requirement that the person under duress "does not intend to cause a greater harm than the one sought to be avoided," which is an element of necessity: "*N'est pas pénalement responsable la personne qui, face à un danger actuel ou imminent qui menace elle-même, autrui ou un bien, accomplit un acte nécessaire à la sauvegarde de la personne ou du bien, sauf s'il y a disproportion entre les moyens employés et la gravité de la menace.*" N. CODE PÉNAL art. 122–7 (Fr.). The Statute appears to reject, at least in part, the holding of the Appeals Chamber in the *Erdemović* case, to the effect that duress may not afford a complete defense to a soldier charged with a war crime or crime against humanity where the underlying offense involved the killing of an innocent human being. The Statute appears to adopt the position of the dissent to the effect that some proportionality between the threat to the accused and the offense is required; but it remains to be seen whether the Court will adopt the other requirements imposed by Judge Cassese and Judge Stephen in their separate opinions in the case, such as the requirement that the situation creating the duress must not have been voluntarily brought about by the person coerced. Prosecutor v. Erdemović (Case No. IT-96-22), Separate and Dissenting Opinion of Judge Cassese (ICTY Appeals Chamber, Oct. 7, 1997); Prosecutor v. Erdemović (Case No. IT-96-22), Separate and Dissenting Opinion of Judge Stephen (ICTY Appeals Chamber, Oct. 7, 1997).

163. MODEL DRAFT STATUTE FOR THE INTERNATIONAL CRIMINAL COURT BASED ON THE PREPARATORY COMMITTEE'S TEXT TO THE DIPLOMATIC CONFERENCE, ROME, JUNE 15–JULY 17, 1998, 13*ter* NOUVELLE ÉTUDES PÉNALES 56 (Leila Sadat Wexler, special ed., 1998).

164. JOSHUA DRESSLER, UNDERSTANDING CRIMINAL LAW 197 (1998).

the accused to protect his or her own life, even at the expense of the victim's life.[165] In addition, considering a conduct to be justified suggests that under particular circumstances, conduct that is ordinarily deemed to be criminal is justified, and perhaps even condoned by society. In contrast, conduct which is excused may still be culpable, but it may be pointless to punish the accused for it because he or she will neither understand the punishment nor be deterred by it (for example, if they are insane, or coerced).[166] While these categories and rationales are far from absolute, thinking about the underlying policy reasons for a particular defense will no doubt be important to the future Court as it shapes its jurisprudence in the context of international prosecutions for crimes of extreme gravity.

Finally, the Statute is silent on the quantum of proof needed to establish particular defenses. Common law jurisdictions have developed doctrines involving affirmative defenses (where the burden of proof lies with the defendant), such as duress.[167] Conversely, other "defenses" such as mistake of fact do not shift the burden to the accused, who must simply offer evidence of the mistake. The ICTY has taken the position that at least some defenses such as diminished or lack of mental capacity must be established by the defense "on the balance of probabilities."[168] The Rome Statute, on the other hand, suggests in article 67(1)(i) that the burden may not be shifted to the accused, a result that may not be desirable given that at least certain defenses are founded upon information which the accused is uniquely positioned to supply.[169] The Statute, however, in referring to the right not to have imposed upon the accused "any reversal of the burden of proof or any onus of rebuttal," does not appear to be addressing the issue of defenses, but only stating a corollary of the presumption of innocence.[170]

---

165. Situations can become much more complex and ambiguous than this, as Professor Dressler points out in his treatment of the subject. *Id.* at 196–97.

166. JOSHUA DRESSLER, UNDERSTANDING CRIMINAL LAW 189 n. 18 and sources cited (1998).

167. *See, e.g.*, U.S. MODEL PENAL CODE § 2.09 (1985).

168. JOHN R.W.D. JONES, THE PRACTICE OF THE INTERNATIONAL CRIMINAL TRIBUNALS FOR THE FORMER YUGOSLAVIA AND RWANDA 143 (2d ed. 2000) (citing *Order on Esad Landzos Submission regarding Diminished or lack of mental capacity issued in Delalić et al., June 18, 1999*).

169. Professor Knoops argues that in the ICTY and the ICTR, the Prosecutor's duty to prove guilt beyond a reasonable doubt "leads to the notion that the defendant is not obliged to prove beyond a reasonable doubt the existence of a legal defense; the accused may merely depend on the criterion of preponderance of the evidence by presenting a *prima facie* case." GEERT-JAN G.J. KNOOPS, DEFENSES IN CONTEMPORARY INTERNATIONAL CRIMINAL LAW 161 (2001).

170. William A. Schabas, *Article 67: Rights of the Accused, in* COMMENTARY ON THE ROME STATUTE OF THE INTERNATIONAL CRIMINAL COURT 845, 862 (Otto Triffterer,

The Draft Rules of Procedure and Evidence provides no guidance on this question.

B. Mistake and Superior Orders

In addition to article 31's general provisions on defenses, articles 32 and 33 of the Statute address two specific additional grounds for excluding criminal responsibility under the Statute: mistake, either of law or fact (article 32), and superior orders (article 33). Because they are closely related, they will be taken up together in this section.

Article 32(1) provides that a mistake of fact, which presumably includes ignorance of a fact as well,[171] excludes criminal responsibility if it negates the mental element required for the crime. The provision is arguably redundant because it is clearly the Prosecutor's burden to prove the mental element in each case. Indeed, it was proposed during the Preparatory Committee's discussions of the subject that any provision on mistake of fact should be eliminated as entirely self-evident.[172] Although the provision is thus relatively uncontroversial, and analogs are found in virtually all legal systems,[173] one potentially problematic aspect of this defense which is not apparent from the text of the Statute is whether or not the mistake must be objectively reasonable or unavoidable for the

---

ed., 1999). As Professor Schabas notes, there is little in the negotiating history to address the question.

171. The two are generally treated as identical and there appears to be no particular reason why a mistaken belief and the absence of any belief should be treated differently. *See, e.g.*, Otto Triffterer, *Mistake of fact or mistake of law, in* COMMENTARY ON THE ROME STATUTE OF THE INTERNATIONAL CRIMINAL COURT 555, 564–65 (Otto Triffterer, ed., 1999); JOSHUA DRESSLER, UNDERSTANDING CRIMINAL LAW 133 n. 2 (1998); U.S. MODEL PENAL CODE §2.04 (1985).

172. *See, e.g.*, *Zutphen Intersessional Draft*, art. 24[K], n. 103. On mistake of fact generally in the common law and under the U.S. Model Penal Code, *see, e.g.*, George P. Fletcher, *Mistake in the Model Penal Code: a False False Problem*, 19 RUTGERS L.J. 649 (1988); Peter W. Low, *The Model Penal Code, the Common Law, and Mistakes of Fact: Recklessness, Negligence, or Strict Liability?*, 19 RUTGERS L.J. 539 (1988); Kenneth W. Simons, *Mistake and Impossibility, Law and Fact, and Culpability: A Speculative Essay*, 81 J. CRIM. L. & CRIMINOLOGY 447 (1990); A.T.H. Smith, *Rethinking the Defence of Mistake*, 2 OXFORD J. OF LEGAL STUDIES 429 (1982). *See also* Stanislaw Pomorski, *Reflections on the First Criminal Code of Post-Communist Russia*, 46 AM. J. COMP. L. 375 (1998).

173. *See, e.g.*, U.S. MODEL PENAL CODE §2.04 (1985); Strafgesetzbuch [StGB] (German Penal Code) § 17, *translated in* THE GERMAN FEDERAL REPUBLIC PENAL CODE 55 (Joseph J. Darby trans. 1987).

accused to prevail. At common law, the reasonableness of the defendant's mistake was irrelevant for purposes of specific intent crimes; however, with crimes having a "lower" *mens rea* requirement, i.e., general intent crimes, the common law typically took the position that the mistake had to be "reasonable" to exculpate the defendant.[174] As noted earlier, the ICC Statute requires all elements of a crime (unless otherwise provided for by the Statute) to be committed with "intent" and "knowledge" pursuant to article 30. This appears to require quite a high threshold for most crimes, consistent with the Court's purpose which is to punish the most serious crimes of concern to the international community as a whole. If, for example, an accused is charged under article 8(2)(b)(ix) with intentionally directing an attack against a hospital, is it a defense to the crime for the accused to argue that he or she did not know it was a hospital if some indicator to that effect is present, such as a symbol on the building, or on a map used by the accused? Although commanders have a duty to inform themselves, and therefore probably should not benefit from "unreasonable" or "avoidable" mistakes of fact, their subordinates may not have the same responsibility, and could therefore be sheltered by the Statute's language, although the Prosecutor could employ extrinsic evidence to refute the accused's assertion that he or she was mistaken as to the true nature of the target.[175] Finally, although the Statute is unclear as to the burden upon the accused to establish defenses, mistake of fact would not appear to be an "affirmative defense" in the common law sense, requiring the accused to prove its existence to overcome his or her culpability. Rather, it probably remains the Prosecutor's job to overcome or disprove the accused's

---

174. In French law mistake of fact may exclude responsibility or may transform a crime into a lesser offense with respect to specific intent crimes, unless the mistake goes to the identity of the victim, in which case the conduct is not excused at all. No excuse is permitted however for crimes where the *mens rea* is imprudence, negligence, or presumably, recklessness. GASTON STEFANI, GEORGES LEVASSEUR & BERNARD BOULOC, DROIT PÉNAL GÉNÉRAL 338–39 (16th ed. 1997).

175. This view is supported by the fact that the words "avoidable" (with respect to mistake of fact and law) and "reasonable" (with respect to mistake of law) appeared in earlier proposals for this article, but were not adopted. *See, e.g., Zutphen Intersessional Draft*, art. 24[K]. The article suggested by the International Law Association's international criminal court committee in its model draft statute took the position that only "unavoidable" mistakes would exculpate a defendant completely; avoidable mistakes could only mitigate punishment. MODEL DRAFT STATUTE FOR THE INTERNATIONAL CRIMINAL COURT BASED ON THE PREPARATORY COMMITTEE'S TEXT TO THE DIPLOMATIC CONFERENCE, ROME, JUNE 15–JULY 17, 1998, 13*ter* NOUVELLE ÉTUDES PÉNALES 54–55 (Leila Sadat Wexler, special ed., 1998).

assertion of mistake, and establish the mental element for the particular crime beyond a reasonable doubt.[176]

If mistake of fact was a relatively uncontroversial proposition, there were widely divergent views on whether, and how, to include mistake of law. Although both common law and civil law jurisdictions have traditionally and dogmatically asserted that "ignorance of the law is no excuse,"[177] nevertheless virtually all domestic criminal codes, including those in common law countries, have exceptions to this principle. Some legal systems require the mistake of law to be "unavoidable,"[178] others require the mistake to be "reasonable,"[179] and still others treat mistake of law no differently than mistake of fact.[180] The Rome Statute takes the position that, generally speaking, ignorance of the law is no excuse, with two exceptions. The first, found in article 32(2) generally tracks the treatment given to mistakes of fact: mistake of law *may* (not *shall*, as we saw in article 32(1)) be a ground for excluding criminal responsibility if it negates the mental element required by the crime.[181]

The second exception is found in article 33, which more generally covers "superior orders and prescription of law."[182] This article varies considerably from prior international instruments, which took the position that orders of a superior were never grounds for exculpation, but could be considered in mitigation of punishment.[183] Although that proposition was somewhat controversial at the time of the Nuremberg trials, it was considered a key component of imposing individual criminal responsibility for the commission of atrocities that subordinates should not be able to escape liability for their acts by hiding behind the chain of command. Commanders, of course, would take the position that obedience to orders is the *sine qua non* of an effective military; that permitting soldiers to "think for themselves" is dangerous not only for the effectiveness of the military unit, but for the unit's safety; split-second obedience may be required to extricate a unit from danger, with few but the overseeing officer seeing the entire picture and able to assess the sit-

---

176. This is the common law view, although the Court could arguably take a different position. *See, e.g.*, JOSHUA DRESSLER, UNDERSTANDING CRIMINAL LAW 135 (1998).

177. *"Nul n'est censé ignorer la loi."* GASTON STEFANI, GEORGES LEVASSEUR & BERNARD BOULOC, DROIT PÉNAL GÉNÉRAL 336 (16th ed. 1997).

178. *See, e.g.*, N. CODE PÉNAL art. 122–3 (Fr.).

179. This was a proposal in the *Zutphen Intersessional Draft*.

180. *See, e.g.*, U.S. MODEL PENAL CODE §2.04(1) (1985).

181. *Rome Statute*, art. 32(2).

182. *Id.* art. 33.

183. *IMT Charter*, art. 8; *ICTY Statute*, art. 7(4); *ICTR Statute*, art. 6(4); *1996 Draft Code of Crimes*, art. 5.

uation.[184] However, as the International Law Commission noted in its commentary to article 6 of the 1996 Draft Code of Crimes:

> The government official who formulates a criminal plan or policy and the military commander or officer who orders the commission of a criminal act in the implementation of such a plan or policy bear particular responsibility for the eventual commission of the crime. However, the culpability and the indispensable role of the subordinate who actually commits the criminal act cannot be ignored. Otherwise the legal force and effect of the prohibition of crimes under international law would be substantially weakened by the absence of any responsibility or punishment on the part of the actual perpetrators of these heinous crimes and thus of any deterrence on the part of the potential perpetrators thereof.[185]

Thus, international criminal tribunals and scholars have generally postulated that if a defendant knew or should have known that an order was illegal, he or she is criminally responsible for carrying it out.[186]

Somewhat surprisingly, the Rome Statute retreats from this position. Although article 33 is phrased as an abolition of the defense, stating that superior orders "shall not relieve a person of criminal responsibility," it in fact permits subordinates who commit war crimes (or eventually aggression, once that crime is within the Court's jurisdiction), to escape liability for their acts on the grounds that they were following orders if three conditions are met:

(1) the person was under a legal obligation to obey the order;
(2) the person did not know the order was unlawful; and
(3) the order was not manifestly unlawful.[187]

Moreover, the exception applies to non-military personnel (as well as to soldiers) who are not subject to the same psychological and institutional pressures that apply to persons in military units. The article would thus appear to favor subordinates in a way that prior instruments, and the jurisprudence on the subject, did not.[188]

---

184. *Cf.* Mark J. Osiel, *Obeying Orders: Atrocity, Military Discipline, and the Law of War,* 86 CAL. L. REV. 939, 1027-45 (1998).

185. *1996 ILC Draft Code of Crimes,* Commentary to article 6, ¶ 3.

186. STEVEN R. RATNER & JASON S. ABRAMS, ACCOUNTABILITY FOR HUMAN RIGHTS ATROCITIES IN INTERNATIONAL LAW 121 (1997).

187. *Rome Statute,* art. 33(1). Orders to commit genocide or crimes against humanity are deemed "manifestly unlawful" by the text. *Id.* art. 33(2).

188. VIRGINIA MORRIS & MICHAEL P. SCHARF, I THE INTERNATIONAL CRIMINAL TRIBUNAL FOR RWANDA 267 (1998).

Four additional points concerning article 33 are worth noting. First, the article is closely linked to article 32 on mistake of law, and, indeed, the second condition a subordinate must fulfill to benefit from article 33's protection is that he or she did not know the order was unlawful. Certainly, low-level subordinates may not know, either due to complexity or circumstances, that a particular order is unlawful.[189] This would negate the mental element of the crime, and would appear to excuse them from liability under article 32(2) even without the operation of article 33. Second, particularly in the military context, the pressure on an individual to commit an illegal act may be so great that the defense of duress could be available even if obedience to orders was not (because, for example, the accused knew the order was illegal). The Nuremberg Tribunal recognized a defense if no "moral choice" was available to the accused: that is, if he or she was put in the position of killing or being killed, for example. As we saw earlier, however, that defense would be asserted under article 31(1)(d), and the accused would have to act proportionately in responding to the threat.[190] Third, national legislation addressing the defense of superior orders could be much more protective of subordinates than the Rome Statute. Reliance on such a provision, however, might run afoul of article 17's requirement that investigations and/or prosecutions in national courts be "genuine" in order to oust the ICC's jurisdiction under the complementarity provisions, requiring States wishing to fully avail themselves of complementarity's protection to amend any such rules to bring them into line with the ICC Statute. Finally, it should be noted that although article 33 is silent on mitigation of punishment, article 78(1) of the Statute would permit mitigation on a case by case basis if the circumstances so warranted.[191]

C. Statute of Limitations

Article 29 of the Rome Statute provides that the "crimes within the jurisdiction of the Court shall not be subject to any statute of limita-

---

189. STEVEN R. RATNER & JASON S. ABRAMS, ACCOUNTABILITY FOR HUMAN RIGHTS ATROCITIES IN INTERNATIONAL LAW 122 (1997).

190. Defendants in non-military and paramilitary situations have had little success with this defense, the kind of compulsion imposed not being of such nature so as to deprive the individual of his or her freedom of action. *See, e.g.*, Leila Nadya Sadat, *The Legal Legacy of Maurice Papon, in* MEMORY AND JUSTICE ON TRIAL 131 (Richard J. Golsan, ed., Routledge, 2000).

191. *Rome Statute*, art. 78(1).

tions."[192] A similar provision has never appeared in any prior international instruments,[193] either because no one had thought very much about it,[194] or because there was no agreement upon it.[195] Indeed, there was considerable doubt as to whether any consensus regarding a statute of limitations existed in customary international law regarding the "core" crimes

---

192. *Rome Statute*, art. 29. This provision does not apply to offenses against the administration of justice under article 70, which are subject to relatively short periods of limitation set forth in Draft RPE 164.

193. There is no provision on Statute of Limitations in either the Nuremberg and Tokyo Charters, or the Statutes of the two ad hoc tribunals. However, Control Council Law No. 10 did implicitly impose a statue of limitations via its express denial of such for violations occurring between January 31, 1933 and July 1, 1945. Allied Control Council Law No. 10, Punishment of Persons Guilty of War Crimes, Crimes Against Peace and Against Humanity, Dec. 20, 1945, art. II(5), Official Gazette of the Control Council for Germany, No. 3, Berlin, Jan. 31, 1946.

194. Leila Sadat Wexler, *The Interpretation of the Nuremberg Principles by the French Court of Cassation: from Touvier to Barbie and Back Again*, 32 COLUM. J. TRANSNAT'L L. 289, 318 (1994). Although it has been argued that its omission suggests that no time bar was intended by the drafters of earlier instruments, this does not appear correct. First, it appears the question simply was not posed during the drafting of the London and Tokyo Charters. Georges Levasseur, *Les crimes contre l'humanité et le problème de leur prescription*, 93 J. D. I. 259, 265 & n. 22 (1966). Second, generally speaking, international tribunals have been constituted to address discrete situations. They are typically established as temporary, not permanent, institutions, and their Statutes define only their own jurisdiction. Thus, the Statutes of the ad hoc tribunals and the Nuremberg and Tokyo Tribunals were probably unconcerned with prescription for the simple reason that it was not contemplated that those tribunals would exist long enough for a statute of limitations to pose any problem.

195. There are two treaties on the subject, but they have not been widely adopted. United Nations Convention on the Non-Applicability of Statutory Limitations to War Crimes and Crimes Against Humanity, Nov. 26, 1968, 754 U.N.T.S. 75. The convention came into force on November 11, 1970 and according to the United Nations web site currently has only 10 signatories and 44 parties. <http://untreaty.un.org/>. Shortly thereafter, the Council of Europe adopted a similar Convention. European Convention on the Non-Applicability of Statutory Limitation to Crimes Against Humanity and War Crimes, Jan. 25, 1974, E.T.S. No. 82, *reprinted in* 13 I.L.M. 540 (1974). The European Convention was only ratified by two States and never entered into force. Interestingly, both conventions were largely a response to German statutes of limitation that would have caused Nazi crimes to prescribe and prevent prosecution. This result, which was apparently perceived as desirable in Germany, was viewed as unacceptable by many other countries. Leila Sadat Wexler, *The Interpretation of the Nuremberg Principles by the French Court of Cassation: From Touvier to Barbie and Back Again*, 32 COLUMBIA J. TRANSNAT'L L. 289, 318–21 (1994).

found in the Statute.[196] Statutes of limitation even for the crimes within the Court's Statute, or their domestic analogs, are widely accepted in many countries, not to justify or excuse the defendant's behavior, but because public policy generally encourages putting an end to litigation and permitting defendants to reintegrate themselves back into society after a certain number of years have passed. Finally, with the passage of time, it may become difficult to prove the defendant's guilt or innocence. Evidence may have been lost and eye witnesses may have disappeared or their memories clouded. The Rome Statute's adoption of a rule on this point thus arguably departs from national practice and represents progressive development rather than simple codification of current law.

It is not clear whether and how this (new) rule of international law is binding upon States as to any rules they might have on the existence (or not) of Statutes of limitation as to the crimes within the jurisdiction of the Court. Presumably, States Parties to the ICC Statute could not apply a domestic statute of limitations to avoid surrendering a defendant to the Court without violating their obligation to the Court under article 86. In addition, although a State could rely upon a domestic statute of limitations to avoid investigating a defendant wanted by the Court, surely this would not be grounds upon which the State in question could invoke the principle of complementarity to block the case's admissibility in the ICC. Thus, the Statute is likely to have the practical effect of requiring States that currently impose a statute of limitations, even as to international crimes, to revise their legislation as part of the ratification and implementation process.

If the rule represented in the Rome Statute evidences customary international law, its reach may be even broader. Arguably, it might mean that even non-States Parties could not, consistent with international law, apply a statute of limitations to the "core" crimes within the jurisdiction of the Court. Although one could argue that the incrimination, and not the pro-

196. For example, although the French Court of Cassation found that crimes against humanity were "imprescriptable by their nature" as a matter of customary international law, Judgment of January 26, 1984, Cass. Crim., 1984 J.C.P. II G, No. 20,197 (Note Ruzié), J.D.I. 308 (1984), it rejected extending the same principle to war crimes, finding that they would prescribe as provided in French municipal law. The various options for this article presented to the Preparatory Committee reflected a similar divergence of views. Indeed, there were five separate proposals for this article contained in the Zutphen Intersessional Draft, which included options for no statute of limitations (Proposal 2), a 10 year limitations period for war crimes, but not other crimes, (Proposal 4) and the possibility for some other limitations period applicable to all crimes to be adopted in subsequent negotiations (Proposal 5).

cedural modalities surrounding it, is the only element of international criminal law that States are required to apply, one might also contend the opposite—that although the manner in which international law is applied by States is generally a question of national law, given that a limitations period is inextricably intertwined with the application of a *jus cogens* norm of fundamental importance, the better rule would be that national legal systems are bound, as a matter of international law, to apply international, and not national, rules as to statutes of limitation.[197] This problem will no doubt surface as to many of the rules in the Rome Statute—indeed, many questions will undoubtedly arise as to the complex relationship between the law of the Court and national legal systems.

---

197. *See* Leila Nadya Sadat, *Custom, Codification and Some Thoughts About the Relationship Between the Two: Article 10 of the ICC Statute*, 35 DEPAUL L. REV. 909 (2000); Leila Nadya Sadat, *Universal Jurisdiction and National Amnesties, Truth Commissions and Other Alternatives to Prosecution: Giving Justice a Chance* (Princeton Project on Universal Jurisdiction, Princeton, N.J., January 2001).

CHAPTER 8

THE PROCEDURAL ASPECTS OF THE STATUTE AND ITS APPLICATION

We must never forget that the record on which we judge these defendants today is the record on which history will judge us tomorrow. To pass these defendants a poisoned chalice is to put it to our own lips as well.

—Justice Robert H. Jackson
Chief Counsel for the United States at Nuremberg

As discussed in the previous Chapter, establishing an international criminal court required more than simply setting out definitions of crimes and specifying the organs of the Court empowered to investigate, prosecute and adjudicate violations of the norms. An entire body of substantive international criminal law had to be articulated, and, as this Chapter explores, inserted into an international procedural regime that would have to be elaborated, in fairly extensive detail.

One of the major differences between the substantive provisions of the Statute and its procedural regime, however, was the degree of flexibility enjoyed by the Framers in its formulation. As Chapter 5 explores, the Statute's assertion of universal international jurisdiction required the Framers to adhere relatively faithfully to existing customary international and treaty norms, permitting only small innovations in terms of "progressive development" of the law. This was particularly true as to definitions of crimes, although the absence of international rules with regard to the general part of the Statute permitted a relatively freer hand in drafting the text of Part 3 of the Statute. Procedure, however, was quite a different matter. To begin with, provisions relating to procedure were few and far between in the ICC Statute's predecessor instruments. The Nuremberg and Tokyo Charters had relatively rudimentary provisions on questions of procedure,[1] many of which, such as the right to hold trials *in*

1. The Tokyo Charter, for example, had only two articles relating to trial procedure: Article 12 on conduct of the trial, and article 15 on the Trial Proceedings.

absentia,[2] were subsequently criticized as insufficiently protective of the rights of the defense. The procedural provisions of the ICTY and ICTR Statutes are similarly understated, although they are complemented by an extensive set of Rules of Procedure and Evidence adopted by the judges of the tribunals,[3] which, along with the practice of the two ad hoc tribunals, proved instructive to the Framers of the Rome Statute. The International Law Commission's 1994 Draft Statute was a great deal more complete than earlier instruments, and approximately half of its sixty articles were devoted to questions of international criminal procedure. Yet even the ILC's Draft did not go far enough. When the Ad Hoc Committee took up the International Law Commission's draft in 1995, questions of procedure became central. Indeed, as the Report indicates, concerns about the Court's procedure went well beyond technical concerns and "touch[ed] upon fundamental aspects of the proposed institution,"[4] including its ultimate credibility and legitimacy. Thus, the stage was set for extensive negotiations on points of procedure that occupied the delegates considerably.[5]

Second, there being little in the way of uniform international rules of procedure (or practice), the Framers were relatively free to erect the procedural regime of their choice, based either on an idealized view of the "best" possible system, or, more parochially, and perhaps more commonly, based upon their own national systems, with which they had the most familiarity.[6] Thus, unlike the substantive law explored in Chapter 6, and

---

2. The Agreement for the Prosecution and Punishment of Major War Criminals of the European Axis, Charter of the International Military Tribunal, August 8, 1945, art. 12, 8 U.N.T.S. 279, *reprinted in* 39 AM. J. INT'L L. 257 (Supp. 1945).

3. *ICTY Statute*, art. 15; *ICTR Statute*, art. 14.

4. *Report of the Ad Hoc Committee on the Establishment of an International Criminal Court*, U.N. GAOR, 50th Sess., Supp. No. 22, at para. 129, U.N. Doc. A/50/22 (1995).

5. Silvia A. Fernández de Gurmendi, *The Process of Negotiations*, *in* THE INTERNATIONAL CRIMINAL COURT: THE MAKING OF THE ROME STATUTE 217, 217–27 (Roy S. Lee, ed., 1999). *See also* Mahnoush H. Arsanjani, *The Rome Statute of the International Criminal Court*, 93 AM. J. INT'L L. 22, 38–39 (1999).

6. Both civil law and common law adherents had difficulty abandoning the view that their own criminal justice procedures were inherently superior. As the great comparative law scholar Rudolf Schlesinger wrote of American lawyers, "when it comes to criminal procedure, they are possessed by a feeling of superiority that seems to grow in direct proportion to the ever-increasing weight of the accumulating evidence demonstrating the total failure of [the U.S.] system of criminal justice." Rudolf B. Schlesinger, *Comparative Criminal Procedure: A Plea for Utilizing Foreign Experience*, 26 BUFF. L. REV. 361, 363 (1977). *See also* Mirjan Damaška, *Evidentiary Barriers to Conviction and Two Models of Criminal Procedure: A Comparative Study*, 121 U. PENN. L. REV. 506, 588–89 (1973).

the general part of the Statute discussed in Chapter 7, we find in the Statute's procedural regime a fairly dramatic departure from past precedent. Indeed, the resulting regime in the Rome Statute is quite unlike any of its predecessors, including the two ad hoc tribunals.

Following the lead of the Ad Hoc Committee's report, the delegates noted the need to avoid excessive reliance on the common law legal tradition, as the ILC Draft had done, and lend balance to the Statute by drawing inspiration from the Civil law and other legal traditions.[7] They also needed to ensure that the procedures adopted would adequately protect the rights of the defendant, and strike an appropriate balance between the requisite independence of the Court and the sovereignty of States.[8] Finally, they were required to craft a Statute that would accomplish all of the above in enough detail so as to satisfy everyone, without including levels of unnecessary detail that would render the Statute, which was after all a Constitutive document, unduly encumbered by minutiae which could have made it impossibly long, difficult to negotiate, overly complex, and, because of the relatively cumbersome amendment process, insufficiently flexible to meet the continually changing needs of a fledgling institution.

The long and protracted negotiations of the procedural aspects of the Statute, and the efforts of the delegates intimately involved, were largely successful in achieving the above goals. The Statute is rich in complexity without being overly verbose; elements of the civil and common law traditions have been blended in a way that would appear to suit the needs of an international criminal justice system; and defendants, as well as per-

---

7. Silvia A. Fernández de Gurmendi, *The Process of Negotiations, in* THE INTERNATIONAL CRIMINAL COURT: THE MAKING OF THE ROME STATUTE 217, 220–224 (Roy S. Lee, ed., 1999). Particularly as regards terminology, the ILC's draft was quite common law in orientation. Prosecution began upon the establishment of a "prima facie case," and the filing of an "indictment" with the Registrar. *1994 ILC Draft Statute*, art. 27(1). This is also true of the two ad hoc tribunals. *ICTY Statute*, art. 18(4); *ICTR Statute*, art. 17(4), which, in response to criticisms that their procedures were excessively adversarial, have adopted at least some rules attempting to strike a better balance between the two. JOHN R.W.D. JONES, THE PRACTICE OF THE INTERNATIONAL CRIMINAL TRIBUNALS 163–64 (2000).

8. One departure from the practice of the ad hoc tribunals suggested by the Ad Hoc Committee, for example, was to have the Rules of Procedure and Evidence prepared and adopted by the States Parties to the Treaty rather than the Court's judges. *1995 Ad Hoc Committee Report*, at ¶ 129. Another crucial issue for many States was the protection of information they considered essential to their national security, an issue not taken up here, but which engendered much controversy during the Statute's negotiation. *See,* Donald K. Piragoff, *Protection of National Security Information, in* THE INTERNATIONAL CRIMINAL COURT: THE MAKING OF THE ROME STATUTE 270 (Roy S. Lee, ed., 1999).

sons under investigation by the Court, should be well-protected by the extensive panoply of rights contained in the Statute. The one glaring but perhaps inevitable exception to the Statute's overall success was the extensive concessions required to the sovereignty of States, which are particularly apparent in Part 9 of the Statute on International Cooperation and Judicial Assistance, and Part 10 on Enforcement.

I. INVESTIGATION AND PROSECUTION

A. Investigation and Initial Proceedings Before the Court

Part 5 of the Statute, entitled "Investigation and Prosecution," addresses the proceedings of the Court from the decision to investigate the possibility that a crime within the jurisdiction of the Court has been committed (article 53 of the Statute), to the confirmation of the charges before trial (article 61). Because many of these provisions were addressed in Chapter 4, they will not be elaborated upon in great detail here. However, a few points bear noting.

To begin with, the foundational principle of the Statute with regard to the investigation and prosecution of crimes within the Court's jurisdiction is prosecutorial independence.[9] This means independence in deciding whether or not to initiate an investigation, and in deciding whether or not to pursue a particular individual. As a legal matter, this independence operates not only against the other organs of the Court, but against States Parties and the Security Council as well.[10] Thus, pursuant to article 53, it is the Prosecutor that decides whether or not to initiate an investigation or to bring a prosecution, and, pursuant to article 54, it is the Prosecutor's duty to ensure the effective investigation and prosecution of crimes within the jurisdiction of the Court.[11]

The Prosecutor's independence, however, is not absolute. Indeed, the ICC Prosecutor is not an all-powerful "independent counsel for the

---

9. *See, e.g., Rome Statute*, 42(1).

10. Of course, the Assembly of States Parties may always remove a Prosecutor it feels to have "committed serious misconduct or a serious breach of his or her duties under this Statute." *Id.* art. 46(1). Although Draft RPE 24 constrains the Assembly's discretion considerably by defining "serious misconduct" and "serious breach of duty" in fairly narrow terms that would appear to preclude political retaliation against an unpopular Prosecutor by the Assembly, it is not clear how such constraints would, as a practical matter, be enforced.

11. *Rome Statute*, art. 54 (1)(a) & (b).

universe,"[12] levying charges at will and able to send his or her operatives out into the world and bring people in to the Hague for questioning.[13] Instead, the Prosecutor's powers are a great deal more modest. Most obviously, the Prosecutor is bound to act under the law of the Statute. Moreover, he or she will be closely supervised by the Pre-Trial Chamber in many regards to see that he or she does so. Thus, if a Prosecutor declines to proceed based solely on his or her estimation that the investigation or prosecution would not serve the interests of justice, the Pre-Trial Chamber may review the Prosecutor's decision, which will not stand unless confirmed.[14] In addition, the Prosecutor is required to pursue the truth.[15] This principle, which departs considerably from the approach taken by many legal systems,[16] requires the Prosecutor to investigate "incriminating and exonerating circumstances equally."[17] The Prosecutor is also duty-bound

---

12. This concern was raised by the United States' delegation during the Statute's negotiation.

13. See the limitations imposed by article 93(7) in this regard.

14. If the Prosecutor concludes, however, that the evidence does not support a finding that there is a reasonable basis to believe a crime within the jurisdiction of the Court has been committed, or that the case is or would be inadmissible, his or her decision not to proceed is not reviewable by the Pre-Trial Chamber. *Rome Statute*, art. 53(3)(b). *See also* Figure 13. Compare article 26 of the ILC's 1994 Draft, which allowed the Prosecutor not to proceed with an investigation or prosecution only if there was "no sufficient basis" to proceed; a decision by the Prosecutor with regard to which the Presidency could request reconsideration, but had no power to annul.

15. Article 54 provides that the Prosecutor's mission is to "establish the truth." *Rome Statute*, art. 54(1)(a).

16. See also Morten Bergsmo & Pieter Kruger, *Duties and powers of the Prosecutor with respect to investigations, in* COMMENTARY ON THE ROME STATUTE OF THE INTERNATIONAL CRIMINAL COURT 715, 716 (Otto Trifftérer, ed., 1999).

17. *Rome Statute*, art. 54(1)(a). The Rome Statute appears to reject the "procedural or formal" truth pursued by adversarial legal systems in favor of "material and absolute" truth. Rachel A. Van Cleave, *An Offer You Can't Refuse? Punishment without Trial in Italy and the United States: The Search for Truth and an Efficient Criminal Justice System*, 11 EMORY INT'L. L. REV. 419, 426 (1997). Adversarial systems place central importance on the trial. In these systems, "procedural truth is the result achieved by following formal rules designed to ensure that the process is fair, and that individual rights have been protected." *Id.* Civil law inquisitorial systems, on the other hand, "marginalize the importance of the trial and the dialectical debate between the parties while exalting the role of the investigative judge in researching, analyzing, and evaluating the evidence." *Id.* at 427. The Rome Statute has many features that would classify it as closer to a civil law than a common law system—the Court will not automatically accept guilty pleas; the Statute provides for an investigative judge to supervise the investigation and pre-

to respect the interests and personal circumstances of victims and witnesses,[18] and is subject to an independent duty to respect the rights of persons under investigation and the accused, rights which are set out in articles 55 and 67 of the Statute, respectively, and discussed further below.[19] Finally, although nominally the Statute grants the Prosecutor relatively extensive investigatory powers, virtually all of those powers must be exercised through or in cooperation with national authorities which may exclude the ICC Prosecutor and his or her staff from their territories,[20] subject to certain limited exceptions.[21]

As shown in figures 12 through 15, the culmination of the Prosecutor's investigative activity will presumably be the arrest of the individual believed to have committed the crime, assuming the conditions for issuing an arrest warrant are satisfied,[22] and the charging of that individual with a crime or crimes within the jurisdiction of the Court. The person in question (the Statute avoids the use of the word suspect entirely as delegates could not agree to its meaning)[23] will not be arrested by the Office of the Prosecutor itself. Instead, national authorities will be requested to apprehend him or her pursuant to Part 9 of the Statute. The arrest may be challenged at the national level, pursuant to article 59—if ultimately surrendered to the Court, the arrestee may challenge his or her detention (and/or apply for interim release) before the Pre-Trial Chamber, under

---

trial proceedings; and the Statute permits both the Prosecutor and the accused to appeal and permits appeal on questions of fact as well as law. On the search for "truth" in criminal proceedings, see also Mirjan Damaška, *Evidentiary Barriers to Conviction and Two Models of Criminal Procedure: A Comparative Study*, 121 U. PENN. L. REV. 506, 578–89 (1973).

18. *Rome Statute*, art. 68(1).

19. *Id.* art. 54(1)(b) & (c).

20. *Id.* arts. 54(2) & 93.

21. *Rome Statute*, art. 57(3)(d) (the Pre-Trial Chamber may authorize the Prosecutor to take specific investigative steps on the territory of a State Party without its cooperation if the State is clearly unable to execute a request for cooperation due to the unavailability of any authority or any component of its judicial system to execute the request). *See also, id.* art. 99(4) (voluntary measures conducted in a territorial State Party where admissibility has already been determined, or following consultations with the requested State Party and respect of reasonable conditions for the conduct of the investigation imposed by it).

22. *See, id.* art. 58(1). The Statute also sets out, in detail, the elements of a proper arrest warrant to be included in the Prosecutor's application to the Pre-Trial Chamber.

23. The ILC's draft distinguished between the "suspect" under investigation and the "accused" who so became upon confirmation of the indictment. *See 1994 ILC Draft Statute*, at 93.

article 60. Finally, the arrestee is entitled "within a reasonable time" after his or her surrender or voluntary appearance before the Court,[24] to a hearing before a Pre-Trial Chamber composed of three judges[25] to confirm the charges on which the Prosecutor intends to seek trial pursuant to article 61 of the Statute.[26] The trial may only take place as to charges which are confirmed by the Pre-Trial Chamber at the hearing, and the Pre-Trial Chamber may confirm charges only if there exist "substantial grounds to believe that the person committed each of the crimes charged,"[27] presumably a higher standard than appears in article 58 (on arrest) which requires "reasonable grounds" to believe the person has committed a crime.[28]

Although the pretrial and investigatory procedures of the ICC differ in many fundamental respects from the investigatory and pre-trial process of the two ad hoc tribunals,[29] two successful procedures of the ICTY

---

24. *Rome Statute*, art. 61(1). "Reasonable time" is not defined by the Statute. Article 60 protects a person from pre-trial detention that is for "an unreasonable period" prior to trial due to inexcusable delay by the Prosecutor, by providing that the Court "shall consider releasing the person, with or without conditions," if such unreasonable and inexcusable detention occurs. Draft RPE 121 provides that a person shall be brought before the Pre-Trial Chamber "promptly upon arriving at the Court," at which time the Court "shall set the date on which it intends to hold a hearing to confirm the charges." Thus, while the Statute and Rules are admittedly vague, it appears that the general thrust is to bring the person before the Court quickly, and to set the date for confirmation of the charges right away.

25. *Rome Statute*, art. 57(2)(a).

26. As shown in figure 16, article 61 sets forth, in extensive detail, the procedure to be followed with respect to confirmation hearings.

27. *Rome Statute*, art. 61(5).

28. To the extent the Rome Statute imposes a higher standard for confirmation of the charges than arrest, it departs from the practice of the ICTY and ICTR which impose the same standard for both confirmation of the indictment and issuance of a warrant for the suspect's arrest—the establishment of a prima facie case. With regard to the confirmation of the indictment, see *ICTY Statute*, art. 19; *ICTR Statute*, art. 18. On the issuance of an arrest warrant, see ICTY Rule 47(A) & (H); ICTR Rule 47(A) & (H). The practice in the Tribunals is to have the indictment confirmed prior to the arrest warrant's issuance. The complexity of the indictment process is detailed in Michael J. Keegan & Daryl A. Mundis, *Legal Requirements for Indictments, in* ESSAYS ON ICTY PROCEDURE AND EVIDENCE IN HONOUR OF GABRIELLE KIRK MCDONALD 123 (Richard May, et. al., eds., 2001). In the ICC, the arrest warrant will be issued prior to confirmation of the charges. *See generally* Kuniji Shibahara, *Confirmation of the Charges before Trial, in* COMMENTARY ON THE ROME STATUTE OF THE INTERNATIONAL CRIMINAL COURT 783, 785 (Otto Triffterer, ed., 1999).

29. On the investigation and indictment procedure of the ICTY see VIRGINIA MORRIS & MICHAEL P. SCHARF, I AN INSIDER'S GUIDE TO THE TRIBUNAL FOR THE FORMER YUGOSLAVIA 175–97, 202–21 (1995); Michael J. Keegan & Daryl A. Mundis, *Legal*

appear to have been retained which address the practical problems faced by an international criminal court with no direct means of police enforcement to obtain the presence of individuals it wishes to try. First, although there will be no "indictments" *per se* in the ICC, suspects may presumably be arrested without prior notice as to the Prosecutor's intentions, as article 58 proceedings are not conducted with notice to the person under investigation.[30] This will permit the Court to operate in relative secrecy to avoid "tipping off" potential defendants that they are likely to be arrested. Secrecy was critical in the former Yugoslavia to convince IFOR to arrest suspects because it provided soldiers an element of surprise with regard to defendants who might otherwise be on their guard and heavily armed, and the Office of the Prosecutor adopted the practice of issuing "sealed indictments" for just that reason.

Conversely, publicity is sometimes desired by the Office of the Prosecutor to enlist the aid of the media and the general public in locating and arresting the accused, to embarrass States harboring fugitives to stop doing so, or to give the defendant an opportunity to come forward voluntarily to face the charges.[31] Thus, while rejecting the possibility of trials *in absentia*, which were highly controversial during the Preparatory Committee's negotiation,[32] article 61(2) of the ICC Statute provides for a procedure similar to the Rule 61 procedure of the two ad hoc tribunals,[33]

Requirements for Indictments, in ESSAYS ON ICTY PROCEDURE AND EVIDENCE IN HONOUR OF GABRIELLE KIRK MCDONALD 123 (Richard May, et. al., eds., 2001); for the ICTR see VIRGINIA MORRIS & MICHAEL P. SCHARF, I THE INTERNATIONAL CRIMINAL TRIBUNAL FOR RWANDA 427–500 (1998).

30. The Draft Rules of Procedure and Evidence are silent on this point. One option for article 61 of the April Draft Statute provided that indictments were to be public documents, except in certain circumstances. With the elimination of the "indictment" stage of the pre-trial process, however, this article was no longer retained, and the simplified procedure proposed for articles 58 to 61 was ultimately adopted. *April Draft Statute*, at 93, n. 25.

31. VIRGINIA MORRIS & MICHAEL P. SCHARF, I AN INSIDER'S GUIDE TO THE TRIBUNAL FOR THE FORMER YUGOSLAVIA 219 (1995).

32. Håkan Friman, *Rights of Persons Suspected or Accused of a Crime, in* THE INTERNATIONAL CRIMINAL COURT: THE MAKING OF THE ROME STATUTE 247, 255–61 (Roy S. Lee, ed., 1999). In 1996 the Preparatory Commission noted that there was general support for the indictment chamber to record evidence or issuing and publishing an international warrant of arrest for a defendant who was deliberately absent. *Report of the Preparatory Committee on the Establishment of an International Criminal Court, Volume I (Proceedings of the Preparatory Committee during March–April and August 1996)*, U.N. GAOR, 51st Sess., Supp. No. 22, at para. 259, U.N. Doc. No. A/51/22.

33. Rule 61 permits the Prosecutor to submit an indictment to the Trial

by permitting the Pre-Trial Chamber to hold a hearing on the confirmation of the charges without the person being present if he or she has either waived his or her right to be present (which waiver must be voluntary),[34] or has fled and all reasonable steps have been taken to secure his or her appearance before the Court.[35] Unlike the practice which evolved under Rule 61 of the ICTY, the Rome Statute does not provide for a publicized hearing and the issuance of a special "international arrest warrant."[36] However, the option of making an evidentiary record is preserved,[37] which may well form the basis for public and moral condemnation of the defendant who has fled or refuses to "be found."

B. Trial

Following confirmation of the charges before trial, the Presidency is to constitute a three judge Trial Chamber[38] to hear the accused's case.[39] The trial proceedings are governed by the 16 articles of Part 6 of the Statute,

---

Chamber without the presence of the accused if the Judge who confirmed the indictment is satisfied that the Prosecutor and the Registrar have taken all reasonable steps to locate and secure the arrest of the accused but have been unsuccessful in doing so. If, based upon evidence submitted by the Prosecutor, reasonable grounds exist for believing the accused committed the crimes charged in the indictment, the Trial Chamber shall have the indictment read aloud by the Prosecutor in conjunction with an account of the attempts to effect service, and will issue an international arrest warrant to be transmitted to all States. In addition, if the failure to effect personal service was due in whole or in part to the failure or refusal of a State to cooperate with the Tribunal, the Trial Chamber, after consultation with the President, shall notify the Security Council thereof. ICTY, Rule 61; ICTR, Rule 61. JOHN R.W.D. JONES, THE PRACTICE OF THE INTERNATIONAL CRIMINAL TRIBUNALS 304–11, 588–90 (2000). Mr. Jones notes that although the Rule 61 proceeding has been employed several times in the ICTY, it has never been used by the ICTR.

34. *See* Draft RPE 124(2) (the Pre-Trial Chamber must be "satisfied that the person concerned understands the right to be present at the hearing and the consequences of waiving this right.").

35. *Id.* art. 61(2).

36. Article 37(4) of the ILC's 1994 Draft Statute provided for a "Rule 61" type procedure, but it was eliminated during the Statute's negotiation.

37. *See also Rome Statute*, art. 56 and figure 14 in this regard.

38. *Rome Statute*, arts. 39(2) & 61(11). Under no circumstances may a judge who participated in the pre-trial phase of the case be eligible to sit on the Trial Chamber hearing that case. *Id.* art. 39(4).

39. The International Law Commission originally proposed five-judge trial chambers, *1994 ILC Draft*, art. 9(5).

which, as one would expect, are much more detailed than the ILC's 1994 Draft. Unsurprisingly, we find in Part 6 a melange of civil law and common law traditions, blended to produce a trial process that is quite unique. Like the ILC Draft,[40] the Rome Statute specifies that the trial is to be held in public,[41] subject to the need to close hearings so as to protect victims and witnesses, or confidential or sensitive information.[42] Trials will generally be held at the seat of the Court in the Hague, unless decided otherwise[43] by the Court's judges "in the interests of justice,"[44] a broad term that the Court will no doubt be called upon to interpret in the future. A special feature of trials in the ICC will necessarily be the linguistic difficulties that surround them.[45] Trials will be held in the presence of the accused[46] and conducted in the language or languages determined by the Trial Chamber in the particular case,[47] subject, of course, to the defen-

---

40. *1994 ILC Draft Statute*, art. 38(4).

41. *Rome Statute*, art. 64(7).

42. *Id.* arts. 64(7), 68, 72(5)(d).

43. *Id.* art. 62.

44. Draft RPE 100(1). A change of venue may be proposed by the Prosecutor, defense or a majority of the judges at any time after the initiation of the investigation. The application is filed with the Presidency. *Id.*

45. The expert group that reviewed the operation of the two ad hoc Tribunals concluded:

> [A]s a general proposition, the impact of which extends to all facets of the work of the Tribunals' three organs, translation is a bottleneck causing delay on a wide scale, including delay in the issuance of Tribunal decisions. . . . Availability of qualified translators is limited as are the budgetary resources available . . .

Report of the Expert Group to Conduct a Review of the Effective Operation and Functioning of the International Tribunal for the Former Yugoslavia and the International Criminal Tribunal for Rwanda, at para. 37, U.N. Doc. S/2000/597.

46. The issue generated extensive debate throughout the Preparatory Committee meetings, and during the Diplomatic Conference. Some delegations such as France and The Netherlands strongly supported the holding of trials in the absence of the accused, whereas others strongly opposed the idea.

47. *Rome Statute*, art. 64(3)(b). Although one interpretation of this provision is that the Trial Chamber is to determine which languages may be used at trial (such as the language of the accused, for example), *in addition to* English and French, which, pursuant to article 50(2) are the two "working" languages of the Court, another possible interpretation is that the Trial Chamber might reduce the number of languages used in a particular case by picking one language as the language to be employed, if all the parties were comfortable with it. One commentator has suggested that the text necessarily requires an increase in the number of languages being used by a Chamber in a particular case. Gilbert Bitti, *Functions and powers of the Trial Chamber, in* COMMENTARY ON THE ROME STATUTE OF THE INTERNATIONAL CRIMINAL COURT 809, 815 (Otto Triffterer, ed., 1999). However, article 64

dant's right to be informed of the charges in a language he or she fully understands and speaks,[48] and the defendant's right to an interpreter and translations as required.[49] The Statute permits the Court to control the proceedings before it and to sanction not only misconduct before the Court,[50] but offenses against its integrity such as giving false testimony, corrupting a witness, or impeding, intimidating or corruptly influencing an official of the Court.[51]

One issue that was the source of extensive debate during the Statute's negotiation and adoption was the problem of guilty pleas and plea bargaining.[52] A key issue before the Preparatory Commission had been whether to permit the Court to accept guilty pleas from defendants that would result in the automatic conviction of the defendant, completely bypassing the trial phase of the procedure and proceeding straight to the sentencing phase of the case.[53] Although pleading permits an efficient and summary disposition of the case, and allows the accused to admit his or her guilt,[54] guilty pleas

---

(3)(b) is ambiguous (referring to the "language" or "languages" to be used), and the Draft Rules of Procedure and Evidence are silent.

48. *Rome Statute*, art. 67(1)(a). Note that neither the Draft Rules nor the Statute give the defendant the right to be "tried" in his or her own language. Although a Court could find that proceedings were "unfair" absent the accused's ability to follow them in his or her own language, given the chaos which could ensue from such a ruling, it is more likely that article 67(1)(f) which guarantees the accused an interpreter and any necessary translations "free of cost" will be considered the total quantum of "fairness" required by the Statute insofar as linguistic rights are concerned.

49. *Rome Statute*, art. 67(1)(f).

50. *Rome Statute*, art. 71. The procedures to be employed with respect to misconduct before the Court are set forth in Draft RPE 170–71. With respect to the problem of misconduct before the ICTY see Gabriël Oosthuizen, *Of Misconduct, Contempt, False Testimony, Rule Mutations and other Interesting Powers: A Potpourri of Questions and Notes*, *in* ESSAYS ON ICTY PROCEDURE AND EVIDENCE IN HONOUR OF GABRIELLE KIRK MCDONALD 387 (Richard May, et. al., eds., 2001).

51. *Rome Statute*, art. 70. The procedures to be employed with respect to offenses against the administration of justice under article 71 are set forth in Draft RPE 162–69.

52. As one delegate observed, "[a] proposal that an accused be permitted to plead guilty led to some puzzled comments from civil and Islamic lawyers." Roger S. Clark, *The Proposed International Criminal Court: Its Establishment and its Relationship with the United Nations*, 8 CRIM. L. F. 411, 430 n. 64 (1997).

53. *See, e.g.*, *Report of the Preparatory Committee on the Establishment of an International Criminal Court*, Vol. 1, paras. 261–64, U.N. GAOR, 51st Sess., Supp. no. 22, U.N. Doc. A/51/22 (1996).

54. *Id.* at para. 261 (suggesting that the guilty plea could be efficient and spare victims and witnesses "any additional suffering.")

are often extracted from defendants through coercive means. The ICTY encountered this problem in the *Erdemović* case, in which a defendant's plea of guilty, while accepted by the Trial Chamber,[55] was ultimately rejected by the Appeals Chamber, which found that the plea had not been fully informed.[56] Moreover, although determining the defendant's ultimate guilt or innocence is an important goal of the criminal process, criminal trials, particularly in the context of mass atrocities, also serve as an official venue for the acknowledgment of the victims' injuries and the making of an historical record. Thus, it is not clear that a defendant's admission alone should bind the Court and prevent it from hearing additional evidence. Finally, although "pleading" is a well-accepted feature of common law jurisdictions,[57] it is less well-accepted in civil law countries,[58] although both systems tend to permit some sort of truncated proceedings following factual stipulations by the accused.[59]

The compromise ultimately adopted tracks neither the common or civil law approach completely. Instead, it follows article 38 of the ILC's 1994 Draft Statute, which permitted, but did not require, an accused to

---

55. Prosecutor v. Erdemović (Case No. IT-96-22-T), Sentencing Judgment (ICTY Trial Chamber I, Nov. 29, 1996). For a critique of the Trial Court's judgment, *see* Sienho Yee, *The Erdemović Sentencing Judgment: A Questionable Milestone for the International Criminal Tribunal for the Former Yugoslavia*, 26 GEORGIA J. INT'L & COMP. L. 263 (1997). *See also* Michael Bohlander, *Plea-Bargaining before the ICTY, in* ESSAYS ON ICTY PROCEDURE AND EVIDENCE IN HONOUR OF GABRIELLE KIRK MCDONALD 151 (Richard May, et. al., eds., 2001).

56. Prosecutor v. Erdemović (Case No. IT-96-22-A), Joint Separate Opinion of Judge McDonald and Judge Vohrah, para. 14–27 (ICTY Appeals Chamber, Oct. 7, 1997).

57. Roger S. Clark, *The Proposed International Criminal Court: Its Establishment and its Relationship with the United Nations*, 8 CRIM. L. F. 411, 430 n. 64 (1997). For the view that plea bargaining is present even in the civil law world, *see* JOHN HENRY MERRYMAN, DAVID S. CLARK & JOHN O. HALEY, THE CIVIL LAW TRADITION: EUROPE, LATIN AMERICA, AND EAST ASIA 180–82 (1994).

58. Germany takes a particulary dim view of plea bargaining. Michael Bohlander, *Plea-Bargaining before the ICTY, in* ESSAYS ON ICTY PROCEDURE AND EVIDENCE IN HONOUR OF GABRIELLE KIRK MCDONALD 151, 159–60 (Richard May, et. al., eds., 2001).

59. On recent attempts to address the problems of an overburdened criminal justice system by implementing "trial-avoidance mechanisms " see Rachel A. Van Cleave, *An Offer You Can't Refuse? Punishment without Trial in Italy and the United States: The Search for Truth and an Efficient Criminal Justice System*, 11 EMORY INT'L. L. REV. 419 (1997). *See also* Fabricio Guariglia, *Proceedings on an admission of guilt, in* COMMENTARY ON THE ROME STATUTE OF THE INTERNATIONAL CRIMINAL COURT 823, 825 (Otto Triffterer, ed., 1999) (many civil law countries have some trial avoidance mechanisms).

plead guilty or not guilty.[60] In the absence of a plea, the accused would be presumed not guilty; in the presence of a plea of guilty, the Trial Chamber would then hear "at a minimum" some or all of the prosecution's case against the accused and "ensure for itself that the guilty plea was freely entered and is reliable."[61] Article 65 of the Rome Statute, entitled "Proceedings on an admission of guilt," follows this general approach, but expands upon it considerably. The accused may admit his or her guilt pursuant to article 64(8)(a), or may plead "not guilty," if he or she desires to enter a plea at all.[62] The Trial Chamber is then required to determine whether the accused truly understands the nature and consequences of the admission of guilt, that it was made voluntarily and after sufficient consultation with defense counsel, and supported by the facts of the case.[63] If the Trial Chamber considers these criteria to have been fulfilled, it may convict the accused of the crime, or may decide that the interests of justice (and in particular the interests of victims), require a more complete presentation of the facts of the case. If so, it will then order either the trial of the accused, or a more summary proceeding involving the presentation of additional evidence by the Prosecutor.[64] Conversely, if the Trial Chamber is not satisfied that these criteria have been met, the accused is presumed innocent and the case proceeds to trial, either before the same or another Trial Chamber.[65] Finally, the Statute is clear that the Prosecutor may not bind the Court by entering into plea bargains with defendants, although nothing in the Statute prevents the Office of the Prosecutor from engaging in such discussions.[66] Presumably, however, if the Prosecutor was to suggest that a recommendation for reduced sentence made in

---

60. *1994 ILC Draft Statute*, art. 38(1)(d).

61. *1994 ILC Draft Statute*, at 111–12.

62. The Statute avoids using the common law terminology of "guilty plea" in favor of the phrase "admission of guilt," which is equally foreign to civil and common law systems. Somewhat inconsistently, however, it refers to pleading "not guilty" in article 64(8)(a).

63. *Rome Statute*, art. 65(1).

64. *Id*. art. 65(4). If a complete trial is ordered, it *may* be sent to a different trial chamber under the Statute, or may be retained by the Trial Chamber before which the case is already pending. *Id*.

65. *Id*. art. 65(3). Some commentators have suggested that the case should automatically proceed before a different Trial Chamber to avoid any hint of bias or partiality in subsequent proceedings. Fabricio Guariglia, *Proceedings on an admission of guilt*, *in* COMMENTARY ON THE ROME STATUTE OF THE INTERNATIONAL CRIMINAL COURT 823, 830 (Otto Triffterer, ed., 1999) (suggesting that this places in the judges' own hands "the somewhat unrealistic task of evaluating their own impartiality or lack of bias.")

66. *Rome Statute*, art. 65(5).

exchange for a guilty plea would be enforceable, any guilty plea so entered would presumably be tainted as "involuntary" or coerced, and subject to rejection by the Trial Chamber.

The Statute also combines elements of common and civil law practice in its treatment of evidentiary issues. Although witnesses will testify under oath, as in many civil law countries the defendant may make an *unsworn* statement to the Court.[67] Pursuant to article 69 of the Statute the Court may hear any evidence it deems relevant to the case, subject to the right to rule inadmissible evidence which might be unduly prejudicial to the accused's right to a fair trial.[68] The broad language of the Statute thus avoids most of the technicalities of common law trial practice, such as the hearsay rule, but the judges could nevertheless rule particular kinds of evidence excessively prejudicial, and therefore inadmissible, under the general rubric of unfairness. Importantly, the Court is not to apply national laws governing the admission of evidence, unless those rules rise to the level of a general principle of international law, consistent with article 21 of the Statute.[69] Furthermore, if ruling upon the relevance or admissibility of evidence collected by a State, the Court may not rule on the application of the State's national law.[70] This should hopefully assist the Court in developing a uniform approach to the admissibility of evidence that will not vary according to the nationality of the presiding judge in question.[71]

---

67. In French law, for example, witnesses (*les témoins*) are called under oath to testify "without hate or fear, and to tell the truth and nothing but the truth." C. PR. PÉN. art. 331 (Fr.). The defendant is not technically a witness, however, and does not testify under oath. *See, id.* art. 331(6). *See also* Rudolf B. Schlesinger, *Comparative Criminal Procedure: A Plea for Utilizing Foreign Experience*, 26 BUFF. L. REV. 361, 367 (1977) (noting that defendants do not testify under oath in criminal trials in civil law countries).

68. *Rome Statute*, art. 69(4). Pursuant to Draft RPE 64, evidentiary rulings shall be accompanied by reasons. In addition, the rules are explicit that corroboration is not legally required to prove any crime within the jurisdiction of the Court, and in particular crimes of sexual violence. Draft RPE 63(4). The Statute also contains an extensive provision on the protection of national security information in article 72, and provides for the protection of privileges on confidentiality as provided for in the Rules of Procedure and Evidence. See *Rome Statute*, art. 69(5); Draft RPE 73. On evidence in the ICTY see generally ESSAYS ON ICTY PROCEDURE AND EVIDENCE 249–339 (Richard May, et al., eds., 2000).

69. Draft RPE 63(5).

70. *Rome Statute*, art. 69(8).

71. Common law and civil law systems have different approaches to the admissibility of evidence in criminal proceedings that stem from three main factors according to one study: the difference between adversary and non-adversary

All three judges are to be present for the entire trial,[72] and their decision is to be issued after secret deliberations. Although judges may take judicial notice of "facts of common knowledge,"[73] they must, otherwise, base their decision only upon the evidence submitted to the Court during the trial.[74] Finally, although unanimity is encouraged by the Statute, the accused may be convicted or acquitted by majority vote, in which case the Trial Chamber's decision must contain the views of the majority and minority,[75] an element of the Statute critiqued in Chapter 4, above.

Following the conclusion of the trial, the accused will either be acquitted or convicted.[76] If acquitted, he or she will be automatically released,[77] subject to the Prosecutor's right to bring an appeal and request the continued detention of the person pending appeal "under exceptional circumstances, and having regard, *inter alia*, to the concrete risk of flight, the seriousness of the offense charged and the probability of success on appeal."[78] If convicted, the Trial Chamber may hold an additional hearing to determine the appropriate sentence to be imposed,[79] as well as make orders directly against the convicted person specifying reparations to be made to or in respect of victims, including restitution, compensation and rehabilitation.[80] He or she shall "remain in custody pending an appeal" unless the Trial Chamber orders otherwise.[81]

---

procedures, the difference in the structure of their adjudicating bodies (a jury of lay men and women as opposed to a judge or mixed tribunal), and whether the trial is preceded by a purportedly non-partisan investigation, the results of which are available to the judge. Mirjan Damaška, *Evidentiary Barriers to Conviction and Two Models of Criminal Procedure: A Comparative Study*, 121 U. PENN. L. REV. 506, 510–11 (1973).

72. As some judges at the two ad hoc tribunals have noted, the practicality of this requirement is questionable, given the lengthy nature of trials involving extremely serious crimes such as genocide, crimes against humanity and war crimes.

73. *Rome Statute*, art. 69(6).

74. *Id*. art. 74(2).

75. *Id*. art. 74(5). Separate or dissenting opinions, however, are not permitted at the trial level, but may only be issued on questions of law heard by the Appeals Chamber. *See id*., art. 83(4). The Trial Chamber must issue its decision in writing.

76. The Statute and Draft Rules do not appear to envisage the possibility of a mistrial being declared.

77. *Rome Statute*, art. 81(3)(c).

78. *Id*. art. 81(3)(c)(i). This decision may be appealed. *Id*. art. 81(3)(c)(ii).

79. *Id*. art. 76.

80. *Id*. art. 75(2).

81. *Id*. art. 81(3)(a).

C. Appeal and Revision

Part 8 of the Statute, entitled appeal and revision, addresses the functions of the Appeals Chamber of the Court, the relationship between the Appeals Chamber and the other Chambers of the Court's judiciary, and the rights of the various parties that may eventually come before the Court, including not only the Office of the Prosecutor and the accused, but States, victims and their representatives, to challenge decisions of the Pre-Trial and Trial Chambers and obtain their reversal. The provisions of the Statute on appeal were initially not subject to extensive debate by the Preparatory Committee,[82] although it became increasingly apparent that the role of the Appeals Chamber and its procedure would be important to the legitimacy, fairness and efficient functioning of the Court. Thus, this Part as finally adopted by the Diplomatic Conference is considerably longer than its earlier incarnations, addressing not only appeals against final judgments of a Trial Chamber either convicting or acquitting an accused, but appeals against sentences, interlocutory appeals against other decisions of either the Pre-Trial Chamber or Trial Chamber, appeals to orders of reparations, and, finally, the revision of convictions or sentences upon the discovery of new and material evidence or some taint to the proceedings before the Trial Chamber. Each of these aspects of the Statute will be briefly discussed below.

1. Appeal against Judgment or Sentence

One of the criticisms often leveled at the Nuremberg and Tokyo Charters is that they provided the defendants no right of appeal. Although one could argue that, at the time, the right to appeal was not required by international law, and indeed the Statutes of other international courts

---

82. The 1995 Ad Hoc Committee Report contained only 4 short comments on issues relating to appeal, one of which was whether the Statute should contain a time limit for the lodging of an appeal, *Report of the Ad Hoc Committee on the Establishment of an International Criminal Court*, U.N. GAOR, 50th Sess., Supp. No. 22, at para. 192, U.N. Doc. A/50/22 (1995); the Preparatory Committee Reports for 1996 are virtually silent on the issue of appeal, and in the 1997 Preparatory Committee Reports a discussion of appeal and revision does not appear until the third session of the Preparatory Committee, in December. *Preparatory Committee on the Establishment of an International Criminal Court, Decisions Taken by the Preparatory Committee at its Session Held from 1 to 12 December*, at 43–49, U.N. Doc. No. A/AC.249/1997/L.9/Rev.1 (Dec. 18, 1997).

such as the ICJ and the European Court of Justice[83] contained no appeals provisions, the right of the defendant to an appeal in criminal cases is now enshrined in many major international human rights instruments,[84] as well as the Statutes of the two ad hoc Tribunals.[85] Thus, it is unsurprising that the 1994 Draft Statute of the International Law Commission provided for a right of appeal against a judgment convicting the accused; what may be surprising to lawyers from common law systems, however, is that the ILC's Draft, like the Statutes of the two ad hoc Tribunals, also permit the Prosecutor to appeal an acquittal under certain circumstances. Although this would violate the defendant's right not to be placed "twice in jeopardy" for the same offense in many common law jurisdictions, appeals of acquittals are commonplace in civil law countries,[86] and do not appear to be impermissible under international human rights law.[87] The International Law Commission as well as the Statutes of the two ad hoc Tribunals take the same position as article 81 of the Rome Statute, and provide for appeals by both the Prosecutor and the convicted person of either the judgment or the sentence. As we have seen with regard to other articles of the Statute, however, the provisions of the Rome Treaty regarding the right of appeal are considerably longer than those found in earlier drafts or predecessor instruments, reflecting the extensive work of the Preparatory Committee and the Diplomatic Conference on reconciling diverse points of view.

---

83. The European Court of Justice was initially a court of first and last resort in all cases. With the establishment of the European Court of First Instance, however, the ECJ has taken on appellate functions in some cases.

84. *See, e.g.*, ICCPR, art. 14(5); American Convention on Human Rights, art. (8)(2)(h); Protocol 7, European Convention for the Protection of Human Rights, art. 2. The Universal Declaration of Human Rights and the African [Banjul] Charter on Human and Peoples' Rights do not provide a right of appeal.

85. *ICTY Statute*, art. 25; *ICTR Statute*, art. 24.

86. Mirjan Damaška, *Structures of Authority and Comparative Criminal Procedure*, 84 YALE L. J. 480, 525 (1974); Joseph M. Snee, S.J. and A. Kenneth Pye, *Due Process in Criminal Procedure: A Comparison of Two Systems*, 21 OHIO STATE L. J. 467, 499 (1960); Rachel A. Van Cleave, *An OfferYou Can't Refuse? Punishment without Trial in Italy and the United States: The Search for Truth and an Efficient Criminal Justice System*, 11 EMORY INT'L. L. REV. 419, 428 (1997).

87. Christopher Staker, *Article 81: Appeal against decision of acquittal or conviction or against sentence, in* COMMENTARY ON THE ROME STATUTE OF THE INTERNATIONAL CRIMINAL COURT 1015, 1017 (Otto Triffterer, ed., 1999). *See also* Rafael Nieto-Navia & Barbara Roche, *The Ambit of the Powers under Article 25 of the ICTY Statute: Three Issues of Recent Interest, in* ESSAYS ON ICTY PROCEDURE AND EVIDENCE 473, 481 (Richard May, et al., eds., 2000).

As shown in figure 18, under article 81 of the Statute both the Prosecutor and the convicted person may appeal either a judgment or a sentence on the grounds of procedural error, error of fact or error of law. In addition, the convicted person (but not the Prosecutor, except on the convicted person's behalf),[88] may appeal a conviction on the grounds that the fairness or reliability of the proceedings or decision is at issue.[89] Article 83 of the Statute qualifies the grounds found in article 81 by providing that any errors must be "material" to justify reversing or amending a decision or sentence, or to require a new trial be held. In addition, if the convicted person appeals on the grounds that the proceedings were unfair in some other way, that unfairness must have "affected the reliability of the decision or sentence" to merit relief.[90] In a concession to States concerned about the propriety of the Prosecutor's right to appeal, article 83(2) provides that if only the defendant appeals, the Court may not amend either the Trial Chamber's decision or the Sentence to the appellant's detriment.[91]

Unlike appellate courts in common law countries, the ICC Appeals Chamber will have the right to hear new evidence on appeal and either remand cases to the original Trial Chamber for determination of factual issues, or determine the issues for itself.[92] Thus, the Appeals Chamber

---

88. The right of the Prosecutor to appeal a conviction on the convicted person's behalf stems from the obligation he or she undertakes to pursue truth and justice in each case. *Rome Statute*, art. 54(1)(a); *see also* Prosecutor v. Kupreskić (Case No. IT-95-16-T), Decision on Communications Between the Parties and their Witnesses, para. (ii) (ICTY Trial Chamber II, Sept. 21, 1998) (". . . the Prosecutor of the Tribunal is not, or not only, a Party to adversarial proceedings but is an organ of the Tribunal and an organ of international criminal justice whose object is not simply to secure a conviction but to present the case for the Prosecution, which includes not only inculpatory, but also exculpatory evidence, in order to assist the Chamber to discover the truth in a judicial setting.")

89. *Rome Statute*, art. 81(1).

90. *Id.* art. 83(2). This paragraph appears to contradict article 81(1)(b)(iv) which suggests that a convicted person may raise either unfairness *or* lack of reliability as a grounds of appeal.

91. On the other hand, the ILC Draft would have limited the power of the Appeals Chamber in appeals brought by the Prosecutor to the grant of a new trial, and would not have permitted the Appeals Chamber to reverse or amend a judgment of acquittal itself. *1994 ILC Draft Statute*, art. 49, Commentary at 126.

92. As one commentator has noted, this review does not amount to a full de novo hearing of the case, but is a "corrective procedure." Christopher Staker, *Article 81: Appeal against decision of acquittal or conviction or against sentence, in* COMMENTARY ON THE ROME STATUTE OF THE INTERNATIONAL CRIMINAL COURT 1015, 1019 (Otto Triffterer, ed., 1999). *See also* Prosecutor v. Delalić (Case No. IT-96-21-A), Dissenting Opinion of Judge Bennouna on the Jurisdiction of the Appeals

serves not only to correct the Trial Chamber on points of law, but sits as an independent trier of fact, unbound by the factual findings of the Trial Chamber. Although it is not intended that the appeal should "amount to a retrial," the appeals process in the ICC will thus combine "some of the functions of *appel* in civil law systems with some of the functions of *cassation*."[93] Like the Trial Chamber, the decision of the Appeals Chamber on factual questions need not be unanimous, and is simply a written decision setting forth the majority and minority views on the factual issues presented (but without separate or dissenting opinions).[94] On questions of law, however, the judges of the Appeals Chamber may write separate or dissenting opinions. Although there are many bases upon which to criticize the appropriateness and utility of dissenting and separate opinions of judges in the ICC, as noted in Chapter 4, this compromise reflected the view of many delegations that dissenting opinions could serve a useful jurisprudential function and contribute to the development of customary international law.[95]

2. *Appeal against other Decisions*

Part 8 of the Statute also outlines the scope of interlocutory appeals under the Statute (article 82(1)-(3)), and provides for appeals of orders of reparations (article 82(4)). Article 82 of the Statute had no equivalent in the International Law Commission's 1994 Draft, but as the procedural regime of what would ultimately be the Rome Statute became increasingly complex, it became apparent that an article on interlocutory appeals was desirable.[96] It was not until the April Draft Statute that the predecessor to article 82 appeared in Part 8, in substantially similar form to the final text, with one or two exceptions. Although there was consensus in permitting

---

Chamber to Hear Provisional Release Matters, para. 3 (ICTY Appeals Chamber, Feb. 20, 1999).

93. *1994 ILC Draft Statute*, at 127.

94. *Id.* art. 83(4).

95. Helen Brady & Mark Jennings, *Appeal and Revision, in* THE INTERNATIONAL CRIMINAL COURT: THE MAKING OF THE ROME STATUTE 294, 301 (Roy S. Lee, ed., 1999).

96. A proposal for what would eventually become article 82 first appeared in the Preparatory Committee's 1997 Report (August), as a proposal under article 38, as noted by the December 1997 Preparatory Committee Report, which included a paragraph in article 48 that the "Appeals Chamber may hear interlocutory appeals on the grounds provided for in article 38." *Decisions Taken by the Preparatory Committee at its Session Held from 1 to 12 December 1997*, at 45 (proposed article 48(4)), U.N. Doc. A/AC.249/1997/L.9/Rev.1 (1997).

immediate appeals as a matter of right against decisions on jurisdiction and admissibility, bail arrangements and decisions of the Pre-Trial Chamber under article 56(3),[97] other grounds for immediate appeal, such as orders confirming or denying the indictment or the exclusion of evidence were more controversial, and were ultimately deleted.[98] Due to some delegates' concerns that some bases for interlocutory appeals on other grounds should be preserved, however, the final article as adopted at the Diplomatic Conference is a compromise between the need for appellate guidance on crucial issues and the need for the trial and pretrial proceedings to proceed expeditiously. Thus, in addition to appeals of right with regard to the three categories mentioned above, article 82 permits appeals by leave of the Court against decisions that involve "an issue that would significantly affect the fair and expeditious conduct of the proceedings or the outcome of the trial, and for which, in the opinion of the Pre-Trial or Trial Chamber, an immediate resolution by the Appeals Chamber may materially advance the proceedings."[99]

3. Revision of Conviction or Sentence

Revision, or *révision*, as originally known in French,[100] is a procedure generally unfamiliar to common law systems, although they have certain equivalents.[101] It is an extraordinary remedy,[102] which, although seldom

---

97. This article provides for an investigation ordered by the Pre-Trial Chamber to preserve evidence on its own initiative.

98. *See April Draft Statute*, art. 81; Helen Brady & Mark Jennings, *Appeal and Revision, in* THE INTERNATIONAL CRIMINAL COURT: THE MAKING OF THE ROME STATUTE 294, 300–301 (Roy S. Lee, ed., 1999).

99. *Rome Statute*, art. 82(1)(d). The procedure governing both appeals of right and appeals requiring leave of the Court is set out in Draft RPE 154 through 158.

100. *Le pourvoi en révision* is an extraordinary proceeding whereby a person may attack a conviction on the grounds they were mistakenly convicted. In French law it only benefits the defendant; the State may not reopen an acquittal on the grounds it was erroneously won. Other countries, however, such as Germany and Norway, take the position that both the State and the defendant may bring an action for revision. JEAN PRADEL, PROCEDURE PÉNALE 768–75 (1997).

101. JEAN PRADEL, DROIT PÉNAL COMPARÉ 557–59 (1995). Of course, common law systems also have mechanisms for post-conviction review after the ordinary time for lodging an appeal has run, such as the writ of habeas corpus.

102. For example in France from 1983 to 1988 only nineteen applications for revision were brought to the *Cour de cassation*. Eleven were granted. JEAN PRADEL, PROCEDURE PÉNALE 769 (1997).

successful, provides the opportunity for a convicted person to challenge, after the ordinary time for an appeal has run, the sentence or judgment of conviction on the grounds that the proceedings were fundamentally tainted in some way or that new evidence has been discovered that, had it been introduced at trial, would likely have changed the outcome.[103] Although a right to revision, unlike the right of appeal,[104] is not generally thought to be imposed by the International Covenant on Civil and Political Rights, the Covenant does require that an individual who ultimately has his or her conviction reversed or receives a pardon on the basis of new evidence be compensated for the punishment he or she has suffered.[105] Some have suggested that this provision suggests an "implicit" right of revision. Whether or not this is so, the ILC took the position in its 1994 draft that it was a "necessary guarantee against the possibility of factual error relating to material not available to the accused and therefore not brought to the attention of the Court at the time of the initial trial or of any appeal."[106] Accordingly, the ILC included a provision on revision in article 50 of its 1994 Draft Statute, which the Rome Statute expanded upon considerably.[107]

The ILC draft and the Framers of the Rome Statute rejected the notion of a Prosecutor's right of revision; although the Prosecution may appeal

---

103. *See, e.g.*, N. Code Proc. Pénal, arts. 622–26 (France); *see also* Christopher Staker, *Article 84: Revision of Conviction or Sentence, in* Commentary on the Rome Statute of the International Criminal Court 1037, 1038 n. 2 (Otto Triffterer, ed., 1999).

104. ICCPR art. 14(5).

105. *Id*. art. 14(6).

106. *1994 ILC Draft Statute*, at 128.

107. The right of compensation in the case of wrongful conviction on the basis of new evidence is also found in the Rome Statute, in article 85(2). The Statutes of the two ad hoc tribunals do not recognize the right of revision, *per se*, but do accord both the convicted person and the Prosecutor a right of review if "a new fact [is] discovered which was not known at the time of the proceedings . . . and which could have been a decisive factor in reaching the decision." *ICTY Statute*, art. 26; *ICTR Statute*, art. 25. Unlike the ICC Statute, however, the Statutes of the two ad hoc tribunals permit the Prosecutor to apply on his or her own behalf for revision, presumably of an acquittal, although the Rules limit the Prosecutor's right to do so to one year—the defense is under no such time constraint. *See, e.g.*, ICTR Rule 120; ICTY Rule 119. *See also* Virginia Morris & Michael P. Scharf, I The International Criminal Tribunal for Rwanda 614–16 (1998); Virginia Morris & Michael P. Scharf, I An Insider's Guide to the Tribunal for the Former Yugoslavia 302–03 (1995). As of this writing, the revision provisions of the ICTY and ICTR Statutes have not been considered by those Tribunals. John R.W.D. Jones, The Practice of the International Tribunals 455, 641(2000).

an acquittal or sentence under article 81 of the Statute, the Prosecutor may not apply to have an acquittal "revised," reflecting the view that to permit a Prosecutor to do so would violate the principle of *ne bis in idem*.[108] The Statute permits convicted persons, or certain individuals on their behalf,[109] to bring a claim for revision on three grounds: new evidence has been discovered that was not available at the time of trial and is sufficiently important that had it been proved at trial it would have likely resulted in a different verdict;[110] decisive evidence taken into account at trial, and upon which the conviction depends, was false, forged or falsified; or one or more of the judges who participated in the person's conviction or confirmation of the charges has committed, in that case, an act of serious misconduct or serious breach of duty of sufficient gravity to justify their removal under the Statute.[111] The Draft Rules of Procedure and Evidence

---

108. *1994 ILC Draft Statute*, at 128. Article 83 of the April Draft Statute contained a provision for the Prosecutor to apply for revision of a final judgment of acquittal within five years on the grounds of new evidence, or the confession of the acquitted person of his or her guilt. *April Draft Statute*, art. 83(2). This provision was strongly opposed by some delegations and was ultimately deleted from the Statute.

109. The Statute permits the convicted person, or, after his or her death, "spouses, children, parents or one person alive at the time of the accused's death who [was] given express written instructions from the accused" to bring the claim, or "the Prosecutor on the person's behalf." *Rome Statute*, art. 84(1).

110. *Rome Statute*, art. 84(1)(a). The commentary to the ILC's 1994 Draft Statute suggests that the right to apply for revisions must be based on "new evidence which could have been a *decisive* factor in the conviction. It does not extend, for example, to alleged errors in the assessment of facts presented at the trial or to errors of law or procedure, which are a matter for the appeals process." *1994 ILC Draft Statute*, at 128. The Statute specifies that revision is unavailable if the evidence was attributable to the party making the application. *Id*. art. 84(1)(a)(i). One commentator, citing recent jurisprudence of the Yugoslavia Tribunal, has suggested that defense counsel's decision not to introduce certain evidence for strategic reasons would prevent the defendant from subsequently claiming that the evidence had been unavailable to him or her at the time of conviction or sentence, unless the failure to introduce the evidence was due to gross negligence on the part of counsel. Christopher Staker, *Article 84: Revision of Conviction or Sentence, in* COMMENTARY ON THE ROME STATUTE OF THE INTERNATIONAL CRIMINAL COURT 1037, 1040 (Otto Triffterer, ed., 1999).

111. *See id*. art. 46. Although other grounds for revision were contained in the penultimate draft of the Statute, delegates were concerned that they would encourage misuse of the process, and permit too many collateral attacks upon the Court's judgments. *See* Helen Brady & Mark Jennings, *Appeal and Revision, in* THE INTERNATIONAL CRIMINAL COURT: THE MAKING OF THE ROME STATUTE 294, 303 (Roy S. Lee, ed., 1999).

impose no time limit for the bringing of such a claim, unlike appeals of convictions and sentences which must be brought within thirty days.[112]

D. Sentencing

The substance of the Statute's provisions on penalties was discussed in Chapter 6. This section briefly considers their implementation.[113] First, in the event of a conviction, the Trial Chamber is to consider the appropriate sentence to be imposed. In doing so, the Court may either base its decision on the evidence and submissions presented during the trial, or hold a separate sentencing hearing.[114] Neither the Statute of the Court nor the Draft Rules appear to permit the Court to consider national law when sentencing defendants.[115] Instead, the Court is to take into account the gravity of the crime and the individual circumstances of the convicted person in determining the sentence.[116] In addition, the Rules incorporate several factors for the Court to consider in determining sentences, providing, *inter alia*, that the Court is to:

(a) Bear in mind that the totality of any sentence of imprisonment and fine must reflect the culpability of the convicted person;

---

112. Draft RPE 150(1). The Appeals Chamber may extend the time limit set out in sub-rule 1 for good cause. Draft RPE 150(2).

113. Enforcement of sentences is addressed in Part IV, below.

114. The Trial Chamber *must* hold a sentencing hearing if either the Prosecutor or Defense Counsel request it. However, the request must be made before the completion of the trial, except in cases covered by article 65 (on admissions of guilt). *Rome Statute*, art. 76(2).

115. Compare *ICTY Statute*, art. 24(1) ("In determining the terms of imprisonment, the Trial Chambers shall have recourse to the general practice regarding prison sentences in the courts of the former Yugoslavia."); *ICTR Statute*, art. 23(1) ("In determining the terms of imprisonment, the Trial Chambers shall have recourse to the general practice regarding prison sentences in the courts of Rwanda."). *See generally* Dylan Cors & Siobhán K. Fisher, *National Law in International Criminal Punishment: Yugoslavia's Maximum Prison Sentences and the United Nations War Crimes Tribunal*, 3 PARKER SCH. J. E. EUR. L. 637 (1996). The International Law Commission's 1994 Draft also provided for the Court to consider the national laws of the State of the defendant's nationality, the State where the crime was committed, and the Statute which had custody of and jurisdiction over the accused. *1994 ILC Draft Statute*, art. 47(2).

116. *Rome Statute*, art. 78(1).

(b) balance all the relevant factors, including mitigating and aggravating factors and consider the circumstances of the convicted person as well as the crime; and

(c) give consideration, *inter alia*, to the extent of the damage caused, in particular the harm to the victims and their families; the nature of the unlawful behavior and the means employed to execute the crime; the degree of participation of the convicted person; the degree of intent; the circumstances of manner, time and location; and the age, education, social and economic condition of the convicted person.[117]

A sentence must be imposed for each crime of which the defendant is convicted, and the Court is to decide whether the sentences are to run concurrently or consecutively by pronouncing a joint sentence specifying the total period of imprisonment, which is to be no less than the highest individual sentence pronounced, and no more than thirty years, unless a life sentence has been imposed in accordance with article 77(1)(b).[118]

It is too early to know what theory the Court's judges will employ in sentencing—whether they will adopt a rehabilitative approach, a retributive approach, a deterrence approach, or, as is likely, some combination of the three. Sentences in the ICTY and ICTR have ranged from two and one-half years for a prison commander convicted of the war crime of inhumane treatment,[119] to life imprisonment for the former prime minister of

117. Draft RPE 145(1). Paragraph 2 of the Rule specifies additional factors, both mitigating and aggravating that the Court must consider. Mitigating factors include the presence of grounds for exclusion of criminal responsibility that are present but fall short of excluding responsibility, and the person's conduct after the act. Aggravating circumstances include relevant prior criminal convictions, abuse of power or official capacity, commission of the crime where the victim is particularly defenseless, commission of the crime with particular cruelty or where there were multiple victims, and commission of the crime for any motive involving discrimination on any of the grounds found in article 21(3) of the Statute. Interestingly, none of the factors include the likelihood of the convicted person's recidivism.

118. *Rome Statute*, art. 78(3). The provision reflected a compromise between those who felt that a single sentence should be imposed, and others who favored the practice of the two ad hoc tribunals, which assigned sentences for each crime of which the defendant was convicted, and then specified whether they were to be served concurrently or consecutively. See ICTY Rule 101(c) ("The Trial Chamber shall indicate whether multiple sentences shall be served consecutively or concurrently.") ICTR Rule 101(c) ("The Trial Chamber shall indicate whether multiple sentences shall be served consecutively or concurrently.").

119. Prosecutor v. Aleksovski (Case No. IT-95-14/1-T), Judgment, paras. 236–38 (ICTY Trial Chamber I, June 25, 1999).

Rwanda convicted of genocide, incitement to commit genocide and conspiracy to commit genocide.[120] Like the two Tribunals, the Court will need to strike a balance between the need for severe sentences to be imposed on those convicted of extremely serious crimes and the need to distinguish between those of differing levels of culpability. While the Statute permits the judges fairly extensive discretion in developing their sentencing practices,[121] it is important that this flexibility does not prevent them from developing consistency in their sentencing judgments over time. As others have noted, the work of the Court is not limited to the prosecution and punishment of individuals, but is intended to contribute to a normative framework to combat impunity, maintain international peace and security, and assist in national reconciliation and truth-finding.[122] A just, consistent and proportionate sentencing practice will advance that goal.[123]

---

120. Prosecutor v. Kambanda (Case No. ICTR-97-23), Judgment and Sentence, paras. 40, 63–82 (ICTR Trial Chamber I, Sept. 4, 1998).

121. This is in direct contrast to trends in some countries such as the United States, for example, where judges' flexibility in sentencing have been recently constrained by legislative initiatives. *See, e.g.*, Roger S. Clark, *The United States Federal Sentencing Guidelines: Who is Watching the Makers of Grids*, 11 CRIM. L. FORUM 249 (2000); Ronald F. Wright, *Rules for Sentencing Revolutions*, 108 YALE L. J. 1355 (1999), *reviewing* KATE STITH & JOSÉ CABRANES, FEAR OF JUDGING: SENTENCING GUIDELINES IN THE FEDERAL COURTS (1998). For a comparative treatment of sentencing *see* Daniel B. Pickard, *Proposed Sentencing Guidelines for the International Criminal Court*, 20 LOY. L. A. INT'L & COMP. L. J. 123, 140–63 (1997).

122. *Accord* Jan Christoph Nemitz and Steffen Wirth, *Some observations on the law of sentencing of the ICC, available at* <http://www/menshenrechte.de/hrww/1nov99/nemitz.htm>.

123. As noted in Chapter 6, the ICTY Appeals Chamber originally held that if an offense was charged and proven as a crime against humanity, it should entail a heavier penalty than if it were proceeded upon on the basis that it was a war crime. It subsequently reversed itself, holding that there was in law no distinction between the seriousness of a crime against humanity and that of a war crime. Prosecutor v. Duško Tadić (Case No. I-94-1A), *Judgment in Sentencing Appeals* (ICTY Appeals Chamber, Jan. 26, 2000). This reversal of position has been criticized on the grounds that the Appeals Chamber's rejection of its own recent jurisprudence could impair the credibility of the Tribunal. Rafael Nieto-Navia & Barbara Roche, *The Ambit of the Powers under Article 25 of the ICTY Statute: Three Issues of Recent Interest, in* ESSAYS ON ICTY PROCEDURE AND EVIDENCE 473, 489–92 (Richard May, et al., eds., 2000).

II. RIGHTS OF PERSONS SUSPECTED OR ACCUSED OF A CRIME

A critical component of any system of criminal justice is the rights it guarantees to those suspected or accused of crimes, and the International Criminal Court is no exception. Article 21(3) of the Statute, as discussed previously, requires the Court to apply and interpret its Statute, as well as any other applicable law, in accordance with "internationally recognized human rights" and without any adverse distinction on the grounds enumerated therein. In addition, the Framers of the Statute have incorporated an extensive set of protections for defendants and potential defendants before the Court. These rights are not only intended to protect the procedural integrity of the criminal process but, hopefully, the substantive fairness of the ultimate result.[124]

As one might expect, however, compiling a list of rights upon which consensus could be reached by the delegates to the Diplomatic Conference was quite difficult. As with other parts of the Statute, each State had a tendency to view the rights guaranteed by its own system of criminal justice as essential. A compromise position had to be found as to the substance of the rights guaranteed as well as when during the investigative and prosecutorial phases they should attach.[125]

In terms of process, the Statute contains many protections for a person suspected or accused of a crime,[126] and at each stage of the investigation or trial certain objections to the proceedings are available. These include the right to challenge the jurisdiction of the Court or the admissibility of a case,[127] to request interim release pending surrender[128] or trial,[129] the right to confirmation of the charges prior to trial,[130] to prompt review upon surrender,[131] to a trial in his or her presence that is fair,

---

124. *See generally* THE RIGHT TO A FAIR TRIAL (David Weissbrodt & Rüdiger Wolfrum, eds., 1996).

125. For the negotiating history of this part of the Statute see Håkan Friman, *Rights of Persons Suspected or Accused of a Crime, in* THE INTERNATIONAL CRIMINAL COURT: THE MAKING OF THE ROME STATUTE 247, 248–55 (Roy S. Lee, ed., 1999).

126. Due to difficulties the delegates had in agreeing to a particular definition of "suspect," the term does not appear in the Statute. The Statute employs the term "accused" but is unclear as to when a person suspected of a crime becomes an accused, although by implication it would appear to be upon confirmation of the charges and their commitment to a trial chamber for trial. *Rome Statute*, art. 61(7).

127. *Id.* art. 19(2)(a).

128. *Rome Statute*, art. 59(3).

129. *Id.* art. 60(2).

130. *Id.* art. 61.

131. *Id.* art. 60(1).

public and expeditious,[132] and to appeal his or her conviction.[133]

In addition, the Statute contains significant substantive protections for those under investigation by the Prosecutor or accused of a crime. Somewhat confusingly, these protections are sprinkled throughout the Statute, and attach at different times.[134] Article 55, for example, which is part of Part 5 (Investigation and Prosecution), specifies the rights of persons during an investigation. Article 67, on the other hand, which is found in Part 6 (The Trial), outlines the rights of the accused. Although the Statute improves on the ILC draft considerably, both in terms of the scope and content of the rights provisions, the Statute takes a less comprehensive approach to the incorporation of protections for defendants and potential defendants than might have been hoped. For example, the Statute provides that defendants before the Court are presumed innocent until proven guilty, and the Prosecutor has the burden of proof to establish the accused's guilt beyond a reasonable doubt in order to obtain a conviction.[135] Presumably those under investigation by the Court benefit from the presumption of innocence as well, but the placement of the article in the section on the trial and its absence from the Statute's provisions on investigation raises the question.[136]

The basic guarantees of article 14 of the International Covenant on Civil and Political Rights have been incorporated into the ICC Statute, and in some instances expanded: the right to a public hearing, to be informed of the charges against him or her, to have counsel and adequate time to

---

132. *Id.* art. 64.

133. *See* Chapter 8, Section I(C).

134. The International Law Commission's draft included the rights of the accused in Part 5 (the Trial) of its 1994 Draft. This was criticized on the grounds that the rights and protections of the defense should apply to the entire process, not just the trial proceedings, and it was suggested that all the rights of the accused be placed together in a separate part of the Statute, or included in some other way so as to make clear that they apply to all the proceedings before the Court, not just the trial. *See, e.g.*, Christopher L. Blakesley, *Commentary on Parts 5 and 6 of the Zutphen Intersessional Draft: Investigation, Prosecution & Trial, in* OBSERVATIONS ON THE CONSOLIDATED ICC TEXT BEFORE THE FINAL SESSION OF THE PREPARATORY COMMITTEE, *13bis* NOUVELLES ÉTUDES PÉNALES 69 (Leila Sadat Wexler, special ed., 1998).

135. *Rome Statute*, art. 66.

136. Another example is article 55(1)(b) which provides that a person shall not be subjected to any form of coercion, duress or threat, to torture or to any other form of cruel, inhuman or degrading treatment or punishment in respect of an investigation. This provision would presumably have broader application, as its prohibitions should also apply to the trial. Its placement in Part 5, however, makes its application to Part 6 less than certain, an inelegance in the Statute that is unfortunate.

prepare a defense, to choose one's counsel freely and to have counsel free of charge for indigent defendants, the right to remain silent,[137] to have the proceedings in a language understood by the accused or to have, free of charge, an interpreter, the right to confront his or her accusers and to be tried without undue delay.[138] These rights, which are expressly stated to be "minimum guarantees" by article 67 of the Statute,[139] receive further elaboration elsewhere. For example, the general and arguably vague right to be "tried without undue delay"[140] is supported by other specific procedural rights found elsewhere in the Statute: not to be detained for an unreasonable period,[141] and to receive a trial that is "fair and expeditious."[142] Each of these enumerated rights, although generally known to most legal systems in some form or another, will no doubt take on a slightly different meaning as employed by the Court.[143] As one delegate noted during the Statute's negotiation, even a term such as fair trial is "capable of as many interpretations as there . . . [are] criminal procedures in the world."[144] Moreover, as is the case in national legal systems, a right is rarely absolute. For example, the Court is only required to appoint counsel for indigent defendants if the "interests of justice" so require, a caveat which has been criticized by scholars.[145] Similarly, the Statute's exclusionary rule, which requires the Court to exclude evidence obtained in violation of this Statute or internationally recognized human rights, applies only if either the violation casts substantial doubt on the reliability of the evidence, or the admission of the evidence would be antithetical

---

137. The Statute also states that the defendant's silence may not be a consideration in the determination of guilt or innocence, which goes further than the corresponding provision of the ICCPR.

138. *Rome Statute*, art. 67.

139. *Id.* art. 67(1).

140. *Id.* art. 67(1)(c).

141. *Id.* art. 60(4).

142. *Id.* art. 64(2).

143. The term "reasonable doubt" for example, although employed by common law countries, is unknown to the civil law.

144. *See* George E. Edwards, *International Human Rights Law Challenges to the International* Criminal *Court: Right to Privacy in the Search and Seizure Context*, 26 YALE J. INT'L L. 1, n. 97 (2001), *quoting* U.N. Doc. A/Conf. 183 (1998).

145. *Rome Statute*, art. 67(d). This provision has been ably criticized on the grounds that although it complies with the text of the ICCPR, the Covenant envisioned situations where offenses might be minor in character, not situations in which the defendants are charged with the most serious crimes of concern to the international community as a whole such as genocide, crimes against humanity and war crimes. Kenneth S. Gallant, *The Role and Powers of Defense Counsel in the Rome Statute of the International Criminal Court*, 34 INT'L LAWYER 21, 25 (2000).

to and would seriously damage the integrity of the proceedings.[146] Thus, the fairness of the system of rights protections embodied in the Statute will ultimately depend upon its interpretation by the personnel of the Court. This may be problematic given that, as discussed earlier, the one institution omitted by the Framers is a "public defenders office," meaning that the protection of the rights of the accused will depend on the zeal and competence of his or her attorney, and will be ad hoc rather than institutionalized. Finally, although the Statute contains certain remedies for wrongful conduct of the Prosecutor which prejudices the accused or individual under investigation,[147] most of the rights within the Statute are not associated with any particular remedies. Again, it will be up to the Court to determine how aggressively to sanction the Prosecutor for any transgressions, and to develop a jurisprudence that will strongly affirm the rights within the Statute. Although some have criticized the proceedings of the two ad hoc Tribunals as "plagued with liberal safeguards,"[148] it is crucial that the proceedings of the Court are both fair and perceived to be fair by the accused and the international community, a point which will be critically important to establishing the legitimacy of the Court's work.

III. THE STATE COOPERATION REGIME

Part 9 of the Statute, entitled "International Cooperation and Judicial Assistance," is one of the most complex sections of the Rome Treaty. The

---

146. *Rome Statute*, art. 69(6). *See* George E. Edwards, *International Human Rights Law Challenges to the International Criminal Court: Right to Privacy in the Search and Seizure Context*, 26 YALE J. INT'L L. 1 (2001).

147. These include (1) a right to compensation for anyone who has been the victim of unlawful arrest or detention, or who has suffered punishment as a result of a miscarriage of justice, *Rome Statute* art. 85; the right to have evidence suppressed if it is obtained by means of a violation of the Statute or international recognized human rights norms *if* the violation causes substantial doubt on the reliability of the evidence or its admission would be antithetical to and would seriously damage the integrity of the proceedings, *id.* art. 69(6); and the right to release pending trial if a person has been detained for an unreasonable period due to inexcusable delay by the Prosecutor, *id.* art. 60(4).

148. Tom Farer, *Restraining the Barbarians: Can International Criminal Law Help?*, 22 HUM. RTS. Q. 90, 92–98 (2000). A slightly different critique has been made by some members of the Office of the Prosecutor, who point out that many of the defendants they pursue are not "small fish" who require protection from the State, but are leaders and military officials who control a State, and whom the Office of the Prosecutor has great difficulty bringing to book.

17 articles of this Part, which are complemented by 22 Draft Rules,[149] address the interaction between the Court and States in the arrest and transfer of suspects to the Court, and in the conduct of investigations or prosecutions by the Court on State territory. Not surprisingly, Part 9 is the least "supranational" section of the Treaty. Although article 86 requires States Parties to "cooperate fully with the Court in its investigation and prosecution of crimes,"[150] and should be accorded at least some normative effect,[151] the articles that follow are so riddled with exceptions and qualifications that it is difficult to view this as anything but an exhortation. The equivocations of the text underscore the fragile consensus that brought the States of the world together in Rome to approve the Treaty; indeed, it suggests that while States agree to the establishment of the Court in principle, and even to its jurisdiction in theory, they are not willing to make the concessions to international cooperation that are needed to make the Court a success in practice.[152]

Without dismissing the complexities of Part 9, a few generalizations can be made. First, the Statute essentially bifurcates the type of assistance the Court may request of States into two categories: requests for the arrest and surrender of persons to the Court, and requests for anything else the Court might need to conduct investigations and prosecutions under the Statute. As shown in Figure 12, as a matter of principle, States Parties must comply with a request from the Court for the arrest and surrender of a

---

149. Draft RPE 176–97.

150. It is the State and not its officials to whom the command is directed. Claus Kreß, *Article 86: General obligation to cooperate, in* COMMENTARY ON THE ROME STATUTE OF THE INTERNATIONAL CRIMINAL COURT 1051, 1052 (Otto Triffterer, ed., 1999). Nevertheless, presumably under certain circumstances an official's refusal to cooperate could engender State Responsibility.

151. Claus Kreß, *Article 86: General obligation to cooperate, in* COMMENTARY ON THE ROME STATUTE OF THE INTERNATIONAL CRIMINAL COURT 1051, 1053 (Otto Triffterer, ed., 1999). Kreß notes that the *principe de l'effet utile*, often employed by the European Court of Justice in its interpretation of the Community Treaties, would suggest that article 86 has more than merely precatory value. This is no doubt correct; but even a teleological reading of article 86 along with the other provisions of Part 9 does not suggest that the cooperation provisions impose particularly firm constraints on State behavior.

152. For a more positive assessment of Part 9, see Claus Kreß, Kimberly Prost, Angelika Schlunck, Peter Wilkitzki, *Part 9, International Cooperation and Judicial Assistance, Preliminary Remarks, in* COMMENTARY ON THE ROME STATUTE OF THE INTERNATIONAL CRIMINAL COURT 1045, 1045–50 (Otto Triffterer, ed., 1999). The authors suggest that the ICC's cooperation regime departs considerably from the purely international law "horizontal" model of interstate cooperation, and adopts at least elements of a more flexible and supranational "vertical" model.

person,[153] while non-States Parties are under no such obligation.[154] The same is true with respect to requests for other forms of assistance. Although States Parties will be required to adapt their national law to ensure that they are able to fulfill their cooperation obligations under the Statute,[155] a significant residual role remains for national law which will continue to control the form and procedure governing requests for assistance,[156] as well as the execution of such requests, with a very few exceptions.[157]

As shown in Figure 21, article 89 sets forth the general framework for arrest and surrender. The text defines "surrender" as "the delivering up of a person by a State to the Court, pursuant to this Statute." By way of contrast, "extradition" means the delivering up of a person by one State to another as provided by treaty, convention, or national legislation."[158] The inclusion of the two definitions,[159] and the adoption of the term "surrender" to describe the rendering of persons to the Court, helped the dele-

---

153. By "persons," the Statute is presumably tracking earlier drafts in which "persons" included "suspects," "accused," and "convicted persons." *Zutphen Intersessional Draft*, at 226 n. 281.

154. *Rome Statute*, art. 79.

155. *Id.* art. 88. Of course, State cooperation is likely to become problematic in practice, if the experience of the two ad hoc Tribunals is any guide. *See, e.g.*, Göran Sluiter, *To Cooperate or not to Cooperate?: The Case of the Failed Transfer of Ntakirutimana to the Rwanda Tribunal*, 11 LEIDEN J. INT'L L. 383 (1998).

156. *See, e.g., id.* arts. 91(2)(c), 96(2)(e), 99(1).

157. One such exception is article 99(4)(a), which permits the Prosecutor to execute requests that can be performed without any compulsory measures directly on the territory of a State Party if the crime is alleged to have been committed on the territory of that State and there has been a determination of admissibility in the case. The Prosecutor must enter into "all possible consultations" with the requested State Party, as well. *Id.* art. 99(4)(a).

158. *Rome Statute*, art. 102. It has been asked whether this language is consistent with the Geneva Conventions of 1949, which allow a Contracting Party to "hand . . . over for trial" to another Contracting Party those who have committed grave breaches of the Conventions. Geneva Convention I, art. 49; Geneva Convention II, art. 50; Geneva Convention III, art. 129; Geneva Convention IV, art. 146. *See* ALFRED P. RUBIN, ETHICS AND AUTHORITY IN INTERNATIONAL LAW 179–80 (1997). Protocol I, however, uses "extradition." Protocol Additional to the Geneva Conventions of 12 August 1949, and Relating to the Protection of Victims of International Armed Conflicts, June 8, 1977, 1125 U.N.T.S. 3. No doubt this will remain an issue for the Court to resolve, as the terminology ultimately adopted by the Framers to describe the rendering of persons to the Court is *sui generis*.

159. In fact, three different terms were proposed—extradite, surrender, and transfer. *See, e.g., April Draft Statute*, art. 87, entitled "[Surrender][Transfer] [Extradition] of persons to the Court."

gates resolve a difficult terminological debate that was much more than semantic.[160] First, it emphasizes the vertical as opposed to the horizontal nature of the cooperation regime established by the Statute. Second, many States would have encountered grave legal and constitutional difficulties "extraditing" their national to the Court, and use of the term "surrender" helped them avoid these difficulties considerably.

The arrest warrant must be in writing and in a form required by the Requested State.[161] Although States may not impose documentary requirements upon the Court that are more burdensome than those they require for extradition requests pursuant to treaties, and the Statute exhorts States to make the requests less burdensome "if possible,"[162] this lack of uniformity will necessarily make it more difficult for the Court by impeding it from developing a "Standard" surrender request.

In addition, as shown in Figure 21, the Statute contemplates eight separate difficulties that might arise with respect to any particular request for arrest and transfer. Some of these are the natural result of the Court's position in a world in which there are many entities that may have overlapping jurisdiction with the Court in a particular case. For example, the person might be already serving a sentence for a different crime, in which case the State has the option of surrendering the individual to the Court.[163] Other problems, however, stem from the complementarity principle, which denies any primacy to the jurisdiction, investigation, and prosecutions of the Court. For example, a State may be prevented from executing a request from the Court if that request "would require a State to breach a pre-existing treaty obligation undertaken with respect to another State."[164] This extremely broad provision appears to permit States Parties to escape their obligations to the Court, and permits States Parties, not the Court, the final word on the obligations a State must satisfy in the event of

160. Phakiso Mochochoko, *International Cooperation and Judicial Assistance, in* THE INTERNATIONAL CRIMINAL COURT: THE MAKING OF THE ROME STATUTE 305, 309–10 (Roy S. Lee, ed., 1999).

161. *Rome Statute*, art. 91(2)(c). The warrant and request for arrest and surrender must be accompanied by a request for transit if a person is being transported to the Court through third party States. Again, only States Parties are required to permit the transit of the detainee through their territories. *Id.* art. 89(3).

162. *Rome Statute*, art. 91(2)(c).

163. *Id.* art. 89(4). Under article 101, the Statute incorporates the "rule of speciality" pursuant to which, the person may be proceeded against only for the conduct that formed the basis of the crimes for which the person was surrendered to the Court, unless a waiver of the rule is obtained from the surrendering State.

164. *Id.* art. 97(c).

a conflict. This fairly broad provision is arguably qualified by article 90 of the Statute, which addresses the most likely preexisting treaty obligation —a competing request for extradition for the person sought by the Court.

The Statute divides competing requests into two categories—requests that address the same conduct that forms the basis of the crime for which the Court seeks the person's surrender;[165] and requests for extradition for conduct other than that which constitutes the crime for which the Court seeks the person's surrender.[166] As to the first category of requests, unless the Court has already determined that the case is admissible, the requested State need not surrender the person to the Court unless the Court ultimately determines the case is admissible, and the State requesting extradition is also a party to the ICC Statute.[167] If the State requesting extradition is not a party to the Statute, the requested State is under no obligation to surrender the person to the Court even though they may be a State Party to the Statute. Rather, the State need only consider "all the relevant factors" in determining whether to extradite the person to the requesting State or surrender the person to the Court.[168] In the case of competing requests that address conduct different from that which constitutes the crime for which the Court is seeking surrender, the requested State is to give priority to the request from the Court unless the competing request represents an existing international obligation to extradite the person to the requesting State, in which case the requested State is to balance the "relevant factors" in determining whether to give priority to the Court.[169]

With respect to other forms of cooperation in relation to investigations or prosecutions, States Parties remain under a general obligation of assistance to the Court.[170] This assistance may take many forms, some of which are listed in article 93(1), and includes the taking of evidence, service of documents, facilitating the voluntary appearance of persons as witnesses or experts before the Court, questioning persons being investigated or prosecuted by the Court, the freezing or seizing of proceeds, property, assets, and instrumentalities of crimes, and other such matters. Conspicuously absent is any subpoena power. That is, neither the judges nor

---

165. *Id.* art. 90(1).
166. *Id.* art. 90(7).
167. *Id.* art. 90(2).
168. *Id.* art. 90(6).
169. *Id.* art. 90(7)(b).
170. *Id.* art. 93(1). *See generally* Kimberly Prost & Angelika Schlunck, *Article 93: Other forms of cooperation, in* COMMENTARY ON THE ROME STATUTE OF THE INTERNATIONAL CRIMINAL COURT 1101, 1101–118 (Otto Triffterer, ed., 1999).

the Prosecutor of the ICC (or defense counsel, presumably) have any power to compel witnesses to appear.[171] Moreover, as shown in Figure 23, States may rely on several provisions of the Statute to either deny or postpone execution of requests for cooperation. Again, most of these provisions, such as the national security exception in article 72, respond to legitimate concerns of States. Many others are vaguely drafted,[172] however, and may provide States unwilling to cooperate with the Court ample justification for refusing the Court's requests.

Interestingly, the Statute makes no provision for circumventing the State Cooperation regime in the event of a Security Council referral, rather than a complaint filed by a State or the Prosecutor *proprio motu*. Thus, while there is a general feeling that Security Council referrals to the Court would be endowed with "primacy" jurisdiction, like those to the ICTY and the ICTR, at least insofar as State Cooperation goes,[173] this is unsupported by a reading of the Statute. While the Security Council could, of course, attempt to assist the Court by using its binding authority pursuant to Chapter VII,[174] it is unclear how "binding orders" from the Security Council would interface with the very specific commands of the Statute that address the problems of State Cooperation. Finally, under the Statute, any failure to cooperate with the Court, even by States Parties, may not be directly sanctioned by the Court.[175] Instead, the Court may only refer the matter to the Assembly of States Parties or to the Security Council, if the Security Council referred the case to the Court.[176]

---

171. Article 93(7) permits the temporary transfer of persons in custody for purposes of identification or for obtaining testimony, however, the State is not required to agree to the transfer, which is subject, in any event, to the consent of the person transferred. *Rome Statute*, art. 93(7).

172. For example, article 93(3) permits States to refuse assistance if it is prohibited on the basis of "an existing fundamental legal principle of general application." *Id*. art. 93(3).

173. Michael P. Scharf, *Results of the Rome Conference for an International Criminal Court*, ASIL INSIGHT (Aug. 1998) <http://www.asil.org/insigh23.htm>.

174. If the Security Council desires primacy, it may so state in its referral.

175. Note that this will also impact on the rights of defendants, as their access to essential information will be severely impacted by non-cooperation.

176. *Rome Statute*, art. 87(7). If the ICC follows the jurisprudence of the ICTY in the *Blaskić* Case, it would not be permitted to make any recommendations of suggestions as to the course of action the Security Council may wish to take. Prosecutor v. Blaskić (Case No. IT-95-14-A), Judgment on the Request of the Republic of Croatia For Review of the Decision of Trial Chamber II of 18 July 1997, para. 36 (ICTY Appeals Chamber, Oct. 29, 1997).

IV. ENFORCEMENT OF SENTENCES

The International Criminal Court will issue a variety of judgments in addition to requests for cooperation, including, *inter alia*, preliminary rulings on matters such as admissibility, final judgments of conviction or acquittal, sentencing judgments imposing terms of imprisonment, judgments imposing fines or forfeitures of proceeds, and judgments ordering reparations to victims. The recognition and enforcement of these judgments by States will be critical to the successful operation of the Court because the Court's own direct enforcement jurisdiction is so weak. Yet, the Statute does not treat recognition of each of these types of judgments comprehensively. Instead, the enforcement regimes applicable to different kinds of judgments are found in different places in the Statute, or are simply implied by virtue of a State's ratification or accession to the ICC Treaty.

Preliminary rulings, for example, are presumptively binding on States Parties through their adherence to the Court's Statute. The Statute makes clear in numerous ways that the Court, and not States Parties, is the final arbiter of its own jurisdiction, the admissibility of a case, and the admissibility of evidence. Thus, any State agreeing to be a party to the Statute must presumably ensure its entire cooperation with the Court in this way. The Statute is silent as to the enforcement of preliminary rulings, however, perhaps because their validity, at least on the merits, may not be questioned by States Parties. Nonetheless, because the Statute does not impose upon States any change in the manner in which they treat international law, leaving it to each State to use its own Constitutional mechanism to recognize the Court's orders, their effect in national legal orders might ultimately require their "conversion" into national law. Acquittals by the Court have a similar status, with one caveat. Pursuant to article 20, States Parties to the Statute have an affirmative obligation to accord finality to acquittals by the Court (as well as convictions), pursuant to the *ne bis in idem* principle incorporated in article 20.

Convictions by the Court receive the same treatment as acquittals, but are, in addition, covered by an extensive procedural regime. Because the Court will not have its own police force or its own jails, it must rely upon the cooperation of States not only to effectuate arrests and gather evidence, but to enforce its sentences and judgments of fines or forfeitures. The nine articles of Part 10 of the Statute address this problem, and cover enforcement of sentences of imprisonment, as well as fines and forfeiture measures imposed by the Court.

Under this Part of the Statute, it is envisioned that States will "volunteer" to accept persons sentenced by the Court, and it is for the

Presidency[177] to designate which State will receive a particular individual, based upon a set of factors included in article 103(3) of the Statute. Additionally, the Court, and not the State of enforcement supervises the sentence and decides any application for appeal and revision,[178] or reduction of sentence.[179] The Court is also directed to ensure that the conditions of imprisonment, which are generally governed by the law of the State of enforcement, comply with widely accepted international treaty standards governing the treatment of prisoners.[180] This regime is predicated, of course, on the cooperativeness of States, which may turn out to be problematic if the experience of the two ad hoc Tribunals is any indication. In a report presented to the Preparatory Commission in April 2000, the ICTY noted that in the seven years since the Tribunal had been established, it had been able to secure only six enforcement agreements with States, many of which had attached significant conditions or restrictions to those agreements.[181] Difficulties reported by the Tribunal include security issues, inadequate domestic implementing legislation, insufficient prison facilities or standards and financial concerns.[182] As of this writing, the situation is not much improved.[183] To address the possibility that States would be slow (or, worse, completely unwilling) to agree to take prisoners from the ICC, the Rome Statute provides in article 103(4) that if no State is designated (or available), then the sentence "shall be served in a prison facility made available by the host State," in which case the costs of enforcement will be borne not by the State of enforcement, but by the Court.[184] This provision should ensure that the Court has the facilities to provide for the detention of convicted individuals. What it may mean in practice, however, is that rather than States sharing the burden of imprisoning the world's war criminals, The Netherlands will not only be host to the world's courts, but the jailer of its most serious criminals.

---

177. Draft RPE 199.

178. *Rome Statute*, art. 105(2).

179. *Id.* art. 110(2).

180. *Id.* arts. 106(1) & (2).

181. *Contributions of the Chambers of the International Tribunal for the Former Yugoslavia on the Provisional rules of procedure and evidence for the Court, submitted to the Prepatory Commission at its 13–31 March 2000 session*, U.N. Doc. PCNICC/2000/WGRPE(10)/INF/1 (April 5, 2000).

182. *Id.* at 3.

183. Mary Margaret Penrose, *It's Good to Be the King!: Prosecuting Heads of State and Former Heads of State Under International Law*, 39 COL. J. TRANSNAT'L L. 193, 213 (2000) (noting seven enforcement agreements with the ICTY and two with the ICTR).

184. *Rome Statute*, art. 103(4).

CHAPTER 9

CUSTOMARY INTERNATIONAL LAW AND THE ICC

> *[I]t is essential, if man is not to be compelled to have recourse, as a last resort, to rebellion against tyranny and oppression, that human rights should be protected by the rule of law . . .*
>
> —Universal Declaration of Human Rights

Many hoped that through the establishment of a permanent international criminal court the normative content of international criminal law would be substantially advanced. Indeed, the prospect of drafting a Statute for the ICC presented a unique opportunity to codify, advance, and refine the existing law.[1] At the very least, an advantage of codifying the law would be that State practice arguably inconsistent with the normative principles of customary law would not comprise evidence that the custom was no longer accepted, but would, instead, constitute a breach of the norm.[2] As the drafting of the ICC treaty proceeded, however, the disadvantages of codification also became clear. Indeed, it began to seem that there might be a fundamental incompatibility between the political agendas of States and the process of codifying, in a progressive manner, the customary international law of war and crimes against humanity. Thus, the codification process was fated to produce a text that represented a set of political compromises, rather than a new set of progressive norms criminalizing behavior on a broad scale.[3]

---

1. Pursuant to article 13 of the U.N. Charter, the General Assembly can "initiate studies . . . encouraging the progressive development of international law and its codification; . . ." U.N. CHARTER art. 13.

2. One of the most articulate and thorough treatments of the interaction between treaty law, state practice, and custom can be found in the *Nicaragua* case before the International Court of Justice. Case Concerning Military and Paramilitary Activities in and Against Nicaragua (Nicaragua v. U.S.) (Merits) 1986 I.C.J. 14.

3. As Otto Triffterer notes, there was little agreement during the drafting

Seemingly to ensure that the codification of some international criminal law in the ICC Statute would not negatively impact either the existing customary international framework or the development of new customary law, a unique provision was introduced during the Preparatory Committee's negotiations on the ICC. This proposal eventually became article 10 of the Court's Statute, and provides: "[n]othing in this Part of the Statute shall be interpreted as limiting or prejudicing in any way existing or developing rules of international law for purposes other than this Statute."[4]

It has been argued that article 10 expresses already accepted principles of international law.[5] Under this view, article 10 merely restates the obvious by emphasizing the linkage between the prescriptive norms of the Statute and the adjudicative mechanism established to apply them. Yet there is more to article 10 than meets the eye. First, it raises many fascinating questions about the relationship between the codified multilateral treaty provisions inside the ICC Statute ("Rome law") and the uncodified norms of customary international law outside the Statute. Second, its application may become problematic when considered in light of the ICC's jurisdictional mechanisms, which, as noted in Chapter 5, permit the Security Council to apply Rome law to all the human beings in the world, whether or not their State of nationality is a party to the Statute. If it is correct that the prescriptive norms of the Statute are universal in application, it appears paradoxical that article 10 of the Statute expressly attempts to deny them the status of custom, at least insofar as they might restrict existing or developing rules of customary international law, which would also bind all States. May the international community of States have it both ways, asserting on the one hand universal "laws" made by treaty, and on the other hand a different universal "law" established by custom?

Having substantive laws inside and outside the Statute that differ from each other seems troubling, at least at first. It disturbs our settled ideas about the unitary nature of international law, raises the specter of

---

process as to whether a codification of international law "should merely declare and systematize existing rules or also include 'progressive development' [of international law]" as the United Nations Charter and Statute of the International Law Commission contemplate. Otto Triffterer, *Article 10, in* COMMENTARY ON THE ROME STATUTE FOR THE INTERNATIONAL CRIMINAL COURT 315, 316 (Otto Triffterer, ed., 1999).

4. A similar provision, article 80, was introduced in respect of the penalties provisions of the Statute, the negotiation of which also required a great deal of compromise.

5. Otto Triffterer, *Article 10, in* COMMENTARY ON THE ROME STATUTE FOR THE INTERNATIONAL CRIMINAL COURT 315, 317 (Otto Triffterer, ed., 1999).

individuals being subject to multiple, overlapping and arguably conflicting legal obligations, and disrupts our theories about how international law is made. But as a practical matter, the nature and substance of the law that is being applied is inseparable from the jurisdiction applying it. The question is what entity is applying the law, to whom, and for what purpose? Ultimately it appears that having law inside the ICC Statute differ from the law outside the Statute is inevitable. Countries may decide to advance the substance of the laws of war and humanity beyond the collection of compromises codified in the Rome Statute. Customary international law is both the product and the source of this evolution—indeed, article 10 underscores the Framers' wish to preserve the role of custom in the development of normative standards of conduct in the area of international criminal justice.

Upon further reflection, article 10 seems both innovative and politically astute. Its theoretical basis, purpose and ultimate effect are best understood if one views the Diplomatic Conference as a quasi-legislative event that produced a criminal code for the world. The Framers recognized the political compromises they were obliged to make in creating this code of minimum conduct, and they therefore expressly decided, *ex ante*, to set out the relationship of Rome law to non-Rome law. That this is perfectly acceptable as a matter of theory seems apparent, even if it is bold. But because the revolution wrought by Rome was achieved *sotto voce*, without an explicit or even implicit recognition by the surrounding infrastructures of the international and domestic legal orders, article 10's effect as a practical matter is likely to be quite limited. Nonetheless, because national law and customary international law will continue to establish rules of conduct in the areas of war crimes and crimes against humanity, article 10 retains tremendous importance not as a rule of decision but as a principle of interpretation. It is an explicit acknowledgment that the Statute establishes *minimum* rules of conduct and that others (and the Court itself) must read it that way.[6] In this way, article 10 stands as a testament to the idealism that propelled the governments and peoples of the world to come to Rome to construct a uniform criminal code for the world—idealism that was tempered by the political reality of difficult diplomatic negotiations.

---

6. Article 80 has a slightly different thrust, simply articulating that the penalty provisions of the Statute are a negotiated compromise, and without prejudice to national rules on penalties, which may be either more or less severe.

I. DEVELOPING DEFINITIONS OF CRIMES

Three years after the General Assembly requested the ILC to resume work on the ICC, a Working Group of the Commission issued a report outlining the general bases upon which, in its opinion, the establishment of the international criminal court could proceed. With respect to the definition of crimes and the jurisdiction of the Court, the Working Group assumed that the customary international law and treaties on the subject would be incorporated by reference into the ICC Statute, rather than codified therein.[7] A complex regime of State consent accompanied the definitional articles, but it is noteworthy that neither article 22 nor article 26 of the 1993 draft statute, which outlined the two strands of the Court's proposed jurisdiction,[8] attempted to define the crimes over which the Court would ultimately have jurisdiction. Rather, the Working Group was apparently content to leave the matter to the Court itself. The Commission, in turn, although substantially simplifying the jurisdictional regime proposed by the Working Group, essentially accepted as unchanged its basic approach to the crimes in the Statute. That is, article 20 of the 1994 draft approved by the International Law Commission simply listed, rather than defined, the crimes within the jurisdiction of the Court. In the words of the Commission:

> The Statute is primarily an adjectival and procedural instrument. It is not its function to define new crimes. Nor is it the function of the Statute authoritatively to codify crimes under general international law. With respect to certain of these crimes, this is the purpose of the Draft Code of Crimes against the Peace and Security of Mankind, although the Draft Code is not intended to deal with all crimes under general international law. To do so would require a substantial legislative effort. Accordingly the Commission has listed the four crimes without further specification. . . .[9]

---

7. *Report of the Working Group on the question of an International Criminal Jurisdiction, in Report of the International Law Commission on the work of its forty-fourth session*, 47 U.N. GAOR Supp. (No. 10), at 106–107, U.N. Doc. No. A/47/10 (1992), *reprinted in* [1992] 2 Y.B. Int'l L. Comm'n 1, U.N. Doc. A/CN.4/SER.A/1992/Add.1 (Part 2).

8. The initial draft produced by a Working Group of the Commission in 1993 laid out two strands of jurisdiction. The first, found in article 22 of the proposed draft, included treaties that themselves defined the crimes to be included in the Statute. The second was incorporated into article 26 of the Statute covering crimes not defined by treaty but found in customary international law (such as aggression or crimes against humanity) and drug-related crimes. *Id.* at 109–10.

9. *1994 ILC Draft Statute*, at 71–72.

The Commission's reluctance to engage in the drafting of an international criminal code as part of the ICC's establishment was understandable. To begin with, the Commission had already produced several versions of its Draft Code of Crimes, none of which had met with a great deal of success, largely due to the political controversies surrounding many of the definitions it had proposed.[10] No doubt the Commission was concerned that the ICC project would be shelved if the substantive law became an issue of contention. In addition, the jurisdiction *ratione materiae* of the Court as originally conceived in the 1994 draft was a great deal broader than the Statute that ultimately emerged from Rome, and included many treaty crimes, the crime of aggression, and the three core crimes. Until some of the difficult political decisions were made as to which crimes would be included in the Statute, it was arguably inefficient to attempt extensive definitions.[11]

Academics and politicians did not, as a general rule, accept the ILC's decision not to define the crimes in the proposed Statute.[12] Many felt that prosecutions in the proposed Court would run afoul of the *nullum crimen, nulla poena, sine lege* principle if crimes were not sufficiently defined in advance. Moreover, governments faced with the prospect of a world criminal court with prospective jurisdiction over a set of international crimes (as yet to be determined) committed anywhere in the world (assuming the preconditions for jurisdiction and admissibility were met) were wary

---

10. In the Thirteenth Report on the Draft Code, Doudou Thiam, the Special Rapporteur, noted that the draft articles "met with a varied reception [from Governments] . . ." *Thirteenth Report on the Draft Code of Crimes Against the Peace and Security of Mankind*, at 5, U.N. GAOR, 50th Sess., U.N. Doc. No. A/CN.4/466 (1995). Indeed, in an admirable display of candor, the *Rapporteur* noted that the draft articles on the threat of aggression, on intervention, on colonial domination and on willful and severe damage to the environment had been so severely criticized that the Commission should "beat a retreat" therefrom. *Id.* The draft produced by the Commission in 1996 was a great deal shorter than earlier versions, but also met with mixed response. *See generally* Rosemary Rayfuse, *The Draft Code of Crimes Against the Peace and Security of Mankind: Eating Disorders at the International Law Commission*, 8 CRIM. L. F. 43 (1997).

11. As others have noted, while the ILC draft was in many respects criticable, "the ILC's perseverance and ingenuity in developing [a] limited mandate . . . into the 1994 Draft Statute . . . merits high praise." M. Cherif Bassiouni, *Historical Survey: 1919–1998, in* STATUTE OF THE INTERNATIONAL CRIMINAL COURT: A DOCUMENTARY HISTORY 1, 17 (M. Cherif Bassiouni, ed., 1998).

12. Leila Sadat Wexler, *International Law Association (American Branch) Committee on a Permanent International Criminal Court, First Committee Report on Jurisdiction, Definition of Crimes and Complementarity*, 25 DENVER J. INT'L L. & POLICY 221, 223–24 (1997) (Rapporteur's Report) 166–67; *see also* Jordan J. Paust, Nullum Crimen *and Related Claims*, 13 NOUVELLES ÉTUDES PÉNALES 275 (1997).

of entering into a treaty that did not sufficiently set out, *ex ante*, which crimes were within the Court's purview. Thus, when the Commission's draft was taken up by the Ad Hoc Committee established by the General Assembly to consider it,[13] it was generally agreed that the crimes within the Court's jurisdiction would have to be defined in the Statute rather than simply enumerated therein.[14] The Ad Hoc Committee's report was presented to the General Assembly, and ultimately to the Conference Preparatory Committee.

The Preparatory Committee struggled enormously with the task of defining the crimes. While many of the problems were of a drafting or technical nature, others were political. As government delegates debated the content of particular provisions, sharp differences as to both content and interpretation surfaced. Indeed, by 1997 the Preparatory Committee had produced an unwieldy compilation of government proposals, affectionately dubbed the "telephone book,"[15] many of which, if adopted, would have substantially narrowed the definitions of crimes beyond what was thought to be the existing customary international law norms. This was true with respect to the definition of crimes against humanity. It was also true of the war crimes provisions. As one delegate noted with regard to the "mind-boggling array" of proposals[16] on the *per se* illegality of weapons of a nature to cause superfluous injury or unnecessary suffering, or which are inherently indiscriminate,[17] some of the proposals repre-

13. *See* Chapter 2.

14. *Report of the Ad Hoc Committee on the Establishment of an International Criminal Court*, U.N. GAOR, 50th Sess., Supp. 22, at para. 57, U.N. Doc. A/50/22 (1995). The Ad Hoc Committee proposed several methods to define the crimes. One possibility was to track the ILC's initial approach by referring to or incorporating the provisions of relevant treaties. Another involved elaborating definitions for the crimes using the Nuremberg Charter and the Statutes of the two ad hoc Tribunals. Finally, the Committee suggested that those drafting the Court's Statute might use the ILC's Draft Code of Crimes as a starting point, and finalize it "as a matter of priority in order to avoid delays in the establishment of the court." *Id.* The Ad Hoc Committee noted three reasons for defining the crimes in the Court's Statute: respect for the principle of legality, the need to avoid ambiguity, and the need to ensure full respect for the rights of the accused. *Id.*

15. M. Cherif Bassiouni, *Negotiating the Treaty of Rome on the Establishment of an International Criminal Court*, 32 CORNELL INT'L L.J. 443, 444 n. 7 (1999).

16. Roger S. Clark, *The Rome Statute of the International Criminal Court and Weapons of a Nature to Cause Superfluous Injury or Unnecessary Suffering, or which are Inherently Indiscriminate, in* INTERNATIONAL HUMANITARIAN LAW: ORIGINS, CHALLENGES AND PROSPECTS (John Carey & R. John Pritchard, eds., 2000).

17. Hague Convention (IV) Respecting the Law and Customs of War on Land, Oct. 18, 1907, Annex, art. 23(e), 36 Stat. 2277 (prohibiting the employment of "arms, projectiles, or material calculated to cause unnecessary suffering").

sented major retreats from the existing law. A similar phenomenon was seen in attempts to introduce into the *chapeau* of the war crimes provisions language that would have brought war crimes within the jurisdiction of the Court "only when committed as part of a plan or policy or as part of a large-scale commission of such crimes,"[18] effectively importing an element from crimes against humanity into the war crimes area as an attempt to further limit the proposed Court's jurisdiction.[19]

The concern arose that the treaty-making process might, rather than advance the cause of international justice, actually produce definitions of crimes that would be "lowest common denominator" definitions far more restrictive than those generally believed to be part of customary international law or found in the statutes of the two ad hoc tribunals. Indeed, this is to some extent what occurred in Rome. Although many provisions of the text on war crimes and crimes against humanity reflect existing law, and a few others advance it (specifically, the gender-related crime provisions which did not have parallels in earlier texts, and the commitment to criminalizing atrocities committed in internal, as well as international armed conflict as war crimes), many provisions of the Rome Statute restrict existing law. As noted in Chapter 6, the Rome Statute, while still more expansive than some delegations would have liked, did not attempt a progressive codification of the elements of crimes against humanity, war crimes, or genocide (the delegates ultimately refusing to extend the definition to protect groups on the basis of social or political affiliations, as some had proposed they do).[20] The most dramatic example of this is perhaps the exclusion of nuclear, chemical, and biological weapons from the list of those weapons whose use is criminal *per se*—an exclusion brought about by the political necessity of achieving consensus among nuclear and non-nuclear weapons States, as well as among large and poor States.

---

18. *Preparatory Committee Decisions December 1997*, at Option I.

19. As Professor Clark notes, a number of countries, all NATO members, met in 1997 prior to the December PrepCom and produced another version of the weapons proposals that used options, rather than brackets, to suggest that no text was "preferred." Some of the options, however, if adopted, would have substantially narrowed the Court's jurisdiction. Roger S. Clark, *The Rome Statute of the International Criminal Court and Weapons of a Nature to Cause Superfluous Injury or Unnecessary Suffering, or Which are Inherently Indiscriminate, in* INTERNATIONAL HUMANITARIAN LAW: ORIGINS, CHALLENGES AND PROSPECTS 3 (John Carey & R. John Pritchard, eds., 2000).

20. For a considerably more optimistic view of the substantive law of the Statute see Roy S. Lee, *Introduction: The Rome Conference and Its Contributions to International Law, in* THE INTERNATIONAL CRIMINAL COURT: THE MAKING OF THE ROME STATUTE 1, 30–31 (Roy S. Lee, ed., 1999).

To respond, at least in part, to the growing concern about the effect the codification process was having on the normative content of the laws of war and humanity, on December 8, 1997, Professor M. Cherif Bassiouni, representing the government of Egypt,[21] proposed the inclusion of a new article, article "Y," the text of which was as follows:

> Without prejudice to the application of the provisions of this Statute, nothing in this part of the Statute shall be interpreted as limiting or prejudicing in any way existing or developing rules of international law.[22]

Article Y was included in the consolidated text presented to the Diplomatic Conference, but the question of its final placement, either in article 5 (on crimes within the jurisdiction of the Court), or as a separate article in the Statute, was left open for determination.[23] The latter option was preferred by the Framers, and it was ultimately included in the Statute as article 10,[24] meaning that it applies to all the crimes defined in the Statute.[25] As far as this writer can determine it is wholly original. A survey of recently concluded multilateral treaties reveals no parallels to article 10, and it had no precursors either in earlier drafts of the ICC Statute or in the Statutes of the two ad hoc tribunals.[26]

---

21. Professor Bassiouni subsequently chaired the Drafting Committee in Rome.

22. Preparatory Committee on the Establishment of an International Criminal Court, *Decisions Taken by the Preparatory Committee at its Session Held from 1 to 12 December*, art. Y, U.N. Doc. No. A/AC.249/1997/L.9/Rev.1 (Dec. 18, 1997).

23. Article Y was included at the tail end of the section on war crimes in the *Zutphen Intersessional Draft Statute*.

24. *Rome Statute*, Annex II.

25. By its terms, article 10 applies to "this Part," meaning Part II of the Statute. Part II includes articles 5 through 21 of the Statute, and is entitled "jurisdiction, admissibility and applicable law." Thus, article 10 applies not only to the definitions of crimes, but the jurisdictional rules of the Court. This chapter limits its consideration of article 10 to the substantive law of the Statute.

26. The article has no title, and was the only article of the Statute included without a heading. Otto Triffterer, *Article 10, in* COMMENTARY ON THE ROME STATUTE FOR THE INTERNATIONAL CRIMINAL COURT 315 (Otto Triffterer, ed., 1999).

II. LAW "INSIDE" AND LAW "OUTSIDE" THE ROME STATUTE

A. Theoretical Dimensions

The Framers of the Rome Treaty apparently intended their creation to be "law" only in cases involving application of the Court's jurisdiction. That is, even though the prescriptive norms of the Statute apply to the entire world in cases referred to the Court by the Security Council, the clear import of the text is that the substantive criminal law definitions of the Statute, insofar as their import might be restrictive, are to have no influence on customary international law outside the Statute.

At the same time, it is generally accepted that a rule of customary international law is established by two factors: the existence of widespread State practice, generally accepted by States as law, or, as the International Court of Justice held in the *North Sea Continental Shelf Cases*, a practice accepted by States out of a sense of legal obligation. As every international lawyer knows, one way to establish State practice is to point to the provisions of widely-accepted multilateral treaties.[27] Thus, had article Y not been included in the Rome Statute, one surely could have argued that much of the substantive criminal law in the Statute was essentially a codification of the customary international law outside the Statute.

In addition, article 10 speaks only of nothing in the Statute "limiting or prejudicing" existing or developing rules of international law. Thus the Framers apparently intended that only the restrictive portions of the definitions of crimes would remain locked within the ICC structure, not the more progressive elements. In other words, to the extent that the Statute makes a progressive contribution to international humanitarian law, the Framers intended for that law to apply to all.[28] A good example would be the provisions of article 8 criminalizing war crimes committed in non-international armed conflict. During the Diplomatic Conference some countries, China in particular, repeatedly argued that these provisions should be deleted.[29] Their inclusion was supported by most

---

27. *See generally* Arthur M. Weisburd, *Customary International Law: The Problem of Treaties*, 21 VAND. J. TRANSNAT'L L. 1 (1988); Gary L. Scott & Craig L. Carr, *Multilateral Treaties and the Formation of Customary International Law*, 25 DENV. J. INT'L L. & POL'Y 71 (1996).

28. Again, article 80 differs in thrust and effect from article 10. It clearly does not purport to allow "progressive" as opposed to "non-progressive" elements (such as the exclusion of the death penalty from the Statute) to be taken either as restatements or progressive elaborations of customary international law. Rather, it is value-neutral.

29. Author's personal notes.

other delegations, however, including the United States. Certainly article 10 was not intended to provide China with a basis upon which to argue that the internal armed conflict provisions were not now (if they were not already) agreed-upon norms of customary international law.

Finally, the Statute itself contemplates that the Court will use customary international law outside the ICC Statute in its decisions. As Chapter 7 has already explored, article 21, on applicable law, permits the Court to apply "where appropriate, applicable treaties and the principles and rules of international law, including the established principles of the international law of armed conflict."[30] The resort to international law outside the Statute is permitted only to supplement the terms of the Statute itself, not to supplant them;[31] presumably then, the Framers were contemplating the use of international law as a gap filler, but explicitly acknowledging the importance of maintaining a corpus of international humanitarian law that would co-exist with the Rome Statute.

A solution to this apparent contradiction, which would suggest that article 10's theoretical basis is weak, may lie in a deeper understanding of the nature of the law made in Rome by the Diplomatic Conference. As noted in chapter 5, the theory on which the Security Council's power permits it to apply Rome law to all the human beings in the world rests not just upon its Chapter VII powers, but upon the *jus cogens* nature of the crimes within the jurisdiction of the Court.[32] Because any State would have jurisdiction to try the perpetrator of such a crime, the establishment of an international criminal court with power to try defendants accused of committing *jus cogens* crimes is seen as an extension of the theory of universal inter-state jurisdiction.

If we accept the Rome Statute as international universal *legislation*, article 10 becomes merely the expression of a legislative intent not to preempt the field. This leaves to the common law (lawmakers other than the ICC) and to States the task of further developing the law outside the Statute. Moreover, the legislation properly acts as a floor, not a ceiling: all States (or at least all citizens of all States, since the Statute imposes *individual* criminal responsibility) have to obey The Law—codes of conduct that the Framers themselves have deemed to be unbounded by geography and applicable to all the citizens of the world.[33]

30. *Rome Statute*, art. 21(1)(b).

31. *Id.*

32. As previously noted, commentators are not unanimous as to the *jus cogens* nature of aggression.

33. Of course, in cases referred by States or the ICC Prosecutor *proprio motu*, the Court will not have jurisdiction *to adjudicate* unless the State consent regime is complied with. *See* Chapter 4.

The Diplomatic Conference, as noted in Chapter 1, effected an uneasy revolution in the sub-structure of international law: a step towards bringing it from an "underdeveloped" legal system in which the sources of law are hard to find and even more difficult to apply, to a "developed" legal system in which rule-makers adopt rules of conduct that are universally binding, and even, in somewhat limited fashion, enforceable.[34] Article 10, which has no parallels in any other multilateral treaty, supports this view of the paradigm shift effected by the Rome Conference. It suggests that not only did the Conference appear to function as a quasi-legislative body when viewed objectively by outside observers, but that some of the participants subjectively believed that they were indeed legislating, and legislating not just rules of conduct, but dictating the relationship those rules would have with sources of law outside of the Treaty that was adopted.

B. Likely Practical Effects

Article 10 reinforces the view that the Rome Conference was qualitatively and quantitatively different from standard international law-making. Yet, the paradigm shift was both largely unacknowledged and incremental in nature. The addition of the ICC to the constellation of bodies which can enforce (and create) norms of international criminal law was not accompanied by amendments to other political and judicial institutions or legal norms.[35] The ICC was not adopted as an amendment to the U.N. Charter and its establishment leaves the statute of the International Court of Justice intact. Finally, national systems of criminal justice are unaffected by the Court's creation. Thus, in considering article 10's effect on customary international law, it is useful to consider how other bodies will tend to view Rome law, particularly courts other than the ICC.

Surely neither in theory nor in practice are courts other than the ICC bound to the provisions of the Statute. Thus, to the extent that the Statute is widely ratified, even the inclusion of article 10 cannot foreclose arguments that customary international law now includes the Statute's definitions.[36] Indeed, Trial Chamber II of the ICTY recently noted in *Prosecutor v. Furundzija:*

---

34. *Cf.* Arthur M. Weisburd, *Customary International Law: The Problem of Treaties*, 21 VAND. J. TRANSNAT'L L. 1, 2 (1988).

35. On the proliferation of international courts and tribunals see generally Jonathan I. Charney, *International Law and Multiple International Tribunals*, 271 RECUEIL DES COURS 101 (1998).

36. This is also true of article 80.

> [n]otwithstanding article 10 of the Statute, . . . , resort may be had . . . to these provisions [of the Rome Statute] to help elucidate customary international law. Depending on the matter at issue, the Rome Statute may be taken to restate, reflect or clarify customary rules or crystallise them, whereas in some areas it creates new law or modifies existing law.[37]

The same approach could be taken by national courts looking to the ICC Statute for guidance, either in application of national legislation adopted as part of the process of ratifying and implementing the Treaty of Rome, or in interpreting pre-Rome statutes criminalizing genocide, crimes against humanity or war crimes. Indeed, at least three different judicial bodies might have the occasion to consider Rome law: national courts, the ad hoc tribunals, and the International Court of Justice. Each is discussed below, in turn.

1. National Courts

Because the International Criminal Court Statute operates on the principle of complementarity, even once the Statute comes into force, national courts will remain the principle vehicles for international criminal law enforcement. Indeed, the ICC is not an extension of national criminal justice systems; instead, the Court will exercise jurisdiction only where "national legal systems are unwilling or unable genuinely to proceed."[38] Thus, national courts retain their autonomy and sovereignty; the ICC in no way supplants them. This formal separation, however, between national and international systems of criminal justice as a matter of prescriptive and adjudicative jurisdiction does not prevent informal relationships from arising between the two legal orders. In fact, it seems clear that in order for States to be able to avail themselves of the complementarity principle to avoid (or to supplement) prosecutions in the ICC, countries ratifying the Rome Statute are likely to enact universal jurisdiction legislation tracking the substantive criminal law in the Statute, laws that can then be used to prosecute war criminals and criminals against humanity whether or not the Rome Statute applies.

---

37. Prosecutor v. Furundzija (Case No. IT-95-17/1-T), Judgment, para. 227 (Trial Chamber II, Dec. 10, 1998). *Furundzija*'s holding was confirmed by the ICTY Appeals Chamber in the *Tadić* Judgment. Prosecutor v. Tadić (Case No. IT 94-1-A), Judgment, para. 223 (ICTY Appeals Chamber, July 15, 1999).

38. Bruce Broomhall, *The International Criminal Court: Overview, and Co-operation with States*, 13*quater* NOUVELLES ÉTUDES PÉNALES 45, 47 (1999).

Certainly, these national laws need not be identical to Rome law. In fact, many aspects of the substantive law in the Rome Statute which are jurisdictional in character have no place (or a lesser place) in national laws, for the prudential and political concerns that are of issue in creating an *international* system of criminal justice would have lesser or no force in adopting national laws. To take one example, national legislation on genocide could criminalize the intent to destroy, in whole or in part, not just the few groups now included in the Convention, but political and social groups as well. Although one might argue that States may not exercise universal jurisdiction over the crime of genocide if they define genocide more broadly than the current treaty law and custom would allow, to forbid them from doing so could undermine the principle upon which the complementarity principle is based, which is that States and not the ICC remain the primary enforcers of international criminal law. Moreover, as we have already seen, the ICC's enforcement mechanisms are quite weak. Thus, it could cripple the enforcement of international criminal law to deny States the right to prosecute offenders for crimes not covered by the ICC Statute. It would be perverse indeed to hold that the ICC Statute, in codifying the crimes within its reach, now prevents States from reaching out with universal jurisdiction legislation to prosecute additional offenses. If enough States had similar legislation, that legislation would be evidence of State practice that could give rise to a new custom. Although the ICC could not apply the new custom, States, ad hoc or regional tribunals, and the International Court of Justice certainly could. It would therefore seem that the substantive law in the Rome Statute provides a floor, but not a ceiling, for criminalizing offenses against the laws of war and humanity.

2. *Ad hoc Tribunals*

Similarly, the two extant ad hoc Tribunals for the Former Yugoslavia and for Rwanda have their own Statutes which differ in some measure from Rome law.[39] Those entities are already borrowing from the ICC Statute because their own Statutes are quite sketchy as to the elements of crimes; but there is no doubt that they could take different views on interpreting texts similar to those found in the ICC Statute that would also be indicative of trends in customary international law "outside" the Rome

---

39. Other Tribunals for Sierra Leone and Cambodia have also been proposed. *See* Chapter 3 for a discussion of the Sierra Leonean Special Court. In a report submitted on February 22, 1999, a United Nations Group of Experts had called for a UN ad hoc tribunal to be established to try surviving leaders of the brutal 1970's Khmer Rouge regime. Letters dated 15 March 1999 from the Secretary-General to the President of the General Assembly and the President of

Statute. With respect to the establishment of new ad hoc tribunals by the Security Council after the ICC Statute enters into force, it would seem odd to permit the Security Council to provide a newly constituted ad hoc tribunal with law that differs from ICC law, particularly as the ICC Statute would apply to the situation assuming the Council wished to refer the case to the Court. On the other hand, one could imagine crimes not now within the jurisdiction of the Court that would be justiciable by an ad hoc tribunal—such as the crime of aggression, for example, which has yet to be rendered justiciable in the ICC, and may not be for the foreseeable future.

3. *The International Court of Justice*

Finally, the International Court of Justice retains an important residual role to play in the development and articulation of rules of customary international law. Whether or not the ICC is seized in a particular case with regard to individual criminal liability, issues of State Responsibility between States may surface in cases not covered (or covered) by the Rome Statute. That is, uses of force that fall short of the definition of war crimes in the Statute might nonetheless be violations of article 2(4) of the U.N. Charter, and justiciable as a matter of State responsibility rather than individual criminal liability. To the extent that the ICJ's jurisprudence supplements, rather than contradicts, the ICC Statute, ICJ cases will be an important source of law for the Court pursuant to article 21 of the Statute, as well as evidence of customary international law "outside" the Statute.[40]

---

the Security Council, U.N. Doc. A/53/1999/231, annex (Group of Experts Report). However, the Cambodian government rejected that option almost immediately. Steven R. Ratner, *The United Nations Group of Experts for Cambodia*, 93 AM. J. INT'L. L. 948, 952 (1999). On May 24, 2000, Cambodia reached an agreement with the United Nations to form an international criminal tribunal with UN-appointed and local judges. *Cambodia and UN Agree to Establish International Criminal Court*, INT'L ENFORCEMENT L. REP. (July 2000), *available in* LEXIS, NEXIS Library, News Group File. Although the special tribunal is not yet operational, leading observers to question Cambodia's commitment to trials, Cambodia's Prime Minister recently pledged to make Cambodia the first southeast Asian nation to ratify the ICC Statute. *Cambodia to ratify Rome Statute on International Criminal Court*, AGENCE FRANCE PRESSE, June 1, 2001, *available in* LEXIS, NEXIS Library, News Group File.

40. Although it would be possible for divergent views on common questions of law to emerge from the two Courts, a recent study demonstrates that the recent proliferation of international courts and tribunals has not led to incoherent interpretations of international law, and suggests that variations that are found may in fact represent healthy innovation. Jonathan I. Charney, *International Law and Multiple International Tribunals*, 271 RECUEIL DES COURS 101, 352 (1998).

CHAPTER 10

A WINDOW TO THE FUTURE

> *Resistance is proportional to the scale of the change one seeks to bring about. It is even the surest sign that change is on the way. . . . To abandon a project because it meets too many obstacles is often a grave mistake: the obstacles themselves provide the friction to make movement possible.*
>
> —Jean Monnet, *Memoirs*

Three times on the night of July 17, 1998, jubilation exploded through packed meetings of the Diplomatic Conference as it drew to a dramatic close.[1] After more than seventy-five years of preparatory work, the impossible had been accomplished: a treaty establishing a permanent international criminal court had been adopted. The setting had all the features of a revolution: it was hot, the negotiations were difficult and emotional, and those with the largest stake in the existing order objected the most vociferously to change. Global civil society weighed in as never before to represent the interests of those not formally parties to the negotiating process. But as the dust from Rome settles and the Preparatory Commission finalizes the Statute's implementing "legislation," it is useful to reflect upon what the Framers wrought.

As for the legal rules comprising the Treaty's substance, several features of the Statute challenge the Westphalian model, and the unwritten "constitution" of international law premised upon it. The Court will exercise jurisdiction over individuals, including Heads of States. The three

1. Fanny Benedetti & John L. Washburn, *Drafting the International Criminal Court Treaty: Two Years to Rome and an Afterword on the Rome Diplomatic Conference, in* 5 GLOBAL GOVERNANCE 1, 26 (1999). *See also* Giovanni Conso, *Epilogue: Looking to the Future, in* THE INTERNATIONAL CRIMINAL COURT: THE MAKING OF THE ROME STATUTE 471 (Roy S. Lee, ed., 1999) (describing the excitement and votes of the Conference's last day).

crimes currently defined within its jurisdiction will cover the internal, as well as the international, commission of atrocities on a wide scale. Their codification in the Rome Statute strains the current conception of international law as consensual and poses a challenge to the content and status of customary international law. The prescriptive jurisdiction of the Court rests on a new theory of universal international jurisdiction which embodies in it the seeds of a new approach to the repartition of competences between national and international legal orders. This should, as a corollary, cause the Court and the Assembly of States Parties, in adopting the elements of crimes, to separate jurisdictional from material elements of crimes as a matter of pleading and proof. Aggression is included, even if not defined, as a direct challenge to the prerogatives of States to use violence to advance national interests.

Institutionally speaking, the Court is a fascinating mix of common law, civil law, and law *sui generis*. The Court is a permanent, not an *ad hoc* institution. Its Prosecutor will be independent, but not completely so; for the most part his or her work will be supervised by the Pre-Trial Chamber. Duty-bound to pursue the truth and not just convict alleged criminals, the Prosecutor may be subject at times to tensions arising from this double role. The Court's judiciary will be highly qualified and independent but not powerful; there is no life tenure or other protection for these judges of individuals charged with the worst atrocities known to humankind.[2] Its Registry, like the Registries of the two ad hoc Tribunals, will be a co-equal organ performing crucial tasks of administration for the Court, as well as maintaining the Victims and Witnesses Unit and facilities for defense counsel. Indeed, the Registrar is the one potentially "permanent" member of the Court.

The Assembly of States Parties will take decisions by supermajority vote, thereby eroding the most sacred of international law principles: the absolute sovereign equality of States. Thus, much of the "law" of the Statute will be supranational in character. *Déracinée* and *délocalisée*, the ICC will be independent from national legal systems, and even, at least partially, from the Security Council. This will be both a weakness and a strength—an Achilles' heel in terms of the actual investigation and prosecution of crimes which must be largely effectuated through the good offices of States; yet, perhaps, a tremendous moral virtue. Legitimacy, something quite different than effectiveness or efficiency, stems not from brute force or power, but from fairness, universality, and powerlessness.[3]

---

2. *Cf.* U. S. CONST. art. III, section 1.

3. *Cf.* THOMAS FRANCK, THE POWER OF LEGITIMACY AMONG NATIONS 16 (1990). Professor Franck writes:

By divorcing the Court from questions of nationality, such that the nationality of the judges, prosecutors, victims and defendants are virtually irrelevant to its proceedings, the justice dispensed should be truly universal in character. While at least some attention to local customs will no doubt be sacrificed in the process, this should permit the ICC to avoid the charges of "victor's justice" or regional or cultural bias which have been leveled at its predecessor institutions.

The Court is not clearly established within the parameters of the existing United Nations system, although its genesis and creation was undertaken by that institution. Instead, it is brought into what may very well be an uneasy relationship with the United Nations, with significant implications for its financing, bureaucratic structure and procedures, control over prosecutions, and enforcement of its commands. From a theoretical perspective, if the United Nations Charter is a nascent constitution, it is not clear where the Rome Treaty fits in the existing structure. Indeed, one might ask whether the Statute's adoption represented a "Constitutional Moment" in international law—a decision to re-equilibrate the organic law governing international relations, albeit *sotto voce*, by making an end run around, rather than a formal amendment to the Charter.

The law of the Statute builds upon a Century of incremental progress in constructing a normative framework for international criminal law, from the modest steps taken at the Hague in 1899 to the more powerful, even if unenforced Conventions adopted after the Second World War. The Statute defines the crime against humanity for the first time in a widely accepted multilateral treaty, and reinforces the right as well as the desire of the international community to prohibit offenses committed against human beings anywhere, including internal atrocities, if they rise to a certain level of gravity and no State is able or willing to step in and prosecute the offenders. In addition to defining the crimes within the Court's jurisdiction, an entire system of general principles of law was elaborated to govern issues of legality, applicable law, individual responsibility for crimes, the elements of crimes and the defenses thereto. The extraordinary

---

> Deployed by students of national legal systems, the concept of legitimacy is often used to postulate and explain what, other than a command and its enforcement, is required to create a propensity among citizens generally to obey the rulers and the rules. The internationalist ought to feel both comfortable with, and stimulated by, this notion of legitimacy as the non-coercive factor, or bundle of factors, predisposing toward voluntary obedience.

See also Adriaan Bos, *The International Criminal Court: A Perspective, in* THE INTERNATIONAL CRIMINAL COURT: THE MAKING OF THE ROME STATUTE 470 (1999).

nature of this achievement cannot be overstated: blending together elements of the civil and common law, as well as specific rules from a myriad of countries into one relatively coherent (even if not perfect) Statute represents an enormous intellectual and creative endeavor. While the Statute might have been even more consistent had the delegates taken more time in its elaboration,[4] given that many of the inconsistencies derive not from difficulties in drafting but from political compromises, it is possible, and perhaps even probable, that having more time would have made the Statute worse instead of better at least from a systemic point of view. Indeed, the collection of compromises contained in the definitions provisions, as well as Part 7 (on Penalties), caused the Framers to insert language into the Statute attempting to separate it from customary international law and national law, and suggests that at least the definitions of crimes may be seen as minimum rules of conduct, beyond which States may legislate freely.

The richness and complexity of the Court's Statute will undoubtedly give rise to difficulties in its interpretation, but these problems are certainly not insurmountable. The Rome Statute takes the form of an international treaty, but has the status of a Constitution. Many of its provisions perform the function of international legislation, while others supply detailed procedural rules that address the Court's operation.[5] The judges will have the extraordinary task of interpreting these provisions, and although the strict rules of the Vienna Convention on the Law of Treaties will apply due to its status as an international treaty, other interpretative techniques will no doubt be needed as well. For example, teleological methods should be applied to constitutive aspects and provisions representing foundational principles of the Statute,[6] while canons of strict con-

---

4. Shabtai Rosenne, *Poor Drafting and Imperfect Organization: Flaws to Overcome in the Rome Statute*, 41 VA. J. INT'L L. 164, 167–72 (2000).

5. *Cf.* GEORGE A. BERMANN, ET AL., CASES AND MATERIALS ON EUROPEAN COMMUNITY LAW 30 (1993).

6. For example, general provisions such as article 86 ("States Parties shall . . . cooperate with the Court in its investigation and prosecution of crimes within [its] jurisdiction"), have a constitutional character and will need to be interpreted in such a manner so as to effectuate the Statute's object and purpose. A teleological or broad reading of provisions such as article 86 would therefore seem perfectly appropriate. Other provisions that the Court will need to interpret broadly in order to effectuate the Statute's purpose include article 21(3). Whether the Court will adopt an "implied powers" doctrine, as the International Court of Justice did for the United Nations in the *Reparations* case remains to be seen. Reparation for Injuries Suffered in the Service of the United Nations, Advisory Opinion, 1949 I.C.J. 174 (Apr. 11). *See* Mustafa Kamil Yasseen, *Création et personnalité juridique des*

struction are the appropriate guide to interpreting the "legislation within the Statute," that is, the definitions of crimes, which should be narrowly interpreted in accordance with the legality principle and article 22(2)'s command that definitions of crimes shall be strictly construed and not extended by analogy. Between these two extremes lie most of the Statute's provisions that will guide the Court's general operation and govern proceedings before it. Despite the diversity of interpretive techniques appropriate to various components of the Statute, it will be important to the legitimacy and credibility of the Court for its decisions to nevertheless be consistent and coherent.

Finally, the Statute's extensive provisions on procedure should provide the Court with a procedural system well-suited to the needs of international criminal justice. Learning from both the problems and the successes of the two ad hoc Tribunals, the Framers attempted to avoid an often criticized bias in favor of common law procedures, choosing instead to blend aspects of the adversarial and inquisitorial systems and innovate where neither system had a rule that fit the Court's needs. They successfully crafted a Statute that is rich in complexity without being overly verbose, confining the Court's personnel sufficiently to ensure fairness and consistency in the meting out of justice, but leaving enough flexibility to avoid excessive rigidity. One issue that is not squarely addressed by the Statute or the Rules of Procedure and Evidence is streamlining the manner in which cases are investigated and tried before the Court, a very difficult problem that has arisen in the two ad hoc tribunals, where long periods of pre-trial detention and lengthy trials are the norm.[7] This is a practical problem for the Court to address from the outset if it is to succeed. In addition, it will be important if investigations and prosecutions before the Court are to be seen as fair that the rights of the accused and those under investigation are scrupulously protected by the Court's personnel. The lack of an institutionalized public defender's office as well as the absence of specific remedies in the Statute for most transgressions against the rights of the accused and persons under investigation by the Court suggests that the judges and prosecutors of the Court will need to be vigilant to properly balance the need for an effective system of criminal justice with the obligations of due process. Justice must be seen to be done, and be done in fact.

---

organisations internationales, in MANUEL SUR LES ORGANISATIONS INTERNATIONALES 37–40 (RENÉ-JEAN DUPUY, ed., 1988).

7. Report of the Expert Group to Conduct a Review of the Effective Operation and Functioning of the International Criminal Tribunal for the Former Yugoslavia and the International Criminal Tribunal for Rwanda, at paras. 36–101, U.N. Doc. S/2000/597.

As a matter of process, the making of the Rome Treaty was extraordinary. Not only was the Statute voted on by States, thereby erasing any illusions one may have held about the continuing relevance of absolute paradigms of sovereignty in modern times, but the law made by the Statute extends to the entire world in cases involving referrals by the Security Council under Chapter VII. The only truly troubling feature of this Revolution is its occult nature. For, to the extent that no explicitly institutional structure existed to accommodate the various interests of States in what is becoming a quasi-legislative process of multilateral treaty-making, there is a certain impropriety in using a one-vote per State paradigm. The United States of America, which has taken an oppositional view of the Statute ever since its adoption, unsuccessfully attempted to counter the quasi-legislative processes of the Diplomatic Conference by dominating it—by working harder and longer, and thereby prevailing, even though as a formal matter the United States was juridically only as powerful as the smallest State in attendance. The United States repeatedly invoked the doctrine of "sovereignty" to support its views, but, in the final analysis, it was simply outvoted. Adopting a system of weighted voting to more properly realign juridical with factual reality seems more than the international community is ready to handle; and so, large and wealthy countries will have to continue to rely on diplomacy as well as strength to achieve their negotiating objectives.

If many features of the Rome Treaty are revolutionary, however, the Revolution is in no sense an easy one. Indeed, as I have written elsewhere, the opposition has a very powerful champion in the guise of the United States of America. As a matter of law, institutional structure and process, many prerogatives of sovereignty remain. The complementarity regime makes the Court one of last, not first, resort. Although this is unobjectionable in theory, the process by which the complementarity regime is to be effectuated in the Court may tie proceedings up in preliminary motions on admissibility which could significantly impede the Court's capacity to render justice. Additionally, the state cooperation regime weakens the Court's effectiveness considerably, and the "voluntary" enforcement of sentences regime may have the effect of requiring the Netherlands, as the host State, to become the world's jailer.

Although the institution is permanent, its personnel generally are not. Fears of a powerful judiciary and an independent prosecutor caused States to substantially complicate the procedural regimes governing the bringing of cases to the Court, to the point that they may threaten the administration of justice. Where the Framers were required to craft "new" law, as in some of the crimes against humanity provisions, the definitions are relatively restrictive, and the process of defining the Elements of Crimes has caused them to become even more so.

Yet with all its imperfections, inconsistencies, flaws and blemishes, the Rome Statute is an extraordinary achievement. Indeed, it opens a window to the future for humanity at the dawn of the third millennium. The seeds of Revolution were sown; the existing power structure resisted; the final product is a fragile compromise that may or may not succeed. A key component of the Court's success is predicated on the good will and cooperation of States, which will be required to finance its operations, support its personnel, and assist in the conduct of investigations, the arrest of suspects, and the imprisonment of its criminals. The international community's record has been mixed with regard to its support of the two ad hoc Tribunals, leading one to wonder whether the permanent court has any chance at all.[8] But even if the Court is ultimately unsuccessful, the transformation of international law wrought by the Diplomatic Conference will, like ancient Rome itself, continue to influence the world profoundly. And for those who suffer from the scourge of war crimes or atrocities that shock the conscience of humankind, whose sufferings were the *raison d'être* of the Conference in the first place, Rome stands once again as the center of the "civilized" world in the truest sense: the place to which the governments of the world came to establish, before the window closed again, the last great international institution of the Twentieth Century.

---

8. *See, e.g.*, Michael P. Scharf, *The Tools for Enforcing International Criminal Justice in the New Millennium: Lessons from the Yugoslavia Tribunal*, 49 DEPAUL L. REV. 925 (2000).

CHARTS

Figure 1
JURISDICTION OF THE COURT

Purpose: Exercise jurisdiction over persons for the most serious crimes of international concern (art. 1)

Jurisdiction

- limited to the most serious crimes of concern to the international community as a whole (art. 5)
- complementary to national criminal jurisdictions (art. 1)
- not retroactive (art. 11)

Crimes within the Jurisdiction of the Court
(article 5)

genocide	**crimes against humanity**	**war crimes**	**aggression**
• defined in art. 6 • tracks art. 2 of the Genocide Convention	• defined in art. 7 • chapeau requires the crime to have been "committed as part of a widespread or systematic attack directed against any civilian population with knowledge of the attack"	• defined in art. 8 • chapeau suggests a preference for, but does not require, a plan, policy or large-scale commission • "grave breaches" of Geneva Conventions of August 12, 1949 (art. 8(2)(a)) • serious violations of laws and customs applicable in international armed conflict (art. 8(2)(b)), and non-international armed conflict (art. 8(2)(c)–(e)) • seven year opt-out (art. 124)	• jurisdiction only to be exercised after adoption of an amendment defining the crime and setting out conditions of the Court's jurisdiction (see arts. 121 and 123, Amendments and Review of the Statute) • adopted provisions to be consistent with relevant provisions of U.N. Charter

Note: "Nothing in [Part II] shall be interpreted as limiting or prejudicing in any way existing or developing rules of international law for purposes other than this Statute." (art. 10)

Figure 2
ORGANS OF THE ICC

	Judiciary (arts. 35–37)	**Presidency (art. 38)**
Purpose	Judicial function	Administering the Court (except for the Office of the Prosecutor) Other functions conferred by Statute, including determining full-time status of Judges (art. 35(3)); receiving applications for the court to sit elsewhere than the Hague (Draft RPE 100)
Composition	18 Judges shall be elected and assigned as follows: Pre-Trial Division—at least 6 Judges (art. 39) Trial Division—at least 6 Judges (art. 39) Appeals Division—5 Judges, including the President (art. 39) For details of judicial organization, see Figure 3.	President 1st Vice-President 2nd Vice-President
Term	One non-renewable 9-year term of office	3 years or end of term of office as Judge, whichever expires earlier; eligible for re-election once
Election	By secret ballot by at least a two-thirds majority of States present and voting in the Assembly of States Parties In electing judges, the Assembly of States Parties shall take into account the need for: • representation of the principal legal systems of the world, • equitable geographic representation, *and* • a fair representation of female and male judges	By absolute majority of Judges

Figure 2
ORGANS OF THE ICC *(continued)*

	Judiciary (arts. 35–37)	**Presidency (art. 38)**
Qualifications	In the first election: • at least 9 Judges must have established competence in criminal law and procedure and the necessary, relevant experience in criminal proceedings, and • at least 5 Judges must have recognized competence in international law and extensive experience in a legal capacity of relevance to the judicial work of the Court • This ratio must be maintained in subsequent elections High moral character, impartiality, integrity, and requisite qualifications for appointment to the highest judicial office in their country of nationality; fluent in at least one of the working languages of the Court	No additional requirements beyond those for Judges in general
Other	No two Judges of the same nationality	N/A

Figure 3
JUDICIAL ORGANIZATION

	Judicial Divisions		
	Appeals Division 5 Judges (President + 4 Judges) art. 39(1)	**Trial Division** (ad hoc) at least 6 Judges art. 39(1)	**Pre-Trial Division** (ad hoc) at least 6 Judges art. 39(1)
Term	Entire term of office; if necessary, judges shall serve through completion of any case in progress	3 years, or until completion of the case in progress	3 years, or until completion of the case in progress
Chambers	The Appeals Chamber is composed of all members of the Appeals Division	Trial Chambers are composed of 3 Judges of the Trial Division	Pre-Trial Chambers are composed of either 1 or 3 Judges of the Pre-Trial Division
Qualifications	Shall reflect the functions of the Chamber	Shall be composed predominantly of Judges with criminal trial experience	Shall be composed predominantly of Judges with criminal trial experience
Decisions	Judgment by majority, delivered in open court. Majority and minority opinions issued if no unanimity; individual separate or dissenting opinions allowed on questions of law (art. 83)	Trial Chamber should attempt to achieve unanimity, but may decide by majority. One written and reasoned decision issued, including majority and minority opinions if no unanimity. Deliberations secret (art. 74)	By majority, if 3 judges See art. 57(2).

Figure 3
JUDICIAL ORGANIZATION *(continued)*

	Judicial Divisions		
	Appeals Division 5 Judges (President + 4 Judges) art. 39(1)	**Trial Division** (ad hoc) at least 6 Judges art. 39(1)	**Pre-Trial Division** (ad hoc) at least 6 Judges art. 39(1)
Other	Members of the Appeals Division may serve only in the Appeals Chamber	Alternate judges may be designated by the Presidency to attend trial and act as members if a judge dies or becomes unavailable Judges of the Trial Division may be temporarily assigned to the Pre-Trial Division	Must confirm charges prior to constitution of a Trial Chamber Judges of the Pre-Trial Division may be temporarily assigned to the Trial Division, except that a judge who participated in the pre-trial phase of a case may not sit on the Trial Chamber hearing that case

Figure 4
ORGANS OF THE ICC

	Office of the Prosecutor (art. 42)	Registry (art. 43)
Purpose	Full-time organ responsible for receiving referrals, investigating complaints and conducting prosecutions	Full-time organ serving a non-judicial administrative function. Also serves as depository of notifications and channel for communications with States
Composition	Headed by the Prosecutor, assisted by 1 or more Deputy Prosecutors who may act in place of Prosecutor if necessary. Prosecutor may appoint other qualified staff as needed. Staff shall be subject to the Staff Regulations drawn up by Registrar	Registrar, Deputy Registrar, Victims and Witnesses Unit; Presidency may appoint or authorize Registrar to appoint other staff as necessary. Staff shall be subject to Staff Regulations drawn up by Registrar
Term	One non-renewable 9-year term, unless a shorter term is decided on at time of election	Registrar: 5 years; eligible for re-election Deputy Registrar: 5 years or less, as decided by absolute majority of Judges
Election	By secret ballot by an absolute majority of the Assembly of States Parties	Registrar: by secret ballot by absolute majority of Judges Deputy Registrar: by secret ballot by absolute majority of Judges, upon recommendation of the Registrar
Qualifications	High moral character, highly competent, extensive practical experience in the prosecution or trial of criminal cases, fluent in at least one of the working languages of the Court	High moral character, highly competent, fluent in at least one of the working languages of the Court Registrar: shall be available on a full-time basis Deputy Registrar: may be elected on basis that he or she is willing to serve as required

Figure 4
ORGANS OF THE ICC *(continued)*

	Office of the Prosecutor (art. 42)	Registry (art. 43)
Other	Presidency may excuse Prosecutor or Deputy Prosecutor at their request from acting in a particular case. They shall be disqualified if their "impartiality might reasonably be doubted on any ground." Appeals Chamber shall decide cases of disqualification Prosecutor and Deputy Prosecutors shall be of different nationalities	Victims and Witnesses Unit provides protective measures, security arrangements, counseling and other appropriate assistance for victims, witnesses and others at risk on account of their testimony

Figure 5
REMOVAL FROM OFFICE

(article 46)
Who may be removed?

- Judge
- Prosecutor
- Deputy Prosecutor
- Registrar
- Deputy Registrar

Causes for removal

- The person is found to have committed serious misconduct or a serious breach of his or her duties under the Statute or as provided for in the Rules of Procedure and Evidence; *or*
- The person is unable to exercise the functions required by the Statute

Procedure for removal

Judge	**Prosecutor**	**Deputy Prosecutor**	**Registrar, Deputy Registrar**
• by a two-thirds majority of the States Parties upon a recommendation adopted by a two-thirds majority of the other Judges	• by an absolute majority of States Parties	• by an absolute majority of States Parties upon a recommendation of the Prosecutor	• by an absolute majority of the Judges

Note: A Judge, Prosecutor, Deputy Prosecutor, Registrar or Deputy Registrar whose conduct or ability to exercise the functions of the office under the Statute is challenged shall have the opportunity to present and receive evidence and to make submissions in accordance with the Rules of Procedure and Evidence, but shall not otherwise participate in the consideration of the matter.

Figure 6
THE ASSEMBLY OF STATES PARTIES
(article 112)

<table>
<tr><td>Composition
(art. 112(1))</td><td colspan="2">One representative from each State Party
Other States that have signed the Statute or the Final Act may be observers in the Assembly</td></tr>
<tr><td>Functions
(art. 112(2))</td><td>• Consider and act on recommendations of the Preparatory Commission
• Provide management oversight regarding administration of the Court's organs
• Consider and act on reports of the Bureau
• Decide the budget for the Court
• Decide whether to alter the number of judges
• Consider questions of non-cooperation (art. 87(5), (7))</td><td>• Perform any other functions consistent with the Statute or the Rules of Procedure and Evidence
• Adopt Elements of Crimes (art. 9)
• Adopt Rules of Procedure and Evidence (art. 51)
• Elect Judges of the Court (art. 36(6))
• Elect Prosecutor and Deputy Prosecutor (art. 42)
• Establish guidelines for employment of gratis personnel and approve Staff Regulations (art. 44)</td></tr>
<tr><td>Administration
(art. 112(3))</td><td colspan="2">The Assembly shall have a Bureau consisting of:
A President,
2 Vice-Presidents, and
18 Members
The Bureau shall be elected by the Assembly for a term of three years
The composition of the Bureau shall take into account equitable geographic representation and representation of the principal legal systems of the world</td></tr>
<tr><td>Voting
(art. 112(7), (8))</td><td colspan="2">Each State Party has one vote
The Assembly shall try to reach a consensus on all matters. In the absence of consensus, voting is as follows, unless otherwise provided in the Statute:
• For substantive matters, a 2/3 majority of States present provided that an absolute majority of States are present
• For procedural matters, a simple majority of States present
State Parties two years or more in arrears in payment of their assessed contribution for funding of the Court (art. 117) shall have no vote in the Assembly or in the Bureau. The Assembly may nevertheless permit the State to vote if it determines that the failure to pay is beyond the State's control.</td></tr>
</table>

Figure 7
REFERRALS TO THE COURT

Situation is referred by Security Council (art. 13(b))	**Situation is referred to the Prosecutor by State Party** (art. 13(a), art. 14)	**Prosecutor has initiated an investigation of the conduct** (art. 13(c))
↓↓	↓↓	↓↓
Security Council acts under Chapter VII of U.N. Charter (art. 13(b))	Referral must specify relevant circumstances and include supporting documentation (art. 14(1), (2))	Prosecutor action governed by art. 15
↓↓	↓↓	↓↓
No State consent required	↓	↓

Preconditions to jurisdiction (art. 12(2))

Court may exercise jurisdiction if one or more of the following States are Parties to the Statute *or* have accepted the jurisdiction of the Court:

(a) The State on the territory of which the conduct in question occurred ("territorial State") or, if the conduct occurred on board a vessel or aircraft, the State of registration of that vessel or aircraft;
(b) The State of the accused's nationality

Note: No investigation or prosecution may be commenced with or proceeded with under this Statute for a period of 12 months after the Security Council, in a resolution adopted under Chapter VII of the U.N. Charter, has requested the Court to that effect; that request may be renewed by the Council (art. 16)

Figure 8
PROSECUTORIAL PROPRIO MOTU INVESTIGATION
(article 15)

Initiation of Investigation

- Upon receipt of information indicating the occurrence of crimes within the jurisdiction of the Court, the Prosecutor may initiate an investigation
- The Prosecutor shall analyze the seriousness of the information and may seek additional information from States, U.N. organs, intergovernmental or non-governmental organizations or other reliable sources, and may receive written or oral testimony at the seat of the Court
- The Prosecutor then determines if there is a reasonable basis for proceeding with an investigation

Determination of Reasonable Basis[1] by Prosecutor

Reasonable basis exists ↓ (to Pre-Trial Chamber)

No reasonable basis exists
↓
Prosecutor informs those who provided the information that an investigation will not be pursued. The Prosecutor may reconsider opening the investigation if additional facts or evidence are presented

Pre-Trial Chamber (PTC)

- Prosecutor submits request for authorization for an investigation to PTC, with supporting material collected
- Victims may make "representations" to the Chamber in accordance with the RPE
- PTC independently determines whether there is a reasonable basis to proceed with the investigation, and that jurisdiction exists without prejudice to subsequent determinations by the Court on jurisdiction and admissibility

Determination of Reasonable Basis by PTC

Reasonable basis exists ↓ (to authorization)

No reasonable basis exists
↓
No investigation is commenced. The Prosecutor may resubmit the request upon discovery of new facts or evidence

The investigation is authorized
The Statute does not provide for appeal of this decision

[1] Reasonable basis is explained in article 53.

Figure 9

COMPLEMENTARY JURISDICTION AND ADMISSIBILITY

(article 17)

Jurisdiction is complementary to national criminal jurisdictions (preamble para. 10, art. 1)

The Court, in accordance with the principle of complementary jurisdiction, shall determine that a case is inadmissible where:

• the case is being investigated by a prosecutor of a State with jurisdiction (art. 17(1)(a)) • *unless* the State is unwilling (art. 17(2)) or unable (art. 17(3)) genuinely to carry out the investigation or prosecution	• the case has been investigated as in (a) and the State has decided not to prosecute (art. 17(1)(b)) • *unless* decision resulted from unwillingness or inability of State to genuinely prosecute	• the person has already been tried for the conduct that is the subject of the complaint, and a trial by the Court is not permitted under article 20 (*ne bis in idem*) (art. 17(1)(c))	• the case is not of sufficient gravity to justify further action by the Court (art. 17(1)(d))

Notes: Article 17(2) further defines unwillingness
Article 17(3) further defines inability

Figure 10

PRELIMINARY RULINGS REGARDING ADMISSIBILITY

(article 18)

Determination that there exists a reasonable basis to commence an investigation, or the Prosecutor initiates an investigation

↓
↓

Notification of all States Parties *and* those States which would normally exercise jurisdiction over the crimes

- The Prosecutor may notify States on a confidential basis
- The Prosecutor may limit the scope of information provided if necessary to protect persons, prevent destruction of evidence or prevent absconding of persons

↓
↓

After notification by the Prosecutor a State may decide to investigate the matter

↓

(within one month)

State decides to investigate	State decides not to investigate
↓ ↓ ↓	↓ Case proceeds in the ICC

Prosecutor may request authorization to investigate from PTC ↓ ↓ ↓ ↓ ↓ ↓	Prosecutor defers to the State. Question of deferral may be reopened six months after the date of deferral or at any time when there has been a significant change in circumstances based on the State's unwillingness or inability genuinely to carry out the investigation

If authorization is granted, the State may appeal	If authorization is denied, the Prosecutor may appeal

Figure 11

CHALLENGES TO ADMISSIBILITY

(article 19)

Who may challenge?

- The Court shall satisfy itself that it has jurisdiction
- The Court may determine *sua sponte* the admissibility of a case under art. 17
- No limits on number of challenges

- The accused or a person for whom a warrant or summons has been issued

- A State which has jurisdiction over the case, on the ground that it is investigating or prosecuting the case or has investigated or prosecuted

- A State from which acceptance of jurisdiction is required under art. 12

- The Prosecutor may seek a ruling on admissibility or jurisdiction

↓

Prosecutor shall suspend the investigation until the Court makes a determination on the challenge in accordance with art. 17

↓

Pending the Court's ruling, the Prosecutor may seek authority from the Court to take measures reasonably necessary to protect evidence and prevent absconding of persons

↓

Ruling of Court

↓

Ruling appealable to Appeals Chamber by all parties

Limits on challenges by States and the accused:

- Challenges shall be brought prior to or at commencement of trial, except by leave of Court
- only one challenge per party, except by leave of Court
- challenges brought before trial, except by leave of Court, and then only on *ne bis in idem* grounds, if admissibility

Figure 12

INVESTIGATION OF PERSONS AND INITIAL PROCEEDINGS BEFORE THE COURT

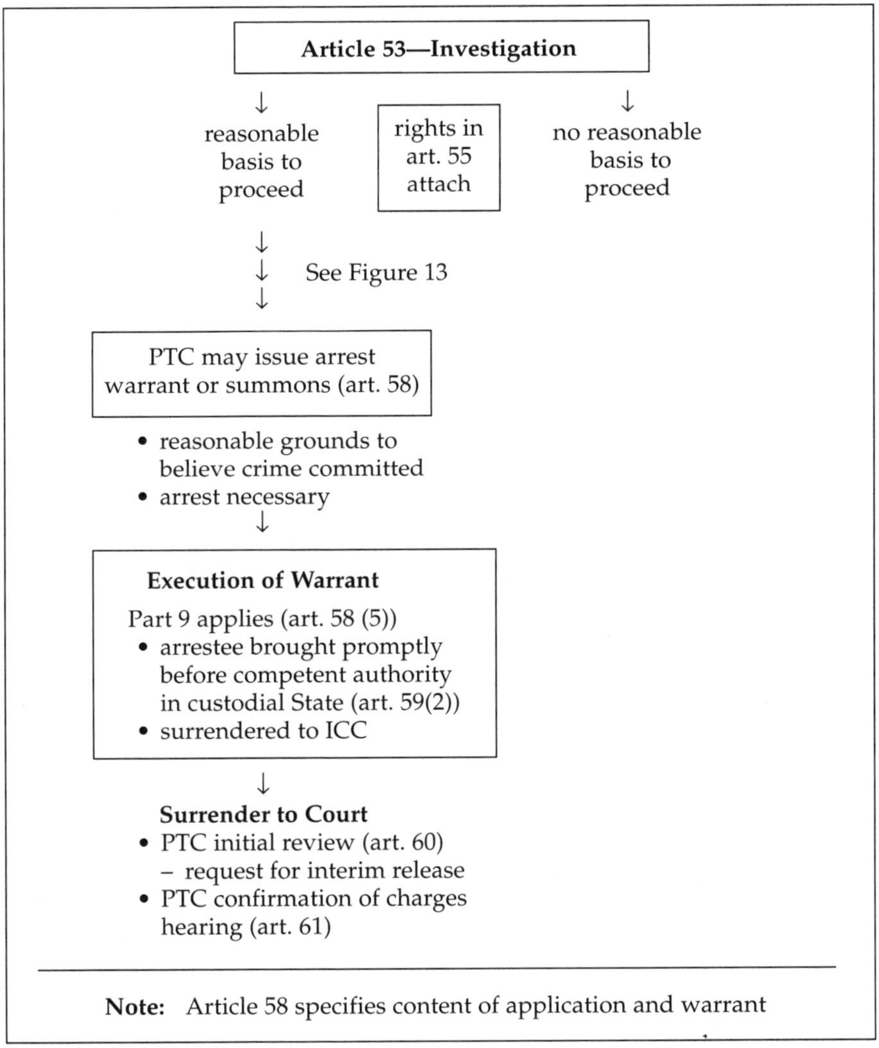

Figure 13
INVESTIGATION

Commencement of Investigation

- referral to Prosecutor by State Party (art. 13(a), art. (14))
- referral to Prosecutor by Security Council (art. 13(b))
- Prosecutor initiates Investigation (art. 13(c), art. 15)

↓

Prosecutor shall investigate unless no reasonable basis to proceed (art. 53). In determining whether to proceed, the Prosecutor shall consider whether:

- The information available to the Prosecutor provides a reasonable basis to believe that a crime within the Court's jurisdiction has been or is being committed (art. 53(1)(a)),
- The case is or would be admissible under art. 17 (art. 53(1)(b)), *and*
- There are substantial reasons to believe that an investigation will not serve the interests of justice, notwithstanding the gravity of the alleged crime and the interests of the victims (art. 53(1)(c))

↓

Prosecutor decides to proceed with investigation
↓
Prosecutorial powers over investigation detailed in art. 54
↓
Rights of persons during an investigation detailed in art. 55

Prosecutor decides not to proceed with investigation
↓
Prosecutor shall inform the PTC and either the State that referred the case or the Security Council, if the Council referred the case, of the decision and the reasons for the decision (art. 53(2))
↓
PTC Review

- The State that referred the case or the Security Council, if the case was referred under art. 13(b), may request that the PTC review the Prosecutor's decision, and may request the Prosecutor to reconsider the decision (art. 53(3)(a))
- The PTC may review the Prosecutor's decision on its own initiative, if the decision is based solely on the Prosecutor's judgment that an investigation or prosecution is not in the interests of justice, in which case the Prosecutor's decision is only effective if confirmed by the PTC (art. 53(3)(b))

Figure 14
UNIQUE INVESTIGATIVE OPPORTUNITY
(article 56)

The Prosecutor shall inform the Pre-Trial Chamber when the Prosecutor considers an investigation to present a unique opportunity, which may not subsequently be available for the purposes of a trial (art. 56(1)(a)), to:

- take testimony or a statement from a witness, or
- to examine, collect or test evidence

↓

Prosecutor may request that the PTC take measures (art. 56(1)(b)) to:

↓

- ensure the efficiency and integrity of the investigation, and
- to protect the rights of the defense

Prosecutor requests measures

↓

PTC may take measures including

- making recommendations or orders regarding procedures to be followed (art. 56(2)(a))
- directing that a record of the proceeding made (art. 56 (2)(b))
- appointing an expert to assist in the investigation (art. 56(2)(c))
- authorizing counsel for a person who has been arrested or who has appeared in response to a summons to participate in the investigation[1] (art.56(2)(d))
- naming one of its members, or another available judge from the Pre-Trial or Trial Division, to observe and make recommendations or orders regarding the collection and preservation of evidence and the questioning of persons (art. 56(2)(e))
- taking other actions necessary for collecting and preserving evidence (art. 56(2)(f))

Prosecutor fails to request measures

↓

If PTC considers measures necessary to preserve evidence essential for trial, it shall consult with the Prosecutor to determine whether failure to request measures is justified (art. 56(3)(a))

Justified

↓

No measures are taken

Unjustified

↓

PTC may take measures on its own initiative (art. 56(3)(a))

↓

Prosecutor may appeal decision of Pre-Trial Chamber (art. 56(3)(b))[2]

---

[1] Where no arrest has been made, or no appearance in response to summons has been made, or counsel has not been designated, the Chamber may appoint another counsel to attend and represent the interests of the defense.

[2] Appeal by Prosecutor of PTC decision to take measures under art. 56 shall be heard on an expedited basis.

Figure 15
REQUESTS FOR WARRANTS AND SUMMONS
(article 58)

Prosecutor
↓

Requests PTC to issue warrant of arrest (art. 58(1))
↓
PTC may issue arrest warrant if, after examining Prosecutor's application, it is satisfied that:

- There are reasonable grounds to believe the person has committed a crime within the jurisdiction of the Court (art. 58(1)(a)), *and*
- Arrest of the person is necessary:
  (i) to ensure the person's appearance at trial (art. 58(1)(b)(i)), *or*
  (ii) to ensure that the person does not obstruct or endanger the investigation (art. 58(1)(b)(ii)), *or*
  (iii) to prevent the person from continuing commission of the crime (art. 58(1)(b)(iii))

↓

Contents of Warrant

- Name of the person and other relevant identifying information (art. 58(3)(a)),
- A specific reference to the crime(s) for which the person is sought (art. 58(3)(b)), *and*
- A concise statement of the facts which are alleged to constitute the crime(s) (art. 58(3)(c))

Requests PTC to issue summons to appear (art. 58(7))
↓
PTC may issue summons to appear if, after examining Prosecutor's application, it is satisfied that:

- There are reasonable grounds to believe the person committed the alleged crime, *and*
- A summons is sufficient to ensure the person's appearance

↓
Summons may impose restrictions on the person's liberty if such restrictions are provided for by national law
↓
↓
↓
↓

Contents of Summons

- Name of the person and other relevant identifying information (art. 58(7)(a)),
- The date on which the person is to appear before the Court (art. 58(7)(b)),
- A specific reference to the crime(s) for which the person is sought (art. 58(7)(c)), *and*
- A concise statement of the facts which are alleged to constitute the crime(s) (art. 58(7)(d))

Figure 16

CONFIRMATION OF CHARGES BEFORE TRIAL

(art. 61)

Hearing held before PTC within reasonable time after the person's surrender or voluntary appearance

accused and counsel present at hearing (art. 61(1))

accused not present if he or she has waived the right to be present or has fled; counsel may be present (art. 61(2); Draft RPE 123, 124, 125, 126)

At hearing:

- Prosecutor shall support each charge with sufficient evidence to establish substantial grounds to believe that the person committed the crime (art. 61(5))
- Accused may object, challenge the evidence, and/or present evidence (art. 61(6)(a)–(c))

↓

Charges Confirmed (art. 61(7)(a))

↓

Prosecutor may amend charges before trial with notice to PTC and accused (art. 61(9); Draft RPE 128)

↓

Presidency constitutes Trial Chamber which is responsible for all subsequent proceedings subject to arts. 64(4) and 61(9) (art. 61(11)). Notification of the same (Draft RPE 129)

Charges Not Confirmed (art. 61(7)(b))

↓

Prosecutor may subsequently seek confirmation with additional evidence (art. 61(8))

Hearing Adjourned (art. 61(7)(c))

↓

PTC requests Prosecutor to consider:

- providing further evidence, or further investigation; or
- amending a charge

Figure 17

TRIAL AND JUDGMENT

3 Judge Trial Chamber

(all 3 Judges, or their alternates, for quorum (art. 74(1))

Powers of the Trial Chamber in conducting Trial set out in art. 64

At commencement of trial, accused has opportunity to admit guilt or not (art. 64(8)(a))

Accused Admits Guilt (art. 65)
↓

- Where Trial Chamber is satisfied the admission of guilt is appropriate (see art. 65(1)), it may convict the accused (art. 65(2))
- Where Trial Chamber is not satisfied as to guilt of the accused, or a more complete presentation of the facts is required, proceed to trial (art. 65(3)–(4))

Accused Does Not Admit Guilt
↓
↓
↓

- All judges shall be present at each stage (art. 74(1))
- Deliberations shall remain secret (art. 74(4))
- Judges shall attempt unanimity failing which the majority shall decide (art. 74(3))
- The single decision shall be fully reasoned and in writing and may contain majority and minority views

↓

Acquit
↓
Accused released immediately unless Trial Chamber detains him for appeal (art. 81(3)(c)(i)))

Convict
↓
Sentencing[1]
↓
Trial Chamber shall consider appropriate sentence[2] (art. 76(1), art. 77(1)–(2)):

- imprisonment
- fines
- forfeiture of assets related to crime

---

[1] "The Court shall establish principles relating to reparations to, or in respect of, victims, including restitution, compensation and rehabilitation." (art. 75(1)). Such awards may come from the Trust Fund provided for in art. 79.

[2] Article 78 presents factors for determination of the sentence.

Figure 18
APPEAL

Appeals Chamber[1]

Decision of Trial Chamber (art. 74)

Sentence (art. 76)

Prosecutor or convicted person may appeal

Grounds for Appeal

- material procedural error
- material error of fact
- material error of law
- any other ground affecting the fairness or reliability of the proceedings or decision[2]

- Disproportion between the crime and the sentence

(Appeals Chamber may)

Reverse or amend the decision or sentence or Order a new trial before a different Trial Chamber

Other Decisions (art. 82)

Either party may appeal a decision

- jurisdiction or admissibility
- granting or denying release of person being investigated or prosecuted
- PTC acts on its own initiative under art. 56(3)
- issue significantly affecting fair and expeditious conduct of proceedings or outcome of trial needing immediate resolution[3]
- PTC decision under art. 57(3)(d)[4]

Order of Reparations (art. 82(4))

- may be appealed by victims' legal representative, the convicted person or a bona fide owner of property adversely affected

No suspensive effect of appeals unless Appeals Chamber so orders (art. 82(3))

Appeals Chamber has all the powers of the Trial Chamber, including the right to hear evidence

Judgment shall state reasons and contain views of majority and minority. Separate or dissenting opinions on questions of law only (art. 83(4))

[1] See Draft RPE 149-158 on proceedings before the Appeals Chamber.
[2] Only the convicted person or the Prosecutor on his or her behalf may bring this claim.
[3] PTC or Trial Chamber must certify need for appeal.
[4] The State concerned or the Prosecutor, with the leave of the PTC, may bring this. Appeal shall be expedited (art. 82)(2))

Figure 19

REVISION OF CONVICTION OR SENTENCE

Appeals Chamber

↓

Revision of Conviction or Sentence

(art. 84, Draft RPE 159–161)

Convicted person or, after death, family member or expressly authorized person or the Prosecutor on the person's behalf may apply for Revision

↓

↓

Grounds for Revision:

- new evidence discovered that was:
  - (i) not available at the time of trial and unavailability not attributed to the party making the application; and
  - (ii) is sufficiently important that had it been proved at trial it would have been likely to have resulted in different verdict
- decisive evidence was forged or falsified
- serious judicial misconduct or breach of duty of sufficient gravity to justify the removal of that/those judge(s) from office has occurred

↓

↓

Appeals Chamber may:

- reject request as unfounded
- reconvene original Trial Chamber
- constitute a new Trial Chamber; or
- retain jurisdiction with a view to determining whether the judgment should be revised

Figure 20

INTERNATIONAL COOPERATION AND JUDICIAL ASSISTANCE

Court issues a request for cooperation

↓

States Parties

↓

- General obligation to cooperate fully with Court's investigation and prosecution (art. 86)
- Shall ensure that procedures are available under national law for all forms of cooperation present in the Statute (art. 88)
- Request transmitted through channel designated by State upon ratification, acceptance, approval or accession (art. 87(1)(a))

↓

If failure to comply, Court may make a finding to that effect and refer the matter to the Assembly of States Parties, or to the Security Council, if Security Council referred the case

Non-States Parties

↓

- No obligation to comply either with request for arrest and surrender or request for transit
- Request handled by ad hoc arrangement or agreement with State (art. 87(5))

↓

If failure to cooperate, Court may so inform the Assembly of States Parties, or the Security Council, if the Security Council referred the matter

IGOs

↓

- May be asked to provide information, documents or cooperation and assistance (art. 87(6))

Figure 21

INTERNATIONAL COOPERATION AND JUDICIAL ASSISTANCE ARREST AND SURRENDER

Court issues a Request for Arrest and Surrender

↓

- need a warrant for arrest and surrender
- must be in writing, and in a form necessary to meet the requirements for surrender in the requested State
- a request for transit to accompany detainee through intermediate States (art. 89(3))

↓

Obstacles to immediate execution of request

↓

- Person may bring challenge before national court on *ne bis in idem* grounds (art. 89(2))
- Person may be serving sentence for a crime different from that for which surrender to the Court is sought; State may or may not decide to surrender (art. 89(4))
- There is insufficient information to execute the request (art. 97(a))
- Despite best efforts, the person sought cannot be located, or the person in the requested State is clearly not the person named in the warrant (art. 97(b))
- Execution of the request in its current form would require the requested State to breach a pre-existing treaty obligation undertaken with respect to another State (art. 97(c))
- There is a competing extradition request (art. 90)[1]
- Court may not proceed with a request for surrender which would require the requested State to act inconsistently with its obligations under international law with respect to the State or diplomatic immunity of a person or property of a third State, unless the Court can first obtain the cooperation of the third State for the waiver of immunity (art. 98(1))
- Court may not proceed with a request for surrender which would require the requested State to act inconsistently with its obligations under international agreements pursuant to which the consent of a sending State is required to surrender a person of that State to the Court, unless the Court can first obtain the cooperation of the sending State for the giving of consent for the surrender (art. 98(2))

---

1 See Figure 22 for further explanation.

Figure 22

INTERNATIONAL COOPERATION AND JUDICIAL ASSISTANCE COMPETING EXTRADITION REQUESTS

Court issues a request for arrest and surrender

↓

For the same conduct that constitutes the crime for which the Court seeks the person's surrender

↓

State Party issues the competing request (art. 90(2)–(3))

↓

State Party shall surrender the person to the Court as a matter of priority if the Court has determined that the case is admissible

or

subsequently, if the Court determines that the case is admissible

Pending determination of admissibility, requested State may deal with extradition request but shall not extradite until Court has determined the case is inadmissible

Non-State Party issues competing request (art. 90(4)–(6))

↓

State Party shall give priority to the request from the Court if:

- the Court has determined the case is admissible, *and*
- State Party is not under an existing international obligation to extradite the person to the requesting State

If the State Party is under an existing international obligation to extradite, it shall decide whether to extradite or surrender, considering "all the relevant factors," including

- the respective dates of the requests;
- the interests of the requesting State, including, where relevant:
  – whether the crime was committed in its territory, and
  – the nationality of the victims and the person sought
- the possibility of subsequent surrender between the Court and the requesting State

For conduct other than that which constitutes the crime for which the Court seeks the person's surrender

↓

- The requested State shall give priority to the request from the Court unless it is under an existing international obligation to extradite the person to the requesting State
- Even if there is an existing international obligation to extradite, the requested State shall, in determining whether to extradite or surrender, consider "all the relevant factors," including those in art. 90(6), but shall give special consideration to the relative nature and gravity of the conduct in question

Figure 23

INTERNATIONAL COOPERATION AND JUDICIAL ASSISTANCE REQUESTS FOR OTHER FORMS OF ASSISTANCE

Court issues a request for cooperation to a State Party

↓

- must be in writing
- must contain information required by article 96(2), as well as any information required under the law of the requested State
- shall be executed in accordance with the relevant procedure under the law of the requested State
- limited to forms of assistance listed in article 93(1)(a)–(k) or any other type of assistance not prohibited by the law of the requested State

↓

Grounds for Denial

- Assistance is prohibited in the requested State on the basis of an existing fundamental legal principle of general application (art. 93(3))
- To protect its national security pursuant to art. 72 (art. 93(4), art. 99(5))
- Assistance would require the State to act inconsistently with its obligations under international law with respect to the State or diplomatic immunity of a person or property of a third State, unless the Court can first obtain the cooperation of that third State for the waiver of immunity (art. 98(1))

Grounds for Postponement

- The immediate execution of the request would interfere with an ongoing investigation or prosecution of a case different from that which the request relates (art. 94)[1]
- An admissibility challenge is under consideration by the Court (art. 95)[1]
- There is insufficient information to execute the request.[2]
- Execution of the request in its current form would require the requested State to breach a pre-existing treaty obligation undertaken with respect to another State (art. 97(c))

[1] In this case, the Prosecutor may nevertheless seek measures to preserve evidence (art. 94(2)) or collect evidence (art. 95).

[2] In this case, the State must consult the Court without delay in order to resolve the matter.

APPENDICES

APPENDIX 1

ROME STATUTE OF THE INTERNATIONAL CRIMINAL COURT

[* as *corrected* by the procés-verbaux of 10 November 1998 and 12 July 1999]

PREAMBLE

The States Parties to this Statute,

Conscious that all peoples are united by common bonds, their cultures pieced together in a shared heritage, and concerned that this delicate mosaic may be shattered at any time,

Mindful that during this century millions of children, women and men have been victims of unimaginable atrocities that deeply shock the conscience of humanity,

Recognizing that such grave crimes threaten the peace, security and well-being of the world,

Affirming that the most serious crimes of concern to the international community as a whole must not go unpunished and that their effective prosecution must be ensured by taking measures at the national level and by enhancing international cooperation,

Determined to put an end to impunity for the perpetrators of these crimes and thus to contribute to the prevention of such crimes,

Recalling that it is the duty of every State to exercise its criminal jurisdiction over those responsible for international crimes,

Reaffirming the Purposes and Principles of the Charter of the United Nations, and in particular that all States shall refrain from the threat or use of force against the territorial integrity or political independence of any State, or in any other manner inconsistent with the Purposes of the United Nations,

Emphasizing in this connection that nothing in this Statute shall be taken as authorizing any State Party to intervene in an armed conflict or in the internal affairs of any State,

Determined to these ends and for the sake of present and future generations, to establish an independent permanent International Criminal Court in relationship with the United Nations system, with jurisdiction over the most serious crimes of concern to the international community as a whole,

Emphasizing that the International Criminal Court established under this Statute shall be complementary to national criminal jurisdictions,

Resolved to guarantee lasting respect for and the enforcement of international justice,

Have agreed as follows:

PART 1. ESTABLISHMENT OF THE COURT

Article 1
The Court

An International Criminal Court ("the Court") is hereby established. It shall be a permanent institution and shall have the power to exercise its jurisdiction over persons for the most serious crimes of international concern, as referred to in this Statute, and shall be complementary to national criminal jurisdictions. The jurisdiction and functioning of the Court shall be governed by the provisions of this Statute.

Article 2
Relationship of the Court with the United Nations

The Court shall be brought into relationship with the United Nations through an agreement to be approved by the Assembly of States Parties to this Statute and thereafter concluded by the President of the Court on its behalf.

Article 3
Seat of the Court

1. The seat of the Court shall be established at The Hague in the Netherlands ("the host State").
2. The Court shall enter into a headquarters agreement with the host State, to be approved by the Assembly of States Parties and thereafter concluded by the President of the Court on its behalf.
3. The Court may sit elsewhere, whenever it considers it desirable, as provided in this Statute.

Article 4
Legal status and powers of the Court

1. The Court shall have international legal personality. It shall also have such legal capacity as may be necessary for the exercise of its functions and the fulfilment of its purposes.

2. The Court may exercise its functions and powers, as provided in this Statute, on the territory of any State Party and, by special agreement, on the territory of any other State.

PART 2. JURISDICTION, ADMISSIBILITY AND APPLICABLE LAW

Article 5

Crimes within the jurisdiction of the Court

1. The jurisdiction of the Court shall be limited to the most serious crimes of concern to the international community as a whole. The Court has jurisdiction in accordance with this Statute with respect to the following crimes:
   (a) The crime of genocide;
   (b) Crimes against humanity;
   (c) War crimes;
   (d) The crime of aggression.
2. The Court shall exercise jurisdiction over the crime of aggression once a provision is adopted in accordance with articles 121 and 123 defining the crime and setting out the conditions under which the Court shall exercise jurisdiction with respect to this crime. Such a provision shall be consistent with the relevant provisions of the Charter of the United Nations.

Article 6

Genocide

For the purpose of this Statute, "genocide" means any of the following acts committed with intent to destroy, in whole or in part, a national, ethnical, racial or religious group, as such:

(a) Killing members of the group;
(b) Causing serious bodily or mental harm to members of the group;
(c) Deliberately inflicting on the group conditions of life calculated to bring about its physical destruction in whole or in part;
(d) Imposing measures intended to prevent births within the group;
(e) Forcibly transferring children of the group to another group.

Article 7

Crimes against humanity

1. For the purpose of this Statute, "crime against humanity" means any of the following acts when committed as part of a widespread or systematic attack directed against any civilian population, with knowledge of the attack:
   (a) Murder;
   (b) Extermination;

(c) Enslavement;
(d) Deportation or forcible transfer of population;
(e) Imprisonment or other severe deprivation of physical liberty in violation of fundamental rules of international law;
(f) Torture;
(g) Rape, sexual slavery, enforced prostitution, forced pregnancy, enforced sterilization, or any other form of sexual violence of comparable gravity;
(h) Persecution against any identifiable group or collectivity on political, racial, national, ethnic, cultural, religious, gender as defined in paragraph 3, or other grounds that are universally recognized as impermissible under international law, in connection with any act referred to in this paragraph or any crime within the jurisdiction of the Court;
(i) Enforced disappearance of persons;
(j) The crime of apartheid;
(k) Other inhumane acts of a similar character intentionally causing great suffering, or serious injury to body or to mental or physical health.

2. For the purpose of paragraph 1:
(a) "Attack directed against any civilian population" means a course of conduct involving the multiple commission of acts referred to in paragraph 1 against any civilian population, pursuant to or in furtherance of a State or organizational policy to commit such attack;
(b) "Extermination" includes the intentional infliction of conditions of life, *inter alia* the deprivation of access to food and medicine, calculated to bring about the destruction of part of a population;
(c) "Enslavement" means the exercise of any or all of the powers attaching to the right of ownership over a person and includes the exercise of such power in the course of trafficking in persons, in particular women and children;
(d) "Deportation or forcible transfer of population" means forced displacement of the persons concerned by expulsion or other coercive acts from the area in which they are lawfully present, without grounds permitted under international law;
(e) "Torture" means the intentional infliction of severe pain or suffering, whether physical or mental, upon a person in the custody or under the control of the accused; except that torture shall not include pain or suffering arising only from, inherent in or incidental to, lawful sanctions;
(f) "Forced pregnancy" means the unlawful confinement of a woman forcibly made pregnant, with the intent of affecting the ethnic composition of any population or carrying out other grave violations of international law. This definition shall not in any way be interpreted as affecting national laws relating to pregnancy;

(g) "Persecution" means the intentional and severe deprivation of fundamental rights contrary to international law by reason of the identity of the group or collectivity;
(h) "The crime of apartheid" means inhumane acts of a character similar to those referred to in paragraph 1, committed in the context of an institutionalized regime of systematic oppression and domination by one racial group over any other racial group or groups and committed with the intention of maintaining that regime;
(i) "Enforced disappearance of persons" means the arrest, detention or abduction of persons by, or with the authorization, support or acquiescence of, a State or a political organization, followed by a refusal to acknowledge that deprivation of freedom or to give information on the fate or whereabouts of those persons, with the intention of removing them from the protection of the law for a prolonged period of time.

3. For the purpose of this Statute, it is understood that the term "gender" refers to the two sexes, male and female, within the context of society. The term "gender" does not indicate any meaning different from the above.

Article 8

War crimes

1. The Court shall have jurisdiction in respect of war crimes in particular when committed as part of a plan or policy or as part of a large-scale commission of such crimes.
2. For the purpose of this Statute, "war crimes" means:
   (a) Grave breaches of the Geneva Conventions of 12 August 1949, namely, any of the following acts against persons or property protected under the provisions of the relevant Geneva Convention:
      (i) Wilful killing;
      (ii) Torture or inhuman treatment, including biological experiments;
      (iii) Wilfully causing great suffering, or serious injury to body or health;
      (iv) Extensive destruction and appropriation of property, not justified by military necessity and carried out unlawfully and wantonly;
      (v) Compelling a prisoner of war or other protected person to serve in the forces of a hostile Power;
      (vi) Wilfully depriving a prisoner of war or other protected person of the rights of fair and regular trial;
      (vii) Unlawful deportation or transfer or unlawful confinement;
      (viii) Taking of hostages.
   (b) Other serious violations of the laws and customs applicable in international armed conflict, within the established framework of international law, namely, any of the following acts:

(i) Intentionally directing attacks against the civilian population as such or against individual civilians not taking direct part in hostilities;
(ii) Intentionally directing attacks against civilian objects, that is, objects which are not military objectives;
(iii) Intentionally directing attacks against personnel, installations, material, units or vehicles involved in a humanitarian assistance or peacekeeping mission in accordance with the Charter of the United Nations, as long as they are entitled to the protection given to civilians or civilian objects under the international law of armed conflict;
(iv) Intentionally launching an attack in the knowledge that such attack will cause incidental loss of life or injury to civilians or damage to civilian objects or widespread, long-term and severe damage to the natural environment which would be clearly excessive in relation to the concrete and direct overall military advantage anticipated;
(v) Attacking or bombarding, by whatever means, towns, villages, dwellings or buildings which are undefended and which are not military objectives;
(vi) Killing or wounding a combatant who, having laid down his arms or having no longer means of defence, has surrendered at discretion;
(vii) Making improper use of a flag of truce, of the flag or of the military insignia and uniform of the enemy or of the United Nations, as well as of the distinctive emblems of the Geneva Conventions, resulting in death or serious personal injury;
(viii) The transfer, directly or indirectly, by the Occupying Power of parts of its own civilian population into the territory it occupies, or the deportation or transfer of all or parts of the population of the occupied territory within or outside this territory;
(ix) Intentionally directing attacks against buildings dedicated to religion, education, art, science or charitable purposes, historic monuments, hospitals and places where the sick and wounded are collected, provided they are not military objectives;
(x) Subjecting persons who are in the power of an adverse party to physical mutilation or to medical or scientific experiments of any kind which are neither justified by the medical, dental or hospital treatment of the person concerned nor carried out in his or her interest, and which cause death to or seriously endanger the health of such person or persons;
(xi) Killing or wounding treacherously individuals belonging to the hostile nation or army;

(xii) Declaring that no quarter will be given;

(xiii) Destroying or seizing the enemy's property unless such destruction or seizure be imperatively demanded by the necessities of war;

(xiv) Declaring abolished, suspended or inadmissible in a court of law the rights and actions of the nationals of the hostile party;

(xv) Compelling the nationals of the hostile party to take part in the operations of war directed against their own country, even if they were in the belligerent's service before the commencement of the war;

(xvi) Pillaging a town or place, even when taken by assault;

(xvii) Employing poison or poisoned weapons;

(xviii) Employing asphyxiating, poisonous or other gases, and all analogous liquids, materials or devices;

(xix) Employing bullets which expand or flatten easily in the human body, such as bullets with a hard envelope which does not entirely cover the core or is pierced with incisions;

(xx) Employing weapons, projectiles and material and methods of warfare which are of a nature to cause superfluous injury or unnecessary suffering or which are inherently indiscriminate in violation of the international law of armed conflict, provided that such weapons, projectiles and material and methods of warfare are the subject of a comprehensive prohibition and are included in an annex to this Statute, by an amendment in accordance with the relevant provisions set forth in articles 121 and 123;

(xxi) Committing outrages upon personal dignity, in particular humiliating and degrading treatment;

(xxii) Committing rape, sexual slavery, enforced prostitution, forced pregnancy, as defined in article 7, paragraph 2 (f), enforced sterilization, or any other form of sexual violence also constituting a grave breach of the Geneva Conventions;

(xxiii) Utilizing the presence of a civilian or other protected person to render certain points, areas or military forces immune from military operations;

(xxiv) Intentionally directing attacks against buildings, material, medical units and transport, and personnel using the distinctive emblems of the Geneva Conventions in conformity with international law;

(xxv) Intentionally using starvation of civilians as a method of warfare by depriving them of objects indispensable to their survival, including wilfully impeding relief supplies as provided for under the Geneva Conventions;

(xxvi) Conscripting or enlisting children under the age of fifteen years into the national armed forces or using them to participate actively in hostilities.

(c) In the case of an armed conflict not of an international character, serious violations of article 3 common to the four Geneva Conventions of 12 August 1949, namely, any of the following acts committed against persons taking no active part in the hostilities, including members of armed forces who have laid down their arms and those placed *hors de combat* by sickness, wounds, detention or any other cause:
   (i) Violence to life and person, in particular murder of all kinds, mutilation, cruel treatment and torture;
   (ii) Committing outrages upon personal dignity, in particular humiliating and degrading treatment;
   (iii) Taking of hostages;
   (iv) The passing of sentences and the carrying out of executions without previous judgement pronounced by a regularly constituted court, affording all judicial guarantees which are generally recognized as indispensable.

(d) Paragraph 2 (c) applies to armed conflicts not of an international character and thus does not apply to situations of internal disturbances and tensions, such as riots, isolated and sporadic acts of violence or other acts of a similar nature.

(e) Other serious violations of the laws and customs applicable in armed conflicts not of an international character, within the established framework of international law, namely, any of the following acts:
   (i) Intentionally directing attacks against the civilian population as such or against individual civilians not taking direct part in hostilities;
   (ii) Intentionally directing attacks against buildings, material, medical units and transport, and personnel using the distinctive emblems of the Geneva Conventions in conformity with international law;
   (iii) Intentionally directing attacks against personnel, installations, material, units or vehicles involved in a humanitarian assistance or peacekeeping mission in accordance with the Charter of the United Nations, as long as they are entitled to the protection given to civilians or civilian objects under the international law of armed conflict;
   (iv) Intentionally directing attacks against buildings dedicated to religion, education, art, science or charitable purposes, historic monuments, hospitals and places where the sick and wounded are collected, provided they are not military objectives;
   (v) Pillaging a town or place, even when taken by assault;
   (vi) Committing rape, sexual slavery, enforced prostitution, forced pregnancy, as defined in article 7, paragraph 2 (f), enforced ster-

ilization, and any other form of sexual violence also constituting a serious violation of article 3 common to the four Geneva Conventions;

(vii) Conscripting or enlisting children under the age of fifteen years into armed forces or groups or using them to participate actively in hostilities;

(viii) Ordering the displacement of the civilian population for reasons related to the conflict, unless the security of the civilians involved or imperative military reasons so demand;

(ix) Killing or wounding treacherously a combatant adversary;

(x) Declaring that no quarter will be given;

(xi) Subjecting persons who are in the power of another party to the conflict to physical mutilation or to medical or scientific experiments of any kind which are neither justified by the medical, dental or hospital treatment of the person concerned nor carried out in his or her interest, and which cause death to or seriously endanger the health of such person or persons;

(xii) Destroying or seizing the property of an adversary unless such destruction or seizure be imperatively demanded by the necessities of the conflict;

(f) Paragraph 2 (e) applies to armed conflicts not of an international character and thus does not apply to situations of internal disturbances and tensions, such as riots, isolated and sporadic acts of violence or other acts of a similar nature. It applies to armed conflicts that take place in the territory of a State when there is protracted armed conflict between governmental authorities and organized armed groups or between such groups.

3. Nothing in paragraph 2 (c) and (e) shall affect the responsibility of a Government to maintain or re-establish law and order in the State or to defend the unity and territorial integrity of the State, by all legitimate means.

Article 9

Elements of Crimes

1. Elements of Crimes shall assist the Court in the interpretation and application of articles 6, 7 and 8. They shall be adopted by a two-thirds majority of the members of the Assembly of States Parties.
2. Amendments to the Elements of Crimes may be proposed by:
   (a) Any State Party;
   (b) The judges acting by an absolute majority;
   (c) The Prosecutor.

Such amendments shall be adopted by a two-thirds majority of the members of the Assembly of States Parties.

3. The Elements of Crimes and amendments thereto shall be consistent with this Statute.

Article 10

Nothing in this Part shall be interpreted as limiting or prejudicing in any way existing or developing rules of international law for purposes other than this Statute.

Article 11

Jurisdiction ratione temporis

1. The Court has jurisdiction only with respect to crimes committed after the entry into force of this Statute.
2. If a State becomes a Party to this Statute after its entry into force, the Court may exercise its jurisdiction only with respect to crimes committed after the entry into force of this Statute for that State, unless that State has made a declaration under article 12, paragraph 3.

Article 12

Preconditions to the exercise of jurisdiction

1. A State which becomes a Party to this Statute thereby accepts the jurisdiction of the Court with respect to the crimes referred to in article 5.
2. In the case of article 13, paragraph (a) or (c), the Court may exercise its jurisdiction if one or more of the following States are Parties to this Statute or have accepted the jurisdiction of the Court in accordance with paragraph 3:
   (a) The State on the territory of which the conduct in question occurred or, if the crime was committed on board a vessel or aircraft, the State of registration of that vessel or aircraft;
   (b) The State of which the person accused of the crime is a national.
3. If the acceptance of a State which is not a Party to this Statute is required under paragraph 2, that State may, by declaration lodged with the Registrar, accept the exercise of jurisdiction by the Court with respect to the crime in question. The accepting State shall cooperate with the Court without any delay or exception in accordance with Part 9.

Article 13

Exercise of jurisdiction

The Court may exercise its jurisdiction with respect to a crime referred to in article 5 in accordance with the provisions of this Statute if:

(a) A situation in which one or more of such crimes appears to have been committed is referred to the Prosecutor by a State Party in accordance with article 14;

(b) A situation in which one or more of such crimes appears to have been committed is referred to the Prosecutor by the Security Council acting under Chapter VII of the Charter of the United Nations; or
(c) The Prosecutor has initiated an investigation in respect of such a crime in accordance with article 15.

Article 14
Referral of a situation by a State Party

1. A State Party may refer to the Prosecutor a situation in which one or more crimes within the jurisdiction of the Court appear to have been committed requesting the Prosecutor to investigate the situation for the purpose of determining whether one or more specific persons should be charged with the commission of such crimes.
2. As far as possible, a referral shall specify the relevant circumstances and be accompanied by such supporting documentation as is available to the State referring the situation.

Article 15
Prosecutor

1. The Prosecutor may initiate investigations *proprio motu* on the basis of information on crimes within the jurisdiction of the Court.
2. The Prosecutor shall analyse the seriousness of the information received. For this purpose, he or she may seek additional information from States, organs of the United Nations, intergovernmental or non-governmental organizations, or other reliable sources that he or she deems appropriate, and may receive written or oral testimony at the seat of the Court.
3. If the Prosecutor concludes that there is a reasonable basis to proceed with an investigation, he or she shall submit to the Pre-Trial Chamber a request for authorization of an investigation, together with any supporting material collected. Victims may make representations to the Pre-Trial Chamber, in accordance with the Rules of Procedure and Evidence.
4. If the Pre-Trial Chamber, upon examination of the request and the supporting material, considers that there is a reasonable basis to proceed with an investigation, and that the case appears to fall within the jurisdiction of the Court, it shall authorize the commencement of the investigation, without prejudice to subsequent determinations by the Court with regard to the jurisdiction and admissibility of a case.
5. The refusal of the Pre-Trial Chamber to authorize the investigation shall not preclude the presentation of a subsequent request by the Prosecutor based on new facts or evidence regarding the same situation.
6. If, after the preliminary examination referred to in paragraphs 1 and 2, the Prosecutor concludes that the information provided does not constitute a reasonable basis for an investigation, he or she shall inform those

who provided the information. This shall not preclude the Prosecutor from considering further information submitted to him or her regarding the same situation in the light of new facts or evidence.

Article 16

Deferral of investigation or prosecution

No investigation or prosecution may be commenced or proceeded with under this Statute for a period of 12 months after the Security Council, in a resolution adopted under Chapter VII of the Charter of the United Nations, has requested the Court to that effect; that request may be renewed by the Council under the same conditions.

Article 17

Issues of admissibility

1. Having regard to paragraph 10 of the Preamble and article 1, the Court shall determine that a case is inadmissible where:
   (a) The case is being investigated or prosecuted by a State which has jurisdiction over it, unless the State is unwilling or unable genuinely to carry out the investigation or prosecution;
   (b) The case has been investigated by a State which has jurisdiction over it and the State has decided not to prosecute the person concerned, unless the decision resulted from the unwillingness or inability of the State genuinely to prosecute;
   (c) The person concerned has already been tried for conduct which is the subject of the complaint, and a trial by the Court is not permitted under article 20, paragraph 3;
   (d) The case is not of sufficient gravity to justify further action by the Court.
2. In order to determine unwillingness in a particular case, the Court shall consider, having regard to the principles of due process recognized by international law, whether one or more of the following exist, as applicable:
   (a) The proceedings were or are being undertaken or the national decision was made for the purpose of shielding the person concerned from criminal responsibility for crimes within the jurisdiction of the Court referred to in article 5;
   (b) There has been an unjustified delay in the proceedings which in the circumstances is inconsistent with an intent to bring the person concerned to justice;
   (c) The proceedings were not or are not being conducted independently or impartially, and they were or are being conducted in a manner which, in the circumstances, is inconsistent with an intent to bring the person concerned to justice.

3. In order to determine inability in a particular case, the Court shall consider whether, due to a total or substantial collapse or unavailability of its national judicial system, the State is unable to obtain the accused or the necessary evidence and testimony or otherwise unable to carry out its proceedings.

Article 18

Preliminary rulings regarding admissibility

1. When a situation has been referred to the Court pursuant to article 13 (a) and the Prosecutor has determined that there would be a reasonable basis to commence an investigation, or the Prosecutor initiates an investigation pursuant to articles 13 (c) and 15, the Prosecutor shall notify all States Parties and those States which, taking into account the information available, would normally exercise jurisdiction over the crimes concerned. The Prosecutor may notify such States on a confidential basis and, where the Prosecutor believes it necessary to protect persons, prevent destruction of evidence or prevent the absconding of persons, may limit the scope of the information provided to States.
2. Within one month of receipt of that notification, a State may inform the Court that it is investigating or has investigated its nationals or others within its jurisdiction with respect to criminal acts which may constitute crimes referred to in article 5 and which relate to the information provided in the notification to States. At the request of that State, the Prosecutor shall defer to the State's investigation of those persons unless the Pre-Trial Chamber, on the application of the Prosecutor, decides to authorize the investigation.
3. The Prosecutor's deferral to a State's investigation shall be open to review by the Prosecutor six months after the date of deferral or at any time when there has been a significant change of circumstances based on the State's unwillingness or inability genuinely to carry out the investigation.
4. The State concerned or the Prosecutor may appeal to the Appeals Chamber against a ruling of the Pre-Trial Chamber, in accordance with article 82. The appeal may be heard on an expedited basis.
5. When the Prosecutor has deferred an investigation in accordance with paragraph 2, the Prosecutor may request that the State concerned periodically inform the Prosecutor of the progress of its investigations and any subsequent prosecutions. States Parties shall respond to such requests without undue delay.
6. Pending a ruling by the Pre-Trial Chamber, or at any time when the Prosecutor has deferred an investigation under this article, the Prosecutor may, on an exceptional basis, seek authority from the Pre-Trial Chamber to pursue necessary investigative steps for the purpose of preserving evidence where there is a unique opportunity to obtain important evidence

or there is a significant risk that such evidence may not be subsequently available.

7. A State which has challenged a ruling of the Pre-Trial Chamber under this article may challenge the admissibility of a case under article 19 on the grounds of additional significant facts or significant change of circumstances.

Article 19

Challenges to the jurisdiction of the Court or the admissibility of a case

1. The Court shall satisfy itself that it has jurisdiction in any case brought before it. The Court may, on its own motion, determine the admissibility of a case in accordance with article 17.
2. Challenges to the admissibility of a case on the grounds referred to in article 17 or challenges to the jurisdiction of the Court may be made by:
   (a) An accused or a person for whom a warrant of arrest or a summons to appear has been issued under article 58;
   (b) A State which has jurisdiction over a case, on the ground that it is investigating or prosecuting the case or has investigated or prosecuted; or
   (c) A State from which acceptance of jurisdiction is required under article 12.
3. The Prosecutor may seek a ruling from the Court regarding a question of jurisdiction or admissibility. In proceedings with respect to jurisdiction or admissibility, those who have referred the situation under article 13, as well as victims, may also submit observations to the Court.
4. The admissibility of a case or the jurisdiction of the Court may be challenged only once by any person or State referred to in paragraph 2. The challenge shall take place prior to or at the commencement of the trial. In exceptional circumstances, the Court may grant leave for a challenge to be brought more than once or at a time later than the commencement of the trial. Challenges to the admissibility of a case, at the commencement of a trial, or subsequently with the leave of the Court, may be based only on article 17, paragraph 1 (c).
5. A State referred to in paragraph 2 (b) and (c) shall make a challenge at the earliest opportunity.
6. Prior to the confirmation of the charges, challenges to the admissibility of a case or challenges to the jurisdiction of the Court shall be referred to the Pre-Trial Chamber. After confirmation of the charges, they shall be referred to the Trial Chamber. Decisions with respect to jurisdiction or admissibility may be appealed to the Appeals Chamber in accordance with article 82.

7. If a challenge is made by a State referred to in paragraph 2 (b) or (c), the Prosecutor shall suspend the investigation until such time as the Court makes a determination in accordance with article 17.
8. Pending a ruling by the Court, the Prosecutor may seek authority from the Court:
   (a) To pursue necessary investigative steps of the kind referred to in article 18, paragraph 6;
   (b) To take a statement or testimony from a witness or complete the collection and examination of evidence which had begun prior to the making of the challenge; and
   (c) In cooperation with the relevant States, to prevent the absconding of persons in respect of whom the Prosecutor has already requested a warrant of arrest under article 58.
9. The making of a challenge shall not affect the validity of any act performed by the Prosecutor or any order or warrant issued by the Court prior to the making of the challenge.
10. If the Court has decided that a case is inadmissible under article 17, the Prosecutor may submit a request for a review of the decision when he or she is fully satisfied that new facts have arisen which negate the basis on which the case had previously been found inadmissible under article 17.
11. If the Prosecutor, having regard to the matters referred to in article 17, defers an investigation, the Prosecutor may request that the relevant State make available to the Prosecutor information on the proceedings. That information shall, at the request of the State concerned, be confidential. If the Prosecutor thereafter decides to proceed with an investigation, he or she shall notify the State to which deferral of the proceedings has taken place.

Article 20

Ne bis in idem

1. Except as provided in this Statute, no person shall be tried before the Court with respect to conduct which formed the basis of crimes for which the person has been convicted or acquitted by the Court.
2. No person shall be tried by another court for a crime referred to in article 5 for which that person has already been convicted or acquitted by the Court.
3. No person who has been tried by another court for conduct also proscribed under article 6, 7 or 8 shall be tried by the Court with respect to the same conduct unless the proceedings in the other court:
   (a) Were for the purpose of shielding the person concerned from criminal responsibility for crimes within the jurisdiction of the Court; or
   (b) Otherwise were not conducted independently or impartially in accordance with the norms of due process recognized by international law

and were conducted in a manner which, in the circumstances, was inconsistent with an intent to bring the person concerned to justice.

Article 21
Applicable law

1. The Court shall apply:
   (a) In the first place, this Statute, Elements of Crimes and its Rules of Procedure and Evidence;
   (b) In the second place, where appropriate, applicable treaties and the principles and rules of international law, including the established principles of the international law of armed conflict;
   (c) Failing that, general principles of law derived by the Court from national laws of legal systems of the world including, as appropriate, the national laws of States that would normally exercise jurisdiction over the crime, provided that those principles are not inconsistent with this Statute and with international law and internationally recognized norms and standards.
2. The Court may apply principles and rules of law as interpreted in its previous decisions.
3. The application and interpretation of law pursuant to this article must be consistent with internationally recognized human rights, and be without any adverse distinction founded on grounds such as gender as defined in article 7, paragraph 3, age, race, colour, language, religion or belief, political or other opinion, national, ethnic or social origin, wealth, birth or other status.

PART 3. GENERAL PRINCIPLES OF CRIMINAL LAW

Article 22
Nullum crimen sine lege

1. A person shall not be criminally responsible under this Statute unless the conduct in question constitutes, at the time it takes place, a crime within the jurisdiction of the Court.
2. The definition of a crime shall be strictly construed and shall not be extended by analogy. In case of ambiguity, the definition shall be interpreted in favour of the person being investigated, prosecuted or convicted.
3. This article shall not affect the characterization of any conduct as criminal under international law independently of this Statute.

Article 23

Nulla poena sine lege

A person convicted by the Court may be punished only in accordance with this Statute.

Article 24

Non-retroactivity ratione personae

1. No person shall be criminally responsible under this Statute for conduct prior to the entry into force of the Statute.
2. In the event of a change in the law applicable to a given case prior to a final judgement, the law more favourable to the person being investigated, prosecuted or convicted shall apply.

Article 25

Individual criminal responsibility

1. The Court shall have jurisdiction over natural persons pursuant to this Statute.
2. A person who commits a crime within the jurisdiction of the Court shall be individually responsible and liable for punishment in accordance with this Statute.
3. In accordance with this Statute, a person shall be criminally responsible and liable for punishment for a crime within the jurisdiction of the Court if that person:
   (a) Commits such a crime, whether as an individual, jointly with another or through another person, regardless of whether that other person is criminally responsible;
   (b) Orders, solicits or induces the commission of such a crime which in fact occurs or is attempted;
   (c) For the purpose of facilitating the commission of such a crime, aids, abets or otherwise assists in its commission or its attempted commission, including providing the means for its commission;
   (d) In any other way contributes to the commission or attempted commission of such a crime by a group of persons acting with a common purpose. Such contribution shall be intentional and shall either:
      (i) Be made with the aim of furthering the criminal activity or criminal purpose of the group, where such activity or purpose involves the commission of a crime within the jurisdiction of the Court; or
      (ii) Be made in the knowledge of the intention of the group to commit the crime;

(e) In respect of the crime of genocide, directly and publicly incites others to commit genocide;
(f) Attempts to commit such a crime by taking action that commences its execution by means of a substantial step, but the crime does not occur because of circumstances independent of the person's intentions. However, a person who abandons the effort to commit the crime or otherwise prevents the completion of the crime shall not be liable for punishment under this Statute for the attempt to commit that crime if that person completely and voluntarily gave up the criminal purpose.

4. No provision in this Statute relating to individual criminal responsibility shall affect the responsibility of States under international law.

Article 26

Exclusion of jurisdiction over persons under eighteen

The Court shall have no jurisdiction over any person who was under the age of 18 at the time of the alleged commission of a crime.

Article 27

Irrelevance of official capacity

1. This Statute shall apply equally to all persons without any distinction based on official capacity. In particular, official capacity as a Head of State or Government, a member of a Government or parliament, an elected representative or a government official shall in no case exempt a person from criminal responsibility under this Statute, nor shall it, in and of itself, constitute a ground for reduction of sentence.
2. Immunities or special procedural rules which may attach to the official capacity of a person, whether under national or international law, shall not bar the Court from exercising its jurisdiction over such a person.

Article 28

Responsibility of commanders and other superiors

In addition to other grounds of criminal responsibility under this Statute for crimes within the jurisdiction of the Court:

(a) A military commander or person effectively acting as a military commander shall be criminally responsible for crimes within the jurisdiction of the Court committed by forces under his or her effective command and control, or effective authority and control as the case may be, as a result of his or her failure to exercise control properly over such forces, where:

(i) That military commander or person either knew or, owing to the circumstances at the time, should have known that the forces were committing or about to commit such crimes; and
(ii) That military commander or person failed to take all necessary and reasonable measures within his or her power to prevent or repress their commission or to submit the matter to the competent authorities for investigation and prosecution.

(b) With respect to superior and subordinate relationships not described in paragraph (a), a superior shall be criminally responsible for crimes within the jurisdiction of the Court committed by subordinates under his or her effective authority and control, as a result of his or her failure to exercise control properly over such subordinates, where:
(i) The superior either knew, or consciously disregarded information which clearly indicated, that the subordinates were committing or about to commit such crimes;
(ii) The crimes concerned activities that were within the effective responsibility and control of the superior; and
(iii) The superior failed to take all necessary and reasonable measures within his or her power to prevent or repress their commission or to submit the matter to the competent authorities for investigation and prosecution.

Article 29

Non-applicability of statute of limitations

The crimes within the jurisdiction of the Court shall not be subject to any statute of limitations.

Article 30

Mental element

1. Unless otherwise provided, a person shall be criminally responsible and liable for punishment for a crime within the jurisdiction of the Court only if the material elements are committed with intent and knowledge.
2. For the purposes of this article, a person has intent where:
   (a) In relation to conduct, that person means to engage in the conduct;
   (b) In relation to a consequence, that person means to cause that consequence or is aware that it will occur in the ordinary course of events.
3. For the purposes of this article, "knowledge" means awareness that a circumstance exists or a consequence will occur in the ordinary course of events. "Know" and "knowingly" shall be construed accordingly.

Article 31

Grounds for excluding criminal responsibility

1. In addition to other grounds for excluding criminal responsibility provided for in this Statute, a person shall not be criminally responsible if, at the time of that person's conduct:
   (a) The person suffers from a mental disease or defect that destroys that person's capacity to appreciate the unlawfulness or nature of his or her conduct, or capacity to control his or her conduct to conform to the requirements of law;
   (b) The person is in a state of intoxication that destroys that person's capacity to appreciate the unlawfulness or nature of his or her conduct, or capacity to control his or her conduct to conform to the requirements of law, unless the person has become voluntarily intoxicated under such circumstances that the person knew, or disregarded the risk, that, as a result of the intoxication, he or she was likely to engage in conduct constituting a crime within the jurisdiction of the Court;
   (c) The person acts reasonably to defend himself or herself or another person or, in the case of war crimes, property which is essential for the survival of the person or another person or property which is essential for accomplishing a military mission, against an imminent and unlawful use of force in a manner proportionate to the degree of danger to the person or the other person or property protected. The fact that the person was involved in a defensive operation conducted by forces shall not in itself constitute a ground for excluding criminal responsibility under this subparagraph;
   (d) The conduct which is alleged to constitute a crime within the jurisdiction of the Court has been caused by duress resulting from a threat of imminent death or of continuing or imminent serious bodily harm against that person or another person, and the person acts necessarily and reasonably to avoid this threat, provided that the person does not intend to cause a greater harm than the one sought to be avoided. Such a threat may either be:
      (i) Made by other persons; or
      (ii) Constituted by other circumstances beyond that person's control.
2. The Court shall determine the applicability of the grounds for excluding criminal responsibility provided for in this Statute to the case before it.
3. At trial, the Court may consider a ground for excluding criminal responsibility other than those referred to in paragraph 1 where such a ground is derived from applicable law as set forth in article 21. The procedures relating to the consideration of such a ground shall be provided for in the Rules of Procedure and Evidence.

Article 32
Mistake of fact or mistake of law

1. A mistake of fact shall be a ground for excluding criminal responsibility only if it negates the mental element required by the crime.
2. A mistake of law as to whether a particular type of conduct is a crime within the jurisdiction of the Court shall not be a ground for excluding criminal responsibility. A mistake of law may, however, be a ground for excluding criminal responsibility if it negates the mental element required by such a crime, or as provided for in article 33.

Article 33
Superior orders and prescription of law

1. The fact that a crime within the jurisdiction of the Court has been committed by a person pursuant to an order of a Government or of a superior, whether military or civilian, shall not relieve that person of criminal responsibility unless:
   (a) The person was under a legal obligation to obey orders of the Government or the superior in question;
   (b) The person did not know that the order was unlawful; and
   (c) The order was not manifestly unlawful.
2. For the purposes of this article, orders to commit genocide or crimes against humanity are manifestly unlawful.

PART 4. COMPOSITION AND ADMINISTRATION OF THE COURT

Article 34
Organs of the Court

The Court shall be composed of the following organs:
(a) The Presidency;
(b) An Appeals Division, a Trial Division and a Pre-Trial Division;
(c) The Office of the Prosecutor;
(d) The Registry.

Article 35
Service of judges

1. All judges shall be elected as full-time members of the Court and shall be available to serve on that basis from the commencement of their terms of office.
2. The judges composing the Presidency shall serve on a fullntime basis as soon as they are elected.

3. The Presidency may, on the basis of the workload of the Court and in consultation with its members, decide from time to time to what extent the remaining judges shall be required to serve on a full-time basis. Any such arrangement shall be without prejudice to the provisions of article 40.
4. The financial arrangements for judges not required to serve on a fullntime basis shall be made in accordance with article 49.

Article 36

Qualifications, nomination and election of judges

1. Subject to the provisions of paragraph 2, there shall be 18 judges of the Court.
2. (a) The Presidency, acting on behalf of the Court, may propose an increase in the number of judges specified in paragraph 1, indicating the reasons why this is considered necessary and appropriate. The Registrar shall promptly circulate any such proposal to all States Parties.
   (b) Any such proposal shall then be considered at a meeting of the Assembly of States Parties to be convened in accordance with article 112. The proposal shall be considered adopted if approved at the meeting by a vote of two thirds of the members of the Assembly of States Parties and shall enter into force at such time as decided by the Assembly of States Parties.
   (c) (i) Once a proposal for an increase in the number of judges has been adopted under subparagraph (b), the election of the additional judges shall take place at the next session of the Assembly of States Parties in accordance with paragraphs 3 to 8, and article 37, paragraph 2;
   (ii) Once a proposal for an increase in the number of judges has been adopted and brought into effect under subparagraphs (b) and (c) (i), it shall be open to the Presidency at any time thereafter, if the workload of the Court justifies it, to propose a reduction in the number of judges, provided that the number of judges shall not be reduced below that specified in paragraph 1. The proposal shall be dealt with in accordance with the procedure laid down in subparagraphs (a) and (b). In the event that the proposal is adopted, the number of judges shall be progressively decreased as the terms of office of serving judges expire, until the necessary number has been reached.
3. (a) The judges shall be chosen from among persons of high moral character, impartiality and integrity who possess the qualifications required in their respective States for appointment to the highest judicial offices.
   (b) Every candidate for election to the Court shall:

(i) Have established competence in criminal law and procedure, and the necessary relevant experience, whether as judge, prosecutor, advocate or in other similar capacity, in criminal proceedings; or

(ii) Have established competence in relevant areas of international law such as international humanitarian law and the law of human rights, and extensive experience in a professional legal capacity which is of relevance to the judicial work of the Court;

(c) Every candidate for election to the Court shall have an excellent knowledge of and be fluent in at least one of the working languages of the Court.

4. (a) Nominations of candidates for election to the Court may be made by any State Party to this Statute, and shall be made either:

(i) By the procedure for the nomination of candidates for appointment to the highest judicial offices in the State in question; or

(ii) By the procedure provided for the nomination of candidates for the International Court of Justice in the Statute of that Court.

Nominations shall be accompanied by a statement in the necessary detail specifying how the candidate fulfils the requirements of paragraph 3.

(b) Each State Party may put forward one candidate for any given election who need not necessarily be a national of that State Party but shall in any case be a national of a State Party.

(c) The Assembly of States Parties may decide to establish, if appropriate, an Advisory Committee on nominations. In that event, the Committee's composition and mandate shall be established by the Assembly of States Parties.

5. For the purposes of the election, there shall be two lists of candidates:

List A containing the names of candidates with the qualifications specified in paragraph 3 (b) (i); and

List B containing the names of candidates with the qualifications specified in paragraph 3 (b) (ii).

A candidate with sufficient qualifications for both lists may choose on which list to appear. At the first election to the Court, at least nine judges shall be elected from list A and at least five judges from list B. Subsequent elections shall be so organized as to maintain the equivalent proportion on the Court of judges qualified on the two lists.

6. (a) The judges shall be elected by secret ballot at a meeting of the Assembly of States Parties convened for that purpose under article 112. Subject to paragraph 7, the persons elected to the Court shall be the 18 candidates who obtain the highest number of votes and a two-thirds majority of the States Parties present and voting.

(b) In the event that a sufficient number of judges is not elected on the first ballot, successive ballots shall be held in accordance with the procedures laid down in subparagraph (a) until the remaining places have been filled.

7. No two judges may be nationals of the same State. A person who, for the purposes of membership of the Court, could be regarded as a national of more than one State shall be deemed to be a national of the State in which that person ordinarily exercises civil and political rights.
8. (a) The States Parties shall, in the selection of judges, take into account the need, within the membership of the Court, for:
   (i) The representation of the principal legal systems of the world;
   (ii) Equitable geographical representation; and
   (iii) A fair representation of female and male judges.
   (b) States Parties shall also take into account the need to include judges with legal expertise on specific issues, including, but not limited to, violence against women or children.
9. (a) Subject to subparagraph (b), judges shall hold office for a term of nine years and, subject to subparagraph (c) and to article 37, paragraph 2, shall not be eligible for re-election.
   (b) At the first election, one third of the judges elected shall be selected by lot to serve for a term of three years; one third of the judges elected shall be selected by lot to serve for a term of six years; and the remainder shall serve for a term of nine years.
   (c) A judge who is selected to serve for a term of three years under subparagraph (b) shall be eligible for re-election for a full term.
10. Notwithstanding paragraph 9, a judge assigned to a Trial or Appeals Chamber in accordance with article 39 shall continue in office to complete any trial or appeal the hearing of which has already commenced before that Chamber.

Article 37
Judicial vacancies

1. In the event of a vacancy, an election shall be held in accordance with article 36 to fill the vacancy.
2. A judge elected to fill a vacancy shall serve for the remainder of the predecessor's term and, if that period is three years or less, shall be eligible for re-election for a full term under article 36.

Article 38
The Presidency

1. The President and the First and Second Vice-Presidents shall be elected by an absolute majority of the judges. They shall each serve for a term of three years or until the end of their respective terms of office as judges, whichever expires earlier. They shall be eligible for re-election once.

2. The First Vice-President shall act in place of the President in the event that the President is unavailable or disqualified. The Second VicenPresident shall act in place of the President in the event that both the President and the First Vice-President are unavailable or disqualified.
3. The President, together with the First and Second Vice-Presidents, shall constitute the Presidency, which shall be responsible for:
   (a) The proper administration of the Court, with the exception of the Office of the Prosecutor; and
   (b) The other functions conferred upon it in accordance with this Statute.
4. In discharging its responsibility under paragraph 3 (a), the Presidency shall coordinate with and seek the concurrence of the Prosecutor on all matters of mutual concern.

Article 39
Chambers

1. As soon as possible after the election of the judges, the Court shall organize itself into the divisions specified in article 34, paragraph (b). The Appeals Division shall be composed of the President and four other judges, the Trial Division of not less than six judges and the Pre-Trial Division of not less than six judges. The assignment of judges to divisions shall be based on the nature of the functions to be performed by each division and the qualifications and experience of the judges elected to the Court, in such a way that each division shall contain an appropriate combination of expertise in criminal law and procedure and in international law. The Trial and Pre-Trial Divisions shall be composed predominantly of judges with criminal trial experience.
2. (a) The judicial functions of the Court shall be carried out in each division by Chambers.
   (b) (i) The Appeals Chamber shall be composed of all the judges of the Appeals Division;
      (ii) The functions of the Trial Chamber shall be carried out by three judges of the Trial Division;
      (iii) The functions of the Pre-Trial Chamber shall be carried out either by three judges of the Pre-Trial Division or by a single judge of that division in accordance with this Statute and the Rules of Procedure and Evidence;
   (c) Nothing in this paragraph shall preclude the simultaneous constitution of more than one Trial Chamber or Pre-Trial Chamber when the efficient management of the Court's workload so requires.
3. (a) Judges assigned to the Trial and Pre-Trial Divisions shall serve in those divisions for a period of three years, and thereafter until the completion of any case the hearing of which has already commenced in the division concerned.

(b) Judges assigned to the Appeals Division shall serve in that division for their entire term of office.

4. Judges assigned to the Appeals Division shall serve only in that division. Nothing in this article shall, however, preclude the temporary attachment of judges from the Trial Division to the Pre-Trial Division or vice versa, if the Presidency considers that the efficient management of the Court's workload so requires, provided that under no circumstances shall a judge who has participated in the pre-trial phase of a case be eligible to sit on the Trial Chamber hearing that case.

Article 40

Independence of the judges

1. The judges shall be independent in the performance of their functions.
2. Judges shall not engage in any activity which is likely to interfere with their judicial functions or to affect confidence in their independence.
3. Judges required to serve on a full-time basis at the seat of the Court shall not engage in any other occupation of a professional nature.
4. Any question regarding the application of paragraphs 2 and 3 shall be decided by an absolute majority of the judges. Where any such question concerns an individual judge, that judge shall not take part in the decision.

Article 41

Excusing and disqualification of judges

1. The Presidency may, at the request of a judge, excuse that judge from the exercise of a function under this Statute, in accordance with the Rules of Procedure and Evidence.
2. (a) A judge shall not participate in any case in which his or her impartiality might reasonably be doubted on any ground. A judge shall be disqualified from a case in accordance with this paragraph if, *inter alia*, that judge has previously been involved in any capacity in that case before the Court or in a related criminal case at the national level involving the person being investigated or prosecuted. A judge shall also be disqualified on such other grounds as may be provided for in the Rules of Procedure and Evidence.
   (b) The Prosecutor or the person being investigated or prosecuted may request the disqualification of a judge under this paragraph.
   (c) Any question as to the disqualification of a judge shall be decided by an absolute majority of the judges. The challenged judge shall be entitled to present his or her comments on the matter, but shall not take part in the decision.

Article 42
The Office of the Prosecutor

1. The Office of the Prosecutor shall act independently as a separate organ of the Court. It shall be responsible for receiving referrals and any substantiated information on crimes within the jurisdiction of the Court, for examining them and for conducting investigations and prosecutions before the Court. A member of the Office shall not seek or act on instructions from any external source.
2. The Office shall be headed by the Prosecutor. The Prosecutor shall have full authority over the management and administration of the Office, including the staff, facilities and other resources thereof. The Prosecutor shall be assisted by one or more Deputy Prosecutors, who shall be entitled to carry out any of the acts required of the Prosecutor under this Statute. The Prosecutor and the Deputy Prosecutors shall be of different nationalities. They shall serve on a full-time basis.
3. The Prosecutor and the Deputy Prosecutors shall be persons of high moral character, be highly competent in and have extensive practical experience in the prosecution or trial of criminal cases. They shall have an excellent knowledge of and be fluent in at least one of the working languages of the Court.
4. The Prosecutor shall be elected by secret ballot by an absolute majority of the members of the Assembly of States Parties. The Deputy Prosecutors shall be elected in the same way from a list of candidates provided by the Prosecutor. The Prosecutor shall nominate three candidates for each position of Deputy Prosecutor to be filled. Unless a shorter term is decided upon at the time of their election, the Prosecutor and the Deputy Prosecutors shall hold office for a term of nine years and shall not be eligible for re-election.
5. Neither the Prosecutor nor a Deputy Prosecutor shall engage in any activity which is likely to interfere with his or her prosecutorial functions or to affect confidence in his or her independence. They shall not engage in any other occupation of a professional nature.
6. The Presidency may excuse the Prosecutor or a Deputy Prosecutor, at his or her request, from acting in a particular case.
7. Neither the Prosecutor nor a Deputy Prosecutor shall participate in any matter in which their impartiality might reasonably be doubted on any ground. They shall be disqualified from a case in accordance with this paragraph if, *inter alia*, they have previously been involved in any capacity in that case before the Court or in a related criminal case at the national level involving the person being investigated or prosecuted.
8. Any question as to the disqualification of the Prosecutor or a Deputy Prosecutor shall be decided by the Appeals Chamber.
   (a) The person being investigated or prosecuted may at any time request

the disqualification of the Prosecutor or a Deputy Prosecutor on the grounds set out in this article;
(b) The Prosecutor or the Deputy Prosecutor, as appropriate, shall be entitled to present his or her comments on the matter;

9. The Prosecutor shall appoint advisers with legal expertise on specific issues, including, but not limited to, sexual and gender violence and violence against children.

Article 43
The Registry

1. The Registry shall be responsible for the non-judicial aspects of the administration and servicing of the Court, without prejudice to the functions and powers of the Prosecutor in accordance with article 42.
2. The Registry shall be headed by the Registrar, who shall be the principal administrative officer of the Court. The Registrar shall exercise his or her functions under the authority of the President of the Court.
3. The Registrar and the Deputy Registrar shall be persons of high moral character, be highly competent and have an excellent knowledge of and be fluent in at least one of the working languages of the Court.
4. The judges shall elect the Registrar by an absolute majority by secret ballot, taking into account any recommendation by the Assembly of States Parties. If the need arises and upon the recommendation of the Registrar, the judges shall elect, in the same manner, a Deputy Registrar.
5. The Registrar shall hold office for a term of five years, shall be eligible for re-election once and shall serve on a full-time basis. The Deputy Registrar shall hold office for a term of five years or such shorter term as may be decided upon by an absolute majority of the judges, and may be elected on the basis that the Deputy Registrar shall be called upon to serve as required.
6. The Registrar shall set up a Victims and Witnesses Unit within the Registry. This Unit shall provide, in consultation with the Office of the Prosecutor, protective measures and security arrangements, counselling and other appropriate assistance for witnesses, victims who appear before the Court, and others who are at risk on account of testimony given by such witnesses. The Unit shall include staff with expertise in trauma, including trauma related to crimes of sexual violence.

Article 44
Staff

1. The Prosecutor and the Registrar shall appoint such qualified staff as may be required to their respective offices. In the case of the Prosecutor, this shall include the appointment of investigators.

2. In the employment of staff, the Prosecutor and the Registrar shall ensure the highest standards of efficiency, competency and integrity, and shall have regard, *mutatis mutandis*, to the criteria set forth in article 36, paragraph 8.
3. The Registrar, with the agreement of the Presidency and the Prosecutor, shall propose Staff Regulations which include the terms and conditions upon which the staff of the Court shall be appointed, remunerated and dismissed. The Staff Regulations shall be approved by the Assembly of States Parties.
4. The Court may, in exceptional circumstances, employ the expertise of gratis personnel offered by States Parties, intergovernmental organizations or non-governmental organizations to assist with the work of any of the organs of the Court. The Prosecutor may accept any such offer on behalf of the Office of the Prosecutor. Such gratis personnel shall be employed in accordance with guidelines to be established by the Assembly of States Parties.

Article 45
Solemn undertaking

Before taking up their respective duties under this Statute, the judges, the Prosecutor, the Deputy Prosecutors, the Registrar and the Deputy Registrar shall each make a solemn undertaking in open court to exercise his or her respective functions impartially and conscientiously.

Article 46
Removal from office

1. A judge, the Prosecutor, a Deputy Prosecutor, the Registrar or the Deputy Registrar shall be removed from office if a decision to this effect is made in accordance with paragraph 2, in cases where that person:
   (a) Is found to have committed serious misconduct or a serious breach of his or her duties under this Statute, as provided for in the Rules of Procedure and Evidence; or
   (b) Is unable to exercise the functions required by this Statute.
2. A decision as to the removal from office of a judge, the Prosecutor or a Deputy Prosecutor under paragraph 1 shall be made by the Assembly of States Parties, by secret ballot:
   (a) In the case of a judge, by a two-thirds majority of the States Parties upon a recommendation adopted by a two-thirds majority of the other judges;
   (b) In the case of the Prosecutor, by an absolute majority of the States Parties;

(c) In the case of a Deputy Prosecutor, by an absolute majority of the States Parties upon the recommendation of the Prosecutor.

3. A decision as to the removal from office of the Registrar or Deputy Registrar shall be made by an absolute majority of the judges.
4. A judge, Prosecutor, Deputy Prosecutor, Registrar or Deputy Registrar whose conduct or ability to exercise the functions of the office as required by this Statute is challenged under this article shall have full opportunity to present and receive evidence and to make submissions in accordance with the Rules of Procedure and Evidence. The person in question shall not otherwise participate in the consideration of the matter.

Article 47
Disciplinary measures

A judge, Prosecutor, Deputy Prosecutor, Registrar or Deputy Registrar who has committed misconduct of a less serious nature than that set out in article 46, paragraph 1, shall be subject to disciplinary measures, in accordance with the Rules of Procedure and Evidence.

Article 48
Privileges and immunities

1. The Court shall enjoy in the territory of each State Party such privileges and immunities as are necessary for the fulfilment of its purposes.
2. The judges, the Prosecutor, the Deputy Prosecutors and the Registrar shall, when engaged on or with respect to the business of the Court, enjoy the same privileges and immunities as are accorded to heads of diplomatic missions and shall, after the expiry of their terms of office, continue to be accorded immunity from legal process of every kind in respect of words spoken or written and acts performed by them in their official capacity.
3. The Deputy Registrar, the staff of the Office of the Prosecutor and the staff of the Registry shall enjoy the privileges and immunities and facilities necessary for the performance of their functions, in accordance with the agreement on the privileges and immunities of the Court.
4. Counsel, experts, witnesses or any other person required to be present at the seat of the Court shall be accorded such treatment as is necessary for the proper functioning of the Court, in accordance with the agreement on the privileges and immunities of the Court.
5. The privileges and immunities of:
    (a) A judge or the Prosecutor may be waived by an absolute majority of the judges;
    (b) The Registrar may be waived by the Presidency;
    (c) The Deputy Prosecutors and staff of the Office of the Prosecutor may be waived by the Prosecutor;

(d) The Deputy Registrar and staff of the Registry may be waived by the Registrar.

Article 49
Salaries, allowances and expenses

The judges, the Prosecutor, the Deputy Prosecutors, the Registrar and the Deputy Registrar shall receive such salaries, allowances and expenses as may be decided upon by the Assembly of States Parties. These salaries and allowances shall not be reduced during their terms of office.

Article 50
Official and working languages

1. The official languages of the Court shall be Arabic, Chinese, English, French, Russian and Spanish. The judgements of the Court, as well as other decisions resolving fundamental issues before the Court, shall be published in the official languages. The Presidency shall, in accordance with the criteria established by the Rules of Procedure and Evidence, determine which decisions may be considered as resolving fundamental issues for the purposes of this paragraph.
2. The working languages of the Court shall be English and French. The Rules of Procedure and Evidence shall determine the cases in which other official languages may be used as working languages.
3. At the request of any party to a proceeding or a State allowed to intervene in a proceeding, the Court shall authorize a language other than English or French to be used by such a party or State, provided that the Court considers such authorization to be adequately justified.

Article 51
Rules of Procedure and Evidence

1. The Rules of Procedure and Evidence shall enter into force upon adoption by a two-thirds majority of the members of the Assembly of States Parties.
2. Amendments to the Rules of Procedure and Evidence may be proposed by:
   (a) Any State Party;
   (b) The judges acting by an absolute majority; or
   (c) The Prosecutor.

   Such amendments shall enter into force upon adoption by a two-thirds majority of the members of the Assembly of States Parties.
3. After the adoption of the Rules of Procedure and Evidence, in urgent cases where the Rules do not provide for a specific situation before the

Court, the judges may, by a two-thirds majority, draw up provisional Rules to be applied until adopted, amended or rejected at the next ordinary or special session of the Assembly of States Parties.

4. The Rules of Procedure and Evidence, amendments thereto and any provisional Rule shall be consistent with this Statute. Amendments to the Rules of Procedure and Evidence as well as provisional Rules shall not be applied retroactively to the detriment of the person who is being investigated or prosecuted or who has been convicted.
5. In the event of conflict between the Statute and the Rules of Procedure and Evidence, the Statute shall prevail.

Article 52
Regulations of the Court

1. The judges shall, in accordance with this Statute and the Rules of Procedure and Evidence, adopt, by an absolute majority, the Regulations of the Court necessary for its routine functioning.
2. The Prosecutor and the Registrar shall be consulted in the elaboration of the Regulations and any amendments thereto.
3. The Regulations and any amendments thereto shall take effect upon adoption unless otherwise decided by the judges. Immediately upon adoption, they shall be circulated to States Parties for comments. If within six months there are no objections from a majority of States Parties, they shall remain in force.

PART 5. INVESTIGATION AND PROSECUTION

Article 53
Initiation of an investigation

1. The Prosecutor shall, having evaluated the information made available to him or her, initiate an investigation unless he or she determines that there is no reasonable basis to proceed under this Statute. In deciding whether to initiate an investigation, the Prosecutor shall consider whether:
   (a) The information available to the Prosecutor provides a reasonable basis to believe that a crime within the jurisdiction of the Court has been or is being committed;
   (b) The case is or would be admissible under article 17; and
   (c) Taking into account the gravity of the crime and the interests of victims, there are nonetheless substantial reasons to believe that an investigation would not serve the interests of justice.

   If the Prosecutor determines that there is no reasonable basis to proceed and his or her determination is based solely on subparagraph (c) above, he or she shall inform the Pre-Trial Chamber.

2. If, upon investigation, the Prosecutor concludes that there is not a sufficient basis for a prosecution because:
   (a) There is not a sufficient legal or factual basis to seek a warrant or summons under article 58;
   (b) The case is inadmissible under article 17; or
   (c) A prosecution is not in the interests of justice, taking into account all the circumstances, including the gravity of the crime, the interests of victims and the age or infirmity of the alleged perpetrator, and his or her role in the alleged crime;

the Prosecutor shall inform the Pre-Trial Chamber and the State making a referral under article 14 or the Security Council in a case under article 13, paragraph (b), of his or her conclusion and the reasons for the conclusion.

3. (a) At the request of the State making a referral under article 14 or the Security Council under article 13, paragraph (b), the Pre-Trial Chamber may review a decision of the Prosecutor under paragraph 1 or 2 not to proceed and may request the Prosecutor to reconsider that decision.
   (b) In addition, the Pre-Trial Chamber may, on its own initiative, review a decision of the Prosecutor not to proceed if it is based solely on paragraph 1 (c) or 2 (c). In such a case, the decision of the Prosecutor shall be effective only if confirmed by the Pre-Trial Chamber.
4. The Prosecutor may, at any time, reconsider a decision whether to initiate an investigation or prosecution based on new facts or information.

Article 54

Duties and powers of the Prosecutor with respect to investigations

1. The Prosecutor shall:
   (a) In order to establish the truth, extend the investigation to cover all facts and evidence relevant to an assessment of whether there is criminal responsibility under this Statute, and, in doing so, investigate incriminating and exonerating circumstances equally;
   (b) Take appropriate measures to ensure the effective investigation and prosecution of crimes within the jurisdiction of the Court, and in doing so, respect the interests and personal circumstances of victims and witnesses, including age, gender as defined in article 7, paragraph 3, and health, and take into account the nature of the crime, in particular where it involves sexual violence, gender violence or violence against children; and
   (c) Fully respect the rights of persons arising under this Statute.
2. The Prosecutor may conduct investigations on the territory of a State:
   (a) In accordance with the provisions of Part 9; or
   (b) As authorized by the Pre-Trial Chamber under article 57, paragraph 3 (d).

3. The Prosecutor may:
   (a) Collect and examine evidence;
   (b) Request the presence of and question persons being investigated, victims and witnesses;
   (c) Seek the cooperation of any State or intergovernmental organization or arrangement in accordance with its respective competence and/or mandate;
   (d) Enter into such arrangements or agreements, not inconsistent with this Statute, as may be necessary to facilitate the cooperation of a State, intergovernmental organization or person;
   (e) Agree not to disclose, at any stage of the proceedings, documents or information that the Prosecutor obtains on the condition of confidentiality and solely for the purpose of generating new evidence, unless the provider of the information consents; and
   (f) Take necessary measures, or request that necessary measures be taken, to ensure the confidentiality of information, the protection of any person or the preservation of evidence.

Article 55

Rights of persons during an investigation

1. In respect of an investigation under this Statute, a person:
   (a) Shall not be compelled to incriminate himself or herself or to confess guilt;
   (b) Shall not be subjected to any form of coercion, duress or threat, to torture or to any other form of cruel, inhuman or degrading treatment or punishment;
   (c) Shall, if questioned in a language other than a language the person fully understands and speaks, have, free of any cost, the assistance of a competent interpreter and such translations as are necessary to meet the requirements of fairness; and
   (d) Shall not be subjected to arbitrary arrest or detention, and shall not be deprived of his or her liberty except on such grounds and in accordance with such procedures as are established in this Statute.
2. Where there are grounds to believe that a person has committed a crime within the jurisdiction of the Court and that person is about to be questioned either by the Prosecutor, or by national authorities pursuant to a request made under Part 9, that person shall also have the following rights of which he or she shall be informed prior to being questioned:
   (a) To be informed, prior to being questioned, that there are grounds to believe that he or she has committed a crime within the jurisdiction of the Court;
   (b) To remain silent, without such silence being a consideration in the determination of guilt or innocence;

(c) To have legal assistance of the person's choosing, or, if the person does not have legal assistance, to have legal assistance assigned to him or her, in any case where the interests of justice so require, and without payment by the person in any such case if the person does not have sufficient means to pay for it; and
(d) To be questioned in the presence of counsel unless the person has voluntarily waived his or her right to counsel.

Article 56

Role of the Pre-Trial Chamber in relation to a unique investigative opportunity

1. (a) Where the Prosecutor considers an investigation to present a unique opportunity to take testimony or a statement from a witness or to examine, collect or test evidence, which may not be available subsequently for the purposes of a trial, the Prosecutor shall so inform the Pre-Trial Chamber.
   (b) In that case, the Pre-Trial Chamber may, upon request of the Prosecutor, take such measures as may be necessary to ensure the efficiency and integrity of the proceedings and, in particular, to protect the rights of the defence.
   (c) Unless the Pre-Trial Chamber orders otherwise, the Prosecutor shall provide the relevant information to the person who has been arrested or appeared in response to a summons in connection with the investigation referred to in subparagraph (a), in order that he or she may be heard on the matter.
2. The measures referred to in paragraph 1 (b) may include:
   (a) Making recommendations or orders regarding procedures to be followed;
   (b) Directing that a record be made of the proceedings;
   (c) Appointing an expert to assist;
   (d) Authorizing counsel for a person who has been arrested, or appeared before the Court in response to a summons, to participate, or where there has not yet been such an arrest or appearance or counsel has not been designated, appointing another counsel to attend and represent the interests of the defence;
   (e) Naming one of its members or, if necessary, another available judge of the Pre-Trial or Trial Division to observe and make recommendations or orders regarding the collection and preservation of evidence and the questioning of persons;
   (f) Taking such other action as may be necessary to collect or preserve evidence.
3. (a) Where the Prosecutor has not sought measures pursuant to this article but the Pre-Trial Chamber considers that such measures are required to preserve evidence that it deems would be essential for

the defence at trial, it shall consult with the Prosecutor as to whether there is good reason for the Prosecutor's failure to request the measures. If upon consultation, the Pre-Trial Chamber concludes that the Prosecutor's failure to request such measures is unjustified, the Pre-Trial Chamber may take such measures on its own initiative.

(b) A decision of the Pre-Trial Chamber to act on its own initiative under this paragraph may be appealed by the Prosecutor. The appeal shall be heard on an expedited basis.

4. The admissibility of evidence preserved or collected for trial pursuant to this article, or the record thereof, shall be governed at trial by article 69, and given such weight as determined by the Trial Chamber.

Article 57

Functions and powers of the Pre-Trial Chamber

1. Unless otherwise provided in this Statute, the Pre-Trial Chamber shall exercise its functions in accordance with the provisions of this article.
2. (a) Orders or rulings of the Pre-Trial Chamber issued under articles 15, 18, 19, 54, paragraph 2, 61, paragraph 7, and 72 must be concurred in by a majority of its judges.
   (b) In all other cases, a single judge of the Pre-Trial Chamber may exercise the functions provided for in this Statute, unless otherwise provided for in the Rules of Procedure and Evidence or by a majority of the Pre-Trial Chamber.
3. In addition to its other functions under this Statute, the Pre-Trial Chamber may:
   (a) At the request of the Prosecutor, issue such orders and warrants as may be required for the purposes of an investigation;
   (b) Upon the request of a person who has been arrested or has appeared pursuant to a summons under article 58, issue such orders, including measures such as those described in article 56, or seek such cooperation pursuant to Part 9 as may be necessary to assist the person in the preparation of his or her defence;
   (c) Where necessary, provide for the protection and privacy of victims and witnesses, the preservation of evidence, the protection of persons who have been arrested or appeared in response to a summons, and the protection of national security information;
   (d) Authorize the Prosecutor to take specific investigative steps within the territory of a State Party without having secured the cooperation of that State under Part 9 if, whenever possible having regard to the views of the State concerned, the Pre-Trial Chamber has determined in that case that the State is clearly unable to execute a request for cooperation due to the unavailability of any authority or any component of its judicial system competent to execute the request for cooperation under Part 9.

(e) Where a warrant of arrest or a summons has been issued under article 58, and having due regard to the strength of the evidence and the rights of the parties concerned, as provided for in this Statute and the Rules of Procedure and Evidence, seek the cooperation of States pursuant to article 93, paragraph 1 (k), to take protective measures for the purpose of forfeiture, in particular for the ultimate benefit of victims.

Article 58

Issuance by the Pre-Trial Chamber of a warrant of arrest or a summons to appear

1. At any time after the initiation of an investigation, the Pre-Trial Chamber shall, on the application of the Prosecutor, issue a warrant of arrest of a person if, having examined the application and the evidence or other information submitted by the Prosecutor, it is satisfied that:
   (a) There are reasonable grounds to believe that the person has committed a crime within the jurisdiction of the Court; and
   (b) The arrest of the person appears necessary:
      (i) To ensure the person's appearance at trial,
      (ii) To ensure that the person does not obstruct or endanger the investigation or the court proceedings, or
      (iii) Where applicable, to prevent the person from continuing with the commission of that crime or a related crime which is within the jurisdiction of the Court and which arises out of the same circumstances.
2. The application of the Prosecutor shall contain:
   (a) The name of the person and any other relevant identifying information;
   (b) A specific reference to the crimes within the jurisdiction of the Court which the person is alleged to have committed;
   (c) A concise statement of the facts which are alleged to constitute those crimes;
   (d) A summary of the evidence and any other information which establish reasonable grounds to believe that the person committed those crimes; and
   (e) The reason why the Prosecutor believes that the arrest of the person is necessary.
3. The warrant of arrest shall contain:
   (a) The name of the person and any other relevant identifying information;
   (b) A specific reference to the crimes within the jurisdiction of the Court for which the person's arrest is sought; and
   (c) A concise statement of the facts which are alleged to constitute those crimes.

4. The warrant of arrest shall remain in effect until otherwise ordered by the Court.
5. On the basis of the warrant of arrest, the Court may request the provisional arrest or the arrest and surrender of the person under Part 9.
6. The Prosecutor may request the Pre-Trial Chamber to amend the warrant of arrest by modifying or adding to the crimes specified therein. The Pre-Trial Chamber shall so amend the warrant if it is satisfied that there are reasonable grounds to believe that the person committed the modified or additional crimes.
7. As an alternative to seeking a warrant of arrest, the Prosecutor may submit an application requesting that the Pre-Trial Chamber issue a summons for the person to appear. If the Pre-Trial Chamber is satisfied that there are reasonable grounds to believe that the person committed the crime alleged and that a summons is sufficient to ensure the person's appearance, it shall issue the summons, with or without conditions restricting liberty (other than detention) if provided for by national law, for the person to appear. The summons shall contain:
   (a) The name of the person and any other relevant identifying information;
   (b) The specified date on which the person is to appear;
   (c) A specific reference to the crimes within the jurisdiction of the Court which the person is alleged to have committed; and
   (d) A concise statement of the facts which are alleged to constitute the crime.

The summons shall be served on the person.

Article 59

Arrest proceedings in the custodial State

1. A State Party which has received a request for provisional arrest or for arrest and surrender shall immediately take steps to arrest the person in question in accordance with its laws and the provisions of Part 9.
2. A person arrested shall be brought promptly before the competent judicial authority in the custodial State which shall determine, in accordance with the law of that State, that:
   (a) The warrant applies to that person;
   (b) The person has been arrested in accordance with the proper process; and
   (c) The person's rights have been respected.
3. The person arrested shall have the right to apply to the competent authority in the custodial State for interim release pending surrender.
4. In reaching a decision on any such application, the competent authority in the custodial State shall consider whether, given the gravity of the alleged crimes, there are urgent and exceptional circumstances to justify interim release and whether necessary safeguards exist to ensure that the custo-

dial State can fulfil its duty to surrender the person to the Court. It shall not be open to the competent authority of the custodial State to consider whether the warrant of arrest was properly issued in accordance with article 58, paragraph 1 (a) and (b).

5. The Pre-Trial Chamber shall be notified of any request for interim release and shall make recommendations to the competent authority in the custodial State. The competent authority in the custodial State shall give full consideration to such recommendations, including any recommendations on measures to prevent the escape of the person, before rendering its decision.
6. If the person is granted interim release, the Pre-Trial Chamber may request periodic reports on the status of the interim release.
7. Once ordered to be surrendered by the custodial State, the person shall be delivered to the Court as soon as possible.

Article 60

Initial proceedings before the Court

1. Upon the surrender of the person to the Court, or the person's appearance before the Court voluntarily or pursuant to a summons, the Pre-Trial Chamber shall satisfy itself that the person has been informed of the crimes which he or she is alleged to have committed, and of his or her rights under this Statute, including the right to apply for interim release pending trial.
2. A person subject to a warrant of arrest may apply for interim release pending trial. If the Pre-Trial Chamber is satisfied that the conditions set forth in article 58, paragraph 1, are met, the person shall continue to be detained. If it is not so satisfied, the Pre-Trial Chamber shall release the person, with or without conditions.
3. The Pre-Trial Chamber shall periodically review its ruling on the release or detention of the person, and may do so at any time on the request of the Prosecutor or the person. Upon such review, it may modify its ruling as to detention, release or conditions of release, if it is satisfied that changed circumstances so require.
4. The Pre-Trial Chamber shall ensure that a person is not detained for an unreasonable period prior to trial due to inexcusable delay by the Prosecutor. If such delay occurs, the Court shall consider releasing the person, with or without conditions.
5. If necessary, the Pre-Trial Chamber may issue a warrant of arrest to secure the presence of a person who has been released.

Article 61

Confirmation of the charges before trial

1. Subject to the provisions of paragraph 2, within a reasonable time after the person's surrender or voluntary appearance before the Court, the Pre-

Trial Chamber shall hold a hearing to confirm the charges on which the Prosecutor intends to seek trial. The hearing shall be held in the presence of the Prosecutor and the person charged, as well as his or her counsel.

2. The Pre-Trial Chamber may, upon request of the Prosecutor or on its own motion, hold a hearing in the absence of the person charged to confirm the charges on which the Prosecutor intends to seek trial when the person has:
   (a) Waived his or her right to be present; or
   (b) Fled or cannot be found and all reasonable steps have been taken to secure his or her appearance before the Court and to inform the person of the charges and that a hearing to confirm those charges will be held.

In that case, the person shall be represented by counsel where the Pre-Trial Chamber determines that it is in the interests of justice.

3. Within a reasonable time before the hearing, the person shall:
   (a) Be provided with a copy of the document containing the charges on which the Prosecutor intends to bring the person to trial; and
   (b) Be informed of the evidence on which the Prosecutor intends to rely at the hearing.

The Pre-Trial Chamber may issue orders regarding the disclosure of information for the purposes of the hearing.

4. Before the hearing, the Prosecutor may continue the investigation and may amend or withdraw any charges. The person shall be given reasonable notice before the hearing of any amendment to or withdrawal of charges. In case of a withdrawal of charges, the Prosecutor shall notify the Pre-Trial Chamber of the reasons for the withdrawal.
5. At the hearing, the Prosecutor shall support each charge with sufficient evidence to establish substantial grounds to believe that the person committed the crime charged. The Prosecutor may rely on documentary or summary evidence and need not call the witnesses expected to testify at the trial.
6. At the hearing, the person may:
   (a) Object to the charges;
   (b) Challenge the evidence presented by the Prosecutor; and
   (c) Present evidence.
7. The Pre-Trial Chamber shall, on the basis of the hearing, determine whether there is sufficient evidence to establish substantial grounds to believe that the person committed each of the crimes charged. Based on its determination, the Pre-Trial Chamber shall:
   (a) Confirm those charges in relation to which it has determined that there is sufficient evidence, and commit the person to a Trial Chamber for trial on the charges as confirmed;
   (b) Decline to confirm those charges in relation to which it has determined that there is insufficient evidence;
   (c) Adjourn the hearing and request the Prosecutor to consider:

(i) Providing further evidence or conducting further investigation with respect to a particular charge; or
(ii) Amending a charge because the evidence submitted appears to establish a different crime within the jurisdiction of the Court.

8. Where the Pre-Trial Chamber declines to confirm a charge, the Prosecutor shall not be precluded from subsequently requesting its confirmation if the request is supported by additional evidence.
9. After the charges are confirmed and before the trial has begun, the Prosecutor may, with the permission of the Pre-Trial Chamber and after notice to the accused, amend the charges. If the Prosecutor seeks to add additional charges or to substitute more serious charges, a hearing under this article to confirm those charges must be held. After commencement of the trial, the Prosecutor may, with the permission of the Trial Chamber, withdraw the charges.
10. Any warrant previously issued shall cease to have effect with respect to any charges which have not been confirmed by the Pre-Trial Chamber or which have been withdrawn by the Prosecutor.
11. Once the charges have been confirmed in accordance with this article, the Presidency shall constitute a Trial Chamber which, subject to paragraph 9 and to article 64, paragraph 4, shall be responsible for the conduct of subsequent proceedings and may exercise any function of the Pre-Trial Chamber that is relevant and capable of application in those proceedings.

PART 6. THE TRIAL

Article 62

Place of trial

Unless otherwise decided, the place of the trial shall be the seat of the Court.

Article 63

Trial in the presence of the accused

1. The accused shall be present during the trial.
2. If the accused, being present before the Court, continues to disrupt the trial, the Trial Chamber may remove the accused and shall make provision for him or her to observe the trial and instruct counsel from outside the courtroom, through the use of communications technology, if required. Such measures shall be taken only in exceptional circumstances after other reasonable alternatives have proved inadequate, and only for such duration as is strictly required.

Article 64
Functions and powers of the Trial Chamber

1. The functions and powers of the Trial Chamber set out in this article shall be exercised in accordance with this Statute and the Rules of Procedure and Evidence.
2. The Trial Chamber shall ensure that a trial is fair and expeditious and is conducted with full respect for the rights of the accused and due regard for the protection of victims and witnesses.
3. Upon assignment of a case for trial in accordance with this Statute, the Trial Chamber assigned to deal with the case shall:
   (a) Confer with the parties and adopt such procedures as are necessary to facilitate the fair and expeditious conduct of the proceedings;
   (b) Determine the language or languages to be used at trial; and
   (c) Subject to any other relevant provisions of this Statute, provide for disclosure of documents or information not previously disclosed, sufficiently in advance of the commencement of the trial to enable adequate preparation for trial.
4. The Trial Chamber may, if necessary for its effective and fair functioning, refer preliminary issues to the Pre-Trial Chamber or, if necessary, to another available judge of the Pre-Trial Division.
5. Upon notice to the parties, the Trial Chamber may, as appropriate, direct that there be joinder or severance in respect of charges against more than one accused.
6. In performing its functions prior to trial or during the course of a trial, the Trial Chamber may, as necessary:
   (a) Exercise any functions of the Pre-Trial Chamber referred to in article 61, paragraph 11;
   (b) Require the attendance and testimony of witnesses and production of documents and other evidence by obtaining, if necessary, the assistance of States as provided in this Statute;
   (c) Provide for the protection of confidential information;
   (d) Order the production of evidence in addition to that already collected prior to the trial or presented during the trial by the parties;
   (e) Provide for the protection of the accused, witnesses and victims; and
   (f) Rule on any other relevant matters.
7. The trial shall be held in public. The Trial Chamber may, however, determine that special circumstances require that certain proceedings be in closed session for the purposes set forth in article 68, or to protect confidential or sensitive information to be given in evidence.
8. (a) At the commencement of the trial, the Trial Chamber shall have read to the accused the charges previously confirmed by the Pre-Trial Chamber. The Trial Chamber shall satisfy itself that the accused understands the nature of the charges. It shall afford him or her the opportu-

nity to make an admission of guilt in accordance with article 65 or to plead not guilty.

(b) At the trial, the presiding judge may give directions for the conduct of proceedings, including to ensure that they are conducted in a fair and impartial manner. Subject to any directions of the presiding judge, the parties may submit evidence in accordance with the provisions of this Statute.

9. The Trial Chamber shall have, *inter alia*, the power on application of a party or on its own motion to:
   (a) Rule on the admissibility or relevance of evidence; and
   (b) Take all necessary steps to maintain order in the course of a hearing.
10. The Trial Chamber shall ensure that a complete record of the trial, which accurately reflects the proceedings, is made and that it is maintained and preserved by the Registrar.

Article 65

Proceedings on an admission of guilt

1. Where the accused makes an admission of guilt pursuant to article 64, paragraph 8 (a), the Trial Chamber shall determine whether:
   (a) The accused understands the nature and consequences of the admission of guilt;
   (b) The admission is voluntarily made by the accused after sufficient consultation with defence counsel; and
   (c) The admission of guilt is supported by the facts of the case that are contained in:
      (i) The charges brought by the Prosecutor and admitted by the accused;
      (ii) Any materials presented by the Prosecutor which supplement the charges and which the accused accepts; and
      (iii) Any other evidence, such as the testimony of witnesses, presented by the Prosecutor or the accused.
2. Where the Trial Chamber is satisfied that the matters referred to in paragraph 1 are established, it shall consider the admission of guilt, together with any additional evidence presented, as establishing all the essential facts that are required to prove the crime to which the admission of guilt relates, and may convict the accused of that crime.
3. Where the Trial Chamber is not satisfied that the matters referred to in paragraph 1 are established, it shall consider the admission of guilt as not having been made, in which case it shall order that the trial be continued under the ordinary trial procedures provided by this Statute and may remit the case to another Trial Chamber.
4. Where the Trial Chamber is of the opinion that a more complete presentation of the facts of the case is required in the interests of justice, in particular the interests of the victims, the Trial Chamber may:

(a) Request the Prosecutor to present additional evidence, including the testimony of witnesses; or
(b) Order that the trial be continued under the ordinary trial procedures provided by this Statute, in which case it shall consider the admission of guilt as not having been made and may remit the case to another Trial Chamber.

5. Any discussions between the Prosecutor and the defence regarding modification of the charges, the admission of guilt or the penalty to be imposed shall not be binding on the Court.

Article 66

Presumption of innocence

1. Everyone shall be presumed innocent until proved guilty before the Court in accordance with the applicable law.
2. The onus is on the Prosecutor to prove the guilt of the accused.
3. In order to convict the accused, the Court must be convinced of the guilt of the accused beyond reasonable doubt.

Article 67

Rights of the accused

1. In the determination of any charge, the accused shall be entitled to a public hearing, having regard to the provisions of this Statute, to a fair hearing conducted impartially, and to the following minimum guarantees, in full equality:
   (a) To be informed promptly and in detail of the nature, cause and content of the charge, in a language which the accused fully understands and speaks;
   (b) To have adequate time and facilities for the preparation of the defence and to communicate freely with counsel of the accused's choosing in confidence;
   (c) To be tried without undue delay;
   (d) Subject to article 63, paragraph 2, to be present at the trial, to conduct the defence in person or through legal assistance of the accused's choosing, to be informed, if the accused does not have legal assistance, of this right and to have legal assistance assigned by the Court in any case where the interests of justice so require, and without payment if the accused lacks sufficient means to pay for it;
   (e) To examine, or have examined, the witnesses against him or her and to obtain the attendance and examination of witnesses on his or her behalf under the same conditions as witnesses against him or her. The accused shall also be entitled to raise defences and to present other evidence admissible under this Statute;

(f) To have, free of any cost, the assistance of a competent interpreter and such translations as are necessary to meet the requirements of fairness, if any of the proceedings of or documents presented to the Court are not in a language which the accused fully understands and speaks;
(g) Not to be compelled to testify or to confess guilt and to remain silent, without such silence being a consideration in the determination of guilt or innocence;
(h) To make an unsworn oral or written statement in his or her defence; and
(i) Not to have imposed on him or her any reversal of the burden of proof or any onus of rebuttal.

2. In addition to any other disclosure provided for in this Statute, the Prosecutor shall, as soon as practicable, disclose to the defence evidence in the Prosecutor's possession or control which he or she believes shows or tends to show the innocence of the accused, or to mitigate the guilt of the accused, or which may affect the credibility of prosecution evidence. In case of doubt as to the application of this paragraph, the Court shall decide.

Article 68

Protection of the victims and witnesses and their participation in the proceedings

1. The Court shall take appropriate measures to protect the safety, physical and psychological well-being, dignity and privacy of victims and witnesses. In so doing, the Court shall have regard to all relevant factors, including age, gender as defined in article 7, paragraph 3, and health, and the nature of the crime, in particular, but not limited to, where the crime involves sexual or gender violence or violence against children. The Prosecutor shall take such measures particularly during the investigation and prosecution of such crimes. These measures shall not be prejudicial to or inconsistent with the rights of the accused and a fair and impartial trial.
2. As an exception to the principle of public hearings provided for in article 67, the Chambers of the Court may, to protect victims and witnesses or an accused, conduct any part of the proceedings *in camera* or allow the presentation of evidence by electronic or other special means. In particular, such measures shall be implemented in the case of a victim of sexual violence or a child who is a victim or a witness, unless otherwise ordered by the Court, having regard to all the circumstances, particularly the views of the victim or witness.
3. Where the personal interests of the victims are affected, the Court shall permit their views and concerns to be presented and considered at stages of the proceedings determined to be appropriate by the Court and in a

manner which is not prejudicial to or inconsistent with the rights of the accused and a fair and impartial trial. Such views and concerns may be presented by the legal representatives of the victims where the Court considers it appropriate, in accordance with the Rules of Procedure and Evidence.

4. The Victims and Witnesses Unit may advise the Prosecutor and the Court on appropriate protective measures, security arrangements, counselling and assistance as referred to in article 43, paragraph 6.
5. Where the disclosure of evidence or information pursuant to this Statute may lead to the grave endangerment of the security of a witness or his or her family, the Prosecutor may, for the purposes of any proceedings conducted prior to the commencement of the trial, withhold such evidence or information and instead submit a summary thereof. Such measures shall be exercised in a manner which is not prejudicial to or inconsistent with the rights of the accused and a fair and impartial trial.
6. A State may make an application for necessary measures to be taken in respect of the protection of its servants or agents and the protection of confidential or sensitive information.

Article 69
Evidence

1. Before testifying, each witness shall, in accordance with the Rules of Procedure and Evidence, give an undertaking as to the truthfulness of the evidence to be given by that witness.
2. The testimony of a witness at trial shall be given in person, except to the extent provided by the measures set forth in article 68 or in the Rules of Procedure and Evidence. The Court may also permit the giving of *viva voce* (oral) or recorded testimony of a witness by means of video or audio technology, as well as the introduction of documents or written transcripts, subject to this Statute and in accordance with the Rules of Procedure and Evidence. These measures shall not be prejudicial to or inconsistent with the rights of the accused.
3. The parties may submit evidence relevant to the case, in accordance with article 64. The Court shall have the authority to request the submission of all evidence that it considers necessary for the determination of the truth.
4. The Court may rule on the relevance or admissibility of any evidence, taking into account, *inter alia*, the probative value of the evidence and any prejudice that such evidence may cause to a fair trial or to a fair evaluation of the testimony of a witness, in accordance with the Rules of Procedure and Evidence.
5. The Court shall respect and observe privileges on confidentiality as provided for in the Rules of Procedure and Evidence.
6. The Court shall not require proof of facts of common knowledge but may take judicial notice of them.

7. Evidence obtained by means of a violation of this Statute or internationally recognized human rights shall not be admissible if:
   (a) The violation casts substantial doubt on the reliability of the evidence; or
   (b) The admission of the evidence would be antithetical to and would seriously damage the integrity of the proceedings.
8. When deciding on the relevance or admissibility of evidence collected by a State, the Court shall not rule on the application of the State's national law.

Article 70

Offences against the administration of justice

1. The Court shall have jurisdiction over the following offences against its administration of justice when committed intentionally:
   (a) Giving false testimony when under an obligation pursuant to article 69, paragraph 1, to tell the truth;
   (b) Presenting evidence that the party knows is false or forged;
   (c) Corruptly influencing a witness, obstructing or interfering with the attendance or testimony of a witness, retaliating against a witness for giving testimony or destroying, tampering with or interfering with the collection of evidence;
   (d) Impeding, intimidating or corruptly influencing an official of the Court for the purpose of forcing or persuading the official not to perform, or to perform improperly, his or her duties;
   (e) Retaliating against an official of the Court on account of duties performed by that or another official;
   (f) Soliciting or accepting a bribe as an official of the Court in connection with his or her official duties.
2. The principles and procedures governing the Court's exercise of jurisdiction over offences under this article shall be those provided for in the Rules of Procedure and Evidence. The conditions for providing international cooperation to the Court with respect to its proceedings under this article shall be governed by the domestic laws of the requested State.
3. In the event of conviction, the Court may impose a term of imprisonment not exceeding five years, or a fine in accordance with the Rules of Procedure and Evidence, or both.
4. (a) Each State Party shall extend its criminal laws penalizing offences against the integrity of its own investigative or judicial process to offences against the administration of justice referred to in this article, committed on its territory, or by one of its nationals;
   (b) Upon request by the Court, whenever it deems it proper, the State Party shall submit the case to its competent authorities for the purpose of prosecution. Those authorities shall treat such cases with diligence and devote sufficient resources to enable them to be conducted effectively.

Article 71

Sanctions for misconduct before the Court

1. The Court may sanction persons present before it who commit misconduct, including disruption of its proceedings or deliberate refusal to comply with its directions, by administrative measures other than imprisonment, such as temporary or permanent removal from the courtroom, a fine or other similar measures provided for in the Rules of Procedure and Evidence.
2. The procedures governing the imposition of the measures set forth in paragraph 1 shall be those provided for in the Rules of Procedure and Evidence.

Article 72

Protection of national security information

1. This article applies in any case where the disclosure of the information or documents of a State would, in the opinion of that State, prejudice its national security interests. Such cases include those falling within the scope of article 56, paragraphs 2 and 3, article 61, paragraph 3, article 64, paragraph 3, article 67, paragraph 2, article 68, paragraph 6, article 87, paragraph 6 and article 93, as well as cases arising at any other stage of the proceedings where such disclosure may be at issue.
2. This article shall also apply when a person who has been requested to give information or evidence has refused to do so or has referred the matter to the State on the ground that disclosure would prejudice the national security interests of a State and the State concerned confirms that it is of the opinion that disclosure would prejudice its national security interests.
3. Nothing in this article shall prejudice the requirements of confidentiality applicable under article 54, paragraph 3 (e) and (f), or the application of article 73.
4. If a State learns that information or documents of the State are being, or are likely to be, disclosed at any stage of the proceedings, and it is of the opinion that disclosure would prejudice its national security interests, that State shall have the right to intervene in order to obtain resolution of the issue in accordance with this article.
5. If, in the opinion of a State, disclosure of information would prejudice its national security interests, all reasonable steps will be taken by the State, acting in conjunction with the Prosecutor, the defence or the Pre-Trial Chamber or Trial Chamber, as the case may be, to seek to resolve the matter by cooperative means. Such steps may include:
   (a) Modification or clarification of the request;
   (b) A determination by the Court regarding the relevance of the information or evidence sought, or a determination as to whether the evi-

dence, though relevant, could be or has been obtained from a source other than the requested State;

(c) Obtaining the information or evidence from a different source or in a different form; or

(d) Agreement on conditions under which the assistance could be provided including, among other things, providing summaries or redactions, limitations on disclosure, use of *in camera* or *ex parte* proceedings, or other protective measures permissible under the Statute and the Rules of Procedure and Evidence.

6. Once all reasonable steps have been taken to resolve the matter through cooperative means, and if the State considers that there are no means or conditions under which the information or documents could be provided or disclosed without prejudice to its national security interests, it shall so notify the Prosecutor or the Court of the specific reasons for its decision, unless a specific description of the reasons would itself necessarily result in such prejudice to the State's national security interests.

7. Thereafter, if the Court determines that the evidence is relevant and necessary for the establishment of the guilt or innocence of the accused, the Court may undertake the following actions:

   (a) Where disclosure of the information or document is sought pursuant to a request for cooperation under Part 9 or the circumstances described in paragraph 2, and the State has invoked the ground for refusal referred to in article 93, paragraph 4:

      (i) The Court may, before making any conclusion referred to in subparagraph 7 (a) (ii), request further consultations for the purpose of considering the State's representations, which may include, as appropriate, hearings *in camera* and *ex parte*;

      (ii) If the Court concludes that, by invoking the ground for refusal under article 93, paragraph 4, in the circumstances of the case, the requested State is not acting in accordance with its obligations under this Statute, the Court may refer the matter in accordance with article 87, paragraph 7, specifying the reasons for its conclusion; and

      (iii) The Court may make such inference in the trial of the accused as to the existence or non-existence of a fact, as may be appropriate in the circumstances; or

   (b) In all other circumstances:

      (i) Order disclosure; or

      (ii) To the extent it does not order disclosure, make such inference in the trial of the accused as to the existence or non-existence of a fact, as may be appropriate in the circumstances.

Article 73

Third-party information or documents

If a State Party is requested by the Court to provide a document or information in its custody, possession or control, which was disclosed to it in confidence by a State, intergovernmental organization or international organization, it shall seek the consent of the originator to disclose that document or information. If the originator is a State Party, it shall either consent to disclosure of the information or document or undertake to resolve the issue of disclosure with the Court, subject to the provisions of article 72. If the originator is not a State Party and refuses to consent to disclosure, the requested State shall inform the Court that it is unable to provide the document or information because of a pre-existing obligation of confidentiality to the originator.

Article 74

Requirements for the decision

1. All the judges of the Trial Chamber shall be present at each stage of the trial and throughout their deliberations. The Presidency may, on a case-by-case basis, designate, as available, one or more alternate judges to be present at each stage of the trial and to replace a member of the Trial Chamber if that member is unable to continue attending.
2. The Trial Chamber's decision shall be based on its evaluation of the evidence and the entire proceedings. The decision shall not exceed the facts and circumstances described in the charges and any amendments to the charges. The Court may base its decision only on evidence submitted and discussed before it at the trial.
3. The judges shall attempt to achieve unanimity in their decision, failing which the decision shall be taken by a majority of the judges.
4. The deliberations of the Trial Chamber shall remain secret.
5. The decision shall be in writing and shall contain a full and reasoned statement of the Trial Chamber's findings on the evidence and conclusions. The Trial Chamber shall issue one decision. When there is no unanimity, the Trial Chamber's decision shall contain the views of the majority and the minority. The decision or a summary thereof shall be delivered in open court.

Article 75

Reparations to victims

1. The Court shall establish principles relating to reparations to, or in respect of, victims, including restitution, compensation and rehabilitation. On this basis, in its decision the Court may, either upon request or on its own motion in exceptional circumstances, determine the scope and extent of

any damage, loss and injury to, or in respect of, victims and will state the principles on which it is acting.

2. The Court may make an order directly against a convicted person specifying appropriate reparations to, or in respect of, victims, including restitution, compensation and rehabilitation.
   Where appropriate, the Court may order that the award for reparations be made through the Trust Fund provided for in article 79.
3. Before making an order under this article, the Court may invite and shall take account of representations from or on behalf of the convicted person, victims, other interested persons or interested States.
4. In exercising its power under this article, the Court may, after a person is convicted of a crime within the jurisdiction of the Court, determine whether, in order to give effect to an order which it may make under this article, it is necessary to seek measures under article 93, paragraph 1.
5. A State Party shall give effect to a decision under this article as if the provisions of article 109 were applicable to this article.
6. Nothing in this article shall be interpreted as prejudicing the rights of victims under national or international law.

Article 76
Sentencing

1. In the event of a conviction, the Trial Chamber shall consider the appropriate sentence to be imposed and shall take into account the evidence presented and submissions made during the trial that are relevant to the sentence.
2. Except where article 65 applies and before the completion of the trial, the Trial Chamber may on its own motion and shall, at the request of the Prosecutor or the accused, hold a further hearing to hear any additional evidence or submissions relevant to the sentence, in accordance with the Rules of Procedure and Evidence.
3. Where paragraph 2 applies, any representations under article 75 shall be heard during the further hearing referred to in paragraph 2 and, if necessary, during any additional hearing.
4. The sentence shall be pronounced in public and, wherever possible, in the presence of the accused.

PART 7. PENALTIES

Article 77
Applicable penalties

1. Subject to article 110, the Court may impose one of the following penalties on a person convicted of a crime referred to in article 5 of this Statute:

(a) Imprisonment for a specified number of years, which may not exceed a maximum of 30 years; or
(b) A term of life imprisonment when justified by the extreme gravity of the crime and the individual circumstances of the convicted person.

2. In addition to imprisonment, the Court may order:
(a) A fine under the criteria provided for in the Rules of Procedure and Evidence;
(b) A forfeiture of proceeds, property and assets derived directly or indirectly from that crime, without prejudice to the rights of bona fide third parties.

Article 78
Determination of the sentence

1. In determining the sentence, the Court shall, in accordance with the Rules of Procedure and Evidence, take into account such factors as the gravity of the crime and the individual circumstances of the convicted person.
2. In imposing a sentence of imprisonment, the Court shall deduct the time, if any, previously spent in detention in accordance with an order of the Court. The Court may deduct any time otherwise spent in detention in connection with conduct underlying the crime.
3. When a person has been convicted of more than one crime, the Court shall pronounce a sentence for each crime and a joint sentence specifying the total period of imprisonment. This period shall be no less than the highest individual sentence pronounced and shall not exceed 30 years imprisonment or a sentence of life imprisonment in conformity with article 77, paragraph 1 (b).

Article 79
Trust Fund

1. A Trust Fund shall be established by decision of the Assembly of States Parties for the benefit of victims of crimes within the jurisdiction of the Court, and of the families of such victims.
2. The Court may order money and other property collected through fines or forfeiture to be transferred, by order of the Court, to the Trust Fund.
3. The Trust Fund shall be managed according to criteria to be determined by the Assembly of States Parties.

Article 80
Non-prejudice to national application of penalties and national laws

Nothing in this Part affects the application by States of penalties prescribed by their national law, nor the law of States which do not provide for penalties prescribed in this Part.

PART 8. APPEAL AND REVISION

Article 81

Appeal against decision of acquittal or conviction or against sentence

1. A decision under article 74 may be appealed in accordance with the Rules of Procedure and Evidence as follows:
   (a) The Prosecutor may make an appeal on any of the following grounds:
      (i) Procedural error,
      (ii) Error of fact, or
      (iii) Error of law;
   (b) The convicted person, or the Prosecutor on that person's behalf, may make an appeal on any of the following grounds:
      (i) Procedural error,
      (ii) Error of fact,
      (iii) Error of law, or
      (iv) Any other ground that affects the fairness or reliability of the proceedings or decision.
2. (a) A sentence may be appealed, in accordance with the Rules of Procedure and Evidence, by the Prosecutor or the convicted person on the ground of disproportion between the crime and the sentence;
   (b) If on an appeal against sentence the Court considers that there are grounds on which the conviction might be set aside, wholly or in part, it may invite the Prosecutor and the convicted person to submit grounds under article 81, paragraph 1 (a) or (b), and may render a decision on conviction in accordance with article 83;
   (c) The same procedure applies when the Court, on an appeal against conviction only, considers that there are grounds to reduce the sentence under paragraph 2 (a).
3. (a) Unless the Trial Chamber orders otherwise, a convicted person shall remain in custody pending an appeal;
   (b) When a convicted person's time in custody exceeds the sentence of imprisonment imposed, that person shall be released, except that if the Prosecutor is also appealing, the release may be subject to the conditions under subparagraph (c) below;
   (c) In case of an acquittal, the accused shall be released immediately, subject to the following:
      (i) Under exceptional circumstances, and having regard, *inter alia*, to the concrete risk of flight, the seriousness of the offence charged and the probability of success on appeal, the Trial Chamber, at the request of the Prosecutor, may maintain the detention of the person pending appeal;

(ii) A decision by the Trial Chamber under subparagraph (c) (i) may be appealed in accordance with the Rules of Procedure and Evidence.

4. Subject to the provisions of paragraph 3 (a) and (b), execution of the decision or sentence shall be suspended during the period allowed for appeal and for the duration of the appeal proceedings.

Article 82
Appeal against other decisions

1. Either party may appeal any of the following decisions in accordance with the Rules of Procedure and Evidence:
   (a) A decision with respect to jurisdiction or admissibility;
   (b) A decision granting or denying release of the person being investigated or prosecuted;
   (c) A decision of the Pre-Trial Chamber to act on its own initiative under article 56, paragraph 3;
   (d) A decision that involves an issue that would significantly affect the fair and expeditious conduct of the proceedings or the outcome of the trial, and for which, in the opinion of the Pre-Trial or Trial Chamber, an immediate resolution by the Appeals Chamber may materially advance the proceedings.
2. A decision of the Pre-Trial Chamber under article 57, paragraph 3 (d), may be appealed against by the State concerned or by the Prosecutor, with the leave of the Pre-Trial Chamber. The appeal shall be heard on an expedited basis.
3. An appeal shall not of itself have suspensive effect unless the Appeals Chamber so orders, upon request, in accordance with the Rules of Procedure and Evidence.
4. A legal representative of the victims, the convicted person or a bona fide owner of property adversely affected by an order under article 75 may appeal against the order for reparations, as provided in the Rules of Procedure and Evidence.

Article 83
Proceedings on appeal

1. For the purposes of proceedings under article 81 and this article, the Appeals Chamber shall have all the powers of the Trial Chamber.
2. If the Appeals Chamber finds that the proceedings appealed from were unfair in a way that affected the reliability of the decision or sentence, or that the decision or sentence appealed from was materially affected by error of fact or law or procedural error, it may:
   (a) Reverse or amend the decision or sentence; or

(b) Order a new trial before a different Trial Chamber.

For these purposes, the Appeals Chamber may remand a factual issue to the original Trial Chamber for it to determine the issue and to report back accordingly, or may itself call evidence to determine the issue. When the decision or sentence has been appealed only by the person convicted, or the Prosecutor on that person's behalf, it cannot be amended to his or her detriment.

3. If in an appeal against sentence the Appeals Chamber finds that the sentence is disproportionate to the crime, it may vary the sentence in accordance with Part 7.
4. The judgement of the Appeals Chamber shall be taken by a majority of the judges and shall be delivered in open court. The judgement shall state the reasons on which it is based. When there is no unanimity, the judgement of the Appeals Chamber shall contain the views of the majority and the minority, but a judge may deliver a separate or dissenting opinion on a question of law.
5. The Appeals Chamber may deliver its judgement in the absence of the person acquitted or convicted.

Article 84

Revision of conviction or sentence

1. The convicted person or, after death, spouses, children, parents or one person alive at the time of the accused's death who has been given express written instructions from the accused to bring such a claim, or the Prosecutor on the person's behalf, may apply to the Appeals Chamber to revise the final judgement of conviction or sentence on the grounds that:
   (a) New evidence has been discovered that:
      (i) Was not available at the time of trial, and such unavailability was not wholly or partially attributable to the party making application; and
      (ii) Is sufficiently important that had it been proved at trial it would have been likely to have resulted in a different verdict;
   (b) It has been newly discovered that decisive evidence, taken into account at trial and upon which the conviction depends, was false, forged or falsified;
   (c) One or more of the judges who participated in conviction or confirmation of the charges has committed, in that case, an act of serious misconduct or serious breach of duty of sufficient gravity to justify the removal of that judge or those judges from office under article 46.
2. The Appeals Chamber shall reject the application if it considers it to be unfounded. If it determines that the application is meritorious, it may, as appropriate:

(a) Reconvene the original Trial Chamber;
(b) Constitute a new Trial Chamber; or
(c) Retain jurisdiction over the matter,

with a view to, after hearing the parties in the manner set forth in the Rules of Procedure and Evidence, arriving at a determination on whether the judgement should be revised.

Article 85

Compensation to an arrested or convicted person

1. Anyone who has been the victim of unlawful arrest or detention shall have an enforceable right to compensation.
2. When a person has by a final decision been convicted of a criminal offence, and when subsequently his or her conviction has been reversed on the ground that a new or newly discovered fact shows conclusively that there has been a miscarriage of justice, the person who has suffered punishment as a result of such conviction shall be compensated according to law, unless it is proved that the non-disclosure of the unknown fact in time is wholly or partly attributable to him or her.
3. In exceptional circumstances, where the Court finds conclusive facts showing that there has been a grave and manifest miscarriage of justice, it may in its discretion award compensation, according to the criteria provided in the Rules of Procedure and Evidence, to a person who has been released from detention following a final decision of acquittal or a termination of the proceedings for that reason.

PART 9. INTERNATIONAL COOPERATION AND JUDICIAL ASSISTANCE

Article 86

General obligation to cooperate

States Parties shall, in accordance with the provisions of this Statute, cooperate fully with the Court in its investigation and prosecution of crimes within the jurisdiction of the Court.

Article 87

Requests for cooperation: general provisions

1. (a) The Court shall have the authority to make requests to States Parties for cooperation. The requests shall be transmitted through the diplomatic channel or any other appropriate channel as may be designated by each State Party upon ratification, acceptance, approval or accession.

Subsequent changes to the designation shall be made by each State Party in accordance with the Rules of Procedure and Evidence.

(b) When appropriate, without prejudice to the provisions of subparagraph (a), requests may also be transmitted through the International Criminal Police Organization or any appropriate regional organization.

2. Requests for cooperation and any documents supporting the request shall either be in or be accompanied by a translation into an official language of the requested State or one of the working languages of the Court, in accordance with the choice made by that State upon ratification, acceptance, approval or accession.

Subsequent changes to this choice shall be made in accordance with the Rules of Procedure and Evidence.

3. The requested State shall keep confidential a request for cooperation and any documents supporting the request, except to the extent that the disclosure is necessary for execution of the request.

4. In relation to any request for assistance presented under this Part, the Court may take such measures, including measures related to the protection of information, as may be necessary to ensure the safety or physical or psychological well-being of any victims, potential witnesses and their families. The Court may request that any information that is made available under this Part shall be provided and handled in a manner that protects the safety and physical or psychological well-being of any victims, potential witnesses and their families.

5. (a) The Court may invite any State not party to this Statute to provide assistance under this Part on the basis of an ad hoc arrangement, an agreement with such State or any other appropriate basis.

(b) Where a State not party to this Statute, which has entered into an ad hoc arrangement or an agreement with the Court, fails to cooperate with requests pursuant to any such arrangement or agreement, the Court may so inform the Assembly of States Parties or, where the Security Council referred the matter to the Court, the Security Council.

6. The Court may ask any intergovernmental organization to provide information or documents. The Court may also ask for other forms of cooperation and assistance which may be agreed upon with such an organization and which are in accordance with its competence or mandate.

7. Where a State Party fails to comply with a request to cooperate by the Court contrary to the provisions of this Statute, thereby preventing the Court from exercising its functions and powers under this Statute, the Court may make a finding to that effect and refer the matter to the Assembly of States Parties or, where the Security Council referred the matter to the Court, to the Security Council.

Article 88

Availability of procedures under national law

States Parties shall ensure that there are procedures available under their national law for all of the forms of cooperation which are specified under this Part.

Article 89
Surrender of persons to the Court

1. The Court may transmit a request for the arrest and surrender of a person, together with the material supporting the request outlined in article 91, to any State on the territory of which that person may be found and shall request the cooperation of that State in the arrest and surrender of such a person. States Parties shall, in accordance with the provisions of this Part and the procedure under their national law, comply with requests for arrest and surrender.
2. Where the person sought for surrender brings a challenge before a national court on the basis of the principle of *ne bis in idem* as provided in article 20, the requested State shall immediately consult with the Court to determine if there has been a relevant ruling on admissibility. If the case is admissible, the requested State shall proceed with the execution of the request. If an admissibility ruling is pending, the requested State may postpone the execution of the request for surrender of the person until the Court makes a determination on admissibility.
3. (a) A State Party shall authorize, in accordance with its national procedural law, transportation through its territory of a person being surrendered to the Court by another State, except where transit through that State would impede or delay the surrender.
   (b) A request by the Court for transit shall be transmitted in accordance with article 87. The request for transit shall contain:
      (i) A description of the person being transported;
      (ii) A brief statement of the facts of the case and their legal characterization; and
      (iii) The warrant for arrest and surrender;
   (c) A person being transported shall be detained in custody during the period of transit;
   (d) No authorization is required if the person is transported by air and no landing is scheduled on the territory of the transit State;
   (e) If an unscheduled landing occurs on the territory of the transit State, that State may require a request for transit from the Court as provided for in subparagraph (b). The transit State shall detain the person being transported until the request for transit is received and the transit is effected, provided that detention for purposes of this subparagraph may not be extended beyond 96 hours from the unscheduled landing unless the request is received within that time.
4. If the person sought is being proceeded against or is serving a sentence in the requested State for a crime different from that for which surrender to the Court is sought, the requested State, after making its decision to grant the request, shall consult with the Court.

Article 90
Competing requests

1. A State Party which receives a request from the Court for the surrender of a person under article 89 shall, if it also receives a request from any other State for the extradition of the same person for the same conduct which forms the basis of the crime for which the Court seeks the person's surrender, notify the Court and the requesting State of that fact.
2. Where the requesting State is a State Party, the requested State shall give priority to the request from the Court if:
   (a) The Court has, pursuant to article 18 or 19, made a determination that the case in respect of which surrender is sought is admissible and that determination takes into account the investigation or prosecution conducted by the requesting State in respect of its request for extradition; or
   (b) The Court makes the determination described in subparagraph (a) pursuant to the requested State's notification under paragraph 1.
3. Where a determination under paragraph 2 (a) has not been made, the requested State may, at its discretion, pending the determination of the Court under paragraph 2 (b), proceed to deal with the request for extradition from the requesting State but shall not extradite the person until the Court has determined that the case is inadmissible. The Court's determination shall be made on an expedited basis.
4. If the requesting State is a State not Party to this Statute the requested State, if it is not under an international obligation to extradite the person to the requesting State, shall give priority to the request for surrender from the Court, if the Court has determined that the case is admissible.
5. Where a case under paragraph 4 has not been determined to be admissible by the Court, the requested State may, at its discretion, proceed to deal with the request for extradition from the requesting State.
6. In cases where paragraph 4 applies except that the requested State is under an existing international obligation to extradite the person to the requesting State not Party to this Statute, the requested State shall determine whether to surrender the person to the Court or extradite the person to the requesting State. In making its decision, the requested State shall consider all the relevant factors, including but not limited to:
   (a) The respective dates of the requests;
   (b) The interests of the requesting State including, where relevant, whether the crime was committed in its territory and the nationality of the victims and of the person sought; and
   (c) The possibility of subsequent surrender between the Court and the requesting State.
7. Where a State Party which receives a request from the Court for the surrender of a person also receives a request from any State for the extradi-

tion of the same person for conduct other than that which constitutes the crime for which the Court seeks the person's surrender:

(a) The requested State shall, if it is not under an existing international obligation to extradite the person to the requesting State, give priority to the request from the Court;

(b) The requested State shall, if it is under an existing international obligation to extradite the person to the requesting State, determine whether to surrender the person to the Court or to extradite the person to the requesting State. In making its decision, the requested State shall consider all the relevant factors, including but not limited to those set out in paragraph 6, but shall give special consideration to the relative nature and gravity of the conduct in question.

8. Where pursuant to a notification under this article, the Court has determined a case to be inadmissible, and subsequently extradition to the requesting State is refused, the requested State shall notify the Court of this decision.

Article 91

Contents of request for arrest and surrender

1. A request for arrest and surrender shall be made in writing. In urgent cases, a request may be made by any medium capable of delivering a written record, provided that the request shall be confirmed through the channel provided for in article 87, paragraph 1 (a).
2. In the case of a request for the arrest and surrender of a person for whom a warrant of arrest has been issued by the Pre-Trial Chamber under article 58, the request shall contain or be supported by:
   (a) Information describing the person sought, sufficient to identify the person, and information as to that person's probable location;
   (b) A copy of the warrant of arrest; and
   (c) Such documents, statements or information as may be necessary to meet the requirements for the surrender process in the requested State, except that those requirements should not be more burdensome than those applicable to requests for extradition pursuant to treaties or arrangements between the requested State and other States and should, if possible, be less burdensome, taking into account the distinct nature of the Court.
3. In the case of a request for the arrest and surrender of a person already convicted, the request shall contain or be supported by:
   (a) A copy of any warrant of arrest for that person;
   (b) A copy of the judgement of conviction;
   (c) Information to demonstrate that the person sought is the one referred to in the judgement of conviction; and
   (d) If the person sought has been sentenced, a copy of the sentence

imposed and, in the case of a sentence for imprisonment, a statement of any time already served and the time remaining to be served.

4. Upon the request of the Court, a State Party shall consult with the Court, either generally or with respect to a specific matter, regarding any requirements under its national law that may apply under paragraph 2 (c). During the consultations, the State Party shall advise the Court of the specific requirements of its national law.

Article 92
Provisional arrest

1. In urgent cases, the Court may request the provisional arrest of the person sought, pending presentation of the request for surrender and the documents supporting the request as specified in article 91.
2. The request for provisional arrest shall be made by any medium capable of delivering a written record and shall contain:
   (a) Information describing the person sought, sufficient to identify the person, and information as to that person's probable location;
   (b) A concise statement of the crimes for which the person's arrest is sought and of the facts which are alleged to constitute those crimes, including, where possible, the date and location of the crime;
   (c) A statement of the existence of a warrant of arrest or a judgement of conviction against the person sought; and
   (d) A statement that a request for surrender of the person sought will follow.
3. A person who is provisionally arrested may be released from custody if the requested State has not received the request for surrender and the documents supporting the request as specified in article 91 within the time limits specified in the Rules of Procedure and Evidence. However, the person may consent to surrender before the expiration of this period if permitted by the law of the requested State. In such a case, the requested State shall proceed to surrender the person to the Court as soon as possible.
4. The fact that the person sought has been released from custody pursuant to paragraph 3 shall not prejudice the subsequent arrest and surrender of that person if the request for surrender and the documents supporting the request are delivered at a later date.

Article 93
Other forms of cooperation

1. States Parties shall, in accordance with the provisions of this Part and under procedures of national law, comply with requests by the Court to provide the following assistance in relation to investigations or prosecutions:

(a) The identification and whereabouts of persons or the location of items;
(b) The taking of evidence, including testimony under oath, and the production of evidence, including expert opinions and reports necessary to the Court;
(c) The questioning of any person being investigated or prosecuted;
(d) The service of documents, including judicial documents;
(e) Facilitating the voluntary appearance of persons as witnesses or experts before the Court;
(f) The temporary transfer of persons as provided in paragraph 7;
(g) The examination of places or sites, including the exhumation and examination of grave sites;
(h) The execution of searches and seizures;
(i) The provision of records and documents, including official records and documents;
(j) The protection of victims and witnesses and the preservation of evidence;
(k) The identification, tracing and freezing or seizure of proceeds, property and assets and instrumentalities of crimes for the purpose of eventual forfeiture, without prejudice to the rights of bona fide third parties; and
(l) Any other type of assistance which is not prohibited by the law of the requested State, with a view to facilitating the investigation and prosecution of crimes within the jurisdiction of the Court.

2. The Court shall have the authority to provide an assurance to a witness or an expert appearing before the Court that he or she will not be prosecuted, detained or subjected to any restriction of personal freedom by the Court in respect of any act or omission that preceded the departure of that person from the requested State.
3. Where execution of a particular measure of assistance detailed in a request presented under paragraph 1, is prohibited in the requested State on the basis of an existing fundamental legal principle of general application, the requested State shall promptly consult with the Court to try to resolve the matter. In the consultations, consideration should be given to whether the assistance can be rendered in another manner or subject to conditions. If after consultations the matter cannot be resolved, the Court shall modify the request as necessary.
4. In accordance with article 72, a State Party may deny a request for assistance, in whole or in part, only if the request concerns the production of any documents or disclosure of evidence which relates to its national security.
5. Before denying a request for assistance under paragraph 1 (l), the requested State shall consider whether the assistance can be provided subject to specified conditions, or whether the assistance can be provided

at a later date or in an alternative manner, provided that if the Court or the Prosecutor accepts the assistance subject to conditions, the Court or the Prosecutor shall abide by them.

6. If a request for assistance is denied, the requested State Party shall promptly inform the Court or the Prosecutor of the reasons for such denial.
7. (a) The Court may request the temporary transfer of a person in custody for purposes of identification or for obtaining testimony or other assistance. The person may be transferred if the following conditions are fulfilled:
   (i) The person freely gives his or her informed consent to the transfer; and
   (ii) The requested State agrees to the transfer, subject to such conditions as that State and the Court may agree.

   (b) The person being transferred shall remain in custody. When the purposes of the transfer have been fulfilled, the Court shall return the person without delay to the requested State.
8. (a) The Court shall ensure the confidentiality of documents and information, except as required for the investigation and proceedings described in the request.

   (b) The requested State may, when necessary, transmit documents or information to the Prosecutor on a confidential basis. The Prosecutor may then use them solely for the purpose of generating new evidence.

   (c) The requested State may, on its own motion or at the request of the Prosecutor, subsequently consent to the disclosure of such documents or information. They may then be used as evidence pursuant to the provisions of Parts 5 and 6 and in accordance with the Rules of Procedure and Evidence.
9. (a) (i) In the event that a State Party receives competing requests, other than for surrender or extradition, from the Court and from another State pursuant to an international obligation, the State Party shall endeavour, in consultation with the Court and the other State, to meet both requests, if necessary by postponing or attaching conditions to one or the other request.
   (ii) Failing that, competing requests shall be resolved in accordance with the principles established in article 90.

   (b) Where, however, the request from the Court concerns information, property or persons which are subject to the control of a third State or an international organization by virtue of an international agreement, the requested States shall so inform the Court and the Court shall direct its request to the third State or international organization.
10. (a) The Court may, upon request, cooperate with and provide assistance to a State Party conducting an investigation into or trial in respect of conduct which constitutes a crime within the jurisdiction of the Court

or which constitutes a serious crime under the national law of the requesting State.

(b) (i) The assistance provided under subparagraph (a) shall include, *inter alia:*

a. The transmission of statements, documents or other types of evidence obtained in the course of an investigation or a trial conducted by the Court; and

b. The questioning of any person detained by order of the Court;

(ii) In the case of assistance under subparagraph (b) (i) a:

a. If the documents or other types of evidence have been obtained with the assistance of a State, such transmission shall require the consent of that State;

b. If the statements, documents or other types of evidence have been provided by a witness or expert, such transmission shall be subject to the provisions of article 68.

(c) The Court may, under the conditions set out in this paragraph, grant a request for assistance under this paragraph from a State which is not a Party to this Statute.

Article 94

Postponement of execution of a request in respect of ongoing investigation or prosecution

1. If the immediate execution of a request would interfere with an ongoing investigation or prosecution of a case different from that to which the request relates, the requested State may postpone the execution of the request for a period of time agreed upon with the Court. However, the postponement shall be no longer than is necessary to complete the relevant investigation or prosecution in the requested State. Before making a decision to postpone, the requested State should consider whether the assistance may be immediately provided subject to certain conditions.
2. If a decision to postpone is taken pursuant to paragraph 1, the Prosecutor may, however, seek measures to preserve evidence, pursuant to article 93, paragraph 1 (j).

Article 95

Postponement of execution of a request in respect of an admissibility challenge

Where there is an admissibility challenge under consideration by the Court pursuant to article 18 or 19, the requested State may postpone the execution of a request under this Part pending a determination by the Court, unless the Court has specifically ordered that the Prosecutor may pursue the collection of such evidence pursuant to article 18 or 19.

Article 96

Contents of request for other forms of assistance under article 93

1. A request for other forms of assistance referred to in article 93 shall be made in writing. In urgent cases, a request may be made by any medium capable of delivering a written record, provided that the request shall be confirmed through the channel provided for in article 87, paragraph 1 (a).
2. The request shall, as applicable, contain or be supported by the following:
   (a) A concise statement of the purpose of the request and the assistance sought, including the legal basis and the grounds for the request;
   (b) As much detailed information as possible about the location or identification of any person or place that must be found or identified in order for the assistance sought to be provided;
   (c) A concise statement of the essential facts underlying the request;
   (d) The reasons for and details of any procedure or requirement to be followed;
   (e) Such information as may be required under the law of the requested State in order to execute the request; and
   (f) Any other information relevant in order for the assistance sought to be provided.
3. Upon the request of the Court, a State Party shall consult with the Court, either generally or with respect to a specific matter, regarding any requirements under its national law that may apply under paragraph 2 (e). During the consultations, the State Party shall advise the Court of the specific requirements of its national law.
4. The provisions of this article shall, where applicable, also apply in respect of a request for assistance made to the Court.

Article 97

Consultations

Where a State Party receives a request under this Part in relation to which it identifies problems which may impede or prevent the execution of the request, that State shall consult with the Court without delay in order to resolve the matter. Such problems may include, *inter alia:*

(a) Insufficient information to execute the request;
(b) In the case of a request for surrender, the fact that despite best efforts, the person sought cannot be located or that the investigation conducted has determined that the person in the requested State is clearly not the person named in the warrant; or
(c) The fact that execution of the request in its current form would require the requested State to breach a pre-existing treaty obligation undertaken with respect to another State.

Article 98

Cooperation with respect to waiver of immunity and consent to surrender

1. The Court may not proceed with a request for surrender or assistance which would require the requested State to act inconsistently with its obligations under international law with respect to the State or diplomatic immunity of a person or property of a third State, unless the Court can first obtain the cooperation of that third State for the waiver of the immunity.
2. The Court may not proceed with a request for surrender which would require the requested State to act inconsistently with its obligations under international agreements pursuant to which the consent of a sending State is required to surrender a person of that State to the Court, unless the Court can first obtain the cooperation of the sending State for the giving of consent for the surrender.

Article 99

Execution of requests under articles 93 and 96

1. Requests for assistance shall be executed in accordance with the relevant procedure under the law of the requested State and, unless prohibited by such law, in the manner specified in the request, including following any procedure outlined therein or permitting persons specified in the request to be present at and assist in the execution process.
2. In the case of an urgent request, the documents or evidence produced in response shall, at the request of the Court, be sent urgently.
3. Replies from the requested State shall be transmitted in their original language and form.
4. Without prejudice to other articles in this Part, where it is necessary for the successful execution of a request which can be executed without any compulsory measures, including specifically the interview of or taking evidence from a person on a voluntary basis, including doing so without the presence of the authorities of the requested State Party if it is essential for the request to be executed, and the examination without modification of a public site or other public place, the Prosecutor may execute such request directly on the territory of a State as follows:
   (a) When the State Party requested is a State on the territory of which the crime is alleged to have been committed, and there has been a determination of admissibility pursuant to article 18 or 19, the Prosecutor may directly execute such request following all possible consultations with the requested State Party;
   (b) In other cases, the Prosecutor may execute such request following consultations with the requested State Party and subject to any rea-

sonable conditions or concerns raised by that State Party. Where the requested State Party identifies problems with the execution of a request pursuant to this subparagraph it shall, without delay, consult with the Court to resolve the matter.

5. Provisions allowing a person heard or examined by the Court under article 72 to invoke restrictions designed to prevent disclosure of confidential information connected with national security shall also apply to the execution of requests for assistance under this article.

Article 100
Costs

1. The ordinary costs for execution of requests in the territory of the requested State shall be borne by that State, except for the following, which shall be borne by the Court:
   (a) Costs associated with the travel and security of witnesses and experts or the transfer under article 93 of persons in custody;
   (b) Costs of translation, interpretation and transcription;
   (c) Travel and subsistence costs of the judges, the Prosecutor, the Deputy Prosecutors, the Registrar, the Deputy Registrar and staff of any organ of the Court;
   (d) Costs of any expert opinion or report requested by the Court;
   (e) Costs associated with the transport of a person being surrendered to the Court by a custodial State; and
   (f) Following consultations, any extraordinary costs that may result from the execution of a request.
2. The provisions of paragraph 1 shall, as appropriate, apply to requests from States Parties to the Court. In that case, the Court shall bear the ordinary costs of execution.

Article 101
Rule of speciality

1. A person surrendered to the Court under this Statute shall not be proceeded against, punished or detained for any conduct committed prior to surrender, other than the conduct or course of conduct which forms the basis of the crimes for which that person has been surrendered.
2. The Court may request a waiver of the requirements of paragraph 1 from the State which surrendered the person to the Court and, if necessary, the Court shall provide additional information in accordance with article 91. States Parties shall have the authority to provide a waiver to the Court and should endeavour to do so.

Article 102

Use of terms

For the purposes of this Statute:

(a) "surrender" means the delivering up of a person by a State to the Court, pursuant to this Statute.

(b) "extradition" means the delivering up of a person by one State to another as provided by treaty, convention or national legislation.

PART 10. ENFORCEMENT

Article 103

Role of States in enforcement of sentences of imprisonment

1. (a) A sentence of imprisonment shall be served in a State designated by the Court from a list of States which have indicated to the Court their willingness to accept sentenced persons.
   (b) At the time of declaring its willingness to accept sentenced persons, a State may attach conditions to its acceptance as agreed by the Court and in accordance with this Part.
   (c) A State designated in a particular case shall promptly inform the Court whether it accepts the Court's designation.
2. (a) The State of enforcement shall notify the Court of any circumstances, including the exercise of any conditions agreed under paragraph 1, which could materially affect the terms or extent of the imprisonment. The Court shall be given at least 45 days' notice of any such known or foreseeable circumstances. During this period, the State of enforcement shall take no action that might prejudice its obligations under article 110.
   (b) Where the Court cannot agree to the circumstances referred to in subparagraph (a), it shall notify the State of enforcement and proceed in accordance with article 104, paragraph 1.
3. In exercising its discretion to make a designation under paragraph 1, the Court shall take into account the following:
   (a) The principle that States Parties should share the responsibility for enforcing sentences of imprisonment, in accordance with principles of equitable distribution, as provided in the Rules of Procedure and Evidence;
   (b) The application of widely accepted international treaty standards governing the treatment of prisoners;
   (c) The views of the sentenced person;
   (d) The nationality of the sentenced person;
   (e) Such other factors regarding the circumstances of the crime or the

person sentenced, or the effective enforcement of the sentence, as may be appropriate in designating the State of enforcement.

4. If no State is designated under paragraph 1, the sentence of imprisonment shall be served in a prison facility made available by the host State, in accordance with the conditions set out in the headquarters agreement referred to in article 3, paragraph 2. In such a case, the costs arising out of the enforcement of a sentence of imprisonment shall be borne by the Court.

Article 104

Change in designation of State of enforcement

1. The Court may, at any time, decide to transfer a sentenced person to a prison of another State.
2. A sentenced person may, at any time, apply to the Court to be transferred from the State of enforcement.

Article 105

Enforcement of the sentence

1. Subject to conditions which a State may have specified in accordance with article 103, paragraph 1 (b), the sentence of imprisonment shall be binding on the States Parties, which shall in no case modify it.
2. The Court alone shall have the right to decide any application for appeal and revision. The State of enforcement shall not impede the making of any such application by a sentenced person.

Article 106

Supervision of enforcement of sentences and conditions of imprisonment

1. The enforcement of a sentence of imprisonment shall be subject to the supervision of the Court and shall be consistent with widely accepted international treaty standards governing treatment of prisoners.
2. The conditions of imprisonment shall be governed by the law of the State of enforcement and shall be consistent with widely accepted international treaty standards governing treatment of prisoners; in no case shall such conditions be more or less favourable than those available to prisoners convicted of similar offences in the State of enforcement.
3. Communications between a sentenced person and the Court shall be unimpeded and confidential.

Article 107
Transfer of the person upon completion of sentence

1. Following completion of the sentence, a person who is not a national of the State of enforcement may, in accordance with the law of the State of enforcement, be transferred to a State which is obliged to receive him or her, or to another State which agrees to receive him or her, taking into account any wishes of the person to be transferred to that State, unless the State of enforcement authorizes the person to remain in its territory.
2. If no State bears the costs arising out of transferring the person to another State pursuant to paragraph 1, such costs shall be borne by the Court.
3. Subject to the provisions of article 108, the State of enforcement may also, in accordance with its national law, extradite or otherwise surrender the person to a State which has requested the extradition or surrender of the person for purposes of trial or enforcement of a sentence.

Article 108
Limitation on the prosecution or punishment of other offences

1. A sentenced person in the custody of the State of enforcement shall not be subject to prosecution or punishment or to extradition to a third State for any conduct engaged in prior to that person's delivery to the State of enforcement, unless such prosecution, punishment or extradition has been approved by the Court at the request of the State of enforcement.
2. The Court shall decide the matter after having heard the views of the sentenced person.
3. Paragraph 1 shall cease to apply if the sentenced person remains voluntarily for more than 30 days in the territory of the State of enforcement after having served the full sentence imposed by the Court, or returns to the territory of that State after having left it.

Article 109
Enforcement of fines and forfeiture measures

1. States Parties shall give effect to fines or forfeitures ordered by the Court under Part 7, without prejudice to the rights of bona fide third parties, and in accordance with the procedure of their national law.
2. If a State Party is unable to give effect to an order for forfeiture, it shall take measures to recover the value of the proceeds, property or assets ordered by the Court to be forfeited, without prejudice to the rights of bona fide third parties.
3. Property, or the proceeds of the sale of real property or, where appropriate, the sale of other property, which is obtained by a State Party as a result of its enforcement of a judgement of the Court shall be transferred to the Court.

Article 110

Review by the Court concerning reduction of sentence

1. The State of enforcement shall not release the person before expiry of the sentence pronounced by the Court.
2. The Court alone shall have the right to decide any reduction of sentence, and shall rule on the matter after having heard the person.
3. When the person has served two thirds of the sentence, or 25 years in the case of life imprisonment, the Court shall review the sentence to determine whether it should be reduced. Such a review shall not be conducted before that time.
4. In its review under paragraph 3, the Court may reduce the sentence if it finds that one or more of the following factors are present:
   (a) The early and continuing willingness of the person to cooperate with the Court in its investigations and prosecutions;
   (b) The voluntary assistance of the person in enabling the enforcement of the judgements and orders of the Court in other cases, and in particular providing assistance in locating assets subject to orders of fine, forfeiture or reparation which may be used for the benefit of victims; or
   (c) Other factors establishing a clear and significant change of circumstances sufficient to justify the reduction of sentence, as provided in the Rules of Procedure and Evidence.
5. If the Court determines in its initial review under paragraph 3 that it is not appropriate to reduce the sentence, it shall thereafter review the question of reduction of sentence at such intervals and applying such criteria as provided for in the Rules of Procedure and Evidence.

Article 111

Escape

If a convicted person escapes from custody and flees the State of enforcement, that State may, after consultation with the Court, request the person's surrender from the State in which the person is located pursuant to existing bilateral or multilateral arrangements, or may request that the Court seek the person's surrender, in accordance with Part 9. It may direct that the person be delivered to the State in which he or she was serving the sentence or to another State designated by the Court.

PART 11. ASSEMBLY OF STATES PARTIES

Article 112

Assembly of States Parties

1. An Assembly of States Parties to this Statute is hereby established. Each State Party shall have one representative in the Assembly who may be

accompanied by alternates and advisers. Other States which have signed this Statute or the Final Act may be observers in the Assembly.

2. The Assembly shall:
   (a) Consider and adopt, as appropriate, recommendations of the Preparatory Commission;
   (b) Provide management oversight to the Presidency, the Prosecutor and the Registrar regarding the administration of the Court;
   (c) Consider the reports and activities of the Bureau established under paragraph 3 and take appropriate action in regard thereto;
   (d) Consider and decide the budget for the Court;
   (e) Decide whether to alter, in accordance with article 36, the number of judges;
   (f) Consider pursuant to article 87, paragraphs 5 and 7, any question relating to non-cooperation;
   (g) Perform any other function consistent with this Statute or the Rules of Procedure and Evidence.
3. (a) The Assembly shall have a Bureau consisting of a President, two Vice-Presidents and 18 members elected by the Assembly for three-year terms.
   (b) The Bureau shall have a representative character, taking into account, in particular, equitable geographical distribution and the adequate representation of the principal legal systems of the world.
   (c) The Bureau shall meet as often as necessary, but at least once a year. It shall assist the Assembly in the discharge of its responsibilities.
4. The Assembly may establish such subsidiary bodies as may be necessary, including an independent oversight mechanism for inspection, evaluation and investigation of the Court, in order to enhance its efficiency and economy.
5. The President of the Court, the Prosecutor and the Registrar or their representatives may participate, as appropriate, in meetings of the Assembly and of the Bureau.
6. The Assembly shall meet at the seat of the Court or at the Headquarters of the United Nations once a year and, when circumstances so require, hold special sessions. Except as otherwise specified in this Statute, special sessions shall be convened by the Bureau on its own initiative or at the request of one third of the States Parties.
7. Each State Party shall have one vote. Every effort shall be made to reach decisions by consensus in the Assembly and in the Bureau. If consensus cannot be reached, except as otherwise provided in the Statute:
   (a) Decisions on matters of substance must be approved by a two-thirds majority of those present and voting provided that an absolute majority of States Parties constitutes the quorum for voting;
   (b) Decisions on matters of procedure shall be taken by a simple majority of States Parties present and voting.

8. A State Party which is in arrears in the payment of its financial contributions towards the costs of the Court shall have no vote in the Assembly and in the Bureau if the amount of its arrears equals or exceeds the amount of the contributions due from it for the preceding two full years. The Assembly may, nevertheless, permit such a State Party to vote in the Assembly and in the Bureau if it is satisfied that the failure to pay is due to conditions beyond the control of the State Party.
9. The Assembly shall adopt its own rules of procedure.
10. The official and working languages of the Assembly shall be those of the General Assembly of the United Nations.

PART 12. FINANCING

Article 113
Financial Regulations

Except as otherwise specifically provided, all financial matters related to the Court and the meetings of the Assembly of States Parties, including its Bureau and subsidiary bodies, shall be governed by this Statute and the Financial Regulations and Rules adopted by the Assembly of States Parties.

Article 114
Payment of expenses

Expenses of the Court and the Assembly of States Parties, including its Bureau and subsidiary bodies, shall be paid from the funds of the Court.

Article 115
Funds of the Court and of the Assembly of States Parties

The expenses of the Court and the Assembly of States Parties, including its Bureau and subsidiary bodies, as provided for in the budget decided by the Assembly of States Parties, shall be provided by the following sources:

(a) Assessed contributions made by States Parties;
(b) Funds provided by the United Nations, subject to the approval of the General Assembly, in particular in relation to the expenses incurred due to referrals by the Security Council.

Article 116
Voluntary contributions

Without prejudice to article 115, the Court may receive and utilize, as additional funds, voluntary contributions from Governments, international organizations, individuals, corporations and other entities, in accordance with relevant criteria adopted by the Assembly of States Parties.

Article 117
Assessment of contributions

The contributions of States Parties shall be assessed in accordance with an agreed scale of assessment, based on the scale adopted by the United Nations for its regular budget and adjusted in accordance with the principles on which that scale is based.

Article 118
Annual audit

The records, books and accounts of the Court, including its annual financial statements, shall be audited annually by an independent auditor.

PART 13. FINAL CLAUSES

Article 119
Settlement of disputes

1. Any dispute concerning the judicial functions of the Court shall be settled by the decision of the Court.
2. Any other dispute between two or more States Parties relating to the interpretation or application of this Statute which is not settled through negotiations within three months of their commencement shall be referred to the Assembly of States Parties. The Assembly may itself seek to settle the dispute or may make recommendations on further means of settlement of the dispute, including referral to the International Court of Justice in conformity with the Statute of that Court.

Article 120
Reservations

No reservations may be made to this Statute.

Article 121
Amendments

1. After the expiry of seven years from the entry into force of this Statute, any State Party may propose amendments thereto. The text of any proposed amendment shall be submitted to the Secretary-General of the United Nations, who shall promptly circulate it to all States Parties.
2. No sooner than three months from the date of notification, the Assembly of States Parties, at its next meeting, shall, by a majority of those present and voting, decide whether to take up the proposal. The Assembly may

deal with the proposal directly or convene a Review Conference if the issue involved so warrants.

3. The adoption of an amendment at a meeting of the Assembly of States Parties or at a Review Conference on which consensus cannot be reached shall require a two-thirds majority of States Parties.
4. Except as provided in paragraph 5, an amendment shall enter into force for all States Parties one year after instruments of ratification or acceptance have been deposited with the Secretary-General of the United Nations by seven-eighths of them.
5. Any amendment to articles 5, 6, 7 and 8 of this Statute shall enter into force for those States Parties which have accepted the amendment one year after the deposit of their instruments of ratification or acceptance. In respect of a State Party which has not accepted the amendment, the Court shall not exercise its jurisdiction regarding a crime covered by the amendment when committed by that State Party's nationals or on its territory.
6. If an amendment has been accepted by seven-eighths of States Parties in accordance with paragraph 4, any State Party which has not accepted the amendment may withdraw from this Statute with immediate effect, notwithstanding article 127, paragraph 1, but subject to article 127, paragraph 2, by giving notice no later than one year after the entry into force of such amendment.
7. The Secretary-General of the United Nations shall circulate to all States Parties any amendment adopted at a meeting of the Assembly of States Parties or at a Review Conference.

Article 122

Amendments to provisions of an institutional nature

1. Amendments to provisions of this Statute which are of an exclusively institutional nature, namely, article 35, article 36, paragraphs 8 and 9, article 37, article 38, article 39, paragraphs 1 (first two sentences), 2 and 4, article 42, paragraphs 4 to 9, article 43, paragraphs 2 and 3, and articles 44, 46, 47 and 49, may be proposed at any time, notwithstanding article 121, paragraph 1, by any State Party. The text of any proposed amendment shall be submitted to the Secretary-General of the United Nations or such other person designated by the Assembly of States Parties who shall promptly circulate it to all States Parties and to others participating in the Assembly.
2. Amendments under this article on which consensus cannot be reached shall be adopted by the Assembly of States Parties or by a Review Conference, by a two-thirds majority of States Parties. Such amendments shall enter into force for all States Parties six months after their adoption by the Assembly or, as the case may be, by the Conference.

Article 123
Review of the Statute

1. Seven years after the entry into force of this Statute the Secretary-General of the United Nations shall convene a Review Conference to consider any amendments to this Statute. Such review may include, but is not limited to, the list of crimes contained in article 5. The Conference shall be open to those participating in the Assembly of States Parties and on the same conditions.
2. At any time thereafter, at the request of a State Party and for the purposes set out in paragraph 1, the Secretary-General of the United Nations shall, upon approval by a majority of States Parties, convene a Review Conference.
3. The provisions of article 121, paragraphs 3 to 7, shall apply to the adoption and entry into force of any amendment to the Statute considered at a Review Conference.

Article 124
Transitional Provision

Notwithstanding article 12, paragraphs 1 and 2, a State, on becoming a party to this Statute, may declare that, for a period of seven years after the entry into force of this Statute for the State concerned, it does not accept the jurisdiction of the Court with respect to the category of crimes referred to in article 8 when a crime is alleged to have been committed by its nationals or on its territory. A declaration under this article may be withdrawn at any time. The provisions of this article shall be reviewed at the Review Conference convened in accordance with article 123, paragraph 1.

Article 125
Signature, ratification, acceptance, approval or accession

1. This Statute shall be open for signature by all States in Rome, at the headquarters of the Food and Agriculture Organization of the United Nations, on 17 July 1998. Thereafter, it shall remain open for signature in Rome at the Ministry of Foreign Affairs of Italy until 17 October 1998. After that date, the Statute shall remain open for signature in New York, at United Nations Headquarters, until 31 December 2000.
2. This Statute is subject to ratification, acceptance or approval by signatory States. Instruments of ratification, acceptance or approval shall be deposited with the Secretary-General of the United Nations.
3. This Statute shall be open to accession by all States. Instruments of accession shall be deposited with the Secretary-General of the United Nations.

Article 126
Entry into force

1. This Statute shall enter into force on the first day of the month after the 60th day following the date of the deposit of the 60th instrument of ratification, acceptance, approval or accession with the Secretary-General of the United Nations.
2. For each State ratifying, accepting, approving or acceding to this Statute after the deposit of the 60th instrument of ratification, acceptance, approval or accession, the Statute shall enter into force on the first day of the month after the 60th day following the deposit by such State of its instrument of ratification, acceptance, approval or accession.

Article 127
Withdrawal

1. A State Party may, by written notification addressed to the Secretary-General of the United Nations, withdraw from this Statute. The withdrawal shall take effect one year after the date of receipt of the notification, unless the notification specifies a later date.
2. A State shall not be discharged, by reason of its withdrawal, from the obligations arising from this Statute while it was a Party to the Statute, including any financial obligations which may have accrued. Its withdrawal shall not affect any cooperation with the Court in connection with criminal investigations and proceedings in relation to which the withdrawing State had a duty to cooperate and which were commenced prior to the date on which the withdrawal became effective, nor shall it prejudice in any way the continued consideration of any matter which was already under consideration by the Court prior to the date on which the withdrawal became effective.

Article 128
Authentic texts

The original of this Statute, of which the Arabic, Chinese, English, French, Russian and Spanish texts are equally authentic, shall be deposited with the Secretary-General of the United Nations, who shall send certified copies thereof to all States.

IN WITNESS WHEREOF, the undersigned, being duly authorized thereto by their respective Governments, have signed this Statute.

DONE at Rome, this 17th day of July 1998.

New York
13–31 March 2000
12–30 June 2000

APPENDIX 2

REPORT OF THE PREPARATORY COMMISSION FOR THE INTERNATIONAL CRIMINAL COURT

Addendum

Part I
Finalized draft text of the Rules of Procedure and Evidence*

Explanatory note

The Rules of Procedure and Evidence are an instrument for the application of the Rome Statute of the International Criminal Court, to which they are subordinate in all cases. In elaborating the Rules of Procedure and Evidence, care has been taken to avoid rephrasing and, to the extent possible, repeating the provisions of the Statute. Direct references to the Statute have been included in the Rules, where appropriate, in order to emphasize the relationship between the Rules and the Rome Statute, as provided for in article 51, in particular, paragraphs 4 and 5.

In all cases, the Rules of Procedure and Evidence should be read in conjunction with and subject to the provisions of the Statute.

The Rules of Procedure and Evidence of the International Criminal Court do not affect the procedural rules for any national court or legal system for the purpose of national proceedings.

In connection with rule 41, the Preparatory Commission considered whether the application of the rule would be facilitated by including a provision in the Regulations of the Court that at least one of the judges of the Chamber in which the case is heard knows the official language used as a working language in a given case. The Assembly of States Parties is invited to give further consideration to this issue.

---

* Incorporating document PCNICC/2000/INF/3/Add.1 and corrections to the Arabic, French and Spanish versions submitted by Governments pursuant to paragraph 16 of the Introduction.

Chapter 1
General provisions

Rule 1
Use of terms

In the present document:

- "article" refers to articles of the Rome Statute;
- "Chamber" refers to a Chamber of the Court;
- "Part" refers to the Parts of the Rome Statute;
- "Presiding Judge" refers to the Presiding Judge of a Chamber;
- "the President" refers to the President of the Court;
- "the Regulations" refers to the Regulations of the Court;
- "the Rules" refers to the Rules of Procedure and Evidence.

Rule 2
Authentic texts

The Rules have been adopted in the official languages of the Court established by article 50, paragraph 1. All texts are equally authentic.

Rule 3
Amendments

1. Amendments to the rules that are proposed in accordance with article 51, paragraph 2, shall be forwarded to the President of the Bureau of the Assembly of States Parties.
2. The President of the Bureau of the Assembly of States Parties shall ensure that all proposed amendments are translated into the official languages of the Court and are transmitted to the States Parties.
3. The procedure described in sub-rules 1 and 2 shall also apply to the provisional rules referred to in article 51, paragraph 3.

Chapter 2
Composition and administration of the Court

Section I
General provisions relating to the composition and administration of the Court

Rule 4
Plenary sessions

1. The judges shall meet in plenary session not later than two months after their election. At that first session, after having made their solemn undertaking, in conformity with rule 5, the judges shall:

   (a) Elect the President and Vice-Presidents;
   (b) Assign judges to divisions.
2. The judges shall meet subsequently in plenary session at least once a year to exercise their functions under the Statute, the Rules and the Regulations and, if necessary, in special plenary sessions convened by the President on his or her own motion or at the request of one half of the judges.
3. The quorum for each plenary session shall be two-thirds of the judges.
4. Unless otherwise provided in the Statute or the Rules, the decisions of the plenary sessions shall be taken by the majority of the judges present. In the event of an equality of votes, the President, or the judge acting in the place of the President, shall have a casting vote.
5. The Regulations shall be adopted as soon as possible in plenary sessions.

Rule 5
Solemn undertaking under article 45

1. As provided in article 45, before exercising their functions under the Statute, the following solemn undertakings shall be made:
   (a) In the case of a judge:
   "I solemnly undertake that I will perform my duties and exercise my powers as a judge of the International Criminal Court honourably, faithfully, impartially and conscientiously, and that I will respect the confidentiality of investigations and prosecutions and the secrecy of deliberations.";
   (b) In the case of the Prosecutor, a Deputy Prosecutor, the Registrar and the Deputy Registrar of the Court:
   "I solemnly undertake that I will perform my duties and exercise my powers as (title) of the International Criminal Court honourably, faithfully, impartially and conscientiously, and that I will respect the confidentiality of investigations and prosecutions."
2. The undertaking, signed by the person making it and witnessed by the President or a Vice-President of the Bureau of the Assembly of States Parties, shall be filed with the Registry and kept in the records of the Court.

Rule 6
Solemn undertaking by the staff of the Office of the Prosecutor, the Registry, interpreters and translators

1. Upon commencing employment, every staff member of the Office of the Prosecutor and the Registry shall make the following undertaking:
   "I solemnly undertake that I will perform my duties and exercise my powers as (title) of the International Criminal Court honourably, faithfully, impartially and conscientiously, and that I will respect the confidentiality of investigations and prosecutions.";

The undertaking, signed by the person making it and witnessed, as appropriate, by the Prosecutor, the Deputy Prosecutor, the Registrar or the Deputy Registrar, shall be filed with the Registry and kept in the records of the Court.

2. Before performing any duties, an interpreter or a translator shall make the following undertaking:
"I solemnly declare that I will perform my duties faithfully, impartially and with full respect for the duty of confidentiality.";
The undertaking, signed by the person making it and witnessed by the President of the Court or his or her representative, shall be filed with the Registry and kept in the records of the Court.

Rule 7
Single judge under article 39, paragraph 2 (b) (iii)

1. Whenever the Pre-Trial Chamber designates a judge as a single judge in accordance with article 39, paragraph 2 (b) (iii), it shall do so on the basis of objective pre-established criteria.
2. The designated judge shall make the appropriate decisions on those questions on which decision by the full Chamber is not expressly provided for in the Statute or the Rules.
3. The Pre-Trial Chamber, on its own motion or, if appropriate, at the request of a party, may decide that the functions of the single judge be exercised by the full Chamber.

Rule 8
Code of Professional Conduct

1. The Presidency, on the basis of a proposal made by the Registrar, shall draw up a draft Code of Professional Conduct for counsel, after having consulted the Prosecutor. In the preparation of the proposal, the Registrar shall conduct the consultations in accordance with rule 20, sub-rule 3.
2. The draft Code shall then be transmitted to the Assembly of States Parties, for the purpose of adoption, according to article 112, paragraph 7.
3. The Code shall contain procedures for its amendment.

Section II
The Office of the Prosecutor

Rule 9
Operation of the Office of the Prosecutor

In discharging his or her responsibility for the management and administration of the Office of the Prosecutor, the Prosecutor shall put in place regulations to govern the operation of the Office. In preparing or amending these regulations, the Prosecutor shall consult with the Registrar on any matters that may affect the operation of the Registry.

Rule 10
Retention of information and evidence

The Prosecutor shall be responsible for the retention, storage and security of information and physical evidence obtained in the course of the investigations by his or her Office.

Rule 11
Delegation of the Prosecutor's functions

Except for the inherent powers of the Prosecutor set forth in the Statute, *inter alia*, those described in articles 15 and 53, the Prosecutor or a Deputy Prosecutor may authorize staff members of the Office of the Prosecutor, other than those referred to in article 44, paragraph 4, to represent him or her in the exercise of his or her functions.

Section III
The Registry

Subsection 1
General provisions relating to the Registry

Rule 12
Qualifications and election of the Registrar and the Deputy Registrar

1. As soon as it is elected, the Presidency shall establish a list of candidates who satisfy the criteria laid down in article 43, paragraph 3, and shall transmit the list to the Assembly of States Parties with a request for any recommendations.
2. Upon receipt of any recommendations from the Assembly of States Parties, the President shall, without delay, transmit the list together with the recommendations to the plenary session.
3. As provided for in article 43, paragraph 4, the Court, meeting in plenary session, shall, as soon as possible, elect the Registrar by an absolute majority, taking into account any recommendations by the Assembly of States Parties. In the event that no candidate obtains an absolute majority on the first ballot, successive ballots shall be held until one candidate obtains an absolute majority.
4. If the need for a Deputy Registrar arises, the Registrar may make a recommendation to the President to that effect. The President shall convene

a plenary session to decide on the matter. If the Court, meeting in plenary session, decides by an absolute majority that a Deputy Registrar is to be elected, the Registrar shall submit a list of candidates to the Court.

5. The Deputy Registrar shall be elected by the Court, meeting in plenary session, in the same manner as the Registrar.

Rule 13
Functions of the Registrar

1. Without prejudice to the authority of the Office of the Prosecutor under the Statute to receive, obtain and provide information and to establish channels of communication for this purpose, the Registrar shall serve as the channel of communication of the Court.
2. The Registrar shall also be responsible for the internal security of the Court in consultation with the Presidency and the Prosecutor, as well as the host State.

Rule 14
Operation of the Registry

1. In discharging his or her responsibility for the organization and management of the Registry, the Registrar shall put in place regulations to govern the operation of the Registry. In preparing or amending these regulations, the Registrar shall consult with the Prosecutor on any matters which may affect the operation of the Office of the Prosecutor. The regulations shall be approved by the Presidency.
2. The regulations shall provide for defence counsel to have access to appropriate and reasonable administrative assistance from the Registry.

Rule 15
Records

1. The Registrar shall keep a database containing all the particulars of each case brought before the Court, subject to any order of a judge or Chamber providing for the non-disclosure of any document or information, and to the protection of sensitive personal data. Information on the database shall be available to the public in the working languages of the Court.
2. The Registrar shall also maintain the other records of the Court.

Subsection 2
Victims and Witnesses Unit

Rule 16
Responsibilities of the Registrar relating to victims and witnesses

1. In relation to victims, the Registrar shall be responsible for the performance of the following functions in accordance with the Statute and these Rules:
   (a) Providing notice or notification to victims or their legal representatives;
   (b) Assisting them in obtaining legal advice and organizing their legal representation, and providing their legal representatives with adequate support, assistance and information, including such facilities as may be necessary for the direct performance of their duty, for the purpose of protecting their rights during all stages of the proceedings in accordance with rules 89 to 91;
   (c) Assisting them in participating in the different phases of the proceedings in accordance with rules 89 to 91;
   (d) Taking gender-sensitive measures to facilitate the participation of victims of sexual violence at all stages of the proceedings.
2. In relation to victims, witnesses and others who are at risk on account of testimony given by such witnesses, the Registrar shall be responsible for the performance of the following functions in accordance with the Statute and these Rules:
   (a) Informing them of their rights under the Statute and the Rules, and of the existence, functions and availability of the Victims and Witnesses Unit;
   (b) Ensuring that they are aware, in a timely manner, of the relevant decisions of the Court that may have an impact on their interests, subject to provisions on confidentiality.
3. For the fulfilment of his or her functions, the Registrar may keep a special register for victims who have expressed their intention to participate in relation to a specific case.
4. Agreements on relocation and provision of support services on the territory of a State of traumatized or threatened victims, witnesses and others who are at risk on account of testimony given by such witnesses may be negotiated with the States by the Registrar on behalf of the Court. Such agreements may remain confidential.

Rule 17
Functions of the Unit

1. The Victims and Witnesses Unit shall exercise its functions in accordance with article 43, paragraph 6.

2. The Victims and Witnesses Unit shall, *inter alia*, perform the following functions, in accordance with the Statute and the Rules, and in consultation with the Chamber, the Prosecutor and the defence, as appropriate:
   (a) With respect to all witnesses, victims who appear before the Court, and others who are at risk on account of testimony given by such witnesses, in accordance with their particular needs and circumstances:
      (i) Providing them with adequate protective and security measures and formulating long- and short-term plans for their protection;
      (ii) Recommending to the organs of the Court the adoption of protection measures and also advising relevant States of such measures;
      (iii) Assisting them in obtaining medical, psychological and other appropriate assistance;
      (iv) Making available to the Court and the parties training in issues of trauma, sexual violence, security and confidentiality;
      (v) Recommending, in consultation with the Office of the Prosecutor, the elaboration of a code of conduct, emphasizing the vital nature of security and confidentiality for investigators of the Court and of the defence and all intergovernmental and non-governmental organizations acting at the request of the Court, as appropriate;
      (vi) Cooperating with States, where necessary, in providing any of the measures stipulated in this rule;
   (b) With respect to witnesses:
      (i) Advising them where to obtain legal advice for the purpose of protecting their rights, in particular in relation to their testimony;
      (ii) Assisting them when they are called to testify before the Court;
      (iii) Taking gender-sensitive measures to facilitate the testimony of victims of sexual violence at all stages of the proceedings.
3. In performing its functions, the Unit shall give due regard to the particular needs of children, elderly persons and persons with disabilities. In order to facilitate the participation and protection of children as witnesses, the Unit may assign, as appropriate, and with the agreement of the parents or the legal guardian, a child-support person to assist a child through all stages of the proceedings.

Rule 18
Responsibilities of the Unit

For the efficient and effective performance of its work, the Victims and Witnesses Unit shall:

(a) Ensure that the staff in the Unit maintain confidentiality at all times;
(b) While recognizing the specific interests of the Office of the Prosecutor, the defence and the witnesses, respect the interests of the witness, including, where necessary, by maintaining an appropriate separation of the services provided to the prosecution and defence witnesses, and act impartially when cooperating with all parties and in accordance with the rulings and decisions of the Chambers;
(c) Have administrative and technical assistance available for witnesses, victims who appear before the Court, and others who are at risk on account of testimony given by such witnesses, during all stages of the proceedings and thereafter, as reasonably appropriate;
(d) Ensure training of its staff with respect to victims' and witnesses' security, integrity and dignity, including matters related to gender and cultural sensitivity;
(e) Where appropriate, cooperate with intergovernmental and non-governmental organizations.

Rule 19
Expertise in the Unit

In addition to the staff mentioned in article 43, paragraph 6, and subject to article 44, the Victims and Witnesses Unit may include, as appropriate, persons with expertise, *inter alia*, in the following areas:
(a) Witness protection and security;
(b) Legal and administrative matters, including areas of humanitarian and criminal law;
(c) Logistics administration;
(d) Psychology in criminal proceedings;
(e) Gender and cultural diversity;
(f) Children, in particular traumatized children;
(g) Elderly persons, in particular in connection with armed conflict and exile trauma;
(h) Persons with disabilities;
(i) Social work and counselling;
(j) Health care;
(k) Interpretation and translation.

Subsection 3
Counsel for the defence

Rule 20
Responsibilities of the Registrar relating to the rights of the defence

1. In accordance with article 43, paragraph 1, the Registrar shall organize the staff of the Registry in a manner that promotes the rights of the

defence, consistent with the principle of fair trial as defined in the Statute. For that purpose, the Registrar shall, *inter alia:*

(a) Facilitate the protection of confidentiality, as defined in article 67, paragraph 1 (b);
(b) Provide support, assistance, and information to all defence counsel appearing before the Court and, as appropriate, support for professional investigators necessary for the efficient and effective conduct of the defence;
(c) Assist arrested persons, persons to whom article 55, paragraph 2, applies and the accused in obtaining legal advice and the assistance of legal counsel;
(d) Advise the Prosecutor and the Chambers, as necessary, on relevant defence-related issues;
(e) Provide the defence with such facilities as may be necessary for the direct performance of the duty of the defence;
(f) Facilitate the dissemination of information and case law of the Court to defence counsel and, as appropriate, cooperate with national defence and bar associations or any independent representative body of counsel and legal associations referred to in sub-rule 3 to promote the specialization and training of lawyers in the law of the Statute and the Rules.

2. The Registrar shall carry out the functions stipulated in sub-rule 1, including the financial administration of the Registry, in such a manner as to ensure the professional independence of defence counsel.
3. For purposes such as the management of legal assistance in accordance with rule 21 and the development of a Code of Professional Conduct in accordance with rule 8, the Registrar shall consult, as appropriate, with any independent representative body of counsel or legal associations, including any such body the establishment of which may be facilitated by the Assembly of States Parties.

Rule 21
Assignment of legal assistance

1. Subject to article 55, paragraph 2 (c), and article 67, paragraph 1 (d), criteria and procedures for assignment of legal assistance shall be established in the Regulations, based on a proposal by the Registrar, following consultations with any independent representative body of counsel or legal associations, as referred to in rule 20, sub-rule 3.
2. The Registrar shall create and maintain a list of counsel who meet the criteria set forth in rule 22 and the Regulations. The person shall freely choose his or her counsel from this list or other counsel who meets the required criteria and is willing to be included in the list.
3. A person may seek from the Presidency a review of a decision to refuse a

request for assignment of counsel. The decision of the Presidency shall be final. If a request is refused, a further request may be made by a person to the Registrar, upon showing a change in circumstances.

4. A person choosing to represent himself or herself shall so notify the Registrar in writing at the first opportunity.
5. Where a person claims to have insufficient means to pay for legal assistance and this is subsequently found not to be so, the Chamber dealing with the case at that time may make an order of contribution to recover the cost of providing counsel.

Rule 22
Appointment and qualifications of Counsel for the defence

1. A counsel for the defence shall have established competence in international or criminal law and procedure, as well as the necessary relevant experience, whether as judge, prosecutor, advocate or in other similar capacity, in criminal proceedings. A counsel for the defence shall have an excellent knowledge of and be fluent in at least one of the working languages of the Court. Counsel for the defence may be assisted by other persons, including professors of law, with relevant expertise.
2. Counsel for the defence engaged by a person exercising his or her right under the Statute to retain legal counsel of his or her choosing shall file a power of attorney with the Registrar at the earliest opportunity.
3. In the performance of their duties, Counsel for the defence shall be subject to the Statute, the Rules, the Regulations, the Code of Professional Conduct for Counsel adopted in accordance with rule 8 and any other document adopted by the Court that may be relevant to the performance of their duties.

Section IV
Situations that may affect the functioning of the Court

Subsection 1
Removal from office and disciplinary measures

Rule 23
General principle

A judge, the Prosecutor, a Deputy Prosecutor, the Registrar and a Deputy Registrar shall be removed from office or shall be subject to disciplinary measures in such cases and with such guarantees as are established in the Statute and the Rules.

Rule 24
Definition of serious misconduct and serious breach of duty

1. For the purposes of article 46, paragraph 1 (a), "serious misconduct" shall be constituted by conduct that:
   (a) If it occurs in the course of official duties, is incompatible with official functions, and causes or is likely to cause serious harm to the proper administration of justice before the Court or the proper internal functioning of the Court, such as:
      (i) Disclosing facts or information that he or she has acquired in the course of his or her duties or on a matter which is *sub judice*, where such disclosure is seriously prejudicial to the judicial proceedings or to any person;
      (ii) Concealing information or circumstances of a nature sufficiently serious to have precluded him or her from holding office;
      (iii) Abuse of judicial office in order to obtain unwarranted favourable treatment from any authorities, officials or professionals; or
   (b) If it occurs outside the course of official duties, is of a grave nature that causes or is likely to cause serious harm to the standing of the Court.
2. For the purposes of article 46, paragraph 1 (a), a "serious breach of duty" occurs where a person has been grossly negligent in the performance of his or her duties or has knowingly acted in contravention of those duties. This may include, *inter alia*, situations where the person:
   (a) Fails to comply with the duty to request to be excused, knowing that there are grounds for doing so;
   (b) Repeatedly causes unwarranted delay in the initiation, prosecution or trial of cases, or in the exercise of judicial powers.

Rule 25
Definition of misconduct of a less serious nature

1. For the purposes of article 47, "misconduct of a less serious nature" shall be constituted by conduct that:
   (a) If it occurs in the course of official duties, causes or is likely to cause harm to the proper administration of justice before the Court or the proper internal functioning of the Court, such as:
      (i) Interfering in the exercise of the functions of a person referred to in article 47;
      (ii) Repeatedly failing to comply with or ignoring requests made by the Presiding Judge or by the Presidency in the exercise of their lawful authority;
      (iii) Failing to enforce the disciplinary measures to which the Registrar or a Deputy Registrar and other officers of the Court

are subject when a judge knows or should know of a serious breach of duty on their part; or

(b) If it occurs outside the course of official duties, causes or is likely to cause harm to the standing of the Court.

2. Nothing in this rule precludes the possibility of the conduct set out in sub-rule 1 (a) constituting "serious misconduct" or "serious breach of duty" for the purposes of article 46, paragraph 1 (a).

Rule 26
Receipt of complaints

1. For the purposes of article 46, paragraph 1, and article 47, any complaint concerning any conduct defined under rules 24 and 25 shall include the grounds on which it is based, the identity of the complainant and, if available, any relevant evidence. The complaint shall remain confidential.
2. All complaints shall be transmitted to the Presidency, which may also initiate proceedings on its own motion, and which shall, pursuant to the Regulations, set aside anonymous or manifestly unfounded complaints and transmit the other complaints to the competent organ. The Presidency shall be assisted in this task by one or more judges, appointed on the basis of automatic rotation, in accordance with the Regulations.

Rule 27
Common provisions on the rights of the defence

1. In any case in which removal from office under article 46 or disciplinary measures under article 47 is under consideration, the person concerned shall be so informed in a written statement.
2. The person concerned shall be afforded full opportunity to present and receive evidence, to make written submissions and to supply answers to any questions put to him or her.
3. The person may be represented by counsel during the process established under this rule.

Rule 28
Suspension from duty

Where an allegation against a person who is the subject of a complaint is of a sufficiently serious nature, the person may be suspended from duty pending the final decision of the competent organ.

Rule 29
Procedure in the event of a request for removal from office

1. In the case of a judge, the Registrar or a Deputy Registrar, the question of removal from office shall be put to a vote at a plenary session.
2. The Presidency shall advise the President of the Bureau of the Assembly of States Parties in writing of any recommendation adopted in the case of a judge, and any decision adopted in the case of the Registrar or a Deputy Registrar.
3. The Prosecutor shall advise the President of the Bureau of the Assembly of States Parties in writing of any recommendation he or she makes in the case of a Deputy Prosecutor.
4. Where the conduct is found not to amount to serious misconduct or a serious breach of duty, it may be decided in accordance with article 47 that the person concerned has engaged in misconduct of a less serious nature and a disciplinary measure imposed.

Rule 30
Procedure in the event of a request for disciplinary measures

1. In the case of a judge, the Registrar or a Deputy Registrar, any decision to impose a disciplinary measure shall be taken by the Presidency.
2. In the case of the Prosecutor, any decision to impose a disciplinary measure shall be taken by an absolute majority of the Bureau of the Assembly of States Parties.
3. In the case of a Deputy Prosecutor:
   (a) Any decision to give a reprimand shall be taken by the Prosecutor;
   (b) Any decision to impose a pecuniary sanction shall be taken by an absolute majority of the Bureau of the Assembly of States Parties upon the recommendation of the Prosecutor.
4. Reprimands shall be recorded in writing and shall be transmitted to the President of the Bureau of the Assembly of States Parties.

Rule 31
Removal from office

Once removal from office has been pronounced, it shall take effect immediately. The person concerned shall cease to form part of the Court, including for unfinished cases in which he or she was taking part.

Rule 32
Disciplinary measures

The disciplinary measures that may be imposed are:
(a) A reprimand; or

(b) A pecuniary sanction that may not exceed six months of the salary paid by the Court to the person concerned.

Subsection 2
Excusing, disqualification, death and resignation

Rule 33
Excusing of a judge, the Prosecutor or a Deputy Prosecutor

1. A judge, the Prosecutor or a Deputy Prosecutor seeking to be excused from his or her functions shall make a request in writing to the Presidency, setting out the grounds upon which he or she should be excused.
2. The Presidency shall treat the request as confidential and shall not make public the reasons for its decision without the consent of the person concerned.

Rule 34
Disqualification of a judge, the Prosecutor or a Deputy Prosecutor

1. In addition to the grounds set out in article 41, paragraph 2, and article 42, paragraph 7, the grounds for disqualification of a judge, the Prosecutor or a Deputy Prosecutor shall include, *inter alia*, the following:
   (a) Personal interest in the case, including a spousal, parental or other close family, personal or professional relationship, or a subordinate relationship, with any of the parties;
   (b) Involvement, in his or her private capacity, in any legal proceedings initiated prior to his or her involvement in the case, or initiated by him or her subsequently, in which the person being investigated or prosecuted was or is an opposing party;
   (c) Performance of functions, prior to taking office, during which he or she could be expected to have formed an opinion on the case in question, on the parties or on their legal representatives that, objectively, could adversely affect the required impartiality of the person concerned;
   (d) Expression of opinions, through the communications media, in writing or in public actions, that, objectively, could adversely affect the required impartiality of the person concerned.
2. Subject to the provisions set out in article 41, paragraph 2, and article 42, paragraph 8, a request for disqualification shall be made in writing as soon as there is knowledge of the grounds on which it is based. The request shall state the grounds and attach any relevant evidence, and shall be transmitted to the person concerned, who shall be entitled to present written submissions.
3. Any question relating to the disqualification of the Prosecutor or a Deputy Prosecutor shall be decided by a majority of the judges of the Appeals Chamber.

Rule 35
Duty of a judge, the Prosecutor or a Deputy Prosecutor to request to be excused

Where a judge, the Prosecutor or a Deputy Prosecutor has reason to believe that a ground for disqualification exists in relation to him or her, he or she shall make a request to be excused and shall not wait for a request for disqualification to be made in accordance with article 41, paragraph 2, or article 42, paragraph 7, and rule 34. The request shall be made and the Presidency shall deal with it in accordance with rule 33.

Rule 36
Death of a judge, the Prosecutor, a Deputy Prosecutor, the Registrar or a Deputy Registrar

The Presidency shall inform, in writing, the President of the Bureau of the Assembly of States Parties of the death of a judge, the Prosecutor, a Deputy Prosecutor, the Registrar or a Deputy Registrar.

Rule 37
Resignation of a judge, the Prosecutor, a Deputy Prosecutor, the Registrar or a Deputy Registrar

1. A judge, the Prosecutor, a Deputy Prosecutor, the Registrar or a Deputy Registrar shall communicate to the Presidency, in writing, his or her decision to resign. The Presidency shall inform, in writing, the President of the Bureau of the Assembly of States Parties.
2. A judge, the Prosecutor, a Deputy Prosecutor, the Registrar or a Deputy Registrar shall endeavour to give notice of the date on which his or her resignation will take effect at least six months in advance. Before the resignation of a judge takes effect, he or she shall make every effort to discharge his or her outstanding responsibilities.

Subsection 3
Replacements and alternate judges

Rule 38
Replacements

1. A judge may be replaced for objective and justified reasons, *inter alia:*
   (a) Resignation;
   (b) Accepted excuse;
   (c) Disqualification;
   (d) Removal from office;
   (e) Death.

2. Replacement shall take place in accordance with the pre-established procedure in the Statute, the Rules and the Regulations.

Rule 39
Alternate judges

Where an alternate judge has been assigned by the Presidency to a Trial Chamber pursuant to article 74, paragraph 1, he or she shall sit through all proceedings and deliberations of the case, but may not take any part therein and shall not exercise any of the functions of the members of the Trial Chamber hearing the case, unless and until he or she is required to replace a member of the Trial Chamber if that member is unable to continue attending. Alternate judges shall be designated in accordance with a procedure pre-established by the Court.

Section V
Publication, languages and translation

Rule 40
Publication of decisions in official languages of the Court

1. For the purposes of article 50, paragraph 1, the following decisions shall be considered as resolving fundamental issues:
   (a) All decisions of the Appeals Division;
   (b) All decisions of the Court on its jurisdiction or on the admissibility of a case pursuant to articles 17, 18, 19 and 20;
   (c) All decisions of a Trial Chamber on guilt or innocence, sentencing and reparations to victims pursuant to articles 74, 75 and 76;
   (d) All decisions of a Pre-Trial Chamber pursuant to article 57, paragraph 3 (d).
2. Decisions on confirmation of charges under article 61, paragraph 7, and on offences against the administration of justice under article 70, paragraph 3, shall be published in all the official languages of the Court when the Presidency determines that they resolve fundamental issues.
3. The Presidency may decide to publish other decisions in all the official languages when such decisions concern major issues relating to the interpretation or the implementation of the Statute or concern a major issue of general interest.

Rule 41
Working languages of the Court

1. For the purposes of article 50, paragraph 2, the Presidency shall authorize the use of an official language of the Court as a working language when:

(a) That language is understood and spoken by the majority of those involved in a case before the Court and any of the participants in the proceedings so requests; or
(b) The Prosecutor and the defence so request.

2. The Presidency may authorize the use of an official language of the Court as a working language if it considers that it would facilitate the efficiency of the proceedings.

Rule 42
Translation and interpretation services

The Court shall arrange for the translation and interpretation services necessary to ensure the implementation of its obligations under the Statute and the Rules.

Rule 43
Procedure applicable to the publication of documents of the Court

The Court shall ensure that all documents subject to publication in accordance with the Statute and the Rules respect the duty to protect the confidentiality of the proceedings and the security of victims and witnesses.

Chapter 3
Jurisdiction and admissibility

Section I
Declarations and referrals relating to articles 11, 12, 13 and 14

Rule 44
Declaration provided for in article 12, paragraph 3

1. The Registrar, at the request of the Prosecutor, may inquire of a State that is not a Party to the Statute or that has become a Party to the Statute after its entry into force, on a confidential basis, whether it intends to make the declaration provided for in article 12, paragraph 3.
2. When a State lodges, or declares to the Registrar its intent to lodge, a declaration with the Registrar pursuant to article 12, paragraph 3, or when the Registrar acts pursuant to sub-rule 1, the Registrar shall inform the State concerned that the declaration under article 12, paragraph 3, has as a consequence the acceptance of jurisdiction with respect to the crimes referred to in article 5 of relevance to the situation and the provisions of Part 9, and any rules thereunder concerning States Parties, shall apply.

Rule 45
Referral of a situation to the Prosecutor

A referral of a situation to the Prosecutor shall be in writing.

Section II
Initiation of investigations under article 15

Rule 46
Information provided to the Prosecutor under article 15, paragraphs 1 and 2

Where information is submitted under article 15, paragraph 1, or where oral or written testimony is received pursuant to article 15, paragraph 2, at the seat of the Court, the Prosecutor shall protect the confidentiality of such information and testimony or take any other necessary measures, pursuant to his or her duties under the Statute.

Rule 47
Testimony under article 15, paragraph 2

1. The provisions of rules 111 and 112 shall apply, *mutatis mutandis*, to testimony received by the Prosecutor pursuant to article 15, paragraph 2.
2. When the Prosecutor considers that there is a serious risk that it might not be possible for the testimony to be taken subsequently, he or she may request the Pre-Trial Chamber to take such measures as may be necessary to ensure the efficiency and integrity of the proceedings and, in particular, to appoint a counsel or a judge from the Pre-Trial Chamber to be present during the taking of the testimony in order to protect the rights of the defence. If the testimony is subsequently presented in the proceedings, its admissibility shall be governed by article 69, paragraph 4, and given such weight as determined by the relevant Chamber.

Rule 48
Determination of reasonable basis to proceed with an investigation under article 15, paragraph 3

In determining whether there is a reasonable basis to proceed with an investigation under article 15, paragraph 3, the Prosecutor shall consider the factors set out in article 53, paragraph 1 (a) to (c).

Rule 49
Decision and notice under article 15, paragraph 6

1. Where a decision under article 15, paragraph 6, is taken, the Prosecutor shall promptly ensure that notice is provided, including reasons for his or her decision, in a manner that prevents any danger to the safety, well-being and privacy of those who provided information to him or her under article 15, paragraphs 1 and 2, or the integrity of investigations or proceedings.
2. The notice shall also advise of the possibility of submitting further information regarding the same situation in the light of new facts and evidence.

Rule 50
Procedure for authorization by the Pre-Trial Chamber of the commencement of the investigation

1. When the Prosecutor intends to seek authorization from the Pre-Trial Chamber to initiate an investigation pursuant to article 15, paragraph 3, the Prosecutor shall inform victims, known to him or her or to the Victims and Witnesses Unit, or their legal representatives, unless the Prosecutor decides that doing so would pose a danger to the integrity of the investigation or the life or well-being of victims and witnesses. The Prosecutor may also give notice by general means in order to reach groups of victims if he or she determines in the particular circumstances of the case that such notice could not pose a danger to the integrity and effective conduct of the investigation or to the security and well-being of victims and witnesses. In performing these functions, the Prosecutor may seek the assistance of the Victims and Witnesses Unit as appropriate.
2. A request for authorization by the Prosecutor shall be in writing.
3. Following information given in accordance with sub-rule 1, victims may make representations in writing to the Pre-Trial Chamber within such time limit as set forth in the Regulations.
4. The Pre-Trial Chamber, in deciding on the procedure to be followed, may request additional information from the Prosecutor and from any of the victims who have made representations, and, if it considers it appropriate, may hold a hearing.
5. The Pre-Trial Chamber shall issue its decision, including its reasons, as to whether to authorize the commencement of the investigation in accordance with article 15, paragraph 4, with respect to all or any part of the request by the Prosecutor. The Chamber shall give notice of the decision to victims who have made representations.
6. The above procedure shall also apply to a new request to the Pre-Trial Chamber pursuant to article 15, paragraph 5.

Section III
Challenges and preliminary rulings under articles 17, 18 and 19

Rule 51
Information provided under article 17

In considering the matters referred to in article 17, paragraph 2, and in the context of the circumstances of the case, the Court may consider, *inter alia*, information that the State referred to in article 17, paragraph 1, may choose to bring to the attention of the Court showing that its courts meet internationally recognized norms and standards for the independent and impartial prosecution of similar conduct, or that the State has confirmed in writing to the Prosecutor that the case is being investigated or prosecuted.

Rule 52
Notification provided for in article 18, paragraph 1

1. Subject to the limitations provided for in article 18, paragraph 1, the notification shall contain information about the acts that may constitute crimes referred to in article 5, relevant for the purposes of article 18, paragraph 2.
2. A State may request additional information from the Prosecutor to assist it in the application of article 18, paragraph 2. Such a request shall not affect the one-month time limit provided for in article 18, paragraph 2, and shall be responded to by the Prosecutor on an expedited basis.

Rule 53
Deferral provided for in article 18, paragraph 2

When a State requests a deferral pursuant to article 18, paragraph 2, that State shall make this request in writing and provide information concerning its investigation, taking into account article 18, paragraph 2. The Prosecutor may request additional information from that State.

Rule 54
Application by the Prosecutor under article 18, paragraph 2

1. An application submitted by the Prosecutor to the Pre-Trial Chamber in accordance with article 18, paragraph 2, shall be in writing and shall contain the basis for the application. The information provided by the State under rule 53 shall be communicated by the Prosecutor to the Pre-Trial Chamber.
2. The Prosecutor shall inform that State in writing when he or she makes an application to the Pre-Trial Chamber under article 18, paragraph 2, and shall include in the notice a summary of the basis of the application.

Rule 55
Proceedings concerning article 18, paragraph 2

1. The Pre-Trial Chamber shall decide on the procedure to be followed and may take appropriate measures for the proper conduct of the proceedings. It may hold a hearing.
2. The Pre-Trial Chamber shall examine the Prosecutor's application and any observations submitted by a State that requested a deferral in accordance with article 18, paragraph 2, and shall consider the factors in article 17 in deciding whether to authorize an investigation.
3. The decision and the basis for the decision of the Pre-Trial Chamber shall be communicated as soon as possible to the Prosecutor and to the State that requested a deferral of an investigation.

Rule 56
Application by the Prosecutor following review under article 18, paragraph 3

1. Following a review by the Prosecutor as set forth in article 18, paragraph 3, the Prosecutor may apply to the Pre-Trial Chamber for authorization in accordance with article 18, paragraph 2. The application to the Pre-Trial Chamber shall be in writing and shall contain the basis for the application.
2. Any further information provided by the State under article 18, paragraph 5, shall be communicated by the Prosecutor to the Pre-Trial Chamber.
3. The proceedings shall be conducted in accordance with rules 54, sub-rule 2, and 55.

Rule 57
Provisional measures under article 18, paragraph 6

An application to the Pre-Trial Chamber by the Prosecutor in the circumstances provided for in article 18, paragraph 6, shall be considered ex parte and in camera. The Pre-Trial Chamber shall rule on the application on an expedited basis.

Rule 58
Proceedings under article 19

1. A request or application made under article 19 shall be in writing and contain the basis for it.
2. When a Chamber receives a request or application raising a challenge or question concerning its jurisdiction or the admissibility of a case in accordance with article 19, paragraph 2 or 3, or is acting on its own motion as

provided for in article 19, paragraph 1, it shall decide on the procedure to be followed and may take appropriate measures for the proper conduct of the proceedings. It may hold a hearing. It may join the challenge or question to a confirmation or a trial proceeding as long as this does not cause undue delay, and in this circumstance shall hear and decide on the challenge or question first.

3. The Court shall transmit a request or application received under sub-rule 2 to the Prosecutor and to the person referred to in article 19, paragraph 2, who has been surrendered to the Court or who has appeared voluntarily or pursuant to a summons, and shall allow them to submit written observations to the request or application within a period of time determined by the Chamber.
4. The Court shall rule on any challenge or question of jurisdiction first and then on any challenge or question of admissibility.

Rule 59
Participation in proceedings under article 19, paragraph 3

1. For the purpose of article 19, paragraph 3, the Registrar shall inform the following of any question or challenge of jurisdiction or admissibility which has arisen pursuant to article 19, paragraphs 1, 2 and 3:
   (a) Those who have referred a situation pursuant to article 13;
   (b) The victims who have already communicated with the Court in relation to that case or their legal representatives.
2. The Registrar shall provide those referred to in sub-rule 1, in a manner consistent with the duty of the Court regarding the confidentiality of information, the protection of any person and the preservation of evidence, with a summary of the grounds on which the jurisdiction of the Court or the admissibility of the case has been challenged.
3. Those receiving the information, as provided for in sub-rule 1, may make representation in writing to the competent Chamber within such time limit as it considers appropriate.

Rule 60
Competent organ to receive challenges

If a challenge to the jurisdiction of the Court or to the admissibility of a case is made after a confirmation of the charges but before the constitution or designation of the Trial Chamber, it shall be addressed to the Presidency, which shall refer it to the Trial Chamber as soon as the latter is constituted or designated in accordance with rule 130.

Rule 61
Provisional measures under article 19, paragraph 8

When the Prosecutor makes application to the competent Chamber in the circumstances provided for in article 19, paragraph 8, rule 57 shall apply.

Rule 62
Proceedings under article 19, paragraph 10

1. If the Prosecutor makes a request under article 19, paragraph 10, he or she shall make the request to the Chamber that made the latest ruling on admissibility. The provisions of rules 58, 59 and 61 shall be applicable.
2. The State or States whose challenge to admissibility under article 19, paragraph 2, provoked the decision of inadmissibility provided for in article 19, paragraph 10, shall be notified of the request of the Prosecutor and shall be given a time limit within which to make representations.

Chapter 4
Provisions relating to various stages of the proceedings

Section I
Evidence

Rule 63
General provisions relating to evidence

1. The rules of evidence set forth in this chapter, together with article 69, shall apply in proceedings before all Chambers.
2. A Chamber shall have the authority, in accordance with the discretion described in article 64, paragraph 9, to assess freely all evidence submitted in order to determine its relevance or admissibility in accordance with article 69.
3. A Chamber shall rule on an application of a party or on its own motion, made under article 64, subparagraph 9 (a), concerning admissibility when it is based on the grounds set out in article 69, paragraph 7.
4. Without prejudice to article 66, paragraph 3, a Chamber shall not impose a legal requirement that corroboration is required in order to prove any crime within the jurisdiction of the Court, in particular, crimes of sexual violence.
5. The Chambers shall not apply national laws governing evidence, other than in accordance with article 21.

Rule 64
Procedure relating to the relevance or admissibility of evidence

1. An issue relating to relevance or admissibility must be raised at the time when the evidence is submitted to a Chamber. Exceptionally, when those issues were not known at the time when the evidence was submitted, it may be raised immediately after the issue has become known. The Chamber may request that the issue be raised in writing. The written motion shall be communicated by the Court to all those who participate in the proceedings, unless otherwise decided by the Court.
2. A Chamber shall give reasons for any rulings it makes on evidentiary matters. These reasons shall be placed in the record of the proceedings if they have not already been incorporated into the record during the course of the proceedings in accordance with article 64, paragraph 10, and rule 137, sub-rule 1.
3. Evidence ruled irrelevant or inadmissible shall not be considered by the Chamber.

Rule 65
Compellability of witnesses

1. A witness who appears before the Court is compellable by the Court to provide testimony, unless otherwise provided for in the Statute and the Rules, in particular rules 73, 74 and 75.
2. Rule 171 applies to a witness appearing before the Court who is compellable to provide testimony under sub-rule 1.

Rule 66
Solemn undertaking

1. Except as described in sub-rule 2, every witness shall, in accordance with article 69, paragraph 1, make the following solemn undertaking before testifying:
   "I solemnly declare that I will speak the truth, the whole truth and nothing but the truth."
2. A person under the age of 18 or a person whose judgement has been impaired and who, in the opinion of the Chamber, does not understand the nature of a solemn undertaking may be allowed to testify without this solemn undertaking if the Chamber considers that the person is able to describe matters of which he or she has knowledge and that the person understands the meaning of the duty to speak the truth.
3. Before testifying, the witness shall be informed of the offence defined in article 70, paragraph 1 (a).

Rule 67
Live testimony by means of audio or video-link technology

1. In accordance with article 69, paragraph 2, a Chamber may allow a witness to give viva voce (oral) testimony before the Chamber by means of audio or video technology, provided that such technology permits the witness to be examined by the Prosecutor, the defence, and by the Chamber itself, at the time that the witness so testifies.
2. The examination of a witness under this rule shall be conducted in accordance with the relevant rules of this chapter.
3. The Chamber, with the assistance of the Registry, shall ensure that the venue chosen for the conduct of the audio or video-link testimony is conducive to the giving of truthful and open testimony and to the safety, physical and psychological well-being, dignity and privacy of the witness.

Rule 68
Prior recorded testimony

When the Pre-Trial Chamber has not taken measures under article 56, the Trial Chamber may, in accordance with article 69, paragraph 2, allow the introduction of previously recorded audio or video testimony of a witness, or the transcript or other documented evidence of such testimony, provided that:

(a) If the witness who gave the previously recorded testimony is not present before the Trial Chamber, both the Prosecutor and the defence had the opportunity to examine the witness during the recording; or
(b) If the witness who gave the previously recorded testimony is present before the Trial Chamber, he or she does not object to the submission of the previously recorded testimony and the Prosecutor, the defence and the Chamber have the opportunity to examine the witness during the proceedings.

Rule 69
Agreements as to evidence

The Prosecutor and the defence may agree that an alleged fact, which is contained in the charges, the contents of a document, the expected testimony of a witness or other evidence is not contested and, accordingly, a Chamber may consider such alleged fact as being proven, unless the Chamber is of the opinion that a more complete presentation of the alleged facts is required in the interests of justice, in particular the interests of the victims.

Rule 70
Principles of evidence in cases of sexual violence

In cases of sexual violence, the Court shall be guided by and, where appropriate, apply the following principles:

(a) Consent cannot be inferred by reason of any words or conduct of a victim where force, threat of force, coercion or taking advantage of a coercive environment undermined the victim's ability to give voluntary and genuine consent;
(b) Consent cannot be inferred by reason of any words or conduct of a victim where the victim is incapable of giving genuine consent;
(c) Consent cannot be inferred by reason of the silence of, or lack of resistance by, a victim to the alleged sexual violence;
(d) Credibility, character or predisposition to sexual availability of a victim or witness cannot be inferred by reason of the sexual nature of the prior or subsequent conduct of a victim or witness.

Rule 71
Evidence of other sexual conduct

In the light of the definition and nature of the crimes within the jurisdiction of the Court, and subject to article 69, paragraph 4, a Chamber shall not admit evidence of the prior or subsequent sexual conduct of a victim or witness.

Rule 72
In camera procedure to consider relevance or admissibility of evidence

1. Where there is an intention to introduce or elicit, including by means of the questioning of a victim or witness, evidence that the victim consented to an alleged crime of sexual violence, or evidence of the words, conduct, silence or lack of resistance of a victim or witness as referred to in principles (a) through (d) of rule 70, notification shall be provided to the Court which shall describe the substance of the evidence intended to be introduced or elicited and the relevance of the evidence to the issues in the case.
2. In deciding whether the evidence referred to in sub-rule 1 is relevant or admissible, a Chamber shall hear in camera the views of the Prosecutor, the defence, the witness and the victim or his or her legal representative, if any, and shall take into account whether that evidence has a sufficient degree of probative value to an issue in the case and the prejudice that such evidence may cause, in accordance with article 69, paragraph 4. For this purpose, the Chamber shall have regard to article 21, paragraph 3, and articles 67 and 68, and shall be guided by principles (a) to (d) of rule 70, especially with respect to the proposed questioning of a victim.

3. Where the Chamber determines that the evidence referred to in sub-rule 2 is admissible in the proceedings, the Chamber shall state on the record the specific purpose for which the evidence is admissible. In evaluating the evidence during the proceedings, the Chamber shall apply principles (a) to (d) of rule 70.

Rule 73
Privileged communications and information

1. Without prejudice to article 67, paragraph 1 (b), communications made in the context of the professional relationship between a person and his or her legal counsel shall be regarded as privileged, and consequently not subject to disclosure, unless:
   (a) The person consents in writing to such disclosure; or
   (b) The person voluntarily disclosed the content of the communication to a third party, and that third party then gives evidence of that disclosure.
2. Having regard to rule 63, sub-rule 5, communications made in the context of a class of professional or other confidential relationships shall be regarded as privileged, and consequently not subject to disclosure, under the same terms as in sub-rules 1 (a) and 1 (b) if a Chamber decides in respect of that class that:
   (a) Communications occurring within that class of relationship are made in the course of a confidential relationship producing a reasonable expectation of privacy and non-disclosure;
   (b) Confidentiality is essential to the nature and type of relationship between the person and the confidant; and
   (c) Recognition of the privilege would further the objectives of the Statute and the Rules.
3. In making a decision under sub-rule 2, the Court shall give particular regard to recognizing as privileged those communications made in the context of the professional relationship between a person and his or her medical doctor, psychiatrist, psychologist or counsellor, in particular those related to or involving victims, or between a person and a member of a religious clergy; and in the latter case, the Court shall recognize as privileged those communications made in the context of a sacred confession where it is an integral part of the practice of that religion.
4. The Court shall regard as privileged, and consequently not subject to disclosure, including by way of testimony of any present or past official or employee of the International Committee of the Red Cross (ICRC), any information, documents or other evidence which it came into the possession of in the course, or as a consequence, of the performance by ICRC of its functions under the Statutes of the International Red Cross and Red Crescent Movement, unless:

(a) After consultations undertaken pursuant to sub-rule 6, ICRC does not object in writing to such disclosure, or otherwise has waived this privilege; or

(b) Such information, documents or other evidence is contained in public statements and documents of ICRC.

5. Nothing in sub-rule 4 shall affect the admissibility of the same evidence obtained from a source other than ICRC and its officials or employees when such evidence has also been acquired by this source independently of ICRC and its officials or employees.
6. If the Court determines that ICRC information, documents or other evidence are of great importance for a particular case, consultations shall be held between the Court and ICRC in order to seek to resolve the matter by cooperative means, bearing in mind the circumstances of the case, the relevance of the evidence sought, whether the evidence could be obtained from a source other than ICRC, the interests of justice and of victims, and the performance of the Court's and ICRC's functions.

Rule 74
Self-incrimination by a witness

1. Unless a witness has been notified pursuant to rule 190, the Chamber shall notify a witness of the provisions of this rule before his or her testimony.
2. Where the Court determines that an assurance with respect to self-incrimination should be provided to a particular witness, it shall provide the assurances under sub-rule 3, paragraph (c), before the witness attends, directly or pursuant to a request under article 93, paragraph (1) (e).
3. (a) A witness may object to making any statement that might tend to incriminate him or her.
   (b) Where the witness has attended after receiving an assurance under sub-rule 2, the Court may require the witness to answer the question or questions.
   (c) In the case of other witnesses, the Chamber may require the witness to answer the question or questions, after assuring the witness that the evidence provided in response to the questions:
      (i) Will be kept confidential and will not be disclosed to the public or any State; and
      (ii) Will not be used either directly or indirectly against that person in any subsequent prosecution by the Court, except under articles 70 and 71.
4. Before giving such an assurance, the Chamber shall seek the views of the Prosecutor, ex parte, to determine if the assurance should be given to this particular witness.

5. In determining whether to require the witness to answer, the Chamber shall consider:
   (a) The importance of the anticipated evidence;
   (b) Whether the witness would be providing unique evidence;
   (c) The nature of the possible incrimination, if known; and
   (d) The sufficiency of the protections for the witness, in the particular circumstances.
6. If the Chamber determines that it would not be appropriate to provide an assurance to this witness, it shall not require the witness to answer the question. If the Chamber determines not to require the witness to answer, it may still continue the questioning of the witness on other matters.
7. In order to give effect to the assurance, the Chamber shall:
   (a) Order that the evidence of the witness be given in camera;
   (b) Order that the identity of the witness and the content of the evidence given shall not be disclosed, in any manner, and provide that the breach of any such order will be subject to sanction under article 71;
   (c) Specifically advise the Prosecutor, the accused, the defence counsel, the legal representative of the victim and any Court staff present of the consequences of a breach of the order under subparagraph (b);
   (d) Order the sealing of any record of the proceedings; and
   (e) Use protective measures with respect to any decision of the Court to ensure that the identity of the witness and the content of the evidence given are not disclosed.
8. Where the Prosecutor is aware that the testimony of any witness may raise issues with respect to self-incrimination, he or she shall request an in camera hearing and advise the Chamber of this, in advance of the testimony of the witness. The Chamber may impose the measures outlined in sub-rule 7 for all or a part of the testimony of that witness.
9. The accused, the defence counsel or the witness may advise the Prosecutor or the Chamber that the testimony of a witness will raise issues of self-incrimination before the witness testifies and the Chamber may take the measures outlined in sub-rule 7.
10. If an issue of self-incrimination arises in the course of the proceedings, the Chamber shall suspend the taking of the testimony and provide the witness with an opportunity to obtain legal advice if he or she so requests for the purpose of the application of the rule.

Rule 75
Incrimination by family members

1. A witness appearing before the Court, who is a spouse, child or parent of an accused person, shall not be required by a Chamber to make any statement that might tend to incriminate that accused person. However, the witness may choose to make such a statement.

2. In evaluating the testimony of a witness, a Chamber may take into account that the witness, referred to in sub-rule 1, objected to reply to a question which was intended to contradict a previous statement made by the witness, or the witness was selective in choosing which questions to answer.

Section II
Disclosure

Rule 76
Pre-trial disclosure relating to prosecution witnesses

1. The Prosecutor shall provide the defence with the names of witnesses whom the Prosecutor intends to call to testify and copies of any prior statements made by those witnesses. This shall be done sufficiently in advance to enable the adequate preparation of the defence.
2. The Prosecutor shall subsequently advise the defence of the names of any additional prosecution witnesses and provide copies of their statements when the decision is made to call those witnesses.
3. The statements of prosecution witnesses shall be made available in original and in a language which the accused fully understands and speaks.
4. This rule is subject to the protection and privacy of victims and witnesses and the protection of confidential information as provided for in the Statute and rules 81 and 82.

Rule 77
Inspection of material in possession or control of the Prosecutor

The Prosecutor shall, subject to the restrictions on disclosure as provided for in the Statute and in rules 81 and 82, permit the defence to inspect any books, documents, photographs and other tangible objects in the possession or control of the Prosecutor, which are material to the preparation of the defence or are intended for use by the Prosecutor as evidence for the purposes of the confirmation hearing or at trial, as the case may be, or were obtained from or belonged to the person.

Rule 78
Inspection of material in possession or control of the defence

The defence shall permit the Prosecutor to inspect any books, documents, photographs and other tangible objects in the possession or control of the defence, which are intended for use by the defence as evidence for the purposes of the confirmation hearing or at trial.

Rule 79
Disclosure by the defence

1. The defence shall notify the Prosecutor of its intent to:
   (a) Raise the existence of an alibi, in which case the notification shall specify the place or places at which the accused claims to have been present at the time of the alleged crime and the names of witnesses and any other evidence upon which the accused intends to rely to establish the alibi; or
   (b) Raise a ground for excluding criminal responsibility provided for in article 31, paragraph 1, in which case the notification shall specify the names of witnesses and any other evidence upon which the accused intends to rely to establish the ground.
2. With due regard to time limits set forth in other rules, notification under sub-rule 1 shall be given sufficiently in advance to enable the Prosecutor to prepare adequately and to respond. The Chamber dealing with the matter may grant the Prosecutor an adjournment to address the issue raised by the defence.
3. Failure of the defence to provide notice under this rule shall not limit its right to raise matters dealt with in sub-rule 1 and to present evidence.
4. This rule does not prevent a Chamber from ordering disclosure of any other evidence.

Rule 80
Procedures for raising a ground for excluding criminal responsibility under article 31, paragraph 3

1. The defence shall give notice to both the Trial Chamber and the Prosecutor if it intends to raise a ground for excluding criminal responsibility under article 31, paragraph 3. This shall be done sufficiently in advance of the commencement of the trial to enable the Prosecutor to prepare adequately for trial.
2. Following notice given under sub-rule 1, the Trial Chamber shall hear both the Prosecutor and the defence before deciding whether the defence can raise a ground for excluding criminal responsibility.
3. If the defence is permitted to raise the ground, the Trial Chamber may grant the Prosecutor an adjournment to address that ground.

Rule 81
Restrictions on disclosure

1. Reports, memoranda or other internal documents prepared by a party, its assistants or representatives in connection with the investigation or preparation of the case are not subject to disclosure.

2. Where material or information is in the possession or control of the Prosecutor which must be disclosed in accordance with the Statute, but disclosure may prejudice further or ongoing investigations, the Prosecutor may apply to the Chamber dealing with the matter for a ruling as to whether the material or information must be disclosed to the defence. The matter shall be heard on an ex parte basis by the Chamber. However, the Prosecutor may not introduce such material or information into evidence during the confirmation hearing or the trial without adequate prior disclosure to the accused.
3. Where steps have been taken to ensure the confidentiality of information, in accordance with articles 54, 57, 64, 72 and 93, and, in accordance with article 68, to protect the safety of witnesses and victims and members of their families, such information shall not be disclosed, except in accordance with those articles. When the disclosure of such information may create a risk to the safety of the witness, the Court shall take measures to inform the witness in advance.
4. The Chamber dealing with the matter shall, on its own motion or at the request of the Prosecutor, the accused or any State, take the necessary steps to ensure the confidentiality of information, in accordance with articles 54, 72 and 93, and, in accordance with article 68, to protect the safety of witnesses and victims and members of their families, including by authorizing the non-disclosure of their identity prior to the commencement of the trial.
5. Where material or information is in the possession or control of the Prosecutor which is withheld under article 68, paragraph 5, such material and information may not be subsequently introduced into evidence during the confirmation hearing or the trial without adequate prior disclosure to the accused.
6. Where material or information is in the possession or control of the defence which is subject to disclosure, it may be withheld in circumstances similar to those which would allow the Prosecutor to rely on article 68, paragraph 5, and a summary thereof submitted instead. Such material and information may not be subsequently introduced into evidence during the confirmation hearing or the trial without adequate prior disclosure to the Prosecutor.

Rule 82
Restrictions on disclosure of material and information protected under article 54, paragraph 3 (e)

1. Where material or information is in the possession or control of the Prosecutor which is protected under article 54, paragraph 3 (e), the Prosecutor may not subsequently introduce such material or information into evidence without the prior consent of the provider of the material or information and adequate prior disclosure to the accused.

2. If the Prosecutor introduces material or information protected under article 54, paragraph 3 (e), into evidence, a Chamber may not order the production of additional evidence received from the provider of the initial material or information, nor may a Chamber for the purpose of obtaining such additional evidence itself summon the provider or a representative of the provider as a witness or order their attendance.
3. If the Prosecutor calls a witness to introduce in evidence any material or information which has been protected under article 54, paragraph 3 (e), a Chamber may not compel that witness to answer any question relating to the material or information or its origin, if the witness declines to answer on grounds of confidentiality.
4. The right of the accused to challenge evidence which has been protected under article 54, paragraph 3 (e), shall remain unaffected subject only to the limitations contained in sub-rules 2 and 3.
5. A Chamber dealing with the matter may order, upon application by the defence, that, in the interests of justice, material or information in the possession of the accused, which has been provided to the accused under the same conditions as set forth in article 54, paragraph 3 (e), and which is to be introduced into evidence, shall be subject *mutatis mutandis* to sub-rules 1, 2 and 3.

Rule 83
Ruling on exculpatory evidence under article 67, paragraph 2

The Prosecutor may request as soon as practicable a hearing on an ex parte basis before the Chamber dealing with the matter for the purpose of obtaining a ruling under article 67, paragraph 2.

Rule 84
Disclosure and additional evidence for trial

In order to enable the parties to prepare for trial and to facilitate the fair and expeditious conduct of the proceedings, the Trial Chamber shall, in accordance with article 64, paragraphs 3 (c) and 6 (d), and article 67, paragraph (2), and subject to article 68, paragraph 5, make any necessary orders for the disclosure of documents or information not previously disclosed and for the production of additional evidence. To avoid delay and to ensure that the trial commences on the set date, any such orders shall include strict time limits which shall be kept under review by the Trial Chamber.

Section III
Victims and witnesses

Subsection 1
Definition and general principle relating to victims

Rule 85
Definition of victims

For the purposes of the Statute and the Rules of Procedure and Evidence:

(a) "Victims" means natural persons who have suffered harm as a result of the commission of any crime within the jurisdiction of the Court;

(b) Victims may include organizations or institutions that have sustained direct harm to any of their property which is dedicated to religion, education, art or science or charitable purposes, and to their historic monuments, hospitals and other places and objects for humanitarian purposes.

Rule 86
General principle

A Chamber in making any direction or order, and other organs of the Court in performing their functions under the Statute or the Rules, shall take into account the needs of all victims and witnesses in accordance with article 68, in particular, children, elderly persons, persons with disabilities and victims of sexual or gender violence.

Subsection 2
Protection of victims and witnesses

Rule 87
Protective measures

1. Upon the motion of the Prosecutor or the defence or upon the request of a witness or a victim or his or her legal representative, if any, or on its own motion, and after having consulted with the Victims and Witnesses Unit, as appropriate, a Chamber may order measures to protect a victim, a witness or another person at risk on account of testimony given by a witness pursuant to article 68, paragraphs 1 and 2. The Chamber shall seek to obtain, whenever possible, the consent of the person in respect of whom the protective measure is sought prior to ordering the protective measure.
2. A motion or request under sub-rule 1 shall be governed by rule 134, provided that:

(a) Such a motion or request shall not be submitted ex parte;
(b) A request by a witness or by a victim or his or her legal representative, if any, shall be served on both the Prosecutor and the defence, each of whom shall have the opportunity to respond;
(c) A motion or request affecting a particular witness or a particular victim shall be served on that witness or victim or his or her legal representative, if any, in addition to the other party, each of whom shall have the opportunity to respond;
(d) When the Chamber proceeds on its own motion, notice and opportunity to respond shall be given to the Prosecutor and the defence, and to any witness or any victim or his or her legal representative, if any, who would be affected by such protective measure; and
(e) A motion or request may be filed under seal, and, if so filed, shall remain sealed until otherwise ordered by a Chamber. Responses to motions or requests filed under seal shall also be filed under seal.

3. A Chamber may, on a motion or request under sub-rule 1, hold a hearing, which shall be conducted in camera, to determine whether to order measures to prevent the release to the public or press and information agencies, of the identity or the location of a victim, a witness or other person at risk on account of testimony given by a witness by ordering, *inter alia:*
   (a) That the name of the victim, witness or other person at risk on account of testimony given by a witness or any information which could lead to his or her identification, be expunged from the public records of the Chamber;
   (b) That the Prosecutor, the defence or any other participant in the proceedings be prohibited from disclosing such information to a third party;
   (c) That testimony be presented by electronic or other special means, including the use of technical means enabling the alteration of pictures or voice, the use of audio-visual technology, in particular video-conferencing and closed-circuit television, and the exclusive use of the sound media;
   (d) That a pseudonym be used for a victim, a witness or other person at risk on account of testimony given by a witness; or
   (e) That a Chamber conduct part of its proceedings in camera.

Rule 88
Special measures

1. Upon the motion of the Prosecutor or the defence, or upon the request of a witness or a victim or his or her legal representative, if any, or on its own motion, and after having consulted with the Victims and Witnesses Unit, as appropriate, a Chamber may, taking into account the views of the victim or witness, order special measures such as, but not limited to,

measures to facilitate the testimony of a traumatized victim or witness, a child, an elderly person or a victim of sexual violence, pursuant to article 68, paragraphs 1 and 2. The Chamber shall seek to obtain, whenever possible, the consent of the person in respect of whom the special measure is sought prior to ordering that measure.

2. A Chamber may hold a hearing on a motion or a request under sub-rule 1, if necessary in camera or ex parte, to determine whether to order any such special measure, including but not limited to an order that a counsel, a legal representative, a psychologist or a family member be permitted to attend during the testimony of the victim or the witness.
3. For *inter partes* motions or requests filed under this rule, the provisions of rule 87, sub-rules 2 (b) to (d), shall apply *mutatis mutandis*.
4. A motion or request filed under this rule may be filed under seal, and if so filed shall remain sealed until otherwise ordered by a Chamber. Any responses to *inter partes* motions or requests filed under seal shall also be filed under seal.
5. Taking into consideration that violations of the privacy of a witness or victim may create risk to his or her security, a Chamber shall be vigilant in controlling the manner of questioning a witness or victim so as to avoid any harassment or intimidation, paying particular attention to attacks on victims of crimes of sexual violence.

Subsection 3
Participation of victims in the proceedings

Rule 89
Application for participation of victims in the proceedings

1. In order to present their views and concerns, victims shall make written application to the Registrar, who shall transmit the application to the relevant Chamber. Subject to the provisions of the Statute, in particular article 68, paragraph 1, the Registrar shall provide a copy of the application to the Prosecutor and the defence, who shall be entitled to reply within a time limit to be set by the Chamber. Subject to the provisions of sub-rule 2, the Chamber shall then specify the proceedings and manner in which participation is considered appropriate, which may include making opening and closing statements.
2. The Chamber, on its own initiative or on the application of the Prosecutor or the defence, may reject the application if it considers that the person is not a victim or that the criteria set forth in article 68, paragraph 3, are not otherwise fulfilled. A victim whose application has been rejected may file a new application later in the proceedings.
3. An application referred to in this rule may also be made by a person acting with the consent of the victim, or a person acting on behalf of a victim,

in the case of a victim who is a child or, when necessary, a victim who is disabled.

4. Where there are a number of applications, the Chamber may consider the applications in such a manner as to ensure the effectiveness of the proceedings and may issue one decision.

Rule 90
Legal representatives of victims

1. A victim shall be free to choose a legal representative.
2. Where there are a number of victims, the Chamber may, for the purposes of ensuring the effectiveness of the proceedings, request the victims or particular groups of victims, if necessary with the assistance of the Registry, to choose a common legal representative or representatives. In facilitating the coordination of victim representation, the Registry may provide assistance, *inter alia*, by referring the victims to a list of counsel, maintained by the Registry, or suggesting one or more common legal representatives.
3. If the victims are unable to choose a common legal representative or representatives within a time limit that the Chamber may decide, the Chamber may request the Registrar to choose one or more common legal representatives.
4. The Chamber and the Registry shall take all reasonable steps to ensure that in the selection of common legal representatives, the distinct interests of the victims, particularly as provided in article 68, paragraph 1, are represented and that any conflict of interest is avoided.
5. A victim or group of victims who lack the necessary means to pay for a common legal representative chosen by the Court may receive assistance from the Registry, including, as appropriate, financial assistance.
6. A legal representative of a victim or victims shall have the qualifications set forth in rule 22, sub-rule 1.

Rule 91
Participation of legal representatives in the proceedings

1. A Chamber may modify a previous ruling under rule 89.
2. A legal representative of a victim shall be entitled to attend and participate in the proceedings in accordance with the terms of the ruling of the Chamber and any modification thereof given under rules 89 and 90. This shall include participation in hearings unless, in the circumstances of the case, the Chamber concerned is of the view that the representative's intervention should be confined to written observations or submissions. The Prosecutor and the defence shall be allowed to reply to any oral or written observation by the legal representative for victims.

3. (a) When a legal representative attends and participates in accordance with this rule, and wishes to question a witness, including questioning under rules 67 and 68, an expert or the accused, the legal representative must make application to the Chamber. The Chamber may require the legal representative to provide a written note of the questions and in that case the questions shall be communicated to the Prosecutor and, if appropriate, the defence, who shall be allowed to make observations within a time limit set by the Chamber.
   (b) The Chamber shall then issue a ruling on the request, taking into account the stage of the proceedings, the rights of the accused, the interests of witnesses, the need for a fair, impartial and expeditious trial and in order to give effect to article 68, paragraph 3. The ruling may include directions on the manner and order of the questions and the production of documents in accordance with the powers of the Chamber under article 64. The Chamber may, if it considers it appropriate, put the question to the witness, expert or accused on behalf of the victim's legal representative.
4. For a hearing limited to reparations under article 75, the restrictions on questioning by the legal representative set forth in sub-rule 2 shall not apply. In that case, the legal representative may, with the permission of the Chamber concerned, question witnesses, experts and the person concerned.

Rule 92
Notification to victims and their legal representatives

1. This rule on notification to victims and their legal representatives shall apply to all proceedings before the Court, except in proceedings provided for in Part 2.
2. In order to allow victims to apply for participation in the proceedings in accordance with rule 89, the Court shall notify victims concerning the decision of the Prosecutor not to initiate an investigation or not to prosecute pursuant to article 53. Such a notification shall be given to victims or their legal representatives who have already participated in the proceedings or, as far as possible, to those who have communicated with the Court in respect of the situation or case in question. The Chamber may order the measures outlined in sub-rule 8 if it considers it appropriate in the particular circumstances.
3. In order to allow victims to apply for participation in the proceedings in accordance with rule 89, the Court shall notify victims regarding its decision to hold a hearing to confirm charges pursuant to article 61. Such a notification shall be given to victims or their legal representatives who have already participated in the proceedings or, as far as possible, to those who have communicated with the Court in respect of the case in question.

4. When a notification for participation as provided for in sub-rules 2 and 3 has been given, any subsequent notification as referred to in sub-rules 5 and 6 shall only be provided to victims or their legal representatives who may participate in the proceedings in accordance with a ruling of the Chamber pursuant to rule 89 and any modification thereof.
5. In a manner consistent with the ruling made under rules 89 to 91, victims or their legal representatives participating in proceedings shall, in respect of those proceedings, be notified by the Registrar in a timely manner of:
   (a) Proceedings before the Court, including the date of hearings and any postponements thereof, and the date of delivery of the decision;
   (b) Requests, submissions, motions and other documents relating to such requests, submissions or motions.
6. Where victims or their legal representatives have participated in a certain stage of the proceedings, the Registrar shall notify them as soon as possible of the decisions of the Court in those proceedings.
7. Notifications as referred to in sub-rules 5 and 6 shall be in writing or, where written notification is not possible, in any other form as appropriate. The Registry shall keep a record of all notifications. Where necessary, the Registrar may seek the cooperation of States Parties in accordance with article 93, paragraph 1 (d) and (l).
8. For notification as referred to in sub-rule 3 and otherwise at the request of a Chamber, the Registrar shall take necessary measures to give adequate publicity to the proceedings. In doing so, the Registrar may seek, in accordance with Part 9, the cooperation of relevant States Parties, and seek the assistance of intergovernmental organizations.

Rule 93
Views of victims or their legal representatives

A Chamber may seek the views of victims or their legal representatives participating pursuant to rules 89 to 91 on any issue, *inter alia*, in relation to issues referred to in rules 107, 109, 125, 128, 136, 139 and 191. In addition, a Chamber may seek the views of other victims, as appropriate.

Subsection 4
Reparations to victims

Rule 94
Procedure upon request

1. A victim's request for reparations under article 75 shall be made in writing and filed with the Registrar. It shall contain the following particulars:
   (a) The identity and address of the claimant;
   (b) A description of the injury, loss or harm;

(c) The location and date of the incident and, to the extent possible, the identity of the person or persons the victim believes to be responsible for the injury, loss or harm;
(d) Where restitution of assets, property or other tangible items is sought, a description of them;
(e) Claims for compensation;
(f) Claims for rehabilitation and other forms of remedy;
(g) To the extent possible, any relevant supporting documentation, including names and addresses of witnesses.

2. At commencement of the trial and subject to any protective measures, the Court shall ask the Registrar to provide notification of the request to the person or persons named in the request or identified in the charges and, to the extent possible, to any interested persons or any interested States. Those notified shall file with the Registry any representation made under article 75, paragraph 3.

Rule 95
Procedure on the motion of the Court

1. In cases where the Court intends to proceed on its own motion pursuant to article 75, paragraph 1, it shall ask the Registrar to provide notification of its intention to the person or persons against whom the Court is considering making a determination, and, to the extent possible, to victims, interested persons and interested States. Those notified shall file with the Registry any representation made under article 75, paragraph 3.
2. If, as a result of notification under sub-rule 1:
   (a) A victim makes a request for reparations, that request will be determined as if it had been brought under rule 94;
   (b) A victim requests that the Court does not make an order for reparations, the Court shall not proceed to make an individual order in respect of that victim.

Rule 96
Publication of reparation proceedings

1. Without prejudice to any other rules on notification of proceedings, the Registrar shall, insofar as practicable, notify the victims or their legal representatives and the person or persons concerned. The Registrar shall also, having regard to any information provided by the Prosecutor, take all the necessary measures to give adequate publicity of the reparation proceedings before the Court, to the extent possible, to other victims, interested persons and interested States.
2. In taking the measures described in sub-rule 1, the Court may seek, in accordance with Part 9, the cooperation of relevant States Parties, and

seek the assistance of intergovernmental organizations in order to give publicity, as widely as possible and by all possible means, to the reparation proceedings before the Court.

Rule 97
Assessment of reparations

1. Taking into account the scope and extent of any damage, loss or injury, the Court may award reparations on an individualized basis or, where it deems it appropriate, on a collective basis or both.
2. At the request of victims or their legal representatives, or at the request of the convicted person, or on its own motion, the Court may appoint appropriate experts to assist it in determining the scope, extent of any damage, loss and injury to, or in respect of victims and to suggest various options concerning the appropriate types and modalities of reparations. The Court shall invite, as appropriate, victims or their legal representatives, the convicted person as well as interested persons and interested States to make observations on the reports of the experts.
3. In all cases, the Court shall respect the rights of victims and the convicted person.

Rule 98
Trust Fund

1. Individual awards for reparations shall be made directly against a convicted person.
2. The Court may order that an award for reparations against a convicted person be deposited with the Trust Fund where at the time of making the order it is impossible or impracticable to make individual awards directly to each victim. The award for reparations thus deposited in the Trust Fund shall be separated from other resources of the Trust Fund and shall be forwarded to each victim as soon as possible.
3. The Court may order that an award for reparations against a convicted person be made through the Trust Fund where the number of the victims and the scope, forms and modalities of reparations makes a collective award more appropriate.
4. Following consultations with interested States and the Trust Fund, the Court may order that an award for reparations be made through the Trust Fund to an intergovernmental, international or national organization approved by the Trust Fund.
5. Other resources of the Trust Fund may be used for the benefit of victims subject to the provisions of article 79.

Rule 99
Cooperation and protective measures for the purpose of forfeiture under articles 57, paragraph 3 (e), and 75, paragraph 4

1. The Pre-Trial Chamber, pursuant to article 57, paragraph 3 (e), or the Trial Chamber, pursuant to article 75, paragraph 4, may, on its own motion or on the application of the Prosecutor or at the request of the victims or their legal representatives who have made a request for reparations or who have given a written undertaking to do so, determine whether measures should be requested.
2. Notice is not required unless the Court determines, in the particular circumstances of the case, that notification could not jeopardize the effectiveness of the measures requested. In the latter case, the Registrar shall provide notification of the proceedings to the person against whom a request is made and so far as is possible to any interested persons or interested States.
3. If an order is made without prior notification, the relevant Chamber shall request the Registrar, as soon as is consistent with the effectiveness of the measures requested, to notify those against whom a request is made and, to the extent possible, to any interested persons or any interested States and invite them to make observations as to whether the order should be revoked or otherwise modified.
4. The Court may make orders as to the timing and conduct of any proceedings necessary to determine these issues.

Section IV
Miscellaneous provisions

Rule 100
Place of the proceedings

1. In a particular case, where the Court considers that it would be in the interests of justice, it may decide to sit in a State other than the host State.
2. An application or recommendation changing the place where the Court sits may be filed at any time after the initiation of an investigation, either by the Prosecutor, the defence or by a majority of the judges of the Court. Such an application or recommendation shall be addressed to the Presidency. It shall be made in writing and specify in which State the Court would sit. The Presidency shall satisfy itself of the views of the relevant Chamber.
3. The Presidency shall consult the State where the Court intends to sit. If that State agrees that the Court can sit in that State, then the decision to sit in a State other than the host State shall be taken by the judges, in plenary session, by a two-thirds majority.

Rule 101
Time limits

1. In making any order setting time limits regarding the conduct of any proceedings, the Court shall have regard to the need to facilitate fair and expeditious proceedings, bearing in mind in particular the rights of the defence and the victims.
2. Taking into account the rights of the accused, in particular under article 67, paragraph (1) (c), all those participating in the proceedings to whom any order is directed shall endeavour to act as expeditiously as possible, within the time limit ordered by the Court.

Rule 102
Communications other than in writing

Where a person is unable, due to a disability or illiteracy, to make a written request, application, observation or other communication to the Court, the person may make such request, application, observation or communication in audio, video or other electronic form.

Rule 103
Amicus curiae and other forms of submission

1. At any stage of the proceedings, a Chamber may, if it considers it desirable for the proper determination of the case, invite or grant leave to a State, organization or person to submit, in writing or orally, any observation on any issue that the Chamber deems appropriate.
2. The Prosecutor and the defence shall have the opportunity to respond to the observations submitted under sub-rule 1.
3. A written observation submitted under sub-rule 1 shall be filed with the Registrar, who shall provide copies to the Prosecutor and the defence. The Chamber shall determine what time limits shall apply to the filing of such observations.

Chapter 5
Investigation and prosecution

Section I
Decision of the Prosecutor regarding the initiation of an investigation under article 53, paragraphs 1 and 2

Rule 104
Evaluation of information by the Prosecutor

1. In acting pursuant to article 53, paragraph 1, the Prosecutor shall, in evaluating the information made available to him or her, analyse the seriousness of the information received.

2. For the purposes of sub-rule 1, the Prosecutor may seek additional information from States, organs of the United Nations, intergovernmental and non-governmental organizations, or other reliable sources that he or she deems appropriate, and may receive written or oral testimony at the seat of the Court. The procedure set out in rule 47 shall apply to the receiving of such testimony.

Rule 105
Notification of a decision by the Prosecutor not to initiate an investigation

1. When the Prosecutor decides not to initiate an investigation under article 53, paragraph 1, he or she shall promptly inform in writing the State or States that referred a situation under article 14, or the Security Council in respect of a situation covered by article 13, paragraph (b).
2. When the Prosecutor decides not to submit to the Pre-Trial Chamber a request for authorization of an investigation, rule 49 shall apply.
3. The notification referred to in sub-rule 1 shall contain the conclusion of the Prosecutor and, having regard to article 68, paragraph 1, the reasons for the conclusion.
4. In case the Prosecutor decides not to investigate solely on the basis of article 53, paragraph 1 (c), he or she shall inform in writing the Pre-Trial Chamber promptly after making that decision.
5. The notification shall contain the conclusion of the Prosecutor and the reasons for the conclusion.

Rule 106
Notification of a decision by the Prosecutor not to prosecute

1. When the Prosecutor decides that there is not a sufficient basis for prosecution under article 53, paragraph 2, he or she shall promptly inform in writing the Pre-Trial Chamber, together with the State or States that referred a situation under article 14, or the Security Council in respect of a situation covered by article 13, paragraph (b).
2. The notifications referred to in sub-rule 1 shall contain the conclusion of the Prosecutor and, having regard to article 68, paragraph 1, the reasons for the conclusion.

Section II
Procedure under article 53, paragraph 3

Rule 107
Request for review under article 53, paragraph 3 (a)

1. A request under article 53, paragraph 3, for a review of a decision by the Prosecutor not to initiate an investigation or not to prosecute shall be

made in writing, and be supported with reasons, within 90 days following the notification given under rule 105 or 106.

2. The Pre-Trial Chamber may request the Prosecutor to transmit the information or documents in his or her possession, or summaries thereof, that the Chamber considers necessary for the conduct of the review.
3. The Pre-Trial Chamber shall take such measures as are necessary under articles 54, 72 and 93 to protect the information and documents referred to in sub-rule 2 and, under article 68, paragraph 5, to protect the safety of witnesses and victims and members of their families.
4. When a State or the Security Council makes a request referred to in sub-rule 1, the Pre-Trial Chamber may seek further observations from them.
5. Where an issue of jurisdiction or admissibility of the case is raised, rule 59 shall apply.

Rule 108
Decision of the Pre-Trial Chamber under article 53, paragraph 3 (a)

1. A decision of the Pre-Trial Chamber under article 53, paragraph 3 (a), must be concurred in by a majority of its judges and shall contain reasons. It shall be communicated to all those who participated in the review.
2. Where the Pre-Trial Chamber requests the Prosecutor to review, in whole or in part, his or her decision not to initiate an investigation or not to prosecute, the Prosecutor shall reconsider that decision as soon as possible.
3. Once the Prosecutor has taken a final decision, he or she shall notify the Pre-Trial Chamber in writing. This notification shall contain the conclusion of the Prosecutor and the reasons for the conclusion. It shall be communicated to all those who participated in the review.

Rule 109
Review by the Pre-Trial Chamber under article 53, paragraph 3 (b)

1. Within 180 days following a notification given under rule 105 or 106, the Pre-Trial Chamber may on its own initiative decide to review a decision of the Prosecutor taken solely under article 53, paragraph 1 (c) or 2 (c). The Pre-Trial Chamber shall inform the Prosecutor of its intention to review his or her decision and shall establish a time limit within which the Prosecutor may submit observations and other material.
2. In cases where a request has been submitted to the Pre-Trial Chamber by a State or by the Security Council, they shall also be informed and may submit observations in accordance with rule 107.

Rule 110
Decision by the Pre-Trial Chamber under article 53, paragraph 3 (b)

1. A decision by the Pre-Trial Chamber to confirm or not to confirm a decision taken by the Prosecutor solely under article 53, paragraph 1 (c) or 2 (c), must be concurred in by a majority of its judges and shall contain reasons. It shall be communicated to all those who participated in the review.
2. When the Pre-Trial Chamber does not confirm the decision by the Prosecutor referred to in sub-rule 1, he or she shall proceed with the investigation or prosecution.

Section III
Collection of evidence

Rule 111
Record of questioning in general

1. A record shall be made of formal statements made by any person who is questioned in connection with an investigation or with proceedings. The record shall be signed by the person who records and conducts the questioning and by the person who is questioned and his or her counsel, if present, and, where applicable, the Prosecutor or the judge who is present. The record shall note the date, time and place of, and all persons present during the questioning. It shall also be noted when someone has not signed the record as well as the reasons therefor.
2. When the Prosecutor or national authorities question a person, due regard shall be given to article 55. When a person is informed of his or her rights under article 55, paragraph 2, the fact that this information has been provided shall be noted in the record.

Rule 112
Recording of questioning in particular cases

1. Whenever the Prosecutor questions a person to whom article 55, paragraph 2, applies, or for whom a warrant of arrest or a summons to appear has been issued under article 58, paragraph 7, the questioning shall be audio- or video-recorded, in accordance with the following procedure:
   (a) The person questioned shall be informed, in a language he or she fully understands and speaks, that the questioning is to be audio- or video-recorded, and that the person concerned may object if he or she so wishes. The fact that this information has been provided and the response given by the person concerned shall be noted in the record. The person may, before replying, speak in private with his or

her counsel, if present. If the person questioned refuses to be audio- or video-recorded, the procedure in rule 111 shall be followed;
(b) A waiver of the right to be questioned in the presence of counsel shall be recorded in writing and, if possible, be audio- or video-recorded;
(c) In the event of an interruption in the course of questioning, the fact and the time of the interruption shall be recorded before the audio- or video-recording ends as well as the time of resumption of the questioning;
(d) At the conclusion of the questioning, the person questioned shall be offered the opportunity to clarify anything he or she has said and to add anything he or she may wish. The time of conclusion of the questioning shall be noted;
(e) The tape shall be transcribed as soon as practicable after the conclusion of the questioning and a copy of the transcript supplied to the person questioned together with a copy of the recorded tape or, if multiple recording apparatus was used, one of the original recorded tapes;
(f) The original tape or one of the original tapes shall be sealed in the presence of the person questioned and his or her counsel, if present, under the signature of the Prosecutor and the person questioned and the counsel, if present.

2. The Prosecutor shall make every reasonable effort to record the questioning in accordance with sub-rule 1. As an exception, a person may be questioned without the questioning being audio- or video-recorded where the circumstances prevent such recording taking place. In this case, the reasons for not recording the questioning shall be stated in writing and the procedure in rule 111 shall be followed.
3. When, pursuant to sub-rule 1 (a) or 2, the questioning is not audio- or video-recorded, the person questioned shall be provided with a copy of his or her statement.
4. The Prosecutor may choose to follow the procedure in this rule when questioning other persons than those mentioned in sub-rule 1, in particular where the use of such procedures could assist in reducing any subsequent traumatization of a victim of sexual or gender violence, a child or a person with disabilities in providing their evidence. The Prosecutor may make an application to the relevant Chamber.
5. The Pre-Trial Chamber may, in pursuance of article 56, paragraph 2, order that the procedure in this rule be applied to the questioning of any person.

Rule 113
Collection of information regarding the state of health of the person concerned

1. The Pre-Trial Chamber may, on its own initiative or at the request of the Prosecutor, the person concerned or his or her counsel, order that a per-

son having the rights in article 55, paragraph 2, be given a medical, psychological or psychiatric examination. In making its determination, the Pre-Trial Chamber shall consider the nature and purpose of the examination and whether the person consents to the examination.

2. The Pre-Trial Chamber shall appoint one or more experts from the list of experts approved by the Registrar, or an expert approved by the Pre-Trial Chamber at the request of a party.

Rule 114
Unique investigative opportunity under article 56

1. Upon being advised by the Prosecutor in accordance with article 56, paragraph 1 (a), the Pre-Trial Chamber shall hold consultations without delay with the Prosecutor and, subject to the provisions of article 56, paragraph 1 (c), with the person who has been arrested or who has appeared before the Court pursuant to summons and his or her counsel, in order to determine the measures to be taken and the modalities of their implementation, which may include measures to ensure that the right to communicate under article 67, paragraph 1 (b), is protected.
2. A decision of the Pre-Trial Chamber to take measures pursuant to article 56, paragraph 3, must be concurred in by a majority of its judges after consultations with the Prosecutor. During the consultations, the Prosecutor may advise the Pre-Trial Chamber that intended measures could jeopardize the proper conduct of the investigation.

Rule 115
Collection of evidence in the territory of a State Party under article 57, paragraph 3 (d)

1. Where the Prosecutor considers that article 57, paragraph 3 (d), applies, the Prosecutor may submit a written request to the Pre-Trial Chamber for authorization to take certain measures in the territory of the State Party in question. After a submission of such a request, the Pre-Trial Chamber shall, whenever possible, inform and invite views from the State Party concerned.
2. In arriving at its determination as to whether the request is well founded, the Pre-Trial Chamber shall take into account any views expressed by the State Party concerned. The Pre-Trial Chamber may, on its own initiative or at the request of the Prosecutor or the State Party concerned, decide to hold a hearing.
3. An authorization under article 57, paragraph 3 (d), shall be issued in the form of an order and shall state the reasons, based on the criteria set forth in that paragraph. The order may specify procedures to be followed in carrying out such collection of evidence.

Rule 116
Collection of evidence at the request of the defence under article 57, paragraph 3 (b)

1. The Pre-Trial Chamber shall issue an order or seek cooperation under article 57, paragraph 3 (b), where it is satisfied:
   (a) That such an order would facilitate the collection of evidence that may be material to the proper determination of the issues being adjudicated, or to the proper preparation of the person's defence; and
   (b) In a case of cooperation under Part 9, that sufficient information to comply with article 96, paragraph 2, has been provided.
2. Before taking a decision whether to issue an order or seek cooperation under article 57, paragraph 3 (b), the Pre-Trial Chamber may seek the views of the Prosecutor.

Section IV
Procedures in respect of restriction and deprivation of liberty

Rule 117
Detention in the custodial State

1. The Court shall take measures to ensure that it is informed of the arrest of a person in response to a request made by the Court under article 89 or 92. Once so informed, the Court shall ensure that the person receives a copy of the arrest warrant issued by the Pre-Trial Chamber under article 58 and any relevant provisions of the Statute. The documents shall be made available in a language that the person fully understands and speaks.
2. At any time after arrest, the person may make a request to the Pre-Trial Chamber for the appointment of counsel to assist with proceedings before the Court and the Pre-Trial Chamber shall take a decision on such request.
3. A challenge as to whether the warrant of arrest was properly issued in accordance with article 58, paragraph 1 (a) and (b), shall be made in writing to the Pre-Trial Chamber. The application shall set out the basis for the challenge. After having obtained the views of the Prosecutor, the Pre-Trial Chamber shall decide on the application without delay.
4. When the competent authority of the custodial State notifies the Pre-Trial Chamber that a request for release has been made by the person arrested, in accordance with article 59, paragraph 5, the Pre-Trial Chamber shall provide its recommendations within any time limit set by the custodial State.
5. When the Pre-Trial Chamber is informed that the person has been granted interim release by the competent authority of the custodial State, the Pre-Trial Chamber shall inform the custodial State how and when it would like to receive periodic reports on the status of the interim release.

Rule 118
Pre-trial detention at the seat of the Court

1. If the person surrendered to the Court makes an initial request for interim release pending trial, either upon first appearance in accordance with rule 121 or subsequently, the Pre-Trial Chamber shall decide upon the request without delay, after seeking the views of the Prosecutor.
2. The Pre-Trial Chamber shall review its ruling on the release or detention of a person in accordance with article 60, paragraph 3, at least every 120 days and may do so at any time on the request of the person or the Prosecutor.
3. After the first appearance, a request for interim release must be made in writing. The Prosecutor shall be given notice of such a request. The Pre-Trial Chamber shall decide after having received observations in writing of the Prosecutor and the detained person. The Pre-Trial Chamber may decide to hold a hearing, at the request of the Prosecutor or the detained person or on its own initiative. A hearing must be held at least once every year.

Rule 119
Conditional release

1. The Pre-Trial Chamber may set one or more conditions restricting liberty, including the following:
   (a) The person must not travel beyond territorial limits set by the Pre-Trial Chamber without the explicit agreement of the Chamber;
   (b) The person must not go to certain places or associate with certain persons as specified by the Pre-Trial Chamber;
   (c) The person must not contact directly or indirectly victims or witnesses;
   (d) The person must not engage in certain professional activities;
   (e) The person must reside at a particular address as specified by the Pre-Trial Chamber;
   (f) The person must respond when summoned by an authority or qualified person designated by the Pre-Trial Chamber;
   (g) The person must post bond or provide real or personal security or surety, for which the amount and the schedule and mode of payment shall be determined by the Pre-Trial Chamber;
   (h) The person must supply the Registrar with all identity documents, particularly his or her passport.
2. At the request of the person concerned or the Prosecutor or on its own initiative, the Pre-Trial Chamber may at any time decide to amend the conditions set pursuant to sub-rule 1.
3. Before imposing or amending any conditions restricting liberty, the Pre-Trial Chamber shall seek the views of the Prosecutor, the person con-

cerned, any relevant State and victims that have communicated with the Court in that case and whom the Chamber considers could be at risk as a result of a release or conditions imposed.

4. If the Pre-Trial Chamber is convinced that the person concerned has failed to comply with one or more of the obligations imposed, it may, on such basis, at the request of the Prosecutor or on its own initiative, issue a warrant of arrest in respect of the person.
5. When the Pre-Trial Chamber issues a summons to appear pursuant to article 58, paragraph 7, and intends to set conditions restricting liberty, it shall ascertain the relevant provisions of the national law of the State receiving the summons. In a manner that is in keeping with the national law of the State receiving the summons, the Pre-Trial Chamber shall proceed in accordance with sub-rules 1, 2 and 3. If the Pre-Trial Chamber receives information that the person concerned has failed to comply with conditions imposed, it shall proceed in accordance with sub-rule 4.

Rule 120
Instruments of restraint

Personal instruments of restraint shall not be used except as a precaution against escape, for the protection of the person in the custody of the Court and others or for other security reasons, and shall be removed when the person appears before a Chamber.

Section V
Proceedings with regard to the confirmation of charges under article 61

Rule 121
Proceedings before the confirmation hearing

1. A person subject to a warrant of arrest or a summons to appear under article 58 shall appear before the Pre-Trial Chamber, in the presence of the Prosecutor, promptly upon arriving at the Court. Subject to the provisions of articles 60 and 61, the person shall enjoy the rights set forth in article 67. At this first appearance, the Pre-Trial Chamber shall set the date on which it intends to hold a hearing to confirm the charges. It shall ensure that this date, and any postponements under sub-rule 7, are made public.
2. In accordance with article 61, paragraph 3, the Pre-Trial Chamber shall take the necessary decisions regarding disclosure between the Prosecutor and the person in respect of whom a warrant of arrest or a summons to appear has been issued. During disclosure:
   (a) The person concerned may be assisted or represented by the counsel of his or her choice or by a counsel assigned to him or her;
   (b) The Pre-Trial Chamber shall hold status conferences to ensure that

disclosure takes place under satisfactory conditions. For each case, a judge of the Pre-Trial Chamber shall be appointed to organize such status conferences, on his or her own motion, or at the request of the Prosecutor or the person;

(c) All evidence disclosed between the Prosecutor and the person for the purposes of the confirmation hearing shall be communicated to the Pre-Trial Chamber.

3. The Prosecutor shall provide to the Pre-Trial Chamber and the person, no later than 30 days before the date of the confirmation hearing, a detailed description of the charges together with a list of the evidence which he or she intends to present at the hearing.
4. Where the Prosecutor intends to amend the charges pursuant to article 61, paragraph 4, he or she shall notify the Pre-Trial Chamber and the person no later than 15 days before the date of the hearing of the amended charges together with a list of evidence that the Prosecutor intends to bring in support of those charges at the hearing.
5. Where the Prosecutor intends to present new evidence at the hearing, he or she shall provide the Pre-Trial Chamber and the person with a list of that evidence no later than 15 days before the date of the hearing.
6. If the person intends to present evidence under article 61, paragraph 6, he or she shall provide a list of that evidence to the Pre-Trial Chamber no later than 15 days before the date of the hearing. The Pre-Trial Chamber shall transmit the list to the Prosecutor without delay. The person shall provide a list of evidence that he or she intends to present in response to any amended charges or a new list of evidence provided by the Prosecutor.
7. The Prosecutor or the person may ask the Pre-Trial Chamber to postpone the date of the confirmation hearing. The Pre-Trial Chamber may also, on its own motion, decide to postpone the hearing.
8. The Pre-Trial Chamber shall not take into consideration charges and evidence presented after the time limit, or any extension thereof, has expired.
9. The Prosecutor and the person may lodge written submissions with the Pre-Trial Chamber, on points of fact and on law, including grounds for excluding criminal responsibility set forth in article 31, paragraph 1, no later than three days before the date of the hearing. A copy of these submissions shall be transmitted immediately to the Prosecutor or the person, as the case may be.
10. The Registry shall create and maintain a full and accurate record of all proceedings before the Pre-Trial Chamber, including all documents transmitted to the Chamber pursuant to this rule. Subject to any restrictions concerning confidentiality and the protection of national security information, the record may be consulted by the Prosecutor, the person and victims or their legal representatives participating in the proceedings pursuant to rules 89 to 91.

Rule 122
Proceedings at the confirmation hearing in the presence of the person charged

1. The Presiding Judge of the Pre-Trial Chamber shall ask the officer of the Registry assisting the Chamber to read out the charges as presented by the Prosecutor. The Presiding Judge shall determine how the hearing is to be conducted and, in particular, may establish the order and the conditions under which he or she intends the evidence contained in the record of the proceedings to be presented.
2. If a question or challenge concerning jurisdiction or admissibility arises, rule 58 applies.
3. Before hearing the matter on the merits, the Presiding Judge of the Pre-Trial Chamber shall ask the Prosecutor and the person whether they intend to raise objections or make observations concerning an issue related to the proper conduct of the proceedings prior to the confirmation hearing.
4. At no subsequent point may the objections and observations made under sub-rule 3 be raised or made again in the confirmation or trial proceedings.
5. If objections or observations referred to in sub-rule 3 are presented, the Presiding Judge of the Pre-Trial Chamber shall invite those referred to in sub-rule 3 to present their arguments, in the order which he or she shall establish. The person shall have the right to reply.
6. If the objections raised or observations made are those referred to in sub-rule 3, the Pre-Trial Chamber shall decide whether to join the issue raised with the examination of the charges and the evidence, or to separate them, in which case it shall adjourn the confirmation hearing and render a decision on the issues raised.
7. During the hearing on the merits, the Prosecutor and the person shall present their arguments in accordance with article 61, paragraphs 5 and 6.
8. The Pre-Trial Chamber shall permit the Prosecutor and the person, in that order, to make final observations.
9. Subject to the provisions of article 61, article 69 shall apply *mutatis mutandis* at the confirmation hearing.

Rule 123
Measures to ensure the presence of the person concerned at the confirmation hearing

1. When a warrant of arrest or summons to appear in accordance with article 58, paragraph 7, has been issued for a person by the Pre-Trial Chamber and the person is arrested or served with the summons, the Pre-Trial Chamber shall ensure that the person is notified of the provisions of article 61, paragraph 2.

2. The Pre-Trial Chamber may hold consultations with the Prosecutor, at the request of the latter or on its own initiative, in order to determine whether there is cause to hold a hearing on confirmation of charges under the conditions set forth in article 61, paragraph 2 (b). When the person concerned has a counsel known to the Court, the consultations shall be held in the presence of the counsel unless the Pre-Trial Chamber decides otherwise.
3. The Pre-Trial Chamber shall ensure that a warrant of arrest for the person concerned has been issued and, if the warrant of arrest has not been executed within a reasonable period of time after the issuance of the warrant, that all reasonable measures have been taken to locate and arrest the person.

Rule 124
Waiver of the right to be present at the confirmation hearing

1. If the person concerned is available to the Court but wishes to waive the right to be present at the hearing on confirmation of charges, he or she shall submit a written request to the Pre-Trial Chamber, which may then hold consultations with the Prosecutor and the person concerned, assisted or represented by his or her counsel.
2. A confirmation hearing pursuant to article 61, paragraph 2 (a), shall only be held when the Pre-Trial Chamber is satisfied that the person concerned understands the right to be present at the hearing and the consequences of waiving this right.
3. The Pre-Trial Chamber may authorize and make provision for the person to observe the hearing from outside the courtroom through the use of communications technology, if required.
4. The waiving of the right to be present at the hearing does not prevent the Pre-Trial Chamber from receiving written observations on issues before the Chamber from the person concerned.

Rule 125
Decision to hold the confirmation hearing in the absence of the person concerned

1. After holding consultations under rules 123 and 124, the Pre-Trial Chamber shall decide whether there is cause to hold a hearing on confirmation of charges in the absence of the person concerned, and in that case, whether the person may be represented by counsel. The Pre-Trial Chamber shall, when appropriate, set a date for the hearing and make the date public.
2. The decision of the Pre-Trial Chamber shall be notified to the Prosecutor and, if possible, to the person concerned or his or her counsel.

3. If the Pre-Trial Chamber decides not to hold a hearing on confirmation of charges in the absence of the person concerned, and the person is not available to the Court, the confirmation of charges may not take place until the person is available to the Court. The Pre-Trial Chamber may review its decision at any time, at the request of the Prosecutor or on its own initiative.
4. If the Pre-Trial Chamber decides not to hold a hearing on confirmation of charges in the absence of the person concerned, and the person is available to the Court, it shall order the person to appear.

Rule 126
Confirmation hearing in the absence of the person concerned

1. The provisions of rules 121 and 122 shall apply *mutatis mutandis* to the preparation for and holding of a hearing on confirmation of charges in the absence of the person concerned.
2. If the Pre-Trial Chamber has determined that the person concerned shall be represented by counsel, the counsel shall have the opportunity to exercise the rights of that person.
3. When the person who has fled is subsequently arrested and the Court has confirmed the charges upon which the Prosecutor intends to pursue the trial, the person charged shall be committed to the Trial Chamber established under article 61, paragraph 11. The person charged may request in writing that the Trial Chamber refer issues to the Pre-Trial Chamber that are necessary for the Chamber's effective and fair functioning in accordance with article 64, paragraph 4.

Section VI
Closure of the pre-trial phase

Rule 127
Procedure in the event of different decisions on multiple charges

If the Pre-Trial Chamber is ready to confirm some of the charges but adjourns the hearing on other charges under article 61, paragraph 7 (c), it may decide that the committal of the person concerned to the Trial Chamber on the charges that it is ready to confirm shall be deferred pending the continuation of the hearing. The Pre-Trial Chamber may then establish a time limit within which the Prosecutor may proceed in accordance with article 61, paragraph 7 (c) (i) or (ii).

Rule 128
Amendment of the charges

1. If the Prosecutor seeks to amend charges already confirmed before the trial has begun, in accordance with article 61, the Prosecutor shall make a written request to the Pre-Trial Chamber, and that Chamber shall so notify the accused.
2. Before deciding whether to authorize the amendment, the Pre-Trial Chamber may request the accused and the Prosecutor to submit written observations on certain issues of fact or law.
3. If the Pre-Trial Chamber determines that the amendments proposed by the Prosecutor constitute additional or more serious charges, it shall proceed, as appropriate, in accordance with rules 121 and 122 or rules 123 to 126.

Rule 129
Notification of the decision on the confirmation of charges

The decision of the Pre-Trial Chamber on the confirmation of charges and the committal of the accused to the Trial Chamber shall be notified, if possible, to the Prosecutor, the person concerned and his or her counsel. Such decision and the record of the proceedings of the Pre-Trial Chamber shall be transmitted to the Presidency.

Rule 130
Constitution of the Trial Chamber

When the Presidency constitutes a Trial Chamber and refers the case to it, the Presidency shall transmit the decision of the Pre-Trial Chamber and the record of the proceedings to the Trial Chamber. The Presidency may also refer the case to a previously constituted Trial Chamber.

Chapter 6
Trial procedure

Rule 131
Record of the proceedings transmitted by the Pre-Trial Chamber

1. The Registrar shall maintain the record of the proceedings transmitted by the Pre-Trial Chamber, pursuant to rule 121, sub-rule 10.
2. Subject to any restrictions concerning confidentiality and the protection of national security information, the record may be consulted by the Prosecutor, the defence, the representatives of States when they participate in the proceedings, and the victims or their legal representatives participating in the proceedings pursuant to rules 89 to 91.

Rule 132
Status conferences

1. Promptly after it is constituted, the Trial Chamber shall hold a status conference in order to set the date of the trial. The Trial Chamber, on its own motion, or at the request of the Prosecutor or the defence, may postpone the date of the trial. The Trial Chamber shall notify the trial date to all those participating in the proceedings. The Trial Chamber shall ensure that this date and any postponements are made public.
2. In order to facilitate the fair and expeditious conduct of the proceedings, the Trial Chamber may confer with the parties by holding status conferences as necessary.

Rule 133
Motions challenging admissibility or jurisdiction

Challenges to the jurisdiction of the Court or the admissibility of the case at the commencement of the trial, or subsequently with the leave of the Court, shall be dealt with by the Presiding Judge and the Trial Chamber in accordance with rule 58.

Rule 134
Motions relating to the trial proceedings

1. Prior to the commencement of the trial, the Trial Chamber on its own motion, or at the request of the Prosecutor or the defence, may rule on any issue concerning the conduct of the proceedings. Any request from the Prosecutor or the defence shall be in writing and, unless the request is for an ex parte procedure, served on the other party. For all requests other than those submitted for an ex parte procedure, the other party shall have the opportunity to file a response.
2. At the commencement of the trial, the Trial Chamber shall ask the Prosecutor and the defence whether they have any objections or observations concerning the conduct of the proceedings which have arisen since the confirmation hearings. Such objections or observations may not be raised or made again on a subsequent occasion in the trial proceedings, without leave of the Trial Chamber in this proceeding.
3. After the commencement of the trial, the Trial Chamber, on its own motion, or at the request of the Prosecutor or the defence, may rule on issues that arise during the course of the trial.

Rule 135
Medical examination of the accused

1. The Trial Chamber may, for the purpose of discharging its obligations under article 64, paragraph 8 (a), or for any other reasons, or at the request of a party, order a medical, psychiatric or psychological examination of the accused, under the conditions set forth in rule 113.
2. The Trial Chamber shall place its reasons for any such order on the record.
3. The Trial Chamber shall appoint one or more experts from the list of experts approved by the Registrar, or an expert approved by the Trial Chamber at the request of a party.
4. Where the Trial Chamber is satisfied that the accused is unfit to stand trial, it shall order that the trial be adjourned. The Trial Chamber may, on its own motion or at the request of the prosecution or the defence, review the case of the accused. In any event, the case shall be reviewed every 120 days unless there are reasons to do otherwise. If necessary, the Trial Chamber may order further examinations of the accused. When the Trial Chamber is satisfied that the accused has become fit to stand trial, it shall proceed in accordance with rule 132.

Rule 136
Joint and separate trials

1. Persons accused jointly shall be tried together unless the Trial Chamber, on its own motion or at the request of the Prosecutor or the defence, orders that separate trials are necessary, in order to avoid serious prejudice to the accused, to protect the interests of justice or because a person jointly accused has made an admission of guilt and can be proceeded against in accordance with article 65, paragraph 2.
2. In joint trials, each accused shall be accorded the same rights as if such accused were being tried separately.

Rule 137
Record of the trial proceedings

1. In accordance with article 64, paragraph 10, the Registrar shall take measures to make, and preserve, a full and accurate record of all proceedings, including transcripts, audio- and video-recordings and other means of capturing sound or image.
2. A Trial Chamber may order the disclosure of all or part of the record of closed proceedings when the reasons for ordering its non-disclosure no longer exist.
3. The Trial Chamber may authorize persons other than the Registrar to take photographs, audio- and video-recordings and other means of capturing the sound or image of the trial.

Rule 138
Custody of evidence

The Registrar shall retain and preserve, as necessary, all the evidence and other materials offered during the hearing, subject to any order of the Trial Chamber.

Rule 139
Decision on admission of guilt

1. After having proceeded in accordance with article 65, paragraph 1, the Trial Chamber, in order to decide whether to proceed in accordance with article 65, paragraph 4, may invite the views of the Prosecutor and the defence.
2. The Trial Chamber shall then make its decision on the admission of guilt and shall give reasons for this decision, which shall be placed on the record.

Rule 140
Directions for the conduct of the proceedings and testimony

1. If the Presiding Judge does not give directions under article 64, paragraph 8, the Prosecutor and the defence shall agree on the order and manner in which the evidence shall be submitted to the Trial Chamber. If no agreement can be reached, the Presiding Judge shall issue directions.
2. In all cases, subject to article 64, paragraphs 8 (b) and 9, article 69, paragraph 4, and rule 88, sub-rule 5, a witness may be questioned as follows:
   (a) A party that submits evidence in accordance with article 69, paragraph 3, by way of a witness, has the right to question that witness;
   (b) The prosecution and the defence have the right to question that witness about relevant matters related to the witness's testimony and its reliability, the credibility of the witness and other relevant matters;
   (c) The Trial Chamber has the right to question a witness before or after a witness is questioned by a participant referred to in sub-rules 2 (a) or (b);
   (d) The defence shall have the right to be the last to examine a witness.
3. Unless otherwise ordered by the Trial Chamber, a witness other than an expert, or an investigator if he or she has not yet testified, shall not be present when the testimony of another witness is given. However, a witness who has heard the testimony of another witness shall not for that reason alone be disqualified from testifying. When a witness testifies after hearing the testimony of others, this fact shall be noted in the record and considered by the Trial Chamber when evaluating the evidence.

Rule 141
Closure of evidence and closing statements

1. The Presiding Judge shall declare when the submission of evidence is closed.
2. The Presiding Judge shall invite the Prosecutor and the defence to make their closing statements. The defence shall always have the opportunity to speak last.

Rule 142
Deliberations

1. After the closing statements, the Trial Chamber shall retire to deliberate, in camera. The Trial Chamber shall inform all those who participated in the proceedings of the date on which the Trial Chamber will pronounce its decision. The pronouncement shall be made within a reasonable period of time after the Trial Chamber has retired to deliberate.
2. When there is more than one charge, the Trial Chamber shall decide separately on each charge. When there is more than one accused, the Trial Chamber shall decide separately on the charges against each accused.

Rule 143
Additional hearings on matters related to sentence or reparations

Pursuant to article 76, paragraphs 2 and 3, for the purpose of holding a further hearing on matters related to sentence and, if applicable, reparations, the Presiding Judge shall set the date of the further hearing. This hearing can be postponed, in exceptional circumstances, by the Trial Chamber, on its own motion or at the request of the Prosecutor, the defence or the legal representatives of the victims participating in the proceedings pursuant to rules 89 to 91 and, in respect of reparations hearings, those victims who have made a request under rule 94.

Rule 144
Delivery of the decisions of the Trial Chamber

1. Decisions of the Trial Chamber concerning admissibility of a case, the jurisdiction of the Court, criminal responsibility of the accused, sentence and reparations shall be pronounced in public and, wherever possible, in the presence of the accused, the Prosecutor, the victims or the legal representatives of the victims participating in the proceedings pursuant to rules 89 to 91, and the representatives of the States which have participated in the proceedings.

2. Copies of all the above-mentioned decisions shall be provided as soon as possible to:
   (a) All those who participated in the proceedings, in a working language of the Court;
   (b) The accused, in a language he or she fully understands or speaks, if necessary to meet the requirements of fairness under article 67, paragraph 1 (f).

Chapter 7
Penalties

Rule 145
Determination of sentence

1. In its determination of the sentence pursuant to article 78, paragraph 1, the Court shall:
   (a) Bear in mind that the totality of any sentence of imprisonment and fine, as the case may be, imposed under article 77 must reflect the culpability of the convicted person;
   (b) Balance all the relevant factors, including any mitigating and aggravating factors and consider the circumstances both of the convicted person and of the crime;
   (c) In addition to the factors mentioned in article 78, paragraph 1, give consideration, *inter alia*, to the extent of the damage caused, in particular the harm caused to the victims and their families, the nature of the unlawful behaviour and the means employed to execute the crime; the degree of participation of the convicted person; the degree of intent; the circumstances of manner, time and location; and the age, education, social and economic condition of the convicted person.
2. In addition to the factors mentioned above, the Court shall take into account, as appropriate:
   (a) Mitigating circumstances such as:
      (i) The circumstances falling short of constituting grounds for exclusion of criminal responsibility, such as substantially diminished mental capacity or duress;
      (ii) The convicted person's conduct after the act, including any efforts by the person to compensate the victims and any cooperation with the Court;
   (b) As aggravating circumstances:
      (i) Any relevant prior criminal convictions for crimes under the jurisdiction of the Court or of a similar nature;
      (ii) Abuse of power or official capacity;
      (iii) Commission of the crime where the victim is particularly defenceless;

(iv) Commission of the crime with particular cruelty or where there were multiple victims;

(v) Commission of the crime for any motive involving discrimination on any of the grounds referred to in article 21, paragraph 3;

(vi) Other circumstances which, although not enumerated above, by virtue of their nature are similar to those mentioned.

3. Life imprisonment may be imposed when justified by the extreme gravity of the crime and the individual circumstances of the convicted person, as evidenced by the existence of one or more aggravating circumstances.

Rule 146
Imposition of fines under article 77

1. In determining whether to order a fine under article 77, paragraph 2 (a), and in fixing the amount of the fine, the Court shall determine whether imprisonment is a sufficient penalty. The Court shall give due consideration to the financial capacity of the convicted person, including any orders for forfeiture in accordance with article 77, paragraph 2 (b), and, as appropriate, any orders for reparation in accordance with article 75. The Court shall take into account, in addition to the factors referred to in rule 145, whether and to what degree the crime was motivated by personal financial gain.
2. A fine imposed under article 77, paragraph 2 (a), shall be set at an appropriate level. To this end, the Court shall, in addition to the factors referred to above, in particular take into consideration the damage and injuries caused as well as the proportionate gains derived from the crime by the perpetrator. Under no circumstances may the total amount exceed 75 per cent of the value of the convicted person's identifiable assets, liquid or realizable, and property, after deduction of an appropriate amount that would satisfy the financial needs of the convicted person and his or her dependants.
3. In imposing a fine, the Court shall allow the convicted person a reasonable period in which to pay the fine. The Court may provide for payment of a lump sum or by way of instalments during that period.
4. In imposing a fine, the Court may, as an option, calculate it according to a system of daily fines. In such cases, the minimum duration shall be 30 days and the maximum duration five years. The Court shall decide the total amount in accordance with sub-rules 1 and 2. It shall determine the amount of daily payment in the light of the individual circumstances of the convicted person, including the financial needs of his or her dependants.
5. If the convicted person does not pay the fine imposed in accordance with the conditions set above, appropriate measures may be taken by the Court pursuant to rules 217 to 222 and in accordance with article 109. Where, in cases of continued wilful non-payment, the Presidency, on its

own motion or at the request of the Prosecutor, is satisfied that all available enforcement measures have been exhausted, it may as a last resort extend the term of imprisonment for a period not to exceed a quarter of such term or five years, whichever is less. In the determination of such period of extension, the Presidency shall take into account the amount of the fine, imposed and paid. Any such extension shall not apply in the case of life imprisonment. The extension may not lead to a total period of imprisonment in excess of 30 years.

6. In order to determine whether to order an extension and the period involved, the Presidency shall sit in camera for the purpose of obtaining the views of the sentenced person and the Prosecutor. The sentenced person shall have the right to be assisted by counsel.
7. In imposing a fine, the Court shall warn the convicted person that failure to pay the fine in accordance with the conditions set out above may result in an extension of the period of imprisonment as described in this rule.

Rule 147
Orders of forfeiture

1. In accordance with article 76, paragraphs 2 and 3, and rules 63, sub-rule 1, and 143, at any hearing to consider an order of forfeiture, Chamber shall hear evidence as to the identification and location of specific proceeds, property or assets which have been derived directly or indirectly from the crime.
2. If before or during the hearing, a Chamber becomes aware of any bona fide third party who appears to have an interest in relevant proceeds, property or assets, it shall give notice to that third party.
3. The Prosecutor, the convicted person and any bona fide third party with an interest in the relevant proceeds, property or assets may submit evidence relevant to the issue.
4. After considering any evidence submitted, a Chamber may issue an order of forfeiture in relation to specific proceeds, property or assets if it is satisfied that these have been derived directly or indirectly from the crime.

Rule 148
Orders to transfer fines or forfeitures to the Trust Fund

Before making an order pursuant to article 79, paragraph 2, a Chamber may request the representatives of the Fund to submit written or oral observations to it.

Chapter 8
Appeal and revision

Section I
General provisions

Rule 149
Rules governing proceedings in the Appeals Chamber

Parts 5 and 6 and rules governing proceedings and the submission of evidence in the Pre-Trial and Trial Chambers shall apply *mutatis mutandis* to proceedings in the Appeals Chamber.

Section II
Appeals against convictions, acquittals, sentences and reparation orders

Rule 150
Appeal

1. Subject to sub-rule 2, an appeal against a decision of conviction or acquittal under article 74, a sentence under article 76 or a reparation order under article 75 may be filed not later than 30 days from the date on which the party filing the appeal is notified of the decision, the sentence or the reparation order.
2. The Appeals Chamber may extend the time limit set out in sub-rule 1, for good cause, upon the application of the party seeking to file the appeal.
3. The appeal shall be filed with the Registrar.
4. If an appeal is not filed as set out in sub-rules 1 to 3, the decision, the sentence or the reparation order of the Trial Chamber shall become final.

Rule 151
Procedure for the appeal

1. Upon the filing of an appeal under rule 150, the Registrar shall transmit the trial record to the Appeals Chamber.
2. The Registrar shall notify all parties who participated in the proceedings before the Trial Chamber that an appeal has been filed.

Rule 152
Discontinuance of the appeal

1. Any party who has filed an appeal may discontinue the appeal at any time before judgement has been delivered. In such case, the party shall

file with the Registrar a written notice of discontinuance of appeal. The Registrar shall inform the other parties that such a notice has been filed.

2. If the Prosecutor has filed an appeal on behalf of a convicted person in accordance with article 81, paragraph 1 (b), before filing any notice of discontinuance, the Prosecutor shall inform the convicted person that he or she intends to discontinue the appeal in order to give him or her the opportunity to continue the appeal proceedings.

Rule 153
Judgement on appeals against reparation orders

1. The Appeals Chamber may confirm, reverse or amend a reparation order made under article 75.
2. The judgement of the Appeals Chamber shall be delivered in accordance with article 83, paragraphs 4 and 5.

Section III
Appeals against other decisions

Rule 154
Appeals that do not require the leave of the Court

1. An appeal may be filed under article 81, paragraph 3 (c) (ii), or article 82, paragraph 1 (a) or (b), not later than five days from the date upon which the party filing the appeal is notified of the decision.
2. An appeal may be filed under article 82, paragraph 1 (c), not later than two days from the date upon which the party filing the appeal is notified of the decision.
3. Rule 150, sub-rules 3 and 4, shall apply to appeals filed under sub-rules 1 and 2 of this rule.

Rule 155
Appeals that require leave of the Court

1. When a party wishes to appeal a decision under article 82, paragraph 1 (d), or article 82, paragraph 2, that party shall, within five days of being notified of that decision, make a written application to the Chamber that gave the decision, setting out the reasons for the request for leave to appeal.
2. The Chamber shall render a decision and shall notify all parties who participated in the proceedings that gave rise to the decision referred to in sub-rule 1.

Rule 156
Procedure for the appeal

1. As soon as an appeal has been filed under rule 154 or as soon as leave to appeal has been granted under rule 155, the Registrar shall transmit to the Appeals Chamber the record of the proceedings of the Chamber that made the decision that is the subject of the appeal.
2. The Registrar shall give notice of the appeal to all parties who participated in the proceedings before the Chamber that gave the decision that is the subject of the appeal, unless they have already been notified by the Chamber under rule 155, sub-rule 2.
3. The appeal proceedings shall be in writing unless the Appeals Chamber decides to convene a hearing.
4. The appeal shall be heard as expeditiously as possible.
5. When filing the appeal, the party appealing may request that the appeal have suspensive effect in accordance with article 82, paragraph 3.

Rule 157
Discontinuance of the appeal

Any party who has filed an appeal under rule 154 or who has obtained the leave of a Chamber to appeal a decision under rule 155 may discontinue the appeal at any time before judgement has been delivered. In such case, the party shall file with the Registrar a written notice of discontinuance of appeal. The Registrar shall inform the other parties that such a notice has been filed.

Rule 158
Judgement on the appeal

1. An Appeals Chamber which considers an appeal referred to in this section may confirm, reverse or amend the decision appealed.
2. The judgement of the Appeals Chamber shall be delivered in accordance with article 83, paragraph 4.

Section IV
Revision of conviction or sentence

Rule 159
Application for revision

1. An application for revision provided for in article 84, paragraph 1, shall be in writing and shall set out the grounds on which the revision is sought. It shall as far as possible be accompanied by supporting material.

2. The determination on whether the application is meritorious shall be taken by a majority of the judges of the Appeals Chamber and shall be supported by reasons in writing.
3. Notification of the decision shall be sent to the applicant and, as far as possible, to all the parties who participated in the proceedings related to the initial decision.

Rule 160
Transfer for the purpose of revision

1. For the conduct of the hearing provided for in rule 161, the relevant Chamber shall issue its order sufficiently in advance to enable the transfer of the sentenced person to the seat of the Court, as appropriate.
2. The determination of the Court shall be communicated without delay to the State of enforcement.
3. The provisions of rule 206, sub-rule 3, shall be applicable.

Rule 161
Determination on revision

1. On a date which it shall determine and shall communicate to the applicant and to all those having received notification under rule 159, sub-rule 3, the relevant Chamber shall hold a hearing to determine whether the conviction or sentence should be revised.
2. For the conduct of the hearing, the relevant Chamber shall exercise, *mutatis mutandis*, all the powers of the Trial Chamber pursuant to Part 6 and the rules governing proceedings and the submission of evidence in the Pre-Trial and Trial Chambers.
3. The determination on revision shall be governed by the applicable provisions of article 83, paragraph 4.

Chapter 9
Offences and misconduct against the Court

Section I
Offences against the administration of justice under article 70

Rule 162
Exercise of jurisdiction

1. Before deciding whether to exercise jurisdiction, the Court may consult with States Parties that may have jurisdiction over the offence.
2. In making a decision whether or not to exercise jurisdiction, the Court may consider, in particular:

(a) The availability and effectiveness of prosecution in a State Party;
(b) The seriousness of an offence;
(c) The possible joinder of charges under article 70 with charges under articles 5 to 8;
(d) The need to expedite proceedings;
(e) Links with an ongoing investigation or a trial before the Court; and
(f) Evidentiary considerations.

3. The Court shall give favourable consideration to a request from the host State for a waiver of the power of the Court to exercise jurisdiction in cases where the host State considers such a waiver to be of particular importance.
4. If the Court decides not to exercise its jurisdiction, it may request a State Party to exercise jurisdiction pursuant to article 70, paragraph 4.

Rule 163
Application of the Statute and the Rules

1. Unless otherwise provided in sub-rules 2 and 3, rule 162 and rules 164 to 169, the Statute and the Rules shall apply *mutatis mutandis* to the Court's investigation, prosecution and punishment of offences defined in article 70.
2. The provisions of Part 2, and any rules thereunder, shall not apply, with the exception of article 21.
3. The provisions of Part 10, and any rules thereunder, shall not apply, with the exception of articles 103, 107, 109 and 111.

Rule 164
Periods of limitation

1. If the Court exercises jurisdiction in accordance with rule 162, it shall apply the periods of limitation set forth in this rule.
2. Offences defined in article 70 shall be subject to a period of limitation of five years from the date on which the offence was committed, provided that during this period no investigation or prosecution has been initiated. The period of limitation shall be interrupted if an investigation or prosecution has been initiated during this period, either before the Court or by a State Party with jurisdiction over the case pursuant to article 70, paragraph 4 (a).
3. Enforcement of sanctions imposed with respect to offences defined in article 70 shall be subject to a period of limitation of 10 years from the date on which the sanction has become final. The period of limitation shall be interrupted with the detention of the convicted person or while the person concerned is outside the territory of the States Parties.

Rule 165
Investigation, prosecution and trial

1. The Prosecutor may initiate and conduct investigations with respect to the offences defined in article 70 on his or her own initiative, on the basis of information communicated by a Chamber or any reliable source.
2. Articles 53 and 59, and any rules thereunder, shall not apply.
3. For purposes of article 61, the Pre-Trial Chamber may make any of the determinations set forth in that article on the basis of written submissions, without a hearing, unless the interests of justice otherwise require.
4. A Trial Chamber may, as appropriate and taking into account the rights of the defence, direct that there be joinder of charges under article 70 with charges under articles 5 to 8.

Rule 166
Sanctions under article 70

1. If the Court imposes sanctions with respect to article 70, this rule shall apply.
2. Article 77, and any rules thereunder, shall not apply, with the exception of an order of forfeiture under article 77, paragraph 2 (b), which may be ordered in addition to imprisonment or a fine or both.
3. Each offence may be separately fined and those fines may be cumulative. Under no circumstances may the total amount exceed 50 per cent of the value of the convicted person's identifiable assets, liquid or realizable, and property, after deduction of an appropriate amount that would satisfy the financial needs of the convicted person and his or her dependants.
4. In imposing a fine the Court shall allow the convicted person a reasonable period in which to pay the fine. The Court may provide for payment of a lump sum or by way of instalments during that period.
5. If the convicted person does not pay a fine imposed in accordance with the conditions set forth in sub-rule 4, appropriate measures may be taken by the Court pursuant to rules 217 to 222 and in accordance with article 109. Where, in cases of continued wilful non-payment, the Court, on its own motion or at the request of the Prosecutor, is satisfied that all available enforcement measures have been exhausted, it may as a last resort impose a term of imprisonment in accordance with article 70, paragraph 3. In the determination of such term of imprisonment, the Court shall take into account the amount of fine paid.

Rule 167
International cooperation and judicial assistance

1. With regard to offences under article 70, the Court may request a State to provide any form of international cooperation or judicial assistance corresponding to those forms set forth in Part 9. In any such request, the

Court shall indicate that the basis for the request is an investigation or prosecution of offences under article 70.

2. The conditions for providing international cooperation or judicial assistance to the Court with respect to offences under article 70 shall be those set forth in article 70, paragraph 2.

Rule 168
Ne bis in idem

In respect of offences under article 70, no person shall be tried before the Court with respect to conduct which formed the basis of an offence for which the person has already been convicted or acquitted by the Court or another court.

Rule 169
Immediate arrest

In the case of an alleged offence under article 70 committed in the presence of a Chamber, the Prosecutor may orally request that Chamber to order the immediate arrest of the person concerned.

Section II
Misconduct before the Court under article 71

Rule 170
Disruption of proceedings

Having regard to article 63, paragraph 2, the Presiding Judge of the Chamber dealing with the matter may, after giving a warning:

(a) Order a person disrupting the proceedings of the Court to leave or be removed from the courtroom; or,
(b) In case of repeated misconduct, order the interdiction of that person from attending the proceedings.

Rule 171
Refusal to comply with a direction by the Court

1. When the misconduct consists of deliberate refusal to comply with an oral or written direction by the Court, not covered by rule 170, and that direction is accompanied by a warning of sanctions in case of breach, the Presiding Judge of the Chamber dealing with the matter may order the interdiction of that person from the proceedings for a period not exceeding 30 days or, if the misconduct is of a more serious nature, impose a fine.
2. If the person committing misconduct as described in sub-rule 1 is an official of the Court, or a defence counsel, or a legal representative of victims, the Presiding Judge of the Chamber dealing with the matter may also

order the interdiction of that person from exercising his or her functions before the Court for a period not exceeding 30 days.

3. If the Presiding Judge in cases under sub-rules 1 and 2 considers that a longer period of interdiction is appropriate, the Presiding Judge shall refer the matter to the Presidency, which may hold a hearing to determine whether to order a longer or permanent period of interdiction.
4. A fine imposed under sub-rule 1 shall not exceed 2,000 euros, or the equivalent amount in any currency, provided that in cases of continuing misconduct, a new fine may be imposed on each day that the misconduct continues, and such fines shall be cumulative.
5. The person concerned shall be given an opportunity to be heard before a sanction for misconduct, as described in this rule, is imposed.

Rule 172
Conduct covered by both articles 70 and 71

If conduct covered by article 71 also constitutes one of the offences defined in article 70, the Court shall proceed in accordance with article 70 and rules 162 to 169.

Chapter 10
Compensation to an arrested or convicted person

Rule 173
Request for compensation

1. Anyone seeking compensation on any of the grounds indicated in article 85 shall submit a request, in writing, to the Presidency, which shall designate a Chamber composed of three judges to consider the request. These judges shall not have participated in any earlier judgement of the Court regarding the person making the request.
2. The request for compensation shall be submitted not later than six months from the date the person making the request was notified of the decision of the Court concerning:
   (a) The unlawfulness of the arrest or detention under article 85, paragraph 1;
   (b) The reversal of the conviction under article 85, paragraph 2;
   (c) The existence of a grave and manifest miscarriage of justice under article 85, paragraph 3.
3. The request shall contain the grounds and the amount of compensation requested.
4. The person requesting compensation shall be entitled to legal assistance.

Rule 174
Procedure for seeking compensation

1. A request for compensation and any other written observation by the person filing the request shall be transmitted to the Prosecutor, who shall have an opportunity to respond in writing. Any observations by the Prosecutor shall be notified to the person filing the request.
2. The Chamber designated under rule 173, sub-rule 1, may either hold a hearing or determine the matter on the basis of the request and any written observations by the Prosecutor and the person filing the request. A hearing shall be held if the Prosecutor or the person seeking compensation so requests.
3. The decision shall be taken by the majority of the judges. The decision shall be notified to the Prosecutor and to the person filing the request.

Rule 175
Amount of compensation

In establishing the amount of any compensation in conformity with article 85, paragraph 3, the Chamber designated under rule 173, sub-rule 1, shall take into consideration the consequences of the grave and manifest miscarriage of justice on the personal, family, social and professional situation of the person filing the request.

Chapter 11
International cooperation and judicial assistance

Section I
Requests for cooperation under article 87

Rule 176
Organs of the Court responsible for the transmission and receipt of any communications relating to international cooperation and judicial assistance

1. Upon and subsequent to the establishment of the Court, the Registrar shall obtain from the Secretary-General of the United Nations any communication made by States pursuant to article 87, paragraphs 1 (a) and 2.
2. The Registrar shall transmit the requests for cooperation made by the Chambers and shall receive the responses, information and documents from requested States. The Office of the Prosecutor shall transmit the requests for cooperation made by the Prosecutor and shall receive the responses, information and documents from requested States.

3. The Registrar shall be the recipient of any communication from States concerning subsequent changes in the designation of the national channels charged with receiving requests for cooperation, as well as of any change in the language in which requests for cooperation should be made, and shall, upon request, make such information available to States Parties as may be appropriate.
4. The provisions of sub-rule 2 are applicable *mutatis mutandis* where the Court requests information, documents or other forms of cooperation and assistance from an intergovernmental organization.
5. The Registrar shall transmit any communications referred to in sub-rules 1 and 3 and rule 177, sub-rule 2, as appropriate, to the Presidency or the Office of the Prosecutor, or both.

Rule 177
Channels of communication

1. Communications concerning the national authority charged with receiving requests for cooperation made upon ratification, acceptance, approval or accession shall provide all relevant information about such authorities.
2. When an intergovernmental organization is asked to assist the Court under article 87, paragraph 6, the Registrar shall, when necessary, ascertain its designated channel of communication and obtain all relevant information relating thereto.

Rule 178
Language chosen by States Parties under article 87, paragraph 2

1. When a requested State Party has more than one official language, it may indicate upon ratification, acceptance, approval or accession that requests for cooperation and any supporting documents can be drafted in any one of its official languages.
2. When the requested State Party has not chosen a language for communication with the Court upon ratification, acceptance, accession or approval, the request for cooperation shall either be in or be accompanied by a translation into one of the working languages of the Court pursuant to article 87, paragraph 2.

Rule 179
Language of requests directed to States not party to the Statute

When a State not party to the Statute has agreed to provide assistance to the Court under article 87, paragraph 5, and has not made a choice of language for such requests, the requests for cooperation shall either be in or be accompanied by a translation into one of the working languages of the Court.

Rule 180
Changes in the channels of communication or the languages of requests for cooperation

1. Changes concerning the channel of communication or the language a State has chosen under article 87, paragraph 2, shall be communicated in writing to the Registrar at the earliest opportunity.
2. Such changes shall take effect in respect of requests for cooperation made by the Court at a time agreed between the Court and the State or, in the absence of such an agreement, 45 days after the Court has received the communication and, in all cases, without prejudice to current requests or requests in progress.

Section II
Surrender, transit and competing requests under articles 89 and 90

Rule 181
Challenge to admissibility of a case before a national court

When a situation described in article 89, paragraph 2, arises, and without prejudice to the provisions of article 19 and of rules 58 to 62 on procedures applicable to challenges to the jurisdiction of the Court or the admissibility of a case, the Chamber dealing with the case, if the admissibility ruling is still pending, shall take steps to obtain from the requested State all the relevant information about the *ne bis in idem* challenge brought by the person.

Rule 182
Request for transit under article 89, paragraph 3 (e)

1. In situations described in article 89, paragraph 3 (e), the Court may transmit the request for transit by any medium capable of delivering a written record.
2. When the time limit provided for in article 89, paragraph 3 (e), has expired and the person concerned has been released, such a release is without prejudice to a subsequent arrest of the person in accordance with the provisions of article 89 or article 92.

Rule 183
Possible temporary surrender

Following the consultations referred to in article 89, paragraph 4, the requested State may temporarily surrender the person sought in accordance with conditions determined between the requested State and the Court. In such case the person shall be kept in custody during his or her presence before the Court and shall be transferred to the requested State once his or her presence before the Court is no longer required, at the latest when the proceedings have been completed.

Rule 184
Arrangements for surrender

1. The requested State shall immediately inform the Registrar when the person sought by the Court is available for surrender.
2. The person shall be surrendered to the Court by the date and in the manner agreed upon between the authorities of the requested State and the Registrar.
3. If circumstances prevent the surrender of the person by the date agreed, the authorities of the requested State and the Registrar shall agree upon a new date and manner by which the person shall be surrendered.
4. The Registrar shall maintain contact with the authorities of the host State in relation to the arrangements for the surrender of the person to the Court.

Rule 185
Release of a person from the custody of the Court other than upon completion of sentence

1. Subject to sub-rule 2, where a person surrendered to the Court is released from the custody of the Court because the Court does not have jurisdiction, the case is inadmissible under article 17, paragraph 1 (b), (c) or (d), the charges have not been confirmed under article 61, the person has been acquitted at trial or on appeal, or for any other reason, the Court shall, as soon as possible, make such arrangements as it considers appropriate for the transfer of the person, taking into account the views of the person, to a State which is obliged to receive him or her, to another State which agrees to receive him or her, or to a State which has requested his or her extradition with the consent of the original surrendering State. In this case, the host State shall facilitate the transfer in accordance with the agreement referred to in article 3, paragraph 2, and the related arrangements.
2. Where the Court has determined that the case is inadmissible under article 17, paragraph 1 (a), the Court shall make arrangements, as appropriate, for the transfer of the person to a State whose investigation or prosecution has formed the basis of the successful challenge to admissibility, unless the State that originally surrendered the person requests his or her return.

Rule 186
Competing requests in the context of a challenge to the admissibility of the case

In situations described in article 90, paragraph 8, the requested State shall provide the notification of its decision to the Prosecutor in order to enable him or her to act in accordance with article 19, paragraph 10.

Section III
Documents for arrest and surrender under articles 91 and 92

Rule 187
Translation of documents accompanying request for surrender

For the purposes of article 67, paragraph 1 (a), and in accordance with rule 117, sub-rule 1, the request under article 91 shall be accompanied, as appropriate, by a translation of the warrant of arrest or of the judgement of conviction and by a translation of the text of any relevant provisions of the Statute, in a language that the person fully understands and speaks.

Rule 188
Time limit for submission of documents after provisional arrest

For the purposes of article 92, paragraph 3, the time limit for receipt by the requested State of the request for surrender and the documents supporting the request shall be 60 days from the date of the provisional arrest.

Rule 189
Transmission of documents supporting the request

When a person has consented to surrender in accordance with the provisions of article 92, paragraph 3, and the requested State proceeds to surrender the person to the Court, the Court shall not be required to provide the documents described in article 91 unless the requested State indicates otherwise.

Section IV
Cooperation under article 93

Rule 190
Instruction on self-incrimination accompanying request for witness

When making a request under article 93, paragraph 1 (e), with respect to a witness, the Court shall annex an instruction, concerning rule 74 relating to self-incrimination, to be provided to the witness in question, in a language that the person fully understands and speaks.

Rule 191
Assurance provided by the Court under article 93, paragraph 2

The Chamber dealing with the case, on its own motion or at the request of the Prosecutor, defence or witness or expert concerned, may decide, after taking into account the views of the Prosecutor and the witness or expert concerned, to provide the assurance described in article 93, paragraph 2.

Rule 192
Transfer of a person in custody

1. Transfer of a person in custody to the Court in accordance with article 93, paragraph 7, shall be arranged by the national authorities concerned in liaison with the Registrar and the authorities of the host State.
2. The Registrar shall ensure the proper conduct of the transfer, including the supervision of the person while in the custody of the Court.
3. The person in custody before the Court shall have the right to raise matters concerning the conditions of his or her detention with the relevant Chamber.
4. In accordance with article 93, paragraph 7 (b), when the purposes of the transfer have been fulfilled, the Registrar shall arrange for the return of the person in custody to the requested State.

Rule 193
Temporary transfer of the person from the State of enforcement

1. The Chamber that is considering the case may order the temporary transfer from the State of enforcement to the seat of the Court of any person sentenced by the Court whose testimony or other assistance is necessary to the Court. The provisions of article 93, paragraph 7, shall not apply.
2. The Registrar shall ensure the proper conduct of the transfer, in liaison with the authorities of the State of enforcement and the authorities of the host State. When the purposes of the transfer have been fulfilled, the Court shall return the sentenced person to the State of enforcement.
3. The person shall be kept in custody during his or her presence before the Court. The entire period of detention spent at the seat of the Court shall be deducted from the sentence remaining to be served.

Rule 194
Cooperation requested from the Court

1. In accordance with article 93, paragraph 10, and consistent with article 96, mutatis mutandis, a State may transmit to the Court a request for cooperation or assistance to the Court, either in or accompanied by a translation into one of the working languages of the Court.
2. Requests described in sub-rule 1 are to be sent to the Registrar, which shall transmit them, as appropriate, either to the Prosecutor or to the Chamber concerned.
3. If protective measures within the meaning of article 68 have been adopted, the Prosecutor or Chamber, as appropriate, shall consider the views of the Chamber which ordered the measures as well as those of the relevant victim or witness, before deciding on the request.
4. If the request relates to documents or evidence as described in article 93, paragraph 10 (b) (ii), the Prosecutor or Chamber, as appropriate, shall obtain the written consent of the relevant State before proceeding with the request.
5. When the Court decides to grant the request for cooperation or assistance from a State, the request shall be executed, insofar as possible, following any procedure outlined therein by the requesting State and permitting persons specified in the request to be present.

Section V
Cooperation under article 98

Rule 195
Provision of information

1. When a requested State notifies the Court that a request for surrender or assistance raises a problem of execution in respect of article 98, the requested State shall provide any information relevant to assist the Court in the application of article 98. Any concerned third State or sending State may provide additional information to assist the Court.
2. The Court may not proceed with a request for the surrender of a person without the consent of a sending State if, under article 98, paragraph 2, such a request would be inconsistent with obligations under an international agreement pursuant to which the consent of a sending State is required prior to the surrender of a person of that State to the Court.

Section VI
Rule of speciality under article 101

Rule 196
Provision of views on article 101, paragraph 1

A person surrendered to the Court may provide views on a perceived violation of the provisions of article 101, paragraph 1.

Rule 197
Extension of the surrender

When the Court has requested a waiver of the requirements of article 101, paragraph 1, the requested State may ask the Court to obtain and provide the views of the person surrendered to the Court.

Chapter 12
Enforcement

Section I
Role of States in enforcement of sentences of imprisonment and change in designation of State of enforcement under articles 103 and 104

Rule 198
Communications between the Court and States

Unless the context otherwise requires, article 87 and rules 176 to 180 shall apply, as appropriate, to communications between the Court and a State on matters relating to enforcement of sentences.

Rule 199
Organ responsible under Part 10

Unless provided otherwise in the Rules, the functions of the Court under Part 10 shall be exercised by the Presidency.

Rule 200
List of States of enforcement

1. A list of States that have indicated their willingness to accept sentenced persons shall be established and maintained by the Registrar.
2. The Presidency shall not include a State on the list provided for in article 103, paragraph 1 (a), if it does not agree with the conditions that such a

State attaches to its acceptance. The Presidency may request any additional information from that State prior to taking a decision.

3. A State that has attached conditions of acceptance may at any time withdraw such conditions. Any amendments or additions to such conditions shall be subject to confirmation by the Presidency.
4. A State may at any time inform the Registrar of its withdrawal from the list. Such withdrawal shall not affect the enforcement of the sentences in respect of persons that the State has already accepted.
5. The Court may enter bilateral arrangements with States with a view to establishing a framework for the acceptance of prisoners sentenced by the Court. Such arrangements shall be consistent with the Statute.

Rule 201
Principles of equitable distribution

Principles of equitable distribution for purposes of article 103, paragraph 3, shall include:

(a) The principle of equitable geographical distribution;
(b) The need to afford each State on the list an opportunity to receive sentenced persons;
(c) The number of sentenced persons already received by that State and other States of enforcement;
(d) Any other relevant factors.

Rule 202
Timing of delivery of the sentenced person to the State of enforcement

The delivery of a sentenced person from the Court to the designated State of enforcement shall not take place unless the decision on the conviction and the decision on the sentence have become final.

Rule 203
Views of the sentenced person

1. The Presidency shall give notice in writing to the sentenced person that it is addressing the designation of a State of enforcement. The sentenced person shall, within such time limit as the Presidency shall prescribe, submit in writing his or her views on the question to the Presidency.
2. The Presidency may allow the sentenced person to make oral presentations.
3. The Presidency shall allow the sentenced person:
   (a) To be assisted, as appropriate, by a competent interpreter and to benefit from any translation necessary for the presentation of his or her views;
   (b) To be granted adequate time and facilities necessary to prepare for the presentation of his or her views.

Rule 204
Information relating to designation

When the Presidency notifies the designated State of its decision, it shall also transmit the following information and documents:

(a) The name, nationality, date and place of birth of the sentenced person;
(b) A copy of the final judgement of conviction and of the sentence imposed;
(c) The length and commencement date of the sentence and the time remaining to be served;
(d) After having heard the views of the sentenced person, any necessary information concerning the state of his or her health, including any medical treatment that he or she is receiving.

Rule 205
Rejection of designation in a particular case

Where a State in a particular case rejects the designation by the Presidency, the Presidency may designate another State.

Rule 206
Delivery of the sentenced person to the State of enforcement

1. The Registrar shall inform the Prosecutor and the sentenced person of the State designated to enforce the sentence.
2. The sentenced person shall be delivered to the State of enforcement as soon as possible after the designated State of enforcement accepts.
3. The Registrar shall ensure the proper conduct of the delivery of the person in consultation with the authorities of the State of enforcement and the host State.

Rule 207
Transit

1. No authorization is required if the sentenced person is transported by air and no landing is scheduled on the territory of the transit State. If an unscheduled landing occurs on the territory of the transit State, that State shall, to the extent possible under the procedure of national law, detain the sentenced person in custody until a request for transit as provided in sub-rule 2 or a request under article 89, paragraph 1, or article 92 is received.
2. To the extent possible under the procedure of national law, a State Party shall authorize the transit of a sentenced person through its territory and the provisions of article 89, paragraph 3 (b) and (c), and articles 105 and

108 and any rules relating thereto shall, as appropriate, apply. A copy of the final judgement of conviction and of the sentence imposed shall be attached to such request for transit.

Rule 208
Costs

1. The ordinary costs for the enforcement of the sentence in the territory of the State of enforcement shall be borne by that State.
2. Other costs, including those for the transport of the sentenced person and those referred to in article 100, paragraph 1 (c), (d) and (e), shall be borne by the Court.

Rule 209
Change in designation of State of enforcement

1. The Presidency, acting on its own motion or at the request of the sentenced person or the Prosecutor, may at any time act in accordance with article 104, paragraph 1.
2. The request of the sentenced person or of the Prosecutor shall be made in writing and shall set out the grounds upon which the transfer is sought.

Rule 210
Procedure for change in the designation of a State of enforcement

1. Before deciding to change the designation of a State of enforcement, the Presidency may:
   (a) Request views from the State of enforcement;
   (b) Consider written or oral presentations of the sentenced person and the Prosecutor;
   (c) Consider written or oral expert opinion concerning, *inter alia*, the sentenced person;
   (d) Obtain any other relevant information from any reliable sources.
2. The provisions of rule 203, sub-rule 3, shall apply, as appropriate.
3. If the Presidency refuses to change the designation of the State of enforcement, it shall, as soon as possible, inform the sentenced person, the Prosecutor and the Registrar of its decision and of the reasons therefor. It shall also inform the State of enforcement.

Section II
Enforcement, supervision and transfer under articles 105, 106 and 107

Rule 211
Supervision of enforcement of sentences and conditions of imprisonment

1. In order to supervise the enforcement of sentences of imprisonment, the Presidency:
   (a) Shall, in consultation with the State of enforcement, ensure that in establishing appropriate arrangements for the exercise by any sentenced person of his or her right to communicate with the Court about the conditions of imprisonment, the provisions of article 106, paragraph 3, shall be respected;
   (b) May, when necessary, request any information, report or expert opinion from the State of enforcement or from any reliable sources;
   (c) May, where appropriate, delegate a judge of the Court or a member of the staff of the Court who will be responsible, after notifying the State of enforcement, for meeting the sentenced person and hearing his or her views, without the presence of national authorities;
   (d) May, where appropriate, give the State of enforcement an opportunity to comment on the views expressed by the sentenced person under sub-rule 1 (c).
2. When a sentenced person is eligible for a prison programme or benefit available under the domestic law of the State of enforcement which may entail some activity outside the prison facility, the State of enforcement shall communicate that fact to the Presidency, together with any relevant information or observation, to enable the Court to exercise its supervisory function.

Rule 212
Information on location of the person for enforcement of fines, forfeitures or reparation measures

For the purpose of enforcement of fines and forfeiture measures and of reparation measures ordered by the Court, the Presidency may, at any time or at least 30 days before the scheduled completion of the sentence served by the sentenced person, request the State of enforcement to transmit to it the relevant information concerning the intention of that State to authorize the person to remain in its territory or the location where it intends to transfer the person.

Rule 213
Procedure for article 107, paragraph 3

With respect to article 107, paragraph 3, the procedure set out in rules 214 and 215 shall apply, as appropriate.

Section III
Limitation on the prosecution or punishment of other offences under article 108

Rule 214
Request to prosecute or enforce a sentence for prior conduct

1. For the application of article 108, when the State of enforcement wishes to prosecute or enforce a sentence against the sentenced person for any conduct engaged in prior to that person's transfer, it shall notify its intention to the Presidency and transmit to it the following documents:
   (a) A statement of the facts of the case and their legal characterization;
   (b) A copy of any applicable legal provisions, including those concerning the statute of limitation and the applicable penalties;
   (c) A copy of any sentence, warrant of arrest or other document having the same force, or of any other legal writ which the State intends to enforce;
   (d) A protocol containing views of the sentenced person obtained after the person has been informed sufficiently about the proceedings.
2. In the event of a request for extradition made by another State, the State of enforcement shall transmit the entire request to the Presidency with a protocol containing the views of the sentenced person obtained after informing the person sufficiently about the extradition request.
3. The Presidency may in all cases request any document or additional information from the State of enforcement or the State requesting extradition.
4. If the person was surrendered to the Court by a State other than the State of enforcement or the State seeking extradition, the Presidency shall consult with the State that surrendered the person and take into account any views expressed by that State.
5. Any information or documents transmitted to the Presidency under sub-rules 1 to 4 shall be transmitted to the Prosecutor, who may comment.
6. The Presidency may decide to conduct a hearing.

Rule 215
Decision on request to prosecute or enforce a sentence

1. The Presidency shall make a determination as soon as possible. This determination shall be notified to all those who have participated in the proceedings.
2. If the request submitted under sub-rules 1 or 2 of rule 214 concerns the enforcement of a sentence, the sentenced person may serve that sentence in the State designated by the Court to enforce the sentence pronounced by it or be extradited to a third State only after having served the full sentence pronounced by the Court, subject to the provisions of article 110.

3. The Presidency may authorize the temporary extradition of the sentenced person to a third State for prosecution only if it has obtained assurances which it deems to be sufficient that the sentenced person will be kept in custody in the third State and transferred back to the State responsible for enforcement of the sentence pronounced by the Court, after the prosecution.

Rule 216
Information on enforcement

The Presidency shall request the State of enforcement to inform it of any important event concerning the sentenced person, and of any prosecution of that person for events subsequent to his or her transfer.

Section IV
Enforcement of fines, forfeiture measures and reparation orders

Rule 217
Cooperation and measures for enforcement of fines, forfeiture or reparation orders

For the enforcement of fines, forfeiture or reparation orders, the Presidency shall, as appropriate, seek cooperation and measures for enforcement in accordance with Part 9, as well as transmit copies of relevant orders to any State with which the sentenced person appears to have direct connection by reason of either nationality, domicile or habitual residence or by virtue of the location of the sentenced person's assets and property or with which the victim has such connection. The Presidency shall, as appropriate, inform the State of any third-party claims or of the fact that no claim was presented by a person who received notification of any proceedings conducted pursuant to article 75.

Rule 218
Orders for forfeiture and reparations

1. In order to enable States to give effect to an order for forfeiture, the order shall specify:
   (a) The identity of the person against whom the order has been issued;
   (b) The proceeds, property and assets that have been ordered by the Court to be forfeited; and
   (c) That if the State Party is unable to give effect to the order for forfeiture in relation to the specified proceeds, property or assets, it shall take measures to recover the value of the same.
2. In the request for cooperation and measures for enforcement, the Court shall also provide available information as to the location of the proceeds, property and assets that are covered by the order for forfeiture.

3. In order to enable States to give effect to an order for reparations, the order shall specify:
   (a) The identity of the person against whom the order has been issued;
   (b) In respect of reparations of a financial nature, the identity of the victims to whom individual reparations have been granted, and, where the award for reparations shall be deposited with the Trust Fund, the particulars of the Trust Fund for the deposit of the award; and
   (c) The scope and nature of the reparations ordered by the Court, including, where applicable, the property and assets for which restitution has been ordered.
4. Where the Court awards reparations on an individual basis, a copy of the reparation order shall be transmitted to the victim concerned.

Rule 219
Non-modification of orders for reparation

The Presidency shall, when transmitting copies of orders for reparations to States Parties under rule 217, inform them that, in giving effect to an order for reparations, the national authorities shall not modify the reparations specified by the Court, the scope or the extent of any damage, loss or injury determined by the Court or the principles stated in the order, and shall facilitate the enforcement of such order.

Rule 220
Non-modification of judgements in which fines were imposed

When transmitting copies of judgements in which fines were imposed to States Parties for the purpose of enforcement in accordance with article 109 and rule 217, the Presidency shall inform them that in enforcing the fines imposed, national authorities shall not modify them.

Rule 221
Decision on disposition or allocation of property or assets

1. The Presidency shall, after having consulted, as appropriate, with the Prosecutor, the sentenced person, the victims or their legal representatives, the national authorities of the State of enforcement or any relevant third party, or representatives of the Trust Fund provided for in article 79, decide on all matters related to the disposition or allocation of property or assets realized through enforcement of an order of the Court.
2. In all cases, when the Presidency decides on the disposition or allocation of property or assets belonging to the sentenced person, it shall give priority to the enforcement of measures concerning reparations to victims.

Rule 222
Assistance for service or any other measure

The Presidency shall assist the State in the enforcement of fines, forfeiture or reparation orders, as requested, with the service of any relevant notification on the sentenced person or any other relevant persons, or the carrying out of any other measures necessary for the enforcement of the order under the procedure of the national law of the enforcement State.

Section V
Review concerning reduction of sentence under article 110

Rule 223
Criteria for review concerning reduction of sentence

In reviewing the question of reduction of sentence pursuant to article 110, paragraphs 3 and 5, the three judges of the Appeals Chamber shall take into account the criteria listed in article 110, paragraph 4 (a) and (b), and the following criteria:

(a) The conduct of the sentenced person while in detention, which shows a genuine dissociation from his or her crime;
(b) The prospect of the resocialization and successful resettlement of the sentenced person;
(c) Whether the early release of the sentenced person would give rise to significant social instability;
(d) Any significant action taken by the sentenced person for the benefit of the victims as well as any impact on the victims and their families as a result of the early release;
(e) Individual circumstances of the sentenced person, including a worsening state of physical or mental health or advanced age.

Rule 224
Procedure for review concerning reduction of sentence

1. For the application of article 110, paragraph 3, three judges of the Appeals Chamber appointed by that Chamber shall conduct a hearing, unless they decide otherwise in a particular case, for exceptional reasons. The hearing shall be conducted with the sentenced person, who may be assisted by his or her counsel, with interpretation, as may be required. Those three judges shall invite the Prosecutor, the State of enforcement of any penalty under article 77 or any reparation order pursuant to article 75 and, to the extent possible, the victims or their legal representatives who participated in the proceedings, to participate in the hearing or to submit written observations. Under exceptional circumstances, this hearing may be con-

ducted by way of a videoconference or in the State of enforcement by a judge delegated by the Appeals Chamber.

2. The same three judges shall communicate the decision and the reasons for it to all those who participated in the review proceedings as soon as possible.
3. For the application of article 110, paragraph 5, three judges of the Appeals Chamber appointed by that Chamber shall review the question of reduction of sentence every three years, unless it establishes a shorter interval in its decision taken pursuant to article 110, paragraph 3. In case of a significant change in circumstances, those three judges may permit the sentenced person to apply for a review within the three-year period or such shorter period as may have been set by the three judges.
4. For any review under article 110, paragraph 5, three judges of the Appeals Chamber appointed by that Chamber shall invite written representations from the sentenced person or his or her counsel, the Prosecutor, the State of enforcement of any penalty under article 77 and any reparation order pursuant to article 75 and, to the extent possible, the victims or their legal representatives who participated in the proceedings. The three judges may also decide to hold a hearing.
5. The decision and the reasons for it shall be communicated to all those who participated in the review proceedings as soon as possible.

Section VI
Escape

Rule 225
Measures under article 111 in the event of escape

1. If the sentenced person has escaped, the State of enforcement shall, as soon as possible, advise the Registrar by any medium capable of delivering a written record. The Presidency shall then proceed in accordance with Part 9.
2. However, if the State in which the sentenced person is located agrees to surrender him or her to the State of enforcement, pursuant to either international agreements or its national legislation, the State of enforcement shall so advise the Registrar in writing. The person shall be surrendered to the State of enforcement as soon as possible, if necessary in consultation with the Registrar, who shall provide all necessary assistance, including, if necessary, the presentation of requests for transit to the States concerned, in accordance with rule 207. The costs associated with the surrender of the sentenced person shall be borne by the Court if no State assumes responsibility for them.
3. If the sentenced person is surrendered to the Court pursuant to Part 9, the Court shall transfer him or her to the State of enforcement.

Nevertheless, the Presidency may, acting on its own motion or at the request of the Prosecutor or of the initial State of enforcement and in accordance with article 103 and rules 203 to 206, designate another State, including the State to the territory of which the sentenced person has fled.

4. In all cases, the entire period of detention in the territory of the State in which the sentenced person was in custody after his or her escape and, where sub-rule 3 is applicable, the period of detention at the seat of the Court following the surrender of the sentenced person from the State in which he or she was located shall be deducted from the sentence remaining to be served.

New York
13–31 March 2000
12–30 June 2000

APPENDIX 3

REPORT OF THE PREPARATORY COMMISSION FOR THE INTERNATIONAL CRIMINAL COURT

Addendum

Part II
Finalized draft text of the Elements of Crimes*

Explanatory note: The structure of the elements of the crimes of genocide, crimes against humanity and war crimes follows the structure of the corresponding provisions of articles 6, 7 and 8 of the Rome Statute. Some paragraphs of those articles of the Rome Statute list multiple crimes. In those instances, the elements of crimes appear in separate paragraphs which correspond to each of those crimes to facilitate the identification of the respective elements.

Elements of crimes

General introduction

1. Pursuant to article 9, the following Elements of Crimes shall assist the Court in the interpretation and application of articles 6, 7 and 8, consistent with the Statute. The provisions of the Statute, including article 21 and the general principles set out in Part 3, are applicable to the Elements of Crimes.
2. As stated in article 30, unless otherwise provided, a person shall be criminally responsible and liable for punishment for a crime within the jurisdiction of the Court only if the material elements are committed with intent and knowledge. Where no reference is made in the Elements of Crimes to a mental element for any particular conduct, consequence or circumstance listed, it is understood that the relevant mental element, i.e., intent, knowledge or both, set out in article 30 applies. Exceptions to the article 30 standard, based on the Statute, including applicable law under its relevant provisions, are indicated below.

---

* Incorporating document PCNICC/2000/INF/3/Add.2 and corrections to the Arabic, French and Spanish versions submitted by Governments pursuant to paragraph 16 of the Introduction.

3. Existence of intent and knowledge can be inferred from relevant facts and circumstances.
4. With respect to mental elements associated with elements involving value judgement, such as those using the terms "inhumane" or "severe", it is not necessary that the perpetrator personally completed a particular value judgement, unless otherwise indicated.
5. Grounds for excluding criminal responsibility or the absence thereof are generally not specified in the elements of crimes listed under each crime.[1]
6. The requirement of "unlawfulness" found in the Statute or in other parts of international law, in particular international humanitarian law, is generally not specified in the elements of crimes.
7. The elements of crimes are generally structured in accordance with the following principles:
   - As the elements of crimes focus on the conduct, consequences and circumstances associated with each crime, they are generally listed in that order;
   - When required, a particular mental element is listed after the affected conduct, consequence or circumstance;
   - Contextual circumstances are listed last.
8. As used in the Elements of Crimes, the term "perpetrator" is neutral as to guilt or innocence. The elements, including the appropriate mental elements, apply, *mutatis mutandis*, to all those whose criminal responsibility may fall under articles 25 and 28 of the Statute.
9. A particular conduct may constitute one or more crimes.
10. The use of short titles for the crimes has no legal effect.

Article 6
Genocide

Introduction

With respect to the last element listed for each crime:

- The term "in the context of" would include the initial acts in an emerging pattern;
- The term "manifest" is an objective qualification;
- Notwithstanding the normal requirement for a mental element provided for in article 30, and recognizing that knowledge of the circumstances will usually be addressed in proving genocidal intent, the appropriate requirement, if any, for a mental element regarding this circumstance will need to be decided by the Court on a case-by-case basis.

---

1. This paragraph is without prejudice to the obligation of the Prosecutor under article 54, paragraph 1, of the Statute.

Article 6 (a)
Genocide by killing

Elements

1. The perpetrator killed[2] one or more persons.
2. Such person or persons belonged to a particular national, ethnical, racial or religious group.
3. The perpetrator intended to destroy, in whole or in part, that national, ethnical, racial or religious group, as such.
4. The conduct took place in the context of a manifest pattern of similar conduct directed against that group or was conduct that could itself effect such destruction.

Article 6 (b)
Genocide by causing serious bodily or mental harm

Elements

1. The perpetrator caused serious bodily or mental harm to one or more persons.[3]
2. Such person or persons belonged to a particular national, ethnical, racial or religious group.
3. The perpetrator intended to destroy, in whole or in part, that national, ethnical, racial or religious group, as such.
4. The conduct took place in the context of a manifest pattern of similar conduct directed against that group or was conduct that could itself effect such destruction.

Article 6 (c)
Genocide by deliberately inflicting conditions of life calculated to bring about physical destruction

Elements

1. The perpetrator inflicted certain conditions of life upon one or more persons.
2. Such person or persons belonged to a particular national, ethnical, racial or religious group.
3. The perpetrator intended to destroy, in whole or in part, that national, ethnical, racial or religious group, as such.

---

2. The term "killed" is interchangeable with the term "caused death".
3. This conduct may include, but is not necessarily restricted to, acts of torture, rape, sexual violence or inhuman or degrading treatment.

4. The conditions of life were calculated to bring about the physical destruction of that group, in whole or in part.[4]
5. The conduct took place in the context of a manifest pattern of similar conduct directed against that group or was conduct that could itself effect such destruction.

Article 6 (d)
Genocide by imposing measures intended to prevent births

Elements

1. The perpetrator imposed certain measures upon one or more persons.
2. Such person or persons belonged to a particular national, ethnical, racial or religious group.
3. The perpetrator intended to destroy, in whole or in part, that national, ethnical, racial or religious group, as such.
4. The measures imposed were intended to prevent births within that group.
5. The conduct took place in the context of a manifest pattern of similar conduct directed against that group or was conduct that could itself effect such destruction.

Article 6 (e)
Genocide by forcibly transferring children

Elements

1. The perpetrator forcibly transferred one or more persons.[5]
2. Such person or persons belonged to a particular national, ethnical, racial or religious group.
3. The perpetrator intended to destroy, in whole or in part, that national, ethnical, racial or religious group, as such.
4. The transfer was from that group to another group.
5. The person or persons were under the age of 18 years.
6. The perpetrator knew, or should have known, that the person or persons were under the age of 18 years.
7. The conduct took place in the context of a manifest pattern of similar conduct directed against that group or was conduct that could itself effect such destruction.

---

4. The term "conditions of life" may include, but is not necessarily restricted to, deliberate deprivation of resources indispensable for survival, such as food or medical services, or systematic expulsion from homes.

5. The term "forcibly" is not restricted to physical force, but may include threat of force or coercion, such as that caused by fear of violence, duress, detention, psychological oppression or abuse of power, against such person or persons or another person, or by taking advantage of a coercive environment.

Article 7
Crimes against humanity

Introduction

1. Since article 7 pertains to international criminal law, its provisions, consistent with article 22, must be strictly construed, taking into account that crimes against humanity as defined in article 7 are among the most serious crimes of concern to the international community as a whole, warrant and entail individual criminal responsibility, and require conduct which is impermissible under generally applicable international law, as recognized by the principal legal systems of the world.
2. The last two elements for each crime against humanity describe the context in which the conduct must take place. These elements clarify the requisite participation in and knowledge of a widespread or systematic attack against a civilian population. However, the last element should not be interpreted as requiring proof that the perpetrator had knowledge of all characteristics of the attack or the precise details of the plan or policy of the State or organization. In the case of an emerging widespread or systematic attack against a civilian population, the intent clause of the last element indicates that this mental element is satisfied if the perpetrator intended to further such an attack.
3. "Attack directed against a civilian population" in these context elements is understood to mean a course of conduct involving the multiple commission of acts referred to in article 7, paragraph 1, of the Statute against any civilian population, pursuant to or in furtherance of a State or organizational policy to commit such attack. The acts need not constitute a military attack. It is understood that "policy to commit such attack" requires that the State or organization actively promote or encourage such an attack against a civilian population.[6]

Article 7 (1) (a)
Crime against humanity of murder

Elements

1. The perpetrator killed[7] one or more persons.

---

6. A policy which has a civilian population as the object of the attack would be implemented by State or organizational action. Such a policy may, in exceptional circumstances, be implemented by a deliberate failure to take action, which is consciously aimed at encouraging such attack. The existence of such a policy cannot be inferred solely from the absence of governmental or organizational action.

7. The term "killed" is interchangeable with the term "caused death". This footnote applies to all elements which use either of these concepts.

2. The conduct was committed as part of a widespread or systematic attack directed against a civilian population.
3. The perpetrator knew that the conduct was part of or intended the conduct to be part of a widespread or systematic attack against a civilian population.

Article 7 (1) (b)
Crime against humanity of extermination

Elements

1. The perpetrator killed[8] one or more persons, including by inflicting conditions of life calculated to bring about the destruction of part of a population.[9]
2. The conduct constituted, or took place as part of,[10] a mass killing of members of a civilian population.
3. The conduct was committed as part of a widespread or systematic attack directed against a civilian population.
4. The perpetrator knew that the conduct was part of or intended the conduct to be part of a widespread or systematic attack directed against a civilian population.

Article 7 (1) (c)
Crime against humanity of enslavement

Elements

1. The perpetrator exercised any or all of the powers attaching to the right of ownership over one or more persons, such as by purchasing, selling, lending or bartering such a person or persons, or by imposing on them a similar deprivation of liberty.[11]
2. The conduct was committed as part of a widespread or systematic attack directed against a civilian population.

---

8. The conduct could be committed by different methods of killing, either directly or indirectly.

9. The infliction of such conditions could include the deprivation of access to food and medicine.

10. The term "as part of" would include the initial conduct in a mass killing.

11. It is understood that such deprivation of liberty may, in some circumstances, include exacting forced labour or otherwise reducing a person to a servile status as defined in the Supplementary Convention on the Abolition of Slavery, the Slave Trade, and Institutions and Practices Similar to Slavery of 1956. It is also understood that the conduct described in this element includes trafficking in persons, in particular women and children.

3. The perpetrator knew that the conduct was part of or intended the conduct to be part of a widespread or systematic attack directed against a civilian population.

Article 7 (1) (d)
Crime against humanity of deportation or forcible transfer of population

Elements

1. The perpetrator deported or forcibly[12] transferred,[13] without grounds permitted under international law, one or more persons to another State or location, by expulsion or other coercive acts.
2. Such person or persons were lawfully present in the area from which they were so deported or transferred.
3. The perpetrator was aware of the factual circumstances that established the lawfulness of such presence.
4. The conduct was committed as part of a widespread or systematic attack directed against a civilian population.
5. The perpetrator knew that the conduct was part of or intended the conduct to be part of a widespread or systematic attack directed against a civilian population.

Article 7 (1) (e)
Crime against humanity of imprisonment or other severe deprivation of physical liberty

Elements

1. The perpetrator imprisoned one or more persons or otherwise severely deprived one or more persons of physical liberty.
2. The gravity of the conduct was such that it was in violation of fundamental rules of international law.
3. The perpetrator was aware of the factual circumstances that established the gravity of the conduct.
4. The conduct was committed as part of a widespread or systematic attack directed against a civilian population.
5. The perpetrator knew that the conduct was part of or intended the conduct to be part of a widespread or systematic attack directed against a civilian population.

---

12. The term "forcibly" is not restricted to physical force, but may include threat of force or coercion, such as that caused by fear of violence, duress, detention, psychological oppression or abuse of power against such person or persons or another person, or by taking advantage of a coercive environment.

13. "Deported or forcibly transferred" is interchangeable with "forcibly displaced".

Article 7 (1) (f)
Crime against humanity of torture[14]

Elements

1. The perpetrator inflicted severe physical or mental pain or suffering upon one or more persons.
2. Such person or persons were in the custody or under the control of the perpetrator.
3. Such pain or suffering did not arise only from, and was not inherent in or incidental to, lawful sanctions.
4. The conduct was committed as part of a widespread or systematic attack directed against a civilian population.
5. The perpetrator knew that the conduct was part of or intended the conduct to be part of a widespread or systematic attack directed against a civilian population.

Article 7 (1) (g)-1
Crime against humanity of rape

Elements

1. The perpetrator invaded[15] the body of a person by conduct resulting in penetration, however slight, of any part of the body of the victim or of the perpetrator with a sexual organ, or of the anal or genital opening of the victim with any object or any other part of the body.
2. The invasion was committed by force, or by threat of force or coercion, such as that caused by fear of violence, duress, detention, psychological oppression or abuse of power, against such person or another person, or by taking advantage of a coercive environment, or the invasion was committed against a person incapable of giving genuine consent.[16]
3. The conduct was committed as part of a widespread or systematic attack directed against a civilian population.
4. The perpetrator knew that the conduct was part of or intended the conduct to be part of a widespread or systematic attack directed against a civilian population.

---

14. It is understood that no specific purpose need be proved for this crime.

15. The concept of "invasion" is intended to be broad enough to be gender-neutral.

16. It is understood that a person may be incapable of giving genuine consent if affected by natural, induced or age-related incapacity. This footnote also applies to the corresponding elements of article 7 (1) (g)-3, 5 and 6.

Article 7 (1) (g)-2
Crime against humanity of sexual slavery[17]

Elements

1. The perpetrator exercised any or all of the powers attaching to the right of ownership over one or more persons, such as by purchasing, selling, lending or bartering such a person or persons, or by imposing on them a similar deprivation of liberty.[18]
2. The perpetrator caused such person or persons to engage in one or more acts of a sexual nature.
3. The conduct was committed as part of a widespread or systematic attack directed against a civilian population.
4. The perpetrator knew that the conduct was part of or intended the conduct to be part of a widespread or systematic attack directed against a civilian population.

Article 7 (1) (g)-3
Crime against humanity of enforced prostitution

Elements

1. The perpetrator caused one or more persons to engage in one or more acts of a sexual nature by force, or by threat of force or coercion, such as that caused by fear of violence, duress, detention, psychological oppression or abuse of power, against such person or persons or another person, or by taking advantage of a coercive environment or such person's or persons' incapacity to give genuine consent.
2. The perpetrator or another person obtained or expected to obtain pecuniary or other advantage in exchange for or in connection with the acts of a sexual nature.
3. The conduct was committed as part of a widespread or systematic attack directed against a civilian population.

---

17. Given the complex nature of this crime, it is recognized that its commission could involve more than one perpetrator as a part of a common criminal purpose.

18. It is understood that such deprivation of liberty may, in some circumstances, include exacting forced labour or otherwise reducing a person to a servile status as defined in the Supplementary Convention on the Abolition of Slavery, the Slave Trade, and Institutions and Practices Similar to Slavery of 1956. It is also understood that the conduct described in this element includes trafficking in persons, in particular women and children.

4. The perpetrator knew that the conduct was part of or intended the conduct to be part of a widespread or systematic attack directed against a civilian population.

Article 7 (1) (g)-4
Crime against humanity of forced pregnancy

Elements

1. The perpetrator confined one or more women forcibly made pregnant, with the intent of affecting the ethnic composition of any population or carrying out other grave violations of international law.
2. The conduct was committed as part of a widespread or systematic attack directed against a civilian population.
3. The perpetrator knew that the conduct was part of or intended the conduct to be part of a widespread or systematic attack directed against a civilian population.

Article 7 (1) (g)-5
Crime against humanity of enforced sterilization

Elements

1. The perpetrator deprived one or more persons of biological reproductive capacity.[19]
2. The conduct was neither justified by the medical or hospital treatment of the person or persons concerned nor carried out with their genuine consent.[20]
3. The conduct was committed as part of a widespread or systematic attack directed against a civilian population.
4. The perpetrator knew that the conduct was part of or intended the conduct to be part of a widespread or systematic attack directed against a civilian population.

Article 7 (1) (g)-6
Crime against humanity of sexual violence

Elements

1. The perpetrator committed an act of a sexual nature against one or more persons or caused such person or persons to engage in an act of a sexual

19. The deprivation is not intended to include birth-control measures which have a non-permanent effect in practice.

20. It is understood that "genuine consent" does not include consent obtained through deception.

nature by force, or by threat of force or coercion, such as that caused by fear of violence, duress, detention, psychological oppression or abuse of power, against such person or persons or another person, or by taking advantage of a coercive environment or such person's or persons' incapacity to give genuine consent.

2. Such conduct was of a gravity comparable to the other offences in article 7, paragraph 1 (g), of the Statute.
3. The perpetrator was aware of the factual circumstances that established the gravity of the conduct.
4. The conduct was committed as part of a widespread or systematic attack directed against a civilian population.
5. The perpetrator knew that the conduct was part of or intended the conduct to be part of a widespread or systematic attack directed against a civilian population.

Article 7 (1) (h)
Crime against humanity of persecution

Elements

1. The perpetrator severely deprived, contrary to international law,[21] one or more persons of fundamental rights.
2. The perpetrator targeted such person or persons by reason of the identity of a group or collectivity or targeted the group or collectivity as such.
3. Such targeting was based on political, racial, national, ethnic, cultural, religious, gender as defined in article 7, paragraph 3, of the Statute, or other grounds that are universally recognized as impermissible under international law.
4. The conduct was committed in connection with any act referred to in article 7, paragraph 1, of the Statute or any crime within the jurisdiction of the Court.[22]
5. The conduct was committed as part of a widespread or systematic attack directed against a civilian population.
6. The perpetrator knew that the conduct was part of or intended the conduct to be part of a widespread or systematic attack directed against a civilian population.

---

21. This requirement is without prejudice to paragraph 6 of the General Introduction to the Elements of Crimes.

22. It is understood that no additional mental element is necessary for this element other than that inherent in element 6.

Article 7 (1) (i)
Crime against humanity of enforced disappearance of persons[23] [24]

Elements

1. The perpetrator:
   (a) Arrested, detained[25] [26] or abducted one or more persons; or
   (b) Refused to acknowledge the arrest, detention or abduction, or to give information on the fate or whereabouts of such person or persons.
2. (a) Such arrest, detention or abduction was followed or accompanied by a refusal to acknowledge that deprivation of freedom or to give information on the fate or whereabouts of such person or persons; or
   (b) Such refusal was preceded or accompanied by that deprivation of freedom.
3. The perpetrator was aware that:[27]
   (a) Such arrest, detention or abduction would be followed in the ordinary course of events by a refusal to acknowledge that deprivation of freedom or to give information on the fate or whereabouts of such person or persons;[28] or
   (b) Such refusal was preceded or accompanied by that deprivation of freedom.
4. Such arrest, detention or abduction was carried out by, or with the authorization, support or acquiescence of, a State or a political organization.
5. Such refusal to acknowledge that deprivation of freedom or to give information on the fate or whereabouts of such person or persons was carried out by, or with the authorization or support of, such State or political organization.
6. The perpetrator intended to remove such person or persons from the protection of the law for a prolonged period of time.

---

23. Given the complex nature of this crime, it is recognized that its commission will normally involve more than one perpetrator as a part of a common criminal purpose.

24. This crime falls under the jurisdiction of the Court only if the attack referred to in elements 7 and 8 occurs after the entry into force of the Statute.

25. The word "detained" would include a perpetrator who maintained an existing detention.

26. It is understood that under certain circumstances an arrest or detention may have been lawful.

27. This element, inserted because of the complexity of this crime, is without prejudice to the General Introduction to the Elements of Crimes.

28. It is understood that, in the case of a perpetrator who maintained an existing detention, this element would be satisfied if the perpetrator was aware that such a refusal had already taken place.

7. The conduct was committed as part of a widespread or systematic attack directed against a civilian population.
8. The perpetrator knew that the conduct was part of or intended the conduct to be part of a widespread or systematic attack directed against a civilian population.

Article 7 (1) (j)
Crime against humanity of apartheid

Elements

1. The perpetrator committed an inhumane act against one or more persons.
2. Such act was an act referred to in article 7, paragraph 1, of the Statute, or was an act of a character similar to any of those acts.[29]
3. The perpetrator was aware of the factual circumstances that established the character of the act.
4. The conduct was committed in the context of an institutionalized regime of systematic oppression and domination by one racial group over any other racial group or groups.
5. The perpetrator intended to maintain such regime by that conduct.
6. The conduct was committed as part of a widespread or systematic attack directed against a civilian population.
7. The perpetrator knew that the conduct was part of or intended the conduct to be part of a widespread or systematic attack directed against a civilian population.

Article 7 (1) (k)
Crime against humanity of other inhumane acts

Elements

1. The perpetrator inflicted great suffering, or serious injury to body or to mental or physical health, by means of an inhumane act.
2. Such act was of a character similar to any other act referred to in article 7, paragraph 1, of the Statute.[30]
3. The perpetrator was aware of the factual circumstances that established the character of the act.
4. The conduct was committed as part of a widespread or systematic attack directed against a civilian population.
5. The perpetrator knew that the conduct was part of or intended the conduct to be part of a widespread or systematic attack directed against a civilian population.

---

29. It is understood that "character" refers to the nature and gravity of the act.
30. It is understood that "character" refers to the nature and gravity of the act.

Article 8
War crimes

Introduction

The elements for war crimes under article 8, paragraph 2 (c) and (e), are subject to the limitations addressed in article 8, paragraph 2 (d) and (f), which are not elements of crimes.

The elements for war crimes under article 8, paragraph 2, of the Statute shall be interpreted within the established framework of the international law of armed conflict including, as appropriate, the international law of armed conflict applicable to armed conflict at sea.

With respect to the last two elements listed for each crime:

- There is no requirement for a legal evaluation by the perpetrator as to the existence of an armed conflict or its character as international or non-international;
- In that context there is no requirement for awareness by the perpetrator of the facts that established the character of the conflict as international or non-international;
- There is only a requirement for the awareness of the factual circumstances that established the existence of an armed conflict that is implicit in the terms "took place in the context of and was associated with".

Article 8 (2) (a)
Article 8 (2) (a) (i)
War crime of wilful killing

Elements

1. The perpetrator killed one or more persons.[31]
2. Such person or persons were protected under one or more of the Geneva Conventions of 1949.
3. The perpetrator was aware of the factual circumstances that established that protected status.[32] [33]

---

31. The term "killed" is interchangeable with the term "caused death". This footnote applies to all elements which use either of these concepts.

32. This mental element recognizes the interplay between articles 30 and 32. This footnote also applies to the corresponding element in each crime under article 8 (2) (a), and to the element in other crimes in article 8 (2) concerning the awareness of factual circumstances that establish the status of persons or property protected under the relevant international law of armed conflict.

33. With respect to nationality, it is understood that the perpetrator needs only to know that the victim belonged to an adverse party to the conflict. This footnote also applies to the corresponding element in each crime under article 8 (2) (a).

4. The conduct took place in the context of and was associated with an international armed conflict.[34]
5. The perpetrator was aware of factual circumstances that established the existence of an armed conflict.

Article 8 (2) (a) (ii)-1
War crime of torture

Elements[35]

1. The perpetrator inflicted severe physical or mental pain or suffering upon one or more persons.
2. The perpetrator inflicted the pain or suffering for such purposes as: obtaining information or a confession, punishment, intimidation or coercion or for any reason based on discrimination of any kind.
3. Such person or persons were protected under one or more of the Geneva Conventions of 1949.
4. The perpetrator was aware of the factual circumstances that established that protected status.
5. The conduct took place in the context of and was associated with an international armed conflict.
6. The perpetrator was aware of factual circumstances that established the existence of an armed conflict.

Article 8 (2) (a) (ii)-2
War crime of inhuman treatment

Elements

1. The perpetrator inflicted severe physical or mental pain or suffering upon one or more persons.
2. Such person or persons were protected under one or more of the Geneva Conventions of 1949.
3. The perpetrator was aware of the factual circumstances that established that protected status.
4. The conduct took place in the context of and was associated with an international armed conflict.

---

34. The term "international armed conflict" includes military occupation. This footnote also applies to the corresponding element in each crime under article 8 (2) (a).

35. As element 3 requires that all victims must be "protected persons" under one or more of the Geneva Conventions of 1949, these elements do not include the custody or control requirement found in the elements of article 7 (1) (e).

5. The perpetrator was aware of factual circumstances that established the existence of an armed conflict.

Article 8 (2) (a) (ii)-3
War crime of biological experiments

Elements

1. The perpetrator subjected one or more persons to a particular biological experiment.
2. The experiment seriously endangered the physical or mental health or integrity of such person or persons.
3. The intent of the experiment was non-therapeutic and it was neither justified by medical reasons nor carried out in such person's or persons' interest.
4. Such person or persons were protected under one or more of the Geneva Conventions of 1949.
5. The perpetrator was aware of the factual circumstances that established that protected status.
6. The conduct took place in the context of and was associated with an international armed conflict.
7. The perpetrator was aware of factual circumstances that established the existence of an armed conflict.

Article 8 (2) (a) (iii)
War crime of wilfully causing great suffering

Elements

1. The perpetrator caused great physical or mental pain or suffering to, or serious injury to body or health of, one or more persons.
2. Such person or persons were protected under one or more of the Geneva Conventions of 1949.
3. The perpetrator was aware of the factual circumstances that established that protected status.
4. The conduct took place in the context of and was associated with an international armed conflict.
5. The perpetrator was aware of factual circumstances that established the existence of an armed conflict.

Article 8 (2) (a) (iv)
War crime of destruction and appropriation of property

Elements

1. The perpetrator destroyed or appropriated certain property.
2. The destruction or appropriation was not justified by military necessity.

3. The destruction or appropriation was extensive and carried out wantonly.
4. Such property was protected under one or more of the Geneva Conventions of 1949.
5. The perpetrator was aware of the factual circumstances that established that protected status.
6. The conduct took place in the context of and was associated with an international armed conflict.
7. The perpetrator was aware of factual circumstances that established the existence of an armed conflict.

Article 8 (2) (a) (v)
War crime of compelling service in hostile forces

Elements

1. The perpetrator coerced one or more persons, by act or threat, to take part in military operations against that person's own country or forces or otherwise serve in the forces of a hostile power.
2. Such person or persons were protected under one or more of the Geneva Conventions of 1949.
3. The perpetrator was aware of the factual circumstances that established that protected status.
4. The conduct took place in the context of and was associated with an international armed conflict.
5. The perpetrator was aware of factual circumstances that established the existence of an armed conflict.

Article 8 (2) (a) (vi)
War crime of denying a fair trial

Elements

1. The perpetrator deprived one or more persons of a fair and regular trial by denying judicial guarantees as defined, in particular, in the third and the fourth Geneva Conventions of 1949.
2. Such person or persons were protected under one or more of the Geneva Conventions of 1949.
3. The perpetrator was aware of the factual circumstances that established that protected status.
4. The conduct took place in the context of and was associated with an international armed conflict.
5. The perpetrator was aware of factual circumstances that established the existence of an armed conflict.

Article 8 (2) (a) (vii)-1
War crime of unlawful deportation and transfer

Elements

1. The perpetrator deported or transferred one or more persons to another State or to another location.
2. Such person or persons were protected under one or more of the Geneva Conventions of 1949.
3. The perpetrator was aware of the factual circumstances that established that protected status.
4. The conduct took place in the context of and was associated with an international armed conflict.
5. The perpetrator was aware of factual circumstances that established the existence of an armed conflict.

Article 8 (2) (a) (vii)-2
War crime of unlawful confinement

Elements

1. The perpetrator confined or continued to confine one or more persons to a certain location.
2. Such person or persons were protected under one or more of the Geneva Conventions of 1949.
3. The perpetrator was aware of the factual circumstances that established that protected status.
4. The conduct took place in the context of and was associated with an international armed conflict.
5. The perpetrator was aware of factual circumstances that established the existence of an armed conflict.

Article 8 (2) (a) (viii)
War crime of taking hostages

Elements

1. The perpetrator seized, detained or otherwise held hostage one or more persons.
2. The perpetrator threatened to kill, injure or continue to detain such person or persons.
3. The perpetrator intended to compel a State, an international organization, a natural or legal person or a group of persons to act or refrain from act-

ing as an explicit or implicit condition for the safety or the release of such person or persons.

4. Such person or persons were protected under one or more of the Geneva Conventions of 1949.
5. The perpetrator was aware of the factual circumstances that established that protected status.
6. The conduct took place in the context of and was associated with an international armed conflict.
7. The perpetrator was aware of factual circumstances that established the existence of an armed conflict.

Article 8 (2) (b)
Article 8 (2) (b) (i)
War crime of attacking civilians

Elements

1. The perpetrator directed an attack.
2. The object of the attack was a civilian population as such or individual civilians not taking direct part in hostilities.
3. The perpetrator intended the civilian population as such or individual civilians not taking direct part in hostilities to be the object of the attack.
4. The conduct took place in the context of and was associated with an international armed conflict.
5. The perpetrator was aware of factual circumstances that established the existence of an armed conflict.

Article 8 (2) (b) (ii)
War crime of attacking civilian objects

Elements

1. The perpetrator directed an attack.
2. The object of the attack was civilian objects, that is, objects which are not military objectives.
3. The perpetrator intended such civilian objects to be the object of the attack.
4. The conduct took place in the context of and was associated with an international armed conflict.
5. The perpetrator was aware of factual circumstances that established the existence of an armed conflict.

Article 8 (2) (b) (iii)
War crime of attacking personnel or objects involved in a humanitarian assistance or peacekeeping mission

Elements

1. The perpetrator directed an attack.
2. The object of the attack was personnel, installations, material, units or vehicles involved in a humanitarian assistance or peacekeeping mission in accordance with the Charter of the United Nations.
3. The perpetrator intended such personnel, installations, material, units or vehicles so involved to be the object of the attack.
4. Such personnel, installations, material, units or vehicles were entitled to that protection given to civilians or civilian objects under the international law of armed conflict.
5. The perpetrator was aware of the factual circumstances that established that protection.
6. The conduct took place in the context of and was associated with an international armed conflict.
7. The perpetrator was aware of factual circumstances that established the existence of an armed conflict.

Article 8 (2) (b) (iv)
War crime of excessive incidental death, injury, or damage

Elements

1. The perpetrator launched an attack.
2. The attack was such that it would cause incidental death or injury to civilians or damage to civilian objects or widespread, long-term and severe damage to the natural environment and that such death, injury or damage would be of such an extent as to be clearly excessive in relation to the concrete and direct overall military advantage anticipated.[36]
3. The perpetrator knew that the attack would cause incidental death or injury to civilians or damage to civilian objects or widespread, long-term

---

36. The expression "concrete and direct overall military advantage" refers to a military advantage that is foreseeable by the perpetrator at the relevant time. Such advantage may or may not be temporally or geographically related to the object of the attack. The fact that this crime admits the possibility of lawful incidental injury and collateral damage does not in any way justify any violation of the law applicable in armed conflict. It does not address justifications for war or other rules related to *jus ad bellum*. It reflects the proportionality requirement inherent in determining the legality of any military activity undertaken in the context of an armed conflict.

and severe damage to the natural environment and that such death, injury or damage would be of such an extent as to be clearly excessive in relation to the concrete and direct overall military advantage anticipated.[37]

4. The conduct took place in the context of and was associated with an international armed conflict.
5. The perpetrator was aware of factual circumstances that established the existence of an armed conflict.

Article 8 (2) (b) (v)
War crime of attacking undefended places[38]

Elements

1. The perpetrator attacked one or more towns, villages, dwellings or buildings.
2. Such towns, villages, dwellings or buildings were open for unresisted occupation.
3. Such towns, villages, dwellings or buildings did not constitute military objectives.
4. The conduct took place in the context of and was associated with an international armed conflict.
5. The perpetrator was aware of factual circumstances that established the existence of an armed conflict.

Article 8 (2) (b) (vi)
War crime of killing or wounding a person hors de combat

Elements

1. The perpetrator killed or injured one or more persons.
2. Such person or persons were *hors de combat*.
3. The perpetrator was aware of the factual circumstances that established this status.
4. The conduct took place in the context of and was associated with an international armed conflict.
5. The perpetrator was aware of factual circumstances that established the existence of an armed conflict.

---

37. As opposed to the general rule set forth in paragraph 4 of the General Introduction, this knowledge element requires that the perpetrator make the value judgement as described therein. An evaluation of that value judgement must be based on the requisite information available to the perpetrator at the time.

38. The presence in the locality of persons specially protected under the Geneva Conventions of 1949 or of police forces retained for the sole purpose of maintaining law and order does not by itself render the locality a military objective.

Article 8 (2) (b) (vii)-1
War crime of improper use of a flag of truce

Elements

1. The perpetrator used a flag of truce.
2. The perpetrator made such use in order to feign an intention to negotiate when there was no such intention on the part of the perpetrator.
3. The perpetrator knew or should have known of the prohibited nature of such use.[39]
4. The conduct resulted in death or serious personal injury.
5. The perpetrator knew that the conduct could result in death or serious personal injury.
6. The conduct took place in the context of and was associated with an international armed conflict.
7. The perpetrator was aware of factual circumstances that established the existence of an armed conflict.

Article 8 (2) (b) (vii)-2
War crime of improper use of a flag, insignia or uniform of the hostile party

Elements

1. The perpetrator used a flag, insignia or uniform of the hostile party.
2. The perpetrator made such use in a manner prohibited under the international law of armed conflict while engaged in an attack.
3. The perpetrator knew or should have known of the prohibited nature of such use.[40]
4. The conduct resulted in death or serious personal injury.
5. The perpetrator knew that the conduct could result in death or serious personal injury.
6. The conduct took place in the context of and was associated with an international armed conflict.
7. The perpetrator was aware of factual circumstances that established the existence of an armed conflict.

---

39. This mental element recognizes the interplay between article 30 and article 32. The term "prohibited nature" denotes illegality.

40. This mental element recognizes the interplay between article 30 and article 32. The term "prohibited nature" denotes illegality.

Article 8 (2) (b) (vii)-3
War crime of improper use of a flag, insignia or uniform of the United Nations

Elements

1. The perpetrator used a flag, insignia or uniform of the United Nations.
2. The perpetrator made such use in a manner prohibited under the international law of armed conflict.
3. The perpetrator knew of the prohibited nature of such use.[41]
4. The conduct resulted in death or serious personal injury.
5. The perpetrator knew that the conduct could result in death or serious personal injury.
6. The conduct took place in the context of and was associated with an international armed conflict.
7. The perpetrator was aware of factual circumstances that established the existence of an armed conflict.

Article 8 (2) (b) (vii)-4
War crime of improper use of the distinctive emblems of the Geneva Conventions

Elements

1. The perpetrator used the distinctive emblems of the Geneva Conventions.
2. The perpetrator made such use for combatant purposes[42] in a manner prohibited under the international law of armed conflict.
3. The perpetrator knew or should have known of the prohibited nature of such use.[43]
4. The conduct resulted in death or serious personal injury.
5. The perpetrator knew that the conduct could result in death or serious personal injury.
6. The conduct took place in the context of and was associated with an international armed conflict.
7. The perpetrator was aware of factual circumstances that established the existence of an armed conflict.

---

41. This mental element recognizes the interplay between article 30 and article 32. The "should have known" test required in the other offences found in article 8 (2) (b) (vii) is not applicable here because of the variable and regulatory nature of the relevant prohibitions.

42. "Combatant purposes" in these circumstances means purposes directly related to hostilities and not including medical, religious or similar activities.

43. This mental element recognizes the interplay between article 30 and article 32. The term "prohibited nature" denotes illegality.

Article 8 (2) (b) (viii)
The transfer, directly or indirectly, by the Occupying Power of parts of its own civilian population into the territory it occupies, or the deportation or transfer of all or parts of the population of the occupied territory within or outside this territory

Elements

1. The perpetrator:
   (a) Transferred,[44] directly or indirectly, parts of its own population into the territory it occupies; or
   (b) Deported or transferred all or parts of the population of the occupied territory within or outside this territory.
2. The conduct took place in the context of and was associated with an international armed conflict.
3. The perpetrator was aware of factual circumstances that established the existence of an armed conflict.

Article 8 (2) (b) (ix)
War crime of attacking protected objects[45]

Elements

1. The perpetrator directed an attack.
2. The object of the attack was one or more buildings dedicated to religion, education, art, science or charitable purposes, historic monuments, hospitals or places where the sick and wounded are collected, which were not military objectives.
3. The perpetrator intended such building or buildings dedicated to religion, education, art, science or charitable purposes, historic monuments, hospitals or places where the sick and wounded are collected, which were not military objectives, to be the object of the attack.
4. The conduct took place in the context of and was associated with an international armed conflict.
5. The perpetrator was aware of factual circumstances that established the existence of an armed conflict.

---

44. The term "transfer" needs to be interpreted in accordance with the relevant provisions of international humanitarian law.

45. The presence in the locality of persons specially protected under the Geneva Conventions of 1949 or of police forces retained for the sole purpose of maintaining law and order does not by itself render the locality a military objective.

Article 8 (2) (b) (x)-1
War crime of mutilation

Elements

1. The perpetrator subjected one or more persons to mutilation, in particular by permanently disfiguring the person or persons, or by permanently disabling or removing an organ or appendage.
2. The conduct caused death or seriously endangered the physical or mental health of such person or persons.
3. The conduct was neither justified by the medical, dental or hospital treatment of the person or persons concerned nor carried out in such person's or persons' interest.[46]
4. Such person or persons were in the power of an adverse party.
5. The conduct took place in the context of and was associated with an international armed conflict.
6. The perpetrator was aware of factual circumstances that established the existence of an armed conflict.

Article 8 (2) (b) (x)-2
War crime of medical or scientific experiments

Elements

1. The perpetrator subjected one or more persons to a medical or scientific experiment.
2. The experiment caused death or seriously endangered the physical or mental health or integrity of such person or persons.
3. The conduct was neither justified by the medical, dental or hospital treatment of such person or persons concerned nor carried out in such person's or persons' interest.
4. Such person or persons were in the power of an adverse party.
5. The conduct took place in the context of and was associated with an international armed conflict.
6. The perpetrator was aware of factual circumstances that established the existence of an armed conflict.

---

46. Consent is not a defence to this crime. The crime prohibits any medical procedure which is not indicated by the state of health of the person concerned and which is not consistent with generally accepted medical standards which would be applied under similar medical circumstances to persons who are nationals of the party conducting the procedure and who are in no way deprived of liberty. This footnote also applies to the same element for article 8 (2) (b) (x)-2.

Article 8 (2) (b) (xi)
War crime of treacherously killing or wounding

Elements

1. The perpetrator invited the confidence or belief of one or more persons that they were entitled to, or were obliged to accord, protection under rules of international law applicable in armed conflict.
2. The perpetrator intended to betray that confidence or belief.
3. The perpetrator killed or injured such person or persons.
4. The perpetrator made use of that confidence or belief in killing or injuring such person or persons.
5. Such person or persons belonged to an adverse party.
6. The conduct took place in the context of and was associated with an international armed conflict.
7. The perpetrator was aware of factual circumstances that established the existence of an armed conflict.

Article 8 (2) (b) (xii)
War crime of denying quarter

Elements

1. The perpetrator declared or ordered that there shall be no survivors.
2. Such declaration or order was given in order to threaten an adversary or to conduct hostilities on the basis that there shall be no survivors.
3. The perpetrator was in a position of effective command or control over the subordinate forces to which the declaration or order was directed.
4. The conduct took place in the context of and was associated with an international armed conflict.
5. The perpetrator was aware of factual circumstances that established the existence of an armed conflict.

Article 8 (2) (b) (xiii)
War crime of destroying or seizing the enemy's property

Elements

1. The perpetrator destroyed or seized certain property.
2. Such property was property of a hostile party.
3. Such property was protected from that destruction or seizure under the international law of armed conflict.
4. The perpetrator was aware of the factual circumstances that established the status of the property.
5. The destruction or seizure was not justified by military necessity.

6. The conduct took place in the context of and was associated with an international armed conflict.
7. The perpetrator was aware of factual circumstances that established the existence of an armed conflict.

Article 8 (2) (b) (xiv)
War crime of depriving the nationals of the hostile power of rights or actions

Elements

1. The perpetrator effected the abolition, suspension or termination of admissibility in a court of law of certain rights or actions.
2. The abolition, suspension or termination was directed at the nationals of a hostile party.
3. The perpetrator intended the abolition, suspension or termination to be directed at the nationals of a hostile party.
4. The conduct took place in the context of and was associated with an international armed conflict.
5. The perpetrator was aware of factual circumstances that established the existence of an armed conflict.

Article 8 (2) (b) (xv)
War crime of compelling participation in military operations

Elements

1. The perpetrator coerced one or more persons by act or threat to take part in military operations against that person's own country or forces.
2. Such person or persons were nationals of a hostile party.
3. The conduct took place in the context of and was associated with an international armed conflict.
4. The perpetrator was aware of factual circumstances that established the existence of an armed conflict.

Article 8 (2) (b) (xvi)
War crime of pillaging

Elements

1. The perpetrator appropriated certain property.
2. The perpetrator intended to deprive the owner of the property and to appropriate it for private or personal use.[47]

---

47. As indicated by the use of the term "private or personal use", appropriations justified by military necessity cannot constitute the crime of pillaging.

3. The appropriation was without the consent of the owner.
4. The conduct took place in the context of and was associated with an international armed conflict.
5. The perpetrator was aware of factual circumstances that established the existence of an armed conflict.

Article 8 (2) (b) (xvii)
War crime of employing poison or poisoned weapons

Elements

1. The perpetrator employed a substance or a weapon that releases a substance as a result of its employment.
2. The substance was such that it causes death or serious damage to health in the ordinary course of events, through its toxic properties.
3. The conduct took place in the context of and was associated with an international armed conflict.
4. The perpetrator was aware of factual circumstances that established the existence of an armed conflict.

Article 8 (2) (b) (xviii)
War crime of employing prohibited gases, liquids, materials or devices

Elements

1. The perpetrator employed a gas or other analogous substance or device.
2. The gas, substance or device was such that it causes death or serious damage to health in the ordinary course of events, through its asphyxiating or toxic properties.[48]
3. The conduct took place in the context of and was associated with an international armed conflict.
4. The perpetrator was aware of factual circumstances that established the existence of an armed conflict.

Article 8 (2) (b) (xix)
War crime of employing prohibited bullets

Elements

1. The perpetrator employed certain bullets.
2. The bullets were such that their use violates the international law of armed conflict because they expand or flatten easily in the human body.

---

48. Nothing in this element shall be interpreted as limiting or prejudicing in any way existing or developing rules of international law with respect to the development, production, stockpiling and use of chemical weapons.

3. The perpetrator was aware that the nature of the bullets was such that their employment would uselessly aggravate suffering or the wounding effect.
4. The conduct took place in the context of and was associated with an international armed conflict.
5. The perpetrator was aware of factual circumstances that established the existence of an armed conflict.

Article 8 (2) (b) (xx)
War crime of employing weapons, projectiles or materials or methods of warfare listed in the Annex to the Statute

Elements
[Elements will have to be drafted once weapons, projectiles or material or methods of warfare have been included in an annex to the Statute.]

Article 8 (2) (b) (xxi)
War crime of outrages upon personal dignity

Elements

1. The perpetrator humiliated, degraded or otherwise violated the dignity of one or more persons.[49]
2. The severity of the humiliation, degradation or other violation was of such degree as to be generally recognized as an outrage upon personal dignity.
3. The conduct took place in the context of and was associated with an international armed conflict.
4. The perpetrator was aware of factual circumstances that established the existence of an armed conflict.

Article 8 (2) (b) (xxii)-1
War crime of rape

Elements

1. The perpetrator invaded[50] the body of a person by conduct resulting in penetration, however slight, of any part of the body of the victim or of

49. For this crime, "persons" can include dead persons. It is understood that the victim need not personally be aware of the existence of the humiliation or degradation or other violation. This element takes into account relevant aspects of the cultural background of the victim.

50. The concept of "invasion" is intended to be broad enough to be gender-neutral.

the perpetrator with a sexual organ, or of the anal or genital opening of the victim with any object or any other part of the body.

2. The invasion was committed by force, or by threat of force or coercion, such as that caused by fear of violence, duress, detention, psychological oppression or abuse of power, against such person or another person, or by taking advantage of a coercive environment, or the invasion was committed against a person incapable of giving genuine consent.[51]
3. The conduct took place in the context of and was associated with an international armed conflict.
4. The perpetrator was aware of factual circumstances that established the existence of an armed conflict.

Article 8 (2) (b) (xxii)-2
War crime of sexual slavery[52]

Elements

1. The perpetrator exercised any or all of the powers attaching to the right of ownership over one or more persons, such as by purchasing, selling, lending or bartering such a person or persons, or by imposing on them a similar deprivation of liberty.[53]
2. The perpetrator caused such person or persons to engage in one or more acts of a sexual nature.
3. The conduct took place in the context of and was associated with an international armed conflict.
4. The perpetrator was aware of factual circumstances that established the existence of an armed conflict.

---

51. It is understood that a person may be incapable of giving genuine consent if affected by natural, induced or age-related incapacity. This footnote also applies to the corresponding elements of article 8 (2) (b) (xxii)-3, 5 and 6.

52. Given the complex nature of this crime, it is recognized that its commission could involve more than one perpetrator as a part of a common criminal purpose.

53. It is understood that such deprivation of liberty may, in some circumstances, include exacting forced labour or otherwise reducing a person to servile status as defined in the Supplementary Convention on the Abolition of Slavery, the Slave Trade, and Institutions and Practices Similar to Slavery of 1956. It is also understood that the conduct described in this element includes trafficking in persons, in particular women and children.

Article 8 (2) (b) (xxii)-3
War crime of enforced prostitution

Elements

1. The perpetrator caused one or more persons to engage in one or more acts of a sexual nature by force, or by threat of force or coercion, such as that caused by fear of violence, duress, detention, psychological oppression or abuse of power, against such person or persons or another person, or by taking advantage of a coercive environment or such person's or persons' incapacity to give genuine consent.
2. The perpetrator or another person obtained or expected to obtain pecuniary or other advantage in exchange for or in connection with the acts of a sexual nature.
3. The conduct took place in the context of and was associated with an international armed conflict.
4. The perpetrator was aware of factual circumstances that established the existence of an armed conflict.

Article 8 (2) (b) (xxii)-4
War crime of forced pregnancy

Elements

1. The perpetrator confined one or more women forcibly made pregnant, with the intent of affecting the ethnic composition of any population or carrying out other grave violations of international law.
2. The conduct took place in the context of and was associated with an international armed conflict.
3. The perpetrator was aware of factual circumstances that established the existence of an armed conflict.

Article 8 (2) (b) (xxii)-5
War crime of enforced sterilization

Elements

1. The perpetrator deprived one or more persons of biological reproductive capacity.[54]
2. The conduct was neither justified by the medical or hospital treatment of the person or persons concerned nor carried out with their genuine consent.[55]

---

54. The deprivation is not intended to include birth-control measures which have a non-permanent effect in practice.

55. It is understood that "genuine consent" does not include consent obtained through deception.

3. The conduct took place in the context of and was associated with an international armed conflict.
4. The perpetrator was aware of factual circumstances that established the existence of an armed conflict.

Article 8 (2) (b) (xxii)-6
War crime of sexual violence

Elements

1. The perpetrator committed an act of a sexual nature against one or more persons or caused such person or persons to engage in an act of a sexual nature by force, or by threat of force or coercion, such as that caused by fear of violence, duress, detention, psychological oppression or abuse of power, against such person or persons or another person, or by taking advantage of a coercive environment or such person's or persons' incapacity to give genuine consent.
2. The conduct was of a gravity comparable to that of a grave breach of the Geneva Conventions.
3. The perpetrator was aware of the factual circumstances that established the gravity of the conduct.
4. The conduct took place in the context of and was associated with an international armed conflict.
5. The perpetrator was aware of factual circumstances that established the existence of an armed conflict.

Article 8 (2) (b) (xxiii)
War crime of using protected persons as shields

Elements

1. The perpetrator moved or otherwise took advantage of the location of one or more civilians or other persons protected under the international law of armed conflict.
2. The perpetrator intended to shield a military objective from attack or shield, favour or impede military operations.
3. The conduct took place in the context of and was associated with an international armed conflict.
4. The perpetrator was aware of factual circumstances that established the existence of an armed conflict.

Article 8 (2) (b) (xxiv)
War crime of attacking objects or persons using the distinctive emblems of the Geneva Conventions

Elements

1. The perpetrator attacked one or more persons, buildings, medical units or transports or other objects using, in conformity with international law, a distinctive emblem or other method of identification indicating protection under the Geneva Conventions.
2. The perpetrator intended such persons, buildings, units or transports or other objects so using such identification to be the object of the attack.
3. The conduct took place in the context of and was associated with an international armed conflict.
4. The perpetrator was aware of factual circumstances that established the existence of an armed conflict.

Article 8 (2) (b) (xxv)
War crime of starvation as a method of warfare

Elements

1. The perpetrator deprived civilians of objects indispensable to their survival.
2. The perpetrator intended to starve civilians as a method of warfare.
3. The conduct took place in the context of and was associated with an international armed conflict.
4. The perpetrator was aware of factual circumstances that established the existence of an armed conflict.

Article 8 (2) (b) (xxvi)
War crime of using, conscripting or enlisting children

Elements

1. The perpetrator conscripted or enlisted one or more persons into the national armed forces or used one or more persons to participate actively in hostilities.
2. Such person or persons were under the age of 15 years.
3. The perpetrator knew or should have known that such person or persons were under the age of 15 years.
4. The conduct took place in the context of and was associated with an international armed conflict.
5. The perpetrator was aware of factual circumstances that established the existence of an armed conflict.

Article 8 (2) (c)
Article 8 (2) (c) (i)-1
War crime of murder

Elements

1. The perpetrator killed one or more persons.
2. Such person or persons were either *hors de combat*, or were civilians, medical personnel, or religious personnel[56] taking no active part in the hostilities.
3. The perpetrator was aware of the factual circumstances that established this status.
4. The conduct took place in the context of and was associated with an armed conflict not of an international character.
5. The perpetrator was aware of factual circumstances that established the existence of an armed conflict.

Article 8 (2) (c) (i)-2
War crime of mutilation

Elements

1. The perpetrator subjected one or more persons to mutilation, in particular by permanently disfiguring the person or persons, or by permanently disabling or removing an organ or appendage.
2. The conduct was neither justified by the medical, dental or hospital treatment of the person or persons concerned nor carried out in such person's or persons' interests.
3. Such person or persons were either *hors de combat*, or were civilians, medical personnel or religious personnel taking no active part in the hostilities.
4. The perpetrator was aware of the factual circumstances that established this status.
5. The conduct took place in the context of and was associated with an armed conflict not of an international character.
6. The perpetrator was aware of factual circumstances that established the existence of an armed conflict.

Article 8 (2) (c) (i)-3
War crime of cruel treatment

Elements

1. The perpetrator inflicted severe physical or mental pain or suffering upon one or more persons.

---

56. The term "religious personnel" includes those non-confessional non-combatant military personnel carrying out a similar function.

2. Such person or persons were either *hors de combat*, or were civilians, medical personnel, or religious personnel taking no active part in the hostilities.
3. The perpetrator was aware of the factual circumstances that established this status.
4. The conduct took place in the context of and was associated with an armed conflict not of an international character.
5. The perpetrator was aware of factual circumstances that established the existence of an armed conflict.

Article 8 (2) (c) (i)-4
War crime of torture

Elements

1. The perpetrator inflicted severe physical or mental pain or suffering upon one or more persons.
2. The perpetrator inflicted the pain or suffering for such purposes as: obtaining information or a confession, punishment, intimidation or coercion or for any reason based on discrimination of any kind.
3. Such person or persons were either *hors de combat*, or were civilians, medical personnel or religious personnel taking no active part in the hostilities.
4. The perpetrator was aware of the factual circumstances that established this status.
5. The conduct took place in the context of and was associated with an armed conflict not of an international character.
6. The perpetrator was aware of factual circumstances that established the existence of an armed conflict.

Article 8 (2) (c) (ii)
War crime of outrages upon personal dignity

Elements

1. The perpetrator humiliated, degraded or otherwise violated the dignity of one or more persons.[57]
2. The severity of the humiliation, degradation or other violation was of such degree as to be generally recognized as an outrage upon personal dignity.
3. Such person or persons were either *hors de combat*, or were civilians, medical personnel or religious personnel taking no active part in the hostilities.
4. The perpetrator was aware of the factual circumstances that established this status.

---

57. For this crime, "persons" can include dead persons. It is understood that the victim need not personally be aware of the existence of the humiliation or degradation or other violation. This element takes into account relevant aspects of the cultural background of the victim.

5. The conduct took place in the context of and was associated with an armed conflict not of an international character.
6. The perpetrator was aware of factual circumstances that established the existence of an armed conflict.

Article 8 (2) (c) (iii)
War crime of taking hostages

Elements

1. The perpetrator seized, detained or otherwise held hostage one or more persons.
2. The perpetrator threatened to kill, injure or continue to detain such person or persons.
3. The perpetrator intended to compel a State, an international organization, a natural or legal person or a group of persons to act or refrain from acting as an explicit or implicit condition for the safety or the release of such person or persons.
4. Such person or persons were either *hors de combat*, or were civilians, medical personnel or religious personnel taking no active part in the hostilities.
5. The perpetrator was aware of the factual circumstances that established this status.
6. The conduct took place in the context of and was associated with an armed conflict not of an international character.
7. The perpetrator was aware of factual circumstances that established the existence of an armed conflict.

Article 8 (2) (c) (iv)
War crime of sentencing or execution without due process

Elements

1. The perpetrator passed sentence or executed one or more persons.[58]
2. Such person or persons were either *hors de combat*, or were civilians, medical personnel or religious personnel taking no active part in the hostilities.
3. The perpetrator was aware of the factual circumstances that established this status.
4. There was no previous judgement pronounced by a court, or the court that rendered judgement was not "regularly constituted", that is, it did not afford the essential guarantees of independence and impartiality, or

---

58. The elements laid down in these documents do not address the different forms of individual criminal responsibility, as enunciated in articles 25 and 28 of the Statute.

the court that rendered judgement did not afford all other judicial guarantees generally recognized as indispensable under international law.[59]

5. The perpetrator was aware of the absence of a previous judgement or of the denial of relevant guarantees and the fact that they are essential or indispensable to a fair trial.
6. The conduct took place in the context of and was associated with an armed conflict not of an international character.
7. The perpetrator was aware of factual circumstances that established the existence of an armed conflict.

Article 8 (2) (e)
Article 8 (2) (e) (i)
War crime of attacking civilians

Elements

1. The perpetrator directed an attack.
2. The object of the attack was a civilian population as such or individual civilians not taking direct part in hostilities.
3. The perpetrator intended the civilian population as such or individual civilians not taking direct part in hostilities to be the object of the attack.
4. The conduct took place in the context of and was associated with an armed conflict not of an international character.
5. The perpetrator was aware of factual circumstances that established the existence of an armed conflict.

Article 8 (2) (e) (ii)
War crime of attacking objects or persons using the distinctive emblems of the Geneva Conventions

Elements

1. The perpetrator attacked one or more persons, buildings, medical units or transports or other objects using, in conformity with international law, a distinctive emblem or other method of identification indicating protection under the Geneva Conventions.
2. The perpetrator intended such persons, buildings, units or transports or other objects so using such identification to be the object of the attack.
3. The conduct took place in the context of and was associated with an armed conflict not of an international character.
4. The perpetrator was aware of factual circumstances that established the existence of an armed conflict.

---

59. With respect to elements 4 and 5, the Court should consider whether, in the light of all relevant circumstances, the cumulative effect of factors with respect to guarantees deprived the person or persons of a fair trial.

Article 8 (2) (e) (iii)
War crime of attacking personnel or objects involved in a humanitarian assistance or peacekeeping mission

Elements

1. The perpetrator directed an attack.
2. The object of the attack was personnel, installations, material, units or vehicles involved in a humanitarian assistance or peacekeeping mission in accordance with the Charter of the United Nations.
3. The perpetrator intended such personnel, installations, material, units or vehicles so involved to be the object of the attack.
4. Such personnel, installations, material, units or vehicles were entitled to that protection given to civilians or civilian objects under the international law of armed conflict.
5. The perpetrator was aware of the factual circumstances that established that protection.
6. The conduct took place in the context of and was associated with an armed conflict not of an international character.
7. The perpetrator was aware of factual circumstances that established the existence of an armed conflict.

Article 8 (2) (e) (iv)
War crime of attacking protected objects[60]

Elements

1. The perpetrator directed an attack.
2. The object of the attack was one or more buildings dedicated to religion, education, art, science or charitable purposes, historic monuments, hospitals or places where the sick and wounded are collected, which were not military objectives.
3. The perpetrator intended such building or buildings dedicated to religion, education, art, science or charitable purposes, historic monuments, hospitals or places where the sick and wounded are collected, which were not military objectives, to be the object of the attack.
4. The conduct took place in the context of and was associated with an armed conflict not of an international character.
5. The perpetrator was aware of factual circumstances that established the existence of an armed conflict.

---

60. The presence in the locality of persons specially protected under the Geneva Conventions of 1949 or of police forces retained for the sole purpose of maintaining law and order does not by itself render the locality a military objective.

Article 8 (2) (e) (v)
War crime of pillaging

Elements

1. The perpetrator appropriated certain property.
2. The perpetrator intended to deprive the owner of the property and to appropriate it for private or personal use.[61]
3. The appropriation was without the consent of the owner.
4. The conduct took place in the context of and was associated with an armed conflict not of an international character.
5. The perpetrator was aware of factual circumstances that established the existence of an armed conflict.

Article 8 (2) (e) (vi)-1
War crime of rape

Elements

1. The perpetrator invaded[62] the body of a person by conduct resulting in penetration, however slight, of any part of the body of the victim or of the perpetrator with a sexual organ, or of the anal or genital opening of the victim with any object or any other part of the body.
2. The invasion was committed by force, or by threat of force or coercion, such as that caused by fear of violence, duress, detention, psychological oppression or abuse of power, against such person or another person, or by taking advantage of a coercive environment, or the invasion was committed against a person incapable of giving genuine consent.[63]
3. The conduct took place in the context of and was associated with an armed conflict not of an international character.
4. The perpetrator was aware of factual circumstances that established the existence of an armed conflict.

---

61. As indicated by the use of the term "private or personal use", appropriations justified by military necessity cannot constitute the crime of pillaging.

62. The concept of "invasion" is intended to be broad enough to be gender-neutral.

63. It is understood that a person may be incapable of giving genuine consent if affected by natural, induced or age-related incapacity. This footnote also applies to the corresponding elements in article 8 (2) (e) (vi)-3, 5 and 6.

Article 8 (2) (e) (vi)-2
War crime of sexual slavery[64]

Elements

1. The perpetrator exercised any or all of the powers attaching to the right of ownership over one or more persons, such as by purchasing, selling, lending or bartering such a person or persons, or by imposing on them a similar deprivation of liberty.[65]
2. The perpetrator caused such person or persons to engage in one or more acts of a sexual nature.
3. The conduct took place in the context of and was associated with an armed conflict not of an international character.
4. The perpetrator was aware of factual circumstances that established the existence of an armed conflict.

Article 8 (2) (e) (vi)-3
War crime of enforced prostitution

Elements

1. The perpetrator caused one or more persons to engage in one or more acts of a sexual nature by force, or by threat of force or coercion, such as that caused by fear of violence, duress, detention, psychological oppression or abuse of power, against such person or persons or another person, or by taking advantage of a coercive environment or such person's or persons' incapacity to give genuine consent.
2. The perpetrator or another person obtained or expected to obtain pecuniary or other advantage in exchange for or in connection with the acts of a sexual nature.
3. The conduct took place in the context of and was associated with an armed conflict not of an international character.
4. The perpetrator was aware of factual circumstances that established the existence of an armed conflict.

---

64. Given the complex nature of this crime, it is recognized that its commission could involve more than one perpetrator as a part of a common criminal purpose.

65. It is understood that such deprivation of liberty may, in some circumstances, include exacting forced labour or otherwise reducing a person to servile status as defined in the Supplementary Convention on the Abolition of Slavery, the Slave Trade, and Institutions and Practices Similar to Slavery of 1956. It is also understood that the conduct described in this element includes trafficking in persons, in particular women and children.

Article 8 (2) (e) (vi)-4
War crime of forced pregnancy

Elements

1. The perpetrator confined one or more women forcibly made pregnant, with the intent of affecting the ethnic composition of any population or carrying out other grave violations of international law.
2. The conduct took place in the context of and was associated with an armed conflict not of an international character.
3. The perpetrator was aware of factual circumstances that established the existence of an armed conflict.

Article 8 (2) (e) (vi)-5
War crime of enforced sterilization

Elements

1. The perpetrator deprived one or more persons of biological reproductive capacity.[66]
2. The conduct was neither justified by the medical or hospital treatment of the person or persons concerned nor carried out with their genuine consent.[67]
3. The conduct took place in the context of and was associated with an armed conflict not of an international character.
4. The perpetrator was aware of factual circumstances that established the existence of an armed conflict.

Article 8 (2) (e) (vi)-6
War crime of sexual violence

Elements

1. The perpetrator committed an act of a sexual nature against one or more persons or caused such person or persons to engage in an act of a sexual nature by force, or by threat of force or coercion, such as that caused by fear of violence, duress, detention, psychological oppression or abuse of power, against such person or persons or another person, or by taking advantage of a coercive environment or such person's or persons' incapacity to give genuine consent.

---

66. The deprivation is not intended to include birth-control measures which have a non-permanent effect in practice.

67. It is understood that "genuine consent" does not include consent obtained through deception.

2. The conduct was of a gravity comparable to that of a serious violation of article 3 common to the four Geneva Conventions.
3. The perpetrator was aware of the factual circumstances that established the gravity of the conduct.
4. The conduct took place in the context of and was associated with an armed conflict not of an international character.
5. The perpetrator was aware of factual circumstances that established the existence of an armed conflict.

Article 8 (2) (e) (vii)
War crime of using, conscripting and enlisting children

Elements

1. The perpetrator conscripted or enlisted one or more persons into an armed force or group or used one or more persons to participate actively in hostilities.
2. Such person or persons were under the age of 15 years.
3. The perpetrator knew or should have known that such person or persons were under the age of 15 years.
4. The conduct took place in the context of and was associated with an armed conflict not of an international character.
5. The perpetrator was aware of factual circumstances that established the existence of an armed conflict.

Article 8 (2) (e) (viii)
War crime of displacing civilians

Elements

1. The perpetrator ordered a displacement of a civilian population.
2. Such order was not justified by the security of the civilians involved or by military necessity.
3. The perpetrator was in a position to effect such displacement by giving such order.
4. The conduct took place in the context of and was associated with an armed conflict not of an international character.
5. The perpetrator was aware of factual circumstances that established the existence of an armed conflict.

Article 8 (2) (e) (ix)
War crime of treacherously killing or wounding

Elements

1. The perpetrator invited the confidence or belief of one or more combatant adversaries that they were entitled to, or were obliged to accord, protection under rules of international law applicable in armed conflict.

2. The perpetrator intended to betray that confidence or belief.
3. The perpetrator killed or injured such person or persons.
4. The perpetrator made use of that confidence or belief in killing or injuring such person or persons.
5. Such person or persons belonged to an adverse party.
6. The conduct took place in the context of and was associated with an armed conflict not of an international character.
7. The perpetrator was aware of factual circumstances that established the existence of an armed conflict.

Article 8 (2) (e) (x)
War crime of denying quarter

Elements

1. The perpetrator declared or ordered that there shall be no survivors.
2. Such declaration or order was given in order to threaten an adversary or to conduct hostilities on the basis that there shall be no survivors.
3. The perpetrator was in a position of effective command or control over the subordinate forces to which the declaration or order was directed.
4. The conduct took place in the context of and was associated with an armed conflict not of an international character.
5. The perpetrator was aware of factual circumstances that established the existence of an armed conflict.

Article 8 (2) (e) (xi)-1
War crime of mutilation

Elements

1. The perpetrator subjected one or more persons to mutilation, in particular by permanently disfiguring the person or persons, or by permanently disabling or removing an organ or appendage.
2. The conduct caused death or seriously endangered the physical or mental health of such person or persons.
3. The conduct was neither justified by the medical, dental or hospital treatment of the person or persons concerned nor carried out in such person's or persons' interest.[68]
4. Such person or persons were in the power of another party to the conflict.

---

68. Consent is not a defence to this crime. The crime prohibits any medical procedure which is not indicated by the state of health of the person concerned and which is not consistent with generally accepted medical standards which would be applied under similar medical circumstances to persons who are nationals of the party conducting the procedure and who are in no way deprived of liberty. This footnote also applies to the similar element in article 8 (2) (e) (xi)-2.

5. The conduct took place in the context of and was associated with an armed conflict not of an international character.
6. The perpetrator was aware of factual circumstances that established the existence of an armed conflict.

Article 8 (2) (e) (xi)-2
War crime of medical or scientific experiments

Elements

1. The perpetrator subjected one or more persons to a medical or scientific experiment.
2. The experiment caused the death or seriously endangered the physical or mental health or integrity of such person or persons.
3. The conduct was neither justified by the medical, dental or hospital treatment of such person or persons concerned nor carried out in such person's or persons' interest.
4. Such person or persons were in the power of another party to the conflict.
5. The conduct took place in the context of and was associated with an armed conflict not of an international character.
6. The perpetrator was aware of factual circumstances that established the existence of an armed conflict.

Article 8 (2) (e) (xii)
War crime of destroying or seizing the enemy's property

Elements

1. The perpetrator destroyed or seized certain property.
2. Such property was property of an adversary.
3. Such property was protected from that destruction or seizure under the international law of armed conflict.
4. The perpetrator was aware of the factual circumstances that established the status of the property.
5. The destruction or seizure was not required by military necessity.
6. The conduct took place in the context of and was associated with an armed conflict not of an international character.
7. The perpetrator was aware of factual circumstances that established the existence of an armed conflict.

BIBLIOGRAPHY

BOOKS

Norman Abrams & Sara Sun Beale, *Federal Criminal Law and Its Enforcement* (2d ed. 1993).

AIDP Draft International Criminal Code (1980).

Amnesty International, *The International Criminal Court: Making the Right Choices—Part V* (1998).

Benedict Anderson, *Imagined Communities: Reflections on the Origin and Spread of Nationalism* (Rev. ed. 1991).

Anthony C. Arend & Robert J. Beck, *International Law and the Use of Force: Beyond the U.N. Charter Paradigm* (1993).

Kelly Dawn Askin, *War Crimes Against Women* (1997).

Benjamin R. Barber, *Jihad vs. McWorld* (1995).

Gary Jonathan Bass, *Stay the Hand of Vengeance* (2000).

M. Cherif Bassiouni, *Crimes Against Humanity in International Criminal Law* (2d ed. 1999).

M. Cherif Bassiouni, *A Draft International Criminal Code and Draft Statute for an International Criminal Tribunal* (1987).

M. Cherif Bassiouni & Edward M. Wise, *Aut Dedere, Aut Judicare: The Duty to Extradite or Prosecute in International Law* (1995).

M. Cherif Bassiouni & Peter Manikas, *The Law of the International Criminal Tribunal for the Former Yugoslavia* (1996).

George A. Bermann et al., *Cases and Materials on European Community Law* (1993).

Black's Law Dictionary (6th Edition, 1990).

William Bourdon, *La Cour pénale internationale* (2000).

Lea Brilmayer, *American Hegemony: Political Morality in a One-Superpower World* (1994).

Ian Brownlie, *Principles of Public international Law* (5th ed. 1998).

E.R. Chamberlin, *The Sack of Rome* (1979).

Joseph H. Choate, *The Two Hague Conferences* (1913).

Commentary on the Rome Statute of the International Criminal Court (Otto Triffterer, ed., 1999).

Melton S. Davis, *Who Defends Rome* (1972).

Yoram Dinstein, *Laws of War* (1983).

Joshua Dressler, *Understanding Criminal Law* (1998).

Essays on ICTY Procedure and Evidence in Honour of Gabrielle Kirk McDonald (Richard May, et. al., eds., 2001).

Europe After Maastricht: American and European Perspectives (Paul Michael Lützeler, ed., 1994).

Werner Feld, *The Court of the European Communities: New Dimension in International Adjudication* (1964).

Benjamin B. Ferencz, *An International Criminal Court* (2 vols., 1980).

Benjamin B. Ferencz, *Defining International Aggression: The Search for World Peace—A Documentary History and Analysis* (1975).

Thomas M. Franck, *Fairness in International Law and Institutions* (1997).

Thomas Franck, *The Power of Legitimacy Among Nations* (1990).

Thomas L. Friedman, *The Lexus and the Olive Tree: Understanding Globalism* (1999).

Richard J. Goldstone, *For Humanity: Reflections of a War Crimes Investigator* (2000).

Priscilla B. Hayner, *Unspeakable Truths: Confronting State Terror and Atrocity* (2001).

Louis Henkin et al., *International Law* (2d ed. 1987).

Marc Henzelin, *Le principe de l'universalité en droit pénal international* (2000).

Rosalyn Higgins, *Problems and Process: International Law and How We Use It* (1994).

André Huet & Renée Koering-Joulin, *Droit pénal international* (1994).

Ijaz Hussain, *Dissenting and Separate Opinions at the World Court* (1984).

William I. Hull, *The Two Hague Conferences and their Contributions to International Law* (1908).

Human Rights Watch, *Commentary for the August 1997 Preparatory Committee Meeting on the Establishment of an International Criminal Court: Materials for Working Groups 1 and 2* (1997).

Human Rights Watch, *Commentary to the Preparatory Commission on the International Criminal Court, Elements of Crimes and Rules of Evidence and Procedure* (June 2000).

Samuel P. Huntington, *The Clash of Civilizations and the Remaking of World Order* (1996).

Impunity and Human Rights in International Law and Practice (Naomi Roht-Arriaza, ed., 1995).

International Humanitarian Law: Origins, Challenges and Prospects (John Carey & R. John Pritchard, eds., 2000).

International Law: A Contemporary Perspective (Richard Falk et al. eds., 1985).

International Law: Achievements and Prospects (Mohammed Bedjaoui, ed., 1991).

International Law Association, Report of the Thirty-Fourth Conference (1927).

Robert H. Jackson, *The Nürnberg Case* (1971).

Mark W. Janis & John W. Noyes, *International Law* (1997).

John R.W.D. Jones, *The Practice of the International Criminal Tribunals* (2000).

John R.W.D. Jones, *The Practice of the International Criminal Tribunals for the Former Yugoslavia and Rwanda* (2d ed. 2000).

Hans Kelsen, *Peace Through Law* (1973).

Paul Kennedy, *The Rise and Fall of the Great Powers: Economic Change and Military Conflict from 1500 to 2000* (1987).

Geert-Jan G.J. Knoops, *Defenses in Contemporary International Criminal Law* (2001).

Wayne R. LaFave & Austin W. Scott Jr., *Criminal Law* (2d ed. 1986).

Wayne R. LaFave & Jerold H. Israel, *Criminal Procedure* (2d ed. 1992).

Law of War Crimes: National and International Approaches (Timothy L.H. McCormack & Gerry J. Simpson, eds., 1997).

Lawyers Committee for Human Rights, *Issues of Jurisdiction and Admissibility* (2000).

Lawyers Committee for Human Rights, *Report Issues of Jurisdiction and Admissibility in the Rules of Procedure and Evidence* (2000).

Lawyer's Committee for Human Rights, *The Accountability of an Ex Officio Prosecutor* (Feb. 1998).

Lawyer's Committee for Human Rights, *The International Criminal Court Trigger Mechanism and the Need for an Independent Prosecutor* (July 1997).

Le petit Robert dictionnaire de la langue française (2d ed. 1992).

Claude Lombois, *Droit Pénal International* (1979).

Farhad Malekian, *The Monopolization of International Criminal Law in the United Nations: A Jurisprudential Approach* (2d ed. 1995).

Manuel sur les organisations internationales (René-Jean Dupuy, ed., 1988).

Lord McNair, *The Law of Treaties* (1961).

Memory and Justice on Trial: The Papon Affair (Richard J. Golsan, ed., Routledge, 2000).

John Henry Merryman, *The Civil Law Tradition* (1969).

John Henry Merryman, David S. Clark & John O. Haley, *The Civil Law Tradition: Europe, Latin America, and East Asia* (1994).

Martha Minow, *Between Vengeance and Forgiveness: Facing History After Genocide and Mass Violence* (1998).

Model Draft Statute for the International Criminal Court Based on the Preparatory Committee's Text to the Diplomatic Conference, Rome, June 15–July 17, 1998 (Association Internationale de Droit Pénal, Nouvelles Études Pénales No. 13*ter*) (Leila Sadat Wexler, ed., 1998).

Virginia Morris & Michael P. Scharf, *The International Criminal Tribunal for Rwanda* (1998).

Virginia Morris & Michael P. Scharf, *An Insider's Guide to the International Criminal Tribunal for the Former Yugoslavia* (1995).

Carlos Santiago Nino, *Radical Evil on Trial* (1996).

Observations on the consolidated ICC Text Before the Final Session of the Preparatory Committee, 13bis Nouvelles Études Pénales (Leila Sadat Wexler, special ed., 1998).

Covey T. Oliver et al., *The International Legal System* (4th ed. 1995).
Mark Osiel, *Mass Atrocity, Collective Memory, and the Law* (1997).
Jean Pradel, *Droit pénal comparé* (1995).
Jean Pradel, *Procedure pénale* (1997).
Steven R. Ratner & Jason S. Abrams, *Accountability for Atrocities in International Law (1997).*
Restatement (Third) of the Foreign Relations law of the United States (1987).
Ahmed M. Rifaat, *International Aggression: A Study of the Legal Concept: Its Development and Definition in International Law* (1979).
Geoffrey Robertson, *Crimes Against Humanity: The Struggle for Global Justice* (2000).
B.V.A. Röling & Antonio Cassese, *The Tokyo Trial and Beyond* (1993).
Shabtai Rosenne, *The World Court: What it is and how it works* (1989).
Alfred P. Rubin, *Ethics and Authority in International Law* (1997).
William A. Schabas, *Genocide in International Law* (2000).
H. G. Schermers, *International Institutional Law* (2d ed., 1980).
Rudolf B. Schlesinger, Hans W. Baade & Peter S. Herzog, *Comparative Law* (6th ed., 1998).
James Brown Scott, *I The Hague Peace Conferences of 1899 and 1907* (1909).
Mohamed Shahabuddeen, *Precedent in the World Court* (1996).
Judith Shklar, *Legalism: Law. Morals and Political Trials* (1964).
Statute of the International Criminal Court: A Documentary History (M. Cherif Bassiouni, ed., 1998).
Gaston Stefani, Georges Levasseur & Bernard Bouloc, *Droit pénal général* (16th ed. 1997).
Kate Stith & José Cabranes, *Fear of Judging: Sentencing Guidelines in the Federal Courts* (1998).
John F. Sweets, *The Politics of Resistance in France* (1976).
Telford Taylor, *The Anatomy of the Nuremberg Trials* (1992).
The German Federal Republic Penal Code (Joseph J. Darby trans. 1987).
The International Criminal Court: Observations and Issues Before the 1997–98 Preparatory Committee; and Administrative and Financial Implications (Association Internationale de Droit Pénal, Nouvelles Études Pénales No. 13)(M. Cherif Bassiouni, ed., 1997).
The International Criminal Court: The Making of the Rome Statute (Roy S. Lee, ed., 1999).
The Law of War Crimes: National and International Approaches (Timothy L.H. McCormack & Gerry J. Simpson, eds., 1997).
The Morality of Truth Commissions: Truth v. Justice (Robert I. Rotberg & Dennis Thompson, eds., 2000).
The Nuremberg Trial and International Law (George Ginsburgs & V.N. Kudriavtsev, eds., 1990).
The Oxford English Dictionary (2d ed. 1991).
The United States and the International Criminal Court (Sarah B. Sewall & Carl Kaysen, eds., 2000).

Toward a Global Civil Society (Michael Walzer, ed., 1995).
Transitional Justice: Country Studies (Neil J. Kritz, ed., 1995).
United Nations Legal Order (Oscar Schacter & Christopher C. Joyner, eds., 1995).
United States Model Penal Code (1985).
N.D. White, *The Law of International Organizations* (1996).
Derek Williams, *The Reach of Rome* (1988).
Women and International Human Rights Law (Kelly D. Askin & Dorean M. Koenig, eds., 2000).
David W. Ziegler, *War, Peace, and International Politics* (7th ed. 1997).

ARTICLES

Bruce Ackerman, *Constitutional Politics/Constitutional Law*, 99 YALE L. J. 453 (1989).
Michael Akehurst, *Jurisdiction in International Law*, 1972–1973 BRITISH Y.B. INT'L L. 145.
Payam Akhavan, *Beyond Impunity: Can International Criminal Justice Prevent Future Atrocities?*, 95 AM. J. INT'L L. 7 (2001).
Payam Akhavan, *Justice and Reconciliation in the Great Lakes Region of Africa: The Contribution of the International Criminal Tribunal for Rwanda*, 7 DUKE J. COMP. & INT'L L. 325 (1997).
Payam Akhavan, *Justice in the Hague, Peace in the Former Yugoslavia*, 20 HUM. RTS. Q. 737 (1999).
Payam Akhavan, *The International Criminal Tribunal for Rwanda: The Politics and Pragmatics of Punishment*, 90 AM. J. INT'L L. 501 (1996).
Babafemi Akinrinade, *International Humanitarian Law and the Conflict in Sierra Leone*, 15 NOTRE DAME J. L. ETHICS & PUB. POL. 391 (2001).
George H. Aldrich and Christine M. Chinkin, *Symposium: The Hague Peace Conferences*, 94 AM. J. INT'L. L. 1 (2000).
José Alvarez, *Crimes of State/Crimes of Hate: Lessons from Rwanda*, 24 YALE J. INT'L L. 365 (1999).
José E. Alvarez, *Rush to Closure: Lessons of the Tadić Judgment*, 96 MICH. L. REV. 2031 (1998).
Kai Ambos, *General Principles of Criminal Law in the Rome Statute*, 10 CRIM. L. FORUM 1 (1999).
Anthony Clark Arend, *International Law and the Recourse to Force: A Shift in Paradigms*, 27 STAN. J. INT'L L. 1 (1990).
Mahnoush H. Arsanjani, *The Rome Statute of the International Criminal Court*, 93 AM. J. INT'L L. 22 (1999).
Kelly D. Askin, *Crimes within the Jurisdiction of the International Criminal Court*, 10 CRIM. L. F. 33 (1999).
M. Cherif Bassiouni, *Combating Impunity for International Crimes*, 71 U. COLO. L. REV. 409 (2000).

M. Cherif Bassiouni, *"Crimes Against Humanity": The Need for a Specialized Convention*, 31 COLUM. J. TRANSNAT'L. L. 457 (1994).

M. Cherif Bassiouni, *From Versailles to Rwanda in Seventy-Five Years: The Need to Establish a Permanent International Criminal Court*, 10 HARV. HUM. RTS. J. 11 (1997).

M. Cherif Bassiouni, *Negotiating the Treaty of Rome on the Establishment of an International Criminal Court*, 32 CORNELL INT'L L. J. 443 (1999).

M. Cherif Bassiouni, *The Normative Framework of International Humanitarian Law: Overlaps, Gaps and Ambiguities*, 8 TRANSNAT'L L. & CONTEMP. PROBS. 199 (1998).

M. Cherif Bassiouni, *The Time has come for an International Criminal Court*, 1 IND. INT'L & COMP. L. REV. 1 (1991).

Fanny Benedetti & John L. Washburn, *Drafting the International Criminal Court Treaty: Two Years to Rome and an Afterword on the Rome Diplomatic Conference*, 5 GLOBAL GOVERNANCE 1 (1999).

Christopher L. Blakesley, *Obstacles to the Creation of a Permanent War Crimes Tribunal*, 18 FLETCHER FORUM WORLD AFF. 77 (1992).

Roman Boed, *The Effect of a Domestic Amnesty on the Ability of Foreign States to Prosecute Alleged Perpetrators of Serious Human Rights Violations*, 33 CORNELL INT'L L. J. 297 (2000).

Michael Bothe, *War-Crimes in Non-International Armed Conflicts*, 24 ISRAEL Y.B. HUM. RTS. 241 (1994) .

D. W. Bowett, *Jurisdiction: Changing Patterns of Authority over Activities and Resources*, 1982 BRITISH Y. B. INT'L L. 1.

Evelyn Bradley, *In Search for Justice—A Truth in Reconciliation [sic] Commission for Rwanda*, 7 J. INT'L L. & PRAC. 129 (1998).

William J. Brennan, *In Defense of Dissents*, 50 HASTINGS L. J. 671 (1999).

Bruce Broomhall, *The International Criminal Court: Overview, and Cooperation with States*, 13*quater* NOUVELLES ÉTUDES PÉNALES 45 (1999).

Christina M. Carroll, *An Assessment of the Role and Effectiveness of the International Criminal Tribunal for Rwanda and the Rwandan National Justice System in Dealing with the Mass Atrocities of 1994*, 18 BOSTON UNIV. INT'L L. J. 163 (2000).

Antonio Cassese, *On the Current Trends Towards Criminal Prosecution and Punishment of Breaches of International Humanitarian Law*, 9 EUR. J. INT'L L. 2 (1998).

Antonio Cassese, *Reflections on International Criminal Justice*, 61 MOD. L. REV. 1 (1998).

Hilary Charlesworth and Christine Chinkin, *The Gender of Jus Cogens*, 15 HUM. RTS. Q. 63 (1993).

Jonathan I. Charney, *International Law and Multiple International Tribunals*, 271 RECUEIL DES COURS 101 (1998).

Roger S. Clark, *The Proposed International Criminal Court: Its Establishment and Its Relationship with the United Nations*, 8 CRIM. L. F. 411 (1997).

Roger S. Clark, *The United States Federal Sentencing Guidelines: Who is Watching the Makers of Grids*, 11 CRIM. L. FORUM 249 (2000).

Stanley Cohen, *State Crimes of Previous Regimes: Knowledge, Accountability and the Policing of the Past*, 20 J. L. & SOC. INQUIRY 1 (1995).

Rhonda Copelon, *Gender Crimes as War Crimes: Integrating Crimes against Women into International Criminal Law*, 46 MCGILL L. J. 217 (2000).

Dylan Cors & Siobhán K. Fisher, *National Law in International Criminal Punishment: Yugoslavia's Maximum Prison Sentences and the United Nations War Crimes Tribunal*, 3 PARKER SCH. J. E. EUR. L. 637 (1996).

Mirjan Damaška, *Structures of Authority and Comparative Criminal Procedure*, 84 YALE L. J. 480 (1974).

Daniel H. Derby, *An International Criminal Court for the Future*, 5 TRANSNAT'L L. & CONTEMP. PROBS. 307 (1995).

David Dolinko, *Three Mistakes of Retributivism*, 39 U.C.L.A. L. REV. 1623 (1992).

Fania Domb, *Treatment of War Crimes in Peace Settlements—Prosecution or Amnesty?*, 24 ISRAEL Y.B. HUM. RTS. 253 (1994).

Joshua Dressler, *Hating Criminals: How can Something That Feels so Good be Wrong?*, 88 MICH. L. REV. 1448 (1990).

Mark A. Drumbl, *Punishment, Postgenocide: From Guilt to Shame to* Civis *in Rwanda*, 75 N.Y.U. L. REV. 1221 (2000).

John Dugard, *Reconciliation and Justice: The South African Experience*, 8 TRANSAT'L L. & CONTEMP. PROBS. 277 (1988).

George E. Edwards, *International Human Rights Law Challenges to the International* Criminal *Court: Right to Privacy in the Search and Seizure Context*, 26 YALE J. INT'L L. 1 (2001).

Catherine Elliott, *The French Law of Intent and its Influence on the Development of International Criminal Law*, 11 CRIM. L. F. 35 (2000).

Richard Falk, *Global Civil Society: Perspectives, Initiatives, Movements*, 26 OXFORD DEV. STUD. 99 (1998).

Richard Falk, *The Grotian Moment: Unfulfilled Promise, Harmless Fantasy, Missed Opportunity?*, 13 INT'L INSIGHTS 3 (1997).

Richard Falk, *The Nuclear Weapons Advisory Opinion and the New Jurisprudence of Global Civil Society*, 7 TRANSNAT'L L. & CONTEMP. PROBS. 333 (1998).

Tom J. Farer, *Restraining the Barbarians: Can International Criminal Law Help?*, 22 HUM. RTS. Q. 90 (2000).

Bardo Fassbender, *The United Nations Charter as Constitution of the International Community*, 36 COLUM. J. TRANSNAT'L L. 529 (1998).

Benjamin B. Ferencz, *Can Aggression be Deterred by Law*, 11 PACE INT'L L. REV. 344 (1999).

George P. Fletcher, *Mistake in the Model Penal Code: a False False Problem*, 19 RUTGERS L. J. 649 (1988).

Thomas M. Franck, *Who Killed Article 2(4): Changing Norms Governing the Use of Force by States*, 64 AM. J. INT'L L. 809 (1970).

Kenneth S. Gallant, *The Role and Powers of Defense Counsel in the Rome Statute of the International Criminal Court*, 34 INT'L LAWYER 21 (2000).

Ruth Bader Ginsburg, *Remarks on Writing Separately*, 65 WASH. L. REV. 133 (1990).

Pricilla B. Hayner, *Fifteen Truth Commissions—1974 to 1994: A Comparative Study*, 16 HUM. RTS. Q. 597 (1994).

Laurence R. Helfer & Anne-Marie Slaughter, *Toward a Theory of Effective Supranational Adjudication*, 107 YALE L. J. 273 (1997).

Louis Henkin, *The Reports of the Death of Article 2(4) are Greatly Exaggerated*, 65 AM. J. INT'L L. 544 (1971).

A.J. J. de Hoogh, *The Relationship between* Jus Cogens, *Obligations* Erga Omnes *and International Crimes: Peremptory Norms in Perspective*, 42 AUSTRIAN J. PUBL. INT'L L. 183 (1991).

Manley O. Hudson, *The Proposed International Criminal Court*, 32 AM. J. INT'L L. 549 (1938).

Samuel P. Huntington, *The Lonely Superpower*, 78 FOREIGN AFF. 35 (1999).

William L. Hurlock, *The International Court of Justice: Effectively Providing a Long Overdue Remedy for Ending State-Sponsored Genocide (Bosnia-Herzogovina v. Yugoslavia)*, 12 AM. U. J. INT'L L. & POL'Y 299 (1997).

Scott C. Idleman, *A Prudential Theory of Judicial Candor*, 73 TEX. L. REV. 1307 (1995).

Jennifer Jackson Preece, *Ethnic Cleansing as an Instrument of National-State Creation: Changing State Practices and Evolving Legal Norms*, 20 HUMAN RTS. Q. 817 (1998).

Jean Paul Jacqué & Joseph H.H. Weiler, *On the Road to European Union—A New Judicial Architecture: An Agenda for the Intergovernmental Conference*, 27 COMMON MKT. L. REV. 185 (1990).

Dan M. Kahan, *The Secret Ambition of Deterrence*, 113 HARV. L. REV. 414 (1999).

Philippe Kirsch & John T. Holmes, *The Rome Conference on an International Criminal Court: The Negotiating Process*, 93 AM. J. INT'L. L. 2 (1999).

Daniel T. Kobil, *The Quality of Mercy Strained: Wrestling the Pardoning Power from the King*, 69 TEX. L. REV. 569 (1991).

Elizabeth S. Kopelman, *Ideology and International Law: The Dissent of the Indian Justice at the Tokyo War Crimes Trial*, 23 N.Y.U. J. INT'L L. & POL. 373 (1991).

Neil J. Kritz, *Coming to Terms with Atrocities: A Review of Accountability Mechanisms for Mass Violations of Human Rights*, 59 J. L. & CONTEMP. PROBS. 127 (1996).

Laura Krugman Ray, *Justice Brennan and the Jurisprudence of Dissent*, 61 TEMPLE L. REV. 307 (1988).

Maurice Lagrange, *La Cour de Justice des Communautés Européennes: du plan Schuman à l'union européenne*, 14 REVUE TRIMESTRIELLE DE DROIT EUROPÉEN 2 (1978).

Georges Levasseur, *Les crimes contre l'humanité et le problème de leur prescription*, 93 J. DU DROIT INT'L [J.D.I] 259 (1966).

Matthew Lippman, *The Convention on the Prevention and Punishment of the Crime of Genocide: Fifty Years Later*, 15 ARIZ. J. INT'L & COMP. L. 415 (1998).

Rory K. Little, *Reading Justice Brennan: Is There a "Right" to Dissent?*, 50 HASTINGS L. J. 683 (1999).

Peter W. Low, *The Model Penal Code, the Common Law, and Mistakes of Fact: Recklessness, Negligence, or Strict Liability?*, 19 RUTGERS L.J. 539 (1988).

Lori Lyman Bruun, *Beyond the 1948 Convention—Emerging Principles of Genocide in Customary International Law*, 17 MD. J. INT'L L. & TRADE 193 (1993).

Konstantinos D. Magliveras, *The Special Court for Sierra Leone: A New Type of Regional Criminal Court for the International Community?*, 17 INT'L ENFORCEMENT L. REP. (Feb. 2001).

John O. McGinnis, *The Decline of the Western Nation State and the Rise of the Regime of International Federalism*, 18 CARDOZO L. REV. 903 (1996).

Lorna McGregor, *Individual Accountability in South Africa: Cultural Optimum or Political Facade?*, 95 AM. J. INT'L L. 32 (2001).

Saul Mendlovitz & Merav Datan, *Judge Weeramantry's Grotian Quest*, 7 TRANSNAT'L L. & CONTEMP. PROBS. 401 (1997).

Theodor Meron, *Is International Law Moving Towards Criminalization?*, 9 EUR. J. INT'L L. 18 (1998).

Theodor Meron, *The Role of Custom in the Formation of International Humanitarian Law*, 90 AM. J. INT'L L. 238 (1996).

Madeline Morris, *The Trials of Concurrent Jurisdiction: The Case of Rwanda*, 7 DUKE J. COMP. & INT'L L. 349 (1997).

Herman Mosler, *The International Society as a Legal Community, in* 140 RECUEIL DES COURS 1(1974).

Kurt H. Nadelmann, *The Judicial Dissent: Publication v. Secrecy*, 8 AM. J. COMP. L. 415 (1959).

Jan Christoph Nemitz and Steffen Wirth, *Some observations on the law of sentencing of the ICC, available at* <http://www/menshenrechte.de/hrww/1nov99/nemitz.htm>.

Carlos S. Nino, *The Duty to Punish Past Abuses of Human Rights Put Into Context: The Case of Argentina*, 100 YALE L. J. 2619 (1991).

James C. O'Brien, *The International Tribunal for Violations of International Humanitarian Law in the Former Yugoslavia*, 87 AM. J. INT'L L. 639 (1993).

Abdullah Omar, *Truth and Reconciliation in South Africa: Accounting for the Past*, 4 BUFFALO HUM. RTS. L. REV. 5 (1997).

Diane F. Orentlicher, *Settling Accounts: The Duty to Prosecute Human Rights Violations of a Prior Regime*, 100 YALE L. J. 2537 (1991).

Mark J. Osiel, *Obeying Orders: Atrocity, Military Discipline, and the Law of War*, 86 CAL. L. REV. 939 (1998).

Mark J. Osiel, *Why Prosecute? Critics of Punishment for Mass Atrocity*, 22 HUM. RTS. Q. 118 (2000).

Panel, *The Transformation of Sovereignty*, 88 AM. SOC'Y INT'L L. PROC. 1 (1994).

Jordan J. Paust, Nullum Crimen *and Related Claims*, 13 NOUVELLES ÉTUDES PÉNALES 275 (1997).

Mary Margaret Penrose, *It's Good to be the King!: Prosecuting Heads of State and*

Former Heads of State Under International Law, 39 COLUM. J. TRANSNAT'L L. 193 (2000).

Lord Phillimore, *An International Criminal Court and the Resolutions of the Committee of Jurists*, 1922–23 BRIT. Y.B. INT'L L. 79.

Daniel B. Pickard, *Proposed Sentencing Guidelines for the International Criminal Court*, 20 LOY. L. A. INT'L & COMP. L. J. 123 (1997).

Mauro Politi, *Le Statute de Rome de la Cour Pénale Internationale: Le point de vue d'un négociateur*, 1999 REVUE GÉNÉRALE DE DROIT INTERNATIONAL PUBLIC 817.

Stanislaw Pomorski, *Reflections on the First Criminal Code of Post-Communist Russia*, 48 AM. J. COMP. L. 375 (1998).

Peter E. Quint, *The Border Guard Trials and the East German Past—Seven Arguments*, 48 AM. J. COMP. L. 541 (2000).

Kenneth C. Randall, *Universal Jurisdiction Under International Law*, 66 TEX. L. REV. 785 (1988).

Steven R. Ratner, *The United Nations Group of Experts for Cambodia*, 93 AM. J. INT'L L. 948 (1999).

Rosemary Rayfuse, *The Draft Code of Crimes Against the Peace and Security of Mankind: Eating Disorders at the International Law Commission*, 8 CRIM. L. F. 43 (1997).

W. Michael Reisman, *Legal Responses to Genocide and Other Massive Violations of Human Rights*, 59 L. & CONTEMP. PROBS. 75 (1996).

Mary Robinson, *Genocide, War Crimes, Crimes Against Humanity*, 23 FORDHAM INT'L L. J. 275 (1999).

Martin A. Rogoff, *Interpretation of International Agreements by Domestic Courts and the Politics of International Treaty Relations: Reflections on Some Recent Decisions of the United States Supreme Court*, 11 AM. U. J. INT'L L. & POL'Y 559 (1996).

Naomi Roht-Arriaza, *State Responsibility to Investigate and Prosecute Grave Human Rights Violations in International Law*, 78 CAL. L. REV. 451 (1990).

Shabatai Rosenne, *Poor Drafting and Imperfect Organization: Flaws to Overcome in the Rome Statute*, 41 VA. J. INT'L L. 164 (2000).

Leila Nadya Sadat, *Custom, Codification and Some Thoughts About the Relationship Between the Two: Article 10 of the ICC Statute*, 35 DEPAUL L. REV. 909 (2000).

Leila Sadat Wexler, *International Law Association (American Branch) Committee on a Permanent International Criminal Court, First Committee Report on Jurisdiction, Definition of Crimes and Complementarity*, 25 DENVER J. INT'L L. & POLICY 221 (1997) (Rapporteur's Report).

Leila Nadya Sadat, Panel Discussion, *Association of American Law School Panel on the International Criminal Court*, 36 AM. CRIM. L. REV. 223 (1999).

Leila Sadat Wexler, *Reflections on the Trial of Vichy Collaborator Paul Touvier for Crimes Against Humanity in France*, 20 J. L. & SOC. INQUIRY 191 (1995).

Leila Nadya Sadat, *The Establishment of the International Criminal Court: From the Hague to Rome and Back Again*, 8 DET. J. INT'L L. & PRAC. 97 (1999).

Leila Sadat Wexler, *The Interpretation of the Nuremberg Principles by the French Court of Cassation: From Touvier to Barbie and Back Again*, 32 COL. J. TRANSNAT'L L. 289 (1994).

Leila Nadya Sadat & S. Richard Carden, *The New International Criminal Court: An Uneasy Revolution*, 88 GEO. L. J. 381 (2000).

Leila Sadat Wexler, *The Proposed Permanent International Criminal Court: An Appraisal*, 29 CORNELL J. INT'L L. 665 (1996).

Leila Nadya Sadat, *Universal Jurisdiction and National Amnesties, Truth Commissions and Other Alternatives to Prosecution: Giving Justice a Chance*, Princeton Project on Universal Jurisdiction (Princeton University, 2001).

Jeremy Sarkin, *The Trials and Tribulations of South Africa's Truth and Reconciliation Commission*, 12 SOUTH AFRICAN J. HUM. RTS. 617 (1996).

William A. Schabas, *Sentencing by International Tribunals: A Human Rights Approach*, 7 DUKE J. COMP. & INT'L L. 461 (1997).

Oscar Schachter, *In Defense of International Rules on the Use of Force*, 53 U. CHI. L. REV. 113 (1986).

Michael P. Scharf, *Results of the Rome Conference for an International Criminal Court*, ASIL INSIGHT (Aug. 1998) <http://www.asil.org/insigh23.htm>.

Michael P. Scharf, *Swapping Amnesty for Peace: Was there a Duty to Prosecute International Crimes in Haiti?*, 31 TEX. INT'L L. J. 1 (1996).

Michael P. Scharf, *The Amnesty Exception to the Jurisdiction of the International Criminal Court*, 32 CORNELL INT'L L. J. 507 (1999).

Michael P. Scharf, *The Special Court for Sierra Leone*, ASIL Insight (Oct. 2000), *available in* <http://www.asil.org/insigh53.htm>.

Michael P. Scharf, *The Tools for Enforcing International Criminal Justice in the New Millennium: Lessons from the Yugoslavia Tribunal*, 49 DEPAUL L. REV. 925 (2000).

Michael P. Scharf, *Trial and Error: An Assessment of the First Judgment of the Yugoslavia War Crimes Tribunal*, 30 N.Y.U. J. INT'L L. & POL. 167 (1997–98).

David J. Scheffer, *A Negotiator's Perspective on the International Criminal Court*, 167 MILITARY L. REV. 1 (2001).

Peter A. Schey, Dinah Shelton and Naomi Roht-Arriaza, *Addressing Human Rights Abuses: Truth Commissions and the Value of Amnesty*, 19 WHITTIER L. REV. 325 (1997).

Rudolf B. Schlesinger, *Comparative Criminal Procedure: A Plea for Utilizing Foreign Experience*, 26 BUFF. L. REV. 361 (1977).

Jean-Eric Schoettl, *Décisions du Conseil Constitutionnel: Cour pénale internationale*, L'ACTUALITÉ JURIDIQUE—DROIT ADMINISTRATIF 230 (Mar. 20, 1999).

Minna Schrag, *The Yugoslav War Crimes Tribunal: An Interim Assessment*, 7 TRANSNAT'L L. & CONTEMP. PROBS. 15 (1997).

Justin M. Schwartz, *South Africa's Truth and Reconciliation Commission: A Functional Equivalent to Prosecution*, 3 DEPAUL DIG. INT'L L. 13 (1997).

Egon Schwelb, *Crimes Against Humanity*, 1946 BRIT. Y.B. INT'L L. 178.

Gary L. Scott & Craig L. Carr, *Multilateral Treaties and the Formation of*

Customary International Law, 25 DENV. J. INT'L L. & POL'Y 71 (1996).

Leslie Sebba, *The Pardoning Power—A World Survey*, 68 J. CRIM. L. & CRIMINOLOGY 83 (1977).

Kenneth W. Simons, *Mistake and Impossibility, Law and Fact, and Culpability: A Speculative Essay*, 81 J. CRIM. L. & CRIMINOLOGY 447 (1990).

Anne-Marie Slaughter, *International Law in a World of Liberal States*, 6 EUR. J. INT'L L. 503 (1995) .

Göran Sluiter, *To Cooperate or not to Cooperate?: The Case of the Failed Transfer of Ntakirutimana to the Rwanda Tribunal*, 11 LEIDEN J. INT'L L. 383 (1998).

A.T.H. Smith, *Rethinking the Defence of Mistake*, 2 OXFORD J. OF LEGAL STUDIES 429 (1982).

Joseph M. Snee, S.J. and A. Kenneth Pye, *Due Process in Criminal Procedure: A Comparison of Two Systems*, 21 OHIO STATE L. J. 467 (1960).

Hansjörg Strohmeyer, *Collapse and Reconstruction of a Judicial System: The United Nations Missions in Kosovo and East Timor*, 95 AM. J. INT'L L. 46 (2001).

Symposium, *War Crimes: Bosnia and Beyond*, 34 VA. J. INT'L L. 255 (1994).

Ruti Teitel, *Transitional Jurisprudence: The Role of Law in Political Transformation*, 105 YALE L. J. 2009 (1997).

Susan W. Tiefenbrun, *The Paradox of International Adjudication: Developments in the International Criminal Tribunals for the Former Yugoslavia and Rwanda, the World Court, and the ICC*, 25 N. CAROLINA J. INT'L L. & COMM. REG. 589 (2000).

Christian Tomuschat, *Crimes Against the Peace and Security of Mankind and the Recalcitrant Third State*, 24 ISRAEL Y.B. HUM. RTS. 41 (1994).

Detlev F. Vagts, *The Hague Conventions and Arms Control*, 94 AM. J. INT'L L. 31 (2000).

Rachel A. Van Cleave, *An Offer You Can't Refuse? Punishment without Trial in Italy and the United States: The Search for Truth and an Efficient Criminal Justice System*, 11 EMORY INT'L L. REV. 419 (1997).

Johan D. van der Vyver, *Prosecution and Punishment of the Crime of Genocide*, 23 FORDHAM INT'L L. J. 286 (1999).

Beth Van Schaack, *The Crime of Political Genocide: Repairing the Genocide Convention's Blind Spot*, 106 YALE L. J. 2259 (1997).

Dirk van Zyl Smith, *Life Imprisonment as the Ultimate Penalty in International Law: A Human Rights Perspective*, 9 CRIM L. F. 5 (1999) .

Vladan A. Vasilijevic, *Crimes Against Peace: Between the Past and the Future*, 43 JUGOSLOVENSKA REVIJA ZA MEDUNARODNO PRAVO 425 (1996).

John Washburn, *The Negotiation of the Rome Statute for the International Criminal Court and International Lawmaking in the 21st Century*, 11 PACE INT'L L. REV. 361 (1999).

Ruth Wedgwood & Harold K. Jacobson, *Foreword: Symposium: State Reconstruction After Civil Conflict*, 95 AM. J. INT'L L. 1 (2001).

Ruth Wedgwood, *The Case for a Permanent War Crimes Court*, THE CHRISTIAN SCIENCE MONITOR, Aug. 16, 1995, at 19.

Joseph H.H. Weiler, *The Transformation of Europe*, 100 YALE L. J. 2403 (1991).
Arthur M. Weisburd, *Customary International Law: The Problem of Treaties*, 21 VAND. J. TRANSNAT' L. 1 (1988).
David Wippman, *Atrocities, Deterrence, and the Limits of International Justice*, 23 FORDHAM INT'L L. J. 473 (1999).
Ronald F. Wright, *Rules for Sentencing Revolutions*, 108 YALE L. J. 1355 (1999).
Sienho Yee, *The Erdemović Sentencing Judgment: A Questionable Milestone for the International Criminal Tribunal for the Former Yugoslavia*, 26 GEORGIA J. INT'L & COMP. L. 263 (1997).
Karl M. ZoBell, *Division of Opinion in the Supreme Court: A History of Judicial Disintegration*, 44 CORNELL L. Q. 186 (1959).

COLLECTED WORKS

Kai Ambos, *Individual Criminal Responsibility, in* COMMENTARY ON THE ROME STATUTE OF THE INTERNATIONAL CRIMINAL COURT 475 (Otto Triffterer, ed., 1999).
Kelly Dawn Askin, *The ICTY: An Introduction to its Origins, Rules and Jurisprudence, in* ESSAYS ON ICTY PROCEDURE AND EVIDENCE IN HONOUR OF GABRIELLE KIRK MCDONALD 13 (Richard May, et. al., eds., 2001).
M. Cherif Bassiouni, *Historical Survey: 1919–1998, in* STATUTE OF THE INTERNATIONAL CRIMINAL COURT: A DOCUMENTARY HISTORY 1 (M. Cherif Bassiouni, ed., 1998).
Morten Bergsmo & Pieter Kruger, *Duties and powers of the Prosecutor with respect to investigations, in* COMMENTARY ON THE ROME STATUTE OF THE INTERNATIONAL CRIMINAL COURT 715 (Otto Triffterer, ed., 1999).
Gilbert Bitti, *Functions and powers of the Trial Chamber, in* COMMENTARY ON THE ROME STATUTE OF THE INTERNATIONAL CRIMINAL COURT 809 (Otto Triffterer, ed., 1999).
Christopher L. Blakesley, *Commentary on Parts 5 and 6 of the Zutphen Intersessional Draft: Investigation, Prosecution & Trial, in* OBSERVATIONS ON THE CONSOLIDATED ICC TEXT BEFORE THE FINAL SESSION OF THE PREPARATORY COMMITTEE, *13bis* NOUVELLES ÉTUDES PÉNALES 69 (Leila Sadat Wexler, special ed., 1998).
Michael Bohlander, *Plea-Bargaining before the ICTY, in* ESSAYS ON ICTY PROCEDURE AND EVIDENCE IN HONOUR OF GABRIELLE KIRK MCDONALD 151 (Richard May, et. al., eds., 2001).
Adriaan Bos, *The International Criminal Court: A Perspective, in* THE INTERNATIONAL CRIMINAL COURT: THE MAKING OF THE ROME STATUTE 470 (Roy S. Lee, ed., 1999).
Helen Brady & Mark Jennings, *Appeal and Revision, in* THE INTERNATIONAL CRIMINAL COURT: THE MAKING OF THE ROME STATUTE 294 (Roy S. Lee, ed., 1999).

Bruce Broomhall, *Article 22, Nullum crimen sine lege, in* COMMENTARY ON THE ROME STATUTE OF THE INTERNATIONAL CRIMINAL COURT 447 (Otto Triffterer, ed., 1999).

Roger S. Clark, *Commentary on Parts 1 and 4 of the Zutphen Intersessional Draft: Establishment of the Court and Composition and Administration of the Court, in* OBSERVATIONS ON THE CONSOLIDATED ICC TEXT BEFORE THE FINAL SESSION OF THE PREPARATORY COMMITTEE, 13*bis* NOUVELLES ÉTUDES PÉNALES 55 (Leila Sadat Wexler, special ed., 1998).

Roger S. Clark, *Crimes Against Humanity, in* THE NUREMBERG TRIAL AND INTERNATIONAL LAW 177 (George Ginsburgs & V.N. Kudriavtsev, eds., 1990).

Roger S. Clark, *The Rome Statute of the International Criminal Court and Weapons of a Nature to Cause Superfluous Injury or Unnecessary Suffering, or Which are Inherently Indiscriminate, in* INTERNATIONAL HUMANITARIAN LAW: ORIGINS, CHALLENGES AND PROSPECTS (John Carey & R. John Pritchard, eds., 2000).

Giovanni Conso, *Looking to the Future, in* THE INTERNATIONAL CRIMINAL COURT: THE MAKING OF THE ROME STATUTE 471 (Roy S. Lee, ed., 1999).

Albin Eser, *Grounds for excluding criminal responsibility, in* COMMENTARY ON THE ROME STATUTE OF THE INTERNATIONAL CRIMINAL COURT 537 (Otto Triffterer, ed., 1999).

Richard Falk, *The Grotian Quest, in* INTERNATIONAL LAW: A CONTEMPORARY PERSPECTIVE 36 (Richard Falk et al. eds., 1985).

William J. Fenrick, *Responsibility of commanders and other superiors, in* COMMENTARY ON THE ROME STATUTE OF THE INTERNATIONAL CRIMINAL COURT 515 (Otto Triffterer, ed., 1999).

Silvia A. Fernández de Gurmendi, *The Process of Negotiations, in* THE INTERNATIONAL CRIMINAL COURT: THE MAKING OF THE ROME STATUTE 217 (Roy S. Lee, ed., 1999).

Rolf Einer Fife, *Penalties, in* THE INTERNATIONAL CRIMINAL COURT: THE MAKING OF THE ROME STATUTE 319 (Roy S. Lee, ed., 1999).

Håkan Friman, *Rights of Persons Suspected or Accused of a Crime, in* THE INTERNATIONAL CRIMINAL COURT: THE MAKING OF THE ROME STATUTE 247 (Roy S. Lee, ed., 1999).

Fabricio Guariglia, *Proceedings on an admission of guilt, in* COMMENTARY ON THE ROME STATUTE OF THE INTERNATIONAL CRIMINAL COURT 823 (Otto Triffterer, ed., 1999).

John T. Holmes, *The Principle of Complementarity, in* THE INTERNATIONAL CRIMINAL COURT: THE MAKING OF THE ROME STATUTE 41 (Roy S. Lee, ed., 1999).

Robert Y. Jennings, *Treaties, in* INTERNATIONAL LAW: ACHIEVEMENTS AND PROSPECTS 135 (Mohammed Bedjaoui, ed., 1991).

Michael J. Keegan & Daryl A. Mundis, *Legal Requirements for Indictments, in* ESSAYS ON THE ICTY PROCEDURE AND EVIDENCE IN HONOUR OF GABRIELLE KIRK MCDONALD 123 (Richard May, et. al., eds., 2001).

Elizabeth Kiss, *Reflections on Restorative Justice, in* THE MORALITY OF TRUTH COMMISSIONS: TRUTH v. JUSTICE 70 (Robert I. Rotberg & Dennis Thompson, eds., 2000).

Dorean M. Koenig & Kelly D. Askin, *International Criminal Law and the International Criminal Court Statute: Crimes Against Women, in* II WOMEN AND INTERNATIONAL HUMAN RIGHTS LAW 3 (Kelly D. Askin & Dorean M. Koenig, eds., 2000).

Claus Kreß, *Article 86: General obligation to cooperate, in* COMMENTARY ON THE ROME STATUTE OF THE INTERNATIONAL CRIMINAL COURT 1051 (Otto Triffterer, ed., 1999).

Claus Kreß & Kimberly Prost, *Article 87: Requests for Cooperation: General provisions, in* COMMENTARY ON THE ROME STATUTE OF THE INTERNATIONAL CRIMINAL COURT 1055 (Otto Triffterer, ed., 1999).

Claus Kreß, Kimberly Prost, Angelika Schlunck, Peter Wilkitzki, *Part 9, International Cooperation and Judicial Assistance, Preliminary Remarks, in* COMMENTARY ON THE ROME STATUTE OF THE INTERNATIONAL CRIMINAL COURT 1045 (Otto Triffterer, ed., 1999).

Roy S. Lee, *The Rome Conference and its Contribution to International Law, in* THE INTERNATIONAL CRIMINAL COURT: THE MAKING OF THE ROME STATUTE 1 (Roy S. Lee, ed., 1999).

Margaret McAuliffe deGuzman, *Article 21: Applicable Law, in* COMMENTARY ON THE ROME STATUTE OF THE INTERNATIONAL CRIMINAL COURT 435 (Otto Triffterer, ed., 1999).

Timothy L.H. McCormack, *From Sun Tzu to the Sixth Committee: The Evolution of an International Criminal Law Regime, in* THE LAW OF WAR CRIMES: NATIONAL AND INTERNATIONAL APPROACHES 37 (Timothy L.H. McCormack & Gerry J. Simpson, eds., 1997).

Phakiso Mochochoko, *International Cooperation and Judicial Assistance, in* THE INTERNATIONAL CRIMINAL COURT: THE MAKING OF THE ROME STATUTE 305 (Roy S. Lee, ed., 1999).

Gabriël Oosthuizen, *Of Misconduct, Contempt, False Testimony, Rule Mutations and other Interesting Powers: A Potpourri of Questions and Notes, in* ESSAYS ON THE ICTY PROCEDURE AND EVIDENCE IN HONOUR OF GABRIELLE KIRK MCDONALD 387 (Richard May, et. al., eds., 2001).

Raul C. Pangalangan, *Non-retroactivity ratione personae, in* COMMENTARY ON THE ROME STATUTE OF THE INTERNATIONAL CRIMINAL COURT 467 (Otto Triffterer, ed., 1999).

Jordan J. Paust, *Commentary on Parts 1 and 2 of the Zutphen Intersessional Draft, in* OBSERVATIONS ON THE CONSOLIDATED ICC TEXT BEFORE THE FINAL SESSION OF THE PREPARATORY COMMITTEE, *13bis* NOUVELLES ÉTUDES PÉNALES 27 (Leila Sadat Wexler, special ed., 1998).

Jordan J. Paust, *Nullem Crimen and Related Claims, in* THE INTERNATIONAL CRIMINAL COURT: OBSERVATIONS AND ISSUES BEFORE THE 1997–98 PREPARATORY COMMITTEE; AND ADMINISTRATIVE AND FINANCIAL IMPLICATIONS, 13*ter* NOUVELLES ÉTUDES PÉNALES 275 (M. Cherif Bassiouni, ed., 1997).

Per Saland, *International Criminal Law Principles, in* THE INTERNATIONAL CRIMINAL COURT: THE MAKING OF THE ROME STATUTE 189 (Roy S. Lee, ed., 1999).

Donald K. Piragoff, *Mental Element, in* COMMENTARY ON THE ROME STATUTE OF THE INTERNATIONAL CRIMINAL COURT 527 (Otto Triffterer, ed., 1999).

Donald K. Piragoff, *Protection of National Security Information, in* THE INTERNATIONAL CRIMINAL COURT: THE MAKING OF THE ROME STATUTE 270 (Roy S. Lee, ed., 1999).

Kimberly Prost & Angelika Schlunck, *Article 93: Other forms of cooperation, in* COMMENTARY ON THE ROME STATUTE OF THE INTERNATIONAL CRIMINAL COURT 1101 (Otto Triffterer, ed., 1999).

S. Rama Rao, *Financing of the Court, Assembly of States Parties and the Preparatory Commission, in* THE INTERNATIONAL CRIMINAL COURT: THE MAKING OF THE ROME STATUTE 399 (Roy S. Lee, ed., 1999).

Naomi Roht-Arriaza, *Punishment, Redress and Pardon: Theoretical and Psychological Approaches, in* IMPUNITY AND HUMAN RIGHTS IN INTERNATIONAL LAW AND PRACTICE 17 (Naomi Roht-Arriaza, ed., Oxford, 1995).

Naomi Roht-Arrizia, *Sources in International Treaties of an Obligation to Investigate, Prosecute and Provide Redress, in* IMPUNITY AND HUMAN RIGHTS IN INTERNATIONAL LAW AND PRACTICE 28 (Naomi Roht-Arriaza, ed., Oxford, 1995).

Medard R. Rwelamira, *Composition and Administration of the Court, in* THE INTERNATIONAL CRIMINAL COURT: THE MAKING OF THE ROME STATUTE 153 (Roy S. Lee, ed., 1999).

Leila Sadat Wexler, *Commentary on Parts 1 and 2 of the Zutphen Intersessional Draft: Establishment of the Court, Complementarity, Jurisdiction and Admissibility, in* OBSERVATIONS ON THE CONSOLIDATED ICC TEXT BEFORE THE FINAL SESSION OF THE PREPARATORY COMMITTEE, 13*bis* NOUVELLES ÉTUDES PÉNALES 17 (Leila Sadat Wexler, special ed., 1998).

Leila Sadat Wexler, *First Committee Report on Jurisdiction, Definition of Crimes and Complementarity, in* THE INTERNATIONAL CRIMINAL COURT: OBSERVATIONS AND ISSUES BEFORE THE 1997–98 PREPARATORY COMMITTEE; AND ADMINISTRATIVE AND FINANCIAL IMPLICATIONS, 13*ter* NOUVELLES ÉTUDES PÉNALES 163 (M. Cherif Bassiouni, ed., 1997).

Leila Nadya Sadat, *The Legal Legacy of Maurice Papon, in* MEMORY AND JUSTICE ON TRIAL: THE PAPON AFFAIR 131 (Richard J. Golsan, ed., Rutledge, 2000).

Leila Sadat Wexler, *The Role of the European Court of Justice on the Way to European Union, in* EUROPE AFTER MAASTRICHT: AMERICAN AND EUROPEAN PERSPECTIVES 159 (Paul Michael Lützeler, ed., 1994).

William A. Schabas, *Article 23, Nulla poena sine lege, in* COMMENTARY ON THE ROME STATUTE OF THE INTERNATIONAL CRIMINAL COURT 463 (Otto Triffterer, ed., 1999).

William A. Schabas, *Article 67: Rights of the Accused, in* COMMENTARY ON THE ROME STATUTE OF THE INTERNATIONAL CRIMINAL COURT 845 (Otto Triffterer, ed., 1999).

Oscar Schacter, *The U.N. Legal Order: An Overview, in* 1 UNITED NATIONS LEGAL ORDER 1 (Oscar Schacter & Christopher C. Joyner, eds., 1995).

Michael P. Scharf, *Justice vs. Peace, in* THE UNITED STATES AND THE INTERNATIONAL CRIMINAL COURT 186 (Sarah B. Sewall & Carl Kaysen, eds., 2000).

Ignaz Seidl-Hohenveldern, *Les organes des organisations internationales: organes pléniers, in* MANUEL SUR LES ORGANISATIONS INTERNATIONALES 81 (René-Jean Dupuy, ed., 1988).

Kuniji Shibahara, *Confirmation of the Charges before trial, in* COMMENTARY ON THE ROME STATUTE OF THE INTERNATIONAL CRIMINAL COURT 783 (Otto Triffterer, ed., 1999).

Gerry J. Simpson, *War Crimes: A Critical Introduction, in* THE LAW OF WAR CRIMES: NATIONAL AND INTERNATIONAL APPROACHES 4 (Timothy L.H. McCormack & Gerry J. Simpson, eds., 1997).

Christopher Staker, *Article 84: Revision of Conviction or Sentence, in* COMMENTARY ON THE ROME STATUTE OF THE INTERNATIONAL CRIMINAL COURT 1037 (Otto Triffterer, ed., 1999).

Christopher Staker, *Article 81: Appeal against decision of acquittal or conviction or against sentence, in* COMMENTARY ON THE ROME STATUTE OF THE INTERNATIONAL CRIMINAL COURT 1015 (Otto Triffterer, ed. 1999).

Cate Steains, *Gender Issues*, in THE INTERNATIONAL CRIMINAL COURT: THE MAKING OF THE ROME STATUTE 357 (Roy S. Lee, ed., 1999).

Irwin P. Stotzky, *Haiti: Searching for Alternatives, in* IMPUNITY AND HUMAN RIGHTS IN INTERNATIONAL LAW AND PRACTICE 185 (Naomi Roht-Arriaza, ed., Oxford, 1995).

Strafgesetzbuch [StGB] (German Penal Code), *translated in* THE GERMAN FEDERAL REPUBLIC PENAL CODE 55 (Joseph J. Darby trans. 1987).

Paul Szasz, *General Law-Making Processes, in* 1 UNITED NATIONS LEGAL ORDER 35 (Oscar Schacter & Christopher C. Joyner, eds., 1995).

Immi Tallgren, *Article 20, Ne bis in idem, in* COMMENTARY ON THE ROME STATUTE OF THE INTERNATIONAL CRIMINAL COURT 419 (Otto Triffterer, ed., 1999).

Santiago Torres Bernárdez, *Subsidiary Organs, in* MANUEL SUR LES ORGANISATIONS INTERNATIONALES 108 (René-Jean Dupuy, ed., 1988).

Otto Triffterer, *Article 10, in* COMMENTARY ON THE ROME STATUTE OF THE INTERNATIONAL CRIMINAL COURT 316 (Otto Triffterer, ed., 1999).

Otto Triffterer, *Irrelevance of official capacity, in* COMMENTARY ON THE ROME STATUTE OF THE INTERNATIONAL CRIMINAL COURT 501 (Otto Triffterer, ed., 1999).

Otto Triffterer, *Mistake of fact or mistake of law, in* COMMENTARY ON THE ROME STATUTE OF THE INTERNATIONAL CRIMINAL COURT 555 (Otto Triffterer, ed., 1999).

Herman von Hebel & Darryl Robinson, *Crimes Within the Jurisdiction of the Court, in* THE INTERNATIONAL CRIMINAL COURT: THE MAKING OF THE ROME STATUTE 79 (Roy S. Lee, ed., 1999).

Michael Walzer, *The Concept of Civil Society, in* TOWARD A GLOBAL CIVIL SOCIETY 7 (Michael Walzer, ed., 1995).

Edith Brown Weiss, *Judicial Independence and Impartiality: A Preliminary Inquiry, in* THE INTERNATIONAL CRIMINAL COURT OF JUSTICE AT A CROSSROADS 123 (1987).

Edward M. Wise, *Commentary on Parts 2 and 3 of the Zutphen Intersessional Draft: General Principles of Criminal Law, in* OBSERVATIONS ON THE CONSOLIDATED ICC TEXT BEFORE THE FINAL SESSION OF THE PREPARATORY COMMITTEE, 13*bis* NOUVELLES ÉTUDES PÉNALES 43 (Leila Sadat Wexler, special ed., 1998).

Edward M. Wise, *General Rules of Criminal Law, in* THE INTERNATIONAL CRIMINAL COURT: OBSERVATIONS AND ISSUES BEFORE THE 1997–98 PREPARATORY COMMITTEE; AND ADMINISTRATIVE AND FINANCIAL IMPLICATIONS, 13*ter* NOUVELLES ÉTUDES PÉNALES 267 (M. Cherif Bassiouni, ed., 1997).

Mustafa Kamil Yasseen, *Création et personnalité juridique des organisations internationales, in* MANUEL SUR LES ORGANISATIONS INTERNATIONALES (RENÉ-JEAN DUPUY, ed., 1988).

UNITED NATIONS DOCUMENTS

Ricardo J. Alfaro, *Question of International Criminal Jurisdiction*, U.N. Doc. No. A/CN.4/15 (1950), *reprinted in* [1950] 2 Y.B. INT'L L. COMM'N 1, U.N. Doc. A/CN.4/SER.A/1950/Add.1.

AN AGENDA FOR PEACE: PREVENTIVE DIPLOMACY, PEACEMAKING AND PEACE-KEEPING [Report of the Secretary-General pursuant to the state adopted by the summit meeting of the Security Council on Jan. 31, 1992], U.N. Doc. A/47/277-S/2411 (1992), U.N. Sales No. E.95.I.15 (1995).

Report of the Secretary-General on the establishment of a Special Court for Sierra Leone, U.N. SCOR, 55th Sess., 4 October 2000, U.N. Doc. S/2000/915.

The Charter and Judgment of the Nuremberg Tribunal: History and Analysis: Memorandum Submitted by the Secretary General, U.N. Sales No. 1949.V.7 (1949).

Comments and Observations on the Draft Code of Crimes Against the Peace and Security of Mankind Adopted on First Reading by the International Law Commission at its Forty-Third Session, U.N. Doc. A/CN.4/448 and Add.1 (1993).

Comments Received from Governments Regarding the Report of the Committee on International Criminal Jurisdiction, U.N. GAOR, 7th Sess., Annex 2, Agenda Item 52, at 1, U.N. Doc. A/2186 and Add.1 (1952).

Compilation of Proposals on the Crime of Aggression, submitted at the Preparatory Committee on the Establishment of an International Criminal Court (1996–1998), the United Nations Diplomatic Conference of Plenipotentiaries on the Establishment of the International Criminal Court (1998), and the Preparatory Commission for the International Criminal Court (1999), U.N. Doc. PCNICC/1999/INF/2 (1999).

Contributions of the Chambers of the International Tribunal for the Former Yugoslavia on the Provisional rules of procedure and evidence for the Court, submitted to the Prepatory Commission at its 13–31 March 2000 session, U.N. Doc. PCNICC/2000/WGRPE(10)/INF/1 (April 5, 2000).

Decisions Taken by the Preparatory Committee at its Session Held from 4 to 15 August 1997, U.N. Doc. A/AC.249/1997/L.8/Rev.1 (1997).

Decisions Taken by the Preparatory Committee at its Session Held from 1 to 12 December 1997, U.N. Doc. A/AC.249/1997/L.9/Rev.1 (1997).

Decisions Taken by the Preparatory Committee at its Session Held from 11 to 21 February 1997, U.N. Doc. A/AC.249/1997/L.5 (1997).

Definition of Aggression, G.A. Res. 3314 (xxix), 29 U.N. GAOR Supp. No. 31, at 142, U.N. Doc. A/9631 (1974).

Draft Agreement on the Privileges and Immunities of the Court, U.N. Doc. PNCICC/2001/WGAPIC/RT.1, March 8, 2001.

Draft Code of Crimes Against the Peace and Security of Mankind, G.A. Res. 43/164, U.N. GAOR, 43d Sess., Supp. (No. 49), U.N. Doc. A/43/49 (1988).

Draft Code of Crimes Against the Peace and Security of Mankind, U.N. Doc. A/CN.4/L.532 (1996).

Draft Code of Crimes against the Peace and Security of Mankind, Report of the International Law Commission on the work of its forty-eighth Session, U.N. GAOR 51st Sess., Supp. No. 10, A/51/10 (1996).

Draft Code of Offenses Against the Peace and Security of Mankind, G.A. Res. 36/106, U.N. GAOR, Dec. 10, 1981.

Draft Financial Regulations and Rules of the International Criminal Court, U.N. Doc. PCNICC/2001/WGFIRR/RT/Rev.1, March 7, 2001.

Draft relationship agreement between the Court and the United Nations, U.N. Doc. PCICC/2001/WGICC-UN/RT.1/Rev.1, March 8, 2001.

Draft Resolution of the Preparatory Commission on the Establishment of the Committe on Budget and Finance: Discussion Paper/ Proposed by the Coordinator, U.N. Doc. PCNICC/2001/WGFIRR/RT.2/Rev.1, March 7, 2001.

Draft Rules of Procedure of the Assembly of States Parties, U.N. Doc. PCNICC/2001/WGRPASP/L.1, December 20, 2000.

Draft Statute for an International Criminal Court: Suggested Modifications to the 1994 ILC Draft Prepared by a Committee of Experts, Done in Siracusa/Freiburg/ Chicago, January 31, 1996.

Establishment of An International Criminal Court, G.A. Res. 50/46, U.N. GAOR 50th Sess., U.N. Doc. A/RES/50/46 (1995).

Final Act of the United Nations Diplomatic Conference of Plenipoteniaries on the Establishment of the International Criminal Court on 17 July 1998, at Annex I, Resolution F, U.N. Doc. A/CONF.183/10.

Final Report of the United Nations Commission of Experts Established Pursuant to Security Council Resolution 780 (1992), U.N. SCOR, 54th Sess., Annex, U.N. Doc. S/1994/674 (1994).

Finalized Draft Text of the Elements of Crimes, Preparatory Commission for the

International Criminal Court, U.N. Doc. PCNICC/2000/INF/3/Add.2, July 6, 2000.

Historical Survey of the Question of International Criminal Jurisdiction: Memorandum Submitted by the Secretary General, U.N. Doc. A/CN.4/7/Rev.1, U.N. Sales No. 1949.V.8 (1949).

1994 ILC Draft Statute for an International Criminal Court With Suggested Modifications (Updated Siracusa-Draft) prepared by a Committee of Experts, Done in Siracusa/ Frieburg/ Chicago, March 15, 1996.

Information Paper submitted by the delegations of Bosnia and Herzegovina, Canada, Colombia, Egypt, Portugal and Spain concerning Part 4 of the Rome Statute: Contributions of the Chambers of the International Tribunal for the Former Yugoslavia on the provisional rules of procedure and evidence for the court, submitted to the Preparatory Commission at its 13–31 March 2000 session, U.N. Doc. PCNICC/2000/WGRPE(4)/INF/1, April 5, 2000.

International Criminal Jurisdiction, G.A. Res. 489 (V), *reprinted in* 3 UNITED NATIONS RESOLUTIONS, SERIES I: RESOLUTIONS OF THE GENERAL ASSEMBLY 151 (Dusan J. Djonovich, ed., 1973).

International Criminal Responsibility of Individuals and Entities Engaged in Illicit Trafficking in Narcotic Drugs Across National Frontiers and Other Transnational Criminal Activities: Establishment of an International Criminal Court with Jurisdiction Over Such Crimes, G.A. Res. 44/39, U.N. GAOR, 44th Sess., Supp. (No. 49), U.N. Doc. A/44/49 (1989).

Letters dated 15 March 1999 from the Secretary-General to the President of the General Assembly and the President of the Security Council, U.N. Doc. A/53/1999/231, annex (Group of Experts Report).

Model Treaty on Extradition, Dec. 14, 1990, art. 4(d), U.N. GAOR, 45th Sess., 68th plen. mtg., U.N. Doc. A/RES/45/116 (1990).

Preparatory Commission for the International Criminal Court, Working Group on the Crime of Aggression, Proposal submitted by Bosnia and Herzegovina, New Zealand and Romania, art. 4, U.N. Doc. PCNICC/2001/WGCA/DP.1, Feb. 23, 2001.

Preparatory Committee on the Establishment of an International Criminal Court, 12–30 August 1996, Drafts Statute of the International Criminal Court, Working paper submitted by France, U.N. Doc. A/AC.249/L.3 (1996).

Prevention and Punishment of the Crime of Genocide, G.A. Res. 260B(III), 2 UNITED NATIONS RESOLUTIONS, SERIES I: RESOLUTIONS OF THE GENERAL ASSEMBLY 241 (Dusan J. Djonovich, ed., 1973).

Proceedings of the Preparatory Commission at its second session (26 July–13 August 1999), Preparatory Commission for the International Criminal Court, U.N. Doc. PCNICC/1999/l.4/Rev.1 (1999).

Proceedings of the Preparatory Commission at its sixth session (27 November–8 December 2000), Annex V, Crime of Aggression, U.N. Doc. PCNICC/ 2000/L.4/Rev.1.

Proposal submitted by Canada, France, Germany and the Netherlands in connection with article 43 of the Rome Statute of the International Criminal Court con-

cerning the Rules of Procedure and Evidence as regards document PCNICC/1999/DP.1, Preparatory Commission for the International Criminal Court, Working Group on Rules of Procedure and Evidence, U.N. Doc PCNICC/1999/WGRPE(4)/DP.2 (1999).

Question of the Impunity of Perpetrators of Human Rights Violations (Civil and Political) U.N. Doc. E/CN.4/Sub.2/1997/20 (1997), at Annex II, Definitions, A.

Reference Document on the Crime of Aggression, Prepared by the Secretariat, Working Group on the Crime of Aggression, U.N. Doc. PCNICC/2000/WGCA/INF/1, June 17, 2000.

Report of the Ad Hoc Committee on the Establishment of an International Criminal Court, U.N. GAOR, 50th Sess., Supp. No. 22, U.N. Doc. A/50/22 (1995).

Report of the Committee on International Criminal Jurisdiction on its Session Held from 1 to 31 August 1951, U.N. GAOR. 7th Sess., Supp. (No. 11), U.N. Doc. A/2136 (1952).

Report of the 1953 Committee on International Criminal Jurisdiction, 27 July–20 August 1953, U.N. GAOR 9th Sess., Supp. (No. 12), U.N. Doc. A/2638 (1954).

Report of the Expert Group to Conduct a Review of the Effective Operation and Functioning of the International Tribunal for the Former Yugoslavia and the International Criminal Tribunal for Rwanda, UN Doc. A/54/634 (1999).

Report of the Expert Group to Conduct a Review of the Effective Operation and Functioning of the International Tribunal for the Former Yugoslavia and the International Criminal Tribunal for Rwanda, UN Doc. S/2000/597.

Report of the International Law Commission on the work of its Forty-Sixth Session, U.N. GAOR, 49th Sess., Supp. No. 10, U.N. Doc. A/49/10 (1994).

Report of the International Law Commission on the work of its Forty-Sixth Session: Report of the Sixth Committee, U.N. GAOR 6th Comm., 49th Sess., U.N. Doc. A/49/738 (Nov. 23, 1994).

Report of the International Law Commission Covering the Work of its Forty-Fourth Session, 4 May–24 July 1992, 47 U.N. GAOR Supp. (No. 10), U.N. Doc. No. A/47/10 (1992), *reprinted in* [1992] 2 Y.B. INT'L L. COMM'N 1, U.N. Doc. A/CN.4/SER.A/1992/Add.1 (Part 2).

Report of the International Law Commission Covering the Work of its Forty-Third Session, 29 April–19 July 1991, 46 U.N. GAOR Supp. (No. 10), U.N. Doc. No. A/46/10 (1991), *reprinted in* [1991] 2 Y.B. INT'L L. COMM'N 1, U.N. Doc. A/CN.4/SER.A/1991/Add.1 (Part 2).

Report of the International Law Commission on the work of its Forty-Second Session, 45 U.N. GAOR, Supp. (No. 10), at 155, U.N. Doc. No. A/45/10 (1990), *reprinted in* [1990] 2 Y.B. INT'L L. COMM'N 1, U.N. Doc. A/CN.4/SER.A/1990/Add.1 (Part 2).

Report of the International Law Commission Covering the Work of its Thirty-Eighth Session, 5 May–11 July 1986, 41 U.N. GAOR Supp. (No. 10), U.N. Doc. No. A/41/10 (1986), *reprinted in* [1986] 2 Y.B. INT'L L. COMM'N 1, U.N. Doc. A/CN.4/SER.A/1986/Add.1 (Part 2).

Report of the International Law Commission Covering the Work of its Thirty-Fifth Session 3 May–22 July 1983, 38 U.N. GAOR Supp. (No. 10), U.N. Doc. No. A/38/10 (1983), *reprinted in* [1983] 2 Y.B. INT'L L. COMM'N 1, U.N. Doc. A/CN.4/SER.A/1983/Add.1 (Part 2).

Report of the International Law Commission Covering the Work of its Sixth Session, 3 June–28 July 1954, 9 U.N. GAOR Supp. (No. 9), U.N. Doc. No. A/2693 (1954), *reprinted in* [1953] 2 Y.B. INT'L L. COMM'N 195, U.N. Doc. A/CN.4/SER.A/1954/Add.1.

Report of the International Law Commission to the General Assembly, U.N. GAOR Supp. (No. 10), U.N. Doc. No. A/1316 (1950), *reprinted in* [1950] 2 Y.B. INT'L L. COMM'N 364, U.N. Doc. A/CN.4/SER.A/1950/Add.1.

Report of the Inter-Sessional Meeting from 19 to 30 January 1998 in Zutphen, The Netherlands, U.N. Doc. A/AC.249/1998/L.13 (1998).

Report of the Office of Internal Oversight Services on the investigation into possible fee-splitting arrangements between defence counsel and indigent detainees at the International Criminal Tribunal for Rwanda and the International Tribunal for the Former Yugoslavia, U.N. Doc. A/55/759, February 1, 2001.

Report of the Preparatory Committee on the Establishment of an International Criminal Court, U.N. Doc. A/CONF.183/2/Add.1 (1998).

Report of the Preparatory Committee on the Establishment of an International Criminal Court (Proceedings of the Preparatory Committee during March–April and August 1996), Vols. I & II, U.N. GAOR, 51st Sess., Supp. No. 22, U.N. Doc. A/51/22 (1996).

Report of the Secretary-General Pursuant to Paragraph 2 of Security Council Resolution 808, U.N. Doc. S/25704/Add.1/Corr. 1 (1993).

Report of the Secretary-General on the establishment of a Special Court for Sierra Leone, U.N. Doc. S/2000/915 (2000).

Report of the Working Group on General Principles of Criminal Law, U.N. Doc. A/CONF. 183/C.1/WGGP/L.4 (June 18, 1998).

Report of the Working Group on the question of an International Criminal Jurisdiction, in Report of the International Law Commission on the work of its forty-fourth session, 47 U.N. GAOR Supp. (No. 10), U.N. Doc. No. A/47/10 (1992), *reprinted in* [1992] 2 Y.B. Int'l L. Comm'n 1, U.N. Doc. A/CN.4/SER.A/1992/Add.1 (Part 2).

Review of the Multilateral Treaty-Making Process, U.N. Doc. ST/LEG/SER.B/21 (1985).

Emil Sandström, *Question of International Criminal Jurisdiction,* U.N. Doc. No. A/CN.4/15 (1950), *reprinted in* [1950] 2 Y.B. INT'L L. COMM'N 18, U.N. Doc. A/CN.4/SER.A/1950/Add.1.

Security Council Resolution 678 (1990) authorizing Member States to use all necessary means to implement Security Council Resolution 660 (on Iraq invasion of Kuwait) and all relevant resolutions, S.C. Res. 678, U.N. SCOR, 45th Sess., 2963d mtg., U.N. Doc. S/RES/678 (1990).

Security Council Resolution 1315 (2000) on establishing a special court in Sierra Leone, S. C. Res. 1315 (2000), U.N. Doc. S/RES/1315 (2000), to be issued in U.N. SCOR, 55th Year, Resolutions and Decisions 2000.

Security Council Resolution 827 (1993) on Establishment of an International Tribunal for Prosecutions of Persons Responsible for Serious Violations of International Humanitarian Law Committed in the Territory of the Former Yugoslavia since 1991, S.C. Res. 827, U.N. SCOR, 3217th mtg., U.N. Doc. S/RES/827 (1993).

Security Council Resolution 808 (1993) on Establishment of an International Tribunal for the Prosecutions of Persons Responsible for Violations of International Humanitarian Law Committed in the Territory of the Former Yugoslavia, U.N. SCOR, 3175mtg., U.N. Doc. S/RES/808 (1993).

Security Council Resolution 955 (1994) on Establishment of an International Tribunal for Rwanda and adoption of the Statute of the Tribunal, S.C. Res. 955, U.N. SCOR, 49th Sess., 3453rd mtg., at 2, U.N. Doc. S/RES/955 (1994).

Set of Principles for the Protection and Promotion of Human Rights Through Action to Combat Impunity, U.N. Subcommission for Prevention of Discrimination and Protection of Minorities, 48th Sess., Annex II, Agenda Item 10, at 12, U.N. Doc. E/CN.4/Sub.2/1996/18 (1996).

Summary Records of the Forty-Second Session, [1990] 1 Y.B. INT'L L. COMM'N, U.N. Doc. A/CN.4/SER.A/1990.

Summary Records of the Thirty-Fifth Session, reprinted in [1983] 1 Y.B. INT'L L. COMM'N, U.N. Doc. A/CN.4/SER.A/1983.

Doudou Thiam, Special Rapporteur, *First Report on the Draft Code of Offenses Against the Peace and Security of Mankind*, U.N. GAOR, 35th Sess., U.N. Doc. No. A/CN.4/364 (1983).

Thirteenth Report on the Draft Code of Crimes Against the Peace and Security of Mankind, U.N. GAOR, 50th Sess., U.N. Doc. No. A/CN.4/466 (1995).

United Nations Diplomatic Conference of Plenipotentiaries on the Establishment of an International Criminal Court, U.N. Doc. A/CON.181/10, July 17, 1998.

OTHER

Commission on the Responsibility of the Authors of the War and on Enforcement of Penalties: Report Presented to the Preliminary Peace Conference, 14 AM. J. INT'L L. 95 (1920).

Conference, *Sovereignty in the North American Context and in a Changing World*, 20 CAN.-U.S. L.J. 1 (1994).

Osama Ghanem Alobaidy, The International Criminal Court: An Arab Perspective in View of Islamic Law and the 1998 Rome Statute (2000) (unpublished J.S.D. dissertation, Washington University School of Law) (on file with the Washington University School of Law Library).

NGO Coalition for an ICC, Report of Outcome of the Key Issues at the Fifth PrepCom, June 6, 2000.

Princeton Project on Universal Jurisdiction, Working Papers, January 26–27, 2001 (Princeton University).

Jennifer Schense, NGO Coalition for an International Criminal Court, *Draft Report on the Fourth Session of the Preparatory Commission, March 13–31, 2000.*

HELPFUL INTERNET SITES

Amnesty International
<http://www.amnesty.org/>.

Human Rights Watch
<http://www.hrw.org>

IPS, *TerraViva, The Conference Daily Newspaper*
<http://www.ips.org/icc>.

No Peace Without Justice—International Committee of parliamentarians, mayors and citizens for the establishment of an effective system of international justice
<http://www.npwj.org>.

Sierra Leone Web site
<http://www.sierra-leone.gov.sl>.

The American Society of International Law
<http://www.asil.org/>.

The American Society of International Law Insights
<http://www.asil.org/insights.htm>

The Coalition for the International Criminal Court (CICC) Web site
<http://www.igc/icc>

The Coalition for the International Criminal Court (CICC) Web site: Rome International Criminal Court Treaty Conference Web Page
<http://www.igc.org/icc/rome/index.html>.

The Coalition for the International Criminal Court (CICC): Rome Statute Signature and Ratification Chart
<http://www.igc.org/icc/rome/html/ratify.html>

Truth and Reconciliation Commission
<http://www.truth.org.za>

United States Department of State
<http://www.state.gov/>.

United States Department of State: Office of the Coordinator For Counterterrorism
<http://www.state.gov/www/global/terrorism>.

United Nations
<http://www.un.org/>.

United Nations: Bringing Peace to Kosovo News Reports
<http://www.un.org/peace/kosovo/news/99/oct00.htm#Anchor16>.

United Nations: Rome Statute of the International Criminal Court
<http://www.un.org/law/icc>

United Nations: The International Criminal Tribunal for the former Yugoslavia

<http://www.un.org/icty>
United Nations: The International Criminal Tribunal for Rwanda
<http://www.un.org/ictr>
United Nations Treaty Collection
<http://www.untreaty.un.org/>

TABLE OF CASES

INTERNATIONAL COURT DECISIONS

International Court of Justice

Case Concerning Military and Paramilitary Activities in and Against Nicaragua (Nicaragua v. U.S.) (Merits) 1986 I.C.J. 14.
Legality of the Threat or Use of Nuclear Weapons, Advisory Opinion, 1996 I.C.J. 226 (July 8).
North Sea Continental Shelf Cases, (F.R.G. v. Den., F.R.G. v. Neth.), 1969 I.C.J. 3 (Feb. 20).
Reservations to the Genocide Convention, International Court of Justice [1951] I.C.J. Rep. 15.

International Criminal Tribunal for the former Yugoslavia

Prosecutor v. Aleksovski, (Case No. IT-95-14/1-T), Judgment (ICTY Trial Chamber I, June 25, 1999).
Prosecutor v. Blaskić, (Case No. IT-95-14), Judgment on the Request of the Republic of Croatia for Review of the Decision of Trial Chamber II of July 18, 1997 (ICTY Appeals Chamber, Oct. 29, 1997).
Prosecutor v. Blaskić, (Case No. IT-95-14-T), Judgment (ICTY Trial Chamber, Mar. 3, 2000).
Prosecutor v. Delalić, (Case No. IT-96-21-T), Judgment (ICTY Trial Chamber II, Nov. 16, 1998).
Prosecutor v. Delalić, (Case No. IT-96-21-A), Dissenting Opinion of Judge Bennouna on the Jurisdiction of the Appeals Chamber to Hear Provisional Release Matters (ICTY Appeals Chamber, Feb. 20, 1999).
Prosecutor v. Erdemović, (Case No. IT-96-22-T), Sentencing Judgment (ICTY Trial Chamber I, Nov. 29, 1996).
Prosecutor v. Erdemović, (Case No. IT-96-22), Separate and Dissenting Opinion of Judge Cassese (ICTY Appeals Chamber, Oct. 7, 1997).
Prosecutor v. Erdemović, (Case No. IT-96-22-A), Separate and Dissenting Opinion of Judge Li (ICTY Appeals Chamber, Oct. 7, 1997).

Prosecutor v. Erdemović, (Case No. IT-96-22-A), Joint Separate Opinion of Judge McDonald and Judge Vohrah (ICTY Appeals Chamber, Oct. 7, 1997).

Prosecutor v. Erdemović, (Case No. IT-96-22), Separate and Dissenting Opinion of Judge Stephen (ICTY Appeals Chamber, Oct. 7, 1997).

Prosecutor v. Furundzija, No. IT-95-17/1-T, Judgment (ICTY Trial Chamber II, Dec. 10, 1998).

Prosecutor v. Jelesić (Case No. IT-95-10-T), Judgment (ICTY Trial Chamber I, Dec. 14, 1999).

Prosecutor v. Kupreskic, (Case No. IT-95-16-T), Decision on Communications Between the Parties and their Witnesses (ICTY Trial Chamber II, Sept. 21, 1998).

Prosecutor v. Msksić, Radić, and Sljivancanin, (Case No. IT-95-13-R61), Review of the Indictment Pursuant to Rule 61 of the Rules of Procedure and Evidence (ICTY Trial Chamber I, Apr. 3, 1996).

Prosecutor v. Tadić, (Case No. IT-94-1-AR72), Decision on the Defence Motion for Interlocutory Appeal on Jurisdiction (ICTY Appeals Chamber Oct. 2, 1995).

Prosecutor v. Tadić, (Case No. IT-94-1-T), Opinion and Judgment (ICTY Trial Chamber II, May 7, 1997).

Prosecutor v. Tadić, (Case No. IT-94-1-A), Judgment (ICTY Appeals Chamber, July 15, 1999).

Prosecutor v. Tadić, (Case No. IT-94-1-A), Judgment in Sentencing Appeals (ICTY Appeals Chamber, Jan. 26, 2000).

International Criminal Tribunal for Rwanda

Prosecutor v. Akayesu, (Case No. ICTR-96-4-A) (ICTR Appeals Chamber, June 1, 2000).

Prosecutor v. Akayesu, (Case No. ICTR-96-4-T), Judgment (ICTR Trial Chamber I, Sept. 2, 1998).

Prosecutor v. Kambanda, (Case No. ICTR-97-23-S), Judgment and Sentence (ICTR Trial Chamber I, Sept. 4, 1998).

Prosecutor v. Kayishema and Ruzindana, (Case No. ICTR-95-1-T), Judgment (ICTR Trial Chamber II, May 21, 1999).

Prosecutor v. Musema, (Case No. ICTR-96-13-T, Judgment (ICTR Trial Chamber I, Jan. 27, 2000).

Prosecutor v. Rutaganda, (Case No. ICTR-96-3-T), Judgment and Sentence (ICTR Trial Chamber I, Dec. 6, 1999).

Prosecutor v. Serashugo, (Case No. ICTR-98-39-S), Sentence (ICTR Trial Chamber I, Feb. 5, 1999).

Other

Garay Hermosilla et al. v. Chile, Inter-Am.C.H.R., Report No. 36/96 (Oct. 15, 1996).
Judgment of October 1, 1946, International Military Tribunal Judgment and Sentences, 41 AM. J. INT'L. L. 172 (1947).
THE TOKYO JUDGMENT: THE INTERNATIONAL MILITARY TRIBUNAL FOR THE FAR EAST (I.M.T.F.E.), 29 April 1946–12 November 1948 (B.V.A. Röling and C.F. Rüter, eds., 1977).
Velásquez Rodríguez, Inter-Am. Ct.H.R. (Ser. C) No. 4 (1988) (July 29, 1988).
X and Y v. The Netherlands, Eur. Ct. H. R. (Feb. 27, 1985).

NATIONAL COURT DECISIONS

France

Cass. Crim., October 21, 1993 (*Touvier Affair*).
Cour d'appel de Paris, 9 Dec. 1992, Gaz. Pal. 1992, 2, somm. 526.
Judgment of April 13, 1992, Cour d'appel de Paris, première chambre d'accusation, *reprinted in part in* 1992 Gaz. Pal. 387 (*Touvier Affair*).
Judgment of December 20, 1985, Cass. crim., 1986 J.C.P. II G, No. 20,655, J.D.I. 127 (1986) (*Barbie Affair*).
Judgment of January 26, 1984, Cass. crim., 1984 J.C.P. II G, No. 20,197 (Note Ruzié), J.D.I. 308 (1934) (*Barbie Affair*).
Judgment of January 23, 1997, Cass. crim., 1997 J.C.P. II G, No. 22,812 (Note Robert) (*Papon Affair*).
Judgment of June 30, 1976, Cass. crim., 1977 D.S. Jur. 1, 1976 Gaz. Pal. Nos. 322, 1976 J.C.P. II G, No. 18,435 (*Touvier Affair*).
Judgment of June 3, 1988, Cass. crim., 1988 J.C.P. II G, No. 21,149 (Report of Counselor Angevin) (*Barbie Affair*).
Judgment of June 2, 1993, Cour d'appel de Versailles, première chambre d'accusation (*Touvier Affair*).
Judgment of November 27, 1992, Cass. crim., 1993 J.C.P. II G, No. 21,977 (*Touvier Affair*).
Judgment of October 27, 1975, Cour d'appel de Paris, 1976 G.P., Nos. 154–55 (*Touvier Affair*).
Judgment of October 6, 1983, Cass. crim., 1984 D.S. Jur. 113, G.P. Nos. 352–54 (Dec. 18–20, 1983), 1983 J.C. P. II G, No. 20,107, J.D. I. 779 (1983) (*Barbie Affair*).
Judgment of September 18, 1996, Chambre d'accusation de la Cour d'appel de Bordeaux (*Papon Affair*).

United States

Bartkus v. Illinois, 359 U.S. 121 (1959).
Brown v. Board of Education, 347 U.S. 483 (1954).
Calder v. Bull, 3 U.S. (3 Dall.) 386 (1798).
Cooper v. Aaron, 358 U.S. 1 (1958).
Crist v. Bretz, 437 U.S. 28 (1978).
Trial of General Tomoyuki Yamashita, United States Military Commission, Manila (8th October–7th December, 1945), 4 LAW REPORTS OF TRIALS 1 (1948).
United States v. Nixon, 418 U.S. 683 (1974).
United States v. Yamashita, 327 U.S. 1 (1946).

Other

Azanian Peoples Organisation (AZAPO) v. The President of the Republic of South Africa, 1996 (4) S.A.L.R. 671 (South African Const. Ct.).
Case No. 4895/96, (South African Cape Provincial Div. Supreme Ct., May 9, 1996).
Regina v. Bow Street Metropolitan Stipendiary Magistrate, *ex parte* Pinochet Ugarte, [1999] 2 W.L.R. 827 (H.L.).
Regina v. Finta [1994] 1 S.C.R. 701 (Canada).

TREATIES

African [Banjul] Charter on Human and Peoples' Rights, June 27, 1981, OAU Doc. CAB/LEG/67/3 rev.5, 21 I.L.M. 58 (1982).
American Convention on Human Rights, Nov. 22, 1969, S. TREATY Doc. No. 95–2, 1144 U.N.T.S. 144.
Convention Against Torture or Other Cruel, Inhuman or Degrading Treatment or Punishment, G.A. Res. 39/46, 39 U.N. GAOR Supp. (No. 51), U.N. Doc. A/39/51 (1984).
Convention [No. III] for the Adaptation to Maritime Warfare of the Principles of the Geneva Conventions of 22 August 1864, July 29, 1899, 32 Stat. 1827, 1 Bevans 263.
Convention for the Creation of an International Criminal Court, *opened for signature*, Nov. 16, 1937, LEAGUE OF NATIONS O.J. Spec. Supp. 156 (1938).
Convention on the Non-Applicability of Statutory Limitations to War Crimes and Crimes Against Humanity, G.A. Res. 2391, 23 U.N. GAOR Supp. No. 18, U.N. Doc. A/7218 (1968).
Convention on the Prohibition of the Use, Stockpiling, Production and Transfer of Anti- Personnel Mines and on Their Destruction, *opened for sig-*

nature Dec. 3, 1997, 36 I.L.M. 1507 (1997) (entered into force Mar. 1, 1999).

Convention on the Rights of the Child, Nov. 20, 1989, G.A. Res. 44/25, U.N. GAOR, 44th Sess., Supp. No. 49, U.N. Doc. A/44/49 (1989).

Convention on the Suppression and Punishment of the Crime of Apartheid, U.N. GAOR Supp. (No. 30), U.N. Doc. A/9030 (1973).

Convention [No. I] Regarding the Pacific Settlement of International Disputes, July 29, 1899, 32 Stat. 1779, 1 Bevans 230.

Convention [No. IV] Respecting The Laws and Customs of War on Land, Oct. 18, 1907, 36 Stat. 2277, T.S. No. 539, 1 Bevans 631.

Convention [No. II] with Respect to the Laws and Customs of War on Land, with annex of regulations, July 29, 1899, 32 Stat. 1803, 1 Bevans 247.

European Convention for the Protection of Human Rights and Fundamental Freedoms, November 4, 1950, Europ. T.S. No. 5, 213 U.N.T.S. 222.

Geneva Convention for the Amelioration of the Condition of the Wounded and Sick in Armed Forces in the Field, Aug. 12, 1949, 75 U.N.T.S. 31.

Geneva Convention for the Amelioration of the Condition of Wounded, Sick and Shipwrecked Members of Armed Forces at Sea, Aug. 12, 1949, 75 U.N.T.S. 85.

Geneva Convention Relative to the Protection of Civilian Persons in Time of War, Aug. 12, 1949, 75 U.N.T.S. 287.

Geneva Convention Relative to the Treatment of Prisoners of War, Aug. 12, 1949, 75 U.N.T.S. 135.

International Covenant on Civil and Political Rights, G.A. Res. 2200A (XXI), U.N. GAOR, 21st Sess., Supp. No. 16, U.N. Doc. A/6316 (1966), 999 U.N.T.S. 171 (*entered into force* Mar. 23, 1976).

International Convention for the Suppression of Terrorist Bombings, U.N. GAOR, 52nd Sess., Annex, U.N. Doc. A/RES/52/164 (1998).

League of Nations Doc. C.547(I)M.384(I)1937V (never entered into force), *reprinted in* 7 INTERNATIONAL LEGISLATION (1935–1937) (Manley O. Hudson, ed., 1941).

Protocol No. 6 to the Convention For the Protection of Human Rights and Fundamental Freedoms, *opened for signature* Apr. 28, 1983, EUROP. T.S. NO. 114, 22 I.L.M. 538 (1938).

Protocol Additional to the Geneva Conventions of 12 August 1949, and Relating to the Protection of Victims of International Armed Conflicts, June 8, 1977, 1125 U.N.T.S. 3.

Second Optional Protocol to the International Covenant on Civil and Political Rights, opened for signature Dec. 15, 1989, 29 I.L.M. 1464 (1990).

Special Proclamation: Establishment of an International Military Tribunal for the Far East, Jan. 19, 1946, T.I.A.S. No. 1589, 4 Bevans 20.

The Agreement for the Prosecution and Punishment of Major War Criminals of the European Axis, Charter of the International Military Tribunal, August 8, 1945, 8 U.N.T.S. 279, *reprinted in* 39 AM. J. INT'L L. 257 (Supp. 1945).

Treaty of Peace Between the Allied and Associated Powers and Germany, June 28, 1919, *reprinted in* 11 MARTENS NOUVEAU RECUEIL (Ser. 3) 323 (Fr.).
Vienna Convention on the Law of Treaties, May 23, 1969, 1155 U.N.T.S. 331.
United Nations Charter.
Universal Declaration of Human Rights, G.A. Res. 217A (III), U.N. GAOR, 3d Sess., Supp. No. 49, U.N. Doc. A/810 (1948).

INDEX